California For Dummies
4th Edition

San Francisco Mass Transit

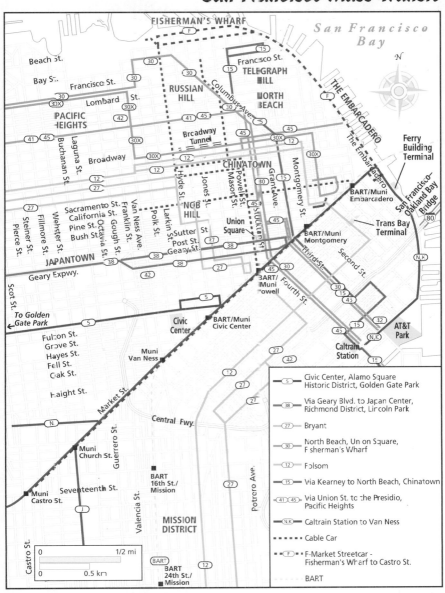

San Diego Trolley System

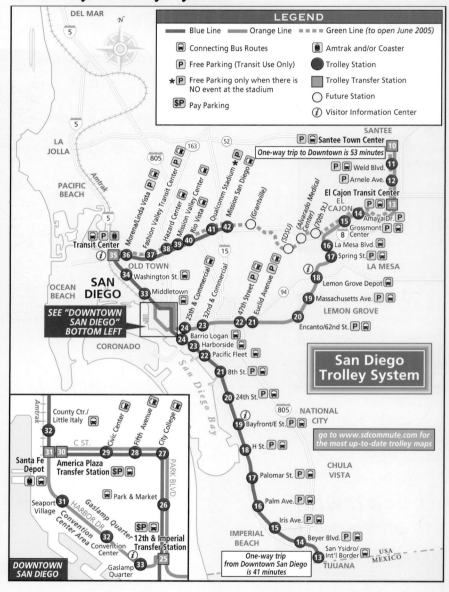

FOR DUMMIES

The fun and easy way™ to travel!

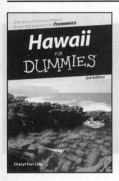
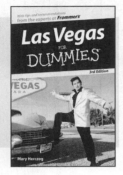
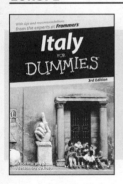

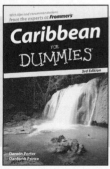
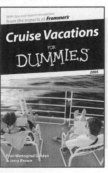

California

FOR

DUMMIES®

4TH EDITION

by Mary Herczog and Paula Tevis

Wiley Publishing, Inc.

California For Dummies®, 4th Edition

Published by
Wiley Publishing, Inc.
111 River St.
Hoboken, NJ 07030-5774
www.wiley.com

WILEY

About the Authors

Mary Herczog is a second-generation California native and is married to Paula Tevis's prom date. She writes for Frommer's and Wiley whenever she can, which is quite a bit (*Frommer's New Orleans, Frommer's Las Vegas, Las Vegas For Dummies, Los Angeles For Dummies,* and more!) and she is so happy she can do it in the California sunshine. The rest of the time, Mary works for the film industry, which is a very California thing to do.

Paula Tevis, also a second-generation Californian, was born and raised in Santa Barbara, attended college in Los Angeles, and then moved to her favorite city, where she could cheer for the San Francisco Giants in peace. After an eclectic but blessedly brief career that included stints in the computer and nonprofit sectors, she and her California-bred husband produced a couple of lovely children, and Paula happily relinquished the 9-to-5 world for the 24/7 one that parenting brings. Upon regaining consciousness, she metamorphosed into a freelance writer, and over the years has contributed articles and essays to *Parenting* and *Family Fun* magazines, the *San Francisco Chronicle,* Citysearch.com, *Frommer's Las Vegas,* and *Frommer's New Orleans.* She is the author of *San Francisco For Dummies,* the *Berlitz Vancouver Pocketguide,* and *Frommer's San Francisco with Kids.* Paula currently lives with her husband and their daughters in London, but reads the *Chronicle* online daily.

Dedication

This book is dedicated to the memory of my brother, Peter Tevis.

Authors' Acknowledgments

I wouldn't write this book if I couldn't write it with Paula Tevis. Without Melissa Sherman Pearl, the San Diego and Laguna chapters would have been skimpy, and Sims Brannon created the Central Coast wine chapter. I am hugely grateful to both. Lisa Derrick helped make sense of Los Angeles, and Rick Garman helps me make sense of everything. California is the golden state because I live here with Steve Hochman.

— *Mary Herczog*

Many thanks to my coauthor, the truly amazing Mary Herczog. Thanks, too, to the wonderful people who assisted me in one way or another as I made my way through the best half of California: Bev Chin, Patience Tevis, Prudence and Steve Handelman, Nick Cann and Peggy Blair, Andrea and Jeff Tobias, Irene Levin Dietz, Ina Levin Gyemant and Leonard Shlain, the imitable Cynde Ahart Woods, Robert Markstein, Donna Joyner, the wonderful Renee Brincks of the Monterey County Convention and Visitors Bureau, and Patricia Unterman. Mark Katz and our daughters, Lili and Madeleine, make living anywhere an adventure and a joy.

— *Paula Tevis*

Mary and Paula also wish to extend great thanks to their editor, Marc Nadeau.

Publisher's Acknowledgments

We're proud of this book; please send us your comments through our Dummies online registration form located at www.dummies.com/register/.

Some of the people who helped bring this book to market include the following:

Editorial

Editors: Marc Nadeau, Development Editor; Heather Wilcox, Production Editor

Copy Editor: Elizabeth Kuball

Cartographer: Anton Crane

Editorial Assistant: Melinda Quintero

Senior Photo Editor: Richard Fox

Cover Photos: *Front:* Carmel: The Lone Cypress Tree (© Michael Howell/Robert Harding World Imagery/Getty Images)

Back: Wall Mural depicting old Hollywood stars seated in movie theater (© David Peevers/ Lonely Planet Images)

Cartoons: Rich Tennant (www.the5thwave.com)

Composition Services

Project Coordinator: Patrick Redmond

Layout and Graphics: Claudia Bell, Stephanie D. Jumper, Barry Offringa, Julia Trippetti

Special Art: Anniversary Logo Design: Richard Pacifico

Proofreaders: David Faust, Techbooks

Indexer: Techbooks

Publishing and Editorial for Consumer Dummies

Diane Graves Steele, Vice President and Publisher, Consumer Dummies

Joyce Pepple, Acquisitions Director, Consumer Dummies

Kristin A. Cocks, Product Development Director, Consumer Dummies

Michael Spring, Vice President and Publisher, Travel

Kelly Regan, Editorial Director, Travel

Publishing for Technology Dummies

Andy Cummings, Vice President and Publisher, Dummies Technology/ General User

Composition Services

Gerry Fahey, Vice President of Production Services

Debbie Stailey, Director of Composition Services

Contents at a Glance

Maps at a Glance

• •

Table of Contents

Part III: Northern California: Redwoods, Wine, and Wonder......89

Introduction

*I*f you reached for *California For Dummies,* 4th Edition, because it
stood out from the overwhelming pack of California guidebooks or
because it just seemed different, pat yourself on the back — you have
good instincts.

This book walks you through the whole process of putting together your
perfect trip, from the ins and outs of laying out a manageable itinerary to
choosing the right places to stay to how much time to allot for which
attractions and activities. Not that one right answer exists for anybody,
of course. This book gives you the tools you need — and only what you
need, not too much — to really help you discover what works for you
and what doesn't. We know your time is valuable, so we strive to get
right to the point and give you the clearest picture of what you need to
know, what choices you have to make, and what your options are so you
can make informed decisions easily and efficiently.

Think of building your vacation less as a step-by-step process and more
as a jigsaw puzzle. This book helps you choose the right puzzle pieces
and assemble them so that they interlock smoothly and the finished
product reflects the picture *you* want, not someone else's image of what
your vacation should be.

About This Book

Some parts of California deserve your valuable time and hard-earned
money, and others don't. For this reason, we've focused not on covering
California comprehensively, but on covering the best that California
offers. This book is a reference tool that answers all your questions
about the state's most terrific destinations — places such as Disneyland
and Napa Valley. The result is a guidebook that directs you to all the
worthiest locales and doesn't bother you with the secondary stuff.

Instead of just throwing out reams of information for you to sift through
until you're too tired to tell Bakersfield from Big Sur, *California For
Dummies,* 4th Edition, cuts to the good stuff. We've done the legwork
for you, and we want you to benefit from our expertise. We know that
you work hard to set aside a few precious weeks of vacation time and
that money doesn't grow on palm fronds. But no matter how much
money you have, you don't want to waste it. Consequently, we're willing
to take a stand so that you will know what to include in your California
vacation — and, even more important, what to pass by. After all, you
want to figure this stuff out now, in the planning stage — not after you
get there, when it's too late.

Dummies Post-it® Flags

As you read this book, you may find information that you want to reference as you plan or enjoy your trip — whether a new hotel, a must-see attraction, or a must-try walking tour. To simplify your trip planning, mark these pages with the handy Post-it® Flags included in this book.

Please be advised that travel information is subject to change at any time — especially prices. We, therefore, suggest that you write or call ahead for confirmation when making your travel plans. The authors, editors, and publisher can't be held responsible for the experiences of readers while traveling. Your safety is important to us, however, so we encourage you to stay alert and be aware of your surroundings.

Conventions Used in This Book

We recently tried to extract some information from a guidebook and found so many symbols that we considered training in hieroglyphics to interpret them all. We are happy to report that the user-friendly *California For Dummies,* 4th Edition, travel guide isn't like that. The use of symbols and abbreviations is kept to a minimum.

The credit-card abbreviations are as follows:

- **AE:** American Express
- **DC:** Diners Club
- **DISC:** Discover
- **MC:** MasterCard
- **V:** Visa

We list the hotels and restaurants in alphabetical order (for the most part — and when we don't, we let you know) so that moving among the maps and descriptions is easy.

We include some general pricing information to help you as you decide where to unpack your bags or dine on the local cuisine, and we use a system of dollar signs to show a range of costs for one night in a hotel or a meal at a restaurant. Check out the following table to decipher the dollar signs:

Cost	Hotel	Restaurant
$	$75 and under	$15 and under
$$	$76 to $150	$16 to $25
$$$	$151 to $225	$26 to $40
$$$$	$226 to $300	$41 to $70
$$$$$	$301 and up	$71 and up

For those hotels, restaurants, and attractions that are plotted on a map, we provide a page reference in the listing information. If a hotel, restaurant, or attraction is outside city limits or in an out-of-the-way area, it may not be mapped.

Foolish Assumptions

Maybe this is your first California vacation — or maybe you haven't been to California since you were a kid, or you haven't visited a particular region within the state. Or maybe you don't want to dedicate your life to trip planning, wading through hundreds of dense pages only to feel more confused than confident about your choices. Maybe you don't like the way that so many conventional guidebooks require you to figure out which hotels, destinations, restaurants, and so on the authors actually like and which they're including because they think quantity outweighs quality.

On the other hand, you may be an experienced traveler, but you don't have a lot of time to devote to trip planning or you don't have a lot of time to spend in California after you get there. You want expert advice on how to maximize your time and enjoy a hassle-free trip.

How This Book Is Organized

California For Dummies, 4th Edition, is divided into six parts. The chapters within each part cover specific travel topics or regions in detail. You can read each chapter or part without reading the one that came before it — no need to read about San Francisco if you're heading to Southern California — but we may refer you to other chapters of the book for more information on certain subjects.

Part I: Introducing California

This part introduces you to the best of California and touches on everything you want to consider before actually getting down to the nitty-gritty of trip planning, including:

  ✔ Lively cultural information

  ✔ When to go (and when you may want to stay home)

✔ Tips on planning your itinerary, plus actual time-tested itineraries that you can use as a proven blueprint for your own vacation

Part II: Planning Your Trip to California

This is where we get down to the nuts and bolts of travel planning, including:

✔ How to get to California and how to get around California after you arrive

✔ How much you can expect your trip to cost, with tips on how to save if money is a concern

✔ Special considerations for families, seniors, travelers with disabilities, and gay and lesbian travelers

✔ The advantages of all-inclusive travel packages

✔ Getting ready to go, from the pluses and minuses of buying travel insurance to making advance dinner reservations to what to pack

Parts III, IV, and V: The Destinations

If you think of this book as a meal, these parts constitute the main course. They form the bulk of the book and cover the destinations you want to visit. Each chapter offers all the specific details and recommendations you need for a given destination, including:

✔ When to go

✔ How much time you'll need

✔ How to get there

✔ Where to stay

✔ Where to eat

✔ What to do after you arrive

Part III covers Northern California: the San Francisco Bay Area; Wine Country; the wild North Coast and tall-tree Redwood Country; and the Sierra Nevada mountains, where you'll find spectacular Lake Tahoe and Yosemite National Park.

Part IV covers California's Central Coast, which includes Santa Cruz and such marvelous destinations as the Monterey Peninsula, Big Sur, Hearst Castle, the Santa Ynez Valley, and that gem of the coast, Santa Barbara.

Part V focuses on Southern California, namely Los Angeles, San Diego, the Disneyland Resort, and parts in between. And, if you're the type who never thinks the weather is too hot or too dry, we cover the desert, including Palm Springs.

For a more thorough overview of California, flip to Chapter 3.

Part VI: The Part of Tens

Every *For Dummies* book contains a Part of Tens. If Parts III, IV, and V are the main course of your meal, think of these fun chapters, each its own top-ten list, as dessert. Go to Chapter 28 to find out where you can get down and wacky the way actual Californians do (when we're not writing travel guides). If the folks back home demand a token of your travels, and you're something of a penny-pincher, read Chapter 29 to get the low-down on inexpensive gifts.

Appendix

The Quick Concierge lists many details for easy reference, putting the facts about California at your fingertips, from locating local American Express offices to finding the most accurate online weather forecasts. You can find this appendix easily because it's printed on yellow paper.

Icons Used in This Book

You'll notice the following icons sprinkled throughout the text. Think of them as signposts; we use them to highlight special tips, draw your attention to must-see destinations, and give you a heads-up on a variety of topics.

This icon points out useful advice on things to do, alternate ways to schedule your time, and other tips you won't want to miss.

This icon helps you spot tourist traps rip-offs, time-wasters, and other details to beware.

These attractions, hotels, restaurants, or activities are especially family-friendly.

Check out this icon for money-saving tips or particularly great values.

This icon points out bits of well-guarded insider advice that give you an edge over those who don't know better.

This icon highlights the best that California has to offer — at least in our humble opinion. Look at Chapter 1 for a brief introduction to each of the places and activities in this book that have earned this icon.

Where to Go from Here

As you read through this book and start to formulate your California vacation, remember this: Planning really is half the fun. Don't think of choosing your destination and solidifying the details as a chore. Make the homebound part of the process a voyage of discovery and you'll end up with an entire vacation experience that is much more rewarding and enriching — really. Let your vacation begin right now.

Part I
Introducing California

The 5th Wave   By Rich Tennant

"I think we should arrange to be there for Garlic-Anchovy-Chili Bean Week, and then shoot over to the Breathmint-Antacid Festival."

In this part . . .

This part introduces you to the best of California, offers some basic tips on timing your trip, and suggests some possible itineraries, all so that your California vacation is as spectacular as the state. The chapters in this part offer a cultural introduction to the state — digging deeper into California's storied history and unique culinary traditions — and also discuss the movies and books that best define the California ethos. This part helps you decide where and when to go and offers several itineraries to follow on your trip.

Chapter 1

Discovering the Best of California

. . . .

In This Chapter

▶ Drawing a bead on California's outstanding experiences
▶ Serving up the best of California's hotels and restaurants
▶ Finding the best family destinations
▶ Taking the scenic tour (even guided ones)
▶ Making your way to California's elite museums

. . . .

California is really an awesome place, in the truest sense (not the surfer-dude sense) of the word. Its jaw-dropping diversity is what continues to amaze us (and we're natives, mind you) more than anything else. With two of the nation's largest megalopolises — the San Francisco Bay Area, which has grown beyond speculator's wildest dreams with the rise of Silicon Valley, and metropolitan Los Angeles, whose urban sprawl has a glamorous heart called Hollywood — California has the largest, wealthiest, and most urbanized population of any state in the nation. Yet it's also an agricultural wonderland with a bounty that runs the gamut from artichokes, raisins, garlic, and asparagus to some of the finest wine-making grapes in the world. And it still manages to be home to much of the country's most striking and varied wilderness — from purple mountains' majesty to arid, marvelously barren desert to coastlines of unsurpassed beauty.

Even with all that, California is so much more — much more than we can possibly include here. So we've designed this book to highlight what we consider the best of the best of this awesome state — at least the best of the best of what we think may appeal to you. In this chapter, you get an added bonus: a quick reference to the experiences, hotels, restaurants, and more that stand out as the absolute best. In the destination chapters in Parts III, IV, and V, we discuss the places and experiences noted here (the ones highlighted in bold) in more detail; just look for the Best of the Best icon you see next to this paragraph.

The Best California Travel Experiences

Without taking the easy way out and suggesting that all travel experiences in the Golden State are the best, here are a few prime cuts to consider adding to your California itinerary:

✔ **Strolling along San Francisco's Embarcadero to Aquatic Park:** This is a quintessential San Francisco activity, ideally experienced on a sunny day. We love to begin near the baseball park, although it's more convenient to take public transportation to the end of Market Street and start there. With the water on your right and city landmarks popping up on your left, a leisurely walk past the piers, through Fisherman's Wharf, leads to Aquatic Park and the Municipal Pier. Be sure to hike all the way to the end of the pier, stopping if you will to see what, if anything, the anglers have caught. You'll be rewarded with million-dollar bay vistas and a spot-on view of the beautiful Golden Gate Bridge. See Chapter 11.

✔ **Hiking in Yosemite Valley during the winter:** Snow covers the ground and clings to the tree branches, the air is crisp, the sky is bright blue, and Yosemite Falls roars with snowmelt. With so few visitors in the park during this low season, you'll feel as though you have this wonderland almost to yourself. Take advantage of winter rates and stay at the grand Ahwahnee Hotel. See Chapter 16.

✔ **Biking along the Monterey coastline:** The Monterey Peninsula's 18-mile Recreation Trail was a brilliant piece of civic planning, a useful and beautiful path for all to enjoy. It ends (or starts, if you like) at Seal Rock past Pebble Beach and wends its way along the coast through Monterey north to Marina. The most traveled section is from Custom House Plaza past Cannery Row, the Aquarium, and on to Lover's Point; however, we suggest you carry on to Pacific Grove, stop for lunch, and dawdle on the beach on your way back. If you're more than just a recreational cyclist, you may want to carry on through the 17-Mile Drive. See Chapter 18.

✔ **Sitting on a beach in Southern California:** This activity's not so active, but there has to be a reason for all those Beach Boys songs, right? You could surf, too, and you probably should get your feet wet in the Pacific. But really, it's all about the imagery, the girls, the boys, the sand, the surf, the sun, the palm trees, and did we mention that it's January? See Part V.

✔ **Cruising Sunset Boulevard:** It's the way to best see all that L.A. has to offer in a short amount of time, as you drive this iconic boulevard from its origins at Olvera Street (L.A.'s oldest) through ethnic neighborhoods, bohemian enclaves, dumps and dives, the dregs of Hollywood, the spick-and-span wealth of Beverly Hills, the subdued hush of Bel Air, past scenes of crime and shame (John Belushi and River Phoenix each died within steps of the street, and the infamous O.J. murder case happened blocks away), and catch glimpses of the Hollywood sign and stars on the sidewalk, all the way to the end at the Pacific Ocean. We love L.A., and this drive is one of the reasons why. See Chapter 23.

✓ **Getting within 6 feet of a star:** We can't promise you'll spot any celebrities while in L.A. (keep your eyes peeled), but we can promise you proximity to some of the biggest names of the past . . . by visiting their graves. Forest Lawn, Hollywood Forever, and Westwood Memorial Park are just some of the resting spots of Gable, Monroe, Disney, Valentino, and more. See Chapter 23.

California's Best Hotels

When vacationing in California, swimming is nearly always an option — for the kids and the adults. So if you're looking for the best hotel pools — or the best hotels for a romantic getaway or for a decidedly unromantic stay with the kids — this section is the right place.

Best all-around family hotels

Traveling with the kids? We know from experience that a good kid-friendly hotel can make all the difference between a classically good vacation and a classically bad one. The following are our favorite family-friendly hotels in the state:

✓ The playful **Argonaut Hotel** in San Francisco shares lobby space with the Maritime Museum, and its enviable location next to the Cannery near Fisherman's Wharf means you'll be close to many kid-pleasing attractions. See Chapter 11.

✓ The moderately priced **Hotel del Sol** in San Francisco has a heated outdoor pool, treats for the kids, and a few units with kitchenettes. Plus, the parking is free! See Chapter 11.

✓ Up in Calistoga, the enormous mineral pool at **Indian Springs** is all that your kids need for happiness. The easygoing resortlike atmosphere is relaxing for the grown-ups as well. See Chapter 12.

✓ The new **Treebones Resort** in Big Sur offers an alternative to both hotels and camping by housing guests in gorgeous yurts. Reserve the yurt with the ping-pong table and then try to get the kids outside to hike. See Chapter 19.

✓ **Asilomar Conference Grounds** in Pacific Grove resembles an organized camp with better sleeping accommodations. Find the kids on the beach or playing ping-pong. See Chapter 18.

Best hotels for a romantic weekend

Not traveling with the kids? Ahh, you're in for a treat at these fine destinations for two:

✔ In San Francisco, romantics have a couple of choices. The new **Hotel Vitale** on the Embarcadero has a small spa with two semi-secluded outdoor baths and rooms with knockout views of the bay. If you need to duck the paparazzi, the **St. Regis Hotel** is a self-contained oasis you and your partner won't want to leave. See Chapter 11.

✔ Cocoon at the ultracomfy and chic **Milliken Creek,** convenient to the town of Napa but providing a sense of being somewhere much more glamorous. If you'd rather really be in the relative country of the Sonoma Valley, hide away at the beautiful **Kenwood Inn and Spa,** our pick for honeymooners. See Chapter 12.

✔ Mendocino is a popular romantic getaway. Lots less fancy than Kenwood, but private, relaxed, and well tended, is the village's **Alegria Oceanfront Inn & Cottages.** The beach access and excellent breakfast make it extra nice. If you're seeking a Mendo retreat with all the extras, wonderful **Stanford Inn by the Sea** has more comforts than you'll find at home, plus on-site spa services and a very good vegetarian restaurant. See Chapter 13.

✔ Our northernmost pick is Ferndale's **Gingerbread Mansion Inn.** We've never seen anything quite like the over-the-top Romanesque (as in Caesar) Empire Suite. See Chapter 14.

✔ For pure pampering and four-star dining, **Château du Sureau** in Oakhurst will not disappoint, plus you'll be close enough to Yosemite to enjoy a day in the park. See Chapter 16.

✔ There's nothing like endless ocean views to stir the senses and you'll find them, as well as a splendid breakfast and unobtrusive service, in Monterey/Pacific Grove at the **Grand View** and **Seven Gables** inns. See Chapter 18.

✔ It's tough to choose between Big Sur's **Post Ranch Inn** and **Ventana Inn & Spa** — both are splendid examples of luxury properties. Post Ranch is smaller and has the ocean view; Ventana is friendlier. See Chapter 19.

✔ Santa Barbara's **Four Seasons Biltmore** is right on the beach and is a divine old (built in 1927) hotel run by the most pampering of hoteliers in the country. See Chapter 22.

✔ When in L.A., consider the **Chateau Marmont,** where the Art Deco and Beaux Arts castle-style main building and individual bungalows remind us of the noir days of Los Angeles, where a rendezvous in a dark corner seems like a very good thing indeed. See Chapter 23.

✔ La Jolla's **Lodge at Torrey Pines** is a dreamy, breathtaking five-diamond resort full of Craftsman furniture and luxe touches; however, as a resort, it may be a bit more bustling than you want. See Chapter 27.

Best hotel pools

Just when you thought a hotel pool is a hotel pool is a hotel pool, along
come these two heavenly respites:

- ✔ Children under 16 aren't actually allowed in the spa at the
  Huntington in San Francisco, so the lovely, large pool, which
  reflects an eastward view of downtown, is the purview of the
  grown-ups. If we had a category for best hotel spa, the Huntington
  would get the nod there as well, although the St. Regis spa is magnificent, too. See Chapter 11.

- ✔ Many Wine Country lodgings have pools, but none as inviting as
  the Olympic-sized mineral pool at **Indian Springs** in Calistoga. The
  view from the deck chairs is awesome as well. See Chapter 12.

California's Best Restaurants

Eating out in California is not quite a competitive sport — but almost. In
this section, check out some of the state's most innovative and most
inexpensive — and many others in between.

Best to impress

Expect no surprises when looking for the meal to die for (or the restaurant to be seen). The Bay Area and L.A. offer the cream of the crop of
California's trendiest restaurants. However, you can find a gem or two in
other parts of the state.

- ✔ In San Francisco, **Gary Danko** runs a smooth operation from the
  kitchen to the front of the house. His prix-fixe menu is unusual in
  that guests do the choosing and it's impossible to make a mistake.
  See Chapter 11.

- ✔ Serious foodies regard the **French Laundry** in the Napa Valley
  village of Yountville as the Holy Grail of Gourmetdom; the problem
  is actually getting a reservation. Of course, if it were easy to get
  into, it would lose some cachet. See Chapter 12 for info on making
  an attempt.

- ✔ If you're near Santa Cruz around dinnertime, try booking a table at
  the tiny **Oswald.** It does everything right, but quietly, which means
  you may not have heard of the place. Take our word for it — the
  food is worth a detour. See Chapter 17.

- ✔ You could get into some serious arguments with Los Angeles food
  critics, daring them to choose between their beloved **Campanile,**
  where owner Mark Peel has long demonstrated his gift with seasonal cooking; **Patina,** which spawned a restaurant empire, and

now in its new Disney Hall–adjacent space, regularly thrills diners; and the new **Providence,** whose French-influenced seafood earned a James Beard nomination for Best New Restaurant, and may be the finest dining option in Los Angeles. See Chapter 23.

Best for families with picky eaters

We don't propose you let anyone starve (although that thought has crossed our minds on occasion); on the other hand, no one ought to be a hostage to chicken fingers in the bountiful state of California. The restaurants in this list should satisfy the dining wish list of everyone in your traveling party:

✔ In San Francisco, there's something good for everyone on the menu at **Chow,** which has two locations — one in the Castro district and one near Golden Gate Park.

Another brilliant suggestion in the Bay Area (if we do say so ourselves) is to let everyone graze to his own taste around the **Ferry Building** on the Embarcadero where Market Street ends. Seafoodies can wait for a stool at the Hog Island Oyster Bar, while those in the mood for Japanese can pick up a bento box at Delica rf-1. The kids (and probably you, too) will gleefully join the lines at Taylor's Refresher, a two-restaurant chain that redefines fast food for health-conscious Northern Californians. See Chapter 11.

✔ In Monterey, **Rosine's** is kind of what a Denny's ought to have aspired to: a plain, let's-please-the-mainstream menu, but with mom in the kitchen and better desserts. See Chapter 18.

✔ L.A. has many options for fussy eaters. The **101 Coffeeshop** (in the Best Western Hollywood Hills Hotel) has serious grown-up food alongside one of the best burgers in the area. The **Farmers Market** features a number of food stalls and restaurants around a central food court area, so there is something for every taste — diner food or homemade pies, doughnuts or Chinese food, deli or Greek, and more. **Angeli Café** will make a simple pasta for your young diners, as well as give them a ball of dough to mash and mold before baking the creation as a take-home souvenir, all while you dine on the cafe's seasonal Italian delights. See Chapter 23.

Best for a lovely, but reasonably priced dinner

Not in the market for a meal to die for? You can dine just as nicely (and also trendily) at any of the following establishments:

✔ **Isa** is one of two San Francisco restaurants we recommend in this category. It serves absolutely delicious meals in a friendly, casual, but professional little place in the Marina. We also adore the more intimate **Tablespoon** on Russian Hill. See Chapter 11.

✔ In the Wine Country, **Angèle** in Napa is run by second-generation restaurateurs and it shows, from the warm design of the lodgelike interior to the carefully crafted menu. Our hands-down favorite in Sonoma is **Café La Haye.** If an eatery can be described as having clarity of purpose, this is it. See Chapter 12.

✔ Adorable Pacific Grove is preferable to Monterey, in our opinion, for dining, and we especially recommend **Passionfish.** The menu has a light Southeast-Asian bent and this is a calm place in which to enjoy excellent food. See Chapter 18.

✔ Santa Barbara's **Sage & Onion** is a little gem with some of the cleverest cooking in Southern California. See Chapter 22.

✔ **Angelini Osteria** in Los Angeles has remarkably authentic Italian food, lovingly and passionately prepared. See Chapter 23.

Best dining with views

Good food and a view don't usually mix; our theory is that, when you're facing a great view, the kitchen figures no one is really concentrating on the meal, but that's not fair, now, is it?

✔ One of San Francisco's most celebrated restaurants, the **Slanted Door,** recently moved to the new Ferry Building, so now you can chow down on stellar Vietnamese and look at Alcatraz while enjoying both. See Chapter 11.

✔ The **Ravens Restaurant** at the Stanford Inn by the Sea in Mendocino overlooks both the gorgeous property and the ocean in the distance. The vegetarian menu will convince even the toughest carnivore that green things are good. See Chapter 13.

✔ The food is just okay at **Nepenthe,** but this is the view to sigh for in Big Sur. For great food and views, splash out at **Cielo** in the Ventana Inn. See Chapter 19.

Best local traditions

Join the local residents and sample a meal at these time-tested eateries, and you'll discover how these establishments came to be so, er, well established:

✔ It's hard to find a single native who, when discussing food in Santa Barbara, won't bring up **La Super-Rica Taqueria.** It's just a taco shack, but one with lines out the door just about any time of day. There's a reason why. See Chapter 22.

✔ "Just" a French-dip sandwich doesn't explain why locals have kept **Philippe's** in Los Angeles open since they created said sandwich in 1918. Join the crowds and become a regular yourself. See Chapter 23.

Best inexpensive meals

Los Angeles's real claim to culinary fame isn't so much brand-name chefs, though it does boast more than a few. In our opinion, where other cities can't compete is with the heavenly and often-shockingly cheap fare found at nondescript hole-in-the-wall restaurants. And, after all, eating a variety of cuisines is a way to pay homage to the melting pot that is California. You won't have time in a short trip to do some serious, daring poking around, so we direct you to two of our standout favorites: **Sanamluang Café,** where you can dine for weeks on a massive Thai menu, and **Zankou Chicken** (with three locations), where the perfect roast chicken would be good enough, but when they add their special garlic paste, it's lifted into perfection. See Chapter 23.

The Best Family Excursions

Assuming you and your family will be unable to schedule several weeks covering the whole of the Golden State, we've highlighted a few can't-miss family destinations for whichever part of the state you target:

✔ We wouldn't have believed it if we hadn't experienced it for our-selves, but taking the ferry to **Alcatraz Island,** trooping up the hill, pulling on the headset for the audio tour, and staring at prison cells turns out to be fascinating. And we did it with a couple of teenage girls. Alcatraz may be one of the biggest tourist attractions in Northern California, but it's actually worth the price of admission. See Chapter 11.

✔ **Humboldt Redwoods State Park** is ideal if you're an outdoorsy type, and a hike amongst the giants is a memorable experience. During the summer, stop by the visitor center for information on ranger-led nature walks and the Junior Ranger's program for kids 7 to 12. See Chapter 14.

✔ The **Santa Cruz Beach Boardwalk,** a cartoon-character-free zone, may not have the glitz or polish of pristine Disneyland, but its manageable size, beachside location, and old-fashioned ambience hearken back to amusement parks such as New York's Coney Island. Bay Area teens flock here in the summer along with vaca-tioning families; we recall bringing the kids when they were still too short to qualify for the more daring rides. Be sure to buy a bag of saltwater taffy, because you can't find that stuff just anywhere. See Chapter 17.

✔ The **Monterey Bay Aquarium** is no glorified fish hostel; few aquar-iums come anywhere close in grandeur to this spectacular com-pound. Stand at the window into the Outer Bay exhibit for a while and we bet you'll agree this is one of the few "educational" stops on a tour of Northern California that probably ought to be mandatory. See Chapter 18.

✔ The original — and still the champion — **Disneyland Resort** remains the must-see family destination in California. It's expensive; it can be crowded and hot; it's magic. Really, did you think there was any way we weren't going to recommend this for children? Actually, there is: if your kids are under the age of 6, do take into consideration any fears or phobias they may have. For example, if your kids are anxious in dark places, many of the rides — even those geared toward the very young — start off in the dark. It would be a shame to spend that much money, time, and effort just to ride the merry-go-round a bunch. See Chapter 24.

✔ Speaking of merry-go-rounds, you can find an all-wood one from the 1920s on the **Santa Monica Pier,** along with other carnival rides, shops, and food stalls. A sweet little excursion right on the edge of not-so-sweet Los Angeles. See Chapter 23.

✔ A couple of L.A. museums may be just the ticket for your kids. If you're the sort of parent who wants an educated holiday, try the **California ScienCenter,** which has all sorts of hands-on interactive displays and, as of this writing, actual human bodies preserved in plastic. Yuck! But we bet kids will remember they saw it, long after they've forgotten about the Grand Canyon. Or if you really want your kids to love you, let them watch TV on their vacation, but do so at the **Museum of Television & Radio,** where an extraordinary number of hours of classic TV, from sitcoms to Moon landings to Olympic moments, are available for viewing on monitors. See Chapter 23.

✔ Kids and zoos go together, and though we're partial to the sometimes overlooked, but still worthy Los Angeles Zoo (see Chapter 23), the **San Diego Zoo** (see Chapter 27) gets a lot of headlines for a reason. One operation is slick and sharp, the other perhaps not so much, but honestly, we don't see enough of a difference to justify the disparity in ticket prices. Pick whichever one you're closest to geographically. But remember that animals are smart, and that's why, when it's hot, they snooze in the shade. If you want to see more than slumber be sure to go early or late or on a generally cool or overcast day.

The Best Scenic Drives

Beauty may be in the eye of the beholder, but California offers so much to behold that we think it's essential to plan for at least one day of just driving. These scenic drives promise the best views, stopovers, and distractions that very quickly fill up that one day of just driving:

✔ **Best in Northern California:** If you're in San Francisco with plans to head south, rent a car the day you're leaving. Say farewell to the city by driving west on **Geary Boulevard** all the way out to the ocean where you'll turn left onto the **Great Highway.** This road leads along the water to the tiny village of Pacifica and to **Highway 1.** Traffic can be dense on weekends, but there's no lovelier way to reach Santa Cruz or points farther south. After you pass the town of Napa, the drive along **Highway 29** up to and past Calistoga is so pretty you'll want to draw straws to determine who gets the passenger seat. Although the drive to Mendocino gets enthusiastic raves from people who love car trips, the 32-mile tour along the **Avenue of the Giants** is easier on folks who get carsick, because the road is comparatively less curvy.

✔ **Best on the Central Coast:** Paying to drive through some of the more expensive real estate in the country may seem counterintuitive, but the fact is, the **17-Mile Drive** through Pebble Beach is a worthy attraction (despite the price of gasoline). We can't ever get enough of the splendid coast however, and the always-toll-free **Highway 1** between Point Lobos State Reserve (just south of Carmel) and San Simeon is on the top-ten list of excitingly gorgeous drives.

✔ **Best in Southern California:** The **Pacific Coast Highway** (Highway 1) runs along some of the most spectacular coastal scenery in the country. Pretty much anywhere is good, from the start at San Juan Capistrano all the way up through San Luis Obispo, although it varies: The stretch alongside Los Angeles County is somewhat developed, but after you get past Malibu and on your way up to (and past) Santa Barbara, you're rewarded with rocky cliffs tumbling into the ocean. The stretch of 19 miles in Santa Barbara County is one of the finest, and while continuing north into Central Coast Wine Country adds green vineyards into the scenic mix, that is technically no longer Southern California.

The Best Museums

You can find some nice little museums in California cities outside of the Bay Area and L.A. — and we introduce you to some of them in the destinations chapters in this book. But for hardcore museum-philes, to the big cities you go.

✔ **Best with kids:** Try San Francisco. The **Exploratorium** benefits from being educational but not boring — all the exhibits are hands-on and there are plenty of them. Science-minded scions will settle in happily for hours. Artsy teens may be intrigued by the **Cartoon Art Museum,** not far from the Sony Metreon. See Chapter 11.

✔ **Best for contemporary-art lovers:** San Francisco's **Museum of Modern Art** (see Chapter 11) is our kind of gallery; the art is well curated, the building is beautiful, the cafe has really good food, and the gift shop is tops. But Los Angeles's two-part **Museum of Contemporary Art/MOCA at the Geffen Contemporary** (see Chapter 23) has significant exhibits, from Lucien Freud retrospectives to a recent Minimal Art exhibit that was featured in *Time* magazine to fantastic permanent collections.

✔ **Best encyclopedic museum oth**e**r than the Met in NYC:** The **Los Angeles County Museum of Ar**t has something for everyone: old masters, young modern artists, antiquities from across the globe and through the centuries, some of the finest collections of Asian art anywhere, and the list goes on. The building is no great shakes, but it's oddly and undeservedly uncrowded much of the time. See Chapter 23.

✔ **Best museum with a message:** The **Museum of Tolerance** in Beverly Hills may be more Holocaust-centric than one would like (only because the tragic consequences of intolerance manifest in many different times and places), but its message is universal, now in these perilous times more than ever. See Chapter 23.

✔ **Best-looking museum:** Listing the very wealthy and powerful **Getty Museum** this way is probably odd, but we know the truth: The collection is boring, but the setting, way up in the hills over West Los Angeles, with views out to the sea, and in a very modern urban space, is anything but. It's worth it just to come here for a snack, and because it's free (albeit with a $7 parking fee), not at all a risk. The newly reopened **Getty Villa,** with an emphasis on Roman and Greek antiquities, styled as a classical Roman villa and set on a Malibu cliffside, is a near-perfect combination of structure and collection. See Chapter 23.

The Best Guided Tours

We generally are reluctant to heartily recommend guided tours — armed with this book and your own intimate knowledge of your personal interests, you're likely to do just about as well as any tour guide. However, we do make some exceptions for the following:

✔ **Best for food and wine lovers:** In San Francisco, we suggest either **Wok Wiz Chinatown Tour** or **Mangia! North Beach** (see Chapter 11). Though expensive, both are scads of fun and offer an opportunity to meet some local characters while walking around the city's more fascinating neighborhoods. In Napa, let the boys from the **Napa Winery Shuttle** (see Chapter 12) show you their favorite wineries, or they can customize a daylong itinerary.

✔ **Best for architecture buffs:** The major sights of Los Angeles are easy to do on your own, but if you want to see the hidden charms of this city, we highly recommend **Architecture Tours L.A.** The owner does two-hour tours of the overviews and highlights of various L.A. neighborhoods (and she can customize for you), from Greene and Greene beauties to the groundbreaking work of Neutra and Schindler.

Chapter 2

Digging Deeper into California

In This Chapter
▶ Having a glance at California's historical roots
▶ Ordering off California's multicultural culinary menu
▶ Taking in the film industry — with its cast of thousands

The smug East Coast believes it has a monopoly on U.S. history, as if California had a gold rush and little else until it sprung, fully formed, from the forehead of the film industry in the 1910s. That's rank arrogance. California's history goes back thousands of years; Native Americans enjoyed it from the mountains to the sea well before the Europeans showed up in the mid–16th century (yes, that's right; about the same time they were settling the East Coast). Of course, this being California, where people have come for centuries to reinvent themselves, hardly anything remains pre-1700-something (much less thousands of years back), although there are some very nice parking lots.

In any event, this chapter invites you to understand a little more about the state's historical and cultural legacy.

History 101

Portuguese explorer Juan Rodrígues Cabrillo is credited with being the first European to "discover" (in 1542) California, beginning the process of newcomers wrecking the state for the natives (a complaint that remains today, although the self-proclaimed "natives" are people whose residency ranges from a couple of years to two whole generations). Over the next 200 years, dozens of sailors mapped the coast, including British explorer Sir Francis Drake, who sailed his *Golden Hind* into what is now called Drake's Bay in 1579, and Spanish explorer Sebastian Vizcano, who, in 1602, bestowed most of the place names that survive today, including San Diego, Santa Barbara, and Carmel.

European colonial competition and Catholic missionary zeal prompted Spain to establish settlements along the Alta (upper) California coast and claim the lands as its own. In 1769, teeny (5-foot-nothing) Father Junípero Serra, accompanied by 300 soldiers and clergy, began forging a path from Mexico to Monterey. A small mission and presidio (fort) were established that year at San Diego, and by 1804, a chain of 21 missions, each a day's walk from the next along a dirt road called *Camino Real* (Royal Road), stretched all the way to Sonoma. Most of the solidly built missions — Mission Delores, Mission San Juan Bautista, Mission San Diego de Alcala, to name just a few — still remain and offer public tours.

The missions are pretty and pious, but their existence resulted in the usual story: Thousands of Native Americans were converted to Christianity and coerced into labor. Many others died from imported diseases. Because not all the natives welcomed their conquerors with open arms, many missions and pueblos (small towns) suffered repeated attacks, leading to the construction of California's now ubiquitous — and fireproof — red-tile roofs.

Embattled at home as well as abroad, the Spanish relinquished their claim to Mexico and California in 1821. Under Mexican rule, Alta California's Spanish missionaries fell out of favor and lost much of their land to the increasingly wealthy *Californios* — Mexican immigrants who had been granted tracts of land.

Beginning in the late 1820s, Americans from the East began to make their way to California via a three-month sail around Cape Horn. Most of them settled in the territorial capital of Monterey and in Northern California.

From the 1830s on, Manifest Destiny led many a pioneer to go west, young man — and woman. The first covered-wagon train made the four-month crossing in 1844. Over the next few years, several hundred Americans made the trek to California over the Sierra Nevada range via Truckee Pass, just north of Lake Tahoe. A memorial to the Donner Party — the most famous tragedy in the history of westward migration, and the subject of many a culinary joke we won't repeat — marks the site of the ill-fated travelers.

In 1846, President James Polk offered Mexico $40 million for California and New Mexico, a sum that will barely get you a shack on the beach in Malibu today. The offer might have been accepted, but the two countries got too busy fighting over Texas, instead. The United States won and simply took over the entire West Coast. (This chain of events throws an interesting light on the attitudes toward Mexican immigrants today.)

In 1848, California's non–Native American population was around 7,000. But then gold was discovered in them thar hills — well, flakes at a sawmill along the American River, anyway. Faster than you can say "Eureka, California!" 300,000 men and women rushed into the state between 1849 and 1851, one of the largest mass migrations in U.S. history. Very few of them found any actual gold, foreshadowing similar migrations trying to hit it big in the movie industry.

In 1850, California was admitted to the Union as the 31st state. The state constitution on which California applied for admission included several noteworthy features that set up California as the progressive (to some, flaky and overly liberal) place it remains. To protect the miners, slavery was prohibited. To attract women from the East Coast, legal recognition was given to the separate property of a married woman (California was the first state to offer such recognition).

Not-so-progressively, by 1870, almost 90 percent of the state's Native American population had been wiped out, and the bulk of the rest were removed to inland reservations.

In 1875, when the Santa Fe Railroad reached Los Angeles, Southern California's population of just 10,000 was divided equally between Los Angeles and San Diego. As San Francisco, around the tenth-largest city in the United States, suffered a serious setback in the form of the infamous 1906 earthquake and subsequent devastating fire (it rallied fast and strong enough to host the 1915 Panama Pacific Exposition), Los Angeles got its own growth spurt, and identity, thanks to the nascent movie industry realizing that in places where it doesn't snow, you can film out-doors year-round. The movies' glamorous, idyllic portrayal of California boosted the region's popularity and population, especially during the Great Depression of the 1930s, when thousands of families (like the Joads in John Steinbeck's novel *The Grapes of Wrath*) packed up their belongings and headed west in search of a better life.

World War II brought heavy industry to California, in the form of muni-tions factories, shipyards, and airplane manufacturing. In the 1950s, California in general, and San Francisco in particular, became popular with artists and intellectuals. The so-called Beat Generation appeared, which later inspired alternative-culture groups — most notably the flower children of the 1960s — in San Francisco's Haight-Ashbury district. During the Summer of Love in 1967, as the war in Vietnam escalated, stu-dent protests increased at Berkeley and elsewhere in California, as they did across the country. A year later, amid rising racial tensions, Martin Luther King, Jr., was killed, setting off riots in the Watts section of Los Angeles and in other cities. Soon thereafter, Robert F. Kennedy was fatally shot in Los Angeles after winning the California Democratic Party presi-dential primary. Antiwar protests continued into the 1970s.

Perhaps in response to an increasingly violent society, the 1970s also gave rise to several exotic religions and cults, which found eager adher-ents in California. The spiritual New Age continued into the 1980s, along with a growing population, environmental pollution, and escalating social ills, especially in Los Angeles. Real-estate values soared, the com-puter industry — centered in Silicon Valley, south of San Francisco — boomed, and banks and businesses prospered.

The late 1980s and early 1990s, however, brought a devastating reces-sion to the state. Los Angeles stayed perpetually in the news, thanks to grave issues such as the race riots spurred by a videotaping and subsequent acquittal of four white police officers beating black motorist Rodney King, along with ultimately trivial if captivating ones like the O.J. Simpson murder case and other celebrity peccadilloes. Two years later, a major earthquake caused billions of dollars in damage to L.A. and left thousands injured and homeless, while Oakland's hills became a raging inferno, killing 26 people and destroying 3,000 homes.

Midway through the 1990s, the U.S. economy slowly began to improve, a welcome relief to recession-battered Californians. Crime and unemployment began to drop, while public schools received millions for much-needed improvements. Computer- and Internet-related industries flourished in the Bay Area, with entrepreneurialism fueling much of the growth. As the stock market continued its record-setting pace, no state reaped more benefits than California, which was gaining new millionaires by the day. At the millennium, optimism in the state's economy and quality of life was at an all-time high.

At the turn of the century, the economy was still strong, the unemployment rate still low, and property rates still rising. Then came some out-of-the-blue sucker punches to California's rosy economy, including the rapid demise of many, if not most, of the dot-coms in the stock-market slump and an energy deregulation scheme gone awry, leaving irate residents with periodic rolling blackouts and escalating energy bills. The terrorist attacks of September 11, 2001, and the following national trauma and economic downturn hit California hard.

And just when things seemed to be getting back to normal, along came the 2003 recall effort to oust Governor Gray Davis, launching California politics into the national news limelight as Arnold "The Terminator" Schwarzenegger unseated the unpopular politician. Not to be outdone, the following year San Francisco elected a 36-year-old supervisor, Gavin Newsom, as mayor. He quickly made national headlines by authorizing city hall to issue marriage licenses to same-sex couples. He even performed a few of the unions. Six months later, the state supreme court invalidated 3,955 gay marriages. California: It's like that. It may be many things, but boring is never one of them.

A Bite of California's Culinary Past and Present

What are the factors that make California such a delightful place to dine (and grocery shop)? Location, location, location. No other state in the union cultivates like the Golden State; in fact, California's farmers produce over half the country's fruit and vegetables on just a measly 3 percent of its farmland. Almonds, olives, lemons, artichokes, all kinds of cruciferous and cabbagey vegetables, figs, dates, and truckloads of grapes and tomatoes are just some of the commercially produced goodies that thrive in the state's mellow Mediterranean climate.

But California's cuisine is greater than the sum of its parts. Along with a rich pantry, immigration has affected what and how Californians and its visitors eat. In Northern California, the Gold Rush attracted an enormous number of Chinese from Canton Province, who stayed to work on the railroad and eventually settled into Chinatowns throughout the state. Chinese eateries opened to feed the largely male population, but by the 1920s, adventuresome Anglos found it fashionable to give Chinese food a try, and soon you could sample chop suey in every city, big or small.

In Southern California, Latino immigrants brought their influence to bear, introducing unfamiliar spices and changing the tastes of a population to such an extent that fast food today means tacos and burritos as much as hamburgers and fries. Los Angeles, in fact, can make its strongest claim to culinary fame (beyond the first and still champion celebrity chef, the highly influential Wolfgang Puck of iconic **Spago** in Beverly Hills) courtesy of its many hole-in-the-wall ethnic restaurants. Reflecting the dozens (if not hundreds) of cultures that have settled in the area, the curious can nosh on Armenian, Nicaraguan, Oaxacan, Ethiopian, Issan Thai, Romanian, Hungarian, and more — a veritable United Nations of dining experiences, and many of them within just a few blocks of each other. And that's not even discussing California rolls, which regrettably (in the minds of some purists) forever changed sushi-eating from a meditative consideration on a choice slice of fish to a circus stunt wrapped in seaweed. And Nancy Silverton's **La Brea Bakery,** originally just a local bread shop, seems to have survived the low-carb phase just fine, bringing the gospel of artisanal bread to restaurants and supermarkets across the country.

Perhaps the greatest modern influence on how tuned-in Californians eat can be traced to food gurus such as Alice Waters. Her restaurant, Berkeley-based **Chez Panisse,** began as an outgrowth of Waters's desire to feed her friends and became a philosophical training ground for many of today's important chefs. Like French cooks — and Waters was profoundly changed by a year living in Paris — she is interested not in the quantity or cost of ingredients, but strictly in quality and freshness.

In Berkeley, Waters created an infrastructure in which her restaurant is dependent on a cadre of small farmers, and vice versa. It wasn't enough, however, to provide customers with the tastiest heirloom tomatoes and organic baby lettuces: the breads must be as delicious and fresh; the meats must be sourced from trusted ranchers; the cheese should complement the fruits and come from local producers as well.

So along with a generation of restaurateurs, Chez Panisse inspired such robust local-artisan producers as Acme Bread and Cowgirl Creamery. California cuisine — which is really about showcasing the flavors of locally grown, seasonal bounty at its peak — has spread throughout and beyond California, thanks to Waters and to the chefs who have made her vision their own.

California on the Page and the Screen

The beauty and metaphor that is California (Gold Rush; Land of Opportunity; Go West, Young Man; Silver Screen — the list goes on) has inspired far too many authors and moviemakers to list in any comprehensive way. But we give you a taste in the sections that follow.

Reading up on California

Quantifying art is odious, but we have to say the greatest California novels were written by John Steinbeck. Oh, c'mon, the man won the Nobel Prize for Literature — that has to count for something. Start with **The Grapes of Wrath,** as the Joad family flees the defeat of Dust Bowl Oklahoma only to find bitter disillusionment in the not-so-Golden State. Then visit with his oddly happy crew of lowlifes who hang around Monterey Bay's **Cannery Row.**

Upton Sinclair didn't get a Nobel Prize (despite the efforts of his admirer, George Bernard Shaw), but his **Oil!** is considered the great novel of 1920s Southern California. Hollywood Noir simply wouldn't be the same without Philip Marlowe, the private-eye protagonist of Raymond Chandler's detective novels such as **The Big Sleep.** His Northern California counterpart Dashiell Hammett brought the world Sam Spade in **The Maltese Falcon** (Spade worked in San Francisco). What does it say about the state when its most famous romantic figures are troubled loners?

Anyone wanting to try his luck in Hollywood should be required to read Nathaniel West's **Day of the Locusts** (because it rips the glitter off Tinseltown and shows the savagery beneath) and Bud Shulberg's **What Makes Sammy Run?** (featuring everyone's favorite amoral, desperate agent Sammy Glick, role model for too many ambitious, if not particularly self-aware, Young Turks). Following in these footsteps is Michael Tolkein's **The Player,** equally unsentimental about This Town and The Industry, to say the least. (At least Sammy Glick never killed anyone — that we know of.) If you ask him, however, Tolkein would say the best novel about Los Angeles is John Fante's 1939 **Ask The Dust,** wherein yet another young writer gets his hopes and dreams crushed.

And while we are recommending downer (if brilliant) books, follow Los Angeles's turbulent history and speculate on its future via Mark Davis's **City of Quartz.** Relive some of the state's most infamous (and brutal) moments with Vincent Bugliosi's **Helter Skelter** (the best version of the Manson murders and the book most responsible for childhood nightmares among a generation), or one of the many books about San Francisco's Zodiac Killer, L.A.'s Hillside Strangler, and, of course, O.J.

One of the more famous and beloved pieces of modern fiction based in San Francisco is Armistead Maupin's **Tales of the City.** If you've seen the miniseries, and especially if you haven't, this is a must read for a leisurely afternoon — Maupin is a Dickens for his time. His 1970s soap opera covers the residents of 28 Barbary Lane (Macondry Lane on

Russian Hill was the inspiration), melding sex, drugs, and growing self-awareness with enormous warmth and humor. A work of fiction featuring San Francisco during the Gold Rush is *Daughter of Fortune* by acclaimed novelist and Marin resident Isabel Allende. The tale begins in Chile and follows the life of Eliza, an orphan adopted by a proper English spinster and her brother. In love with a boy who has sailed for the gold fields, a pregnant Eliza runs away from home to search for the lad and is befriended by a Chinese doctor. Allende's vivid depiction of life in California during the mid–19th century is one of the novel's strengths.

Going to the California picture show

Perhaps we should turn to movies to lighten things up. San Francisco and Northern California, landscape and residents both, are God's gift to filmmakers.

✔ The film version of *The Grapes of Wrath* (1940). The John Ford–directed, Academy Award–winning film of dispossessed Okie Dust Bowl farmers who migrate west to the promised land — California — wins a spot on this list not for its tremendous footage of the Golden State, but because it beautifully evokes California's agrarian story.

✔ *Vertigo* (1958) is the work of possibly the greatest movie director of all time, Alfred Hitchcock, who always used locations well — remember Mount Rushmore in *North by Northwest?* In *Vertigo,* the suspense master uses San Francisco to dizzying effect (pun intended).

✔ *Monterey Pop* (1969), D.A. Pennebaker's first-rate rockumentary, chronicles the glorious three-day music festival that was actually a better realization of the Summer of Love dream than Woodstock ever hoped to be. The film wonderfully captures '60s' San Francisco's Haight-Ashbury vibe and the California sound, including groups such as the Mamas and the Papas (whose leader, the late John Phillips, was the brains behind the event), Jefferson Airplane, Janis Joplin with Big Brother and the Holding Company, Jimi Hendrix, Canned Heat, The Who, and others, including a stunning performance by Otis Redding.

✔ With *Play Misty for Me* (1971), Clint Eastwood made his directorial debut, a winningly creepy thriller costarring Jessica Walter (and Donna Mills, of quintessentially Californian *Knots Landing* fame). Young, studly Clint looks mighty fine, but the real star of the show is stunning Carmel, which Clint films with a genuine hometown love and a master's eye. (You may remember that Eastwood was elected mayor of Carmel-by-the-Sea in 1986; he still owns the Mission Ranch, an elegant country inn, and resides in town.) Watch for the great footage of Big Sur's Bixby Bridge.

✔ *What's Up, Doc?* (1972) is a Peter Bogdanovich–directed, Buck Henry–scribed gem starring Barbra Streisand and Ryan O'Neal that shows off the hilly streets of San Francisco — especially Chinatown — at their most colorful and romantic.

Of course, the film industry in Southern California has spent some time concentrating on itself as well, as in the following gems:

✔ A more light-hearted view of California comes from *Gidget* (1965). Perky Sally Field is the ultimate California beach girl in the ultimate California beach movie. This innocent romp is really a joy to watch — far superior to the Frankie Avalon/Annette Funicello beach movies — with excellent footage of Malibu Beach and Pacific Coast Highway (cruisin' with the top down, of course).

✔ Staying South, *Chinatown* (1974) is possibly the finest noir ever committed to film, using L.A. in the '70s to re-create L.A. in the '30s impeccably. Not only did director Roman Polanski (pre-exile) capture the City of Angels masterfully, but writer Robert Towne worked in an essential slice of city history: the dirty dealing and power grabbing of water rights that allowed — for better or worse — the infant desert city to blossom into the sprawling metropolis you see today. And, of course, this true classic features Jack Nicholson as the hard-boiled detective embroiled with femme fatale Faye Dunaway, plus legendary Hollywood heavyweight John Huston as the evil genius behind the Chandleresque web of intrigue. Its modern-day noir and crime successor is the Oscar winning *L.A. Confidential* (1997).

✔ *Valley Girl* (1983), starring a teenage Nicolas Cage, is an underdog in a teen genre that includes *Fast Times at Ridgemont High* and *Clueless,* but it comes out a winner because of its New-Wave-Boy-meets-mall-lovin'-Valley-Girl love story at the height of Valley Girl mania.

✔ *The Big Picture* (1989) is director Christopher Guest's first feature, a dead-on and deadly satire of the movie industry, filmed presumably on a shoestring around Hollywood and just outside in the desert. It's hilarious — we watch it once a year just to laugh ourselves silly, and wince over how recognizable it all is — and we don't just mean the locations.

✔ Steve Martin's *L.A. Story* (1991) is a romantic look at everything that's wonderfully silly about life in contemporary Tinseltown.

✔ *The Player* (1992) all-too-realistically captures the seedy underbelly and soul-selling seductive power of Hollywood influence and celebrity. Everybody who's anybody in the movie industry knows how scarily close to home Tim Robbins's portrayal of beleaguered studio exec Griffin Mill hits.

✔ Finally, check out any movie with "Beverly Hills" in the title *(Slums of Beverly Hills, Down and Out in Beverly Hills, Beverly Hills Cop . . .).*

Chapter 3

Deciding Where and When to Go

California isn't like any state in the Union. In fact, it's hardly like a state at all. Even national politicians tend to refer to the 31st state as "the nation of California" — a sovereign country all its own, an immense and diverse dominion to be conquered above and beyond the other 49 states.

Their outsize view isn't far from the truth. With nearly 159,000 square miles of land and a 1,264-mile coastline, California is the third largest state in the United States. Sure, both Alaska and Texas are bigger — but California's uniqueness stems from much more than size. California is like the high-school homecoming queen whose natural beauty and innate poise make the rest of the student body sneer at her while wanting to bask in her glow at the very same time. They don't call this the Golden State for nothing, after all.

Within the natural landscape alone, the contrast is unparalleled. Take Mount Whitney and Death Valley as a case in point: At 14,494 feet above and 282 feet below sea level, respectively, they are the highest and lowest points in the continental United States — and just 85 miles separates them. Wow.

Going Everywhere You Want to Be

Unless you have a couple of months to spare for vacation (lucky you!), you're not going to see everything this marvelous, multifaceted state has to offer. You know what? Don't even waste time trying. Frankly, some parts of California are much worthier of your valuable time and hard-earned money than others.

The destinations in this chapter (shown on the inside front cover of this book) comprise the best of California. You discover more about them throughout this book as you plan your trip.

The San Francisco Bay Area

The metropolitan San Francisco Bay Area grew by leaps and bounds with the Silicon Valley revolution; even with the dot-com bust, the city and environs have remained coveted real estate. The prime draw, however, is still the loveliest and most beguiling city in America, **San Francisco** (see Chapter 11). "The city" (as locals call it — never, ever "Frisco") is smaller than you may expect, loaded with personality in all corners, and pleasant to visit year-round. It's also the one destination in the Driving State where you can easily get around without a car.

If San Francisco is the ultimate urban destination, then the gorgeous **Wine Country** of Napa and Sonoma counties — America's premier wine-growing region (see Chapter 12) — is the embodiment of pastoral escape. These superfertile valleys brim with world-class wine-tasting rooms and some of the country's finest restaurants and inns.

The North Coast

The wild and woolly coastal region north of the San Francisco Bay Area (see Part III) offers some of California's most breathtaking scenery. It's quiet, remote, and ruggedly handsome, with spectacular nature broken only by the occasional picturesque village. Of those villages, none is lovelier than romantic **Mendocino** (see Chapter 13), a postage stamp of a town situated on a majestic headland. Rife with elegant bed-and-breakfasts (B&Bs), upscale restaurants, and pricey boutiques and galleries, it's definitely built for two — but families with kids find plenty of outdoor activities to occupy them in the surrounding area. Beware the weather, though, which can be cold and misty at any time of the year — all part of the dreamy Mendocino vibe, aficionados say.

Mendocino also serves as a good jumping-off point for exploring the regal **Redwood Country** (see Chapter 14), which starts just inland and north of Mendocino. The towering coast redwoods — the tallest trees on the planet — extend all the way to the Oregon border, but you don't need to travel that far to get your fill of their majesty. You can follow the scenic 32-mile **Avenue of the Giants** to the midpoint as a day trip from Mendocino or dedicate a couple of days to the drive, depending on your sightseeing goals.

The Sierra Nevadas

Travel inland from the Bay Area or North Coast and you'll soon reach the **Sierra Nevadas,** the magnificently rugged, granite-peaked mountain range that defines northeast and east-central California. This high-altitude region is so uniquely stunning that such geniuses as Mark Twain and Ansel Adams considered it one of their greatest inspirations. The

Sierra Nevadas stirred John Muir to do no less than found the U.S. National Park system.

Possibly the greatest of the national parks is spectacular **Yosemite National Park** (see Chapter 16), whose natural wonders include such record-setters as **Yosemite Falls** (North America's tallest waterfall) and **El Capitan** (the world's largest granite monolith). Beware, though, because Yosemite is the superstar of California's natural attractions, drawing theme-park-worthy crowds in summer — but we tell you in Chapter 16 how to do your best to lose them. Just to the south of Yosemite is the year-round recreational playground resort of **Mammoth Mountain,** where you can ski from November to July.

Also in the High Sierras rests the biggest and most beautiful alpine lake in the United States, sparkling **Lake Tahoe** (see Chapter 15) — California's finest outdoor playground. Come in the winter to ski, in the summer to hike, bike, kayak, sail . . . you name it. If you're a history buff and on your way to or from Tahoe, consider taking a day to visit **Sacramento,** California's capital, or the **Gold Country** (see Chapter 15), the epicenter of California's 19th-century gold-rush hysteria.

The Central Coast

If you ask us (and you did), the Central Coast — the stretch between San Francisco and Los Angeles — represents California at its very best (see Part IV). The drive along Highway 1 — the world-famous Pacific Coast Highway — is one of the most scenic in the world. Keep in mind, however, that the drive is slow going and quite curvy — real Dramamine territory, so stock up if you're queasy.

Where the San Francisco Bay Area meets the Monterey Peninsula sits **Santa Cruz** (see Chapter 17), California's quintessential, and kinda wacky, surf town. Kids (and kids at heart) will love Santa Cruz — especially the genuine old-fashioned boardwalk, the West Coast's only beachfront amusement park. Santa Cruz is at its best in summer and early fall, when the beach party is going strong.

Pristine nature meets unbridled commercialism on the **Monterey Peninsula** (see Chapter 18) — and fortunately, nature wins out. This stunning knob of land jutting out to sea cradles Monterey Bay, one of the richest and most diverse marine habitats on Earth. On land you'll find the **Monterey Bay Aquarium,** one of California's all-time top attractions, plus a collection of delightful communities, from family-friendly Monterey itself to golf mecca **Pebble Beach** to ultraromantic **Carmel-by-the-Sea.** The marriage of natural beauty and man-made diversions doesn't get any better than this.

In **Big Sur** (see Chapter 19), on the other hand, the spectacular wilderness and breathtaking views are unhindered by all but the most minimal development. Dedicate a full day to the natural splendor of Big Sur even if you don't want to stay in one of the region's funky hotels; you won't regret a minute of it.

Hearst Castle (see Chapter 20), one of the most outrageous private homes ever built and a real hoot to tour, lies on the other end of the man-versus-nature continuum. Even if this monument to excess isn't your style, you'll enjoy the surrounding countryside — neither Northern California nor Southern, it has a distinct, golden-hued beauty all its own — and the amiable village of **Cambria**, a great place to soak up some small-town charm.

Driving farther down the coast puts you squarely in Southern California. Adults enjoy meandering through the charming Central Coast Wine Country towns of Paso Robles, San Luis Obispo, Ballard, and others, sampling the region's concerted efforts to demonstrate that not all California wine comes from Napa Valley (see Chapter 21). If you have little ones in tow or a strong affinity for good pastry, head inland to Danish **Solvang** (also in Chapter 21), a storybook town straight out of Scandinavia. Or visit **Santa Barbara** (see Chapter 22), a seaside jewel that embodies the Southern California dream — perfect for clocking in some top-quality relaxation time — and then take a break in the restful surrounds of California's own Shangri-La, the **Ojai Valley.**

The Southern California cities

Southern California is where things get crazy, in a good way. Certainly, **Los Angeles** (see Chapter 23), the poster child for urban sprawl, isn't for everybody. But think twice before you reject it out of hand. L.A.'s charms may be subtle (after all, it's easy to be popular when all your goods are in your shop windows, so to speak), but they do exist. In addition to being celeb-rich and gloriously silly, it also happens to be the state's finest museum town. Really.

Do you really need us to tell you to go to **Disneyland** (see Chapter 24)? Oh, all right. Just south of L.A. (behind the Orange Curtain, as Angelenos are fond of saying), in Anaheim (Orange County), it is the Happiest Place on Earth and the original theme park, and it's an unadulterated blast for kids of all ages (even grown-up ones with jobs and mortgages). Consider visiting again even if you've been before, because you're sure to find plenty of new things to see and do — including the latest Disney park, called California Adventure.

Almost midway between L.A. and San Diego are two spots to catch your breath after a hectic urban odyssey. Beach lovers can park themselves in the sand in quaint and calm **Laguna Beach,** perhaps occasionally getting up long enough to browse the goods created by one of the area's many artists. Then follow the swallows to the hauntingly lovely adobe ruins of **San Juan Capistrano's** fabled mission (see Chapter 25).

In **San Diego** (see Chapter 27), you'll find a wonderfully mellow vibe, golden beaches galore, and plenty of memory-making diversions, most notably three terrific animal parks: the **San Diego Zoo, SeaWorld,** and the **Wild Animal Park.** If that's not enough to keep you and the kids happy and busy, also consider the multifaceted joys of **Balboa Park** (the second-largest city park in the country, after the Big Apple's Central Park) and the metro area's youngest theme-park addition, **LEGOLAND,** which opened in 1999.

The Desert

Unlike the other destinations in this book — which are generally most popular in summer and largely pleasant to visit year-round — California's desert is most fun to visit in any season *except* summer, when the scorching heat can be a bit much to bear. Still, some people enjoy summer in the desert, when prices are low and crowds are minimal (just pack your sunscreen — SPF 30 or higher, preferably).

The **Palm Springs** area (see Chapter 26) is the place to go for desert cool. This is the manicured side of the desert, where streets bear names such as Frank Sinatra Drive, and golf greens, swimming pools, spa treatments, and martinis rule the day. What's more, easy access to unspoiled nature makes Palm Springs appealing even to those who couldn't care less about the prefabricated glamour or retro-groovy stuff.

Scheduling Your Time

You gain no particular advantage by starting at one end of the state over the other, so don't worry about it. Just head north or south based on what's most convenient, appealing, and/or cost-efficient for you. Following are some tips to help you map out your travel strategy. For suggested itineraries that we've mapped out for you, see Chapter 4.

✔ **Embrace the hugeness of California.** You'll drive a lot moving from one destination to another, so factor that in when plotting your strategy. If you're the road-trip type, planning an ambitious itinerary is fine. But if getting to really know a place is important to you, you'll want to make plans to settle in for a few days. Or if spending too much time in the car with the kids is more like a chore than a vacation, plan accordingly for that, too.

✔ **If you have only one week, limit yourself to no more than three destinations.** If you don't limit yourself, you'll suffer from the "If it's Tuesday, it must be Big Sur" syndrome. If, for example, you're touring Southern California, start with two days in San Diego, then two days in Disneyland, and wrap it up with three days in L.A.

✔ **Consider flying in to one airport and leaving from another.** The time saved by flying into L.A. and leaving from San Francisco, say, or flying into San Jose and departing from Palm Springs, may be worth the extra airline charges and/or rental-car drop-off charges. What's more, depending on your points of arrival and departure, you may not even incur extra fees. Consider a couple of options and price them out with the airlines and car companies (or put your travel agent to work) before you decide.

✔ **Consider your drive part of the adventure.** You can either drive straight through without stopping or take a leisurely meander off the beaten path — it depends on how adventurous you are and how much unassigned time you have. California is a gorgeous state, with lots to admire along just about any route you take. Be sure to make time for unplanned stops and serendipitous side trips.

✔ **Don't try to cram too many activities into a day when you'll be making a long drive.** Driving long distances can really sap your energy. Estimated drive times in this book don't include rest stops, unforeseen traffic, or detours; unfortunately, traffic is only getting worse, especially in L.A., one of the most congested cities in the country. If you have time and energy to do more than drive and check into your new hotel on big drive days, consider it a gimme; use the time to relax. (After all, this is a vacation, remember?)

✔ **Avoid ending up at a super-popular weekend destination on the weekends.** Restful destinations such as Napa Valley, Mendocino, Carmel, Hearst Castle, Solvang, and Santa Barbara become human zoos when urban dwellers escape the city for the weekend. Many also require two-night minimums over the weekend, which can throw a monkey wrench in your plans. Try, instead, to schedule your city visits over the weekends and your retreat destinations during the week.

Understanding California's Climate

W.C. Fields once said, "California is the only state in the Union where you can fall asleep under a rose bush in full bloom and freeze to death." Surely a gross exaggeration, right? Actually, no.

Don't be fooled by what you think you know about California's weather. "Really," you say, "I've seen *Baywatch* and *The O.C.* What's there to understand? California is all buffed bikini-clad bods and perpetual sun." Well, yes and no. Sometimes the reality lives up to the myth; sometimes it doesn't. Frankly, the weather isn't that predictable.

The most important weather predictor is your location: coast or inland, north or south. As a general rule, the weather is cool and windy along the coastline — even in July and August — and warmer and perpetually sunnier as you move inland. The climate is always warmer and sunnier in inland Sacramento than in famously foggy San Francisco. (The temperature drops again as you climb into the mountains to high-elevation places such as Lake Tahoe.) Believe it or not, the rule even holds true in the same city: Downtown Los Angeles is more often than not 10°F to 20°F warmer than L.A.'s oceanside beach community, Santa Monica, which benefits from cooling ocean breezes. Latitude matters, too; in general, the southern coast — Santa Barbara and points south — sees better beach weather than its northern counterparts.

One thing you can say for sure about California weather is how change-able it is. The temperature may drop at night more than you're used to; in many places, both along the coast and inland, daytime temperatures of 80°F and above may routinely drop into the low 40s in the evening. Cool fog covers much of the coastline in the mornings, but if the sun breaks through, temperatures soar by noon or so. The bottom line: Be prepared for dramatic daily changes, even in summer. Layering your clothes is always a good idea.

Revealing the Secret of the Seasons

California is seasonless to a certain degree — any time is a good time to visit. The state benefits from glorious conditions year-round, with the weather being generally warmer than most other mainland U.S. spots in winter, and cooler and drier than most in summer.

One of the most surprising ticks in California's weather pattern is that summer generally starts late. As the temperature charts in Table 3-1 show, both San Francisco and Los Angeles (and virtually all points in between) don't really start warming up until July. Even blessedly sunny L.A. is notorious for *June gloom:* Morning gray rolls in and stays until afternoon.

Table 3-1   Average Temperatures around the State (°F)

	Jan	Feb	Mar	Apr	May	June	July	Aug	Sep	Oct	Nov	Dec
Lake Tahoe												
High	40	42	44	51	60	69	77	77	69	59	47	41
Low	20	21	23	27	33	39	45	45	39	32	26	21
San Francisco												
High	58	60	60	61	62	63	64	65	67	67	63	58
Low	43	46	46	47	49	51	53	54	54	52	48	44
Napa Valley												
High	57	62	65	69	75	80	82	82	81	77	65	57
Low	37	41	42	43	48	52	54	54	52	48	42	38
Monterey												
High	60	62	62	63	64	67	68	69	72	70	65	60
Low	43	45	45	46	48	50	52	53	53	51	47	43

	Jan	Feb	Mar	Apr	May	June	July	Aug	Sep	Oct	Nov	Dec
Santa Barbara												
High	65	66	66	69	69	72	75	77	76	74	69	66
Low	43	45	47	49	52	55	58	59	58	54	49	44
Los Angeles (downtown)												
High	68	69	70	72	73	78	84	85	83	79	72	68
Low	49	50	52	54	58	61	65	66	65	60	54	49
Palm Springs												
High	70	76	80	87	95	104	109	107	101	92	79	70
Low	43	46	49	54	61	68	75	75	69	60	49	42

On the upside, when the warm weather comes, it almost always stays through September and usually well into October. (Unfortunately, in L.A., "warm" often means several days of really stinkin' hot.) Indian summer is common, and fall is universally the best season, weatherwise. In September and October, the fog even lifts from perpetually misty spots along the coast, such as Monterey and Mendocino. In places where the weather starts to crisp in the fall, such as Tahoe, clear air and beautiful colors make for gorgeous conditions.

If you're coming to California to hit the beach in your bikini in January, don't count on it — this is not Hawaii. Still, the weather will likely be milder here than where you're from — swimming may not happen, but strolling the sands under cloudless brilliant blue skies probably will. No wonder so many people love visiting in winter — 50°F in San Francisco is way better than Chicago's, or even New York's, parka weather. Tahoe is a prime spot for skiing, and snow-blanketed Yosemite is crowd-free and magnificent. And we've often found the coastal destinations — particularly Monterey and Big Sur — to be more pleasant, with clearer skies, in December or January than in June or July. If you're lucky, you may even get a beach day in L.A. or San Diego in those months, when the occasional 80°F day takes a bow.

Perusing a California Calendar of Events

Here's a brief rundown of the Golden State's top annual events:

- ✔ **December–March:** This is **whale-watching season** all along the California coast. Mammoth gray whales migrate from the cold Alaskan waters to warmer climes for their birthing season and then transport their new pups back home. Just look out to sea for a blow; the puff of steam can rise 12 feet from the whale's blowhole.

The best place to watch for whales is **Monterey,** which celebrates the annual migration with a two-week party in January called Whalefest. For information, call ☎ 831-649-6544 or go to www. whalefestmonterey.com.

Mendocino holds its own celebration, the Mendocino Whale and Wine Festival, usually in early March (☎ 707-961-6303; www. mendocinocoast.com).

✔ **January 1:** New Year's Day sees the **Tournament of Roses Parade,** the mother of all college bowl parades, descend upon Pasadena (near Los Angeles) almost at the crack of dawn. Outrageous floats constructed entirely of fresh roses and other flora compete for the spotlight with high-volume marching bands and high-wattage celebs making appearances. Although the festivities happen on New Year's Day, arrive the night before (bring supplies for sleeping on the sidewalk, and remember, it gets quite nippy) if you want a spot that lets you see anything. Call ☎ 626-449-4100 or visit www.tournamentofroses.com for grandstand tickets, official tour packages, and other information.

✔ **January–February:** The **Chinese New Year Festival and Parade** in San Francisco, the largest Chinese New Year's celebration in the United States, encompasses two weeks of excitement, the highlight of which is a magnificent parade featuring the legendary Golden Dragon. Events range from the Miss Chinatown USA pageant to street and flower fairs. The Chinese New Year begins in late January or February. Call ☎ 415-982-3071 for exact details and dates, or go to www.chineseparade.com.

✔ **Late January–March:** The **Napa Valley Mustard Festival,** a celebration of the petite yellow-petaled mustard flowers that bloom in late winter (and everyone's favorite gourmet condiment), has grown into the Wine Country's biggest event. Two full months of high-end hoopla run the gamut from wine auctions to gallery shows to gourmet-food competitions. The festival runs from the end of January through the end of March. Call ☎ 707-944-1133 or check www.mustard festival.org for details.

✔ **Late February–early March:** Snowfest in North Lake Tahoe, a ten-day celebration of the ski season, is the largest of its kind in the world. Features include snow- and ice-sculpture contests, a polar-bear swim in Lake Tahoe, the Incredible Dog Snow Challenge (in which man's best friend competes in freestyle Frisbee, search-and-rescue, and sledding competitions), and more. It's the most fun you'll ever have in Polartec. Call ☎ 530-583-7167 or visit the Web site at www.tahoesnowfestival.com.

✔ **Early May:** Celebrate **Cinco de Mayo,** Mexico's favorite holiday, in San Diego's historic Old Town, the original Spanish birthplace of California, or in the Mexican heart of Los Angeles, El Pueblo de Los Angeles State Historic Monument. Expect festive mariachi music, folk dancing, and lots of yummy eats. Events usually take place over the weekend closest to May 5. Call ☎ 213-625-5045 for L.A. information, ☎ 619-296-3161 or 619-220-5422 for San Diego information.

✔ **Mid-May:** The **ING Bay to Breakers** in San Francisco, the world's largest and zaniest footrace, is actually more fun than run. More than 70,000 runners race across the park in their costumed best. For information, call ☎ 415-359-2800, or point your Web browser to www.ingbaytobreakers.com.

✔ **Late June:** San Francisco hosts the **Lesbian, Gay, Bisexual, and Transgender Pride Parade,** the world's largest and most outrageous gay-pride parade. Call ☎ 415-864-3733 or visit www.sf pride.org. L.A.'s own **Gay and Lesbian Pride Day parade,** also in late June, is a close second. It's in West Hollywood. Call ☎ 323-969-8302 or go to www.lapride.org.

✔ **Fourth of July:** Virtually all of California's communities hold their own style of Independence Day celebrations, from San Francisco's (fog-shrouded) fireworks to Monterey's Living History Festival to the Redwood Country's old-fashioned parade and picnic in Victorian-era Ferndale. Contact local visitor bureaus to find out what's on in the town you plan to visit (see the "Gathering More Information" section at the end of each destination chapter in Parts II, III, and IV).

✔ **Late August or early September:** The **San Diego Street Scene** is a three-day festival of food, music, and fun. Call ☎ 619-557-8490 or visit the Web site at www.street-scene.com.

✔ **Mid-September:** Solvang's Scandinavian glory reaches its tacky-genuine zenith with **Danish Days,** a historic three-day extravaganza celebrating Solvang's heritage. For details, call ☎ 800-468-6765 or 805-688-6144.

✔ **Third weekend in September:** The **Monterey Jazz Festival,** the world's longest-running jazz festival (44 years and counting), hosts the biggest names in traditional and contemporary jazz. If you want more information, call ☎ 925-275-9255 or point your Web browser to www.montereyjazzfestival.org.

✔ **Mid-October: Coloma Gold Rush Live** in Marshall Gold Discovery State Historic Park, Coloma, tells the gold-rush story in living color through demonstrations, story-telling, and entertainment. Call ☎ 530-622-3470 or 530-295-2170 for information.

✔ **October 31:** Join the 400,000 costumed revelers in **Los Angeles** who flood the streets of West Hollywood for some mighty creative merriment. Call ☎ **310-289-2525.**

✔ **Late November:** The stars brighten Hollywood Boulevard the Sunday after Thanksgiving in the **Hollywood Christmas Parade** in Los Angeles, a classic celebrity-studded parade that launches the holiday season in glittering Tinseltown style. For details, call ☎ **323-469-8311.**

Considering all that goes on every year in California, this brief list is merely a drop in the bucket. For a complete rundown of events, call the **California Division of Tourism** (☎ **800-462-2543**) and request a copy of *California Celebrations,* or point your Web browser to www.culture california.com.

Chapter 4

Following an Itinerary: Five Great Trips

*U*nderstand this right now: You will not see all of California. We know actual native Californians who've lived here all their lives and who continue to stumble upon new discoveries.

Still, it's easy to see quite a bit of the Golden State, even if your vacation time is short. In this chapter, we offer a few specific itineraries — ten-day jaunts through Northern and Southern California, romantic idylls for two, kid-friendly road trips, and forays into the wilds of the state — to help you plan your own California dream of a trip.

The itineraries we suggest in this chapter give you an idea of what you can see and do comfortably in the time you have. But remember that no one ideal vacation plan exists. Use the itineraries in this chapter as you see fit — either as proven, hard-and-fast plans, or simply as starting blueprints that you can then customize to your own needs.

Seeing Northern California's Highlights in Ten Days

On **Day 1,** fly in to **San Francisco.** Spend **Day 2** and **Day 3** enjoying the City by the Bay (see Chapter 11 for more details on San Francisco).

Itinerary #1

After spending **Day 4** in **San Francisco,** head to the **Wine Country** (see Chapter 12) early on **Day 5** and spend **Day 5** and **Day 6** getting to know the area. For the ideal introduction, plan on a late-morning or early-afternoon winery tour, perhaps one of the reservation-only tours at Schramsberg or Robert Mondavi, or one of the terrific first-come, first-served tours offered by Clos Pegase or St. Supéry. See two more wineries after lunch, and mix it up with a little sightseeing or shopping before resting up for a gourmet feast at one of the valley's stellar restaurants. Book two months ahead if you want to eat at **French Laundry,** often named the best restaurant in the United States. On the morning of **Day 6,** stop at one of the valley's gourmet markets to assemble a lunchtime picnic. Plan some additional activities to mix in with your winery-going, such as a hot-air balloon ride, a bit of bicycling, and/or a mud bath and massage.

On **Day 7,** head north from the Wine Country in the afternoon for **Redwood Country** (see Chapter 14). Follow Highway 128 north to U.S. 101, and spend the night along the Redwood Highway, perhaps in charming, Victorian **Ferndale.** On **Day 8,** meander down the Redwood Highway, reaching Mendocino in time for dinner. Spend **Day 9** exploring **Mendocino** (see Chapter 13), hiking the headlands, shopping, or just enjoying the wild beauty of the misty North Coast.

On **Day 10,** drive back to **San Francisco** for your flight home.

 You can easily trim this itinerary to eight days by cutting a day off your time in San Francisco and limiting your Redwood Country exploring to a day trip.

Itinerary #2

Depart San Francisco on **Day 4** for the **Monterey Peninsula.** Leave in the morning and spend the day playing on the boardwalk and the beach in **Santa Cruz,** arriving in Monterey in time for dinner. If there are just the two of you and you're looking for romance, consider **Carmel** as a base. If your budget is generous, go all out and spend your nights on some of the most spectacular real estate in the nation: **Pebble Beach,** the California destination for golfers.

The Monterey Peninsula (see Chapter 18) deserves a good chunk of time, so spend the evening of **Day 4** and the following two nights here. Start **Day 5** at the **Monterey Bay Aquarium.** (Don't forget to buy your aquarium tickets in advance to save aggravating time in line.) In the afternoon, rent bikes and follow Monterey's gorgeous bayfront bike path (suitable for all riders) for some spectacular views.

Spend **Day 6** exploring the rest of the peninsula by car, including the justifiably famous **17-Mile Drive** (viewable from that rented bike if you have the energy). Spend the afternoon strolling through charming Carmel; if the weather is chilly, bundle up for a walk along cypress-lined Carmel Beach, one of the world's most beautiful stretches of sand.

On **Day 7,** drive through gorgeous **Big Sur** (see Chapter 19) to **San Simeon** and **Hearst Castle,** which we discuss in Chapter 20. Resist the urge to stop much along the way (you'll have time for that later). Arrive at your base in nearby **Cambria** in time to see the elephant seals basking in the sun just north of San Simeon and do a little exploring in Cambria before a leisurely dinner.

Dedicate **Day 8** to **Hearst Castle.** Book yourself a morning tour and an afternoon tour, with time for a flick in the five-story-high iWERKS format at the castle visitor center in between (this makes for good resting-your-tootsies time).

Day 9 is for exploring awesome **Big Sur.** In fact, spend the night along the Big Sur coast so that you have plenty of hiking and/or contemplation time.

Fly home on **Day 10.** Consider flying out of **San Jose** to avoid the drive back to the San Francisco airport.

Seeing Southern California's Highlights in Ten Days

On **Day 1,** fly into Los Angeles. Spend **Day 2** and **Day 3** enjoying Tinseltown. Check out Chapter 23 for additional details about Los Angeles.

Itinerary #1

On **Day 4,** go to **Disneyland** (see Chapter 24). In fact, consider making the hour's drive south on the evening of **Day 3** so that you can be first in the park in the morning. (You may even be able to get a jump-start on the masses with an early entrance, a perk currently enjoyed by Disneyland Resort hotel guests, though that may be dropped by the time you read this.) Spend the evening of **Day 4** in Anaheim so that you'll have an entire day in the park. In fact, you may want to consider spending the better part of **Day 5** at Disneyland as well, especially if you want to see the California Adventure park. You may also want to split up your park time if you have little kids who'll tire out easily, if your own theme-park stamina is low, or if you're visiting at a peak time with long lines and wait times for rides. If you've had your fill of Disneyland by **Day 5,** spend that day relaxing by the pool, soaking up some of those California rays.

In any case, head south to **San Diego** (see Chapter 27) in time for dinner on **Day 5** so that you can start your animal-park adventures early on **Day 6.** Whether you have the kids with you or not, don't miss the **San Diego Zoo;** hyped though it may be, there is a reason it's a major attraction. On **Day 7,** choose between spending the day at **SeaWorld,** taking your lit-tlest ones on an excursion to **LEGOLAND,** or treating your older kids to the **Wild Animal Park.** Or, if you've had enough theme-park fun for one trip, split your day between San Diego's culture-rich **Balboa Park** and the beach.

After all this running around, you deserve some rest-and-relaxation time. On **Day 8,** head to **Palm Springs** and spend **Day 9** relaxing under the desert sun. You can also get in some quality time on the fairway or some pampering at the spa (or both, if you're so inclined). If the desert isn't your bag, try the small seaside town of **Laguna Beach** or check out the fabled mission of **San Juan Capistrano** (see Chapter 25).

If you'd rather avoid a lot of running around, simply stay put in **San Diego** on **Day 8** and **Day 9** — it's another terrific place to kick back — and fly out from there on **Day 10.** Either way, you'll be relaxed and contented enough to head home on **Day 10,** whether you leave from Palm Springs International or San Diego's airport (if you've stayed put) or take the easy two-hour drive back to Los Angeles.

Itinerary #2

If theme parks aren't your style, head to **Palm Springs** (see Chapter 26) in the late afternoon of **Day 4,** arriving in time for an alfresco dinner. On **Day 5,** take a desert excursion with Desert Adventures Jeep Eco-Tours. Spend **Day 6** golfing, spa-ing, or just sitting by the pool sipping fruity drinks garnished with umbrellas.

On **Day 7,** head west again, skirting L.A. as you head northwest to lovely **Santa Barbara** (see Chapter 22), arriving in time for dinner.

If you're driving on a weekday, be sure to pass through L.A. before 3 p.m. to avoid getting stuck in rush-hour traffic.

Spend **Day 8** and **Day 9** hanging out in **Santa Barbara,** Southern California's loveliest beach town. If you're not the beach type (or if the weather's just not beachy), and you feel as if you've seen and done it all by midday on **Day 9,** explore Santa Barbara's Wine Country or head to **Solvang** (see Chapter 21) for a slice of Scandinavia, Southern California–style. Or consider spending a night in the small town of **Ojai** (about half an hour southeast of Santa Barbara — see Chapter 22), where artists congregate and the setting sun turns the bluffs pink every night.

The drive is an easy 100 miles back to L.A. on **Day 10,** your day to fly home.

Discovering California with Kids

Kids love California as much as adults do — it's sort of like a giant playground with all the latest toys. If you're traveling with kids, you won't have a problem finding things to do; the trick is fitting it all in.

Itinerary #1

On **Day 1**, fly the brood in to **San Diego**. Spend **Day 2** and **Day 3** enjoying the local animal parks.

Check out of your San Diego hotel on the morning of **Day 4** and head north to either **LEGOLAND** in nearby Carlsbad with the little ones or the **San Diego Wild Animal Park**, in Escondido, with older kids

Both parks make easy stops along the way to **Anaheim**, where you want to check in to your hotel, have an early dinner, and rest up for your big day at **Disneyland**. Spread your park time over two days, **Day 5** and **Day 6**, to avoid burnout — your own and the kids'.

On the morning of **Day 7**, head north to **L.A.** Base yourself at the beach for maximum fun. Visit **Universal Studios** on **Day 8**.

On **Day 9**, make the short (two-hour) drive north to cutesy, Danish-themed **Solvang**, which your younger kids are bound to enjoy — especially if they like pastries

On **Day 10**, head north to **Monterey**, stopping in **San Luis Obispo** for a pleasant lunch break (it's just about exactly at the midpoint of the four-hour drive). The peninsula features plenty to entertain you and the kids on **Day 11** and **Day 12**; the **Aquarium**, of course, is a must.

Spend **Day 13** on the beach and boardwalk at **Santa Cruz**, California's historic seaside amusement park (see Chapter 17). It's a real joy, and a must-do for families. You can see the boardwalk in a few ways: You can make it a day trip from your base in Monterey or enjoy it on your way to **San Francisco** (from where you're presumably flying out on **Day 14**). However, we recommend spending the night in Santa Cruz so that you can enjoy the neon-lit rides and lively arcades after dark, which is especially fun in summer.

Only a half-hour or so from Santa Cruz, **San Jose** makes the perfect departure point for your homebound flight on **Day 14**.

Itinerary #2

Fly into **San Francisco** on **Day 1**. The City by the Bay has plenty of kid appeal — in fact, more than enough to occupy **Day 2** and **Day 3**. Chapter 11 can help you formulate a sightseeing plan.

On **Day 4**, drive to **Yosemite National Park**, where you can spend **Day 5** and **Day 6**. It's an ideal place for kids to discover and enjoy the natural world. (If the weather's warm, consider staying in the tent cabins, which offer both creature comforts and a kid-friendly resemblance to camping.)

On **Day 7**, head back to the coast, basing everyone in **Monterey** or **Santa Cruz** on **Day 8** and **Day 9** for area exploring.

Drive south on **Day 10,** spending the night in **Solvang.** If you choose to spend the day at L.A.'s **Universal Studios,** leave this mini-Denmark early on **Day 11.**

The distance from Monterey all the way to L.A. is one heckuva drive, so if you'd like to wake up in L.A. on the morning of **Day 11,** we recommend departing **Monterey** or **Santa Cruz** on the afternoon of **Day 9** and basing yourself in the **Hearst Castle** area before heading south on **Day 10.** In fact, you'll even have time to catch a castle tour in the morning before you set out, if you want.

Head to **Anaheim** on the evening of **Day 11** to spend **Day 12** at **Disneyland** (see Chapter 24).

Depart Anaheim early on **Day 13** to make the hour's drive south to **San Diego** with plenty of time to enjoy **LEGOLAND,** the **San Diego Zoo,** the **Wild Animal Park,** or SeaWorld — pick one for your pleasure. Schedule a late flight out on **Day 14** to finish up at another park — and the kids will sleep on the way home like the angels they are.

If you'd like to spend more time in San Diego without adding another day to your trip, consider cutting back a day in San Francisco; leave the city on the afternoon of **Day 3,** arriving at **Yosemite** in time for dinner.

California in Two Weeks for Romance-Seeking Couples

Fly in to **San Francisco** on **Day 1.** Spend **Day 2** and **Day 3** enjoying the most romantic city in the United States. See Chapter 11 for a recommended sightseeing plan of San Francisco.

Itinerary #1

Head north on **Day 4.** If you don't mind a long drive, consider the coastal route on your way up, which winds through lovely, artsy seaside towns. Stop at misty **Mendocino** (see Chapter 13), where picnicking, bike riding, strolling the charming seaside village, and snuggling up in front of a roaring fire in the evening are the primary orders of business. Frankly, towns don't get any more romantic, so spend **Day 5** here, too.

On the afternoon of **Day 6,** pick up curvaceous Highway 128 just south of Mendocino and follow it into the **Wine Country** (see Chapter 12). Set up camp at one of the valleys' romantic B&Bs (the Milliken Creek Inn is a great choice), and wine and dine on **Day 7** and **Day 8.**

On **Day 9,** cut south, back toward the coast, and make magical **Carmel-by-the-Sea** your love nest from which to explore the **Monterey Peninsula** over **Day 10** and **Day 11.** If the weather's good, work in an afternoon kayaking among the elephant seals and sea otters in **Monterey Bay** (see Chapter 18). And don't forget to take a romantic stroll along jaw-droppingly beautiful **Carmel Beach.**

Leave the Monterey area early on **Day 12** to give you the entire day to meander through **Big Sur** (see Chapter 19) on your way to **Hearst Castle** (see Chapter 20). Make **Cambria** your area base and dedicate **Day 13** to touring Xanadu.

On **Day 14,** drive back to San Francisco (or the **San Jose** or the **Monterey** airport, both a tad closer) to catch a late-day flight home.

Itinerary #2

Spend **Day 4** in San Francisco, and on **Day 5** head directly to the **Wine Country.** Dedicate **Day 5** and **Day 6** to touring the romantic, adult-oriented region (see Chapter 12).

On **Day 7,** drive to **Carmel** (or to the **Casa Palermo** in Pebble Beach, if you have the bucks) and settle in for **Monterey Peninsula** sightseeing on **Day 8** and **Day 9** (see Chapter 18).

On **Day 10,** meander through **Big Sur** country, arriving in **Cambria** (see Chapter 20) in time for a candlelit dinner (the **Sow's Ear** makes a good choice). Make **Day 11** your castle day — and because you're in the romantic mood, ask your guide for tales of Clark Gable and Carole Lombard's visits to "the ranch."

Take **Day 12** to drive south along the Central Coast to **Santa Barbara** (see Chapter 22), a great place to spend **Day 13** at the beach.

On **Day 14,** drive the easy two hours south to the Los Angeles airport to catch a flight home.

California in Two Weeks for Nature Lovers

These two nature-loving itineraries start from Los Angeles.

Itinerary #1

Fly into **Los Angeles** on **Day 1** — and leave immediately. Drive two hours east to discover the desert beauty of **Palm Springs** (see Chapter 26). (Or avoid the drive by flying directly into Palm Springs.) Spend **Day 2** exploring wild, fascinating, untrammeled **Joshua Tree National Park** (see Chapter 26), an excursion that should take the entire day.

Spend the morning of **Day 3** lazing by the pool. After lunch, head out of Palm Springs, skirting L.A. again as you head northwest to **Santa Barbara** (see Chapter 22).

If you're traveling on a weekday, make sure you pass through L.A. before 3 p.m. to avoid getting stuck in rush-hour traffic.

Spend **Day 4** relaxing in the lovely beach town of Santa Barbara, and then head to **Big Sur** (see Chapter 19) on **Day 5.** We highly recommend spending at least one night here among the trees, so that you can enjoy this spectacular coast on **Day 6,** too.

On **Day 7,** head to the **Monterey Peninsula** (see Chapter 18), where you should park yourself in **Pacific Grove** for the best outdoors experience today and on **Day 8.**

On **Day 9,** make the drive to **Yosemite National Park** (see Chapter 16), and spend **Day 10** and **Day 11** exploring the park; head for the High Country if you want to avoid crowds, but be sure to dedicate a half-day to seeing the icons of Yosemite Valley first.

On **Day 12,** head north to **Lake Tahoe** (see Chapter 15). Spend **Day 13** admiring this magnificent lake and its surroundings. Schedule a late-day flight out of **Reno** so that you have most of **Day 14** to play, too.

Itinerary #2

Fly in to **Los Angeles** on **Day 1** and get a good night's rest for the mammoth 300-mile drive to **Death Valley National Park** (see Chapter 26) on **Day 2.** Expect it to be a *looooong* driving day.

Spend **Day 3** and **Day 4** exploring the vast expanses of the park. (Consider renting a four-wheel-drive vehicle if you want to explore some of the primitive park's backcountry roads.)

On **Day 5,** drive out of Death Valley on the western side and take the I-395 route north to the east (Tioga Pass) entrance of **Yosemite National Park** (see Chapter 16). Again, plan on another full day of driving. Spend **Day 6** and **Day 7** exploring the park.

 Yosemite's Tioga Pass entrance is closed from the first snowfall, which usually occurs in November, until mid- to late June. Call ahead (☎ 209-372-0200) to check road conditions around these times.

On **Day 8,** drive out of the park's south entrance and head to the **Monterey Peninsula** (see Chapter 18). Make forested **Pacific Grove** your base here on **Day 8** and **Day 9** for the best outdoors experience.

On **Day 10,** head to **Big Sur** (see Chapter 19), staying to enjoy this wonderful wilderness on **Day 11** as well.

On **Day 12,** meander south along the view-endowed Pacific Coast Highway to **Santa Barbara** (see Chapter 22), one of the most naturally blessed towns in the United States; it's a good place to rest up on **Day 13** for the flight home from Los Angeles on **Day 14.**

Part II
Planning Your Trip to California

The 5th Wave   By Rich Tennant

In this part . . .

In this part, we discuss your travel options: how to get to California and how to get around after you arrive; how to plan a trip around your budget; and whether to go the package-tour route. This part offers savvy travel advice for travelers with special needs. This part also helps you finalize those little last-minute details, such as making dinner reservations at hot local restaurants and weighing your travel-insurance options. No glamour here — but all necessary.

Chapter 5

Managing Your Money

"So — how much is this trip going to cost me, anyway?"

The question is a reasonable one, no matter where your budget sits on the spending ladder. A vacation is a considerable endeavor, with costs that can add up before you know it — especially if you're traveling with kids, when expensive admission tickets and pricier-than-you-thought meals can multiply the damage in the blink of an eye. Therefore, knowing what to expect before you go makes sense.

Planning Your Budget

The good news is that structuring a California trip to suit any budget is relatively easy. Sure, you can rub elbows with high-profile celebs or dot-com millionaires by choosing to stay at ultraluxurious resorts and dine at elegant restaurants, but you don't have to; plenty of affordable choices exist in every destination. Sure, you can spend tons of money at many excellent high-ticket attractions, from the **Monterey Bay Aquarium** to **Disneyland,** but pursuing such pleasures as a stroll on the beach or a mountain hike carries no admission price whatsoever. Whatever your tastes, this section helps you figure out where your money's going to go and what you can afford to do.

Totaling transportation costs

Most visitors to California fly in and rent a car to get around this mammoth state. The following sections help you budget enough for comfortable transportation wherever you want to go.

Booking airfare

Airfare is one of the two big-ticket items of your California trip (the other is lodging). Predicting airfares is almost impossible, because they can fall to new lows or go through the roof at the drop of a hat. We can tell you, however, that California's main airports — San Francisco, Los Angeles, and San Diego — tend to get so much air traffic (and, therefore, generate so much competition) that airfares are usually lower than if you're flying into less competitive markets elsewhere in the country. And both Northern and Southern California have alternative airports that are even cheaper, especially with the expansion of low-fare carriers. Oakland, for example, is generally cheaper to fly in and out of than San Francisco. Southwest Airlines serves Oakland, and United has lower fares in and out of Oakland (again, generally). In Southern California, Burbank is another smaller airport beloved by Southwest, and Long Beach is the tiny home to JetBlue and its amazing deals from New York City.

Don't quote us, because prices can always vary, but expect to pay in the neighborhood of $400 to $600 per person for a coast-to-coast flight. You'll pay less if you plan well in advance, stay over on a Saturday night, or get lucky and catch a fare sale; see Chapter 6 for tips on getting the best airfare.

Be sure to check out airfares within California as well. Thanks to the variety of low-fare carriers, prices are usually quite reasonable. At press time, for example, the advance-purchase fare between Oakland and San Diego was just $73 one-way. One of these lower fares may allow you to fly into California through one airport and return home via a second airport. (But don't forget to factor in any rental-car drop-off charges before booking.)

Renting a car

Rental cars are relatively cheap in the Driving State. You can often get a compact car for between $100 and $200 a week, depending on your dates and where you pick up your car. (Southern California rentals are usually cheaper.) If you want a vehicle meant to haul your family, expect to pay more like $200 to $300 a week — frankly, still quite reasonable.

 Do yourself a favor and book a rental car with unlimited mileage. You'll be doing a lot of driving as you travel within California, and you don't want to end up paying for your rental on a per-mile basis — you'll end up on the short end of this stick.

And because you'll probably cover a good deal of ground, don't forget to factor in gas, which at press time was hovering around $3 a gallon (in California, prices vary greatly in different parts of the state). Parking is another cost factor, especially in the cities; play it safe and budget $10 to $20 a day, more if you're spending lots of time in the cities. Also remember to account for any additional insurance costs.

For further details on renting a car in California, see Chapter 7.

What things cost in San Francisco

An average latte in North Beach	$3
Shuttle from San Francisco International Airport SFO) to any hotel	$15 (plus tip)
Taxi from SFO to city center	$30–$45 (plus tip)
One-way Muni/bus fare to any destination within the city (adult)	$1.50
Ferry ride and admission to Alcatraz	$19
Admission to Exploratorium	$13
A stroll across the Golden Gate Bridge	Free!
A drive across the Golden Gate Bridge	$5 toll to get back to the city
Luxury room for two at the Huntington	$350–$500
Romantic room for two at Petite Auberge	$150–$245
Budget room for two at the Cow Hollow Motor Inn & Suites	$72–$125
Dinner for two at Boulevard (with wine)	$200
Dinner for two at A-16 (with wine)	$100
Dinner for two at Chow (no wine)	$40
An Anchor Steam beer at Johnny Foley's	$4.75
A tall martini at Top of the Mark	$10
Theater ticket for *Beach Blanket Babylon*	$25–$80

Paying for lodging

California has a wealth of luxury hotels and resorts, but it also offers plenty of affordable choices. The cities specialize in business- and tourist-oriented hotels, while the smaller destinations feature standard hotels, bed-and-breakfasts, and motels, plus destination resorts in some locales. We recommend a range of choices in each of the destinations covered in this book so that you have suitable options, no matter what your needs or budget.

In the destination chapters in this book, a number of dollar signs, ranging from one ($) to five ($$$$$), follows each hotel name. These dollar signs represent the median price for a double room per night, as follows:

Symbol	Meaning
$	Super-cheap: $75 or less per night
$$	Still affordable: $76 to $150
$$$	Moderate: $151 to $225
$$$$	Expensive but not ridiculous: $226 to $300
$$$$$	Ultraluxurious: more than $300 per night

In general, you'll find that if you budget between $100 and $175 to spend per night, you'll be able to balance your costs. Make economical choices in the more affordable locations so that you can comfortably handle any pricier destinations down the road, such as Carmel. Staying cheaply when possible will make digging a little deeper into your pockets later on easier to bear.

So that you don't encounter any unwanted surprises at payment time, be sure to account for the taxes that will be added to your final bill. The base hotel tax is 14 percent, but some municipalities add an additional surcharge, bringing taxes as high as 25 percent in some cities. We note the taxes you can expect to pay in the hotel section of each destination chapter in Parts II, III, and IV.

Dining with dollars

California prides itself on its culinary prowess, but prepare to pay for that prowess; dining out tends to be rather expensive, especially in tourist-targeted destinations such as the Wine Country. Main courses can run from $12 to $22 on the average dinner menu. Throughout this book, however, we make an effort to recommend a range of choices in every destination so that you have options, no matter what your needs or budget.

In the destination chapters, a number of dollar signs, ranging from one ($) to five ($$$$$), follows each restaurant name. The dollar signs are meant to give you an idea of what a complete dinner for one person — including appetizer, main course, one drink, tax, and tip — will likely set you back. The price categories go like this:

Symbol	Meaning
$	Cheap eats: $15 or less per person
$$	Still inexpensive: $16 to $25
$$$	Moderate: $26 to $40
$$$$	Pricey: $41 to $70
$$$$$	Ultraexpensive: more than $70 per person

Of course, just about any menu has a range of prices, and the final tally depends on how you order. The wine or bar tab is more likely to jack up the bill quicker than anything else; desserts also add to the total.

What things cost in Los Angeles

An average cup of coffee	$1.75
A ride aboard the Metro Rail subway	$1.25
Parking your rental car	$2–$40
Viewing hand- and footprints at Grauman's and stars on Hollywood Boulevard	Free!
Map to the stars' homes	$7
Admission to Los Angeles County Museum of Art	$9
Admission to the Getty Center	Free! ($7 for parking, though)
A day at the beach	Free!
Luxury room for two at the Chateau Marmont	$320 and up
Romantic room for two at the Venice Beach House	$144–$300
Dinner for two at Patina (with wine)	$155
Dinner for two at Border Grill (with beer)	$65
Dinner for two at Zankou Chicken	$15
Two tickets to a concert at Walt Disney Concert Hall	$78 and up
Two tickets to a Dodgers game, upper level	$12

Saving on sightseeing and activities

Sightseeing admission charges and other activity fees can add up quickly, especially if you're traveling with kids. Of course, how much you spend depends on what you want to do. If you're traveling to California largely to discover its scenic towns and natural wonders, you won't have to budget much for sightseeing. Admission to national and state parks is minimal, and activities such as hiking, picnicking, and beachcombing are absolutely free (except for the cost of refreshments). Even bike and kayak rentals are inexpensive.

But if you're planning to visit the big-name sightseeing attractions — especially the theme parks — know what your budget can handle. These destinations can be expensive: Expect to pay about $41 per person just to get in the door at **Disneyland,** the same at **Universal Studios,** $39 at **SeaWorld,** $18 at the **San Diego Zoo,** and $20 at the **Monterey Bay Aquarium.** (Needless to say, the Southern California theme-park loop won't be cheap.) Admission is slightly cheaper for kids — but don't worry, they'll find plenty of ways to spend the difference and then some.

In the destination chapters in this book, we tell you how much you can expect to pay for admission fees and activities so that you can budget your sightseeing money realistically.

Allotting funds for shopping and entertainment

Shopping is a huge temptation in California. Many of the state's finest small towns are rich in unique boutiques and other shopping opportunities. We dare you to escape Napa Valley (see Chapter 12) without spending money on wine or other goodies. But places such as Mendocino (see Chapter 13) and Carmel (see Chapter 18) are so pleasant just to stroll through that, if your budget's tight, you won't suffer if you limit yourself to window-shopping while you're there.

 Don't blow a wad at the theme-park souvenir stands. Anything you buy at **Disneyland** is available at your local mall's Disney Store. And your teenager doesn't need another **Hard Rock Cafe** T-shirt. Save your dough for something special — a one-of-a-kind souvenir that will recall vivid memories of happy vacation times. Or a really good pair of shoes, at least.

The cities are loaded with nightlife and entertainment options. You can spend a hundred bucks on a pair of theater tickets or nurse a couple of $3 beers in a friendly bar all night — the choice is entirely up to you and your wallet. Outside of the cities, California tends to be quiet after dark, although college towns such as Santa Barbara and resort destinations such as Palm Springs are exceptions.

Keeping a Lid on Expenses

We don't care how much money you have, but we do know that you don't want to spend more than you have to. In this section, we help you rein in your expenses before they get out of control.

Getting the best airfare

This is such a huge topic that we've dedicated the better part of a chapter to it. Before you even start scanning for fares, see Chapter 6 (also see Chapter 7 if you're interested in traveling *within* California by plane).

Booking accommodations — and avoiding the rack-rate scam

The *rack rate* is the equivalent of the suggested retail price for your hotel room. Don't be unduly alarmed by the prices listed for some of the hotels — many a $300 hotel never charges $300 a night for a room. The best way to avoid paying the full rack rate when booking your hotels is stunningly simple: Just ask for a cheaper or discounted rate. You may be pleasantly surprised. But you have to take the initiative and ask, because no one is going to volunteer to save you money.

Taking the AAA advantage

 If you aren't already a member, consider taking a few minutes to join the **American Automobile Association (AAA)** before you launch your California vacation. Unfamiliar roads, unpredictable drivers, unforeseen circumstances (a flat that needs fixing, a battery that needs jump-starting), and unexplainable moments of stupidity (hello, lockout!) are just a few of the reasons for hooking into the club's roadside assistance network before you leave home.

But AAA membership offers much more than the occasional roadside rescue. Membership can save you money on hotel rates and admission to attractions throughout California (and other locations). Also included in the annual dues is a mind-boggling array of travel-related and general lifestyle services, as well as comprehensive maps. The **AAA Travel Agency** can help you book air, hotel, and car arrangements as well as all-inclusive tour packages — and the staff will always let you know when a AAA member discount is available. American Express traveler's checks are available to members at no charge (see the "Handling Money" section later in this chapter for more information on traveler's checks).

To find the AAA office nearest you, log on to www.aaa.com, where you'll be linked to your regional club's home page after you enter your home zip code. You can get instant membership by calling the national 24-hour emergency roadside service number (☎ 800-AAA-HELP), which can connect you to any regional membership department during expanded business hours (only roadside assistance operates 24 hours a day). If you live in Canada, the **Canadian Automobile Association** (☎ 613-247-0117; www.caa.ca) offers similar services (plus reciprocal benefits with AAA).

Cutting costs, but not the fun

In addition to the suggestions we discuss in the preceding sections, here are some other potential money-saving tips:

- ✔ **Always mention membership in AAA, AARP, or frequent-flier/ frequent-traveler programs.** You may also qualify for corporate, student, military, or senior discounts.

- ✔ **Call the hotel directly and also call the central reservations toll-free number.** We've found that it's worth the extra pennies to make both calls and find out which one gives you the better deal. Sometimes the local reservationist knows about special deals or packages, but the hotel may neglect to tell the central booking line. We think phoning the hotel directly is especially important if you have questions about room configurations and amenities. The nice folks manning the phones at central reservations don't actually know anything more about the individual hotels than what they may have read on a brochure. For the most accurate information, talk to the reservations manager at the hotel.

✔ **Consult a reliable travel agent.** Even if you've already booked your own airfare, you may find that a travel agent can negotiate a better price with certain hotels than you can get on your own. For more advice on the pros and cons of using an agent, see Chapter 6.

✔ **Bed-and-breakfasts are generally nonnegotiable on price.** However, always ask whether a price break is available midweek or during the off-season; in fact, you'll find that many B&Bs publish discounted midweek and off-season rates.

✔ **Study this book.** Keep your eyes posted for the Bargain Alert icon as you read this book. This icon highlights money-saving opportunities and especially good values throughout the Golden State.

✔ **Travel midweek to popular weekending destinations.** Rates to destinations such as the Wine Country, Carmel, the Hearst Castle area, Solvang, and Santa Barbara are at their highest on the weekends. Schedule your visits to the cities on weekends, when business travelers abandon San Francisco, L.A., and San Diego hotels, leaving them open to bargain-hunting vacationers.

✔ **Check the hotel listings in this book.** In the destination chapters, we note the types of discounts that each hotel, B&B, or motel tends to offer. We can't guarantee what discounts may apply when you reserve, of course, but these tips should give you a heads-up on the kinds of special deals or discounted rates to ask for when you book.

✔ **Remember that summer — June through mid-September — is the busy season.** If you haven't decided on a travel time yet, consider the off-seasons, which are not only cheaper and less crowded but often more pleasant, weather-wise. See Chapter 3 for lots of helpful guidance.

✔ **Try a package tour.** For many destinations, you can book airfare, hotel, ground transportation, and even some sightseeing just by making one call to a travel agent or packager, for a price much less than if you put the trip together yourself. (See Chapter 6 for more on package tours.)

✔ **Try expensive restaurants at lunch instead of dinner.** Lunch tabs are usually a fraction of what dinner would cost at a top restaurant, and the menu often boasts many of the same specialties.

✔ **Get out of town.** In many places, big savings are just a short drive or taxi ride away. Hotels just outside the city, across the river, or less conveniently located are great bargains. Outlying motels often have free parking, with lower rates than downtown hotels offering amenities that you may never use. Sure, at a motel you'll be carrying your own bags, but the rooms are often just as comfortable and a whole lot cheaper.

✔ **Walk a lot.** A good pair of walking shoes can save money on taxis and other local transportation. As a bonus, you'll get to know your destination more intimately, as you explore at a slower pace.

Handling Money

You're the best judge of how much cash you feel comfortable carrying or what alternative form of currency is your favorite. That's not going to change much on your vacation. True, you'll probably be moving around more and incurring more expenses than you generally, and you may let your mind slip into vacation gear and not be as vigilant about your safety as when you're in work mode. But, those factors aside, the only type of payment that won't be quite as available to you away from home is your personal checkbook.

Using ATMs and carrying cash

The easiest and best way to get cash away from home is from an ATM (automated teller machine). The **Cirrus** (☎ **800-424-7787;** www. mastercard.com) and **PLUS** (☎ **800-843-7587;** www.visa.com) networks span the globe; look at the back of your bank card to find out which network you're on, and then call or check online for ATM locations at your destination.

Charging ahead with credit cards

Credit cards are a safe way to carry money: They also provide a convenient record of all your expenses, and they generally offer relatively good exchange rates. You can also withdraw cash advances from your credit cards at banks or ATMs, provided you know your PIN, but most banks charge their highest rate of interest on cash advances. If you've forgotten yours, or didn't know you had one, call the number on the back of your credit card and ask the bank to send it to you.

Toting traveler's checks

These days, traveler's checks are less necessary than in the past because most cities have 24-hour ATMs that allow you to withdraw cash as needed.

You can get traveler's checks at almost any bank. You'll pay a service charge ranging from 1 percent to 4 percent. You can also get **American Express** traveler's checks over the phone by calling ☎ **800-221-7282;** Amex gold and platinum cardholders who use this number are exempt from the 1 percent fee.

 If you choose to carry traveler's checks, be sure to keep a record of their serial numbers separate from your checks, in case they're stolen or lost. You'll get a refund faster if you know the numbers.

Dealing with a Lost or Stolen Wallet

Be sure to contact all your credit-card companies the minute you discover your wallet has been lost or stolen and file a report at the nearest police precinct. Your credit-card company or insurer may require a police-report number or a record of the loss. Most credit-card companies have an emergency toll-free number to call if your card is lost or stolen; the company may be able to wire you a cash advance immediately or deliver an emergency credit card in a day or two. Call the following emergency numbers in the United States:

- ✔ **American Express:** ☎ **800-221-7282** (for cardholders and traveler's check holders)

- ✔ **MasterCard:** ☎ **800-307-7309** or 636-722-7111

- ✔ **Visa:** ☎ **800-847-2911** or 410-581-9994

For other credit cards, call the toll-free number directory at ☎ **800-555-1212.**

If you need emergency cash over the weekend when all banks and American Express offices are closed, you can have money wired to you via **Western Union** (☎ **800-325-6000;** www.westernunion.com).

Identity theft and fraud are potential complications of losing your wallet, especially if you've lost your driver's license along with your cash and credit cards. Notify the major credit-reporting bureaus immediately; placing a fraud alert on your records may protect you against liability for criminal activity. The three major U.S. credit-reporting agencies are **Equifax** (☎ **800-766-0008;** www.equifax.com), **Experian** (☎ **888-397-3742;** www.experian.com), and **TransUnion** (☎ **800-680-7289;** www.transunion.com). Finally, if you've lost all forms of photo ID, call your airline and explain the situation; the airline may allow you to board the plane if you have a copy of your passport or birth certificate and a copy of the police report you've filed.

Chapter 6

Getting to California

*G*etting there may not *really* be half the fun, but it's a necessary step and a big part of the planning process. Should you use a travel agent or go the independent route? Should you book a package deal or book the elements of your vacation separately?

In this chapter, we give you the information you need to decide what's right for you.

Who Flies Where

The major California airports include

- ✔ **San Francisco International Airport (SFO)**, 14 miles south of downtown San Francisco via U.S. 101 (☎ **650-821-8211**; www. flysfo.com)

- ✔ **Sacramento International Airport**, north of downtown Sacramento on I-5, just past the junction with Highway 99 (☎ **916-929-5411**; www.sacairports.org)

- ✔ **San Jose International Airport**, gateway to the Silicon Valley, just north of the U.S. 101/I-880/Highway 17 junction, at the intersection of U.S. 101 and Highway 87 (☎ **408-501-7600**; www.sjc.org)

- ✔ **Los Angeles International Airport (LAX)**, at the intersection of the I-405 and I-105 freeways, 9½ miles south of Santa Monica and 16 miles southwest of Hollywood (☎ **310-646-5252**; www.lawa.org)

- ✔ **San Diego International Airport**, locally known as Lindbergh Field, on I-5 right in the heart of San Diego (☎ **619-400-2400**; www. san.org)

Chances are good that one of these major airports will be your gateway. In addition, major carriers also serve good-size or smaller airports in Oakland, just across the bay from San Francisco (see Chapter 11); in the middle of the state in Fresno, close to the southern gateway to Yosemite (see Chapter 16); in Reno, Nevada, less than an hour's drive from Lake Tahoe (see Chapter 15); on the northern Central Coast in Monterey (see Chapter 18); in Orange County, just a stone's throw from Disneyland (see Chapter 24); and in Palm Springs (see Chapter 26).

 Because the Golden State is so darn big and has so many major airports, you need to work out a basic itinerary for yourself before you book your airline tickets. The destination chapters in this book help you do that, as do the itineraries in Chapter 4.

 Seriously consider flying into one California airport and leaving from another. The time you save by flying into San Diego and leaving from San Francisco, say, or flying into San Jose and departing from Palm Springs, may justify the extra airline charges and/or rental-car drop-off charges. What's more, depending on your points of arrival and departure, you may happily discover that no extra charges apply. Your best bet is to have a couple of options and price them out with the airlines and car companies (or put your travel agent to work) before you make a final decision.

Tips for getting the best airfare

Competition among the major U.S. airlines is unlike that of any other industry. Every airline offers virtually the same product (basically, a coach seat is a coach seat is a . . .), yet prices can vary by hundreds of dollars.

 Business travelers who need the flexibility to buy their tickets at the last minute and change their itineraries at a moment's notice — and who want to get home before the weekend — often pay (or at least their companies pay) the premium rate, known as the *full fare*. But if you can book your ticket far in advance, stay over Saturday night, and are willing to travel midweek (Tuesday, Wednesday, or Thursday), you can qualify for the least expensive price — usually a fraction of the full fare. On most flights, even the shortest hops within the United States, the full fare is close to $1,000 or more, but a 7- or 14-day advance-purchase ticket may cost less than half of that amount. Obviously, planning ahead pays.

The airlines also periodically hold sales, in which they lower the prices on their most popular routes. These fares have advance-purchase requirements and date-of-travel restrictions, but you can't beat the prices. As you plan your vacation, keep your eyes open for these sales, which tend to take place in seasons of low travel volume — for California, that's the winter months. You almost never see a sale around the peak summer-vacation months of July and August, or around Thanksgiving or Christmas, when many people fly, regardless of the fare they have to pay.

Consolidators, also known as *bucket shops,* are great sources for international tickets, although they usually can't beat the Internet on fares within North America. Start by looking in Sunday newspaper travel sections; U.S. travelers should focus on the *New York Times, Los Angeles Times,* and *Miami Herald.*

Booking your flight online

The "big three" online travel agencies, **Expedia** (www.expedia.com), **Travelocity** (www.travelocity.com), and **Orbitz** (www.orbitz.com), sell most of the air tickets bought on the Internet. (Canadian travelers should try www.expedia.ca and www.travelocity.ca; U.K. residents can go for expedia.co.uk and opodo.co.uk.) Each has different business deals with the airlines and may offer different fares on the same flights, so shopping around is wise. Expedia and Travelocity will also send you an **e-mail notification** when a cheap fare becomes available to your favorite destination. Of the smaller travel-agency Web sites, **SideStep** (www.sidestep.com) receives good reviews from users.

Great **last-minute deals** are available through free weekly e-mail services provided directly by the airlines. Most of these deals are announced on Tuesday or Wednesday and must be purchased online. Most are only valid for travel that weekend, but some (such as Southwest's) can be booked weeks or months in advance. Sign up for weekly e-mail alerts at airline Web sites or check mega-sites that compile comprehensive lists of last-minute specials, such as **Smarter Travel** (www.smartertravel.com). For last-minute trips, www.site59.com in the United States and www.lastminute.com in Europe often have better deals than the major-label sites.

 Great last-minute deals are also available directly from the airlines themselves through a free e-mail service called *E-savers.* Each week, the airline sends you a list of discounted flights, usually leaving the upcoming Friday or Saturday and returning the following Monday or Tuesday. You can sign up for all the major airlines at one time by logging on to **Smarter Travel** (www.smartertravel.com), or you can go to each individual airline's Web site. Airline sites also offer schedules, flight booking, and information on late-breaking bargains.

Driving to California

Driving yourself to California can be a smart move, especially if you live relatively close by and you'd prefer to tour the state in your own car.

The major interstates that lead into the state are as follows:

- **I-5,** which enters California from Oregon at the northern border and runs south through the middle of the state all the way to San Diego
- **I-80,** which arrives from the east via Reno, Nevada, and runs west through Sacramento to San Francisco

✔ **I-15,** which connects Las Vegas, Nevada, with I-10 just east of Los Angeles

✔ **I-40,** which runs across the northern half of the southern states, cutting through the Texas panhandle; Albuquerque, New Mexico; and Flagstaff, Arizona, before entering California in Needles, California (where Snoopy's cousin Spike is from, if you're a *Peanuts* fan) — otherwise known as the middle of nowhere — and heading west until it connects to I-15 northeast of Los Angeles

✔ **I-10,** the most popular route into Southern California, which runs from New Orleans, Louisiana, to Los Angeles, passing through Houston, Texas; Phoenix, Arizona; and Palm Springs along the way.

✔ **I-8,** which links Tucson and Yuma, Arizona, with San Diego

Table 6-1 has some handy drive times for your road trip, not including any delays for traffic, weather, or mishaps:

Table 6-1   Counting the Miles and Hours to California

City	Distance	Drive Time
To San Francisco from:		
Portland, Oregon	636 miles	10¼ hours
Reno, Nevada	220 miles	3¾ hours
Boise, Idaho	641 miles	11½ hours
Salt Lake City, Utah	737 miles	11¾ hours
Las Vegas, Nevada	574 miles	9½ hours
To Los Angeles from:		
Salt Lake City, Utah	690 miles	11 hours
Las Vegas, Nevada	270 miles	4½ hours
Albuquerque, New Mexico	789 miles	12½ hours
Phoenix, Arizona	373 miles	6¼ hours
To San Diego from:		
Las Vegas, Nevada	332 miles	5½ hours
El Paso, Texas	725 miles	11½ hours
Tucson, Arizona	407 miles	6½ hours

Taking the train

Amtrak (☎ 800-USA-RAIL; www.amtrak.com) serves multiple California cities, including San Francisco, San Jose, Santa Barbara, L.A., and San Diego.

Arriving by train from another state is much slower and not significantly cheaper than traveling by plane. Therefore, explore this option only if you hate flying, saving a little money means more to you than speed of travel, or you're drawn to the romanticism of a train journey. You'll still need to rent a car to do any significant sightseeing, unless you'd prefer to travel around California by train, too; for details, see Chapter 7.

Joining an Escorted Tour

You may be one of the many people who love escorted tours. The tour company takes care of all the details and tells you what to expect at each leg of your journey. You know your costs upfront and, in the case of the tame ones, you don't get many surprises. Escorted tours can take you to the maximum number of sights in the minimum amount of time with the least amount of hassle.

 If you decide to go with an escorted tour, we strongly recommend purchasing travel insurance, especially if the tour operator asks you to pay upfront. But don't buy insurance from the tour operator! If the tour operator doesn't fulfill its obligation to provide you with the vacation you paid for, there's no reason to think that it'll fulfill its insurance obligations either. Get travel insurance through an independent agency. (We tell you more about the ins and outs of travel insurance in Chapter 10.)

When choosing an escorted tour, along with finding out whether you have to put down a deposit and when final payment is due, ask a few simple questions before you buy:

- ✔ **What is the cancellation policy?** Can the tour operator cancel the trip if it doesn't get enough people? How late can you cancel if you're unable to go? Do you get a refund if you cancel? If the tour operator cancels?

- ✔ **How jam-packed is the schedule?** Does the tour schedule try to fit 25 hours into a 24-hour day, or does it give you ample time to relax by the pool or shop? If getting up at 7 a.m. every day and not returning to your hotel until 6 or 7 p.m. at night sounds like a grind, certain escorted tours may not be for you.

- ✔ **How large is the group?** The smaller the group, the less time you spend waiting for people to get on and off the bus. Tour operators may be evasive about this, because they may not know the exact size of the group until everybody has made reservations, but they should be able to give you a rough estimate.

✔ **Is there a minimum group size?** Some tours have a minimum group size and may cancel the tour if they don't book enough people. If a quota exists, find out what it is and how close the company is to reaching it. Again, tour operators may be evasive in their answers, but the information may help you select a tour that's sure to happen.

✔ **What exactly is included?** Don't assume anything. You may have to pay to get yourself to and from the airport. A box lunch may be included in an excursion, but drinks may be extra. Beer may be included but not wine. How much flexibility do you have? Can you opt out of certain activities, or does the bus leave once a day, with no exceptions? Are all your meals planned in advance? Can you choose your entree at dinner, or does everybody get the same chicken cutlet?

Choosing a Package Tour

For lots of destinations, package tours can be a smart way to go. In many cases, a package tour that includes airfare, hotel, and transportation to and from the airport costs less than the hotel alone on a tour you book yourself. That's because packages are sold in bulk to tour operators, who resell them to the public. It's kind of like buying your vacation at a buy-in-bulk store — except the tour operator is the one who buys the 1,000-count box of garbage bags and resells them 10 at a time at a cost that undercuts the local supermarket.

Package tours can vary as much as those garbage bags, too. Some offer a better class of hotels than others; others provide the same hotels for lower prices. Some book flights on scheduled airlines; others sell charters. In some packages, your choice of accommodations and travel days may be limited. Some let you choose between escorted vacations and independent vacations; others allow you to add on just a few excursions or escorted day trips (also at discounted prices) without booking an entirely escorted tour.

To find package tours, check out the travel section of your local Sunday newspaper or the ads in the back of national travel magazines such as *Travel + Leisure, National Geographic Traveler,* and *Condé Nast Traveler.* **Liberty Travel** (☎ 888-271-1584; www.libertytravel.com) is one of the biggest packagers in the Northeast, and usually boasts a full-page ad in Sunday papers.

Another good source of package deals is the airlines themselves. Most major airlines offer air/land packages, including **American Airlines Vacations** (☎ 800-321-2121; www.aavacations.com), **Delta Vacations** (☎ 800-221-6666; www.deltavacations.com), **Continental Airlines Vacations** (☎ 800-301-3800; www.covacations.com), and **United Vacations** (☎ 888-854-3899; www.unitedvacations.com). Several big

online travel agencies — Expedia, Travelocity, Orbitz, Site59, and Lastminute.com — also do a brisk business in packages. If you're unsure about the pedigree of a smaller packager, check with the Better Business Bureau in the city where the company is based, or go online to www. bbb.org. If a packager won't tell you where it's based, don't fly with it.

If you're considering either arriving in California by train or traveling around the state by train — or both — check into the all-inclusive travel packages offered by **Amtrak Vacations** (☎ 800-654-5748; www.amtrak vacations.com).

If you're an Amex customer, consider going through **American Express Travel** (☎ 800-AXP-6898 or 800-346-3607; www.americanexpress.com/ travel), which can book packages through various vendors, including Continental and Delta.

If you're heading to Disneyland, you may want to contact the official Disney travel agency, **Walt Disney Travel Co.** (☎ 800-225-2024 or 714-520-5050; www.disneyland.com). The company offers Disney-focused packages that can also include a wide range of Southern California extras, depending on your wants and needs. For more on this, see Chapter 24.

Universal Studios Vacations offers all-inclusive L.A. vacation deals that include a visit to its park; call ☎ 800-711-0080 or go online to www. universalstudiosvacations.com.

The well-conceived escorted tours of California offered by **Tauck Tours** (☎ 800-788-7885; www.tauck.com) are more luxurious and less structured than your average escorted tour. They're pricey but worth the cost if you'd rather let someone else do the driving.

Be advised that most travel packagers don't offer comprehensive California vacations. They tend to focus on the large-volume destinations — San Francisco, Los Angeles, San Diego, Disneyland, and sometimes Lake Tahoe and Palm Springs. If you want to hit other destinations, you'll likely have to (or have your travel agent) book those legs of your trip directly. Still, don't give up on the package route; with a little planning, you (or your travel agent) may manage to link a few smaller packages into the good-value vacation of your dreams.

Chapter 7

Getting Around California

• •

In This Chapter

▶ Traveling around California by car (a rental or your own)
▶ Following the rules of the road
▶ Touring the Golden State by plane or train

• •

Forget the Golden State moniker — California is really the Driving State. You need a car to get yourself around, no two ways about it. Even if you choose to move from destination to destination using planes and trains, you likely need an automobile after you get to your destination. The only California destinations that you can easily navigate via other means of transportation are San Francisco, San Diego (some attractions, not all), and Santa Barbara. It's unfortunate, given that California has perhaps the highest gas prices in the country.

Getting Around by Car

If you don't bring your own car to California, you'll probably need to rent one. The following companies rent cars at locations throughout California, including at all the major airports and in the cities:

- ✔ **Alamo:** ☎ **800-462-5266;** www.goalamo.com

- ✔ **Avis:** ☎ **800-230-4898;** www.avis.com

- ✔ **Budget:** ☎ **800-527-0700;** https://rent.drivebudget.com

- ✔ **Dollar:** ☎ **800-800-4000;** www.dollar.com

- ✔ **Enterprise:** ☎ **800-325-8007;** www.enterprise.com

- ✔ **Hertz:** ☎ **800-654-3131;** www.hertz.com

- ✔ **National:** ☎ **800-227-7368;** www.nationalcar.com

- ✔ **Thrifty:** ☎ **800-847-4389;** www.thrifty.com

Rental cars are relatively cheap in the Driving State. Of course, we can't guarantee what you'll pay when you book, but you can often get a compact car for between $100 and $200 a week, depending on your dates and where you pick up your car. (Southern California rentals are usually cheaper.) If you want a car large enough for an entire family, expect to pay more like $200 to $300 a week, which is still quite reasonable.

We advocate flying into one airport and leaving from another so that you can see as much of California as possible. And depending on your pickup and drop-off points, you may find that you won't have to pay extra for your one-way car rental. No promises, but we've found that more often than not, you won't pay more than if you had picked up and dropped off at the same location.

Price car rentals at the same time you price airfares to make sure that flying into one city and out of another is cost-effective on both counts. Check with a few companies before you make a final decision. If you get a rate quote you like and decide that this is the way you want to go, make your reservation (which will lock in your rate) immediately. This will save you from getting taken to the cleaners after the fact — because policies and prices can change at any time.

Getting the best deal on a rental car

Car-rental rates vary even more than airline fares. The price depends on the size of the car, the length of time you keep it, where and when you pick it up and drop it off, where you take it, and a host of other factors. Finding out about a few key details may save you hundreds of dollars.

✔ Weekend rates may be lower than weekday rates. If you're keeping the car five or more days, a weekly rate may be cheaper than the daily rate. Ask whether the rate is the same for pickup Friday morning as it is Thursday night.

✔ Some companies may assess a drop-off charge if you don't return the car to the same rental location; others, notably National, don't.

✔ Check whether the rate is cheaper if you pick up the car at a location in town rather than at the airport.

✔ Find out whether age is an issue. Many car-rental companies add on a fee for drivers younger than 25, while some don't rent to them at all.

✔ If you see an advertised price in your local newspaper, be sure to ask for that specific rate; otherwise, you may be charged the standard (higher) rate. And don't forget to mention membership in AAA, AARP, and trade unions. These memberships usually entitle you to discounts ranging from 5 to 30 percent.

✔ Check your frequent-flier accounts. Not only are your favorite (or at least most-used) airlines likely to send you discount coupons, but most car rentals add at least 500 miles to your account.

✔ As with other aspects of planning your trip, using the Internet can make comparison shopping for a car rental much easier. You can check rates at most of the major agencies' Web sites. Plus, all the major travel sites — **Travelocity** (www.travelocity.com), **Expedia** (www.expedia.com), **Orbitz** (www.orbitz.com), and **Smarter Travel** (www.smartertravel.com), for example — have search engines that can dig up discounted car-rental rates.

In addition to the standard rental prices, other optional charges (and some not-so-optional charges, such as taxes) apply to most car rentals. The *Collision Damage Waiver* (CDW), which requires you to pay for damage to the car in a collision, is covered by many credit-card companies. Check with your credit-card company before you go so that you can avoid paying this hefty fee (as much as $20 a day).

The car-rental companies also offer additional *liability insurance* (if you harm others in an accident), *personal-accident insurance* (if you harm yourself or your passengers), and *personal-effects insurance* (if your luggage is stolen from your car). Your insurance policy on your car at home probably covers most of these unlikely occurrences. However, if your own insurance doesn't cover you for rentals or if you don't have auto insurance, definitely consider the additional coverage (ask your car-rental agent for more information). Unless you're toting around the Hope diamond — and you don't want to leave that in your car trunk, anyway — you can probably skip the personal-effects insurance, but driving around without liability or personal-accident coverage is never a good idea. Even if you're a good driver, other people may not be, and liability claims can be complicated.

Some companies also offer *refueling packages,* in which you pay for your initial full tank of gas upfront and then can return the car with an empty gas tank. The prices can be competitive with local gas prices, but you don't get credit for any gas remaining in the tank. If you reject this option, you pay only for the gas you use, but you have to return the car with a full tank or face charges of $3 to $4 a gallon for any shortfall. If you usually run late and a fueling stop may make you miss your plane, you're a perfect candidate for the fuel-purchase option.

Following the rules of the road

Know these rules of the road before you drive around California:

- ✔ **All passengers must wear seatbelts at all times.** No cheating in the back seat. You must harness children under 4 years old or 40 pounds into an approved safety seat (some car-rental agencies now rent these seats; ask when you reserve your car).

- ✔ **Motorcyclists must wear helmets.**

- ✔ **You can turn right on red as long as a posted sign doesn't say otherwise.** Make sure you make a full stop first — no rolling.

- ✔ **The maximum speed limit on most California freeways is 65 mph, although some freeways carry a posted limit of 70 mph.** For two-lane undivided highways, the maximum speed limit is 55 mph, unless otherwise posted. Speed limits vary in populated areas; defaulting to 25 mph is smart if you're not sure. California law states that you must never drive faster than is safe for the present conditions, regardless of the posted speed limit.

✔ **You can pass on the right on the freeway as long as you act safely and use a properly marked lane.**

✔ **Pedestrians always have the right of way both on crosswalks and at uncontrolled intersections.**

✔ **Those kids you brought with you can come in handy.** Some freeways, especially those in Southern California, have a High Occupancy Vehicle (HOV) lane (otherwise known as a carpool lane), which lets you speed past some of the congestion if three people are in the car (sometimes two; read the signs). Don't flout the rules; if you do, expect to shell out close to $300 for the ticket.

✔ **Always read street-parking signs and keep plenty of quarters on hand for meters.** Popular destinations and smaller towns with parking crunches often have some of the most stringent rules and gung-ho meter readers. Be extra-vigilant in metropolitan areas.

Save yourself some hassle and just get a roll of dedicated parking quarters at your bank before you leave home.

✔ **Check the Web for a complete rundown of California state driving guidelines.** The complete *California Driver Handbook* is available online (www.dmv.ca.gov), and you can also find rules of the road for motorcycles, RVs, and trailers.

In addition to following the rules of the road, include the following tips among your driving practices:

✔ **Always have a good statewide map on hand.** You can get good maps from AAA or the California Division of Tourism (you can even download the official state map from the CDT Web site at www.visitcalifornia.com).

✔ **Know more about the direction you're heading than simply "north" or "south."** California's freeway and highway signs indicate direction, more often than not, by naming a town rather than a compass point: To head east on I-10 to Palm Springs, say, you follow the signs that say "Ontario" as you drive out of L.A., not the ones that say "Santa Monica." Review your map carefully so that you know which way to go before you hit the road.

✔ **Prepare your vehicle for the weather.** If you're heading to Yosemite or Tahoe in winter, top off on antifreeze and bring snow chains. If renting a car, ask the agency if chains are provided. Also, check road conditions before you set out. Call the California Department of Transportation (CALTRANS) at ☎ 800-427-7623, which can fill you in on conditions throughout the state at any time of year. You can also check road and traffic conditions online at www.dot.ca.gov.

✔ **Take along your cellphone or rent one.** A cellphone can be an invaluable lifeline as you drive throughout California. If you're renting a car, you're often able to rent a cellphone along with your vehicle; ask when you call. You can also rent cellphones at airport kiosks. Or, you can rent a phone before you leave home by calling **InTouchUSA** (☎ **800-872-7626;** www.intouchusa.com), which rents wireless products and even evaluates your own phone's calling capabilities for free before you leave home. (Call ☎ **703-222-7161** 9 a.m.–4 p.m.)

✔ **Know how far you have to go.** See Table 7-1 for some sample distances between California destinations.

Table 7-1 Sample Mileage between California Destinations

From San Francisco to	*From Los Angeles to*	*From San Diego to*
Eureka: 261 miles	Mendocino: 528 miles	San Francisco: 504 miles
Yosemite: 202 miles	Lake Tahoe: 189 miles	Yosemite: 345 miles
Napa Valley: 48 miles	Monterey: 323 miles	Death Valley: 324 miles
Monterey: 119 miles	Hearst Castle: 231 miles	Los Angeles: 122 miles
Hearst Castle: 211 miles	Death Valley: 262 miles	Disneyland: 98 miles
Santa Barbara: 328 miles	Santa Barbara: 97 miles	Palm Springs: 141 miles
Los Angeles: 382 miles	Disneyland: 27 miles	Tijuana: 16 miles
Disneyland: 408 miles	Palm Springs: 108 miles	
Palm Springs: 488 miles	San Diego: 122 miles	
San Diego: 504 miles		

Winging Your Way around California

If time is short and you want to cover great distances without the long drive, consider flying between California locations. After all, an hour-long flight can save you the entire travel day that driving between San Francisco and Los Angeles or San Diego would consume. Even shorter distances — L.A. to Monterey, say — can save you a good chunk of valuable vacation time. Airfares are generally reasonable, too, often between $60 and $100 per leg.

The following airlines are well versed in shuttling passengers between multiple California destinations:

- ✔ **Alaska Airlines:** ☎ 800-252-7522; www.alaskaair.com
- ✔ **American/American Eagle:** ☎ 800-433-7300; www.aa.com
- ✔ **America West:** ☎ 800-235-9292; www.americawest.com
- ✔ **Delta:** ☎ 800-221-1212; www.delta.com
- ✔ **Southwest:** ☎ 800-435-9792; www.southwest.com
- ✔ **United/United Express:** ☎ 800-241-6522; www.united.com
- ✔ **US Airways:** ☎ 800-428-4322; www.usairways.com

For a rundown of California airports, see Chapter 6.

 We can't promise who'll have the best deals when you're booking, but we've found that Southwest Airlines is often the cheapest and most convenient airline for traveling within California. Why? Three reasons:

- ✔ Tickets are sold by segments, which makes it cheap and easy to buy one-way fares.
- ✔ Southwest's full fares are comparatively low, so you may be able to change your itinerary without paying a ridiculous markup or penalty, and you can often get a full refund (or at least a credit for a future flight taken within one year of the original purchase) if you can't use the ticket.
- ✔ Internet specials often make the already low fares even lower.

Keep in mind that the airline saves money by skipping certain frills, including seat assignments. You get a seat by using a boarding card, and passengers are boarded in groups.

Going the Amtrak Way

Amtrak (☎ 800-USA-RAIL; www.amtrak.com) runs trains throughout California, including up and down the coast, serving destinations such as Sacramento, San Francisco, San Jose, Santa Barbara, Los Angeles, and San Diego, and numerous points in between. Using Amtrak won't save you any time over driving and may not even save you money over flying. Still, it's an option if you'd rather not drive yourself and don't like to fly, or if you're just enamored with the nostalgia of train travel.

Chapter 8

Booking Your Accommodations

*O*n the one hand, you aren't going to spend much time in your hotel room if you're doing even half the things we recommend in this book. On the other hand, it is nice to know you have some place soft — or cheap, depending on your priorities — to land when you drop at the end of the day. This chapter helps you get the best deals on the right place for your stay in California.

Getting to Know Your Options

Throughout California you have a range of accommodations to choose from — something for every taste, need, budget, and even, in the case of San Luis Obispo's Madonna Inn, fantasy. The larger the city, the greater the range — although, perhaps not in all categories. Unlike San Francisco, for example, Los Angeles has little in the way of adorable B&Bs. L.A. also has little in the way of anything fabulous for those of us whose wallets aren't lined with gold. The smaller the town, the more quaint the offerings — although generic chain hotels are still readily available everywhere. Decide what's important for you — price, style, service — and go from there. See Table 8-1.

Table 8-1	Key to Hotel Dollar Signs	
Dollar Sign(s)	Price Range	What to Expect
$	Less than $75	With a few precious exceptions — and we do go on about them at great length — this gets you basically a bed and motel-room furniture — unless, of course, you scored a good deal on an otherwise pricey room usually found in a higher category. Towels are likely to be of the depressingly thin variety, and don't expect top-brand toiletries. Remind yourself that you're there for the sunshine.
$$	$76–$150	This is a mixed-bag category. You could have a very nice (though perhaps generic-looking) hotel room in a fine establishment with all the amenities. Or it could be even more posh. Or it could be less so. Check each listing carefully.
$$$	$151–$225	The rooms move up in size and in stature — stature of amenities, that is. You're also likely to be in a more convenient (and potentially safer) neighborhood, and you're almost sure to have a lobby to walk through to get to your room — another safety necessity.
$$$$	$226–$300	Now we're talkin'. The service may be snooty, but the linens are soft and you get bathrobes and high-end amenities (nice shampoo, lotion, shoe buffer). We're also willing to bet that the grounds are fabulously landscaped.
$$$$$	$301 and up	In theory, you should have everything your little heart could desire in this category, but this is California, and sometimes you pay that price just for the privilege of staying somewhere that pampers Jennifer Lopez. Not being Jennifer Lopez, you may wonder what the fuss is all about.

Finding the Best Room at the Best Rate

The *rack rate* is the maximum rate a hotel charges for a room. It's the rate you get if you walk in off the street and ask for a room for the night. You sometimes see these rates printed on the fire/emergency-exit diagrams posted on the back of your door.

Hotels are happy to charge you the rack rate, but you can almost always do better. Perhaps the best way to avoid paying the rack rate is surprisingly simple: Just ask for a cheaper or discounted rate. You may be pleasantly surprised. We encourage you not to fret about any rack rate listed in this book. Often, reality differs dramatically.

Finding the best rate

In all but the smallest accommodations, the rate you pay for a room depends on many factors — chief among them being how you make your reservation. A travel agent may be able to negotiate a better price with certain hotels than you can get by yourself. (That's because the hotel often gives the agent a discount in exchange for steering his business toward that hotel.)

Reserving a room through the hotel's toll-free number may also result in a lower rate than calling the hotel directly. On the other hand, the central reservations number may not know about discount rates at specific locations. For example, local franchises may offer a special group rate for a wedding or family reunion, but they may neglect to tell the central booking line. Your best bet is to call both the local number and the toll-free number and see which one gives you a better deal.

Room rates (even rack rates) change with the season, as occupancy rates rise and fall. You can expect higher prices during popular summer in California, in addition to still sunny Christmastime, and any school holiday. Lower rates should turn up during the winter. But even within a given season, room prices are subject to change without notice, so the rates quoted in this book may be different from the actual rate you receive when you make your reservation. When you call to book, be sure to mention membership in AAA, AARP, frequent-flier programs, or any other corporate rewards programs you can think of — or your Uncle Joe's Elks Lodge in which you're an honorary inductee, for that matter. You never know when the affiliation may be worth a few dollars off your room rate.

Surfing the Web for hotel deals

Shopping online for hotels is generally done one of two ways: by booking through the hotel's own Web site or by booking through an independent booking agency (or a fare-service agency such as Priceline). Of the "big three" booking agencies, **Expedia** offers a long list of special deals and "virtual tours" or photos of available rooms so you can see what you're paying for (a feature that helps counter the claims that the best rooms are often held back from bargain-booking Web sites). **Travelocity** posts unvarnished customer reviews and ranks its properties according to the AAA rating system. **Orbitz** features a handy tool to let you search for specific amenities you may be interested in. Also reliable are **Hotels.com** and **Quikbook.com**. An excellent free program, **TravelAxe** (www.travelaxe.net), can help you search multiple hotel sites at once, even ones you may never have heard of — and conveniently lists the total price of the room, including the taxes and service charges.

Another booking site, **Travelweb** (www.travelweb.com), is partly owned by the hotels it represents (including the Hilton, Hyatt, and Starwood chains) and is therefore plugged directly into the hotels' reservations systems — unlike independent online agencies, which have to fax or e-mail reservation requests to the hotel, a good portion of which get misplaced in the shuffle. More than once, travelers have arrived at the hotel, only to be told that they have no reservation.

Many of the major sites are undergoing improvements in service and ease of use, and Expedia will soon be able to plug directly into the reservations systems of many hotel chains — none of which can be bad news for consumers. In the meantime, it's a good idea to get a confirmation number and make a printout of any online-booking transaction.

In the opaque Web site category, **Priceline** and **Hotwire** are even better for hotels than for airfares; with both, you're allowed to pick the neighborhood and quality level of your hotel before offering up your money. Priceline's hotel product even covers Europe and Asia, though it's much better at getting five-star lodging for three-star prices than at finding anything at the bottom of the scale. On the downside, many hotels stick Priceline guests in their least desirable rooms. Be sure to go to the BiddingForTravel Web site (www.biddingfortravel.com) before bidding on a hotel room on Priceline; it features a fairly up-to-date list of hotels that Priceline uses in major cities. For both Priceline and Hotwire, you pay upfront, and the fee is nonrefundable. *Note:* Some hotels do not provide loyalty-program credits or points or other frequent-stay amenities when you book a room through opaque online services.

Reserving the best room

After you make your reservation, asking one or two more pointed questions can go a long way toward making sure you get the best room in the house.

- ✓ **Always ask for a corner room.** They're usually larger, quieter, and have more windows and light than standard rooms, and they don't always cost more.

- ✓ **Ask whether the hotel is renovating.** If it is, request a room away from the renovation work.

- ✓ **Inquire about the location of the restaurants, bars, and discos in the hotel — all sources of annoying noise.**

- ✓ **Ask whether you're paying more for the view.** Rooms with views — of the water in San Francisco and Santa Monica, or any mountain or sterling city vista — often run a bit more, so if you're trying to save money, ask yourself how often you look out the window. (During a slow period, you may be able to score that view room for less than it usually goes for, if you ask nicely enough.)

- ✓ **If you aren't happy with your room when you arrive, talk to the front-desk staff.** If they have another room, they should be happy to accommodate you, within reason.

Chapter 9

Catering to Special Travel Needs or Interests

In This Chapter

▶ Taking the kids along
▶ Going to the Golden State in your golden years
▶ Dealing with disabilities
▶ Traveling tips for gays and lesbians

*G*enerally speaking, California is a forward-thinking state, and plenty accommodating if you have special requirements. But you may want to know more; specifically, how welcoming will California be to you and . . . (pick one or more)

✔ Your kids

✔ Your senior status

✔ Your disability

✔ Your same-sex partner

If you need answers, you've come to the right chapter.

Traveling with the Brood: Advice for Families

With its wealth of parks — both the theme kind, a la Disneyland, and the natural kind, a la Yosemite — California is the ultimate family-vacation state. Knowing on which side its bread is buttered, the Golden State offers a wealth of family-friendly accommodations — from luxury resorts to budget motels — restaurants, and other activities. We note the best kid-friendly spots throughout this book.

Some destinations suit families better than do others. Skip romantic Carmel, for example, and head for kid-friendly Monterey. Your kids will probably prefer San Diego to Palm Springs, if you have to choose. Still, families are as individual as snowflakes, and no single blueprint exists for the ultimate family vacation.

Your vacation will go well if you remember to tailor your trip around the things you and your kids like to do. Check out the itineraries in Chapter 4, a number of which take family travel into consideration.

Following are a few tips to help you with your family travel plans:

- ✔ **Don't be too ambitious.** We can't say this too strongly: Too much time spent in the car moving from one place to another will result in a trip from hell — for both you and the kids. When you can't avoid a long car trip, try to book a rental car with a DVD player. We wish our parents had one when we were kids on long family driving vacations.

- ✔ **Take it slow at the start.** Give the entire family time to adjust to a new time zone or to just being on the road. The best way to do this is to arrive at your initial destination and budget a couple of days that don't require strict itineraries or lots of moving around.

- ✔ **Look for the Kid Friendly icon as you flip through this book.** We use it to highlight hotels, restaurants, and attractions that your family will find particularly welcoming. Zeroing in on these listings helps you plan your trip more efficiently.

- ✔ **Bring plenty of road-trip supplies.** Bring healthy snacks, car-friendly books and games, and a pillow and blanket for nap time. Books on tape are great for entertaining the entire family.

- ✔ **Book some private time for mom and dad.** Most hotels can hook you up with a reliable baby sitter who will entertain the kids while you enjoy a romantic dinner or another adults-only activity. Ask about babysitting services when you make your reservations.

If you have enough trouble getting your kids out of the house in the morning, dragging them thousands of miles away may seem like an insurmountable challenge. But family travel can be immensely rewarding, giving you new ways of seeing the world through smaller pairs of eyes.

Familyhostel (☎ 800-733-9753; www.learn.unh.edu/familyhostel) takes the whole family, including kids ages 8 to 15, on moderately priced domestic and international learning vacations. Lectures, field trips, and sightseeing are guided by a team of academics.

You can find good family-oriented vacation advice on the Internet from sites such as the **Family Travel Forum** (www.familytravelforum.com), a comprehensive site that offers customized trip planning; **Family Travel Network** (www.familytravelnetwork.com), an award-winning site that offers travel features, deals, and tips; **Traveling Internationally with Your Kids** (www.travelwithyourkids.com), a comprehensive site that offers customized trip planning; and **Family Travel Files** (www.thefamily travelfiles.com), which offers an online magazine and a directory of off-the-beaten-path tours and tour operators for families.

Making Age Work for You: Tips for Seniors

Mention the fact that you're a senior citizen when you make your travel reservations. Although all the major U.S. airlines except America West have cancelled their senior-discount and coupon-book programs, many hotels still offer discounts for seniors. In most cities, people over the age of 60 qualify for reduced admission to theaters, museums, and other attractions, as well as discounted fares on public transportation.

Members of **AARP** (formerly known as the American Association of Retired Persons), 601 E St. NW, Washington, DC 20049 (☎ **888-687-2277** or 202-434-2277; www.aarp.org), get discounts on hotels, airfares, and car rentals. AARP offers members a wide range of benefits, including *AARP: The Magazine* and a monthly newsletter. Anyone over 50 can join.

The **U.S. National Park Service** offers a **Golden Age Passport** that gives seniors 62 years or older lifetime entrance to all properties administered by the National Park Service — national parks, monuments, historic sites, recreation areas, and national wildlife refuges — for a one-time processing fee of $10, which must be purchased in person at any NPS facility that charges an entrance fee (for example, Yosemite National Park). Besides free entry, a Golden Age Passport also offers a 50 percent discount on federal-use fees charged for such facilities as camping, swimming, parking, boat launching, and tours. For more information, go online to www.nps.gov/fees_passes.htm or call ☎ **888-467-2757.**

Many reliable agencies and organizations target the 50-plus market. **Elderhostel** (☎ **877-426-8056;** www.elderhostel.org) arranges study programs for those age 55 or older (and a spouse or companion of any age) in the United States and in more than 80 countries around the world. Most courses last five to seven days in the United States (two to four weeks abroad), and many include airfare, accommodations in university dormitories or modest inns, meals, and tuition. **ElderTreks** (☎ **800-741-7956;** www.eldertreks.com) offers small-group tours to off-the-beaten-path or adventure-travel locations, restricted to travelers 50 or older. **INTRAV** (☎ **800-456-8100;** www.intrav.com) is a high-end tour operator that caters to the mature, discerning traveler, not specifically seniors, with trips around the world that include guided safaris, polar expeditions, private-jet adventures, and small-boat cruises down jungle rivers.

Recommended publications offering travel resources and discounts for seniors include: the quarterly magazine *Travel 50 & Beyond* (www.travel50andbeyond.com); *Travel Unlimited: Uncommon Adventures for the Mature Traveler,* by Alison Gardner (Avalon); *101 Tips for Mature Travelers,* available from Grand Circle Travel (☎ **800-221-2610** or 617-350-7500; www.gct.com); and *Unbelievably Good Deals and Great Adventures That You Absolutely Can't Get Unless You're Over 50,* by Joann Rattner Heilman (McGraw-Hill).

Accessing California: Advice for Travelers with a Disability

These days, a disability shouldn't stop anyone from traveling. In fact, California was at the forefront of making sure all public buildings were made wheelchair accessible and were equipped with accessible restrooms. Most hotels and sightseeing attractions (except those grandfathered by landmark status through the Americans with Disabilities Act, or ADA) are outfitted with wheelchair ramps and extra-wide doorways and halls. Many city-sidewalk corners have dropped curbs, and some public-transit systems are equipped with lifts. Your best bet is to contact local visitor bureaus, because they can provide you with all the specifics on accessibility in their locale; see the "Gathering More Information" sections at the end of each destination chapter in Parts II, III, and IV.

Because so many of California's hotels are on the newer side, a good number feature rooms dedicated to the needs of disabled travelers, outfitted with everything from extra-large bathrooms with low-set fixtures to fire-alarm systems adapted for deaf travelers. Still, before you book a hotel room, ask lots of questions based on your needs. After you arrive, always call restaurants, attractions, and theaters before you go to make sure they re fully accessible.

The U.S. National Park Service offers a **Golden Access Passport** that gives free lifetime entrance to all properties administered by the National Park Service — national parks, monuments, historic sites, recreation areas, and national wildlife refuges — for persons who are visually impaired or permanently disabled, regardless of age. You may pick up a Golden Access Passport at any NPS entrance-fee area by showing proof of medically determined disability and eligibility for receiving benefits under federal law. Besides free entry, the Golden Access Passport also offers a 50 percent discount on federal-use fees charged for such facilities as camping, swimming, parking, boat launching, and tours. For more information, go online to www.nps.gov/fees_passes.htm or call ☎ 888-467-2757.

Many travel agencies offer customized tours and itineraries for travelers with disabilities. **Flying Wheels Travel** (☎ 507-451-5005; www.flying wheelstravel.com) offers escorted tours and cruises that emphasize sports and private tours in minivans with lifts. **Access-Able Travel Source** (☎ 303-232-2979; www.access-able.com) offers extensive access information and advice for traveling around the world with disabilities. **Accessible Journeys** (☎ 800-846-4537 or 610-521-0339) assists wheelchair travelers and their families and friends.

Avis Rent a Car has an "Avis Access" program that offers such services as a dedicated 24-hour toll-free number (☎ 888-879-4273) for customers with special travel needs. Special cars feature amenities such as swivel seats, spinner knobs, and hand controls.

Organizations that offer assistance to disabled travelers include **MossRehab** (www.mossresourcenet.org), which provides a library of accessible-travel resources online; SATH (**Society for Accessible Travel and Hospitality;** ☎ 212-447-7284; www.sath.org; annual membership fees: $45 adults, $30 seniors and students), which offers a wealth of travel resources for all types of disabilities and informed recommendations on destinations, access guides, travel agents, tour operators, vehicle rentals, and companion services; and the **American Foundation for the Blind** (**AFB;** ☎ 800-232-5463; www.afb.org), a referral resource for the blind or visually impaired that includes information on traveling with Seeing Eye dogs.

For more information specifically targeted to travelers with disabilities, the community Web site iCan (www.icanonline.net/channels/travel/index.cfm) has destination guides and several regular columns on accessible travel. Also check out the quarterly magazine *Emerging Horizons* ($14.95 per year, $19.95 outside the United States; www.emerginghorizons.com); **Twin Peaks Press** (☎ 360-694-2462; http://disabilitybookshop.virtualave.net/blist84.htm), offering travel-related books for travelers with special needs; and *Open World Magazine,* published by SATH (subscription: $13 per year, $21 outside the United States).

Following the Rainbow: Advice for Gay or Lesbian Travelers

In the Golden State, homosexuality is squarely in the mainstream, especially in the cities. San Francisco is a mecca for gays, with Los Angeles running neck-and-neck with New York for a close second as the gay-friendliest city in the United States. Even relatively conservative San Diego has a huge gay contingent (the Hillcrest neighborhood is the base). Palm Springs is hugely popular with gay travelers, but, by and large, the entire state is welcoming to gays and lesbians.

The **International Gay and Lesbian Travel Association** (IGLTA; ☎ 800-448-8550 or 954-776-2626; www.iglta.org) is the trade association for the gay and lesbian travel industry and offers an online directory of gay- and lesbian-friendly travel businesses.

Many agencies offer tours and travel itineraries specifically designed for gay and lesbian travelers. **Above and Beyond Tours** (☎ 800-397-2681; www.abovebeyondtours.com) is the exclusive gay and lesbian tour operator for United Airlines. **Now, Voyager** (☎ 800-255-6951; www.nowvoyager.com) is a well-known San Francisco–based gay-owned and -operated travel service. **Olivia Cruises & Resorts** (☎ 800-631-6277 or 510-655-0364; www.olivia.com) charters entire resorts and ships exclusively for lesbian vacationers and offers smaller group experiences for both gay and lesbian travelers.

The following travel guides are available at most travel bookstores and gay and lesbian bookstores, or you can order them from **Giovanni's Room** bookstore, 1145 Pine St., Philadelphia, PA 19107 (☎ **215-923-2960**; www.giovannisroom.com): *Out and About* (☎ **800-929-2268** or 415-644-8044; www.outandabout.com), which offers guidebooks and a newsletter ($20 per year; 10 issues) packed with solid information on the global gay and lesbian scene; *Spartacus International Gay Guide* (Bruno Gmünder Verlag; www.spartacusworld.com/gayguide) and *Odysseus,* both good, annual English-anguage guidebooks focused on gay men; the *Damron* guides (www.damron.com), with separate, annual books for gay men and lesbians; and *Gay Travel A to Z: The World of Gay & Lesbian Travel Options at Your Fingertips* by Marianne Ferrari, a very good gay and lesbian guidebook series.

Chapter 10

Taking Care of the Remaining Details

● ●

In This Chapter

▶ Buying insurance and making reservations before you leave home
▶ Staying healthy when you travel
▶ Staying connected by cellphone or e-mail
▶ Keeping up with airline security measures

● ●

*T*his chapter helps you shore up the final details — keeping you healthy, offering advice for how to find help when you need it, and other things we're sure you won't need during your fabulous and easy trip. But it never hurts to have contingency plans.

Playing It Safe with Travel and Medical Insurance

Three kinds of travel insurance are available: trip-cancellation insurance, medical insurance, and lost-luggage insurance. The cost varies widely, depending on the cost and length of your trip, your age and health, and the type of trip you're taking, but expect to pay between 5 and 8 percent of the vacation itself. Here is our advice on all three:

✔ **Trip-cancellation insurance** helps you get your money back if you have to back out of a trip, if you have to go home early, or if your travel supplier goes bankrupt. Allowable reasons for cancellation can range from sickness to natural disasters to the State Department declaring your destination unsafe for travel. (Insurers usually won't cover vague fears, though, as many travelers discovered who tried to cancel their trips in October 2001 because they were wary of flying.)

A good resource is **Travel Guard Alerts,** a list of companies considered high-risk by Travel Guard International (www.travelinsured.com). Protect yourself further by paying for the insurance with a credit card — by law, you can get your money back on goods and services not received if you report the loss within 60 days after the charge is listed on a credit-card statement.

Many tour operators include insurance in the cost of the trip or can arrange insurance policies through a partnering provider, a convenient and often cost-effective way for you to get insurance. However, we believe you should avoid this; you're better off buying from a third-party insurer if you decide to get insurance.

✔ For domestic travel, buying **medical insurance** for your trip doesn't make sense for most travelers. Most existing health policies cover you if you get sick away from home — but check before you go, particularly if you're insured by an HMO.

✔ **Lost-luggage insurance** is not necessary for most travelers. On domestic flights, checked baggage is covered up to $2,500 per ticketed passenger. On international flights (including U.S. portions of international trips), baggage coverage is limited to approximately $9.07 per pound, up to approximately $635 per checked bag. If you plan to check items more valuable than the standard liability, find out whether your valuables are covered by your homeowner's policy, get baggage insurance as part of your comprehensive travel-insurance package, or buy Travel Guard's BagTrak product. Don't buy insurance at the airport — it's usually overpriced. Take any valuables or irreplaceable items with you in your carry-on luggage, as many valuables (including books, money, and electronics) aren't covered by airline policies.

If your luggage is lost, immediately file a lost-luggage claim at the airport, detailing the luggage contents. For most airlines, you must report delayed, damaged, or lost baggage within four hours of arrival. The airlines are required to deliver luggage, once found, directly to your house or destination free of charge.

For more information, contact one of the following recommended insurers: Access America (☎ 866-807-3982; www.accessamerica.com), Travel Guard International (☎ 800-826-4919; www.travelguard.com), Travel Insured International (☎ 800-243-3174; www.travelinsured.com), or Travelex Insurance Services (☎ 888-457-4602; www.travelex-insurance.com).

Staying Healthy When You Travel

Getting sick will ruin your vacation, so we strongly advise against it. (Of course, last time we checked, the bugs weren't listening to us any more than they probably listen to you.) You don't have to worry about much in California, other than a bad sunburn, although if you plan on doing much hiking, beware of Lyme disease, and, probably increasingly, like everywhere else, West Nile Virus. A little Off (or other bug juice of your choice) should handle the really minimal risk of either.

For domestic trips, most reliable healthcare plans provide coverage if you get sick away from home. For travel abroad, you may have to pay all medical costs upfront and be reimbursed later. For more on getting additional medical insurance for your trip, see the preceding section.

Talk to your doctor before leaving on a trip if you have a serious and/or chronic illness. For conditions such as epilepsy, diabetes, or heart problems, wear a **MedicAlert identification tag** (☎ **888-633-4298**; www. medicalert.org), which immediately alerts doctors to your condition and gives them access to your records through MedicAlert's 24-hour hot line.

Staying Connected by Cellphone

Just because your cellphone works at home doesn't mean it'll work elsewhere in the country (thanks to our nation's fragmented cellphone system). It's a good bet that your phone will work in major cities. But take a look at your wireless company's coverage map on its Web site before heading out — T-Mobile, Sprint, and Nextel are particularly weak in rural areas. If you need to stay in touch at a destination where you know your phone won't work, **rent** a phone that does from **InTouch USA** (☎ **800-872-7626**; www.intouchglobal.com) or a rental-car location, but beware that you'll pay $1 a minute or more for airtime.

If you're venturing deep into national parks, you may want to consider renting a **satellite phone** *(satphone)*, which is different from a cellphone in that it connects to satellites rather than ground-based towers. A satphone is more costly than a cellphone but works where there's no cellular signal and no towers. Unfortunately, you pay at least $2 per minute to use the phone, and it works only where you can see the horizon (that is, usually not indoors). In North America, you can rent Iridium satellite phones from **RoadPost** (☎ **888-290-1606** or 905-272-5665; www.roadpost.com). InTouch USA offers a wider range of satphones but at higher rates.

If you're not from the United States, you'll be appalled at the poor reach of our **GSM (Global System for Mobiles) wireless network,** which is used by much of the rest of the world. Your phone will probably work in most major U.S. cities; it definitely won't work in many rural areas. And you may or may not be able to send SMS (text messaging) home. Assume nothing — call your wireless provider and get the full scoop. In a worst-case scenario, you can rent a phone; InTouch USA delivers to hotels.

Accessing the Internet away from Home

You have any number of ways to check your e-mail and access the Internet on the road. Of course, using your own laptop — or even a personal digital assistant (PDA) or electronic organizer with a modem — gives you the most flexibility. But even if you don't have a computer, you can access your e-mail or your office computer from cybercafes.

Checking in publicly

It's hard nowadays to find a city that doesn't have a few **cybercafes.**
That's especially the case in the major (and not-so-major) California
cities. Although there's no definitive directory for cybercafes — these
are independent businesses, after all — two places to start looking are
www.cybercaptive.com and www.cybercafe.com.

Aside from formal cybercafes, most **public libraries** offer Internet access
free or for a small charge. Avoid **hotel business centers** unless you're
willing to pay exorbitant rates.

 Most major airports now have **Internet kiosks** scattered throughout
their gates. These kiosks, which you'll also see in shopping malls, hotel
lobbies, and tourist-information offices, give you basic Web access for a
per-minute fee that's usually higher than cybercafe prices. The kiosks
are clunky and costly, so avoid them whenever possible.

Getting online with your home provider

To retrieve your e-mail, ask your **Internet service provider (ISP)**
whether it has a Web-based interface tied to your existing e-mail
account. If your ISP doesn't have such an interface, you can use the
free **mail2web** service (www.mail2web.com) to view and reply to your
home e-mail. For more flexibility, you may want to open a free, Web-
based e-mail account with **Yahoo! Mail** (http://mail.yahoo.com).
(Microsoft's Hotmail is another popular option, but Hotmail has severe
spam problems.) Your home ISP may be able to forward your e-mail to
the Web-based account automatically.

In addition, major ISPs have **local access numbers** around the world,
allowing you to go online by simply placing a local call. Check your ISP's
Web site or call its toll-free number and ask how you can use your current account away from home, and how much it will cost. If you're
traveling outside the reach of your ISP, the **iPass** network has dial-up
numbers in most of the world's countries. You'll have to sign up with an
iPass provider, who tells you how to set up your computer for your des-
tination(s). For a list of iPass providers, go to www.ipass.com and click
on "Individual Purchase." One solid provider is **i2roam** (☎ **866-811-6209**
or 920-235-0475; www.i2roam.com).

If you need to access files on your office computer, look into a service
called **GoToMyPC** (www.gotomypc.com). The service provides a Web-
based interface for you to access and manipulate a distant PC from anywhere — even a cybercafe — provided your "target" PC is on and has an
always-on connection to the Internet (such as with Road Runner cable).
The service offers top-quality security, but if you're worried about hack-
ers, access the GoToMyPC system using your own laptop rather than a
cybercafe computer.

Most business-class hotels throughout the world offer dataports for
laptop modems, and a few thousand hotels in the United States and

Europe now offer free high-speed Internet access using an Ethernet network cable. You can bring your own cables, but most hotels rent them for around $10. **Call your hotel in advance** to see what your options are.

Wherever you go, bring a **connection kit** of the right power and phone adapters, a spare phone cord, and a spare Ethernet network cable — or find out whether your hotel supplies them to guests.

Going the wireless route

If you are bringing your own computer, the buzzword in computer access to familiarize yourself with is *Wi-Fi* (wireless fidelity), and more and more hotels, cafes, and retailers are signing on as wireless hotspots from where you can get a high-speed connection without cable wires, networking hardware, or a phone line. You can get a Wi-Fi connection one of several ways. Many laptops sold in the last year have built-in Wi-Fi capability (an 802.11b wireless Ethernet connection). Mac owners have their own networking technology, Apple AirPort. If you have an older computer, an 802.11b/**Wi-Fi card** (around $50) can be plugged into your laptop. You sign up for wireless access service much as you do cellphone service, through a plan offered by one of several commercial companies that have made wireless service available in airports, hotel lobbies, and coffee shops, primarily in the United States (followed by the United Kingdom and Japan). **T-Mobile Hotspot** (www.t-mobile.com/hotspot) serves up wireless connections at more than 1,000 Starbucks coffee shops nationwide. **Boingo** (www.boingo.com) and **Wayport** (www.wayport.com) have set up networks in airports and high-class hotel lobbies. iPass providers also give you access to a few hundred wireless hotel lobby setups. Best of all, you don't need to be staying at the Four Seasons to use the hotel's network; just set yourself up on a nice couch in the lobby. The companies' pricing policies can be Byzantine, with a variety of monthly, per-connection, and per-minute plans, but, in general, you pay around $30 a month for limited access — and as more and more companies jump on the wireless bandwagon, prices are likely to get even more competitive.

Keeping Up with Airline Security

With the federalization of airport security, security procedures at U.S. airports are more stable and consistent than ever. Generally, you'll be okay if you arrive at the airport **one hour** before a domestic flight and **two hours** before an international flight; if you show up late, tell an airline employee and she'll probably whisk you to the front of the line. But don't rely on that. We've noticed, and this is strictly our own observation, that Southwest lines tend to be particularly long at Los Angeles International and at Oakland International.

Bring a **current, government-issued photo ID** such as a driver's license or passport. Keep your ID at the ready to show at check-in, the security checkpoint, and sometimes even the gate. (Children under 18 do not need government-issued photo IDs for domestic flights, but they do for international flights to most countries)

In 2003, the TSA phased out **gate check-in** at all U.S. airports. And **E-tickets** have made paper tickets nearly obsolete. If you have an E-ticket, you can beat the ticket-counter lines by using airport **electronic kiosks** or even **online check-in** from your home computer. Online check-in involves logging on to your airline's Web site, accessing your reservation, and printing out your boarding pass — and the airline may even offer you bonus miles to do so! If you're using a kiosk at the airport, bring the credit card you used to book the ticket or your frequent-flier card; you'll need it to access your ticket information. Print out your boarding pass from the kiosk and simply proceed to the security checkpoint with your pass and a photo ID. If you're checking bags or looking to snag an exit-row seat, you'll be able to do so using most airline kiosks. Smaller airlines are also employing the kiosk system; call your airline to make sure these alternatives are available. **Curbside check-in** is also a good way to avoid lines, although a few airlines still ban curbside check-in; call before you go.

Security checkpoint lines are getting shorter than they were during 2001 and 2002, but some doozies remain. If you have trouble standing for long periods of time, tell an airline employee; the airline will provide a wheelchair. Speed up security by **not wearing metal objects** such as big belt buckles, and remember that many leather shoes (other than sneakers) can also contain buzzer-triggering metal. If you have metallic body parts, a note from your doctor can prevent a long chat with the security screeners. Keep in mind that only **ticketed passengers** are allowed past security, except for folks escorting disabled passengers or children.

Federalization has stabilized **what you can carry on** and **what you can't.** The general rule is that sharp things, gels, and liquids are okay in small quantities, nail clippers are okay, and food must be passed through the X-ray machine. Bring food in your carry-on rather than checking it, as explosive-detection machines used on checked luggage have been known to mistake food (especially chocolate, for some reason) for bombs. Travelers in the United States are allowed one carry-on bag, plus a personal item such as a purse, briefcase, or laptop bag. Carry-on hoarders can stuff all sorts of things into a laptop bag; as long as it has a laptop in it, it's still considered a personal item. The Transportation Security Administration (TSA) has issued a list of restricted items; check its Web site (www.tsa.gov/travelers/index.shtm) for details.

Part III
Northern California: Redwoods, Wine, and Wonder

The 5th Wave   By Rich Tennant

SAN FRANCISCO'S AMAZING CABLE CARS

Travelers can ride from Market Street to the Financial District, through the Rocky Mountains and on to Denver, all for the price of one Muni Passport.

In this part . . .

San Francisco is the ultimate urban destination, while the gorgeous Wine Country makes for a wonderfully pastoral getaway. This part includes detailed information on both destinations, as well as travel tips for the wild-and-woolly coastal region north of the San Francisco Bay Area, which offers some of California's most breathtaking scenery. It is quiet, remote, and ruggedly handsome, with spectacular nature broken only by the occasional picturesque village. Travel inland from the Bay Area or North Coast, and you'll soon reach the Sierra Nevadas, the magnificently rugged, granite-peaked mountain range that inspired the U.S. National Park system, of which Yosemite National Park is a grand example. Also awe inspiring is sparkling Lake Tahoe, host to California's finest outdoor-recreation center.

Chapter 11

San Francisco

- -

In This Chapter

▶ Knowing when to go and how to get there
▶ Getting to know the neighborhoods — and how to get around
▶ Choosing the best places to stay and dine
▶ Seeing the sights, shopping, and finding good times in the night

- -

San Francisco continues to be one of America's most enticing destinations. This former gold-rush rowdy may not always bask in the
sunny weather of its Southern California sisters, but where else can you
sample a touch of Asia, a bit of Parisian *joie de vivre,* a taste of Central
America, a hint of Italy, and a good dollop of West Coast style and eccentricity in a single day? San Francisco's secret weapon is its winning combination of big-city sophistication and small-town accessibility. You can
always discover something new in the unique neighborhoods of this
walking town, from restored Victorian homes to amusing shops to some
of the greatest restaurants in the country.

The dot-com implosion, the terrorist attacks of September 11, 2001,
and the general economic malaise that followed certainly left the city
reeling — but only for a while. Office space no longer goes begging and
long-awaited civic improvements have been completed. Market Street,
at Fifth Street, now sports a spiffy new shopping center that rivals . . .
nothing, actually. The new **de Young Museum** in Golden Gate Park
opened to appreciative crowds in October 2005; **Union Square,** in the
heart of downtown, looks glorious after a much-needed nip and tuck;
and the exquisite glass **Conservatory of Flowers,** also in Golden Gate
Park, is back in business after a violent storm nearly destroyed it in
1995. San Francisco's impressive brick-and-concrete **baseball park,** the
"miracle on Third Street," has changed the face of a once-neglected
corner of the bay, and the **waterfront** lined with palm trees, awash in
views, and traversed by vintage trolley cars, is a picture of urban glory,
starring the remodeled and revitalized **Ferry Building.**

What never fails to beguile visitors and locals alike are the much-loved
symbols that are synonymous with the city. The **Golden Gate Bridge,
Golden Gate Park,** the **Palace of Fine Arts,** the **cable cars,** and
Chinatown have changed little over the decades, thank goodness. And
despite good-natured grumbling from the natives regarding the "good
old days," the city of San Francisco has never looked so vibrant.

Timing Your Visit

San Francisco is a year-round city, usually draped in mild to cool temperatures and fog-bound mornings, especially during the summer. If weather is a factor — warm weather, that is — come in September or early October when the city traditionally experiences a hot spell. These, naturally, are the busiest months in the hotel trade, right up there with summer vacation. Be sure to book lodgings ahead of time to ensure a decent place to stay, and inquire about air conditioning if that's important to you — older hotel buildings don't have it. Winter tends to be cold and drizzly (although we've enjoyed fair skies and mild temperatures in Jan), but you can often get fantastic deals on hotel rooms after the holidays. In early spring, the flowering plum trees are in bloom and, though the skies may pour, you may also find drought conditions. Ya just never know.

It's always an excellent idea to check dates with the **San Francisco Convention and Visitors Bureau** (☎ 800-220-5747 or 415-391-2000; www.onlyinsanfrancisco.com) to avoid scheduling your vacation during MacWeek or any other large convention, when hotels and restaurants are jammed.

Getting There

Although you can meander to San Francisco by car or by rail, flying into the region is the recommended option. And the Bay Area has two convenient airports to make flying an even more palatable choice:

- ✔ **San Francisco International** (SFO; ☎ 650-821-8211; www.flysfo.com), 14 miles south of downtown

- ✔ **Oakland International Airport** (☎ 510-563-3300; www.flyoakland.com), across the Bay Bridge off I-880

More airlines fly into the considerably larger SFO, but navigating the less crowded, two-terminal Oakland airport is easier. Plus, getting to Oakland International from downtown San Francisco can take just a half-hour, traffic permitting. You'll find tourist information desks on the first floor (baggage level) of both airports, as well as ATMs located in every terminal on the upper levels.

Making your way downtown from SFO

Travel time from San Francisco International to downtown San Francisco is dependent on the traffic; during rush hour, the trip can take 40 minutes or more, and at other times can run from 20 to 30 minutes. **Super Shuttle** (☎ 415-558-8500; www.supershuttle.com) and other similar companies offer door-to-door service into the city from the airport. The services are located at center islands outside the upper level, and a guide will direct you to the right area. Fares are around $15; advance reservations are not necessary.

Taxis line up at well-marked yellow columns on the center island outside the lower level of the airport. The fare is about $35 to downtown, plus tip.

Probably the smartest new addition to the San Francisco Airport in recent years is the BART station, which allows travelers to use public transport to reach the city and some suburbs. **Bay Area Rapid Transit, or BART** (☎ 510-465-2278; www.bart.gov), ferries travelers from SFO into San Francisco, the East Bay, and the Millbrae Caltrain Station, a few miles south of the airport. BART fares into San Francisco are $5.15. BART airport stations are located on Level 3 of the International Terminal, or from the domestic terminals you can take the automated AirTrain to the Garage G/BART Station stop. If you're renting a car, a free **AirTrain** takes you to the vast building where all the counters and cars are located. Catch the AirTrain on Level 5 in any domestic terminal parking garage.

Making your way to San Francisco from Oakland International

The routine is similar from Oakland International, except that all ground transportation is on one level. **Bayporter Express Shuttles** (☎ 415-467-1800; www.bayporter.com) pick up passengers from Terminal 1 at the center island, and from Terminal 2 around the corner from baggage claim. The fare for the 30- to 40-minute ride to San Francisco is $26 for one person, $38 for two people in the same party, and $7 for kids younger than 12. Reservations aren't necessary.

A 30- to 40-minute **taxi** ride into the city runs you about $45.

BART (☎ 510-465-2278) also runs from Oakland into the city. Take the **AirBART Shuttle** (☎ 510-430-9440) in front of Terminal 1 or 2, which runs every 20 minutes. The fare is $2 for the 15- to 30-minute ride to the Oakland Coliseum BART station. From there, transfer to a BART train into San Francisco; the fare is about $3.35. Purchase your ticket from well-marked kiosks inside the airport or at the BART station. If you're staying around Union Square, the city's commercial hub, exit the BART on Powell Street.

Driving to the Bay Area

Two major highways lead to San Francisco: **I-5** runs north-south through the center of the state. Drivers traveling along this route are deposited onto **I-80**, which comes in from the northeast and leads over the Bay Bridge into the city. The drive to San Francisco from Los Angeles along I-5 takes six hours.

The other major route is **U.S. 101,** which heads up from Los Angeles through the city to Marin County, Napa and Sonoma valleys, and other points north. A prettier, more scenic coastal route, **Highway 1,** takes travelers heading north closer to Monterey and Santa Cruz, but the driving time up from L.A. is approximately eight to ten hours.

Traveling by train to . . . Emeryville?

Amtrak (☎ 800-872-7245; www.amtrak.com) trains arrive in Emeryville, just north of Oakland. Buses then drop passengers off at one of six stops in San Francisco, including the Ferry Building (approximately a 30-minute ride), at the foot of Market Street on the Embarcadero, or the Caltrain station (approximately a 40-minute ride), at Fourth and King streets.

Orienting Yourself and Finding Transportation

San Francisco covers just 7 square miles. The streets are laid out in a traditional grid pattern, except for two major diagonal arteries, Market Street and Columbus Avenue. Market cuts a swath through town from the Embarcadero up to the bottom of Twin Peaks. Columbus runs at an angle through North Beach, starting at the Transamerica Pyramid in the Financial District and ending near the Hyde Street Pier. The "San Francisco Neighborhoods" map on p. 96 offers a glimpse of the city's layout and its major neighborhoods.

Numbered *streets* are downtown; numbered *avenues* are in the Richmond and Sunset districts southwest of downtown.

Other important thoroughfares include Van Ness Avenue, which begins in the Mission District as South Van Ness and terminates at Aquatic Park; and Geary Street, which begins at Market and winds through the city to Ocean Beach.

San Francisco's neighborhoods

Along with the lovely natural setting, the neighborhoods — each with its own quirky personality — are what invest San Francisco with so much charm. This isn't a big city, size-wise, so you're no more than 20 minutes or so by taxi from all the major sites, shopping areas, and restaurants no matter where you stay.

Union Square

The center of tourist activity, Union Square is tucked inside Sutter, Grant, Market, and Mason streets. Big department stores, expensive boutiques, theaters, many good restaurants, and the greatest concentration of hotels in the city surround the actual square, which has become a pleasant place to stroll through. If you stay here, Chinatown, Nob Hill, the Financial District, and SoMa are all within walking distance.

A few blocks west is the **Tenderloin** neighborhood, a gritty patch of poverty bounded by Sutter and Mason streets and Van Ness and Golden Gate avenues. The only reason to linger in the 'loin is to visit **Glide Memorial Church,** 330 Ellis St. (☎ 415-771-6300), for rousing Sunday services. The multicultural choir sings soulful hymns that bring the congregation to its collective feet. Come early to secure a seat.

Chinatown

This densely packed area roughly bordered by Broadway, Taylor, Bush, and Montgomery streets is as colorful and exotic as advertised. The **Dragon Gate** entrance on Grant Avenue leads to touristy shops, but wander up and around Stockton Street; you'll feel as if you're in another country. See "The top attractions" section later in this chapter, for Chinatown's sightseeing and shopping highlights.

Nob Hill

Posh Nob Hill is a rather rarefied residential district, crowned by **Grace Cathedral,** the magnificent Episcopal church at the top of California Street. A string of pricey hotels cascades down the hill toward the Financial District, along with the **California Street cable car line.** If you're prepared for the challenge of walking up and down steep grades, Nob Hill is just a short stroll from Union Square.

The Financial District

The Financial District encompasses prime bay real estate roughly between Montgomery Street and the Embarcadero, on either side of Market Street. Major corporations call this area home and the **Transamerica Pyramid,** at Montgomery and Clay streets, is a skyline landmark. Seek out **Belden Place,** an alley between Kearny, Bush, and Pine streets, which is full of outdoor dining opportunities.

The Embarcadero

Liberated from the pylons and cement of the Embarcadero Freeway, which was damaged by the 1989 Loma Prieta earthquake and subsequently torn down, this area runs along the bay from the eastern edge of Fisherman's Wharf to the beginning of China Basin. **Embarcadero Center,** a collection of five multiuse buildings connected by bridges and walkways at the end of Market Street from Drumm to Sansome, houses upscale chain stores, restaurants, and movie theaters. The Ferry Building at the foot of Market Street is filled with glorious gourmet food shops. Take the F streetcar from Union Square.

South of Market Street (SoMa)

Although the dot-com bust tempered the frenzy, temporarily, South of Market Street (SoMa for short) has exploded in the past 15 years, particularly along Mission Street between Second and Fifth streets. Attractions include the **San Francisco Museum of Modern Art,** the **Museum of the African Diaspora,** the **Cartoon Art Museum, Yerba Buena Gardens,** and the **Metreon** (see "The top attractions" section later in this chapter).

North Beach

North Beach isn't an actual beach; it's the former Italian enclave that Chinatown is encroaching upon. This is the place to hop from one cafe to another, to browse for books and Italian pottery, and to examine the

San Francisco Neighborhoods

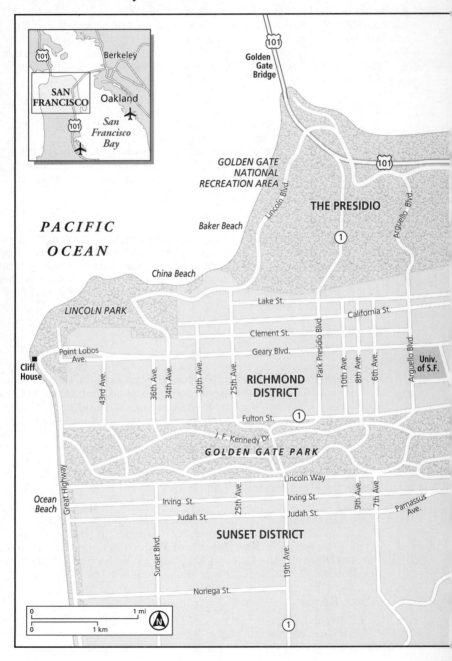

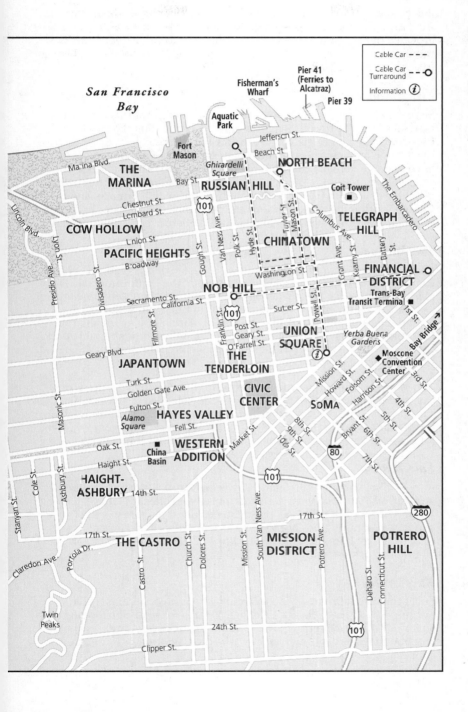

Cable Car - - -
Cable Car
Turnaround - - -o
Information *i*

San Francisco Bay

Fisherman's Wharf

Pier 41 (Ferries to Alcatraz)

Pier 39

Aquatic Park

Jefferson St.

Fort Mason

Beach St.

NORTH BEACH

Marina Blvd.

THE MARINA

Ghirardelli Square

Bay St.

RUSSIAN HILL

Coit Tower

Lincoln Blvd.

Chestnut St.
Lombard St.

101

TELEGRAPH HILL

The Embarcadero

COW HOLLOW

Union St.

Hyde St.

CHINATOWN

Columbus Ave.

PACIFIC HEIGHTS

Broadway

Van Ness Ave.

Polk St.

Taylor St.

Mason St.

Grant Ave.

Kearny St.

Battery St.

Washington St.

FINANCIAL DISTRICT

NOB HILL

Sacramento St.
California St.

Sutter St.

Trans-Bay Transit Terminal

Presidio Ave.

Divisadero St.

Gough St.

Franklin St.

Fillmore St.

101

Post St.
Geary St.
O'Farrell St.

UNION SQUARE

Powell St.

1st St.

Bay Bridge

Geary Blvd.

JAPANTOWN

THE TENDERLOIN

Yerba Buena Gardens

Moscone Convention Center

Turk St.

Golden Gate Ave.

CIVIC CENTER

Mission St.
Howard St.
Folsom St.
Harrison St.

3rd St.

Masonic St.

Fulton St.

SoMa

4th St.
5th St.

Alamo Square

HAYES VALLEY

Fell St.

Market St.

Bryant St.

6th St.

7th St.

Oak St.

China Basin

WESTERN ADDITION

8th St.
9th St.
10th St.

80

Cole St.

Ashbury St.

Haight St.

HAIGHT-ASHBURY

14th St.

101

Stanyan St.

17th St.

280

17th St.

Portola Dr.

THE CASTRO

Church St.
Dolores St.

Mission St.

South Van Ness Ave.

MISSION DISTRICT

Potrero Ave.

POTRERO HILL

Claredon Ave.

Castro St.

Deharo St.
Connecticut St.

Twin Peaks

24th St.

101

Clipper St.

delectables at the various Italian delis and pastry shops. **Columbus Avenue** is the main thoroughfare, but family-style restaurants and crowded bars dot the streets from Washington to Grant, while the XXX-rated clubs stick together on Broadway. Use the Powell-Mason cable car to get here from Union Square.

Fisherman's Wharf

Sixteen million tourists per year can't all be wrong, but this mostly commercial section of town is a matter of taste. Located on Bay Street between Powell and Polk streets, the former working piers have been turned into an embarrassment of commercialism — although you *do* have to come here in order to get to **Alcatraz** (see "The top attractions" section later in this chapter). Step gingerly past Pier 39 and the plethora of schlock shops to the **Hyde Street Pier, Ghirardelli Square,** and the **Cannery,** other legitimate reasons to spend time near the docks. Parking is difficult and/or expensive, so take the F streetcar from Union Square.

The Marina

Many must-see sites are within walking distance of this high-priced district, including the excellent science museum, the **Exploratorium.** The Marina's commercial blocks along Chestnut Street, between Franklin and Lyon streets, are full of coffeehouses, restaurants, and shops. Take a walk to the **Golden Gate Bridge** by way of Marina Boulevard and the redeveloped Crissy Fields, San Francisco's fabulous new shoreline park. Get to the Marina by the 30-Stockton, 22-Fillmore, 41-Union, or 45-Union/Stockton bus.

The Marina is the gateway to the **Presidio,** 1,500 partly wild acres on the westernmost point of the city that once belonged to the U.S. Army. They're now part of the **Golden Gate National Recreation Area.** Stop at the visitor center, in the Main Post at Fort Mason on Montgomery Street, for maps and suggestions for hikes. Take the 29-Sunset bus to get here.

Cow Hollow

A residential paradise surrounded by Broadway, Lyon, and Lombard streets and Van Ness Avenue, the district's main claim to fame — among locals and tourists alike — is **Union Street,** a fashionable haven of shops, restaurants, and those young, urban professionals we all love to hate. To get here, take the 30-Stockton, 22-Fillmore, 41-Union, or 45-Union/Stockton bus.

Russian Hill

Polk Street from Broadway up to around Greenwich Street is a chic avenue with a French flair. It's a delightful area for relaxed shopping and snacking with some terrific little restaurants, bakeries, antiques shops, and boutiques. From Union Square, take the California or Hyde Street cable car.

Civic Center

Bordered by Van Ness and Golden Gate avenues and Franklin, Hyde, and Market streets, Civic Center is home to local politicians, city offices, and cultural centers including the **San Francisco Ballet,** the **San Francisco Symphony,** the **San Francisco Opera,** and the **Asian Art Museum.** **City Hall,** on Van Ness Avenue between McAllister and Grove streets, underwent a spectacular renovation a few years ago, and its glittering black-and-gold dome makes a splendid landmark. You can reach this area via the F streetcar. Note that Civic Center also attracts a sizable homeless contingent.

The Castro

The Castro is famous for its ties to an activist gay community, and a walk through the neighborhood will show off beautifully restored Victorian homes and shops catering to buff guys. Shopping and people-watching take place mainly on Castro Street between Market and 18th streets. Check the schedule at the Art Deco **Castro Theatre,** and consider joining in a Sing-A-Long *Sound of Music* if one's on the calendar. Take the F streetcar from Union Square.

Haight-Ashbury

Commonly known as the Haight and bounded by **Golden Gate Park** and Divisadero, Fulton, and Waller streets. Haight-Ashbury hasn't fully recovered from what must have been a real bummer to some — the demise of the '60s. Haight (rhymes with "fate") Street — where the action is — continues to hold a magical spell over scruffy groups of youngsters campaigning for handouts.

If you're curious enough to drop by, you'll stumble upon a multitude of new and used clothing stores competing for space with all kinds of commercial endeavors, most of which are perfectly legal. The stretch from Masonic to Stanyon is particularly good for vintage wearables, hip fashion, and shoes. The N-Judah Muni Metro line will take you to Haight Street.

Japantown

Japantown consists of some downright unattractive indoor shopping centers off Geary Street between Webster and Laguna streets. It's a shame that this area isn't more visually appealing, because the dismal gray buildings attached by a pedestrian walkway house some good, inexpensive, noodle restaurants and interesting shops. **Kabuki Springs and Spa** is a great place to have a massage and a soak. Across Sutter Street, between Fillmore and Webster streets, look for **Cottage Row,** all that's left of the real Japantown before redevelopment gutted the neighborhood. Catch the 38-Geary or 22-Fillmore bus to get here.

The Mission District

This busy, largely Hispanic community spans the area from César Chávez (formerly Army) Street to Market Street between Dolores and Potrero avenues. The city's most historic building, **Mission Dolores,** founded in 1776 (on Dolores and 16th streets), attracts visitors, as do a wealth of inexpensive restaurants and dramatic murals that burst out from the landscape. Valencia Street between 16th and 23rd streets has become a serious destination for foodies. Take BART to the 24th Street exit.

Telegraph Hill

This residential neighborhood lies just to the east of North Beach, behind **Coit Tower** and the **Filbert Steps. Russian Hill** is just to the northwest, where you'll find the wiggly part of **Lombard Street** and Macondry Lane, fictionalized in Armistead Maupin's *Tales of the City*. You can reach Telegraph Hill via the Powell-Mason cable car.

Pacific Heights

Pacific Heights, bordered by Broadway, Pine, Divisadero, and Franklin streets, is where the city's wealthy elite lounge in lavish, beautifully land-scaped mansions. The 22-Fillmore, 12-Folsom, 27-Bryant, 47-Van Ness, 49-Van Ness/Mission, and 83-Pacific all motor through here.

The Richmond District

Largely residential, the Richmond District is partially framed by **Golden Gate Park** at one edge — *aah*-inspiring, and a great place to walk — and by the Pacific Ocean on another. The N-Judah Muni Metro line provides the easiest way to get here.

The Western Addition

 We mention this old neighborhood between Geary, Haight, Gough, and Divisadero streets because people studying their maps often believe it's an easy walk from Civic Center to Golden Gate Park by way of Oak or Fell streets in the heart of this neighborhood. That's not entirely accurate. First, it's hilly. Second, it's farther than it looks.

Getting around

San Francisco is relatively compact and offers acceptable public trans-portation, so you really don't need to drive around the city. Traffic is heavy downtown, and one-way streets confuse drivers who are unfamil-iar with the territory. That, combined with the lack of street parking and the heavy-handed meter maids, makes leaving your car in a parking garage the sensible thing to do.

 If you're starting your California trip with a few days in San Francisco and then setting out to explore, arriving carless in the city and picking up your rental just before you leave town is a sound idea. Renting a car downtown is simple and smart. See Chapter 7 for more information about renting a car.

From Union Square, where most hotels are located, it's an easy walk to Chinatown, North Beach, SoMa, and the Financial District. Buses, Muni streetcars, and cable cars are convenient and inexpensive ways to reach outlying neighborhoods, but taxis usually require a phone call.

Hoofing it

Walking is the preferred method of travel in San Francisco and the only way to catch the nuances of the neighborhoods. Be careful, however, because vehicle/pedestrian accidents occur with alarming regularity. Although pedestrians have the right-of-way, watch for drivers running red lights or turning right on a red light. Make sure that bus drivers see you entering crosswalks.

Catching cabs

Taxis are easy to hail downtown, especially in front of hotels, but you have to call a cab to come get you almost anywhere else. Reaching the taxi companies by phone can take a while, so keep this in mind, and have these numbers handy:

- ✔ **Desoto Cab:** ☎ 415-970-1300
- ✔ **Luxor Cabs:** ☎ 415-282-4141
- ✔ **Veteran's Cab:** ☎ 415-648-1313
- ✔ **Yellow Cab:** ☎ 415-626-2345

Rates are about $2.85 for the first mile and $2.25 for each additional mile.

Taking the Muni Metro streetcars

The San Francisco Municipal Railway, known as **Muni** (call ☎ 415-673-6864 for gracious directions on how to get where you want to go; www.sfmuni.com), is much maligned by locals for inefficiency, but tens of thousands of commuters rely daily on its buses and electric streetcars for a lift. For information on getting an official Muni map, see the "Transit tips" section.

Muni Metro streetcars run underground downtown and aboveground in the outlying neighborhoods. The five streetcar lines, the J, K, L, M, and N, make the same stops as BART (see the upcoming "Going underground with BART" section) along Market Street, including Embarcadero Station, Montgomery and Powell streets (both near Union Square), and Civic Center. Past Civic Center, the routes branch off in different directions. The **N-Judah** line services Haight-Ashbury and parallels Golden Gate Park on its way down Judah Street to the ocean. The **J-Church** line passes near Mission Dolores and the Castro. Our personal favorite is the **F-Market**, whose antique streetcars run from the Castro Street station down Market Street, over to Mission Street, then down the Embarcadero to Fisherman's Wharf. Muni cars marked "Mission Bay" end their journey at the Caltrain Station on King Street just past the glorious San Francisco Giants' baseball park.

The **fare** to ride a bus or streetcar anywhere in the system is $1.50 for adults and 50¢ for seniors and children, and includes a transfer good for 90 minutes; exact change is required. For information on multiday passes, see the "Transit tips" section.

Riding the bus

A fleet of buses chugs throughout the city from 6 a.m. to midnight. Street-corner signs and painted yellow bands on utility poles and on curbs mark bus stops, and buses are clearly numbered on the front. Depending on your destination and the time of day, buses arrive every 5 to 20 minutes. They aren't the quickest means of transportation, but with 80 transit lines, they are the most complete. During rush hour (7–9 a.m. and 4–6 p.m.), buses are often sardine-can crowded.

Going underground with BART

Bay Area Rapid Transit (☎ 415-989-2278; www.bart.gov) is different from Muni, although visitors often get the two systems mixed up because they share the same underground stations (but different platforms) downtown. Within the city limits, that's not a problem. BART, however, runs all over the Bay Area, and more than one unsuspecting traveler has ended up in Oakland when he intended to exit at the Embarcadero.

Purchase BART tickets from machines at the station. **Fares** to and from any point in the city are $1.40 each way; outside the city, fares vary depending on how far down the line you go.

Hopping aboard the cable cars

No trip to San Francisco would be complete without a ride on a cable car. Three lines traverse the downtown area. The **Powell-Hyde line** — the most scenic and exciting run — begins at Powell Street and ends at the turnaround across from Ghirardelli Square. The **Powell-Mason line** goes through North Beach and ends near Fisherman's Wharf. The **California Street line** — the tamest and least scenic — crests at Nob Hill and ends at Van Ness Avenue. Rides are $5 one-way. You may board a cable car only at specific, clearly marked stops. Cable cars operate from 6:30 a.m. to 12:30 a.m.

Transit tips

Here are a few transit tips and information on multiday passes that will make your life much easier and can even save you money in the process:

  ✔ Buy a copy of the **official Muni map.** It costs $3 and is invaluable for public-transportation users. It shows all the bus, streetcar, cable-car, and BART routes and stations. Maps are available at the Convention and Visitors Bureau Information Center and cable-car ticket booths.

If you want to be proactive, you can find Muni system maps online at www.sfmuni.com, though we don't suggest downloading any without a fast Internet connection.

✔ The one-stop-shopping number to call for **local traffic** or **public-transit information** is ☎ 415-817-1717. This number connects you to whatever information line you need, be it BART or Muni routes, or the latest on traffic conditions. You can also find public-transit schedules on the Web at www.sfmuni.com.

✔ **Muni Passports,** which are accepted on buses, streetcars, and even cable cars, but not BART, are a bargain for visitors. A one-day pass is $11, a three-day pass is $18, and a seven-day pass is $24. You can purchase passes at the Convention and Visitors Bureau Information Center at Hallidie Plaza, at the Powell and Market or Beach and Hyde streets Cable Car Turnaround Police booth, or online at www.sfmuni.com. You may also purchase single-day passes on board the cable cars.

✔ Save a few dollars by buying a **CityPass,** which gives you admission to six major city attractions for nine days as well as seven days' consecutive travel on all Muni transportation, including cable cars. Buy the CityPass at the first attraction you visit or online at www.citypass.com. For more information, see the "Exploring San Francisco" section later in this chapter.

Where to Stay

The following listings reflect our preferences for the city's best accommodations in various price categories (see the "San Francisco Accommodations" map on p. 104 for their locations). You won't find the biggest hotels in town mentioned, though — we're leaving those for the conventioneers.

Hotel room rates fluctuate hugely depending on supply and demand. Historically, in San Francisco, demand is high almost all year, and, in fact, hotel occupancy rates have been increasing steadily since 2003. If you're seeking a break on your accommodations, vacation in the winter months or ask about weekend packages at hotels that cater to business travelers. Be advised that lots of hotels in older buildings, especially around Union Square, have surprisingly tiny rooms and baths and no air-conditioning (only a potential problem in Sept). If you plan to keep a car downtown, prepare yourself for hefty parking fees.

Count on an extra 14 percent in taxes being tacked on to your hotel bill and your parking garage fees.

San Francisco Accommodations

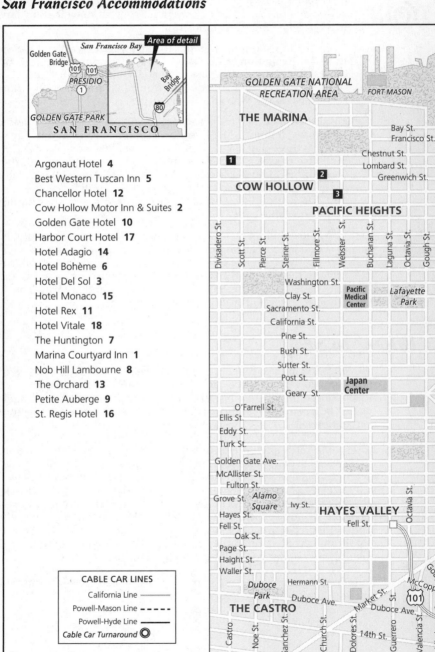

Argonaut Hotel **4**
Best Western Tuscan Inn **5**
Chancellor Hotel **12**
Cow Hollow Motor Inn & Suites **2**
Golden Gate Hotel **10**
Harbor Court Hotel **17**
Hotel Adagio **14**
Hotel Bohème **6**
Hotel Del Sol **3**
Hotel Monaco **15**
Hotel Rex **11**
Hotel Vitale **18**
The Huntington **7**
Marina Courtyard Inn **1**
Nob Hill Lambourne **8**
The Orchard **13**
Petite Auberge **9**
St. Regis Hotel **16**

CABLE CAR LINES
California Line ————
Powell-Mason Line – – – –
Powell-Hyde Line ●
Cable Car Turnaround ◉

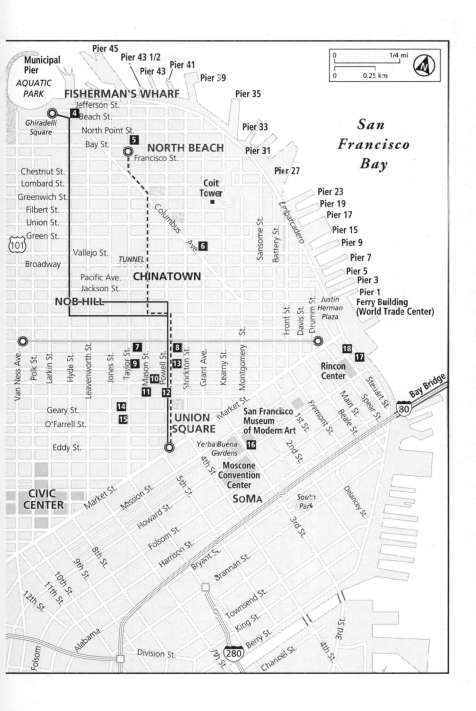

Municipal Pier
AQUATIC PARK
Ghiradelli Square
FISHERMAN'S WHARF
Pier 45
Pier 43 1/2
Pier 43
Pier 41
Pier 39
Pier 35
Pier 33
Pier 31
Pier 27
Pier 23
Pier 19
Pier 17
Pier 15
Pier 9
Pier 7
Pier 5
Pier 3
Pier 1
Jefferson St.
Beach St.
North Point St.
Bay St.
Francisco St.
NORTH BEACH
Chestnut St.
Lombard St.
Greenwich St.
Filbert St.
Union St.
Green St.
Vallejo St.
Broadway
Pacific Ave.
Jackson St.
CHINATOWN
NOB HILL
Coit Tower
Columbus Ave.
TUNNEL

San Francisco Bay

Justin Herman Plaza
Ferry Building (World Trade Center)

Van Ness Ave.
Polk St.
Larkin St.
Hyde St.
Leavenworth St.
Jones St.
Taylor St.
Mason St.
Powell St.
Stockton St.
Grant Ave.
Kearny St.
Montgomery St.
Front St.
Davis St.
Drumm St.
Steuart St.
Main St.
Spear St.
Beale St.
Fremont St.
1st St.
2nd St.

Geary St.
O'Farrell St.
Eddy St.
UNION SQUARE
Rincon Center
Market St.
San Francisco Museum of Modern Art
Yerba Buena Gardens
Moscone Convention Center
SoMa
South Park

CIVIC CENTER
Market St.
Mission St.
Howard St.
Folsom St.
Harrison St.
Bryant St.
Brannan St.
Townsend St.
King St.
Berry St.
Channel St.
Division St.
8th St.
9th St.
10th St.
11th St.
12th St.
Alabama
Folsom
4th St.
5th St.
3rd St.
Delancey St.
Bay Bridge
80
280
19th St.
Sansome St.
Battery St.
Embarcadero

0   1/4 mi
0   0.25 km

Argonaut Hotel
$$$–$$$$ Fisherman's Wharf

In an enviable position next to the Cannery, this perky boutique hotel makes the innumerable chains around Fisherman's Wharf blush in comparison. Many of the nautical-themed rooms have a view of either Alcatraz or the Golden Gate Bridge, while the lesser-priced interior rooms are touted as being quieter. Bedrooms are fairly spacious, but we were surprised by the ordinary-looking bathrooms with shallow tubs. Amenities are generous, including Aveda products, DVD players, robes, well-stocked minibars, and coffeemakers. The hotel's restaurant, **Blue Mermaid Chowder House**, serves all day and is better than average for wharf food.

See map p. 104. 495 Jefferson St. (at Hyde Street). ☎ **866-415-0704** *or 415-563-0800. Fax: 415-563-2800.* www.argonauthotel.com. *Valet parking $36. Rack rates: $179–$299 double. AE, DC, DISC, MC, V.*

Best Western Tuscan Inn
$$$–$$$$ North Beach/Fisherman's Wharf

This is the other wonderful Fisherman's Wharf hotel. The hotel is personable and the just-remodeled rooms are fairly large by local standards. The concierge is friendly and enthusiastic, and all the expected amenities are available including complimentary beverages served in the morning and an evening wine reception in the lobby. This is a pet-friendly hotel as well. The Argonaut has a bit better location in our opinion (plus view rooms), but you may find the rates here lower.

See map p. 104. 425 Northpoint St. (between Mason and Taylor streets). ☎ **800-648-4626** *or 415-561-1100. Fax: 415-561-1199.* www.tuscaninn.com. *Valet parking: $35. Rack rates: $159–$239 double. AE, DC, DISC, MC, V.*

Chancellor Hotel
$$$ Union Square

This 137-room, nonsmoking, family-owned hotel offers a level of intimacy and value you just won't find in many other comparable inns. It's also right on the Powell Street cable-car line, a stone's throw from Saks Fifth Avenue. The little bathrooms are well stocked, the bedrooms are brightly decorated and comfortably furnished, and management recently added a "pillow menu," a nice touch if you're allergic to goose down or if you like a soft pillow. Kids are considered, too: Each room has a Nintendo Game System and the front desk always has cookies. For views, request front rooms ending in 00 to 05 on as high a floor as possible. The hotel has ceiling fans rather than air-conditioning.

See map p. 104. 433 Powell St. (between Post and Sutter streets). ☎ **800-428-4748** *or 415-362-2004. Fax: 415-362-1403.* www.chancellorhotel.com. *Valet parking: $30. Rack rates: $155–$185 double. AE, DC, DISC, MC, V.*

Cow Hollow Motor Inn & Suites
S–$$ The Marina/Cow Hollow

These serviceable, nonsmoking motel rooms, unfortunately accessed by elevators inside the parking garage, are clean and quiet, thanks to a diligent staff and double-paned windows, respectively. The early Sears-Roebuck furnishings may not yet have made a style comeback, but you'll appreciate the in-room coffeemaker and hair dryer, relatively spacious baths, free parking, free Wi-Fi, and low rates. Plus, the inn is around the corner from the best blocks of Chestnut Street, where the shopping and dining set high standards. Families can settle into one of six suites with kitchens and a separate entrance right on Chestnut Street. Try to avoid rooms ending in 28, which are next to noisy ice machines.

See map p. 104. 2190 Lombard St. ☎ 415-921-5800. Fax: 415-922-8515. www.cow hollowmotorinn.com. Free parking. Rack rates: $72–$125 double, $225–$275 suite. AE, MC, V.

Harbor Court Hotel
$$$–$$$$ The Embarcadero

Located just steps from the bay and now under Kimpton Hotel management, this is an especially romantic and sophisticated property, lower key than the Hotel Vitale, but equally as stylish. Rooms were all remodeled in 2005, and although they are pretty small, they're so warmly decorated and comfy we can imagine moving in for a long weekend. Reserve or upgrade to a queen or king bay room, which features dramatic views of the water and the Bay Bridge. Guests have free access to the state-of-the-art Embarcadero YMCA pool and health club next door. Trendy **Ozumo,** an excellent Japanese restaurant, is accessible from the lobby.

See map p. 104. 165 Steuart St., between Mission and Howard streets. ☎ 866-792-6283 or 415-882-1300. Fax: 415-882-1313. www.harborcourthotel.com. Parking: $38. Rack rates: $159–$259 double. AE, DC, DISC, MC, V.

Hotel Adagio
$$ Union Square

In a previous incarnation, this 1929 Colonial Revival building housed the tired Shannon Court Hotel, but a total facelift in 2003 turned Joan Crawford into Cindy Crawford. The modern bedrooms and clean, masculine lines won't appeal to frill-seekers, but the hotel is closer in spirit to the more expensive W and Clift hotels. A nicely fitted fitness center, wireless Internet access, high-end bath products, complimentary afternoon tea, executive-level guest rooms with views, and a continental breakfast bring the hotel squarely into the here and now.

See map p. 104. 550 Geary St, between Taylor and Jones streets. ☎ 800-228-8830 or 415-775-5000. Fax: 415-775-9388. www.jdvhospitality.com. Parking: $33. Rack rates: $129–$299 double. AE, DC, DISC, MC, V.

Hotel Bohème
$$$ North Beach

North Beach is the most European-like neighborhood in the city and is our personal favorite. If you fancy stepping out of your hotel into an Italian-style cafe for your morning latte, the Bohème is for you. The 15 recently refreshed rooms, with pretty iron beds and vivid wall colors, are small; bathrooms have showers only, but in-room amenities are generous. The accommodating staff will assist with restaurant reservations, tours, and rental cars, but you'll have to schlep your own luggage up a flight of narrow stairs. There's no air-conditioning, but the windows open.

See map p. 104. 444 Columbus Ave. (between Vallejo and Green streets). ☎ *415-433-9111. Fax: 415-362-6292.* www.hotelboheme.com. *Self-parking: $31 in a garage a few blocks away. Rack rates: $159–$179 double. AE, DC, DISC, MC, V.*

Hotel Del Sol
$$–$$$ The Marina

Paint, mosaic tiles, and a lively imagination can do a lot to reinvent a motel, and you won't find a better example of how well this works than the Del Sol. You'll think you're in Southern California (after the fog lifts, anyway), but here, pedestrians can walk around without getting startled looks from drivers. A heated pool and a hammock suspended between palm trees complete the hallucination. Multicolor guest rooms and suites contain quality amenities such as designer soap. Kids are treated to free kites and beach balls and can even check out a teddy bear from the Pillow Library. Some rooms include kitchenettes.

See map p. 104. 3100 Webster St. (at Filbert Street). ☎ *877-433-5765 or 415-921-5520. Fax: 415-931-4137.* www.thehoteldelsol.com. *Free parking. Rack rates: $109–$179 double, suites from $189. AE, DC, DISC, MC, V.*

Hotel Monaco
$$$–$$$$$ Union Square

Scare up a vintage Vuitton steamer trunk and a foxtail-trimmed scarf, then sashay into the Art Deco–inspired Monaco. The medium-size rooms are replete with canopied beds, floral prints, and modern furniture. All the amenities — a fitness center, room service, robes, and so on — are available, along with the appropriately named **Grand Cafe** restaurant. It's also close to theaters and is pet-friendly.

See map p. 104. 501 Geary St. (at Taylor Street). ☎ *866-622-5284 or 415-292-0100. Fax: 415-292-0111.* www.monaco-sf.com. *Valet parking: $39. Rack rates: $219–$599 double, from $399 suite. AE, DC, DISC, MC, V.*

Hotel Rex
$$$–$$$$ Union Square

At this attractive, sophisticated 94-room gem, room sizes vary from small-ish doubles on up, so if you want extra space, be sure to request an executive king. All accommodations are colorfully decorated and smartly designed. This is a full-service hotel, with a concierge, a new cafe, and such thoughtful amenities as CD players.

See map p. 104. 562 Sutter St. (between Powell and Mason streets). ☎ *800-433-4434 or 415-433-4434. Fax: 415-433-3695.* www.thehctelrex.com. *Valet parking: $30. Rack rates: $199–$245 double. Rates include evening wine. AE, DC, DISC, MC, V.*

Hotel Vitale
$$$$–$$$$$ The Embarcadero

Expensive, but not over-the-top extravagant, this new property claims the most coveted patch of earth in town, across the boulevard from the Ferry Building. Spoiled by delicious views, an F-Market streetcar stop behind the building, and its location within walking distance to well-regarded restaurants, the hotel delights inside as well. You'll notice, first, how good the place smells (small vials with dried lavender grace the hallways), and attention to detail continues inside the guestrooms. Deluxe waterfront sanctuaries feature a sexy walk-in shower rather than skimpy bathtub/shower combos in the still-spacious, but viewless interior rooms. It's contemporary, chic, and full of vitality.

See map p. 104. 8 Mission St. (at Steuart Street). ☎ *888-890-8688 or 415-278-3700. Fax: 415-278-3750.* www.hotelvitale.com. *Parking: $42. Rack rates: $309–$699 double. AE, DC, DISC, MC, V.*

The Huntington
$$$$$ Nob Hill

The Boston Brahmin in you will adore this quiet, refined oasis with its subtle elegance, impeccable service, and the most gorgeous spa we've seen in this town. The 1924 building originally housed apartments, so guest rooms (most are suites) and baths are larger than average; by the end of 2007, all will have been updated. Rooms above the eighth floor offer views; the ones below are extra-spacious. Children are welcome, and the staff, concierge included, will anticipate your every need. Manicured Huntington Park, complete with playground, is across the street.

See map p. 104. 1075 California St. (at Taylor Street). ☎ *800-227-4683 or 415-474-5400. Fax: 415-474-6227.* www.huntingtonhotel.com. *Parking: $29. Rack rates: $350–$500 double, $600–$1,350 suite. AE, DC, DISC, MC, V.*

The Marina Courtyard Motel
$–$$ The Marina/Cow Hollow

Because this was originally an apartment building, 15 of the rentals in this funky, flower-bedecked, courtyard-style budget motel feature fully equipped kitchens. A granddaughter of the original owner redecorated the medium-size studios with Italian bathroom tiles, Mission-style furniture, and pretty quilts, making this one of the few places on Lombard Street with even a hint of charm. Families can reserve two connecting rooms with a shared bathroom. Surprisingly, considering the location, rooms off the street are remarkably quiet. The front desk clerk will arrange tours or rental cars at your request. It is the definition of cheap and cheerful.

See map p. 104. 2576 Lombard St. (near Divisadero Street). ☎ *800-346-6118 or 415-921-9406. Fax: 415-921-0364.* www.marinamotel.com. *Parking: Free in little garages on the premises. Rack rates: $85–$135 double, $99–$135 family room. AE, MC, V. Dogs welcome.*

Nob Hill Lambourne
$$–$$$ Nob Hill

An intimate 20-room hotel, the relaxed and soothing, nonsmoking Lambourne has spacious rooms with compact kitchenettes and many amenities. Suites are available for vacationing families — and they're beauties. Massages and other on-site spa treatments can be scheduled by the front-desk staff, and nightly turndown service substitutes vitamins for chocolates on your buckwheat-hull-filled pillow. Continental breakfast is included in the rates, and a fresh fruit basket is in the hallway for your pleasure. You won't find a better deal on Nob Hill.

See map p. 104. 725 Pine St. (at Stockton Street). ☎ *800-274-8466 or 415-433-2287. Fax: 415-433-0975.* www.nobhilllambourne.com. *Parking: $32. Rack rates: $139–$209. Rates include continental breakfast and evening wine reception. AE, DC, DISC, MC, V.*

The Orchard
$$$$ Union Square

Opened in 2001, the 105-room Orchard boasts some of the largest bedrooms and most luxurious baths in the area, as well as a charming staff to assist you. Conservatively decorated rooms will satisfy you as a business traveler or as a vacationer, because the rooms include CD/DVD players, high-speed Internet access, and top amenities, including room service. Cable cars stop just around the corner.

See map p. 104. 665 Bush St. (between Stockton and Powell streets). ☎ *888-717-2881 or 415-362-8878. Fax: 415-362-8088.* www.theorchardhotel.com. *Valet parking: $34. Rack rates: $229–$299 double. Rates include continental breakfast. AE, DC, MC, V.*

Petite Auberge
$$$–$$$$ Union Square

Romantics will find true love here among the florals and French-country effects. The high-end rooms are enormous; the less-expensive rooms are cozy and have showers only, but are equally comfortable. Along with a full breakfast served downstairs in the homey dining room, the hotel offers complimentary tea, wine, and hors d'oeuvres in the afternoon. It's exceedingly popular, so if you want to experience the charms of a Provençal-style inn, book way ahead.

See map p. 104. 863 Bush St. (between Mason and Taylor streets). ☎ *800-365-3004* or 415-928-6000. Fax: 415-673-7214. www.petiteaubergesf.com. *Valet parking: $30. Rack rates: $150–$245 double. Rates include full breakfast. AE, DC, MC, V.*

St. Regis Hotel
$$$$$ SoMa

With the entry of the 40-story St. Regis Hotel onto the five-star scene, you can rest assured that pampering has reached, well, new heights. The hotel itself (floors 22 to 40 are residences) is awash in understated, unquestionable great taste and comfort, from the handsome lobby bar to the lose-yourself-in-luxe bedrooms with deep soaking tubs, huge plasma-screen TVs, and digitized remote controls to close the window coverings or signal the butler. The fitness center and spa are the finest in town. Views begin from the eighth floor. **Ame,** the hotel's fine-dining restaurant, is now a destination in itself.

See map p. 104. 125 Third St. (between Market and Mission streets). ☎ *415-284-4000.* Fax: 415-284-4100. www.starwoodhotels.com/stregis. *Parking: $45. Rack rates: $407–$749 double. AE, DC, DISC, MC. V.*

Where to Dine

Eating is not beside the point when you visit San Francisco. The number of restaurants in the city (around 3,300) is astonishing, and the quality of the food in many of them is equally so. You can locate the restaurants reviewed in this section on the "San Francisco Dining" map on p. 112.

So much food and so little time . . . but there is plenty of competition for seats. Call for reservations before arriving at any but the most casual of restaurants. Easier still, log on to the restaurant reservations Web site www.opentable.com and book a table through the Internet.

Want to eat at the most sought-after tables in town? Try calling the day you'd like to go, right after the reservation line opens. The most popular restaurants often require that guests confirm their intentions by noon, so you may luck out and get in on a cancellation.

A16
$$–$$$ The Marina/Cow Hollow SOUTHERN ITALIAN

The name refers to the highway through the Campanga region of Italy (Naples being the major city), and the menu at this stylishly spare restaurant not only reflects the cuisine of the south but also uses ingredients from the area. Favorite dishes include *burrata,* a delicious mozzarella with a creamy center; various house-cured salami; and among a handful of excellent main courses, halibut trimmed with Meyer lemons and almonds. You'll also find a choice lineup of authentic Neapolitan pizzas and pasta dishes.

San Francisco Dining

A16 **2**
Absinthe **17**
Ame **15**
Boulevard **14**
Butterfly **6**
Canteen **12**
Chow **19**
Foreign Cinema **20**
Gary Danko **5**
Grand Cafe **13**
Greens **1**
Isa **3**
Kokkari Estiatorio **9**
Lichee Garden **8**
Lulu **16**
R&G Lounge **11**
Range **20**
The Slanted Door **10**
Tablespoon **4**
Teatro ZinZanni **7**
Zuni Cafe **18**

CABLE CAR LINES

California Line ——————
Powell-Mason Line ――――
Powell-Hyde Line ——
Cable Car Turnaround ⭕

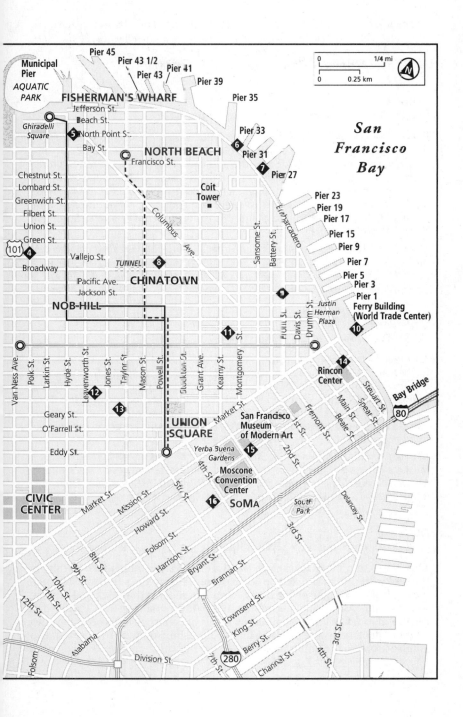

Pier 45
Pier 43 1/2
Pier 43
Pier 41
Pier 39
Pier 35

Municipal
Pier

AQUATIC
PARK

FISHERMAN'S WHARF

Jefferson St.
Beach St.
North Point St.
Bay St.
Francisco St.

Ghiradelli
Square

5

NORTH BEACH

Chestnut St.
Lombard St.
Greenwich St.
Filbert St.
Union St.
Green St.

101 **4**

Vallejo St.
Broadway

TUNNEL **8**

Pacific Ave.
Jackson St.

CHINATOWN

NOB HILL

Coit
Tower

Columbus Ave.

Pier 33
Pier 31
Pier 27
Pier 23
Pier 19
Pier 17
Pier 15
Pier 9
Pier 7
Pier 5
Pier 3
Pier 1

Sansome St.
Battery St.
Embarcadero

6
7

9

Justin
Herman
Plaza

Ferry Building
(World Trade Center)

10

Front St.
Davis St.
Drumm St.

11

San
Francisco
Bay

0   1/4 mi
0   0.25 km

Van Ness Ave.
Polk St.
Larkin St.
Hyde St.
Leavenworth St.
Jones St.
Taylor St.
Mason St.
Powell St.
Stockton St.
Grant Ave.
Kearny St.
Montgomery St.

12
13

Geary St.
O'Farrell St.
Eddy St.

UNION
SQUARE

Market St.

San Francisco
Museum
of Modern Art

Yerba Buena
Gardens

Moscone
Convention
Center

15

Rincon
Center

14

Steuart St.
Main St.
Spear St.
Beale St.
Fremont St.
1st St.
2nd St.

Bay Bridge

80

CIVIC
CENTER

Market St.
Mission St.
Howard St.
Folsom St.
Harrison St.

5th St.
4th St.

16

SoMa

South
Park

Delancey St.
3rd St.

8th St.
9th St.
10th St.
11th St.
12th St.

Bryant St.
Brannan St.

Townsend St.
King St.
Berry St.

280

Division St.
Channel St.

Alabama
Folsom

3rd St.
4th St.
7th St.

See map p. 112. 2355 Chestnut St. (near Scott Street). ☎ *415-771-2216.* www.a16sf.com. *Reservations accepted. To get there: 22-Fillmore, 28-19th Avenue, 30-Stockton, and 43-Masonic buses. Main courses: $8–$19. AE, MC, V. Open: Wed–Fri 11:30 a.m.–2:30 p.m., Sun–Thurs 5–10 p.m., Fri–Sat until 11 p.m.*

Absinthe
$$$–$$$$ Civic Center/Hayes Valley   FRENCH

For a lovely meal around Civic Center, this warmly decorated dining room is a great choice. You can't miss with a selection from the oyster bar or a crisp Caesar salad to start. Some days, the chef cooks like a French *grand-mére*, with coq au vin, a confit of duck, or house-made sausage and pork ready to satisfy your hunger pangs. A hot spot for preconcert dining, book a table after 7:30 p.m. in order to savor the romantic room and seasonal menu. Weekend brunch is busy, but drop in for lunch if you're shopping in the neighborhood.

See map p. 112. 398 Hayes St. (at Gough Street). ☎ *415-551-1590. Reservations recommended, especially on weekends. To get there: Muni to Van Ness Avenue, walk north 2 blocks to Hayes Street, and turn left. Main courses: $20–$27. AE, DC, MC, V. Open: Tues–Fri 11:30 a.m.–midnight, Sat 11 a.m.–midnight, Sun 11 a.m.–10 p.m.*

Boulevard
$$$$ The Embarcadero   CALIFORNIA

An elegant turn-of-the-century setting and generous plates of seasonal California-French cuisine combine to ensure a rousing good time at this deservedly popular restaurant. Entrees of particular note include the Sonoma duck breast wrapped in applewood-smoked bacon and the thick pork chop roasted in the wood-fired oven. Guests without reservations can take a seat at the counter, but you should phone three or four weeks in advance to get a prime-time table.

See map p. 112. 1 Mission St. (at Steuart Street). ☎ *415-543-6084. Reservations a must. To get there: Muni Metro to the Embarcadero Station; walk 1 block east to Mission Street. Main courses: $29–$35. AE, DC, DISC, MC, V. Open: Thurs–Sat 5:30–10:30 p.m., Sun–Wed 5:30–10 p.m., Mon–Fri 11:30 a.m.–2 p.m.*

Butterfly
$$$$ The Embarcadero   PAN-ASIAN

This is a beautiful restaurant on the water, a comfortable place to take in the bay, with drinks and maybe some oysters before the sun sets. The chef-owner, Robert Lam, uses local ingredients in recipes that pick and choose from various Asian cuisines, which makes for unusual eating. If you're in the mood to try something different, order his crispy, fried whole fish with kimchi, black bean sauce, and Chinese sausage. You won't know what to admire more — the shimmering water or your dinner plate.

See map p. 112. Pier 33 on the Embarcadero at Bay Street. ☎ *415-864-8999.* www. butterflysf.com. *Reservations recommended. To get there: F-Market streetcar. Main courses: $16–$38. AE, MC, V. Open: Mon–Fri 11:30 a.m.–3 p.m. and happy hour 3–5 p.m., Sun–Wed 5–10 p.m., Thurs–Sat 5–11 p.m., Sat–Sun 11 a.m.–3 p.m.*

Canteen
$$$ Union Square   CALIFORNIA

Miniscule Canteen is the domain of the much-admired Chef Dennis Leary, whose bona fides include four years at Rubicon prior to opening this 20-seat upscale diner. Leary does the shopping as well as all the cooking, and his menu changes to reflect what appeals on a weekly basis. If you're staying around Union Square, note that breakfast here is stellar, especially the smoked salmon omelet or stuffed pancake. Work the phones to land a dinner seat or come for lunch and see what all the fuss is about.

See map p. 112. 817 Sutter St. (next to the Commodore Hotel). ☎ *415-928-8870.* www.canteensf.com. *Reservations accepted (and needed) for dinner only. Main courses: $20–$25. AE, DC, MC, V. Open: Mon–Fri 7–11 a.m., weekend brunch 8 a.m.–2 p.m., Wed–Fri 11:30 a.m.–2 p.m. and 6–10 p.m.*

Chow
$–$$ The Castro   AMERICAN

Pasta dishes, crispy brick-oven-roasted chicken, and thin-crusted pizzas make this great price performer ideal for kids and grown-ups alike. The wood-paneled room is casual and comfortable, the service is kind, and patrons are happy. With the same menu, **Park Chow,** 1240 Ninth Ave. (☎ **415-665-9912**), by Golden Gate Park, is also terrific.

See map p. 112. 215 Church St. (at Market Street). ☎ *415-552-2469. Reservations not accepted. To get there: Muni Metro J-Church or F-Market to Church Street. Main courses: $7.75–$15. MC, V. Open: Sun–Thurs 11 a.m.–11 p.m., Fri–Sat 11 a.m.–midnight.*

Foreign Cinema
$$$–$$$$ Mission District   CALIFORNIA/MEDITERRANEAN

Mission District regulars nearly lost their empanadas when the shiny, chic Foreign Cinema opened in 1999. The expansive dining room — plus outdoor patio where foreign films are screened on a concrete wall — would throw anyone at first, but some shellfish from the raw bar help to lower resistance to the inevitable changes in the neighborhood. The menu changes regularly, but expect to find entrees such as a roast chicken seasoned with Spanish paprika or an imaginative King salmon "B.L.T."

See map p. 112. 2534 Mission St. (between 21st and 22nd streets). ☎ *415-648-7600. Reservations highly recommended. To get there: BART to 24th Street, then head north on Mission. Main courses: $16–$30. AE, DISC, MC, V. Open: Mon–Thurs 6–10 p.m. (until 11 p.m. Fri–Sat), Sat–Sun 11 a.m.–3 p.m.*

Gary Danko
$$$$–$$$$$ Russian Hill NEW AMERICAN/FRENCH

The ovens were barely lit at this fine-dining center before the food and wine cognoscenti were all over Danko's like hollandaise, proclaiming it among the best restaurants in the country. Choose your own three-course (or more if you like) meal from the menu — perhaps a composed lobster salad followed by day-boat scallops and ending with a mango Napoleon or selections from the cheese cart — then let the kitchen make magic. You can walk in without a booking if you don't mind eating at the bar.

See map p. 112. 800 Northpoint, at Hyde Street. ☎ *415-749-2060.* www.garydanko. com. *Reservations advised four weeks in advance. To get there: Powell-Hyde cable-car line. Prix-fixe menu from $61–$89. DC, DISC, MC, V. Open: Daily 5:30–10 p.m.*

Grand Cafe
$$$ Union Square CALIFORNIA/FRENCH

Living up to its name in every aspect, this vast, high-ceilinged, muraled bistro is abuzz with activity and energy. People gravitate to the Petit Café pre- and post-theater for brick-oven pizzas, sandwiches, and desserts; and they head to the larger dining room for a rib-eye steak or a lovely, fragrant bouillabaisse.

See map p. 112. 501 Geary St. (at Taylor Street). ☎ *415-292-0101. Reservations accepted. To get there: Muni Metro to Powell Street, walk 2 blocks west to Geary and 2 blocks south to Taylor. Main courses: $14–$25; Petit Café $7–$12. AE, DC, DISC, MC, V. Open: Mon–Fri 7–10:30 a.m. and 11:30 a.m.–2:30 p.m., Sat 8 a.m.–2:30 p.m., Sun 9 a.m.–2:30 p.m., Sun–Thurs 5:30–10 p.m., Fri–Sat 5:30–11 p.m.; Petit Café open daily 11:30 a.m.–11 p.m., until midnight Fri–Sat.*

Greens
$$$ The Marina/Cow Hollow VEGETARIAN

If you've never eaten in a gourmet vegetarian restaurant, or if your past encounters with vegetarian dining have been less than inspired, you're in for a marvelous culinary experience. The Saturday evening prix-fixe menu is enticing, especially when you see the gorgeous bay view that comes with the meal.

See map p. 112. Fort Mason, Building A, off Marina Boulevard at Buchanan Street. ☎ *415-771-6222.* http://greensrestaurant.com. *Reservations highly recommended at least two weeks in advance. To get there: 30-Stockton bus to Laguna, transfer to 28-19th Avenue bus into Fort Mason. Main courses: $16–$23; prix-fixe menu (Sat only) $48. AE, DISC, MC, V. Open: Sun 10 a.m.–2 p.m., Tues–Sat noon–2:30 p.m., Mon–Sat 5:30–9 p.m., Sun10:30–2 p.m.*

Isa
$$ Marina/Cow Hollow FRENCH

I (Paula, here) had a running argument with my cousin Irene over who made the wisest picks at this stellar find. My crab salad was full of toothsome, freshly cracked crabmeat, but Irene's baked goat cheese, surrounded by pesto and perfectly ripe tomato, started a fork fight. We reached an impasse over the grilled flat-iron steak and the potato-wrapped sea bass, but we agreed that based on price, atmosphere, service, and taste, this was among the best meals we've eaten in town. Chef-owner Luke Sung has been recognized as a Rising Star Chef of the Year by the James Beard Foundation two years in a row, and we can't argue with that.

See map p. 112. 3324 Steiner St. (at Chestnut Street). ☎ *415-567-9588. Reservations recommended. To get there: 30-Stockton bus. Main courses: $12–$18. MC, V. Open: Mon–Thurs 5:30–10 p.m., Fri–Sat until 10:30 p.m.*

Kokkari Estiatorio
$$$$ **Financial District**   **GREEK**

Your average Mediterranean shipping tycoon would feel perfectly comfortable seated beneath the beamed ceilings of this richly appointed tavern. The California-meets-Greece menu takes familiar dishes to Mount Olympus–style heights. Order the *Yiaourti Graniti* (yogurt sorbet with tangerine ice) for dessert, even if you're full.

See map p. 112. 200 Jackson St. (at Front Street). ☎ *415-981-0983. Reservations a must. To get there: 2, 3, or 4 bus; transfer to 42-Downtown Loop, exit at Sansome and Jackson streets, and walk 2 blocks west to Front. Main courses: $16–$34. AE, DISC, MC, V. Open: Mon–Fri 11:30 a.m.–2:30 p.m., Mon–Thurs 5:30–10 p.m., Fri–Sat 5:30–11 p.m.*

Lichee Garden
$–$$ **Chinatown**   **CHINESE**

This is a particularly reliable family-style Cantonese restaurant, in a quieter part of Chinatown, with a huge menu filled with familiar dishes (such as egg foo yung), lots of seafood, and every Chinese dish you remember from childhood (unless you were raised in China). They also serve a good dim sum lunch. Prices aren't high (Peking duck being the biggest extravagance), service is fine, and the room is bright and lively because this place is popular with the locals — and kids, too.

See map p. 112. 1416 Powell St. (near Broadway). ☎ *415-397-2290. Reservations accepted. To get there: Powell-Mason cable car. Main courses: $6.50–$25. MC, V. Open: Daily 7 a.m.–9:15 p.m.*

Lulu
$$ **SoMa**   **MEDITERRANEAN**

With the buoyant feel of a lively Provençal bistro, the mouthwatering scent of the oak-fired rotisserie, and a lengthy menu of appealing dishes, Lulu seduces on many levels. If you're anywhere near Yerba Buena Center, don't think twice about having lunch or dinner at this local institution. Most dishes should be shared, such as the daily rotisserie specials, the wonderful rosemary-scented chicken, and antipasti plate of your own design. Dinnertime can be pretty noisy, but you'll be surrounded by a buzz of happiness.

See map p. 112. 816 Folsom St. (at Fourth Street). ☎ *415-495-5775.* www.restaurant lulu.com. *Reservations advised. To get there: 45-Union/Stockton or 30-Stockton bus. Main courses: $16–$30. AE, DC, DISC, MC, V. Open: Mon–Thurs 5:30 a.m.– 10 p.m., Fri–Sat 11:30 a.m.–3 p.m. and 5–11 p.m., Sun 11:30 a.m.–3 p.m. and 5–10 p.m.*

R&G Lounge
$–$$ Chinatown   CHINESE

You'll find superb Hong Kong Chinese dishes here, downstairs in a setting reminiscent of an airport lounge, or upstairs in a more attractive dining room, so talk your way to a table there. Make room for salt-and-pepper crab and fresh, crisp vegetables such as Chinese broccoli and *yin choy* (a leafy green vegetable with a red root that's often boiled, then braised with garlic). Bring the family and order a few dishes for all to share. Kids love it.

See map p. 112. 631 Kearny St. (between Sacramento and Clay streets). ☎ *415-982-7877. Reservations accepted. To get there: 15-Third bus. Main courses: $7.25–$9.50. AE, MC, V. Open: Daily 11 a.m.–9:30 p.m.*

Range
$$ Mission District   CALIFORNIA

Range is a prime example of the modern San Francisco neighborhood restaurant. Opened by a kitchen-savvy husband-and-wife team (Phil and Cameron West), their small, seasonal menu features flavor over flash, backed by charming service. The coffee-rubbed pork shoulder is a favorite, while Range's delicate take on meat and potatoes — pan-roasted, thinly sliced bavette steak (cut from the short loin) with narrow fingerlings — satisfies on a more primal level. Two simple yet warm dining rooms, fronted by an attractive bar, allow for conversation, a nice touch given how often restaurants seem designed to make it impossible.

See map p. 112. 842 Valencia St. (between 19th and 20th streets). ☎ *415-282-8283.* www.rangesf.com. *Reservations recommended. To get there: 14 bus or taxi (parking is difficult). Main courses: $17–$20. MC, V. Open: Sun–Thurs 5:30–10 p.m., Fri–Sat 5:30–11 p.m.*

The Slanted Door
$$–$$$ The Embarcadero   VIETNAMESE

The city's premier Vietnamese eatery moved to what we consider a premier location — the new Ferry Building. Savvy travelers and locals rushed on over, and they continue to pour in for the buttery steamed sea bass, caramelized chicken, and plates of "shaking" beef. Even if dinner reservations seem impossible to come by, call at 5:30 p.m. the evening you want to dine, in case of a cancellation. You may get lucky. You even need a reservation for lunch, especially since Chef Charles Phan was named Best Chef in California by the James Beard Foundation in 2004.

See map p. 112. 1 Ferry Building, the Embarcadero and Market. ☎ *415-861-8032. Reservations a must. To get there: BART or Muni to the Embarcadero Station. Main* *courses: $16–$30. AE, MC, V. Open: Daily 11:30 a.m.–2:30 p.m., Sun–Thurs 5:30–10 p.m., Fri–Sat 5:30–10:30 p.m.*

Tablespoon
$$$ **Russian Hill   AMERICAN**

This urbane, Manhattan-like dining room seats only 45 (plus 12 at the bar), and in such close confines, you'll have a chance to examine what the guy next to you is eating. Chances are it'll be delectable, as the chef/co-owner, Robert Riescher, left the renowned Erna's Elderberry House in Oakhurst (see Chapter 16) for an opportunity to operate on his own. The menu changes daily, but with luck he'll be plating a topless ravioli dish with tender shreds of braised lamb shank and mustard greens in a pool of onion broth. It's awesome.

See map p. 112. 2209 Polk St. (at Vallejo Street). ☎ 415-268-0140. Reservations recommended. To get there: Powell-Hyde cable car to Vallejo and walk 2 blocks northwest to Polk. Main courses: $18–$21. AE, MC, V. Open: Mon–Sat 6 p.m.–midnight, Sun to 10 p.m.

Zuni Cafe
$$$ **Civic Center   CALIFORNIA**

You can always detect a palpable buzz from the smartly dressed crowd hanging around Zuni's copper bar drinking vodka and scarfing down oysters. Everything from the brick oven is great, but the roast chicken and bread salad for two is simply divine. Don't opt for an outside table, because the view on this section of Market Street isn't all that pleasant.

See map p. 112. 1658 Market St. (between Franklin and Gough streets). ☎ 415-552-2522. Reservations recommended. To get there: Muni Metro F-Market to Van Ness, and walk 2 blocks southwest. Main courses: $13–$29. AE, MC, V. Open: Tues–Sat 11:30 a.m.–midnight, Sun 11 a.m.–11 p.m.

Dinner as theater

Down at **Pier 29** on the Embarcadero, look for a stylized 1926 *Spiegeltent* (a circular, tented pavilion), the home of **Teatro ZinZanni** (☎ 415-438-2668; www.teatro zinzanni.org). This is an immensely hilarious dinner show with a twist: The audience is part of the proceedings. Don't worry — you won't be asked to get up and recite. Along with an acceptable, if not stellar, five-course meal (it reminds us of hotel wedding suppers), diners are regaled by a talented group of performers who combine cabaret, opera, acrobatics, comedy, and improv in most-unusual ways. The cast changes periodically, and, strangely enough, Joan Baez has appeared in the show off and on; it's worth investigating who's in the lineup when you come to town. This isn't a cheap date — tickets range from $110 to $135 — but it's something to consider if you're celebrating or looking for an evening out of the ordinary. Doors open Wednesday through Saturday at 6 p.m. for a 7 p.m. show (one hour earlier on Sun evenings).

Exploring San Francisco

CityPass (www.citypass.net), a booklet of discounted tickets to six major attractions (**Museum of Modern Art, Palace of the Legion of Honor/de Young museums, California Academy of Sciences** *or* **Asian Art Museum, the Aquarium of the Bay,** and the **Exploratorium**) and a Blue & Gold Bay Cruise, includes a seven-day Muni Passport, making it quite a bargain if you're ambitious enough to use all the coupons. It's $49 for adults, $39 for kids, and you can purchase it online or at the participating attractions.

To locate the attractions reviewed in the upcoming sections, check out the "San Francisco's Top Attractions" map on p. 122.

The top attractions

Alcatraz Island

If not for the movies, Alcatraz Island (aka "The Rock") would never have morphed from a derelict, deserted maximum-security prison into a must-see tourist attraction. Self-guided two-and-a-half-hour audio tours and talks facilitated by National Park rangers are full of interesting anecdotes. The walk uphill to the Cell House is steep, so wear comfortable shoes. A tram runs once every hour to take wheelchair users or anyone unable to make the walk up to the prison. In the summer, order tickets far in advance for the ferry ride to the island — and don't forget to bring a jacket, because the island gets windy. Plan on at least three hours for the entire excursion.

See map p. 122. Pier 33, at Fisherman's Wharf for location of ferry departures. ☎ *415-981-ROCK.* www.AlcatrazCruises.com *or* www.nps.gov/alcatraz. *Open: Winter daily 9:30 a.m.–2:15 p.m., summer daily 9:30 a.m.–4:15 p.m. Night tours offered Thurs–Sun at 6:15 and 7 p.m., and at 4:20 p.m. during the winter. Ferries run approximately every half-hour; arrive at least 20 minutes before sailing time. To get there: F-Market streetcar, Powell-Mason cable car (the line ends a few blocks away), or 30-Stockton bus. Admission (includes ferry and audio tour): $19 adults and kids 12–17, $17 seniors 62 and older, $11 children 5–11; night-tour fares $26 adults, $23 seniors and kids 12–17, $14 children 5–11.*

Asian Art Museum

The Asian Art Museum has one of the largest collections of Asian art in the Western world, covering 6,000 years and encompassing the cultures of Japan, China, Korea, and Southeast Asia. Although the collection itself remains more than enough reason to visit, its newly renovated Beaux Arts building has also attracted plenty of attention. It was designed by Gae Aulenti, the Milanese architect who renovated the former d'Orsay train station in Paris into the wildly popular Musée d'Orsay. The Asian is compact and it won't take you more than a few hours to see all the galleries. Cafe Asia on the first floor is open from 10 a.m. for drinks and Asian-influenced dishes served cafeteria-style.

See map p. 122. 200 Larkin St. (at Fulton Street). ☎ *415-581-3500.* www.asianart. crg. *To get there: Muni or BART to Civic Center station. Public parking lot across the street. Open: Tues–Sun 10 a.m.–5 p.m., Thurs until 9 p.m. Admission: $10 adults, $7 seniors 65 and older, $5 students and kids 12–17, free for kids younger than 12; $5 every Thurs after 5 p.m and free first Tues of the month.*

The Cable Cars

These cherished wooden cars creak and squeal up and around hills as unwitting passengers lean out into the wind, running the risk of getting their heads removed by passing buses. San Francisco's three existing lines comprise the world's only surviving system of cable cars. (Brown signs with a white cable car on them indicate stops.) All three routes are worth your time — and kids will demand at least one ride — but the Powell-Mason line conveniently wends its way from the corner of Powell and Market streets through North Beach and ends near Fisherman's Wharf. The Powell-Hyde line starts at the same intersection and ends up near the Maritime Museum and Ghirardelli Square. The less-thrilling California line begins at the foot of Market Street and travels along California Street over Nob Hill to Van Ness Avenue.

Cars run 6:30 a.m.–12:30 a.m. Fare: $5 per person one-way, payable on board; Muni passports are accepted. For more information, see the "Getting around" section earlier in this chapter.

Chinatown

Crowded with pedestrians and crammed with exotic-looking shops and vegetable markets whose wares spill onto the sidewalks, Chinatown is genuinely fascinating. If you want an authentic experience, veer off Grant Avenue and explore the side streets and alleys. On weekends, Chinatown is extra-jammed with shoppers examining fruits and vegetables piled on outdoor tables. Just walking down the street is an experience.

The **Golden Gate Fortune Cookies Company,** 956 Ross Alley (between Jackson and Washington streets near Grant Avenue), is a working factory where you can purchase inexpensive fresh almond cookies and crispy fortune cookies (terrific gifts for the folks back home!). It's very tight quarters, but you can stand for a few minutes watching rounds of dough be transformed and stuffed with fortunes. Open daily 10 a.m. to 7 p.m.

Portsmouth Square a park above the Portsmouth Square parking garage on Kearny Street (between Washington and Clay streets), is the site of the first California public school, which opened in 1848, and marks the spot where San Francisco was originally settled. A compact but complete playground attracts all the neighborhood preschoolers and, in the morning, elderly Chinese who come to practice tai chi exercises. The landscape includes comfortable benches, attractive lampposts, and young trees. The distinctly San Francisco view includes the Transamerica Pyramid looming above the skyline.

San Francisco's Top Attractions

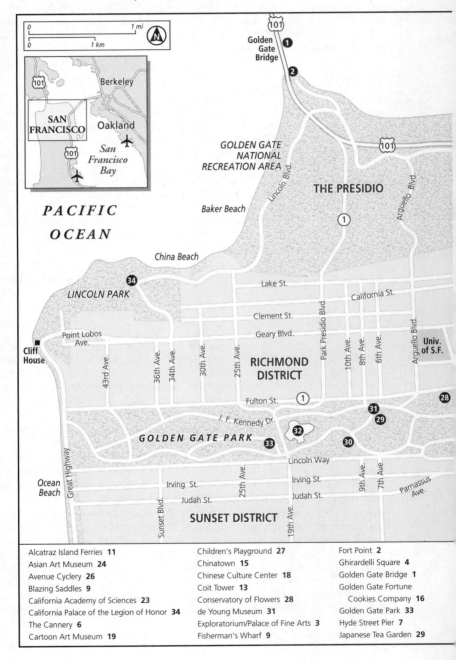

Alcatraz Island Ferries **11**	Children's Playground **27**	Fort Point **2**
Asian Art Museum **24**	Chinatown **15**	Ghirardelli Square **4**
Avenue Cyclery **26**	Chinese Culture Center **18**	Golden Gate Bridge **1**
Blazing Saddles **9**	Coit Tower **13**	Golden Gate Fortune
California Academy of Sciences **23**	Conservatory of Flowers **28**	Cookies Company **16**
California Palace of the Legion of Honor **34**	de Young Museum **31**	Golden Gate Park **33**
The Cannery **6**	Exploratorium/Palace of Fine Arts **3**	Hyde Street Pier **7**
Cartoon Art Museum **19**	Fisherman's Wharf **9**	Japanese Tea Garden **29**

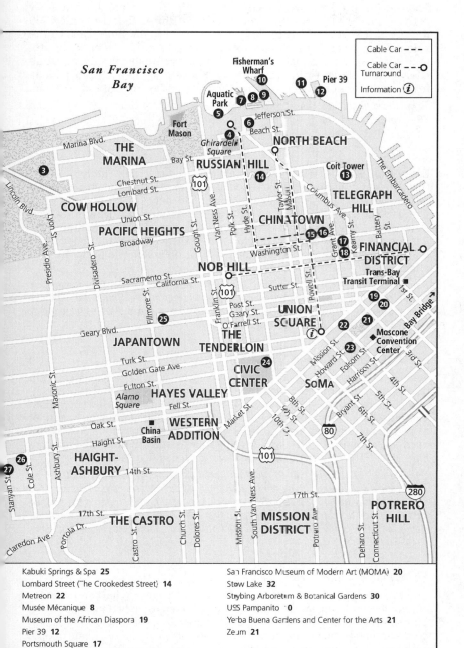

San Francisco Bay

Fisherman's Wharf 10

Pier 39 11

Pier 39 12

Aquatic Park 7 8 9 5

Fort Mason 4

Ghirardelli Square

Jefferson St.

Beach St. 6

NORTH BEACH

THE MARINA

Marina Blvd.

Bay St.

RUSSIAN HILL 14

Coit Tower 13

Chestnut St.

Lombard St.

101

COW HOLLOW

Union St.

CHINATOWN

TELEGRAPH HILL

PACIFIC HEIGHTS

Broadway

Washington St. 15 16

17 18

FINANCIAL DISTRICT

Sacramento St.

California St.

NOB HILL

Trans-Bay Transit Terminal

Geary Blvd.

101

Post St.

Geary St.

O'Farrell St.

Sutter St.

UNION SQUARE

19 20

21

JAPANTOWN

THE TENDERLOIN

22

Moscone Convention Center

Turk St.

Golden Gate Ave.

Fulton St.

CIVIC CENTER 24

Mission St.

Howard St.

Folsom St.

SoMA 23

Bay Bridge

Alamo Square

HAYES VALLEY

Fell St.

Harrison St.

Oak St.

Haight St.

China Basin

WESTERN ADDITION

Market St.

80

HAIGHT-ASHBURY 14th St.

26

27

101

17th St.

17th St.

THE CASTRO

Church St.

Dolores St.

Mission St.

South Van Ness Ave.

MISSION DISTRICT

Potrero Ave.

Deharo St.

Connecticut St.

POTRERO HILL

280

Castro St.

Claredon Ave.

Portola Dr.

Cable Car - - -
Cable Car - - -o
Turnaround
Information (i)

Kabuki Springs & Spa **25**
Lombard Street (The Crookedest Street) **14**
Metreon **22**
Musée Mécanique **8**
Museum of the African Diaspora **19**
Pier 39 **12**
Portsmouth Square **17**
San Francisco Maritime National Historical Park **5**

San Francisco Museum of Modern Art (MOMA) **20**
Stow Lake **32**
Strybing Arboretum & Botanical Gardens **30**
USS Pampanito **0**
Yerba Buena Gardens and Center for the Arts **21**
Zeum **21**

The pedestrian bridge over Kearny Street leads directly into the third floor of the Chinatown Hilton, where you'll find the **Chinese Culture Center,** 750 Kearny St. (☎ **415-986-1822;** www.c-c-c.org). A gift shop leads to the sole gallery, where changing exhibits may feature, for example, photographs from pre-earthquake Chinatown, Chinese brush painting, or exquisitely embroidered antique clothing and household items. Admission is free, and the center is open Tuesday through Sunday from 10 a.m. to 4 p.m.

To get there: Take Muni bus 1-California, 9AX-San Bruno "A" Express, 9BX-San Bruno "B" Express, or 15-Third.

Coit Tower

Erected in 1933 with funds bequeathed to the city by Lillie Hitchcock Coit, this 210-foot concrete landmark is visible from much of the city. But take a closer look to see the beauty of the tower. The décor inside features walls with dramatic murals inspired by and commissioned during the Great Depression. Be warned that the drive up Telegraph Hill and the free parking lot are always a mass of cars. Ride the elevator to the top for panoramic views of the city and the bay. This diversion will probably take about 30 minutes from start to finish.

See map p. 122. Atop Telegraph Hill. ☎ 415-362-0808. To get there: Take the 39-Coit bus or walk from Lombard Street where it meets Telegraph Hill Boulevard (2 blocks east of Stockton Street). Free parking. Open: Daily 10 a.m.–5 p.m. Admission to top of tower: $4.50 adults, $2.50 seniors, $1.50 kids 6–12.

Exploratorium/Palace of Fine Arts

One of the finest hands-on science museums anywhere, this attraction makes an interesting stop for all ages. The changing exhibits explore technology, human perception, and natural phenomena with well-written text. Visiting with kids can be humbling if you're science-impaired, but a staff of alert volunteers is on hand to help with the tough questions. When you need to decompress, stroll the lovely grounds surrounding the Palace of Fine Arts. If the weather's balmy, bring a picnic and stay a while.

See map p. 122. 3601 Lyon St. (at Marina Boulevard). ☎ 415-561-0360. www.exploratorium.edu. *To get there: 30-Stockton bus to Marina stop. Parking: Free and easy. Admission: $13 adults; $10 seniors, kids 13–17, and students over 18; $8 kids 4–12; free for kids under 4; free to all first Wed of the month. Open: Memorial Day–Labor Day, daily 10 a.m.–6 p.m., Wed until 9 p.m.; Labor Day–Memorial Day, Tues–Sun 10 a.m.–5 p.m.*

Fisherman's Wharf

Don't be disappointed when you arrive at Fisherman's Wharf and see lots of people wandering around, none of whom seem to be fishing for a living. This was once a working set of piers, but today it's a seemingly endless outdoor shopping mall masquerading as a bona-fide destination. Some people really enjoy examining the refrigerator magnets and cable-car bookends stocked in one olde shoppe after another; others, dazed in the presence of so much kitsch, hastily plan their escape. Still, because most folks make their way to the wharf for one reason or another, here's a rundown of what's there.

Even when the weather is cold and gray, tourists pack **Pier 39,** a multilevel Disneyesque shopper's fantasy (or nightmare, depending on your point of view). Arcade halls lined with deafening video games anchor the pier on each end, with T-shirt shops and fried food filling the void. The only plausible reasons to join the mob are for the golden view of Alcatraz from the end of the pier, and to watch the sea lions loitering on the west side of the pier (follow the sound of barking). If you're arriving by car, park on adjacent streets or on the wharf between Taylor and Jones streets. (Be advised: The parking garage charges $5.50 per hour! Do your best to avoid these price-gougers or just don't bring a car here.)

The **National Park Service** has opened a new **visitor center,** Hyde and Jefferson streets (☎ 415-447-5000; www.nps.gov/safr/local), inside the Argonaut Hotel, which partners with the Maritime National Historical Park (closed for remodeling through 2008). Along with exhibits and an educational center, the ranger-staffed desk can answer questions about special events on the Hyde Street Pier. Admission is free and it's open daily from 9:30 a.m. to 5:30 p.m.

If you have little kids in tow (or anyone interested in history), you won't want to miss touring the *USS Pampanito,* Pier 45 (☎ 415-561-6662). This submarine saw active duty during World War II and helped save 73 British and Australian prisoners of war. The $20 family pass (for two adults and up to four children) also gets you into the Hyde Street Pier (see the following paragraph). Otherwise, submarine-only admission is $9 for adults, $5 for seniors and students, and $3 children 6 to 12 (kids under 6 are free). Open daily from 9 a.m. to 6 p.m. in winter, and until 8 p.m. in summer.

The **Hyde Street Pier,** at the foot of Hyde Street (at Beach Street, 2 blocks east of the Maritime Museum), houses seven refurbished historic ships (six are national landmarks) on which you can roam around. Of particular note is the *Balclutha,* a square-rigger with a past that began with its 1887 launch. During the year, activities that take place on the *Balclutha* include concerts, sea-chantey singalongs, and children's events. Call ☎ 415-556-6435 for a schedule. You'll spend at least an hour or so touring the vessels. In summer, admission is $5 adults, free for kids 17 and younger. Open daily from 9:30 a.m. to 5 p.m.

Ghirardelli Square, the former chocolate factory across the street from the Maritime Park at 900 North Point, between Polk and Larkin streets (☎ 415-775-5500), is one of the more pleasant shopping malls in the area. Granted landmark status in 1982, the series of brick buildings hosts a roster of special events, including an annual chocolate-tasting benefit in September. Street performers entertain regularly in the West Plaza. Open daily from 10 a.m. to 6 p.m., to 9 p.m. in summer.

One block east in what was once a peach-canning facility is the **Cannery at Del Monte Square,** 2801 Leavenworth St., at Beach Street (☎ 415-771-3112), with yet more shops, jugglers, musicians, and food. Open daily from 10 a.m. to 6 p.m., until 9 p.m. summer

See map p. 122. At the foot of Polk Street, on the western edge of the Embarcadero. To get there: Powell-Hyde cable-car line to the last stop; F-Market streetcar; or 19-Polk, 30-Stockton, 32-Embarcadero, 42-Downtown Loop, or 47-Van Ness bus. Parking: Pricey lots and garages; street parking is difficult.

Golden Gate Bridge

It's the quintessential San Francisco landmark. A walk across the windy, 1¾-mile-long span, hundreds of feet above the water, underscores the point that San Francisco really is like no other city. Bundle up, then set out from the historic Roundhouse visitor center/gift shop on the south end of the bridge. The stroll is noisy and chilly, but exhilarating. The only way to return from the other side is on foot, so assess your fatigue in the middle of the span before continuing on toward Marin. After your stroll, climb below the bridge to walk through the 5-acre garden.

See map p. 122. No phone. www.goldengate.org. *To get there: The 28-19th Avenue or the 29-Sunset bus will deposit you across from the viewing area, right by a parking lot. Open: To pedestrians daily 6 a.m.–6 p.m.*

Lombard Street

The part of Lombard with the moniker "crookedest street in the world" begins at Hyde Street below Russian Hill. The whimsical, flower-lined block attracts thousands of visitors each year. If you intend to drive this redbrick street (it's one-way, downhill, so take the curves slowly), go early in the morning before everyone else revs up their Chevys. Better yet, walk down the stairs to fully admire the flowers, the houses with their long-suffering tenants, and the stellar view.

See map p. 122. Lombard Street between Hyde and Leavenworth streets. To get there: Powell-Hyde cable-car line.

Museum of the African Diaspora (MoAD)

If you walk down Third Street toward Yerba Buena Center, you can't fail to notice the multistory photo mosaic marking one of the latest additions to the South of Market culture klatch. MoAD packs quite a bit into its relatively small exhibition space, and although it won't take more than an hour to tour, you'll find much to think about. Photographs, video, and some very cool interactive displays and technological touches focus upon the themes of origins, movement, adaptation, and transformation in relation to Africa, and thus, in relation to our own selves and communities. Take the kids.

See map p. 122. 685 Mission St. (at Third Street). ☎ **415-358-7200.** www.moadsf. org. *To get there: Take any Muni streetcar to the Montgomery Street Station or the 15-Third, 30-Stockton, or 45-Union/Stockton bus. Admission: $8 adults, $5 seniors and students. Open: Wed–Mon 10 a.m.–6 p.m., until 9 p.m. Thurs.*

San Francisco Museum of Modern Art (MOMA)

It was a big deal when the city finally built a handsome, grown-up museum to house its collection of modern paintings, sculptures, and photographs. The interior is especially beautiful and exudes a warmth that makes viewing the exhibits — including works by Henri Matisse, Jackson Pollock, and Ansel Adams — even more enjoyable.

See map p. 122. 151 Third St. (2 blocks south of Market Street, near Howard Street). ☎ *415-357-4000.* www.sfmoma.org. *To get there: Take any Muni Metro to the Montgomery Street Station and walk 1 block south to Third Street, then 2 blocks east; or take the 15-Third, 30-Stockton, or 45-Union/Stockton bus. Admission: $13 adults, $8 seniors, and $7 students with ID; half-price Thurs 6–9 p.m.; free for kids under 12; free to all first Tues of the month. Open: Thurs 11 a.m.–8:45 p.m., Fri–Tues 11 a.m.– 5:45 p.m., from 10 a.m. in summer.*

Golden Gate Park and its attractions

The 1,017 rectangular acres of greenery and cultural attractions that comprise **Golden Gate Park** contain something for everyone. Locals use the park for everything from soccer practice to wedding receptions to flycasting lessons. On Sundays, when John F. Kennedy Drive is closed to street traffic, bicyclists ride with impunity and in-line skaters converge for dance parties.

 A grand park entrance on Stanyan and Waller streets will lead you to the massive **Children's Playground** and its beautifully restored carousel. The imaginative structures and swings will occupy kids for as long as you allow. Remodeling this entrance cut down on the rather large numbers of street people who used to hang out there, but you never know whether that will change. In any case, don't let it keep you from enjoying the park; the street folks can look a little scary to the uninitiated, but they're generally harmless.

Another entrance at Ninth Avenue on Lincoln Way brings you to the **Strybing Arboretum** and the **Japanese Tea Garden**. The **California Academy of Sciences** is closed for renovations until 2008. However, the **de Young Museum** has been completely rebuilt and boasts even more space for its collections of American art. The **Conservatory of Flowers,** a Victorian glass greenhouse located northeast of the Academy of Sciences off John F. Kennedy Drive, reopened in spring of 2003. Modeled after the conservatory in London's Kew Gardens, it was nearly destroyed in 1995 after a horrific storm all but tore it apart; since then, $25 million has been raised to repair and reinvent this San Francisco landmark.

Joggers and parents pushing baby strollers make regular use of the path around manmade **Stow Lake.** The boathouse (☎ 415-752-0347) rents paddle boats, bikes and in-line skates by the hour, half-day, and full day. If you aren't driving, walking to the boathouse is a bit of a hike. The boathouse is west of the Japanese Tea Garden on Martin Luther King Drive; it's open daily from 9 a.m. to 4 p.m.

The N-Judah Muni Metro streetcar drops you off on Ninth Avenue and Judah Street; walk 3 blocks to the park from there. Numerous bus lines drive close to or into the park, including the 44-O'Shaughnessy, which you can catch on Ninth Avenue; the 21-Hayes; and the 5-Fulton.

Golden Gate Park houses the following museums and attractions.

The Conservatory of Flowers

A fixture in guidebooks and tourist brochures, and nearly as recognizable as the Golden Gate Bridge, the postcard-perfect Victorian Conservatory of Flowers closed in 1995 after sustaining massive damage during a wild storm. Prefabricated in Ireland in 1875 and erected in the park around 1878, reconstruction was finished in 2003, and the conservatory is back to its exquisite self, with lines of delighted visitors snaking past the entrance. Rare orchids, ferns, tropical plants, and a 100-year-old philodendron rescued from the wreckage are among the exhibits.

See map p. 122. Off John F. Kennedy Drive (near the Stanyan Street entrance). ☎ *415-666-7001.* www.conservatoryofflowers.org. *Admission: $5 adults, $3 seniors and youth 12–17, $1.50 kids 5–11, under 5 free. Open: Tues–Sun 9 a.m.–4:30 p.m.*

The de Young Museum

An eclectic permanent collection includes American paintings as well as sculpture, textiles, African and Oceanic objects, furniture, and contemporary crafts housed in a sprawling, copper-clad three-story complex that opened in October 2005. If you want to make some sense of the collection, consider taking one of the free docent tours offered daily at 10 a.m., 11 a.m., 1 p.m., and 2 p.m. A highlight of the building is the 144-foot tower offering unobstructed views (if the sky is clear) of the neighborhoods beyond the park. Access to the tower is free, even if you don't intend on touring the museum.

See map p. 122. 50 Hagiwara Tea Garden Dr. (off John F. Kennedy Drive). ☎ *415-863-3330.* www.deyoungmuseum.org. *Admission: $10 adults, $7 seniors, $6 students and kids 13–17, free for children under 13; $2 discount with Muni transfer. Open: Tues–Sun 9:30 a.m.–5 p.m., until 8:45 p.m. Fri.*

Japanese Tea Garden

This tranquil spot includes colorful pagodas, koi ponds, bridges, and a giant bronze Buddha. Young children find this piece of the park particularly memorable because they can climb over a steeply arched wooden bridge. Passengers spill through the entry gate of this major tour-bus destination with alarming regularity. To avoid the onslaught, arrive before 10 a.m. or after 4 p.m. in summer. Japanese tea, accompanied by a few paltry snacks, is served in the teahouse for $2.95 per person. Although the garden is certainly worth the small admission fee, the food is not.

See map p. 122. 75 Tea Garden Dr. (to the left of the de Young Museum). ☎ *415-752-4227. Admission: $3.50 adults, $1.25 seniors and children 6–12. Open: Oct–Feb 8:30 a.m.–dusk; Mar–Sept 8:30 a.m.–6:30 p.m.*

Strybing Arboretum and Botanical Gardens

This splendid oasis contains more than 6,000 species of well-tended plants. It's exceptionally lovely in late winter, when the rhododendrons blossom and wild irises poke up in corners, and no more peaceful a place exists when the skies are drizzling. We recommend the guided tours — offered daily at 1:30 p.m. — for anyone who finds identifying any but the most basic of flowers and trees difficult. Plan to spend at minimum a half-hour just wandering around.

See map p. 122. Ninth Avenue at Lincoln Way (turn left out of the tour-bus parking lot by the Music Concourse). ☎ *415-661-1316, ext. 314 for guided-tour information.* www.strybing.org. *Admission: Free. Open: Mon–Fri 8 a.m.–4:30 p.m., Sat–Sun 10 a.m.–5 p m.; free guided walks daily at 1:30 p.m.*

Yerba Buena Gardens and Center for the Arts

Where once sat nothing but parking lots and derelicts, this 22-acre complex now stands as a micro-destination. Interactive amusements include an ice-skating rink, a bowling alley, a children's garden and carousel, and an arts/technology studio for older kids (**Zeum**). An entertainment behemoth in a separate building across the street — the **Metreon** — houses restaurants, retail shops, an IMAX theater, and multiplex movie screens.

The center includes a collection of galleries showing a rotating exhibition of contemporary visual and performance art by local artists, lovely gardens, a stage for dance troupes including ODC/San Francisco and Smuin Ballets/SF, and a film/video theater. If you take in all that Yerba Buena Center has to offer, you can easily spend the entire day here. Parking's expensive; use public transportation, f possible.

See map p. 122. 701 Mission St. (between Third and Fourth streets). ☎ *415-978-2700, or 415-978-ARTS for the box office.* www.yerbabuenaarts.org. *To get there: Muni Metro to Powell Street or Montgomery Street and walk 2 blocks east on Third Street; or 14-Mission or 15-Third bus. Admission to the galleries: $6 adults and $3 seniors and students. Open: Tues–Sun 11 a.m.–6 p.m.*

Zeum

This modern art/technology center is probably the only attraction specifically designed for older kids and teens that doesn't rely on video games. The hands-on labs give visitors the opportunity to create animated video shorts with clay figures; learn about graphics, sound, and video in the production studio; and interact with the changing gallery exhibits. Even bored adolescents have difficulty resisting the Zeum offerings.

See map p. 122. Corner of Fourth and Howard. ☎ *415-820-3320.* www.zeum.org. *Admission: $8 adults, $7 seniors and students, $6 kids 5–18. Open: Wed–Sun 11 a.m.–5 p.m. Sept–June; Tues–Sun 11 a.m.–5 p.m. during the summer.*

Pursuing the arts and other cool stuff to see and do

The **California Palace of the Legion of Honor,** in Lincoln Park between Clement Street and 34th Avenue in the outer Richmond

District (☎ 415-863-3330; www.legionofhonor.org), exhibits an impressive collection of paintings, drawings, sculpture, and decorative arts. The grounds around the palace are a draw as well, and there is a very nice cafe. The museum is open Tuesday through Sunday from 9:30 a.m. to 5 p.m., and admission is $10 adults, $7 seniors, $6 kids 13 to 17, free for kids younger than 13 (free for everyone on the second Wed of the month). Take the 38-Geary bus to 33rd and Geary, then transfer to the 18-46th Avenue bus for a ride to the museum entrance.

The **Cartoon Art Museum,** 655 Mission St., near Third Street in SoMa (☎ 415-227-8666; www.cartoonart.org), produces exhibits on all forms of cartoon art and often showcases local cartoonists. It's open Tuesday through Sunday from 11 a.m. to 5 p.m.; admission is $6 adults, $4 seniors, $2 children 6 to 12.

At Fisherman's Wharf, the **Musée Mécanique** (☎ 415-346-2000; www.museemecanique.org) contains a fantastic collection of lovingly restored and maintained mechanical marvels that were the forerunners to pinball machines. Among the treasures, you can try your hand at World Series Baseball, have your fortune told, and giggle wildly with Laughing Sal, all for a quarter a pop. The museum is housed close to Pier 39 (actually at Pier 45 at the end of Taylor Street), having moved from smaller, more charming quarters near the Cliff House. Open Monday through Friday from 11 a.m. to 7 p.m. and Saturday and Sunday from 10 a.m. to 8 p.m., admission is free — but bring along a roll of quarters.

Taking a hike

Fort Point (☎ 415-556-1693), underneath the Golden Gate Bridge at the tip of the peninsula, dates from 1857. It is an easy 3½-mile stroll to Fort Point from the Hyde Street Pier along the paved **Golden Gate Promenade,** which hugs the coast as it passes through the Marina Green and the newly relandscaped Crissy Fields through the Presidio. Alternatively, you can reach Fort Point by taking the 28-19th Avenue or the 29-Sunset bus to the Golden Gate Bridge and climb down from the viewing area to a short trail leading to the fort. Open Friday through Sunday from 10 a.m. to 5 p.m.

Named in honor of Sierra Club founder and conservationist John Muir, 553-acre **Muir Woods** (☎ 415-388-2595; www.nps.gov/muwo) is what's left locally of the redwood forests that once dominated the coast of Northern California. Although not as sizable as Redwood National Forest farther north, these old-growth redwoods are beautiful, and a range of trails here suits hikers of all levels. From the Golden Gate Bridge, take the Stinson Beach/Highway 1 exit west and follow the signs. Parking is limited, so try setting out early in the day on weekends or go during the week. Muir Woods is open from 8 a.m. until sunset.

Riding a bike

If you plan to ride in Golden Gate Park, your best bet for a rental is one of the bike stores nearby, such as **Avenue Cyclery,** 756 Stanyan St.

(☎ 415-387-3155; www.avenuecyclery.com). Open daily from 10 a.m. to 6 p.m., you can rent mountain, city, or kid bikes for $5 per hour or $25 per day.

The **Bike Hut** at South Beach, on the Embarcadero at Pier 40 (☎ 415-543-4335), is the place to find high-quality bikes to pedal along the waterfront. It's open daily from 10 a.m. to 6 p.m. Rentals are $5 per hour or $20 per day.

And if you're considering a bike trip across the Golden Gate Bridge, the nice guys at **Blazing Saddles** at either the North Beach (1095 Columbus Ave.) or Fisherman's Wharf location (Pier 41; ☎ 415-202-8888; www.blazingsaddles.com) can provide you with all the information and encouragement you need to tackle this route. The equipment for kids and adults is shiny and well maintained. Rental prices are $7 per hour or $28 per day and include helmets, locks, front packs, rear racks, maps, and advice.

Walking the beach

Ocean Beach, at the end of Geary Bou evard on the Great Highway, attracts picnicking families and teenagers looking for a place to swill some beer. It's great for oceanside strolls if the tide is low, and the waves can be magnificent. Swimming is dangerous and prohibited, however. The 38-Geary bus gets you within walking distance of the beach, or you can take the N-Judah Muni Metro streetcar to the end of the line.

Soaking it up

For some pampering with a Japanese twist, take the 38-Geary bus to **Kabuki Springs & Spa,** 1750 Geary Blvd., at Webster Street in Japantown (☎ 415-922-6000; www.kabukisprings.com). This is a most respectable communal bathhouse, where you can soak your feet, have a massage, or take a steam bath. Women may use the bathhouse on Sundays, Wednesdays, and Fridays; men are accommodated on Mondays, Thursdays, and Saturdays; Tuesdays are coed. Massages and other spa services are by appointment daily from 10 a.m. to 9:45 p.m.

Sampling the local airwaves — live!

Kind of a poor man's version of *A Prairie Home Companion,* **West Coast Live** (☎ 415-664-9500; www.wcl.org) is a homegrown public radio show broadcast in the Bay Area on Saturdays from 10 a.m. to noon. Hosted by the honey-voiced Sedge Thomson, guests have included writers such as David Sedaris and Calvin Trillin, local musicians, and a tiny cast of regulars. The show is broadcast from a rotating group of venues in San Francisco and Berkeley; check the Web site for schedule and ticket information.

Seeing San Francisco by Guided Tour

An introductory tour is always a good bet if you have limited time to explore the city. A variety of bus tours pass by the highlights and can certainly provide an overview of the city, but there's nothing to compare to a few hours devoted to pounding the pavement. We also strongly recommend that you spend an hour or two out on the bay — it's brisk, beautiful, and will put a nice glow on your cheeks.

Puttin' on that old soft shoe (s)

Friends of the Library sponsors **City Guides** walking tours (☎ 415-557-4266; www.sfcityguides.org). These tours trod 26 different paths each week, all for free — that's right, no charge! All you have to do is decide which tour appeals to you and show up at the proper corner on time. You can explore the haunts of the original 49ers on the "Gold Rush City" tour, admire the Painted Ladies (San Francisco's collection of beautifully resorted Victorian homes) on the "Landmark Victorians of Alamo Square" tour, or get an insider's view of Chinatown. We highly recommend any of these tours.

Local cookbook writer and luminary Shirley Fong-Torres operates Chinatown food tours that will have you classifying noodles like an expert. **Wok Wiz Chinatown Walking Tours and Cooking Center,** 654 Commercial St., between Kearny and Montgomery streets (☎ 650-355-9657; www.wokwiz.com), offers daily tours for $40 for adults and $35 for kids younger than 11. Tours include a seven-course dim sum lunch.

The popular North Beach neighborhood reaches new heights of giddiness on Saturdays when food writer GraceAnn Walden leads **Mangia! North Beach** (☎ 415-397-8530; www.graceannwalden.net), a four-and-a-half-hour, $80 walking, eating, shopping, and history tour. GraceAnn and her followers traipse in and out of a deli, chocolate shop, bakery, bookshop, pottery store, and two very fine churches before ending with a multicourse, family-style lunch at one of her favorite restaurants. This tour offers lots of samples, lots of tidbits about the Italians, and lots of fun. Reservations are a must.

The **Victorian Home Walk** (☎ 415-252-9485; www.victorianwalk.com) combines a trolley-car excursion with a walking tour through a number of celebrated neighborhoods. During the two-and-a-half-hour tour, you see an array of houses in areas where tour vans are prohibited. The cost is $20. Tours leave daily at 11 a.m. from the lobby of the Westin St. Francis, 335 Powell St., between Geary and Post streets in Union Square.

Bay cruises

The bright yellow amphibious vehicles you may see bouncing around bayside neighborhoods belong to **Bay Quackers San Francisco Duck Tours** (☎ 415-431-3825; www.bayquackers.com). Its 80-minute tours leave every two hours beginning at 9 a.m. from the Anchorage Mall at

Fisherman's Wharf and ends up in the bay motoring around McCovey Cove. If you time it right, you could enjoy an unusual view of a Giants' baseball game. Tickets are $35 adults, $32 seniors/students, $25 kids younger than 13. For $100 you can get a family ticket for two adults and two children.

 Our very own **Golden Gate Transit** (☎ 415-455-2000; www.goldengate. org) operates ferry cruises from the Ferry Building at the foot of Market Street to Sausalito or Larkspur in Marin. A round-trip cruise to the pretty, but admittedly touristy, town of Sausalito sets adults back $13; kids 6 to 18 are $6.40; kids younger than 6 are free. You have the thrill of riding the waves past the Golden Gate Bridge, albeit without the onboard commentary provided by the **Blue & Gold Fleet** (☎ 415-705-5555; www. blueandgoldfleet.com; $20 for adults, $16 for seniors and kids 12–18, $12 for kids 5–11) on their one-hour bay cruise.

Shopping 'til You Drop

Most people think of Union Square as the hub of San Francisco shopping, but downtown has plenty of competition. Nearly every neighborhood boasts a thriving "Main Street" of locally owned boutiques, cafes, and bookstores. You can find shops with unique arts and crafts, clothing stores that eschew chain-mentality fashion, even housewares havens that reflect the style of the local clientele. Depending on where you head, you can try on a different attitude as easily as a different outfit.

Union Square

With all big department stores within shouting distance of one another, Union Square gets a body in the mood for retail therapy faster than you can say, "Charge it!" Stand in the square and turn around slowly; you'll see **Saks Fifth Avenue** on the corner of Powell and Post streets (☎ 415-986-4300), **Neiman Marcus** at Stockton and Geary streets (☎ 415-362-3900), and **Macy's** (☎ 415-397-3333) everywhere else.

A half-block north of Neiman's on Stockton Street is **Maiden Lane,** which is lined with designer shops. **Gump's,** 135 Post St. (☎ 415-982-1616; www.gumps.com), sells decorative goods, collectibles, and home furnishings in a 1910 landmark building. Parallel to Stockton eastward is Grant Avenue, with shoe-leather-halting stores such as **Anne Fontaine,** 118 Grant Ave. (☎ 415-677-0911), and the flagship **Banana Republic,** 256 Grant Ave. (☎ 415-788-3087).

Market Street continues its upward trajectory with the opening of the humongous **Bloomingdale's,** centerpiece of the new **Westfield San Francisco Centre.** It's next to the older one where Nordstrom's is located on Fifth and Market streets. Along with all the usual suspects you find in an upscale mall, this one also has a day spa on the fifth floor, a gourmet grocer in the basement, movie theaters, and dining establishments with good pedigrees.

Chinatown

Grubby curio shops line Grant Avenue, selling all manner of cheap trin-kets and clothing. If you venture off Grant, you'll find herbal shops and jewelry stores filled with jade of varying quality. The merchants in the less touristy stores don't always speak English and may not seem friendly, but don't let that keep you from looking around.

Chong Imports, in the Empress of China building at 838 Grant Ave., between Clay and Washington streets (☎ 415-982-1432), stocks a little of everything. **Tai Yick Trading Company,** 1400 Powell St., at Broadway (☎ 415-986-0961), sells porcelain and pottery at reasonable prices; locals swear this is the best store of its kind in town, and the owners are helpful and friendly. The **Imperial Tea Court,** 1411 Powell St., near Broadway (☎ 415-788-6080), displays everything you'll need to brew a proper pot of Chinese tea — plus, it's a nice place to stop and sip a cup.

Haight Street

Clothing is the big draw for shoppers — whether vintage or cutting edge — and you'll locate apparel and shoes for all ages and stages. In particular, look for **Behind the Post Office,** 1510 Haight St. (☎ 415-861-2507), for accessories from local designers; **Kids Only,** 1608 Haight St. (☎ 415-552-5445), for your flower child; **Ambiance,** 1458 Haight St. (☎ 415-552-5095), for pretty dresses, stylish shoes, and somewhat retro handbags; and **Villians Vault,** 1653 and 1672 Haight St. (☎ 415-864-7727 or 415-626-5939), for streetwear and shoes.

Hayes Street

Naming the hippest shopping street in the city would be difficult, but if forced, we'd have to say Hayes Street. Start at Grove and Gough where you'll find the expanded **MAC** (Modern Appealing Clothing) store at 387 Grove St. (☎ 415-837-0615). From there, head 1 block south to Hayes Street and start walking toward the Pacific. You can find a wealth of stuff here, for all facets of your life, unless you live like a spartan or a monk; if that's the case, you may want to stop at the **Gaia Tree,** 575 Hayes St. (☎ 415-255-4848), for a yoga mat or maybe a facial or massage. If your feet hurt, look for a more comfortable pair of shoes at one of the many shoe stores here, including **Paolo Iantorno,** 524 Hayes St. (☎ 415-552-4580), selling beautiful Italian-made creations for men and women to decorate whatever's below your ankles. Many of the stores on these blocks are open Sunday afternoons.

North Beach

Completely different from the street of the same name in Chinatown or Union Square, Grant Avenue from Green to Greenwich streets has a bohemian feel, with many stylish boutiques for clothes and accessories. **Biordi Art Imports,** 412 Columbus Ave., at Vallejo Street (☎ 415-392-8096), stocks the most beautiful hand-painted Majolica dishes and serv-ing pieces — as close as you can get to eating off a work of art. **City**

Going to market

Farmer's market aficionados will find Saturdays at the **Ferry Building** at the foot of Market Street more than satisfying. The majority of producers bring organically grown foodstuffs, and you'll discover unusual varieties of fruits and vegetables. The perfume of the salt air, ripe fruit, and a whiff of lavender wafting past your nostrils is deeply pleasurable; combined with the bay views, a busker playing standards on his saxophone, and a plethora of tastes, the scene is magical. Inside the building, permanent shops, most of which are open seven days a week, stock everything you need for a feast plus all kinds of tempting items including books, chocolates, olive oil, kitchen necessities, wine, and imported packaged foods. If you actually find yourself hungry, this is where the **Slanted Door** (reviewed in the "Where to Dine" section earlier in this chapter) has moved, or you can sit down at the **MarketBar** on the east end, stop at **Taylor's Refreshers** for fast food we approve of, or attempt to get a counter seat at the **Hog Island Oyster Bar.**

Lights Bookstore, the famous Beat-generation bookstore founded by renowned poet and Ginsberg crony Lawrence Ferlinghetti, sits on Columbus Avenue at Broadway (☎ 415-362-8193), and is still a bastion of left-of-center literature.

Union Street

Union Street between Fillmore Street and Van Ness Avenue in the Marina District is the happy valley for folks who love wandering in and out of specialty shops. Muni buses 22-Fillmore, 41-Union, 42-Downtown Loop, and 45-Union/Stockton will get you here.

Carol Doda, who shaped a career out of her chest long before implants were considered accessories, runs a lingerie shop, **Carol Doda's Champagne and Lace,** 1850 Union St. (☎ 415-776-6900). Outside your sweater, cover yourself with beautiful adornments crafted by local artists at **Gallery of Jewels,** 2101 Union St. (☎ 415-929-0259). Because man does not live by cashmere alone, you may be interested in perusing the **Collectors Cave,** 2072 Union St. (☎ 415-929-0231), which displays all kinds of new and old comic books, action figures, and sports cards for serious and not-so-serious collectors. **Mudpie,** 1694 Union St. (☎ 415-771-9262), sells incredibly expensive children's clothes and gifts. Sticker shock is slightly alleviated in the downstairs salesroom.

Enjoying the Nightlife

Still have energy after all that sightseeing? Great; there's lots to do. For up-to-the-minute nightlife listings, pick up a free copy of the *San Francisco Bay Guardian* from sidewalk kiosks or in cafes (or check online at www.sfbg.com).

Beach Blanket Babylon, baby

A veritable institution, *Beach Blanket Babylon* is the only-in-San-Francisco musical revue famous for outrageous costumes and wildly inventive hats that appear to lead lives of their own. The spectacle is so popular that even after celebrating over 30 years of poking fun at stars, politicians, and San Francisco itself, seats for the constantly updated shows are always sold out. Purchase tickets ($25–$80) through the TIX in Union Square (☎ 415-433-7827; www.theatrebayarea.org), online (www.beachblanket babylon.com), by mail, or by fax at least three weeks in advance, especially if you want to attend a weekend performance. If you're under 21, you're relegated to Sunday matinees, when liquor isn't sold.

At Club Fugazi, 678 Green St. (between Powell Street and Columbus Avenue), North Beach. ☎ *415-421-4222. Fax: 415-421-4187.* www.beachblanketbabylon.com. *To get there: 15-Third, 30-Stockton, or 45 to Columbus and Union streets; Green Street is 1 block south of Union.*

Play it loud: Live music

The city has no lack of clubs serving up bone-shaking live music, from jazz to blues to indie rock. This section gives you some recommended venues.

Biscuits and Blues

This all-ages jazz-and-blues venue is in a basement room near the theater district. The Southern-style food is inexpensive, and the musicians range from local faves to legends. Cover ranges from $5 to $15.

410 Mason St. (at Geary Street), Union Square. ☎ *415-292-2583. To get there: 38-Geary bus to Mason Street.*

Boom Boom Room

The Boom Boom Room is open every night for dancing to live music, cocktails, and jiving. Lines often form on the weekends, so arrive on the early side and sip your drink slowly. Cover charge ranges from free to $12.

1601 Fillmore St. (at Geary Street), Japantown. ☎ *415-673-8000.* www.boomboom blues.com. *To get there: 38-Geary bus to Fillmore Street.*

The Empire Plush Room

This intimate showroom books local and national cabaret acts for runs lasting from a weekend to a few weeks. Expect torch and standards singers, musical revues, duos of some repute, even the occasional comedian. You can purchase tickets ranging from $20 to $55 through the Web site.

In the York Hotel, 940 Sutter St. (between Hyde and Leavenworth streets, 4 blocks west of Union Square). ☎ *866-468-3399.* www.yorkhotel.com/plushroom.htm.

The Great American Music Hall

This venue presents big-name acts in an ornate and comfortable setting. Call for an events calendar. This is another all-ages venue. Ticket prices range from $15 to $25.

859 O'Farrell St. (near Polk Street), the Tenderloin. ☎ *415-885-0750.* www.music hallsf.com. *To get there: Take a cab to avoid the excitement of the Tenderloin by night.*

Jazz at Pearl's

Pearl's showcases the 17-piece big band Contemporary Jazz Orchestra every Monday and local jazz musicians Tuesday through Saturday. Dinner (Spanish-inspired dishes including tapas) and show packages are $35 to $50. Show tickets are $5 to $10.

256 Columbus Ave. (at Broadway), North Beach. ☎ *415-291-8255.* www.jazzat pearls.com. *To get there: 15-Third, 30-Stockton, or 45 bus to Columbus and Union streets; walk south on Columbus 3 blocks to Broadway.*

Come here often? Bars and lounges

You may be so intoxicated by the city's natural beauty that cocktails seem redundant. Nevertheless, here are some of our favorite tippling spots in San Francisco.

Amber

If you smoke and drink, or don't mind people who do both at the same time, this is your bar. It's one of the few in town where inside smoking is allowed. A local's hangout, the booze and the lighting are both excellent.

718 14th St. (between Church and Sanchez streets). ☎ *415-626-7827. To get there: Muni to Church and Market streets.*

Edinburgh Castle Pub

Chief among our expat watering holes is this popular pub, which hosts live music, readings, and even a Tuesday Quiz Night.

950 Geary St. (near Polk Street). ☎ *415-885-4074.*

Martuni's

Fancy yourself an undiscovered singing sensation? Make your way to the back room, where customers croon and the piano player is kind.

4 Valencia St. (at Market Street). The F-Market streetcar passes by. ☎ *415-241-0205.*

Top of the Mark

The Top of the Mark has it all — views, music from 9 p.m., dancing, and a convivial crowd of suits. The hotel serves a "Sunset" three-course prix-fixe dinner on Friday and Saturday nights; with 7:30 p.m. reservations, a night on the town is a done deal.

In the Mark Hopkins Intercontinental Hotel, 1 Nob Hill (at Mason and California streets). ☎ *415-616-6916. To get there: For fun, take the California Street cable car and exit at the top of Nob Hill.*

The Independent

True music fans will tell you that this club has the best sound system in town and books the hottest indie and pop bands. It's a regular venue for Noise Pop (www.noisepop.com), the indie music festival scheduled around the last week in March.

628 Divisadero St. (between Grove and Hayes streets). ☎ *415-771-1421.* www.the independentsf.com. *To get there: Easiest by taxi.*

Experiencing the finer side of the arts

San Francisco has a thriving cultural scene, offering opera, dance, music, and edgy theater. For tickets to any performance, call the appropriate box office directly or head online and order with a credit card.

Around Civic Center, **City Box Office,** 180 Redwood St., Suite 100 (☎ 415-392-4400; www.cityboxoffice.com), sells tickets to shows playing at the Nob Hill Masonic Center, Project Artaud Theater, Herbst Theatre, and other lesser-known stages. Hours are Monday through Friday 9:30 a.m. to 5 p.m. and Saturday 10 a.m. to 4 p.m.

If you arrive in town without plans, visit **TIX Bay Area** (☎ 415-433-7827; www.theatrebayarea.org/tix) for half-price tickets for same-day performances (a $1–$3 service charge is tacked on). TIX, which is also a **BASS Ticketmaster** outlet, is located on Union Square between Post and Geary streets; open Tuesday through Thursday 11 a.m. to 6 p.m., Friday 11 a.m. to 7 p.m., Saturday 10 a.m. to 7 p.m., and Sunday 10 a.m. to 3 p.m.

Theater

Union Square houses at least ten professional theaters of varying sizes, and experimental theaters are scattered about the SoMa and Mission districts in converted warehouses and gallery spaces. The preeminent company in town is the **American Conservatory Theater (ACT),** which produces a little of everything during its October to June season. The sets and costumes are universally brilliant, and the acting is first-rate. Productions take place in the lovely Geary Theater, 415 Geary St., at Mason Street (☎ 415-749-2228; www.act-sfbay.org).

Opera

The **San Francisco Opera** season opens with a gala in September and ends quietly in early January. Performances are produced in the War Memorial Opera House, 301 Van Ness Ave., at Grove Street (☎ 415-864-3330; www.sfopera.com), in the Civic Center.

Classical music

The **San Francisco Symphony** performs in the Louise M. Davies Symphony Hall, 201 Van Ness Ave., at Grove Street (☎ **415-864-6000;** www.sfsymphony.org), in the Civic Center. For more symphonic options in the Bay Area, check into **San Francisco Performances** (☎ **415-398-6449;** www.performances.org).

Dance

Classical and modern dance groups abound, the most recognized being the **San Francisco Ballet,** whose season runs from February to June. The troupe performs in the **War Memorial Opera House,** 301 Van Ness Ave., at Grove Street (☎ **415-865-2000;** www.sfballet.org). Some of the most interesting dance companies, including **Smuin Ballets/SF,** appear on stage at the **Yerba Buena Center for the Arts,** 700 Howard St. (☎ **415-978-2787;** www.ybca.org).

Fast Facts

AAA

The office at 150 Van Ness Ave. in Civic Center provides maps and other information to members. Call ☎ 800-222-4357 for emergency service or ☎ 415-565-2012 for information.

Baby Sitters

Your hotel concierge can probably arrange for a baby sitter. Otherwise, try American Child Care Service (☎ 415-285-2300; www.americanchildcare.com), with rates starting at $19 per hour.

Emergencies

For police, fire, or other emergencies, phone ☎ 911. From cellphones, call ☎ 415-553-8090.

Hospitals

Saint Francis Memorial Hospital, 900 Hyde St., between Bush and Pine streets (☎ 415-353-6000), offers 24-hour emergency-care service. The hospital's physician-referral service number is ☎ 415-353-6566. San Francisco General Hospital, 1001 Potrero Ave. (☎ 415-206-8111), accepts uninsured

emergency patients, but the wait can be brutally long and uncomfortable. The patient-assistance number is ☎ 415-206-5166.

Newspapers and Magazines

The *San Francisco Chronicle* is the major daily newspaper; its Sunday Datebook section lists goings-on about town. The weekly *Bay Guardian,* free at sidewalk kiosks and in bookstores, bars, and coffeehouses, is an excellent source for entertainment listings.

Police

Dial ☎ 911 in an emergency. For nonemergencies, call ☎ 415-553-0123.

Post Office

The Rincon Center houses a post office at 180 Steuart St., in the Embarcadero. Call ☎ 800-ASK-USPS or log on to www.usps.gov to find the branch nearest you.

Taxes

Sales tax is 8.5 percent. Hotel and parking-garage taxes are 14 percent.

Taxis

Desoto Cab (☎ 415-970-1300); Luxor Cabs (☎ 415-282-4141); Veteran's Cab (☎ 415-648-1313); Yellow Cab (☎ 415-626-2345).

Transit Info

☎ 415-817-1717.

Gathering More Information

The **San Francisco Convention and Visitors Bureau Information Center** is on the lower level of Hallidie Plaza, 900 Market St., at Powell Street (☎ **800-220-5747** or 415-391-2000). It's open Monday through Friday from 9 a.m. to 5:30 p.m., Saturday from 9 a.m. to 3 p.m., and Sunday from 10 a.m. to 2 p.m.

You can find the **city's official Web site** at www.onlyinsanfrancisco. com. For up-to-date information on the city and surrounding areas, try **Citysearch** (www.sanfrancisco.citysearch.com), the *San Francisco Chronicle* Web site (www.sfgate.com), or the *San Francisco Bay Guardian* Web site (www.sfbg.com).

Chapter 12

Napa and Sonoma Valleys: California's Premier Wine Country

*J*ust an hour's drive north of San Francisco is the gorgeous **Napa Valley,** the most celebrated wine-growing region in the United States. Less than 30 miles from end to end, this extraordinarily fertile area brims with world-class wine-tasting rooms, excellent restaurants, and marvelous resorts and country inns.

Visiting Napa Valley is akin to taking a trip to the south of France, without the jet lag or the language barrier (or the lousy exchange rate). The stresses and strains of regular life just fade away as you cruise gentle Highway 29, the verdant valley's main thoroughfare, stopping in at wineries, pausing between tastings for a gourmet picnic and a bit of boutique shopping.

Just to the west of Napa Valley along Highway 12 is the peaceful **Sonoma Valley.** Sonoma Valley is quieter and less tourist-oriented — but equal to its neighbor as a wine-growing region. First-time visitors may suspect that there's more to see and do in Napa, and they'll be correct. But travelers looking for a place in which to do nothing but eat, drink, and thank their favorite deity that such a paradise exists will be happy as can be in and around Sonoma.

You certainly don't need to be a wine connoisseur to enjoy this section of the state, but we guarantee that if you tour one or two of the wineries we've mentioned, you'll arrive home knowing a lot more about viticulture than your average wine drinker. And if it happens that you don't know much about wine (except you know what you like), don't feel intimidated. Sure, some pretentious wine-tasting rooms do dwell among the grape arbors, but the valleys are completely visitor-friendly and downright welcoming to casual wine drinkers.

Another point worth mentioning: Neither Napa nor Sonoma valley will be the bargain destination of your vacation. If you choose carefully, however, you'll discover affordable places to stay, eat, and drink.

Timing Your Visit

Summer and autumn are the most popular seasons for touring the Wine Country. The valleys are especially gorgeous in fall, and September and October bustle during the grape harvest, or *crush,* which fills the air with the sweet fragrance of *must* (the pulp and skins of crushed grapes). If you plan to visit during these seasons, make reservations early.

As long as the weather is dry, the area is a treat during the winter and spring, when the roads, restaurants, and tasting rooms are relatively unclogged, and the hotels actually offer lower rates. With the vines stripped of their heavy fruit, the valleys are not quite so beautiful, however, and touring can be a downright drag in the rain.

 Weekends are always more crowded than weekdays, and the traffic heading north on the Golden Gate Bridge from San Francisco on Friday afternoons (and south on Sun afternoons) can be torture. Do what you can to plan your visit midweek, while the weekenders are at work; not only will you avoid the crowds and enjoy your stay more, but you're bound to save a few bucks on accommodations.

Although you can easily entertain yourself for a week here, three days and two nights can provide an ideal introduction to the Wine Country. That gives you plenty of time to start with a winery tour (you need to take in only one to get a flavor of the wine-making process), spread out your winery visits over the next couple of days, and work in some other local pleasures — a hot-air balloon ride, perhaps, or some leisurely bicycling or a spa treatment or two.

A single day simply can't do the area justice and will leave you wanting more. But if you can only spare a day out of your San Francisco time, choose Napa Valley over Sonoma Valley. Start out from San Francisco early, because virtually all the wine-tasting rooms shut their doors by 5 p.m. Drive immediately to Calistoga, at the north end, and work your way down the valley along Highway 29 to make your return to San Francisco a bit shorter. Plan to visit no more than three to four wineries (all anyone can really handle in a day, anyway), followed by an early dinner before you head back to the city.

 Don't make this day trip on a summer weekend, because the bumper-to-bumper traffic on Highway 29 will ruin it.

Getting There

You'll have to drive if you want the best experience. If you're a day-tripper, you can take a guided tour from San Francisco, if need be.

Driving yourself

From San Francisco, two roads take you to the Wine Country:

- ✔ If you decide to take the **San Francisco–Oakland Bay Bridge,** head east from downtown over the bridge (I-80) and north to the Napa/Highway 29 exit near Vallejo; follow Highway 29 north into the heart of the valley. The trip takes about 70 minutes.

- ✔ From the **Golden Gate Bridge,** continue on U.S. 101 north to Novato, where you pick up Highway 37 east. Take Highway 121 (the Sonoma Highway) north toward Sonoma and continue north on Highway 12, or stay on 121 east to Napa, if that's your destination, where you end up on Highway 29. Make sure to have a map handy. This drive is more scenic and takes about 90 minutes.

If you're coming from the **North Coast,** take Highway 128 out of Mendocino and follow the road straight into the north end of the valley, which will take a little more than two hours.

From **Lake Tahoe,** pick up I-80 west and take it to Highway 12 for Sonoma. This also will lead you in about 6 miles to Highway 29 north, Napa's main drag. Expect the drive to take about three and a half hours, whether you're coming from the north or south shore.

Along for the ride: Guided tours

If you don't want to drive yourself to or around the Wine Country, you can join an organized tour. Taking a tour is a good alternative if you need a designated driver; otherwise, we strongly suggest the do-it-yourself option. On a tour, you cover a lot of ground in way too short a time, you don't have the freedom to linger in places that catch your fancy, you don't have much of a choice as to where you eat, and you miss some great wineries that aren't part of the package.

That being said, the best tour operator is **Great Pacific Tour Company** (☎ 415-626-4499; www.greatpacifictour.com), which picks you up and delivers you back to your San Francisco hotel after tastings at two Sonoma wineries, a restaurant or picnic lunch, and a tour of **Domaine Chandon,** a sparkling-wine producer in Napa. The cost is $83 for adults, $81 for seniors, and $71 for kids 5 to 11.

Another option is to ride the **Napa Valley Wine Train** (☎ 800-427-4124 or 707-253-2111; www.winetrain.com), basically a gourmet restaurant on wheels that chugs 36 miles through the valley from end to end. Lunch, brunch, and dinner tours range in price from $89 to $140 per person. These are dining and take-in-the-scenery rides only; if you'd rather make a stop, ask about the **Grgich Hills Private Winery Tour and Tasting,** a lunchtime ride ($110 per person), or the **Domaine Chandon Winery** lunch excursion ($115 per person). The train sports a wine-tasting car with an attractive bar and knowledgeable host. The three-hour tours depart from 1275 McKinstry St. in downtown Napa, at the south end of the valley. Reservations are essential.

If you don't want to drive to Napa to pick up the train, **Grayline** (☎ 888-428-6937; www.graylinesanfrancisco.com) arranges passage via bus from San Francisco.

 If you're staying in Napa and just want some local guidance and a designated driver, **Napa Winery Shuttle** (☎ 707-257-1950; www.wineshuttle.com), a small family-run enterprise, gets our vote for value and flexibility. You and your shuttle driver plan the itinerary, although the company does have some favorite wineries it likes to show off. The price is $52 per person for the day, which lasts from approximately 10:15 a.m. to 4 or 5 p.m.

Orienting Yourself

Napa Valley is compact and easy to explore. The town of **Napa** at the south end is just 26 miles from **Calistoga** at the north end. Take a look at the "Napa Valley" map on p. 145, and you find that the valley resembles a ladder, with two main roads running (roughly) north-south — Highway 29, the main drag, along the west side and the Silverado Trail along the east side — with east-west cross streets at regular intervals, every half-mile or so. The valley is more commercial and developed at the south end, growing increasingly bucolic and spread out as you move north.

The town of Napa is the commercial center of the Wine Country and the gateway to Napa Valley. This is where the real people live — hence the fast-food joints and strip malls. Stop by the visitor center (see the "Gathering More Information" section at the end of this chapter) to pick up a winery map, but don't be in a big hurry to leave — there's lots going on in town, including **Copia,** the new temple to food, wine, and the arts.

Just north of Napa is **Yountville.** Both St. Helena and Calistoga boast more old-fashioned charm, but Yountville wins in the convenience department. Exciting restaurants abound, and you can't be more centrally located.

Immediately north of Yountville is **Oakville,** then **Rutherford,** two blink-and-you'll-miss-them towns that really just qualify as map markers. Next is **St. Helena,** about 18 miles north of Napa, an attractive little town with upscale shops tucked away in beautifully restored wooden storefronts.

Around St. Helena, the terrain starts to open up and look like the agricultural landscape it is. In another 8 miles, you reach Calistoga, California's version of Saratoga Springs, the east coast's favorite spa town (the name

Napa Valley

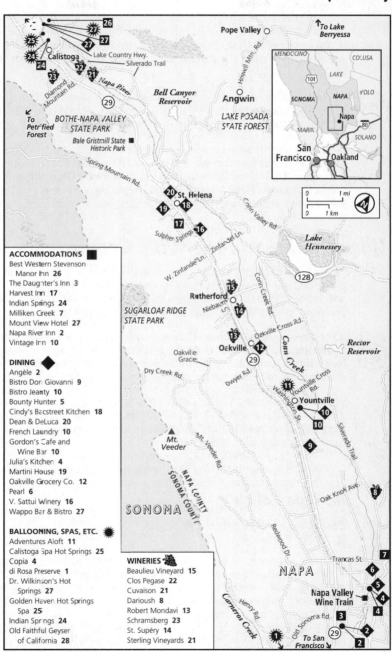

ACCOMMODATIONS ■
Best Western Stevenson
 Manor Inn **26**
The Daughter's Inn **3**
Harvest Inn **17**
Indian Springs **24**
Milliken Creek **7**
Mount View Hotel **27**
Napa River Inn **2**
Vintage Inn **10**

DINING ◆
Angèle **2**
Bistro Don Giovanni **9**
Bistro Jeanty **10**
Bounty Hunter **5**
Cindy's Backstreet Kitchen **18**
Dean & DeLuca **20**
French Laundry **10**
Gordon's Cafe and
 Wine Bar **10**
Julia's Kitchen **4**
Martini House **19**
Oakville Grocery Co. **12**
Pearl **6**
V. Sattui Winery **16**
Wappo Bar & Bistro **27**

BALLOONING, SPAS, ETC. ☀
Adventures Aloft **11**
Calistoga Spa Hot Springs **25**
Copia **4**
di Rosa Preserve **1**
Dr. Wilkinson's Hot
 Springs **27**
Golden Haven Hot Springs
 Spa **25**
Indian Springs **24**
Old Faithful Geyser
 of California **28**

WINERIES 🍇
Beaulieu Vineyard **15**
Clos Pegase **22**
Cuvaison **21**
Darioush **8**
Robert Mondavi **13**
Schramsberg **23**
St. Supéry **14**
Sterling Vineyards **21**

Calistoga is a cross of the two: *Cali*fornia and *Sara*toga). This well-preserved, extremely charming gold-rush town boasts the natural hot springs that make the Wine Country a first-class spa destination, too. It's our favorite place to stay, although you spend a bit more time in the car if you base yourself here. Because the driving is so gorgeous, it's easily worthwhile — but be aware of the distance, especially if your time is limited.

Be very careful while driving always-busy Highway 29. Even if you're a teetotaler, remember that virtually everybody else has imbibed a bit. This two-lane road is the scene of many accidents, especially at night.

Sonoma Valley is smaller and even more rural than Napa Valley, which guarantees that you can see it all in two days (see the "Sonoma Valley" map on p. 147). It includes the towns of **Sonoma, Glen Ellen, Kenwood, Santa Rosa,** and **Healdsburg;** two state parks; a few resorts, hotels, and B&Bs scattered among the country roads; and some fine restaurants.

Where to Stay in the Wine Country

Despite a wealth of choices, high demand keeps room rates on the pricey side. Almost all lodgings have a two-night minimum on weekends and three nights during holidays. Make reservations as far in advance as possible, especially for stays between May and October.

If the places we recommend are full, call **Napa Valley Reservations Unlimited** (☎ 800-251-NAPA; www.napavalleyreservations.com), a free central-reservations service. You can find other credible Napa Valley reservations bureaus online at www.napavalleyonline.com.

The **Sonoma Valley Visitors Bureau** is located in Sonoma on the Sonoma Plaza at 453 First St. E. (☎ 707-996-1090; www.sonomavalley.com). The bureau has an "availability sheet" of rooms in case you forgot to make reservations.

Count on 9 to 12 percent in taxes being tacked on to your hotel bill.

In Napa Valley

Best Western Stevenson Manor Inn
$$–$$$$ Calistoga

Situated just east of town, this pleasant motel offers great value in an expensive neighborhood. The basic, but spacious, rooms are all non-smoking, and boosted up a notch by fireplaces or whirlpool tubs, cable TV, fridges, coffeemakers, and hair dryers, as well as on-property extras including a pool, hot tub, and sauna and steam rooms. You can also get 10 percent off services at the nearby Calistoga Village Inn & Spa. Guest rooms with two queen beds won't crowd the family, and kids younger than 12 stay free.

Sonoma Valley

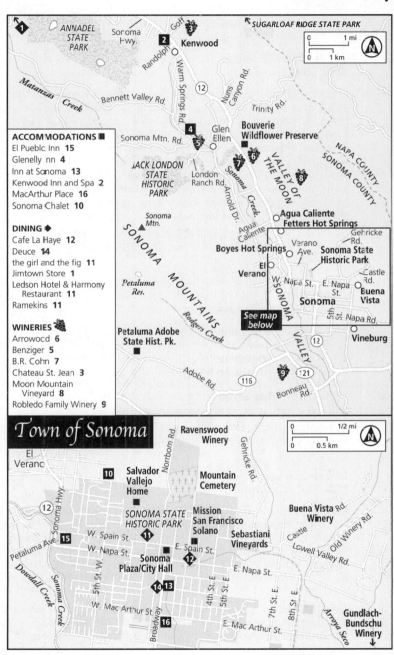

ANNADEL STATE PARK

Sonoma Hwy.

Goff

3

2 Kenwood

← SUGARLOAF RIDGE STATE PARK

0   1 mi
0   1 km

Matanzas Creek

Randolph

Warm Springs Rd.

Bennett Valley Rd.

12

Nuns Canyon Rd.

Trinity Rd.

ACCOMMODATIONS ■
El Pueblo Inn **15**
Glenelly nn **4**
Inn at Sonoma **13**
Kenwood Inn and Spa **2**
MacArthur Place **16**
Sonoma Chalet **10**

DINING ◆
Cafe La Haye **12**
Deuce **14**
the girl and the fig **11**
Jimtown Store **1**
Ledson Hotel & Harmony Restaurant **11**
Ramekins **11**

WINERIES 🍇
Arrowood **6**
Benziger **5**
B.R. Cohn **7**
Chateau St. Jean **3**
Moon Mountain Vineyard **8**
Robledo Family Winery **9**

Sonoma Mtn. Rd.

4 Glen Ellen

5

Bouverie Wildflower Preserve ■

JACK LONDON STATE HISTORIC PARK

London Ranch Rd.

7 **6**

Sonoma Creek

Arnold Dr.

VALLEY OF THE MOON

8

NAPA COUNTY

SONOMA COUNTY

Sonoma Mtn.

Agua Caliente

Agua Caliente

Agua Caliente Fetters Hot Springs

Boyes Hot Springs

Verano Ave.

Gehricke Rd.

Sonoma State Historic Park

S O N O M A

M O U N T A I N S

Rodgers Creek

Petaluma Res.

El Verano

W. Napa St. E. Napa St.

Sonoma

Castle Rd.

Buena Vista

5th St.

Napa Rd.

Petaluma Adobe State Hist. Pk. ■

Adobe Rd.

See map below

115

S O N O M A   V A L L E Y

12

Vineburg

9 **121**

Bonneau Rd.

Town of Sonoma

El Verano

Norrbom Rd.

Ravenswood Winery

Gehricke Rd.

0   1/2 mi
0   0.5 km

10 Salvador Vallejo Home ■

Mountain Cemetery

12

15

Sonoma Hwy.

Petaluma Ave.

Dowdall Creek

Sonoma Creek

W. Spain St.

W. Napa St.

5th St. W.

SONOMA STATE HISTORIC PARK

Mission San Francisco Solano ■

11 E. Spain St.

Sonoma Plaza/City Hall

12

Sebastiani Vineyards

E. Napa St.

Buena Vista Rd.

Buena Vista Winery

Castle

Lowell Valley Rd.

Old Winery Rd.

14 **13**

W. Mac Arthur St.

4th St. E.

5th St. E.

E. Mac Arthur St.

7th St. E.

8th St. E.

Arroyo Seco

16

Broadway

Gundlach-Bundschu Winery

See map p. 145. 1830 Lincoln Ave. (west of Silverado Trail). ☎ **707-942-1112.** *Fax: 707-942-0381.* www.callodging.com. *Free parking. Rack rates: $99–$229 double. Rates include continental breakfast. AE, DC, DISC, MC, V.*

The Daughter's Inn
$$$$ Napa

Downtown Napa has a good selection of B&Bs in converted Victorians, and this family-run inn is among the best. It's a smart choice for couples seeking a little romance, but who also want a location that's close to restaurants and whatever nightlife is available in the revitalized town of Napa. The inn is completely nonsmoking and has a total of ten individually designed, TV-free rooms — five in the mansion and five in a slightly more private new building in the garden. The focal points in all are the cushy beds and in-room Jacuzzis. In the heat of the summer, a more resortlike hotel with a pool would probably be preferable, but in snuggling weather, the Daughter's Inn provides nearly everything you need.

See map p. 145. 1938 First St. ☎ **866-253-1331.** *Fax: 707-255-3772.* www.daughters inn.com. *Street parking. Rack rates: $225–$329 double. Rates include a full breakfast. MC, V.*

Harvest Inn
$$$$–$$$$$ St. Helena

This Tudor-inspired complex was renovated in 1999, and all the rooms are light, attractive, and spacious enough for a family. Recently, 20 new rooms were added. Two pools and two Jacuzzis are set in lovely gardens against a dramatic backdrop of mountains and vineyards. Lots of little luxuries help justify the price, including feather beds, fireplaces, CD players, and VCRs. The mid-valley location is central to everything.

See map p. 145. 1 Main St. ☎ **800-950-8466** *or 707-963-9463. Fax: 707-963-4402.* www.harvestinn.com. *Free parking. Rack rates: $259–$499 double, $399–$675 suite. Rates include continental breakfast. AE, DC, DISC, MC, V.*

Indian Springs
$$$–$$$$ Calistoga

Booking these comfortable, old-fashioned bungalows in summer is not easy; you have to edge out the families that come here year after year, drawn by the excellent location and great value. (***Hint:*** Call 48 hours ahead to find out whether you can get in on a cancellation.) Guests can use the Olympic-size mineral pool until late in the evening (day visitors must leave by 6 p.m.). The wonderful spa offers a full range of treatments, including mud baths.

See map p. 145. 1712 Lincoln Ave. ☎ **707-942-4913.** *Fax: 707-942-4919.* www.indian springscalistoga.com. *Free parking. Rack rates: $185–$325 double studio or one-bedroom, $265–$375 two-bedroom, $450–$600 three-bedroom. MC, V.*

Milliken Creek
$$$$–$$$$$ Napa

Cushy, chic, and romantic, the large, airy rooms in this intimate new inn could have come straight out of *Metropolitan Home*. No luxury has been overlooked, from Frette bed linens and L'Occitane bath products to candlelight turndown service. The 3-acre creekside gardens are equally stunning and private; you'll find it difficult to tear yourself away, although many excellent small wineries await along the Silverado Trail. The facility is completely nonsmoking, and children younger than 16 are not accepted.

See map p. 145. 1815 Silverado Trail. ☎ 886-622-5775 or 707-255-1197. Fax: 707-942-2653. www.millikencreekinn.com. Free parking. Rack rates: $325–$675 double. Rates include breakfast and afternoon wine and cheese. DC, MC, V.

Mount View Hotel
$$$–$$$$$ Calistoga

Ideally situated in the heart of Calistoga, this charming and attractively restored historic hotel is a pleasing place to stay. Done in a cozy California-country style, the rooms are comfortable and well appointed. The secluded cottages, which have private patios with Jacuzzis, are worth the tariff for romance-seeking couples. A pool and Jacuzzi in the cute courtyard and a well-regarded spa round out the appeal.

See map p. 145. 1457 Lincoln Ave. ☎ 800-816-6877 or 707-942-6877. Fax: 707-942-6904. www.mountviewhotel.com. Free parking. Rack rates: $169–$339 double, suite, or cottage. Rates include continental breakfast (delivered to your room). AE, DISC, MC, V.

Napa River Inn
$$$–$$$$$ Napa

The first boutique hotel to reach the city of Napa, the Victorian-influenced Napa River Inn is housed in a converted 1884 warehouse complex that's part of a spiffy redevelopment project along the river. Sixty-six beautifully designed and equipped rooms are situated in three buildings; our favorite is the Embarcadero for its relative privacy. Standard rooms are dark; superior rooms have smaller bathrooms than deluxe rooms, but all include robes, fridges, spa products, and other goodies. The location near Copia (see the "Immersing yourself in food and wine" section later in this chapter) and downtown Napa is also handy.

See map p. 145. 500 Main St. ☎ 877-251-8500 or 707-251-8500. Fax: 707-251-8504. www.napariverinn.com. Free parking. Rack rates: $189–$375 double, $399–$500 suite. Rates include breakfast and wine tasting at the Napa General Store. AE, DISC, MC, V.

Vintage Inn
$$$–$$$$$ Yountville

This big, attractive French-country inn is conveniently situated near some of the finest restaurants in the valley. Recently refurbished in a French

Renaissance décor, rooms are clustered throughout the lovely flowering grounds, and are equipped with fireplaces, fridges, Jacuzzi tubs, coffeemakers, and terry robes. Tennis courts and a heated pool make this a comfortable miniresort, good for couples exploring the area. Spa services are available next door at the Villagio, its sister inn. Check for specials and packages, which can make this a relative bargain.

See map p. 145. 6541 Washington St. ☎ *800-351-1133 or 707-944-1112. Fax: 707-944-1617.* www.vintageinn.com. *Free parking. Rack rates: $230–$630 double. Rates include continental champagne breakfast and afternoon tea. AE, DC, DISC, MC, V.*

In Sonoma Valley

El Pueblo Inn
$–$$$ Sonoma

This lovable, way-better-than-average motel is almost within walking distance of the Sonoma Plaza and is very well located for touring. Family owned and run, it has an affable vibe, supported by comfortable, spacious rooms in the buildings closest to reception. The corner units here have fireplaces. Guest rooms in the original two-story building in the back are less expensive given that the bathrooms are older and smaller. A pretty garden and pool is next to a shaded patio and fitness room; it can get noisy in the summer because the property abuts Highway 12. If we were bringing the kids, we'd stay here without question. And if we were seeking affordable lodgings, ditto.

See map p. 147. 896 West Napa St. ☎ *800-900-8844 or 707-996-3651.* www.elpuebloinn.com. *Free parking. Rack rates: $120–$235 double; includes continental breakfast. MC, V.*

Glenelly Inn
$$$–$$$$ Glen Ellen

A secluded and peaceful family-run B&B, the modest rooms here are small but quaintly decorated, designed solely for relaxation. Each room has a private entry, terry robes, and down comforters, and most have claw-foot tubs with shower heads, but no phones or TV. If you happen to need those modern gadgets, book one of the two spacious cottages that were recently added to the property. A spa in the garden adds to the magic, and you can sit on the verandas and gaze at the mountains.

See map p. 147. 5131 Warm Springs Rd. ☎ *707-996-6720. Fax: 707-996-5227.* www.glenelly.com. *Free parking. Rack rates: $165–$295 doubles, suites, and cottages. Rates include breakfast. MC, V.*

Inn at Sonoma
$$–$$$ Sonoma

This attractive three-year-old Four Sisters Inn offers terrific value for the money. Public and guest rooms are graciously decorated and smartly maintained. Guests are treated to a generous breakfast, afternoon happy hour, and cookies. With just 19 rooms you'll get as much attention as you require from the staff, although actually obtaining a room in summer will take advanced planning because this is a popular hotel for wedding parties. Less than 2 blocks from the Sonoma Plaza, the location makes walking to dinner a simple treat. For romantic occasions, we'd prefer a more secluded and luxurious hideaway such as the Kenwood Inn or Milliken Creek, otherwise, a room here more than satisfies.

See map p. 147. 630 Broadway. ☎ *888-566-9818 or 707-939-1340. Fax: 707-996-5227.* www.foursisters.com. *Free parking Rack rates: $145–$275 double. Rates include full breakfast and afternoon wine. MC, V.*

Kenwood Inn and Spa
$$$$$ **Kenwood**

If price is no object, or you want an all-out splurge, this gorgeous inn — reminiscent of villas on the Italian Riviera — is our pick over any hotel we've visited in either valley. The faux-painted buildings appear almost miragelike as you drive up the Sonoma Highway, the pale yellow stucco blending into the landscape on a sunny day. Once inside, you'll have no desire to leave. Rooms have wood-burning fireplaces, feather beds, and sensuous fabrics; the facilities — an inviting saline pool, a separately situated Jacuzzi, a cozy bar and cafe (for guests only), and spa rooms that overlook vineyards — guarantee a feeling of sublime, luxurious seclusion.

See map p. 147. 10400 Sonoma Hwy. ☎ *800-353-6966 or 707-833-1293. Fax: 707-833-1247.* www.kenwoodinn.com. *Free parking. Rack rates: $350–$700 double. Rates include three-course breakfast. AE, MC, V.*

MacArthur Place
$$$$–$$$$$ **Sonoma**

This divine, small hotel is a renovated Victorian that's masterfully connected to newer buildings. The rooms are spacious and comfy, with wonderful four-poster beds that'll make you think twice about getting up. Contented guests relax at the small, well-staffed spa where the practiced hands of a masseuse work out prevacation tension. Manicured gardens surround a swimming pool, and a steakhouse restaurant in the 100-year-old barn supplies room service.

See map p. 147. 29 E. MacArthur St. ☎ *800-722-1866 or 707-938-2929. Fax: 707-933-9833.* www.macarthurplace.com. *Free parking. Rack rates: $299–$399 double, $375–$499 suite. Rates include continental breakfast. AE, MC, V.*

Sonoma Chalet
$$–$$$ **Sonoma**

Although the views from this private Swiss-inspired farmhouse encompass the mountains and the ranch next door, it's located less than a mile from Sonoma's town square. Antiques and collectibles decorate three big, delightful cottages; inside the house, two pretty upstairs rooms have private facilities and the two downstairs rooms share a bathroom. A simple and delicious breakfast, including fresh pastries, is included, and you can borrow bikes for your explorations.

See map p. 147. 18935 Fifth St. W. ☎ 800-938-3129 or 707-938-3129. Fax: 707-996-0190. www.sonomachalet.com. Free parking. Rack rates: $110–$225 double. Rates include continental breakfast. MC, V.

Where to Dine in the Wine Country

With excellent restaurants at every turn, the Wine Country is a wonderful place to eat well. However, the best dining rooms often book up ahead, so reserve in advance. If you're visiting on a weekend, calling before you even leave home is a good idea.

In Napa Valley

Angèle
$$–$$$ Napa   FRENCH

Napa is experiencing a major growth spurt in hotels and especially in restaurants, none with more to recommend it than this warm, casual brasserie overlooking the Napa River. Part of the historic Hatt Building development, Angèle serves typical French fare as interpreted by a chef with access to the bounty of Northern California (although on one visit, one of us had a craving for a hamburger, and Angèle's was perfection on a gourmet bun). A high level of professionalism at every turn makes this spot a standout.

See map p. 145. 540 Main St. ☎ 707-252-8115. Reservations recommended. Main courses: $19–$32. AE, MC, V. Open: Sun–Thurs 11:30 a.m.–10 p.m., Fri–Sat 11:30 a.m.–11 p.m.

Bistro Don Giovanni
$$–$$$ Napa   ITALIAN

Share a pizza, some antipasto, and a bottle of chardonnay for a delightful, light Italian meal, or go all out with the aged Porterhouse for two. This inviting place, easily the most popular restaurant in the valley, for all the right reasons, attracts a crowd that gathers at tables on the porch over-looking vineyards — just heavenly.

See map p. 145. 4110 Howard Lane (off Highway 29). ☎ 707-224-3300. Reservations recommended. Main courses: $12–$28. AE, DISC, MC, V. Open: Sun–Thurs 11:30 a.m.–10 p.m., Fri–Sat 11:30 a.m.–11 p.m.

Bistro Jeanty
$$$–$$$$ Yountville   FRENCH

This very French bistro is much applauded around the Bay Area for its authenticity, great menu, and vivacious dining room. Eating here satisfies both the appetite and the spirit. The seasonal menu includes rustic dishes such as lamb cheeks and potato salad, or rabbit and sweetbread ragout, plus typical bistro items including coq au vin and steak frites. Adventuresome and timid eaters alike will find something to enjoy and remember here.

See map p. 145. 6510 Washington St. ☎ *707-944-0103.* www.bistrojeanty.com. *Reservations recommended. Main courses: $15–$29. MC, V. Open: Daily 11:30 a.m.– 10:30 p.m.*

Bounty Hunter
$$ Napa   AMERICAN

Foremost a wine shop, the wealth of bottles available here pretty much obviates the need to ever drive Highway 29 again. Surrounded by the best wines available, your other difficult choice will be what to eat — the grilled whole chicken stuffed with Tecate beer? The barbecued ribs, smoky and succulent? A plate groaning with artisan cheeses and meats? This cozy former grocery in downtown Napa knows how to elevate eating its first-rate Southwestern-influenced cooking into a rousing good time.

See map p. 145. 975 First St. ☎ *707-255-0622.* www.bountyhunterwine.com. *No reservations. Main courses: $12–$39. MC, V. Open: Sun–Thurs 11 a.m.–10 p.m., Fri–Sat 11 a.m.–midnight.*

Cindy's Backstreet Kitchen
$$ St. Helena   CALIFORNIA

Cindy Pawlcyn (of Mustards Grill fame) opened this smaller, more low-key eatery in 2001. Given that St. Helena gets its fair share of weekend wine tasters, it's a testament to her sensibility how much this two-story house feels like a neighborhood hangout. A table in the garden is the ideal spot for a Cobb salad or curried chicken and something cold (Cindy has a full bar as well as fresh juice drinks). In the evening, small plates, such as rabbit tostados or Piquillo peppers stuffed with cumin-scented beef seem made for a local lager. Large plates include specials from the wood-burning oven, fish of the day, and steak frites that'll have you hunkered over your dish. Use one of Cindy's root beer floats, featuring homemade vanilla ice cream, to teach kids the difference between ordinary and extraordinary.

See map p. 145. 1327 Railroad Ave. (between Hunt and Adams). ☎ *707-963-1200.* www.cindysbackstreetkitchen.com. *Reservations recommended. Main courses: $11–$21. AE, DC, DISC, MC, V. Open: Daily 11:30 a.m.–9 p.m., Fri–Sat until 10 p.m. Apr–Nov.*

French Laundry
$$$$$ Yountville   FRENCH

Regarded as the finest chef in the United States, Thomas Keller prepares superb multicourse meals for a lucky crowd in his intimate, elegant, universally celebrated restaurant. If you're serious about food, mark your calendar, because reservations are taken two months in advance, between

10 a.m. and 5:30 p.m. The French Laundry experience is sublime on every front — but it's nearly impossible to get a table.

See map p. 145. 6640 Washington St. (at Creek Street). ☎ *707-944-2380.* www. frenchlaundry.com. *Reservations required. Prix-fixe meals: $135–$150. AE, MC, V. Open: Sat 11 a.m.–1 p.m., Tues–Sat 5:30–9:30 p.m.*

Gordon's Cafe and Wine Bar
$–$$$$ Yountville   CREATIVE AMERICAN

Chef-owner Sally Gordon's delicious food is served in a congenial atmosphere reminiscent of a general store. Besides comfort-food favorites at breakfast (perfect for kids) and creative sandwiches at lunch, Gordon's serves a three-course prix-fixe dinner on Friday nights, making the cafe a prime destination for food lovers.

See map p. 145. 6770 Washington St. ☎ *707-944-8246. Reservations essential at dinner. Main courses: $3.50–$8 at breakfast and lunch; $45 prix-fixe dinner. AE, MC, V. Open: Tues–Thurs and Sat–Sun 7:30 a.m.–6 p.m., Fri 7:30 a.m.–5 p.m. and 6–8:30 p.m.*

Julia's Kitchen
$$$ Napa   CALIFORNIA/FRENCH

Food preferences are entirely personal, but we think this bustling restaurant inside Copia (see "Immersing yourself in food and wine," later in this chapter) served the most delicious meal we ate on a working trip to the valley. Named in honor of Julia Child, the kitchen uses organic produce raised on the grounds, so even a simple green salad shines with bright flavor, and life only gets better from there. The menu changes often, but we loved the seared day-boat scallops and the roasted winter-squash skewer. Portions are moderate, which is kind because desserts must be given their due. You can eat here without paying an entrance fee to Copia.

See map p. 145. 500 First St. (at Copia). ☎ *707-265-5700.* www.copia.org. *Reservations recommended. Main courses: $17–$30. AE, MC, V. Open: Wed–Mon 11:30 a.m.–3 p.m., Thurs–Sun 5:30–9:30 p.m.*

Martini House
$$$–$$$$ St. Helena   AMERICAN

A collaboration between Chef Todd Humphries (Campton Place, CIA Greystone) and designer Pat Kuleto (Boulevard and Jardinière, among others), Martini House exudes a sexy, masculine, Old California air that works handsomely with the solid menu. Humphries uses locally grown produce and meats; you'll usually find steak, grilled pork chops, salmon, and pasta dishes — all of which sound a tad boring but aren't because the kitchen knows what it's doing. A separate entrance or the central staircase takes you to the downstairs bar where you don't need reservations to eat.

See map p. 145. 1245 Spring St. (off Highway 29). ☎ *707-963-2233.* www.martini house.com. *Reservations recommended. Main courses: $16–$26 at lunch, $29–$37 at dinner. AE, DC, DISC, MC, V. Open: Fri–Sun 11:30 a.m.–3 p.m., daily 5:30–10 p.m.*

Pearl
$-$$ Napa CALIFORNIA

Probably the most low-key and certainly the most affordable, good restaurant in the valley, Pearl specializes in oysters (naturally) prepared in four different ways (we can vouch for the barbecued ones). The Napa locals consider this cheerful little place an adjunct to their home kitchens, so you'll see families tucking into healthy portions of linguini and clams, soft tacos with two flavorful dipping sauces, or a straightforward roasted chicken and mashed potatoes. This is absolutely the place to eat if one more expensive gourmet meal threatens to finish you off. Enjoy patio dining in fine weather.

See map p. 145. 1339 Pearl St. ☎ *707-224-9161.* www.therestaurantpearl.com. *Reservations accepted. Main courses: $12–$27. MC, V. Open: Tues–Sat 11:30 a.m.– 2 p.m. and 5:30–9:30 p.m.*

Wappo Bar & Bistro
$$$ Calistoga INTERNATIONAL

We like this friendly pair of restaurants off the main drag for an unusual menu that spans a good part of the globe. Start an international culinary tour with spiced chickpea fritters and Vietnamese spring rolls, head to South America with a marvelous Brazilian seafood stew that is layered with flavors, or opt for a soft landing in Italy over some tender *osso buco*. Wappo also serves on a pretty patio that lies in between its two storefronts. A glass of white wine, the Turkish *mezze* (appetizers) plate, and a table in the warmth of a Napa Valley afternoon defines one version of happiness.

See map p. 145. 1226 Washington St. ☎ *707-942-4712. Reservations accepted. Main courses: $14–$24. AE, MC, V. Open: Wed–Mon 11:30 a.m.–2:30 p.m. and 6–9:30 p.m.*

In Sonoma Valley

Cafe La Haye
$$ Sonoma CALIFORNIA

This casual little cafe serves some of the best food around, and unlike many other Wine Country restaurants, it makes no attempt to pretend it's in the Mediterranean. Plain tables and chairs are carefully set about, as if not to disturb the art that fills the walls, making La Haye's single room resemble a gallery. The menu selection, spare but complete, features whatever's seasonal and offers organic produce. The daily risotto is fabulous, but you truly can't go wrong no matter what you order.

See map p. 147. 140 E. Napa St. ☎ *707-935-5994.* www.sterba.com/sonoma/ lahaye. *Reservations advised. Main courses: $16–$29. AE, MC, V. Open: Tues–Sat 5:30–9 p.m.*

Deuce
$$ Sonoma CALIFORNIA

With so many valley restaurants and chefs vying for attention, Deuce, a popular stop for county residents, gets overlooked by travelers. Inside the yellow Craftsman-style house, which sits on the main road heading toward Sonoma Plaza, you'll be treated to especially friendly service and well-prepared food that doesn't require any translation. Lots of diners (especially those who want dessert) make do with a couple of starters, in particular the tender/crispy calamari or the irresistible lobster pot pie. For mains, the smart money is on the thick, perfectly grilled pork chop although the cassoulet is hard to pass up. Kids are welcome here and the kitchen will prepare something to their liking if you ask.

See map p. 147. 691 Broadway. ☎ *707-933-3823.* www.dine-at-deuce.com. *Reservations recommended. Main courses: $19–$25. AE, MC, V. Open: Daily 11:30 a.m.–2:30 p.m. and 5–9 p.m.*

the girl and the fig
$$–$$$ Sonoma COUNTRY FRENCH

This upscale Country French bistro moved to the Sonoma Hotel from its Glen Ellen location in 2001 and, to the delight of its many admirers, added outdoor dining. The seasonal menu meets the needs of seafoodies, vegetarians, and carnivores alike with one or two dishes in each category. The grilled fig salad with arugula and local goat's cheese is a must-order when fresh figs are available.

See map p. 147. 110 West Spain St. ☎ *707-938-3634.* www.thegirlandthefig. com. *Reservations accepted. Main courses: $12–$25. MC, V. Open: Daily 11:30 a.m.– 10 p.m.*

Ledson Hotel & Harmony Restaurant
$$ Sonoma CALIFORNIA/FRENCH

You can't miss this new restaurant and hotel on Sonoma's square, although the designers did such a great job blending the new building with the old architecture that it looks like it's always been here. Ledson's hotel dining room sensibility seems at odds with the casual Wine Country atmosphere everywhere else — servers line up by the kitchen door and the plates of admittedly tasty food can be self-conscious in their presentation. But with a pianist nightly and a jazz vocalist on weekends, Ledson's has definitely enlivened the town.

See map p. 147. 480 First St. ☎ *707-996-9779.* www.ledsonhotel.com. *Reservations recommended. Main courses: $23–$30. AE, MC, V. Open: Daily 11:30 a.m.–10 p.m.*

Touring the Wine Country

Napa Valley is home to more than 380 wineries (Sonoma has over 200), some owned by corporations, and others the domain of individuals so seduced by the grape that they abandoned successful careers to devote themselves to viticulture. Although no correlation exists between the size of a winery and the quality of the product — which has more to do with the talents of the vintners and variables such as weather and soil conditions — the bigger wineries offer more to visitors in terms of education and entertainment.

Wineries in Napa (less so in Sonoma) are developing new ways to market wine tasting as an educational/culinary event — and an expensive one at that. In what we think is an effort to eradicate the notion that this is a great way to cage free alcohol, most wineries charge at least a nominal tasting fee and many are promoting sit-down food and wine pairings for real money. Rubicon Estate (formerly Niebaum-Coppola) is a case in point: You can't even drive onto the property without paying $25 at the gate per adult, just so they know you really, *really* want to be there (the fee covers a tour and five tastes). Wine tasting has become serious business in these parts.

If you want to find out more about grape growing and the blending and bottling process, make the first winery you visit one that offers an in-depth tour. **Robert Mondavi** offers an excellent introductory tour, as does **St. Supéry**. Book the superb tour offered by **Schramsberg** if you're interested in the production of sparkling wine (aka champagne, although only French winemakers from the Champagne region fundamentally have the right to call it that).

 Don't expect a deal on wine purchased directly from the producers. Wineries sell at full retail so as not to undercut their primary market, wine merchants. Buy and carry only what you think you can't get at home. If you're concerned that you won't be able to locate a particular vintage back at the ranch, most wineries offer mail-order service.

How to tell a cab from a zin

The most prominent varieties of grapes produced in the area include cabernet sauvignon, pinot noir, and zinfandel grapes grown for red wines, and chardonnay and sauvignon or fume blanc grapes grown for white wines.

Of course, the best way to really tell a cab from a zin, in laidback California wine-speak, is to read the label on the bottle. The label identifies the type of grape used if the wine contains at least 75 percent of that particular variety. The appellation of origin indicates where the grapes were grown — either a viticulture area such as the Carneros region of the Napa Valley, a county, or the state itself. The vintage date is important because it explains when at least 95 percent of the grapes were crushed. Because many wines taste better as they get older, and some years produce better grapes than others, you want to make a note of the vintage.

You can greatly enhance your knowledge of wine by tasting correctly — and what better classroom than a French-style chateau smack in the

middle of a vineyard? Remember that wine appreciation begins by ana-
lyzing color, followed by aroma, then taste. You do this with your eyes
first, then your nose, then your mouth. Don't be shy about asking questions of the person pouring — he'll cheerfully answer your questions
because the more you discover about his product, the more likely you
are to become a steady customer. And that makes everybody happy!

Here are a few wine-tasting do's and don'ts:

- ✔ **Before the pour, sniff your glass.** It should have a clean aroma. If
  not, ask for a fresh glass.

- ✔ **Never pour the wine yourself.**

- ✔ **Taste wines in the proper order: whites first, reds second, dessert
  wines last.** This reflects the order in which food is generally
  served — white wines with a first course, reds with a hearty main
  course, and dessert wines with sweets.

- ✔ **Swirl the wine to coat the inside of the glass.** This introduces
  more oxygen and helps open up the wine flavors and aromas.

- ✔ **Smell the wine.** Think about what the different aromas bring to
  mind — spice, fruit, flowers, and so forth.

- ✔ **Take a sip and coat the back of your tongue with the wine.**

- ✔ **Keep in mind that, along with baseball, wine tasting is one of the
  few sports where spitting is not only allowed, it's encouraged.**
  Just make sure you hit the target — a bucket or some other con-
  tainer will be available for this purpose. Spitting is a nifty way to
  sample many wines without becoming fuzzy-headed.

- ✔ **Don't mistake a tasting room for your friendly neighborhood
  bar — this is not the time to swill with drunken abandon.** And
  lose the chewing gum.

If you really want to get into this wine thing, pick up a copy of *Wine For
Dummies,* by Mary Ewing Mulligan and Ed McCarthy (published by Wiley
Publishing, Inc.).

The best Napa Valley wineries for first-time visitors

The Napa Valley is winery central, so the handful discussed here represent only the tip of the vine. But the valley contains plenty of other worthwhile wineries, so get a map (they are easily available throughout the
region — or contact one of the visitor bureaus noted in the "Gathering
More Information" section near the end of this chapter) and explore those
back roads.

In the listings in this section, we note current wine-tasting fees and touring policies; keep in mind that wineries can — and do — change their
policies. In any case, the tasting fee should always be clearly posted at
the tasting counter; if you're not sure, ask.

Beaulieu Vineyard

The vintners at this well-regarded, hospitable establishment, founded in 1900 and Napa's third-oldest winery, aim to set visitors at ease the moment they walk through the door by passing out glasses of sauvignon blanc. After you relax, take the free half-hour tour through the production facility, given daily from 11 a.m. to 4 p.m. Each tasting thereafter is $5, or $25 for five delicious reserve vintages; be ready to shell out if you want to take home one of these special bottles.

See map p. 145. 1960 St. Helena Hwy. (Highway 29, just north of Rutherford Cross Road), Rutherford. ☎ *800-264-6918 or 707-967-5230.* www.bvwines.com. *Open: Daily 10 a.m.–5 p.m.*

Clos Pegase

Attention, architecture buffs: Even if you're not interested in the free 30-minute tour (given daily at 11 a.m. and 2 p.m.; no reservations needed), come to see the house. This stunning Michael Graves–designed winery is a temple to modern winemaking. It's plenty easy to while away a happy hour or more here studying the terrific art collection, walking around the sculpture garden, and picnicking on the vast lawn (you must reserve a picnic table). Wine tasting costs $2.50 for current releases, and $2 each for reserve wines. Bottles don't come cheap here, but this is a good place to pick up something special.

See map p. 145. 1060 Dunaweal Lane (west of Silverado Trail), Calistoga. ☎ *800-726-6136 or 707-942-4981.* www.clospegase.com. *Open: Daily 10:30 a.m.–5 p.m.*

Cuvaison

Headquartered in a wonderful Mission-style house, this intimate, excellent winery is a great place to sip and learn. The tasting room is one of the most hospitable in the valley; tastings are $8 ($10 for Estate selections), and you even get to keep your logo glass as a souvenir. A $15-per-person tour and tasting daily at 10:30 a.m. will take you into the state-of-the-art wine cave. Picnic tables are there for your use.

See map p. 145. 4550 Silverado Trail (just south of Dunaweal Lane), Calistoga. ☎ *707-942-2468.* www.cuvaison.com. *Open: 10 a.m.–5 p.m.*

Darioush

A Persian palace (think Persepolis) in Napa? No, you haven't had one too many, you've found Darioush. This eye-catching — to say the least — building, clad in travertine stone mined in Iran, opened in 2004; the winery itself has been producing since 1997. Tastings are offered, of course ($15 for a flight of four wines), but tours must be arranged in advance. We'd make the call if only to peek at Darioush Khaledi's private wine cellar. If it's available, try the 2004 signature Chardonnay, which has an amazing pear-ish, creamy consistency from start to finish. Saturday through Thursday a wine and cheese tasting is offered ($35) and every Friday is a cheese intensive featuring Cowgirl Creamery ($65). A tip from one of the staff is to try to avoid visiting on a Saturday in the summer. The valley is lots calmer during the week.

See map p. 145. 4240 Silverado Trail, Napa. ☎ *707-257-2345.* www.darioush.com. *Open: Daily 10:30 a.m.–5 p.m.*

Robert Mondavi

You'll recognize this grand Mission-style winery from the labels on Mondavi's popular wines. It's a bit corporate, but excellent if you're a novice. The first to conduct public tastings, Mondavi continues its dedication to wine education. To this end, the winery offers a menu of tours, from the daily 75-minute To Kalon tour at $25 a pop (☎ **888-RMONDAVI,** ext. 82001, for same-day reservations) to a $100 Harvest of Joy tour that includes a three-course lunch. For fees ranging from $50 to $110, you can benefit from seminars on grape growing, essence tasting, and wine and food pairing. Reservations are required for tours and seminars. During July and August, you can catch a Saturday-evening concert. The shows sell out quickly, so call ☎ **888-769-5299** or visit Mondavi's Web site for a schedule and tickets.

See map p. 145. 7801 St. Helena Hwy. (Highway 29, just north of Oakville Cross Road), Oakville. ☎ *888-RMONDAVI or 707-226-1395.* www.robertmondaviwinery.com. *Open: Daily 10 a.m.–5 p.m.*

Schramsberg

You can't just stop by this elegant and completely unpretentious 200-acre champagne estate — but advance booking one of the free, 90-minute by-appointment-only tours is well worth the trouble. Schramsberg is the best sparkling-wine producer in the United States, and the guided talk (followed by a $25 tasting) is the country's best sparkling-wine tour. You can explore caves that were hand-dug a hundred years ago and get the lowdown on the whole bottling process, which has hardly changed a whit since then. Afterward, take a walk through the impeccable gardens. Book at least a week in advance on weekends.

See map p. 145. 1400 Schramsberg Rd. (turn off Highway 29 at Peterson Drive), Calistoga. ☎ *707-942-2414.* www.schramsberg.com. *Open: Daily 10 a.m.–4 p.m.*

St. Supéry

If you want an excellent introductory tour that's a little more intimate than the one offered by Mondavi, come to this friendly, first-class winery. Everybody makes a big deal about "SmellaVision," which teaches you about aromas common to certain varietals, but the real highlights are in the demonstration vineyard, where you witness growing techniques up close and get an excellent lesson in tasting at the end of the one-hour tour, offered at 3 p.m. daily. The cost is $10 per person. Self-guided tours are free, but have $10 on hand for the tasting. Weekends only, reserve tastings are in the "Divine Wine" room, where $15 gets you half glasses of the really good stuff (the Meritages are well worth the price). A Winemaker's tour and tasting is now offered for $45 per person at 1 p.m. Monday through Thursday. Tickets can be purchased online.

See map p. 145. 8440 St. Helena Hwy. (between Oakville and Rutherford Cross roads), Rutherford. ☎ *800-942-0809 or 707-963-4507.* www.stsupery.com. *Open: Daily 9:30 a.m.–6 p.m. (to 5 p.m. Nov–Apr).*

Sterling Vineyards

Arrive at this hilltop winery by aerial tram and swoon over the spectacular vista. Wine tasting is included in the ticket price of $15 ($20 weekends and holidays; $10 for those younger than 21). After you reach the winery, take the self-guided tour that leads you through the entire operation and into the tasting room, where the friendly staff serves you wine at tables rather than at a bar. For grander palates, a $45 reserve tasting and guided tour is offered at 11 a.m. daily.

See map p. 145. 1111 Dunaweal Lane (½ mile east of Highway 29), Calistoga. ☎ *800-726-6136 or 707-942-3349.* www.sterlingvineyards.com. *Open: Daily 10:30 a.m.–4:30 p.m.*

Wineries in Sonoma Valley

Arrowood

Arrowood is an intimate, high-end, and somewhat exclusive winery with a small production but national distribution. You need to make an appointment for daily tours of 40 to 90 minutes in duration at fees from $20 to $30. Call a day or two in advance. If you don't care for a tour, you can still sit on the verandah overlooking grapevines and mountains and try some great wines for a $3 tasting fee.

See map p. 147. 14347 Sonoma Hwy., Glen Ellen. ☎ *800-938-5170.* www.arrowood vineyards.com. *Open: Daily 10 a.m.–4:30 p.m.*

Benziger

Tractor-pulled trams take visitors up a flower-lined path at this beautiful 85-acre ranch near Jack London State Park for a 45-minute guided tour ($10; reservations required). The ranch has belonged to the Benziger family since 1981. The tram operators discuss nearly everything you need to know about viticulture, including insect control, and how the sun and soil together affect the taste of the final product. You can choose from two tasting opportunities, one of which is complimentary; the other costs $10 for the reserve wines.

See map p. 147. 1883 London Ranch Rd., Glen Ellen (take Highway 12 to Arnold Drive and turn left on London Ranch Road). ☎ *888-490-2739.* www.benziger.com. *Open: Daily 10 a.m.–5 p.m.*

B.R. Cohn

Cohn's remodeled tasting room, gift shop, and new picnic area flanked by olive trees is just down the road from Arrowood. Tasting fees are a modest

$5 for current releases and $10 for limited-release wines, including the signature 2002 Olive Hill Estate Cabernet. Along with the wines, some of which are only available at the winery, the olive oil produced here is of the highest quality and makes a great gift. Friendly staff members who are happy to talk wine and olives preside over the relaxed tasting room. Doobie Brothers recordings play on the speakers and are available in the gift shop because owner Bruce Cohn is their manager.

See map p. 147. 15000 Sonoma Hwy., Glen Ellen. ☎ *800-330-4064.* www.brcohn. com. *Open: Daily 10 a.m.–5 p.m.*

Chateau St. Jean

Driving back on Warm Springs Drive toward Kenwood, turn left on Highway 12 to find a Mediterranean-style mansion on a 250-acre estate. With an expansive front lawn and shady groves, this winery is a great place for a picnic. (You can pick up picnic food inside the winery.) The magnificent magnolia tree here was planted by famed botanist Luther Burbank. Tours are self-guided only; you can climb the observation tower for a view of the valley. Downstairs, wine tasting is complimentary; $5 is charged for three tastes of reserve wines.

See map p. 147. 8555 Sonoma Hwy., Kenwood. ☎ *800-543-7572 or 707-833-4134.* www. chateaustjean.com. *Open: Daily 10 a.m.–4:30 p.m.*

Moon Mountain Vineyard

A long drive up the mountain rewards with stunning views and some delicious organic estate wines only available on-site. You must make an appointment to visit, but the phone call is well worth the effort. The tasting room is inside a turret, too intimate to accommodate the busloads that flock to more accessible wineries. You'll have a chance to ask questions while touring the tank room and caves or tasting the Bordeaux-style offerings. Fellow tasters are likely to be serious wine students who have sought out what is one of the less ostentatious yet sophisticated wineries in either Napa or Sonoma. The tasting fee is just $10.

See map p. 147. 1700 Moon Mountain Rd., Sonoma (take Highway 12 toward Glen Ellen; Moon Mountain Road is between Agua Caliente and Madrone roads). ☎ *707-996-5870.* www.moonmountainvineyard.com. *Open: Mon–Sat 10 a.m.–4 p.m. by appointment.*

Robledo Family Winery

This modest little tasting room, comfortably furnished with handsome pieces from Michoacán, Mexico, represents an old-fashioned American success story. Reynaldo Robledo, Sr., who arrived in the valley as a 16-year-old migrant worker, combined hard work and a gift for nurturing grapevines into ownership of three vineyards, a vineyard-management company, and this winery. His children are actively involved in the business, and you'll meet at least one behind the bar, pouring tastes of their Estate sauvignon blanc, pinot grigio, pinot noir, and merlot (the tasting fee is $5). A small producer, it sells bottles directly to consumers through its wine club or at the winery.

See map p. 147. 21901 Bonness Rd., Sonoma (take Arnold Drive and turn on Highway 116 toward Petaluma). ☎ *707-939-6903.* www.robledofamilywinery.com. *Open: Mon–Sat 10 a.m.–5 p.m., Sun 11 a.m–4 p.m.*

More Cool Stuff to See and Do

Tasting wine isn't the only thing to keep you occupied on your trip to the Wine Country. The following sections share the myriad other activities the region has to offer.

Picnicking the valleys

Sure, the restaurant scene is great — but hardly a better place on the planet exists for picnicking than the Wine Country. A number of fabulous gourmet grocers can supply the delicacies, and many friendly wineries provide pastoral picnic grounds.

✔ Our favorite picnic supplier is the **Oakville Grocery Co.,** 7856 St. Helena Hwy. (Highway 29), at Oakville Cross Road (☎ **707-944-8802;** www.oakvillegrocery.com). Here you can put together your own gourmet picnic from the excellent bread selection, the deli counter (which runs from first-rate cold cuts to top-quality foie gras), and yummy pastries.

✔ A lot less country store-ish is **Dean & DeLuca,** 607 St. Helena Hwy. (Highway 29, north of Zinfandel Lane). St. Helena (☎ **707-967-9980;** www.deandeluca.com), the Big Apple's favorite gourmet grocer. Everything at this first-class mega-mart is beautifully displayed — and very pricey. Still, you'll get your money's worth.

✔ Just across the street from Dean & DeLuca is **V. Sattui Winery,** 1111 White Lane (at Highway 29), St. Helena (☎ **707-963-7774;** www.vsattui.com), whose mammoth tasting room also serves as a bountiful gourmet shop. If you buy here, you can also dine here on the popular picnic grounds.

✔ It may be a bit out of your way (it's north of Santa Rosa in Healdsburg), but a most memorable stop is the **Jimtown Store,** 6706 State Hwy. 128, Healdsburg (☎ **707-433-1212;** www.jimtown.com). This former gas station supplies charm and country atmosphere along with delicious food and a fun, eclectic assortment of wares. You can make a delicious picnic out of the boxed lunches (try the home-baked ham sandwich with Jimtown's sweet red pepper and tomato spread), daily specials such as Basque ragout or corn chowder, or the homemade spreads (spicy chipotle, Asian peanut, fig, and olive) and breads. They even have their own Jimtown label wine to add to your picnic basket.

After you put your picnic together, where should you go? In addition to V. Sattui, **Clos Pegase, Cuvaison, Oakville Ranch,** and **St. Supéry** are among the many wineries that offer pleasant picnic spots (remember to reserve a table ahead at Clos Pegase).

Bringing a bottle of wine from one winery to enjoy at another is considered poor form. If you're going to use a winery's picnic grounds, buy a bottle of wine inside first to enjoy during your alfresco meal.

Getting pampered in Calistoga

People have been taking to Calistoga's rejuvenating mud baths — a blend of ancient volcanic ash, imported peat, and naturally boiling mineral water, which simmers at a comfy 104°F — for more than 150 years. Calistoga's spas are generally friendly, rustic, comfortable places borne out of a therapeutic tradition — nothing like the marble-tiled glamfests that are most resort spas.

Treatments are relatively affordable. Expect to pay around $150 for a mud bath and one-hour massage. You can reserve a tub, followed by a mineral shower and a massage or a facial, at the following locations:

- ✔ **Dr. Wilkinson's Hot Springs,** 1507 Lincoln Ave. (☎ 707-942-4102; www.drwilkinson.com), probably the most well-known of Calistoga's spas

- ✔ **Indian Springs,** 1712 Lincoln Ave. (☎ 707-942-4913; www.indian springscalistoga.com), a tad pricier but you get pool privileges

- ✔ **Golden Haven Hot Springs Spa,** 1713 Lake St. (☎ 707-942-6793; www.goldenhaven.com), which boasts late hours and private mud-bath rooms for couples

- ✔ **Calistoga Spa Hot Springs,** 1006 Washington St. (☎ 707-942-6269; www.calistogaspa.com), whose mud bath/massage packages are a very good buy

Check for Internet specials. And if mud just sounds icky to you, these spas all offer alternatives, such as salt baths and aromatherapy wraps.

Hot-air ballooning

Soaring over the vineyards under a colorful balloon, with just a few other souls sharing your basket, is an experience. **Bonaventura Balloon Company** (☎ 800-FLY-NAPA or 707-944-2822; www.bonaventura balloons.com) is one of Napa's most trusted hot-air balloon operators, with a range of packages available from $198 per person. Or call **Napa Valley Aloft/Adventures Aloft** (☎ 800-944-4408 or 707-944-4408; www.nvaloft.com), whose early-morning lift-off includes a preflight snack and a postflight brunch with bubbly. At $195 to $250 per person (depending on the number of persons and extras you choose), however, you may want to keep those feet on the ground.

Heeding the call of the wild and the outdoors

Jack London State Historic Park, 2400 London Ranch Rd., near Glen Ellen in Sonoma County (☎ 707-938-5216; www.parks.ca.gov), is where the prolific author of *The Call of the Wild* lived before his death in 1916 at age 40. You can walk on trails to the ruins of Wolf House, London Lake, and Bath House. A museum/library with first editions of London's works and personal memorabilia are on the grounds, as well. It's open daily from 9:30 a.m. to dusk.

Art turns up in the most unexpected places, but none more so than the **di Rosa Preserve** (☎ 707-226-5991 Ext 25; www.dirosapreserve.org). This 217-acre indoor/outdoor gallery located 6½ miles west of Napa on Highway 121, displays over 2,000 works amid meadows, hanging from trees, and throughout the former winery. Rene di Rosa, a former journalist and viticulturist, owns the property. Guides conduct one-hour introductory and two-and-a-half-hour tours Tuesday through Saturday. You must make a reservation for the tours; admission is $10 for the one-hour tour and $15 for the longer version.

The **Old Faithful Geyser of California,** off of Highway 29 north of Calistoga at 1299 Tubbs Lane (☎ 707-942-6463; www.oldfaithful geyser.com), is one of only three "old faithful" geysers in the world. This one has been blowing off steam at regular intervals for just about as long as anyone can remember. The 350°F water spews out to a height of about 60 feet every 30 minutes or so (depending on barometric pressure, the moon, tides, and tectonic stresses). Is it worth the price of admission ($8 for adults, $7 for seniors, $3 for children 6–12)? Well, when we were standing in the ratty tract of yard surrounding the "natural wonder," a Japanese tourist visiting with her young son turned to us and asked plaintively, "Is this it?" Old Faithful is open daily from 9 a.m. to 6 p.m. (to 5 p.m. in winter).

Immersing yourself in food and wine

Copia: The American Center for Wine, Food and the Arts, 500 First St., Napa (☎ 707-259-1600; www.copia.org), opened in the fall of 2001 in the city of Napa and has quickly become one of the must-see attractions in the valley. Reasons for its immediate popularity are obvious: Copia celebrates the finer things in life in a modern, museum-like setting, although it's neither solemn nor overly reverential. One permanent exhibit, an interactive presentation on the role of food and wine in U.S. society, is both accessible and amusing. In addition, a state-of-the-art theater hosts concerts, lectures, and films; a full roster of wine and food courses is offered year-round; and a 500-seat concert terrace overlooking the Napa River, surrounded by Copia's orchard and organic gardens, provides warm-weather amusement. A great restaurant (Julia's Kitchen — see the "Where to Dine in the Wine Country" section earlier in this chapter), a wine bar, and, of course, a gift shop complete the experience. Check the Web site for current activities during your trip and try to take in an exhibit, a class, a concert, or a meal — or all four, if time allows! Admission is $5 adults, $4 seniors and students, and free for children 12 and younger. It's open Wednesday through Monday from 10 a.m. to 5 p.m.

Many olive trees are planted at wineries and in groves around Sonoma Valley. Olives have become an important crop, and olive-oil tastings are a popular activity now. You can debate the merits of various extra-virgin olive oils in Glen Ellen at the **Olive Press,** 14301 Arnold Dr. (☎ **888-965-4839** or 707-939-8900; www.theolivepress.com). The press works 24 hours a day between October and March. Watch the process from the tasting room, while sampling the award-winning olive oil and checking out the olive-themed merchandise.

If you have an abiding interest in cooking, sign up for a three- to four-hour class at **Ramekins,** 450 W. Spain St., Sonoma (☎ **707-933-0450;** www.ramekins.com), a small B&B and culinary school next to the General's Daughter restaurant. During the day, take in the demonstration classes; in the evening, glean culinary tips from some major Bay Area chefs. Students have ample opportunity to sample the goods with a few glasses of wine. Call for a catalog.

Gathering More Information

Call the **Napa Valley Conference and Visitors Bureau (NVCVB)** at ☎ **707-226-7459,** or go online to www.napavalley.com. After you arrive, stop by the NVCVB's office at 1310 Napa Town Center in downtown Napa (exit Highway 29 at First Street), where you'll find helpful counselors on staff as well as a wealth of information.

The **Sonoma Valley Visitors Bureau** is located in Sonoma on the Sonoma Plaza at 453 First St. E. (☎ **707-996-1090;** www.sonomavalley.com). Stop by for maps, lodging information, and winery-tour information.

Chapter 13

Mendocino

• •

In This Chapter

▶ Planning your visit to the rugged North Coast's most refined little town
▶ Finding the ideal places to stay and dine
▶ Taking in the town and surrounding area

• •

For a taste of California's wild and wonderful North Coast, Mendocino is the perfect place. This secluded, artsy, and enchanting town is a West Coast version of a New England seashore village (it actually served as the location for Cabot Cove, Maine, in the old television series *Murder, She Wrote*). Mendocino is magically situated atop craggy headlands that jut out into the Pacific, giving the town a ruggedly gorgeous coastline on three sides. The spectacular setting — a world apart from the seaside landscape farther south, even near San Francisco — makes it an ideal spot for a bit of nature-inspired relaxation.

Hugely popular as a romantic getaway from the Bay Area, the town is dedicated to the laid-back, weekending life. You won't find a whole lot to do in Mendocino — and that suits weary travelers just fine. Couples come to stroll, shop, bike, hike, and generally take it easy. Families are welcome, naturally, although kids may not be happy campers among the expensive shops and arts-and-crafts galleries.

Mendocino also offers a good starting point for exploration of California's one-of-a-kind Redwood Country (see Chapter 14).

Timing Your Visit

Summer or early fall is the best time to come. Mendocino is lovely from May through mid-October. Don't expect warmth, though: Average highs run between 59°F and 66°F, and lows can dip below 50°F even in August. Mornings are misty and generally give way to afternoon sun; fog prevails in July and August and sometimes early September. Dress warmly and in layers. Leave your bathing suit in your suitcase, because these waters are never warm enough for swimming. If you travel inland, up the Redwood Highway, expect temperatures to increase as much as 15 or 20 degrees.

Visit during the week to avoid the maximum-capacity crowds, highest room rates, and mandated two-night minimum stays.

The weather can be a crapshoot in winter (frankly, this far up the coast, it can be a crapshoot at any time of year). Still, winter's not much colder on average than summer — about 10° across the board — and you'll save a bundle on accommodations. You'll also find yourself in **prime whale-watching territory** if you visit between mid-December and mid-April. If you happen to be traveling at the end of January, you can enjoy two of our favorite California pastimes — dining on crab and tasting wine — when Mendocino restaurants celebrate **Dungeness crab season.** Don't be surprised if you run into some rain, though.

How much time do you need? Two nights will do the trick. You may want to stop by just for one night, to sample the vibe on your way up to the Avenue of the Giants (see Chapter 14), but if you aren't in a hurry, a second night is worthwhile.

Getting There and Getting Around

Mendocino's seclusion is a big part of its charm (see the "Mendocino and Redwood Country" map on p. 169) — but that also makes reaching it a slight challenge. The town is 155 miles from San Francisco and 95 miles from the north end of Napa Valley. No major highway runs to Mendocino; you have to battle either the slow-going mountains or the even-slower-going coastal roads to get there.

> ✔ **From San Francisco:** The fastest route is to take U.S. 101 north to Cloverdale, take Highway 128 west to Highway 1, and then go north along the coast. The drive takes about four hours.

> ✔ **From Napa Valley:** The valley's main highway, 129, meets up with Highway 128 in Calistoga, at the north end. Follow 128 West all the way to the coast, which takes two and a half to three hours.

Highway 128, which crosses the mountains, is a curving, nausea-inducing route all the way from U.S. 101 to the coast, which is the bulk of the trip no matter what your starting point. If you have a sensitive tummy and would prefer to keep your nausea in check, take U.S. 101 to Willits, pick up Highway 20 west to the coast, and head south on Highway 1. This alternative route adds 45 minutes or an hour to your trip — and Highway 20 is no joy, either — but it's an appreciably smoother ride.

The most scenic drive from the Bay Area is to take the coastal route, Highway 1, all the way. The drive is stunning, but expect it to take six long hours.

After you've arrived in Mendocino, park your car and set out on foot. The town is entirely walkable and easy to get a handle on. Main Street runs perpendicular to Highway 1 along the oceanfront. Lansing is the

Mendocino and Redwood Country

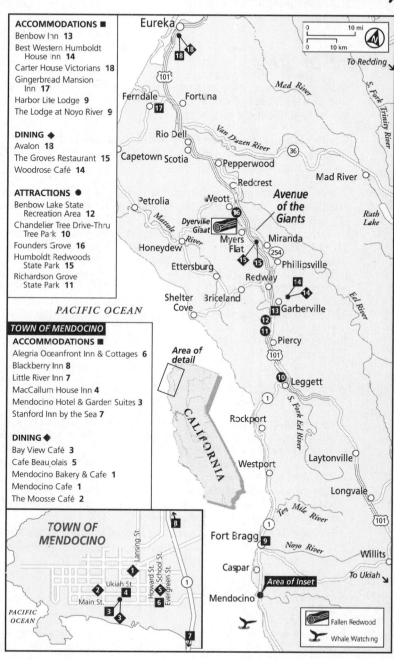

ACCOMMODATIONS ■
Benbow Inn **13**
Best Western Humboldt
House Inn **14**
Carter House Victorians **18**
Gingerbread Mansion
Inn **17**
Harbor Lite Lodge **9**
The Lodge at Noyo River **9**

DINING ◆
Avalon **18**
The Groves Restaurant **15**
Woodrose Café **14**

ATTRACTIONS ●
Benbow Lake State
Recreation Area **12**
Chandelier Tree Drive-Thru
Tree Park **10**
Founders Grove **16**
Humboldt Redwoods
State Park **15**
Richardson Grove
State Park **11**

PACIFIC OCEAN

TOWN OF MENDOCINO
ACCOMMODATIONS ■
Alegria Oceanfront Inn & Cottages **6**
Blackberry Inn **8**
Little River Inn **7**
MacCallum House Inn **4**
Mendocino Hotel & Garden Suites **3**
Stanford Inn by the Sea **7**

DINING ◆
Bay View Café **3**
Cafe Beaujolais **5**
Mendocino Bakery & Cafe **1**
Mendocino Cafe **1**
The Moosse Café **2**

0   10 mi
0   10 km

To Redding

Eureka

Ferndale   Fortuna

Rio Dell

Capetown Scotia   Pepperwood

Mad River

Redcrest

Petrolia   Weott   **Avenue of the Giants**

Ruth Lake

Dyerville Giant

Honeydew   Myers Flat   Miranda

Ettersburg   Phillipsville

Redway

Shelter Briceland
Cove   Garberville

Piercy

Area of detail

Leggett

Rockport

CALIFORNIA

Westport   Laytonville

Longvale

Ten Mile River

Fort Bragg   Noyo River   Willits

Caspar   *Area of Inset*   To Ukiah

Mendocino

Mad River
Van Duzen River
Eel River
S. Fork Eel River
S. Fork Trinity River
Mattole River

TOWN OF MENDOCINO

Lansing St.
Ukiah St.
Howard St.
School St.
Evergreen St.
Main St.

PACIFIC
OCEAN

Fallen Redwood
Whale Watching

main north-south street in town, meeting Main at the ocean. The rest of the town unfolds along a basic grid from there, no more than 6 blocks deep or wide.

Where to Stay

Most lodgings require a two-night minimum stay on weekends and three nights over holidays. Count on 10 percent in taxes being tacked on to your hotel bill at checkout time.

Contact **Mendocino Coast Reservations** (☎ 800-262-7801 or 707-937-5033; www.mendocinovacations.com), a free central reservations service, if our favorites are full.

If Mendocino's high rates are too much for you, trek 10 miles up Highway 1 to Fort Bragg and the value-minded **Harbor Lite Lodge,** 120 N. Harbor Dr. (☎ 800-643-2700 or 707-964-0221; www.harborlitelodge.com). From the highway, this rustic motel hasn't much in the way of curb appeal, but the spacious rooms, for $75 to $163 depending on the season, have pretty river views. Ask for a room away from the bridge to avoid traffic noise. Just down the road and a giant step up is the **Lodge at Noyo River,** 500 Casa del Noyo Dr. (☎ 800-628-1126 or 707-964-8045; www.noyolodge.com). The accommodations in this attractive Craftsman-style B&B cost a bit more dough — anywhere from $99 to $175 double with special rates in the winter — but rates include a lavish buffet breakfast, authentic Victorian décor, and a much more secluded location along the river.

Alegria Oceanfront Inn & Cottages
$$$–$$$$ Mendocino

This charming former sea captain's home is the only accommodation in town with direct beach access. Gorgeous ocean views, pretty gardens, and two of the mellowest innkeepers in the business set a warm, relaxing coastal tone. Each comfortable room has a private entrance, a coffeemaker and fridge, a TV, and either a fireplace or a wood-burning stove. The copious redwood decks with Adirondack chairs offer views galore and are a fine place to retire while digesting breakfast made from organic and local products. It's truly Mendo marvelous!

See map p. 169 44781 Main St. (west of Evergreen Street). ☎ *800-780-7905 or 707-937-5150. Fax: 707-937-5151.* www.oceanfrontmagic.com. *Free parking. Rack rates: $209–$279 double. Rates include full breakfast. AE, MC, V.*

Blackberry Inn
$$–$$$ Mendocino

If you can get past the hokey Old West theme (and few kids can, so bring 'em), you'll enjoy one of the best values on the coast. The motel is designed as a frontier town — the rooms have names like the Barber Shop, the Millinery (one of the best for ocean views), and the Livery Stable. Inside, rooms are bright, pretty, spacious, and spotless; even the cheapest has a sitting area, a well-dressed king-size bed, and the Pacific in the distance. Set on a bluff on the inland side of Highway 1, it's a long walk or a two-minute drive into town. Resident deer contribute to the storybook ambience.

See map p 169. 44951 Larkin Rd. (on the inland side of Highway 1). ☎ **800-950-7806** *or 707-937-5281. Fax: 707-937-5281.* www.mendocinomotel.com. *Free parking. Rack rates: $140–$270 double. MC, V.*

Little River Inn
$$–$$$$$ **Little River**

One of our favorite places to stay in Mendocino, the main buildings are situated off Highway 1, a few minutes' drive from the village. With the feel of a resort, but completely unpretentious, this family-owned and -operated inn encompasses a 9-hole golf course and pro shop, two lighted tennis courts, a spa, a restaurant, and a most congenial bar. Many rooms have ocean views and range from motel-like simple to outrageously luxe with full-on views, stereos, Jacuzzis, and hot tubs on private decks. Room service is available, which is unique in this part of the woods.

See map p. 169. Two miles south of Mendocino on Highway 1, Little River. ☎ **888-INN-LOVE** *or 707-937-5942. Fax: 707-937-3944.* www.littleriverinn.com. *Free parking. Rack rates: $95–$350 double. AE, MC, V.*

MacCallum House Inn
$$–$$$$ **Mendocino**

An attractive mixture of Victorian romance and modern-day amenities (such as wireless Internet access and a popular cocktail lounge) has turned the MacCallum House (remodeled in 2002) into the village hot spot. Guestrooms, some inside the mansion and the rest scattered around the manicured grounds, have DVD players, sleigh beds with down comforters, and private bathrooms. Suites in the barn also include sofa beds if you need extra sleeping space. A trio of young owners — two of whom worked in the highly regarded MacCallum House restaurant as high-schoolers — has infused this historic inn with great energy and attention, and guests can expect a high level of service.

See map p. 169. 45020 Albion St. (between Lansing and Ford streets). ☎ **800-609-0492** *or 707-937-0289. Fax: 707-937-2243.* www.maccallumhouse.com. *Free parking. Rack rates: $150–$295 double, $280–$395 suite. Rates include full breakfast and wine hour. AE, MC. V.*

Mendocino Hotel & Garden Suites
$$–$$$$ **Mendocino**

This 1878 hotel (a leftover from Mendocino's logging days) is a popular choice in the heart of town, especially if the sometimes-stifling intimacy of a B&B isn't your thing. A mix of antiques and reproductions evokes the gold-rush spirit, yet all modern comforts are available. Rooms are spread throughout a 2-block complex; those in the actual hotel aren't equipped with televisions — and some are pretty tiny. Many of the preferable garden rooms feature fireplaces or wood-burning stoves as well as TVs. Avoid rooms in the back over the kitchen, because they can be noisy early in the morning.

See map p. 169. 45080 Main St. (between Kasten and Lansing streets). ☎ *800-548-0513 or 707-937-0511. Fax: 707-937-0513.* www.mendocinohotel.com. *Free parking. Rack rates: $95–$115 double with shared bathroom, $135–$275 double with private bathroom, $265–$395 suite. Rates include morning coffee. AE, MC, V.*

Stanford Inn by the Sea
$$$$–$$$$$ Mendocino

If you intend to spend the big bucks on lodging, this rustic-sophisticated, family-owned and -managed lodge is the place to do so. It sits on extraordinary tiered grounds populated by llamas, horses, and other critters in a woodsy setting near the Big River, a five-minute drive from town. The wood-paneled rooms are done in a supremely comfy California-country style and boast working fireplaces, fridges, and VCRs; the suites are great for families. The grounds feature a gorgeous greenhouse with a lap pool, sauna, and Jacuzzi; a gym; a spa; a fantastic vegetarian restaurant (The Ravens); and canoes and mountain bikes for rent. It's one of the pet-friendliest hotels in California, too. If views are important to you, ask for a room in the original building; if you prefer more square footage, request a room in the newer Forest Building.

See map p. 169. At Highway 1 and Comptche-Ukiah Road. ☎ *800-331-8884 or 707-937-5615. Fax: 707-937-0305.* www.stanfordinn.com. *Free parking. Rack rates: $195–$305 double, $215–$785 one- or two-bedroom suite. Rates include full breakfast, afternoon tea, and evening hors d'oeuvres. AE, DC, DISC, MC, V.*

Where to Dine

Far be it for us to encourage hotel dining, but this area has four quality exceptions. See the hotel listings in the preceding section for contact information.

✔ The **MacCallum House Restaurant** at the MacCallum House Inn is wonderful for breakfast, lunch, or dinner. It's a bit more formal than most restaurants in town, with exemplary service and pleasing continental cuisine with California flair. Main courses run $24 to $37.

✔ Mendocino Hotel's **Victorian Dining Room Restaurant and Garden Café** has kept its historic feel but the cooking is up-to-date. The $49 tasting menu ($65 with wine) is quite the bargain. Otherwise, entrees are from $19 to $38.

✔ Stanford Inn by the Sea also has a pretty dining room, **The Ravens,** which serves creative vegetarian cuisine prepared with organic homegrown veggies; entrees cost $18 to $35.

✔ The **Little River Inn** is the place to eat during crab season in particular, when crab cakes and local Dungeness — steamed, cracked, and served with two dipping sauces — are available. The Mediterranean-influenced menu is well executed; entrees range from $19 to $28.

From mid-November through January, some well-known Mendocino restaurants, including Cafe Beaujolais and the Moosse Café, close for weeks or even months depending on demand. If you're visiting during the winter, phone ahead if you have your heart set on eating in these halls of fame. But don't worry about going hungry if your timing is off — the hotel restaurants serve year-round.

Bay View Cafe
$–$$ Mendocino   AMERICAN

This casual, second-story restaurant serves up just-fine food and excellent views. Expect sandwiches, burgers, home-style breakfasts, and liberal use of the fryer, plus Southwestern-style selections at dinner. This restaurant is hugely popular, especially at breakfast, so anticipate a wait on weekends.

See map p. 169. 45040 Main St. (between Kasten and Lansing streets). ☎ *707-937-4197. No reservations. Main courses: $5–$8 breakfast, $6.50–$15 lunch and dinner. No credit cards. Open: Daily 8 a.m.–3 p.m., and Fri–Sat 7–9 p.m.*

Mendocino Bakery & Cafe
$–$$ Mendocino   CALIFORNIA

Perfect for a quick bite — a slice of pizza, a baked potato, or just coffee and dessert. Settle down at the counter and try to identify who's a local and who's a tourist. Vegetarians have a selection of dishes to choose from, and your dog is welcome at a patio table. You won't find a more laid-back hangout, and the bill won't disrupt your peace of mind.

See map p. 169. 10483 Lansing St. (between Ukiah Street and Little Lake Road). ☎ *707-937-0836. No reservations. Main courses: $2.50–$20. No credit cards. Open: Daily 7:30 a.m.–7:30 p.m.*

Mendocino Cafe
$–$$$ Mendocino   INTERNATIONAL

Popular for its innovative and eclectic menu, this is a great place to choose if you're craving a big delicious salad (the Vietnamese chicken salad is yummy) but your traveling companion wants Mexican or maybe some pasta. The kids — should there be kids involved — will be pleased as well, even if they happen to be picky eaters, for who would turn up their little noses at noodles, chicken wings, or a cheese quesadilla? Plain and casual, with really good cooking, the Mendocino Cafe has the gift of making everyone happy.

See map p. 169. 10451 Lansing St. (between Ukiah Street and Little Lake Road). ☎ *707-937-6141.* www.mendocinocafe.com. *Reservations not needed. Main courses: $12–$26; kids' menu $7–$8. MC, V. Open: Daily 11 a.m.–3.p.m. and 5–9 p.m.*

The Moosse Café
$$–$$$ Mendocino   CALIFORNIA

A bit more informal, and less romantic than its compatriots, this charming restaurant is housed in a simple warren of rooms clad with contemporary art. The short but smart, regularly changing menu features a yummy pasta du jour, an excellent selection of fresh fish, and perhaps a lavender-smoked double pork chop. Prices are relatively moderate for Mendocino.

See map p. 169. In the Blue Heron Inn, 390 Kasten St. (at Albion Street). ☎ *707-937-4323.* www.themoosse.com. *Reservations recommended. Main courses: $18–$27. MC, V. Open: Daily 11:30 a.m.–3:15 p.m. and 5:30–9 p.m.*

Exploring around Mendocino

The primary occupation of most visitors to Mendocino is . . . well, nothing. Most people come to stroll through town, enjoy the charming seacoast vibe, soak up the views, and separate themselves from some of their disposable income.

Sampling the arts (and shops)

Gallery hoppers should head to the visitor center at the Ford House Museum to pick up the *Mendocino Gallery Guide,* which offers a good gallery map. If local lore interests you, visit the **Ford House Museum,** 735 Main St., at the end of Kasten Road (☎ 707-937-5397), and the **Kelley House Museum,** 45007 Albion St., just a few doors down and across Main Street (☎ 707-937-5791), both legacies from Mendocino's 19th-century boomtown days as the logging capital of the North Coast.

A great place to start gallery-hopping is the **Mendocino Art Center,** 45200 Little Lake St., 1 block west of Kasten Street (☎ 707-937-5818), Mendocino's unofficial cultural headquarters. Multiple gallery exhibits are always on display; you can find plenty of art to buy and lovely gardens.

Straightforward shopping highlights include **Mendocino Gift Company,** 321 Kasten St., just off Main Street (☎ 707-937-5298), which features the work of local craftspeople. Also stop in at **Moore Used Books/Main Street Bookshop,** 990A Main St., across from the Presbyterian church (☎ 707-937-1537), a pleasing shop that used-book hounds seek out.

Exploring the headlands

Basically, all the waterfront territory that surrounds town makes up **Mendocino Headlands State Park.** In spring, wildflowers blanket the spectacular area; winter is a great time to watch for California gray whales that cruise close to shore between mid-December and mid-April. Three miles of easy trails wind through the park; stop by the visitor center at the Ford House (described in the preceding section) for an access map. Easiest access is behind Mendocino Presbyterian Church, on Main Street, where a trail leads to stairs that take you down to a small but picturesque beach.

Drive out to Heeser Drive (via Little Lake Road) to reach more remote areas of the park. A number of parking lots along the route lead to short trails and magnificent views along the wild coast, which reminds us very much of Scotland. (Aye!)

Big River Beach, the park's finest stretch of sand, is accessible from the highway just south of Comptche-Ukiah Road. The beach is good for picnicking, walking, and sunbathing, but don't even think about going in the frigid water.

Big River Beach meets the mouth of the Big River, which you can explore via top-sitting kayak or canoe. Double kayaks rent for $20 per hour ($60 for the full day) from **Catch a Canoe & Bicycles, Too!,** just below the Stanford Inn at Highway 1 and Comptche-Ukiah Road (☎ **707-937-0273;** www.stanfordinn.com). They'll also rent you a top-flight mountain bike for $10 per hour ($30 a day).

Visiting Russian Gulch

Several state parks dot the rugged coastline around Mendocino. The best of the bunch is **Russian Gulch State Park** (☎ **707-937-5804** or 707-937-4296; www.parks.ca.gov), located off Highway 1 about 2 miles north of Mendocino. It's more remote and forested than Mendocino Headlands, and quite spectacular. Picnic Area Drive leads right to the park's main attraction, a churning collapsed sea cave with swirling tides called the **Devil's Punchbowl** that's well worth checking out. The well-marked, 3-mile **Falls Loop Trail** is an easy walk through the redwoods to a lovely waterfall. The day-use fee ranges from $4 to $6.

Riding the Skunk Train

Riding the Skunk Train is an easy way to see the redwoods without having to drive yourself. Founded in 1885 as a logging railroad, the **Skunk Trains** (☎ **800-866-1690** or 707-964-6371; www.skunktrain.com) are vintage train cars that take you through gorgeous — and otherwise inaccessible — North Coast redwood territory. (Originally gas powered, the trains emitted a distinctive odor that prompted locals to claim "you can smell 'em before you can see 'em" — hence the name.) The line runs 40 miles between Fort Bragg and Willits to the north. The costs vary by route, season, and the type of train you're riding in (be it steam, diesel, or a motorcar), but generally run between $20 and $45 for adults and $10 to $20 for children. Book summer excursions a month in advance. The depot is west of Main Street between Laurel and Pine streets in downtown Fort Bragg.

Speaking of Fort Bragg . . .

Fort Bragg is the commercial hub of North Coast life (car dealerships, fast-food joints — you get the picture). It's also home to the **Mendocino Coast Botanical Gardens,** 18220 N. Hwy. 1 (☎ **707-964-4352;** www. gardenbythesea.org). This lovely public garden blooms year-round and features gentle trails with terrific ocean views — well worth a couple of hours for green thumbs. Admission is $7.50 for adults, $6 for seniors, $3 for kids 13 to 17, $1 for younger kids. The gardens are open March through October daily from 9 a.m. to 5 p.m., and November through February daily from 9 a.m. to 4 p.m. The main trails are wheelchair accessible.

You can book winter whale-watching excursions and deep-sea fishing charters for tuna, halibut, and salmon at Fort Bragg's Noyo Harbor. Call the **Noyo Fishing Center** (☎ **707-964-3000;** www.fortbraggfishing. com).

Gathering More Information

Before you arrive, call the **Fort Bragg/Mendocino Coast Chamber of Commerce** (☎ **800-726-2780** or 707-961-6300) or point your Web browser to www.mendocinocoast.com. You can visit the chamber's walk-in center in Fort Bragg at 332 N. Main St. (Highway 1), between Laurel and Redwood streets, across from the Guest House Museum. For other online information, the Mendocino County Alliance gives an excellent overview of the area on its Web site at www.gomendo.com.

In Mendocino, stop at the **Ford House Museum,** on the ocean side of Main Street near Kasten (☎ **707-937-5397**). Free publications and maps are available at shops and restaurants around town, and your hotel can also supply you with a wealth of information.

For more information on Mendocino's state parks, visit the official California State Parks Web site at www.parks.ca.gov; follow the "Find a Park" link to search for parks by name, county, region, or even activity. At the visitor center, ask for a copy of the *Mendocino Coastal Parks Guide,* an informative newspaper well worth the 25¢ price tag.

Chapter 14

Redwood Country

- -

In This Chapter

▶ Deciding on the length of your visit

▶ Separating the trees from the cheese along the Avenue of the Giants

▶ Finding a place to stay and dining among the redwoods

- -

*Y*ou need not drive all the way up to **Redwood National and State Parks,** in the far reaches of Northern California near the Oregon border, to experience the state's giant redwoods. Frankly, by the time you get there, some 300 miles north of San Francisco, you'll have already seen enough of the towering trees to last a long while. A day excursion from Mendocino (see Chapter 13) that takes you partway up the famed **Avenue of the Giants** — or a trip that incorporates one night in Mendocino with a second night farther north along the route — provides plenty of exposure to the majestic trees. The Avenue of the Giants is a 32-mile scenic byway that follows a portion of the old two-lane Highway 101, and parallels the modern freeway (as well as the Eel River) from Phillipsville at the south end to Pepperwood at the north. The "giants" are the magnificent coast redwoods, the tallest trees on Earth, which often exceed 300 feet in height. These trees are the longer, lankier cousins to the stout giant sequoias of the Sierra Nevadas. The Avenue is a relatively easy drive, curvaceous but not too challenging, that passes through some of the most spectacular territory in California. If you drive to **Humboldt Redwoods State Park** (roughly the midpoint of the route), you'll witness the largest stand of virgin redwoods in the world.

Unfortunately, you won't see just pristine nature. Tourist traps blight the route, peppering the gorgeous highway with a schlocky sideshow. From drive-through trees to a statue of Bigfoot, many of the attractions feel like leftovers from the Eisenhower era — a '50s B-movie that's lost its kitschy kick. The good news is that the sheer majesty of the trees makes stomaching this cheesiness easy.

Refer to the "Mendocino and Redwood Country" map in Chapter 13 to get your bearings and locate accommodations, dining, and attractions in Redwood Country.

That being said, we don't want to pay short shrift to the remainder of the state. Should you have a desire to explore past Eureka, Highway 101 plays tag with the Pacific above Humboldt Bay through the Redwood

National and State Park to Crescent City. You'll find miles of sandy beaches, tide pools, hiking trails galore, elk herds roaming around Prairie Creek Redwoods State Park (just above the town of Orick, 45 minutes north of Eureka), and a lovely 10-mile drive along the coast and within the redwoods on the Newton Drury Scenic Parkway.

Timing Your Visit

Whether you visit the Avenue of the Giants on a day trip or stretch this part of your holiday into an overnighter, try to set aside plenty of daylight hours to truly appreciate the mammoth redwoods.

Day-tripping from Mendocino

You can make the Avenue of the Giants a day trip from Mendocino, leaving in the morning and returning for dinnertime. (This timetable works best in summer, when you have more daylight hours to enjoy.)

You don't have to follow the entire route to get an eyeful of the tall trees. You can stop for lunch at a number of towns along the way; getting back on U.S. 101 is easy at about a half-dozen points if you tire of the meandering roadway. If you have good day-trip stamina, you can travel as far as **Humboldt Redwoods State Park** and back in a day, with time to stop for some communing with nature. The drive is just less than 100 miles (two and a half hours in each direction, not counting stops).

If that sounds like too much for you, just go as far as **Richardson Grove State Park,** off Highway 101 before the start of the Avenue, about 68 miles (one and a half to two hours) north of Mendocino. This park makes a great place to discover the coastal redwoods, which serve as the area's main tourist attraction. Also, the first leg of the drive takes you past some spectacular coastline. Beyond the park lies more of the same, with one-horse logging towns and souvenir stands thrown in. However, you find some marvelous pristine stretches if you venture farther, with pullouts to hiking trails and day-use areas.

 Because pickings are slim along the route, putting together a picnic lunch at **Mendocino Market** or **Tote Fête,** 10450 Lansing St., at Albion Street, before you leave Mendocino is a good idea, especially if you'd like more than a grilled-cheese sandwich from a lunch counter. Or stop off in Fort Bragg at the excellent **Harvest Market,** 171 Boatyard Dr., where Highway 1 meets Highway 20, which has a gourmet deli and a sushi bar. The drive presents plenty of picnic spots from which to choose.

Finding options for overnighters

If you want to spend more time among the trees, you can (see the "Where to Stay along the Route" section later in this chapter). If you want to take it slow, consider setting aside a full day to meander north from Mendocino and up the Avenue of the Giants; then stay in a Ferndale or Eureka B&B for a night (it's 134 miles to Ferndale, 145 to Eureka). In the morning, hop on U.S. 101 for a speedy return south.

 If your goal is the redwoods and you don't care about the coast — or someone in your party forgot her Dramamine and Highway 1 just isn't going to cut it — skip Mendocino altogether. The weather is much warmer and sunnier inland, and you save time and energy (not to mention a few bucks on accommodations) by sticking to U.S. 101 for northern destinations. Garberville makes a great southern base (especially the comfy **Benbow Inn;** see review later in this chapter) if you follow this strategy. You can also zip your way to the top, stay in Eureka or Ferndale, and meander down the Avenue the next day. Driving the route northbound presents no particular advantage.

Getting There

From Mendocino, follow Highway 1 north along the shoreline to Leggett, where you'll pick up U.S. 101 (the Redwood Highway) northbound. The distance to Leggett is about 53 miles, with the first 30 or so winding along the coast; the scenery becomes truly spectacular after you pass through Fort Bragg. It's slow going, so be prepared. Pick up U.S. 101, and 15 miles later you'll reach **Richardson Grove State Park.** The Garberville exit is another 8½ miles. Six miles beyond Garberville you can pick up the southern end of the Avenue of the Giants, formally known as Highway 254.

If you're bypassing Mendocino and coming from the south, take speedy U.S. 101 all the way north to the Avenue of the Giants exit at Phillipsville (6 miles north of Garberville). This exit is 211 miles from San Francisco straight up the 101, 158 miles from Calistoga (at the north end of Napa Valley) via Highway 128 to U.S. 101.

Driving the Avenue of the Giants

You can see the following highlights as you proceed north on the Redwood Highway, U.S. 101, picking up the Avenue of the Giants, Highway 254, at its southernmost gateway. Much more of both the sublime and the obscure lie on the route: unspoiled woodland stretches with pullouts that lead to wonderful hiking trails and day-use areas in the woods, plus all those silly attractions. Watch for any number of one-horse towns along the road, where you can stop to buy a casual lunch or a carved hunk of redwood.

✔ At the junction of Highway 1 and U.S. 101 sits the **Chandelier Tree Drive-Thru Tree Park** in Leggett (☎ **707-925-6363**), the first of many such attractions on the Redwood Highway. Other corn-pone variations along the route include the "world-famous" treehouse and the one-log house, which has been mounted on wheels and hauled to Garberville. If you're doing the cheeky Roadside Americana version of this tour, don't worry about missing any.

Each attraction sports a massive sign that's more attention-getting than a 10-foot-tall carnival barker.

Lest you think this drive-through tree business is anything natural, Chandelier will dispel that notion right quick. Sometime back in the 1930s, somebody cut a car-size hole in the base of a mammoth redwood, and now you pay five bucks for the right to drive your car through. This cheesy activity is not really worth the $5, but if you're curious, this is as good a place as any to get it out of your system. And we defy you to bypass it with a small child in your car.

✔ Any itinerary should include a visit to **Richardson Grove State Park,** 15 miles north of Leggett (7 miles south of Garberville) on U.S. 101 (☎ **707-247-3318** or 707-247-3415; www.parks.ca.gov). Here's where things really start to get good. The park includes a terrific visitor center with a grocery store and a handy shop, where you can pick up maps and pamphlets covering the entire region. A short (ten-minute) interpretive loop offers an excellent introduction to the towering trees, complete with explanatory placards. More extensive trails include an easy 1.6-mile woodland loop; stop in at the staffed center for a map. The day-use fee is $6.

✔ Even if you're not staying at the Benbow Inn, the adjacent **Benbow Lake State Recreation Area** (☎ **707-247-3318** or 707-923-3238; www.parks.ca.gov) makes an excellent stop for picnicking, sunning, and lake swimming in summer, and includes grassy areas and a rocky beach. The dining room over at the Benbow Inn (see the "Where to Stay along the Route" section in this chapter) makes a good stop for lunch (served in summer only).

✔ About 14½ miles from Phillipsville, the first access point for the Avenue of the Giants is **Humboldt Redwoods State Park** (☎ **707-946-2263;** www.humboldtredwoods.org). Much larger than Richardson Grove, this 53,000-acre park is the real heart of the Avenue. Humboldt Redwoods features the Redwood Highway's main visitor center, plus 100 miles of hiking trails. You can pick up a trail map in the visitor center. If you plan to spend some serious time here, check out the extensive Web site. The day-use parking fee is $6.

✔ About 2 miles north of the visitor center, still in Humboldt Redwoods State Park, is **Founders Grove,** one of the most impressive redwood groves in the region. Its name honors the enlightened folks who founded the Save-the-Redwoods League way back in 1917. A gentle, half-mile interpretive loop meanders through the grove. This walk is an enjoyable introduction to coast redwood ecology, and also takes you past the **Dyerville Giant** — a 370-foot monster of a tree that was designated the "Champion Coast Redwood" before it fell over a decade ago. Here it remains, lying on the forest floor, its root ball alone measuring three stories long.

Where to Stay along the Route

If you want to spend quality time among the redwoods, you have a few choices that offer good places to stay. **Garberville** remains a charm-free bend in the road off Highway 101 near the southern gateway of the Avenue of the Giants. The town is perfectly serviceable if you'd like to skip the coastline altogether and head straight for the trees. You can also stop here for a bite of lunch (see the "Where to Dine along the Route" section later in this chapter).

The tiny but stately burg of **Ferndale** presents a picture-perfect ginger-bread slice of authentic Victoriana just past the north end of the drive. A visit to the town is well worth the 5-mile detour off U.S. 101.

Eureka is about 45 miles north of the Avenue's northern gateway. The largest town on the North Coast doesn't look like much at first glance, but if you turn west off U.S. 101 between B and M streets, you'll discover a charming Victorian Old Town along the waterfront.

For more choices, contact the visitors bureau (see the "Gathering More Information" section at the end of this chapter), whose Web site offers an excellent rundown of options throughout the area.

Hotel taxes in this neck of the woods vary; count on 7.9 to 10 percent being tacked on to your bill at checkout time.

Benbow Inn
$$–$$$$ Garberville

This wonderful Tudor-style hotel is tucked away in the woods on swim-mable Benbow Lake. The appealing Americana-style rooms vary from petite to grand, but all are homey and comfy with pretty, tiled bathrooms; some have VCRs, pullout sofas, terraces, and/or fireplaces. The hotel has lovely lakefront grounds, a terrace restaurant, and attentive service. All in all, it's a great value — and an ideal place to base yourself as you frolic among the redwoods. The dining room specializes in fresh regional cuisine and offers a children's menu.

See map p. 169. 445 Lake Benbow Dr. (off Highway 101). ☎ *800-355-3301 or 707-923-2124. Fax: 707-923-2897.* www.benbowinn.com. *Free parking. Rack rates: $130–$305 double, $375–385 cottage. Rates include afternoon tea and scones and evening hors d'oeuvres. Closed Jan–Mar. AE, DISC, MC, V.*

Carter House Victorians
$$$ Eureka

This grand collection of Victorians is well-situated in Eureka's Old Town. Let price and taste dictate your booking, which may be in the magnificent Carter House mansion, which also houses the highly regarded **Restaurant 301**; the full-service Hotel Carter; or one of two quaint cottages. No matter which you choose, you can count on impeccable accommodations, plush bedding, and terry robes — the works.

See map p. 169. 301 L St. (at Third Street). ☎ *800-404-1390 or 707-444-8062. Fax: 707-444-8067.* www.carterhouse.com. *Free parking. Rack rates: $155–$193 double, $250–$326 suite, $497 cottage. Rates include two-course breakfast and evening wine and hors d'oeuvres. AE, DC, DISC, MC, V.*

Gingerbread Mansion Inn
$$$–$$$$ Ferndale

In a town of pristinely preserved Victorian homes, the Gingerbread Mansion stands head and shoulders above the rest. It has been exquisitely restored and furnished in high Victorian style. Each of the 11 unique rooms includes a private bathroom (some with claw-foot tub and/or a fireplace; one with two claw-foot tubs!) and luxurious extras such as plush bathrobes and turndown service. Honeymooners (or even would-be honeymooners) may want to blow the budget and book the Empire Suite, probably the most over-the-top room we've visited.

See map p. 169. 400 Berding St. (use the Fernbridge/Ferndale exit off U.S. 101 and go 5 miles). ☎ *800-952-4136 or 707-786-4000.* www.gingerbread-mansion.com. *Free parking. Rack rates: $100–$225 double, $155–$400 suite. Rates include full breakfast and afternoon tea. AE, MC, V.*

Where to Dine along the Route

This area is not quite a gourmet ghetto, but you can dine supremely well if you like. The Carter House dining room, **Restaurant 301** (entrees $20–$35), regularly receives *Wine Spectator* awards, as does the restaurant at the Benbow Inn (see information for both in the preceding section). Here are a couple more recommended dining choices.

Avalon
$$–$$$ Eureka CALIFORNIA/FRENCH

A refugee from the nerve-wracking San Francisco restaurant scene, Avalon's owner, Beverley Wolfe, remodeled a historic building in Eureka's old town and opened a sophisticated bistro. The Avalon showcases the works of local artists on the walls and often local jazz musicians on the CD player, but the delicious food takes a back seat to neither. If it's on the seasonal menu, you can't go wrong with the grilled local lamb chops or a filet mignon cooked rare with a generous dollop of hollandaise. The bar area is comfy and inviting; the tables are set far enough apart to allow for intimate conversation.

See map p. 169. Third and G streets. ☎ *707-445-0500.* www.geocities.com/ avaloneureka. *Reservations recommended on weekends. Main courses: $22–$28. MC, V. Open: Tues–Sat cocktails and appetizers from 4:30 p.m., dinner from 5:30 p.m.*

The Groves Restaurant
$$ Myers Flat SOUTHERN FRENCH

Located inside the Riverbend Cellars tasting room, about a 15-minute drive north of Garberville, is this surprisingly sophisticated cafe (we are, after all, in the middle of the woods). Opened in the spring of 2005, this welcome addition to the neighborhood features wood-fired pizzas, sandwiches, and salads for lunch. Dinner guests may find Alaskan salmon in season, steaks, the popular pizzas, and our favorite, lamb chops dressed up with a cherry *demi-glace*. The class cally trained chef sources as much local meat, produce, and fish as possible. Riverbend Cellars' wines may be sampled (there's a $4.50 tasting fee) until 6 p.m. and you may find just the right vintage to enhance your meal.

See map p. 169. 13065 Avenue of the Giants. ☎ 707-943-9930. Reservations accepted. Main courses: Lunch $9–$15, dinner $26–$32. AE, DISC, MC, V. Open: Thurs–Mon 11:30 a.m.–3 p.m., 5–9 p.m. Closed Jan–Mar.

Woodrose Cafe
$ Garberville HEALTHY

Sure, it's Garberville, but you don't have to go hungry. This small diner is a haven for tasty sandwiches, soups, salads, and, if your timing is right, breakfast. Organic ingredients are used when possible, vegans are catered to, and this is the place to go to get a good look at the locals. It's Humboldt County at its purest.

See map p. 169. 911 Redwood Dr. (the main street in town). ☎ 707-923-3191. www. woodrosecafe.com. *No reservations. Main courses: $4.95–$6.95. No credit cards. Open: Mon–Fri 8 a.m.–2:30 p.m., Sat–Sun 8 a.m.–1 p.m.*

Gathering More Information

Your best bet for area information is to contact the **Eureka! Humboldt County Convention and Visitors Bureau** (☎ **800-346-3482** or 707-443-5097; www.redwoodvisitor.org).

For more on the region's state parks, including campground information, visit the official California State Parks Web site at www.parks.ca.gov and follow the "Find a Park" link.

The main visitor center is midway along the route, at **Humboldt Redwoods State Park** (☎ **707-946-2409**), 2 miles south of Weott (near the Burlington Campground) and 20 miles north of Garberville, but you can get any maps you'll need at **Richardson Grove State Park.**

Chapter 15

Lake Tahoe

● ●

In This Chapter

▶ Deciding when to visit, where to go, and how long to stay

▶ Finding the perfect places to dine and dream

▶ Getting active on shore — and out on the water — in any season

▶ Mixing it up with lady luck at the casinos

▶ Stepping back in time with a side trip to the Gold Country

▶ Making a fast getaway to Sacramento, California's capital city

● ●

*I*f you're looking for the Golden State's biggest and best playground, look no further — you've found it. When we Californians — who have more than our fair share of beautiful places to visit — want to get outside and ski, snowmobile, boat, hike, mountain-bike, ride horseback, fish, kayak, or jet-ski (the list goes on), we go to Tahoe.

Lake Tahoe isn't just any old hole in the ground; it's one of the more spectacular bodies of water in the world, and definitely one of the most beautiful that we've ever seen. Tahoe is the largest alpine lake in North America — 22 miles long and 12 miles wide, with a surface area of nearly 192 square miles, which means it can hold about a half-dozen Manhattans (the *borough,* darling, not the cocktail).

To refer to it as "sparkling" barely does this crystalline lake justice. Science even has an explanation for it: The water is 99.9 percent pure, about the same purity as distilled water. It's so clear that a white dinner plate resting 75 feet below the surface would be visible to the naked eye. What's more, Lake Tahoe is the eighth-deepest lake in the world; it holds so much water that, if you tipped it on its side, the contents would flood the entire state of California to a depth of 14 inches.

Evergreens and snowy peaks rising from the shoreline make the lake look that much deeper, broader, and majestic. But don't just take our word for it; listen to Mark Twain, who described Lake Tahoe as "the beautiful relic of fairy-land forgotten." Although Tahoe certainly isn't forgotten anymore, Twain's flight of fancy continues to hold true.

Timing Your Visit

When's the best time to visit? Simple: Come in winter if cross-country or alpine skiing is your game. This is also the time, at least during the week, when you'll have Tahoe to yourself. Otherwise, come in summer. Or try autumn, the secret season in Tahoe. The colors are beautiful, the air is crisp, activities abound, and hotel rates are low, low, low. Skip yucky spring altogether. The snowmelt turns the terrain into mud.

Even in summer, prepare yourself for cool weather. In July, average highs don't hit the 80s, and evenings can dip well below 50°F. And because the upper 12 feet of the lake warms only to about 68°F, don't expect to splash around in your floaties. Chances are, it'll be all you can do to dip your toes in.

 Tahoe is a favorite weekend getaway among San Franciscans, so you'll always save money — and, even more important, avoid the crowds — by scheduling your stay for Monday through Thursday.

Three nights in Tahoe will give you plenty of time to fully explore the area and play. If you cut your stay back to two, you risk spending too much time in the car (getting there and leaving), and not enough time in Tahoe. Budget four nights if you want to experience both shores. For more on this topic, check out the following section.

Choosing between Two Shores

The 30-mile drive between Lake Tahoe's north and south shores can become a two-hour bumper-to-bumper (or snowstormy) nightmare in the high seasons, so choose your shore carefully. Both boast first-rate skiing, good restaurants, lake views, and plenty of on-the-water fun — but that's pretty much where the similarities end.

South Lake Tahoe is more developed and generally cheaper; more hotels mean more competition, so you'll get better accommodations for your money. The big Nevada casinos are at hand (in town for all intents and purposes), so this is the shore for nightlife. Getting out on the water is easier from the south shore, too, because it boasts more marinas, more outfitters, plus some excellent shoreline state parks not far from town.

If Mark Twain could wax poetic about today's Tahoe, he'd write about the north shore. **North Lake Tahoe** is much, much prettier than its southern shore. It's more remote and countrylike, with a variety of ski resorts and first-class accommodations — but you can still find slot machines close by if you feel the urge. **Squaw Valley**, 6 miles from the lakeshore, is one of the best outdoor recreation centers ever, poised to become a one-stop destination, with its alpine-style village. **Tahoe City** is not as commercially spoiled as South Lake Tahoe, but it's way too crowded for its own good in the high seasons. And if affordability is a concern, you won't get as much value for your dollar here.

Although we prefer the north shore, skiers find either one convenient. Our best advice: Avoid the weekends and *never* drive to Tahoe on a Friday afternoon unless you want to sit in traffic on a two-lane highway with no escape. On weekdays, you'll also have an opportunity to enjoy the wonderful drive along Highway 89 at an easy pace so that you can investigate both shores for yourself.

Getting There

Lake Tahoe straddles the California/Nevada border, a four-hour drive east (slightly northeast, actually) from San Francisco. Here's how to get there:

✔ **If you're coming from San Francisco:** Take I-80 east to Sacramento, then U.S. 50 to South Lake Tahoe on the south shore, or stay on I-80 east to Highway 89 south to reach Tahoe City on the north shore.

✔ **If you're coming from Yosemite:** Take Highway 120 east out of the park to I-395 north to U.S. 50 east; at the U.S. 50/Highway 28 split, follow U.S. 50 to South Lake Tahoe, or Highway 28 to Tahoe City on the north shore.

The three-and-a-half-hour drive from Yosemite is doable only between late June and the first snowfall (usually early November), because the park's east gate closes in winter. Otherwise, the drive becomes a five- or six-hour trek north on winding Highway 49 to I-50, which can be slow going in bad weather.

✔ **If you're coming from points south:** Take I-5 through central California to Sacramento, and then pick up I-80 east to the north shore or U.S. 50 east to the south shore.

Whether you take I-80 to the north shore or U.S. 50 to the south shore, you can easily work in a side trip to the Gold Country on your way to Tahoe. All you need is a few hours to spare and the desire to see some small towns; for details, see the "Side-Tripping to the Gold Country" section later in this chapter. The same goes for Sacramento, our state capital, where you can spend a day steeping yourself in history or walking in the footsteps of Governor *Ahhnold;* see the "Prospecting for History in Sacramento" section later in this chapter.

✔ **If you're heading to Squaw Valley:** Follow Highway 89 (River Road) at the 89/28 split in Tahoe City. Go 5 miles and turn left at Squaw Valley Road.

Reno/Tahoe International Airport is at U.S. 395 just south of I-80 in Reno, Nevada (☎ 775-328-6400; www.renoairport.com). All the national car-rental companies have airport locations. The drive takes

Lake Tahoe

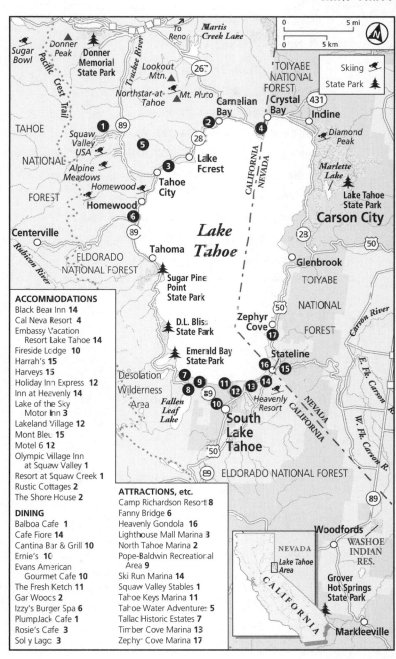

ACCOMMODATIONS
Black Bear Inn **14**
Cal Neva Resort **4**
Embassy Vacation
 Resort Lake Tahoe **14**
Fireside Lodge **10**
Harrah's **15**
Harveys **15**
Holiday Inn Express **12**
Inn at Heavenly **14**
Lake of the Sky
 Motor Inn **3**
Lakeland Village **12**
Mont Bleu **15**
Motel 6 **12**
Olympic Village Inn
 at Squaw Valley **1**
Resort at Squaw Creek **1**
Rustic Cottages **2**
The Shore House **2**

DINING
Balboa Cafe **1**
Cafe Fiore **14**
Cantina Bar & Grill **10**
Ernie's **10**
Evans American
 Gourmet Cafe **10**
The Fresh Ketch **11**
Gar Woods **2**
Izzy's Burger Spa **6**
PlumpJack Cafe **1**
Rosie's Cafe **3**
Sol y Lago **3**

ATTRACTIONS, etc.
Camp Richardson Resort **8**
Fanny Bridge **6**
Heavenly Gondola **16**
Lighthouse Mall Marina **3**
North Tahoe Marina **2**
Pope-Baldwin Recreational
 Area **9**
Ski Run Marina **14**
Squaw Valley Stables **1**
Tahoe Keys Marina **11**
Tahoe Water Adventures **5**
Tallac Historic Estates **7**
Timber Cove Marina **13**
Zephyr Cove Marina **17**

50 minutes to Tahoe City on the north shore; take U.S. 395 north to I-80 west to Highway 89 south. For South Lake Tahoe, take U.S. 395 south to U.S. 50 west, a 70-minute drive.

These airlines fly into Reno/Tahoe:

- ✓ **Alaska Airlines:** ☎ **800-426-0333;** www.alaska-air.com

- ✓ **Aloha Airlines:** ☎ **800-367-5250;** www.alohaairlines.com

- ✓ **American:** ☎ **800-433-7300;** www.aa.com

- ✓ **Continental:** ☎ **800-525-0280;** www.continental.com

- ✓ **Delta Connection/Skywest:** ☎ **800-453-9417;** www.skywest.com

- ✓ **Frontier Airlines:** ☎ **800-432-1359;** www.flyfrontier.com

- ✓ **Horizon Air:** ☎ **800-547-9308;** www.horizonair.com

- ✓ **Northwest:** ☎ **800-225-2525;** www.nwa.com

- ✓ **Southwest:** ☎ **800-435-9792;** www.southwest.com

- ✓ **United:** ☎ **800-241-6522;** www.united.com

- ✓ **US Airways:** ☎ **800-428-4322;** www.usairwaysinfo.com

Getting Your Bearings

On the south shore, two main highways meet at a prominent *Y* intersection in South Lake Tahoe: U.S. 50, which continues up the east (Nevada) shore of the lake to midpoint and then shoots off east; and Highway 89, which runs up the west (California) side of the lake to Tahoe City, and then turns northwest away from the lake. Highway 28 picks up where 89 leaves off, running along the north shore from Tahoe City to midpoint on the Nevada side, where it meets up with U.S. 50, completing the continuous 72-mile circle around the lake. (To get your visual bearings, look for the "Lake Tahoe" map on p. 187.)

Lake Tahoe's biggest town is South Lake Tahoe, which runs along the south shore. Its main drag is U.S. 50, which is called Lake Tahoe Boulevard in town. After you cross the California/Nevada line, you're immediately in Stateline, Nevada. It's easy to tell: The casinos practically trip you after your toes pass over the border.

Follow Highway 89 about 31 miles north along the west shore, past camplike resorts and stunning lakefront homes, and you reach Tahoe City, the commercial hub of the north shore. Go 6 miles northwest on Highway 89 to breathtaking Squaw Valley, whose thriving Olympic Village was built for the 1960 Winter Games.

Along with a few other casino/hotels, another prominent community sits on the northeast shore, Nevada's Incline Village. But we've concentrated on the California side because we're partisans — this *is* a book about California, after all.

Where to Stay

For additional choices throughout the region, contact **Lake Tahoe Central Reservations** (☎ 888-434-1262 or 530-583-3494; www.mytahoevacation. com). The service charges $15 to $20 to make your reservations, and you won't get the best room prices, but the staff is knowledgeable. You can also try **TahoeReservations.com** (www.tahoereservations.com), a free, real-time service that specializes in South Tahoe. For ski packages, contact **Ski Tahoe** (☎ 888-982-1088; www.skitahoe.com).

Expect to see 10 to 12 percent in taxes added to your hotel bill.

On the south shore

The big-name casinos at Stateline, Nevada, resemble unattractive office complexes, and display none of the outrageousness of Las Vegas, but they offer gaming, entertainment, and amenities such as indoor pools and spa facilities. They're fairly similar in middle-of-the-road comforts and prices, which can range from $69 to $289 and up depending on the day and season. These places thrive on packages, so always ask.

- ✔ **Harrah's** (☎ 800-427-7247 or 775-588-6611; www.harrahs.com/ our_casinos/tah) is attractive and low-key, comparatively speaking, and appeals to a slightly less raucous vacationer.

- ✔ **Harveys** (☎ 800-427-8397 or 775-588-2411; www.harrahs.com) is the rock-'n'-roll casino and draws a young, sophisticated crowd.

- ✔ **MontBleu** (☎ 800-648-3353 or 775-588-3515; www.montbleu resort.com) recently replaced the mighty tired Caesars and has brought contemporary glamour to the area.

In addition to the more unique choices detailed in the following listings, South Lake Tahoe also has some excellent-value motels:

- ✔ **Holiday Inn Express,** 3961 Lake Tahoe Blvd. (☎ 800-544-5288 or 530-544-5900; www.holidayinnexpresstahoe.com), has high-quality rooms and is tucked among the trees to ensure quiet. Rooms, including continental breakfast, run $69 to $209, family-size suites $149 to $269.

- ✔ **Motel 6,** 2375 Lake Tahoe Blvd. (☎ 800-466-8356 or 530-542-1400; www.motel6.com), is the best motel value in town for penny-pinching travelers. Rooms run $30 to $105.

Black Bear Inn
$$$$ South Lake Tahoe

Wow! This stunning lodgelike B&B looks like it rambled straight out of a Ralph Lauren advertisement, complete with gleaming knotty-pine woodwork, bearskins, and a two-story river-stone fireplace in the soaring living room. Extraordinary craftsmanship, witty rustic-goes-chic décor, beautifully outfitted rooms (gorgeous bathrooms!), lots of lounging space, and charming hosts add up to the most gracious place to stay on the south shore, period. Geared toward adults and kids older than 16.

See map p. 187. 1202 Ski Run Blvd. ☎ *877-232-7466 or 530-544-4451.* www.tahoe blackbear.com. *Free parking. Rack rates: $200–$320 double; $260–$525 cabin. Rates include full breakfast. AE, MC, V.*

Fireside Lodge
$$ South Lake Tahoe

Recently renovated, these nine tidy little country-pine suites are cozy (read: small), but equipped with kitchenettes, gas fireplaces, and TV/VCRs. Owned and operated by a local family (who also owns the Inn at Heavenly), the location is unbeatable — close to some great restaurants and the marvelous facilities of Camp Richardson, but far enough from the main drag to keep your mind on the mountains. Dogs and kids are most welcome. The staff even lends you bicycles, kayaks, float tubes, and videos.

See map p. 187. 515 Emerald Bay Rd. ☎ *800-692-2246 or 530-544-5515.* www.tahoe firesidelodge.com. *Free parking. Rack rates: $89–$159 double. Rates include continental breakfast. AE, DISC, MC, V.*

Inn at Heavenly
$$–$$$ South Lake Tahoe

These upscale motel rooms are low-ceilinged and teensy, but they're decorated in a dreamy-cute wooden-beam style, each with a gas fireplace, VCR, ceiling fan, and kitchenette with microwave, fridge, and coffeemaker. Swings and picnic sets dot the lovely grounds. Amenities include steam room and sauna, warm-hearted innkeepers, and a cozy common room with games and videos. It's pet-friendly, so bring Fido.

See map p. 187. 1261 Ski Run Blvd. (downhill from Heavenly Mountain Resort). ☎ *800-692-2246 or 530-544-4244. Fax: 530-544-5213.* www.inn-at-heavenly.com. *Free parking. Rack rates: $135–$155 double, $165–$495 cabin (sleeps 8 to 12). Rates include expanded continental breakfast and snacks. AE, DISC, MC, V.*

Lake Tahoe Vacation Resort
$$–$$$$ South Lake Tahoe

Skip the bland Embassy Suites hotel at Stateline and book this lakefront condo resort instead. The sun-filled suites are gorgeously decorated in subdued Southwest colors and high-quality everything. Each one comes with a cute balcony and a fully equipped kitchenette or kitchen. This hotel offers an excellent indoor/outdoor pool, pretty grounds, exercise room, video-game room, coin-op laundry, and far more style and value for your dollar than you'd expect. A winner!

See map p. 187. 901 Ski Run Blvd. ☎ *800-438-2929 or 530-541-6122. Fax: 530-541-2028.* www.sunterraresorts.com. *Free parking. Rack rates: $135–$510 studio, one- and two-bedroom suites (one-bedroom suite from $160, two-bedroom suite from $200). AE, DISC, MC, V.*

On the north shore

Shooting craps actually gives us hives — unless we're winning — but one more casino straddling the north-shore border merits mention. Once owned by Frank Sinatra (until the gaming authorities intervened), the **Cal Neva Resort,** 2 Stateline Rd., Crystal Bay, Nevada (☎ **800-CAL-NEVA** or 775-832-4000; www.calnevaresort.com; $129–$249 double), is our personal choice for a Tahoe gambling den. Though the others are much flashier and have more gaming tables, the Cal Neva offers some history and a little soul, and the spacious guest rooms have glorious lake views.

Lake of the Sky Motor Inn
$–$$ Tahoe City

This '60s-era motel is a walk from restaurants, but far enough from the tourist fray to offer some measure of peace. Expect only the basics, but rooms (all nonsmoking) have been recently remodeled, beds are firm, housekeeping is neat, and beamed ceilings add a lodgelike touch. The lake-view rooms include fridges. The friendly owners keep the coffeepot on all day. The motel offers a pool and free local calls, too.

See map p. 187. 955 N. Lake Blvd. (Highway 28). ☎ *530-583-3305. Fax: 530-583-7621. Free parking. Rack rates: $69–$139 double. Rates include continental breakfast. AE, DC, DISC, MC, V.*

Olympic Village Inn at Squaw Valley
$$–$$$$$ Squaw Valley

This Swiss-chalet-style all-suite hotel is the best value in the gorgeous Olympic Valley. The suites sleep four, are attractively done in a country accent, and boast fully equipped minikitchens, VCRs, and stereos. The lovely grounds are a stone's throw from Squaw Valley USA activities. Timeshare owners get first dibs, so call early; your best bet is to book a midweek stay.

See map p. 187. 1909 Chamonix Place (off Squaw Valley Road). ☎ *800-845-5243 or 530-581-6000. Fax: 530-583-4165.* www.olympicvillageinn.com. *Free parking. Rack rates: $149–$349 one-bedroom suite. AE, DISC, MC, V.*

Resort at Squaw Creek
$$$–$$$$$ Squaw Valley

This 626-acre destination resort was built to take prime advantage of the valley and forest views. Now, after a multimillion-dollar renovation, the rooms are up to par with the location and the unparalleled facilities, which include a wonderful pool complex, spa, first-rate dining, golf, tennis, biking, cross-country ski center, ice-skating in season, private chairlift at Squaw Valley USA, great kids' program, and more.

See map p. 187. 400 Squaw Creek Rd. ☎ 800-327-3353 or 530-583-6300. Fax: 530-581-6632. www.squawcreek.com. *Parking: $15 to valet, free self-parking. Rack rates: $199–$549 double, $249–$849 suite, $399–$2,000 penthouse; off-season rates are lower. AE, DC, DISC, MC, V.*

Rustic Cottages
$–$$$ Tahoe Vista

Originally converted in 1925 from sawmill company housing to holiday duty, these 19 stand-alone cottages have an authentic Tahoe aura. Within walking distance to some nice beaches (and the local Safeway), it's a convenient location for a family vacation: The larger one-bedroom cabins can accommodate up to six people. All the cabins contain microwave ovens, fridges, coffeemakers, and TVs with DVD players; the bigger ones have fireplaces. The friendly staff will help with directions and advice, and you can borrow bikes in the summer and snowshoes and sleds in the winter. Although we think it's perfect for a homey getaway, this isn't a luxury resort. If that's what you're after, head to Squaw Valley.

See map p. 187. 7449 N. Lake Blvd. (Highway 28). ☎ 530-546-3523. Fax: 530-546-0146. Free parking. Rack rates: $59–$169 studio cottage, $139–$199 one-bedroom cottage. Rates include continental breakfast and afternoon treats. MC, V.

The Shore House
$$$–$$$$ Tahoe Vista

A great choice for lakefront amour, this wonderful B&B is 15 minutes from Tahoe City in gorgeous, upscale Tahoe Vista. The rustic-romantic rooms are built for two and have private entrances, knotty-pine walls, cuddly Scandia down comforters on custom-built log beds, gas fireplaces, and TVs and CD players. The B&B offers a new massage studio (with views), a sandy beach next door with kayaks to rent, lots of restaurants nearby, welcoming and attentive innkeepers, and plenty of lake-facing lounge spaces — including a lakeside hot tub.

See map p. 187. 7170 North Lake Blvd. ☎ 800-207-5160 or 530-546-7270. Fax: 530-546-7130. www.shorehouselaketahoe.com. *Rack rates: $190–$290 double. Rates include delicious full breakfast and evening wine and appetizers. DISC, MC, V.*

Where to Dine

Tahoe is at full capacity most weekends, so book Friday and Saturday dinners in advance to avoid disappointment.

On the south shore

Cafe Fiore
$$$ South Lake Tahoe ITALIAN

A low-profile but top-notch restaurant, Cafe Fiore's dining room is rustic yet lovely, with just seven white-linen-dressed tables, plus a handful more on the alfresco terrace in summer. The creative Italian fare is prepared with culinary expertise and care; the garlic bread alone is enough to bring us back, begging for more. A regular winner of the *Wine Spectator* Award of Excellence, this restaurant is ultraromantic and simply divine.

See map p. 187. 1169 Ski Run Blvd. #5 (between U.S. 50 and Pioneer Trail). ☎ *530-541-2908.* www.cafefiore.com. *Reservations highly recommended. Main courses: $16–$32. AE, MC, V. Open: Daily from 5:30 p.m.*

Cantina Bar & Grill
$$–$$$ South Lake Tahoe CAL-MEXICAN

A local fave, this Southwestern cantina is attractive and lively, with first-rate margaritas and 30 different beers during the weekday happy hour and beyond. The kitchen gets creative with specialties such as rock shrimp quesadillas and calamari rellenos, but you won't be disappointed by the tried-and-true: top-notch burritos, taco combos, and the like.

See map p. 187. 765 Emerald Bay Rd. (at Highway 89 and Tenth Street). ☎ *530-544-1233.* www.cantinatahoe.com. *No reservations. Main courses: $10–$16. MC, V. Open: Daily 11:30 a.m.–10 p.m.*

Ernie's Coffee Shop
$ South Lake Tahoe AMERICAN

More than just a mere coffee shop, we happen to love Ernie's for great java, sizable portions of hearty breakfast fare — the scrambled eggs being our favorite — and the excellent milkshakes at lunch. This spot is popular with locals and savvy visitors for all the right reasons.

See map p. 187. 1146 Emerald Bay Rd. (on Highway 89, a mile north of U.S. 50). ☎ *530-541-2161. No reservations. Main courses: $6–$11. MC, V. Open: Daily 6 a.m.–2 p.m.*

Evan's American Gourmet Cafe
$$$–$$$$ South Lake Tahoe CONTEMPORARY AMERICAN

Tucked away in a vintage ski cabin in the woods is Tahoe's best restaurant, on any shore. It's intimate and sophisticated, but completely unpretentious.

Ingredients are fresh and top-quality. Preparations are somewhat complex, yet light enough that even the foie gras starter doesn't seem too heavy. Desserts are swell, too. This terrific restaurant could stand on its own in New York or San Francisco.

See map p. 187. 536 Emerald Bay Rd. (on Highway 89, a mile north of U.S. 50). ☎ *530-542-1990.* www.evanstahoe.com. *Reservations highly recommended. Main courses: $21–$29. AE, DISC, MC, V. Open: Daily from 5:30 p.m.*

The Fresh Ketch
$$–$$$$ South Lake Tahoe   SEAFOOD

The well-worn, casual downstairs bar offers first-rate seafood and good views, while the pretty upstairs dining room maintains a more formal atmosphere. We like the bar for lunch; golden-wood backgammon tables even let you settle in for a game as you nosh on oysters on the half shell, delicately breaded calamari with a zippy dipping sauce, fish and chips, and ahi tacos. The New England clam chowder may be the best you'll find west of the Mississippi.

See map p. 187. At Tahoe Keys Marina, 2433 Venice Dr. (off U.S. 50 at the end of Tahoe Keys Boulevard). ☎ *530-541-5683.* www.thefreshketch.com. *Reservations recommended for dining room. Main courses: $9–$12 at downstairs bar, $18–$36 in upstairs dining room. AE, DC, DISC, MC, V. Open: Daily from 11:30 a.m. (dining room dinner only from 5:30 p.m.).*

On the north shore

Balboa Cafe
$$–$$$ Squaw Valley   CALIFORNIA

The PlumpJack boys got a jump on the competition at the new Village at Squaw Valley, opening the brasserie-style Balboa Cafe before the paint was even dry in the first of the new condos. They serve the identical nearly famous hamburgers here as in the San Francisco haunt of the same name, along with a good steak frites and delicious roast chicken nicely accompanied with potato-mushroom gratin and our personal love, Brussels sprouts. The décor is western eclectic, the bar is fun, and it's the hippest spot in Squaw, a magnet for ski bums of all persuasions. Takeout is available from a little counter next door.

See map p. 187. 1995 Squaw Valley Rd. (directly across from the base lifts in the village). ☎ *530-583-5850.* www.plumpjack.com. *Reservations recommended. Main courses: $11–$29. AE, MC, V. Open: Daily noon–10 p.m. (bar open till 2 a.m.).*

Gar Woods
$$–$$$$ Carnelian Bay   AMERICAN

The large lakefront deck is a popular gathering spot in summer, but this friendly restaurant/bar draws the crowds every season. Along with the grand views, patrons suck up creative cocktails, enjoy live music Friday and Saturday nights, and party down with their pals. The menu, though not particularly creative, covers familiar surf/turf/pasta territory and includes such toothsome appetizers as beer-battered coconut prawns. Quite the scene.

See map p. 187. 5000 North Lake Blvd. (Highway 28, between Tahoe City and Tahoe Vista). ☎ 530-546-3366. www.garwoods.com. *Reservations recommended. Main courses: $13–$19 lunch, $19–$35 dinner; bar menu $13–$19. AE, MC, V. Open: Mon–Thurs 5–9:30 p.m., Fri–Sun 5–10 p.m. (bar open till 1:30 a.m.), Fri–Sun 11:30 a.m.– 2 p.m. Mon–Fri until 5 p.m. (lunch hours daily during summer); Sun brunch in summer (10 a.m.–2 p.m.).*

PlumpJack Cafe
$$$$ Squaw Valley   CONTEMPORARY MEDITERRANEAN

The best restaurant in Squaw Valley is this first-rate resort version of the San Francisco favorite. The Mediterranean-accented modern cuisine revolves around seasonal ingredients, always a good sign (and if the duckling trio is on the menu, order it). The room is 100 percent high-design chic but utterly comfortable nonetheless. Service is impeccable in a not-too-formal way, and the wine list boasts well-chosen labels at reasonable markups. And for a fondue break between ski runs, this is the place.

See map p. 187. 1920 Squaw Valley Rd. (At PlumpJack Squaw Valley Inn). ☎ 530-583-1576. www.plumpjack.com. *Reservations highly recommended for dinner. Main courses: $22–$32, bar menu $9–$16. AE, MC, V. Open: Mon–Fri 7:30–10 a.m., Sat–Sun until 10:30 a.m., Fri–Sat 11:30 a.m.–10 p.m., Sun 11:30 a.m.–9 p.m.*

Rosie's Café
$–$$ Tahoe City   AMERICAN

Two floors of tables usually ensure a short wait, if at all, at this shingled, lodge-style family-owned restaurant. It's noisy and casual, perfect for families, and servings are plentiful. A big menu offers breakfasts designed to rev up skiers, as well as hamburgers, grilled chicken sandwiches, and chef-type salads for lunch, and two-course dinners starring meat (the pot roast is hard to resist) and fish. You won't mistake it for gourmet, but you'll probably appreciate the value and ethos.

See map p. 187. 571 North Lake Blvd. ☎ 530-583-8504. www.rosiescafe.com. *Reservations accepted for dinner. Main courses: $7–$12 lunch, $10–$20 dinner. DISC, MC, V. Open: Daily 6:30 a.m.–10 p.m.*

Sol y Lago
$$$ Tahoe City   LATIN/SPANISH

One of San Francisco's favorite chefs, Johnny Alamilla, packed up his knives and snowboard and relocated to Tahoe in 2005. With a partner, he opened this sleek-yet-casual dinner house, where customers delight in both the excellent views and his wonderful Latino-tinged cooking. Our suggestion is to start with a *mojito* while deciding on either the ceviche or butternut squash and *queso fresco empanaditas.* Follow the small plates with Alamilla's Basque-inspired cassoulet if it's on the menu. Tahoe really lucked out here. *See map p. 187. 760 N. Lake Blvd. (upstairs in the Boatworks Mall).* ☎ *530-583-0358. Reservations accepted. Main courses: $16–$19. AE, MC, V. Open: Sun–Thurs 5:30– 10 p.m., Fri–Sat until 10:30 p.m.*

Enjoying Lake Tahoe

You have to get out on the water to truly appreciate the grandeur of Lake Tahoe.

The 570-passenger *M.S. Dixie II* (☎ 775-589-4906 or 800-238-2463; www. tahoedixie2.com), an authentic paddle-wheeler, offers lake cruises year-round from Zephyr Cove Marina, on U.S. 50, 4 miles east of the Nevada state line. We like the two-hour Emerald Bay Sightseeing Cruise best; it gives you a general feel for the lake and takes you into the stunning bay where you can see Fanette Island and Vikingsholm up close without having to take the difficult walk (see the "Driving along the spectacular west shore" section later in this chapter). Fares are $33 for adults, $9 for kids under 12; reservations are recommended.

If you'd like a more intimate ride, book with **Woodwind Sailing Cruises** (☎ 888-867-6394; www.sailwoodwind.com). Trips, which originate from Camp Richardson Resort or Zephyr Cove, start at $28 for adults, $24 for seniors, $12 for kids 12 and under. The sunset champagne cruise is smooch-worthy.

On the north shore, catch a ride aboard the *Tahoe Gal* (☎ 800-218-2464 or 530-583-0141; www.tahoegal.com), which offers tours from the Lighthouse Mall Marina, 850 N. Lake Blvd., in Tahoe City, from May through September. Prices start at $26 adults, $14 kids. The Happy Hour Cruise is $15 adults and $11 kids.

Boating for do-it-yourselfers

Expect to pay in the neighborhood of $109 to $139 per hour for a power-boat and between $100 and $140 for a jet ski; the fourth hour is often free. Always reserve ahead.

Rental options on the south shore include:

- ✔ **Zephyr Cove Resort Marina,** on U.S. 50, 4 miles east of the Nevada state line (☎ 775-589-4908 or 775-588-3833; www.tahoedixie2.com), rents late-model 16- to 28-foot boats, plus runabouts, ski boats, pontoons, pedal-boats, kayaks, and canoes.

- ✔ **Tahoe Keys Boat Rentals** (☎ 530-544-8888) rents powerboats from Tahoe Keys Marina, conveniently located in South Lake Tahoe off Lake Tahoe Boulevard (U.S. 50) at the end of Tahoe Keys Road.

✔ A great place to launch a kayak is **Timber Cove Marina,** on Lake Tahoe Boulevard at the end of Johnson Boulevard, which has the largest public beach on the south shore. Rentals are available from **Kayak Tahoe** (☎ 530-544-2011; www.kayaktahoe.com). Call ahead to arrange for a guided tour.

✔ **Camp Richardson Marina** at Camp Richardson Resort, 2 miles west of the U.S. 50/Highway 89 junction (☎ 530-541-1801 or 800-544-1801; www.camprichardson.com), rents a full slate of boating equipment similar to that at Zephyr Cove.

For rentals on the north shore, check out the following:

✔ **North Tahoe Marina,** 7360 N. Lake Blvd. (Highway 28, 1 mile west of Highway 267), in Tahoe Vista (☎ 530-546-8248; www.northtahoe marina.com), rents 19- to 24-foot powerboats, plus skis and tow lines.

✔ **Tahoe Water Adventures** at the Lakehouse Mall, just off North Lake Boulevard at the end of Grove Street, in Tahoe City (☎ **530-583-3225**), rents powerboats with wakeboards or skis, canoes, kayaks, jet skis, or environmentally friendly inflatable watercraft.

Sportfishing

The most respected charter company around is **Tahoe Sport Fishing** (www.tahoesportfishing.com), which operates from two south-shore locations: **Ski Run Marina,** off U.S. 50 at the end of Ski Run Boulevard, a mile west of the state line (☎ **800-696-7797** or 530-541-5448); and **Zephyr Cove,** on U.S. 50, 4 miles east of the state line (☎ **800-696-7797** or 775-586-9338). Four- to seven-hour trips run $85 to $135 per person, including all gear, tackle, and bait. If you're lucky enough to hook a salmon or a big Mackinaw lake trout, the fee includes cleaning and sacking.

Driving along the spectacular west shore

The entire drive along Highway 89 offers spectacular scenery. It's worth dedicating the better part of a day to explore (be sure to make your exploration day a bright, clear weekday to avoid traffic). Here are your best stops, from south to north:

✔ The best public-access beaches are part of the **Pope-Baldwin Recreational Area,** which begins just west of the *Y* intersection with U.S. 50. Expect to pay $3 to $5 to park at most public beaches, such as pretty **Pope Beach** and the beach at **Camp Richardson.** Camp Richardson's **Beacon Bar & Grill** is the ideal place to enjoy a sunset Rum Runner (practically the official Tahoe cocktail) because the patio is right on the sand, just a stone's throw — literally — from the water.

✔ Next up is the **Tallac Historic Estates,** three landmarked 1920s homes open for tours in summer. More interesting is **Visitors Center Beach** (turn right at the USFS Lake Tahoe Visitors Center sign). Follow the **Rainbow Trail,** an easy ten-minute walk along a paved walkway dotted with interpretive placards, to the **Stream Profile Chamber,** which offers an eco-lesson in water clarity and the freshwater food chain through a submerged window onto **Taylor Creek.** The view is like looking into an aquarium, only it's the real thing — very cool. Walk ten minutes in the opposite direction from the visitor center, following the "Beach Access" sign, to a very nice stretch of beach.

You can hike a section of the 165-mile Tahoe Rim Trail, which celebrated its 25th birthday in 2006, in a day. Download the route online at www.tahoerimtrail.org. Stop in the visitor center to pick up a copy of the invaluable *Lake of the Sky Journal,* which details other great hikes throughout the area.

✔ From the **Visitors Center Beach,** the highway begins to climb northward. Soon you see the aptly named **Emerald Bay,** a 3-mile-long finger of sparkling green water jutting off the lake. This bay also has the lake's only island — tiny **Fanette Island** — where you find the ruins of an old stone teahouse.

Pull into the lot marked "Emerald Bay State Park/Vikingsholm" for the favorite lake photo-op, bar none. The walk to the lakeshore is 1½ miles long, but at the end you find **Vikingsholm,** a Danish-style castle built by the same (kinda wacky) lady behind the teahouse on Fanette Island. Back in 1928, the lake so reminded her of a Scandinavian fjord that she decided to drive the theme home. The castle is a sight to see — but remember, you have to walk back up that steep 1½-mile hill. The mansion is open for tours in summer only (☎ 530-525-7277).

✔ A couple of miles farther up the road sits **D. L. Bliss State Park** (☎ 530-525-7277), a gorgeous spot with one of the lake's finest beaches (come early in summer to ensure a parking space). If you're a hiker, moderate-level **Rubicon Trail** is a worthy 5-mile hike along Emerald Bay.

✔ Another 7 miles on is **Sugar Pine Point State Park** (☎ 530-525-7982). This terrific park offers 1¾ miles of shoreline with sandy beaches, more than 2,000 forested acres laced with hiking trails, the historic Ehrman Mansion (open for guided tours in summer), and a nature center. Parking starts at $5.

✔ After you reach Tahoe City, take note of **Fanny Bridge,** so named for the view of derrieres as folks bend over the rail to catch sight of the leaping trout below. It's on Highway 89 just south of the *Y* intersection with Highway 28, next to **Izzy's Burger Spa,** a great spot for juicy burgers and thick shakes.

Golfing

Hitting the links is a very big deal in North Tahoe. A half-dozen excellent courses lie within easy reach of Tahoe City, including the award-winning Robert Trent Jones, Jr.–designed links-style course at the **Resort at Squaw Creek** (see the "Where to Stay" section earlier in this chapter), honored by *Golf* magazine as one of the top ten resort courses in America. For tee times here or at another course, contact **North Lake Tahoe Central Reservations** (☎ 888-434-1262 or 530-583-3494; www. tahoefun.org). These friendly folks can also direct south-shore vacationers to great courses, too.

Taking a heavenly ride

Heavenly operates a **gondola** a half-block west of Stateline, right on U.S. 50, between two new Marriott timeshare developments. The ride ($24 for adults, $22 for kids 13 to 18, $15 for kids 5 to 12) takes you 2½ miles up the mountain to an observation deck at 9,123 feet. The views are breathtaking, but there's not much to do up there except eat at the cafe or continue to the top and eat at the Adventure Peak Grill. You'll also find a few hiking trails and a climbing wall, which confuses us but might make the kids happy. You may get more for your money taking the cable car at Squaw Valley High Camp.

River rafting

Truckee River Rafting (☎ 888-584-7238 or 530-583-7238; www.truckee riverrafting.com) offers one cool north-shore activity: a leisurely float along a 5-mile stretch down the Truckee River from Tahoe City to River Ranch Pond. You even hit a couple of baby rapids for a few thrills; kids just love it. The ride is $32 for adults, $27 for kids 6 to 12, including all equipment and pickup at the end. Reserve ahead (and save $7 per person); allow two to four hours for the adventure.

Playing at Squaw Valley High Camp

Squaw Valley High Camp (☎ 530-583-6955; www.squaw.com) is a wonderful place to play in summer, and a great way to experience the Olympic Village. After a scenic cable-car ride to 8,200 feet, you can ice-skate at the mountaintop Olympic Ice Pavilion, or swim and spa in the Swimming Lagoon. If you're a hiker, pick up a trail map at the base information desk and follow any one of a half-dozen mountain trails, ranging from easy to difficult. Mountain bikers can rent a front-suspension bike at the **Squaw Valley Sport Shop,** in the Olympic Village (☎ **530-583-3356**), take it to the top, and explore the snowless slopes. Expect half-day rentals around $30, and full-day rentals in the neighborhood of $40, helmets included; call to book a bike and avoid disappointment. Round-trip cable-car tickets are $20 adults, $16 teens 13 to 15, $5 kids 3 to 12; swim/skate/ride packages are available.

Hitting the slopes in ski season

Tahoe is more popular as a ski resort than anything else. It's home to the state's best skiing and the country's largest concentration of downhill slopes. The ski season usually lasts from November through April but has been known to extend into the early summer. Most resorts welcome snowboarders, but always check first.

Lift tickets for adults cost between $23 and $63 for a full day, depending on the resort, with convenient Heavenly and Squaw Valley on the high end. Resorts often issue money-saving multiday tickets, and kids and seniors always qualify for discounts. Your lodge will probably have discounted tickets on hand as well.

Contact the local **visitor centers** (see the "Gathering More Information" section later in this chapter) or go to www.tahoesbest.com/Skiing for more about the area ski resorts. Also inquire about ski packages, which can usually save you a small fortune, especially if you ski midweek.

The top south-shore slopes

Heavenly (☎ 775-586-7000; www.skiheavenly.com) is off U.S. 50 at the top of Ski Run Boulevard (turn left). It features the region's steepest vertical drop (3,500 ft.) and one of its largest ski terrains (4,800 acres), not to mention one of the world's largest snowmaking systems. A third of the trails are set aside for envelope-pushers, but the rest are dedicated to beginners and intermediates. Excellent for families, with everything from kiddie ski schools to daycare.

Kirkwood (☎ 209-258-7254; www.kirkwood.com) is a 30- to 45-minute drive outside of South Lake Tahoe on Highway 88 (from U.S. 50, take Highway 89 south to 88 west). This resort ranks among *Ski* magazine's top ten in North America for snow, terrain, and challenge. It's a terrific choice for spring skiers thanks to high average snowfall. It's now a destination resort, so inquire if you want to stay.

The top north-shore slopes

Midsize **Alpine Meadows** (☎ 800-441-4423 or 530-583-4232; www.ski alpine.com), 8 miles west of Tahoe City, has the best spring skiing around. Many years, Alpine Meadows is still going strong into May, when everybody else (even Kirkwood) has closed for the season. A local favorite, it maintains a committed following.

Diamond Peak (☎ 775-832-1177; www.diamondpeak.com) is 17 miles east of Tahoe City in Incline Village, Nevada. Diamond Peak has taken great care to target families, and it's the north shore's best resort for kids. It's also smaller and less expensive than most resorts. Kids as young as 3 can learn to ski, and the resort maintains a terrific snow-play area.

If you want spectacular lake views while you ski, take to the slopes at **Homewood** (☎ 530-525-2992; www.skihomewood.com), right on the lake's west shore, 6½ miles south of Tahoe City. It's small, intimate, and a local favorite. Weekday lift tickets are a great value.

Northstar-at-Tahoe (☎ 800-466-6784 or 530-562-1010; www.northstar tahoe.com), 11 miles east of Tahoe City, is under construction midmountain with a Ritz-Carlton resort scheduled to open in 2009. Northstar, which has always been a terrific choice for families, devotes about 75 percent of the ski terrain to beginner and intermediate runs. Skiing will continue during the building, of course, and new lifts should help move the crowds more quickly and efficiently.

Ever dream of Olympic glory? **Squaw Valley USA** (☎ 530-583-6985; www.squaw.com), 9 miles from Tahoe City, was the site of the 1960 Olympic Winter Games. Spanning six Sierra peaks, gorgeous, excellently outfitted Squaw Valley is Tahoe's most state-of-the-art ski area with the most challenging array of runs. A must for serious skiers.

Cross-country skiing and snowmobiling

The north shore offers the most — and best — cross-country options. **Tahoe Cross-Country Ski Area** (☎ 530-583-5475; www.tahoexc.org) has 65 kilometers of groomed trails, a full-service day lodge, state-of-the-art equipment, and a convenient location, 2 miles east of Tahoe City off Highway 28 at Dollar Hill (turn at Fabian Way).

Northstar-at-Tahoe (☎ 530-562-2475; www.northstartahoe.com) has a new cross-country, telemark, and snowshoe center with 50 kilometers of groomed trails. The **Resort at Squaw Creek** (☎ 530-583-6300; www.squawcreek.com) is much smaller, with just 18 kilometers of trails, but the Squaw Valley setting is unparalleled — and the resort was the site of the 2004 U.S. Snowshoeing National Championships.

On the south shore, head to the 35 kilometers of trails at the **Cross-Country Ski Center** at Camp Richardson Resort, on Highway 89 which is 2½ miles north of the U.S. 50/89 Y intersection (☎ 530-542-6584; www.camprich.com).

The south shore's **Zephyr Cove Snowmobile Center,** on U.S. 50, 4 miles east of the state line (☎ 775-588-3833; www.tahoedixie2.com), is the largest snowmobiling center in the United States. You can rent and set out on your own (kids as young as 5 can accompany you on a double machine), or take a guided tour (recommended if you're a newbie). Reservations recommended.

On the north shore, contact **Snowmobiling Unlimited** (☎ 530-583-7192). Tahoe's oldest snowmobile touring company, this company leads two- and three-hour guided tours.

Trying your luck at the casinos

One of the great advantages of a Tahoe vacation is the proximity to the casinos — just a skip across the border in either Stateline or Crystal Bay, Nevada. You can throw a snowball and hit any of them from the California side. These are the best of the bunch:

- ✔ **Cal Neva Resort** (☎ 800-225-6382 or 775-832-4000; www.calneva resort.com), once co-owned by Frank Sinatra, has its diehard fans, including soft-hearted us, who prefer the north-shore location and low-key atmosphere. The showroom, built to the specifications of Ol' Blue Eyes himself, isn't used much anymore and the medium-size gaming room has only blackjack, roulette, craps, and slot machines. However, photos of Marilyn Monroe, Sinatra, and his cronies line the walls, providing a cool piece of history and a hint of past glamour that may be irresistible.

- ✔ The jam-packed showroom at **Harrah's** (☎ 800-427-7247 or 775-588-6611; www.harrahstahoe.com) offers a wide array of entertainment, from comics to big-name headliners, including many baby-boomer faves (the Yardbirds, Pat Benatar, and so forth). The hotel/casino has opened a new nightclub as well.

- ✔ **Harveys** (☎ 800-427-8397 or 775-588-2411; www.harrahs.com) rocks, with video monitors and speakers blasting radio-friendly sounds throughout the largest casino in Tahoe. With its terrific racing and sports book, Harveys draws a young, sophisticated crowd. The showroom focuses on cabaret-style shows and sexy revues, while the **Hard Rock Cafe** hosts live music on Friday and Saturday nights.

- ✔ **MontBleu Resort and Spa** (☎ 800-648-3353 or 775-586-7771; www.montbleuresort.com), targets the 21-to-40 demographic with a nightclub, slick lounge, theater, seven restaurants, and a poker room to complement a full range of gaming tables. It's as close to Vegas as you can get in Tahoe.

If you hope to catch a big-name headliner, check the schedule before you leave home and make reservations to avoid disappointment.

The casinos make sure families feel welcome. Harrah's and Harveys, offer sizable video arcades where classics such as Pac-Man and Donkey Kong buzz and beep alongside the latest virtual-reality games. In addition, the casino showrooms often offer all-ages entertainment, such as magic shows, at earlier family hours.

Side-Tripping to the Gold Country

California's gold-rush country is rich in color and history. Dotted with 19th-century-mining-towns-turned-cutesy-B&B havens, the region is a big weekend destination for Northern Californians. The area has plenty to see and do, but nothing so major that you should devote the half-week you'd need to drive the region's main thoroughfare, Highway 49, from end to end. Leave that for a future vis t, after you've covered so many of California's highlights that you have t he time to dedicate to it.

However, a portion of the Gold Country is so easy to reach on the drive to or from Lake Tahoe that we highly recommend you dedicate half a day to seeing its main (and most fascinating) attraction, the **Marshall Gold Discovery State Historic Park,** where the gold rush began. You can also stop in a gold-rush town or two. Keep in mind, though, that the Gold Country can be brutally hot in summer, so dress accordingly.

Getting there

We suggest you focus on the **Gold Chain Highway;** this section of Highway 49 runs roughly north-south between I-80 (the road to North Tahoe) and U.S. 50 (the road to South Tahoe). I-80 connects with Highway 49 at **Auburn,** 35 miles east of Sacramento and 78 miles (a gorgeous one-and-a-half-hour drive) west of Tahoe City. U.S. 50 connects with this section of Highway 49 on the south end, in **Placerville** (originally dubbed Hangtown for its single-minded justice system), 43 miles east of Sacramento and 55 miles west of South Lake Tahoe.

The roughly 23-mile drive between Auburn and Placerville along the Gold Chain Highway takes about an hour thanks to one narrow lane in each direction and more than a few hairpin turns. **Coloma,** the hairsbreadth of a town where you'll find the Marshall Gold Discovery State Historic Park, is roughly midway between the two.

> ✔ **If you're heading to South Tahoe:** Pick up I-80 (which you may already be on if you're coming from the Bay Area) in Sacramento, turn south on Highway 49 to do your exploring, and then head east to South Tahoe after you meet up with U.S. 50. If you're leaving from South Tahoe, reverse the process by taking U.S. 50 west, Highway 49 north for exploring, then I-80 west when you're done.

> ✔ **If you're heading to North Tahoe:** Take U.S. 50 east from Sacramento, then take Highway 49 north, then I-80 east to Tahoe City. From North Tahoe? You got it — I-80 west, Highway 49 south, U.S. 50 west to your destination

Marshall's gold and Sutter's mill

The **Marshall Gold Discovery State Historic Park** is nestled in the golden Sierra foothills on Highway 49 between Auburn and Placerville at Coloma (☎ **530-622-3470;** www.parks.ca.gov). Actually, about 70 percent of Coloma *is* the park. This is where James Marshall, a carpenter, discovered two itsy-bitsy gold nuggets on January 24, 1848, at John Sutter's mill on the dusty banks of the American River. This discovery managed to launch gold-rush mania and redirect California history in the process.

A working re-creation of Sutter's mill, a few intact gold-rush-era build-ings, and enlightening exhibits capture the pioneering spirit and excite-ment of that day and the '49ers get-rich-quick craze that followed. This place is very cool, and kids will enjoy it more than you may expect. To take maximum advantage of this historic site, start at the **Gold Discovery Museum Visitors Center,** just off Highway 49 at Bridge Street. Come early and ask the rangers about guided discovery tours and sawmill demonstra-tions (usually Thursday through Sunday at 11 a.m. and 1 p.m. in summer). You may even get a chance to pan for gold yourself! The buildings are open daily from 10 a.m. to 5 p.m. (4:30 p.m. in winter), and the fee is $4 to $6 per car. Bring a picnic lunch or snack.

By the way: James Marshall, poor soul, never saw a dime of the gold in them thar hills.

Old Town Auburn

In Auburn, the area just off I-80 at Nevada Street (bounded by Court Street, Lincoln Way, Washington Street, and Maple and Commercial streets) is **Old Town Auburn.** This is an ideal example of an Old West gold town transformed into a boutiqued downtown. Nevertheless, it still maintains a strong historic feel with original buildings boasting false storefronts along steep, cobbled streets. Head to the **Bootleggers Old Town Tavern & Grill,** 210 Washington St. (☎ **530-889-2229**), for a lunch stop with an appealing local vibe.

To get some background history on the area, stop at the **Placer County Courthouse,** the notable neoclassical building with a mismatched hat — a Renaissance gold dome — at the top of the hill at 101 Maple St. (at Court Street and Lincoln Way). Inside is the petite **Placer County Museum** (☎ **530-889-6500**), which tells the story of Auburn's rise as a mother-lode gold-rush town, and is a great place to pick up information on other attractions in the area. Across Maple Street is Latitudes Bistro (☎ **530-885-9535**), one of the better places to eat in the area; the menu spotlights a different area of the world each month.

Where to stay in the Gold Country

If you want to spend more time in Gold Country, the following places are good bets for lodging:

✔ Located within the bounds of the Marshall Gold Discovery Park, the **Coloma Country Inn Bed & Breakfast** (☎ **530-622-6919;** www.colomacountryinn.com) captures the spirit of the locale in a lovely and well-appointed 1852 farmhouse.

✔ In Auburn, your best bet is the **Holiday Inn of Auburn,** on Highway 49 (☎ **800-814-8787** or 530-887-8787; www.holiday-inn.com).

Certain accommodations near **Yosemite National Park** make ideal bases for exploring the region, especially the **Groveland Hotel** and hotels in Oakhurst, such as the posh **Château du Sureau.** See Chapter 16 for details.

Prospecting for History in Sacramento

California's state capital is, admittedly, not the most exciting destination in this book. The nearest "real" city, San Francisco, has always held an iron grip on sophistication and glamour and that won't change no matter who's sitting in the governor's office. Snobbery aside, however, the town is absolutely worth a one-day or overnight detour, especially if you have kids on board. Our governor, Arnold Schwarzenegger, has become a tourist draw (not that he's available to sign autographs), and Old Sacramento, with a terrific train museum and riverside location, is quaint and walkable. Just a 90-minute drive from South Lake Tahoe (two hours from North Lake Tahoe), Sacto is a practical stop on the way to or from Tahoe for an overnight or a side trip if you're skipping the Gold Country but still want to sample state history.

Getting there

Vast housing tracts and freeways surround the city, but finding your way to Old Sacramento and the downtown area is easy. From I-5, take the J Street exit and follow the signs. Highway 80 from the Bay Area intersects I-5 just south of downtown. If you're driving from Tahoe, head west on Highway 50 to Highway 80 and north on I-5.

What do the locals do on their way to visit the relatives in Sacramento? We stop at the factory outlets in Vacaville off Highway 80. No fab designer dubs unfortunately, but you can pick up Levi's, all kinds of athletic shoes, baby OshKosh, and imperfect Jelly Belly candies (as if there were such a thing!).

Where to stay and dine

If you decide to spend the night, you'll have a reasonable selection of chain hotels and motels to choose from. The Hyatt Regency on L Street is where the governor stays when he's in town (he still lives in Los Angeles), but our suggestion, just for the fun of it, is to book a room on the **Delta King,** 1000 Front St. (☎ **916-444-5464** or 800-825-5464; www. deltaking.com). A 1927 riverboat docked in Old Sacramento, the staterooms are tiny but cute, and the boat is outfitted with a restaurant and a 115-seat theater presenting shows nightly. Room rates are $169 to $219 for two ($550 for the Captain's Suite)

Restaurants dot Old Sacramento and the locals are happy with all the new places to dine around the capitol building. Rumor has it that the guv likes the **Esquire Grill,** 1213 K St. (☎ **916-448-8900**), but even if that's unsubstantiated, the classic American chophouse is as good as it gets around here.

When you need a break from exploring the city's attractions, check out the cafeteria in the basement of the State Capitol. You won't find a better value in town for Tex-Mex specials; we tried the food and found it more than satisfying. You can also pick up a sandwich for $4.95 that comes with chips and a soda. The décor down there is dreadful and dark, but you can order lunch to go and eat it outside in the beautiful park.

Exploring California's capital city

Sacramento's highlights center on a downtown core that includes the State Capitol and Old Sacramento. Also worth a visit is Sutter's Fort State Historical Park.

 Street parking is metered and will require a handful of quarters if you choose to go that route. Otherwise, there are parking garages around Old Sacramento. Trolleys make 40-minute round-trip drives around the Capitol Mall and Old Sacramento; the fare is 50¢, and this is a cheap, stress-free way to get your bearings.

Old Sacramento

When elementary school kids in San Francisco make the annual train trip to the state capital, this is where they disembark. Old Sacramento, along the Sacramento River, was the center of commerce around the time of the gold rush, when Sam Brannan opened a general store here. Flooding and fires decimated most of the buildings in the 1850s; in the 1860s, a plan to raise the area above flood level was instituted, but eventually businesses moved east closer to the state capitol buildings. Forty years ago, the city decided to reinvest in the area, renovating the buildings that could be salvaged and reconstructing others. Pick up a map at the visitor center on Second Street, which includes a walking tour of these 20 blocks. Yes, this is a tourist-driven area with way too many sweet shops, useless trinkets, and annoyingly stupid T-shirts; on the other hand, it's no more offensive than Pier 39 in San Francisco or Cannery Row in Monterey. Plus, it's kind of pretty down there by the river.

The great attraction if you have the slightest interest in the railroad is the **California State Railroad Museum,** Second and I streets (☎ **916-445-6645;** www.californiastaterailroadmuseum.org). A gigantic building filled with 19th-century trains, you can watch a film that traces the history of railroading, and clamber aboard to view the elegant dining and sleeping accommodations. The exhibit on the Chinese laborers who essentially built the transcontinental railroad is especially touching. Between April and September, steam-train rides are offered on the weekends. It's open daily from 10 a.m. to 5 p.m. Admission is $8 for adults, $3 for kids 6 to 17.

The State Capitol Building

The last of California's eight capitol buildings (the first five being located in other cities) was occupied near the end of 1869, but actually completed in 1874. The classical Roman-Corinthian structure is stately and grand, especially compared to the modern buildings now housing the majority of the government's offices. The capitol sits at one end of a Victorian-styled park with 40 acres of trees, war memorials, and a fragrant rose garden.

You can take guided tours on the hour or wander around the historic offices and exhibit rooms. The Assembly and Senate galleries on the third floor are open for viewing as well. Strangely enough, you can even walk into the governor's outer office and check out the big, framed photograph of Arnold and Maria, prominently featuring the largest, toothiest grins in California.

Tenth Street, between L and N streets. ☎ *916-324-0333.* www.assembly.ca.gov/museum. *Free admission. Open: Daily 8:30 a.m.–5 p.m.; hourly tours start at 9 a.m.*

Sutter's Fort State Historic Park

An entrepreneur with a history of failed businesses, the Swiss immigrant Captain Johann Augustus Sutter temporarily left his wife and five children behind in Basel, Switzerland, in 1834 to escape his creditors and seek his fortune in America. After travels across the states, and sailing as far as Honolulu, Sutter made his way up the Sacramento and American rivers, landing finally just a mile from the eventual site of his fort. California history — notably Northern California's — is shaped in large part by the discovery of gold at Sutter's Coloma mill. But Sutter, an educated, intelligent, and uncommonly decent man, first built a fort in 1840 that was the center of trade and farming in the area he named "New Helvetia." Much of the fort today has been reconstructed and belongs to the California State Park system. Along with a self-guided audio tour that covers this remarkable man's life, you see examples of the compound's workshops and living quarters. Living-history events and pioneer demonstration days are often scheduled on Saturdays throughout the year. It's a must for kids, but we thought the place was pretty cool ourselves.

Between K and L streets and 26th and 28th streets. ☎ *916-445-4422.* www.parks.ca.gov. *Admission: $6 adults 17 and over, $3 kids. Open: Daily 10 a.m.–5 p.m.*

Gathering More Information

The regions covered in this chapter offer far more to do beyond what's mentioned here. Contact one of the local visitor organizations for more information, especially if you're interested in an activity not discussed.

Lake Tahoe

The **Lake Tahoe Visitors Authority** (☎ 800-AT-TAHOE or 530-544-5050; www.bluelaketahoe.com) has the information you need on South Lake Tahoe and environs. After you arrive, stop by the **South Lake Tahoe Chamber of Commerce,** 3066 S. Lake Tahoe Blvd., east of Altahoe Boulevard (☎ 530-541-5255; www.tahoeinfo.com), open Monday through Saturday from 9 a.m. to 5 p.m.

For information on the north shore, contact the **North Lake Tahoe Resort Association** (☎ 888-434-1262 or 530-583-3494; www.tahoefun.org). After you arrive, stop by their terrific visitor center at 380 North Lake Blvd. in Tahoe City (on the south side of Highway 28; the sign says

"Chamber of Commerce"), open Monday through Friday from 8:30 a.m. to 5 p.m., Saturday and Sunday from 8:30 a.m. to 4 p.m. (hours vary seasonally).

If you'd like information on the Nevada side of the north shore, contact the **Incline Village/Crystal Bay Visitors Bureau** (☎ 775-832-1606; www. gotahoe.com).

 For Tahoe **road conditions,** call ☎ 800-427-7623; for **weather,** call ☎ 800-752-1177 or 530-546-5253.

The Gold Country

For more information on the Auburn area, including local B&B recommendations, contact the **Placer County Visitors Council** (☎ 530-887-2111; www.visitplacer.com).

If you plan to spend more time in the region, consider heading south to cute-as-a-button Sutter Creek (whose **Chatterbox Cafe** the *New York Times* noted "may be the finest luncheonette in North America"), and nearby Jackson. The **Amador County Chamber of Commerce** (☎ 209-223-0350; www.amadorcountychamber.com) has more information.

To the far north end of Highway 49 are Nevada City and Grass Valley, which many consider to be the finest tourist towns in the Gold Country. Contact the **Grass Valley/Nevada County Chamber of Commerce** (☎ 800-655-4667 or 530-273-4667; www.grassvalleychamber.com) or the **Nevada City Chamber of Commerce** (☎ 800-655-6569 or 530-265-2692; www.ncgold.com).

Sacramento

For maps, travel packages, hotel reservations, and brochures, call or stop by the **Old Sacramento Visitors Center,** 1004 Second St. at J Street (☎ 916-442-7644; www.oldsacramento.com). It's open daily from 10 a.m. to 5 p.m.

Chapter 16

Yosemite National Park

In This Chapter

▶ Planning your trip to America's favorite national park

▶ Deciding where to stay and dine within Yosemite

▶ Weighing your options in the nearby gateway towns

▶ Exploring Yosemite — on, and preferably off, the beaten path

▶ Discovering the delights of Mammoth Mountain

*P*repare to meet one of the most spectacular places in the world. Yosemite National Park encompasses nearly 1,200 square miles and a wildly diverse landscape that soars from 2,000 feet to an awesome 13,000 feet above sea level. It's a blue-ribbon destination all the way, home to the world's most impressive glacier-carved canyon (Yosemite Valley); three of the world's ten tallest waterfalls, including North America's tallest (2,425-ft. Yosemite Falls); the world's largest granite monolith (El Capitan); and the world's biggest and oldest trees (the giant sequoias). However, those nature-bending records don't even begin to describe the wonder of Yosemite — you must come and see this breathtaking place for yourself.

The mile-wide, 7-mile-long **Yosemite Valley** is the attraction-laden heart of the mammoth park — much of the rest is unreachable wilderness. When you arrive, you see why this valley is called the ultimate example of a glacier-carved canyon: Its flat, open meadows and oak and mixed-conifer woodlands come to an abrupt halt on all sides, where sheer walls suddenly soar to the sky. The towering cliffs, craggy monoliths, rounded domes, and tumbling waterfalls will have you craning your neck in wide-eyed amazement. Between Memorial and Labor days, however, the mammoth crowds may give you a migraine, because 90 percent of the park's visitors congregate in the valley floor. Think of it as the Waikiki Beach of Yosemite.

You shouldn't miss the valley, but schedule some time to poke around the quieter areas of the park, too, especially if you crave a more genuine wilderness experience. Head for the serene, (largely) crowd-free **High Country** in the summer. The entire Sierra Nevada doesn't get any more beautiful than this splendid mix of verdant subalpine meadows and forest, crystal-blue glacial lakes, granite spires, and domes. Or make time for **Mariposa Grove,** the sky-scraping stand of giant sequoias at the lovely, woodsy, civilized south end.

The beauty of Yosemite is that it's a foolproof park. To accommodate all those tourists, the Park Service has become extremely visitor-friendly, offering lots of available guidance, great facilities, and easy hikes and river access, making Yosemite an ideal place to vacation with children. The summer madness horning in on your communion with nature will seem like the biggest, best summer camp in the world to a kid.

Even at the height of summer chaos you can have a genuine wilderness experience in Yosemite. You don't have to be a survivalist to venture out of the valley and into one of the more remote areas of the park. Whenever you visit, give yourself the space and time (at least two days; more is ideal) to truly appreciate this humbling, awe-inspiring place.

Timing Your Visit

Most people visit Yosemite in June, July, and August — which means that if you don't have to come during those months, don't. The Yosemite Valley is so crowded in the summer that it seems more like a theme park than a natural wonderland. But if your vacation falls during these months, you don't have to stay away.

If you're not staying in the park, enter early (the superintendent has been known, on a few occasions, to close the gates when the park reaches maximum capacity) and plan to spend much of your visit in areas other than the Yosemite Valley, where most visitors congregate. On the upside, summer is the best time to visit **Tuolumne** (too-*all*-oh-mee) **Meadows,** glorious subalpine meadows at an altitude of 8,600 feet, and take the drive to the summit of **Glacier Point,** at 7,214 feet, for spectacular views over the valley.

Mid-September through October is a magical season. Visitor numbers drop, but the park remains fully accessible; the roads to Tuolumne Meadows and Glacier Point generally don't close until November.

If you really want the park all to yourself, visit in winter. The valley is marvelously peaceful, and the snow provides an exquisite contrast to all that granite. (The average annual accumulation on the valley floor is about 4 ft.) If the weather gods are with you, you'll wonder why anyone bothers to visit in the summer. Plus, accommodations are usually discounted. The **High Country** is under about 20 feet of snow from November through May, however, and pretty much off limits.

When deciding how much time to spend touring Yosemite, go with more rather than less. One day, even a full one, is simply not enough. Give yourself at least two days; three full days comes closer to the ideal.

Accessing the Park

You can enter the park through any one of four main entrances (locate each in the "Yosemite National Park" map on p. 212):

✔ The most commonly used entrance (and most traffic-congested in summer) is the **Arch Rock Entrance,** on the west side of the park via Highway 140, through the "Hey, where'd it go?" town of El Portal. (This entrance closes nightly between 10:30 p.m. and 6:30 a.m.) This gateway offers the most direct access to Yosemite Valley, where your first stop should be the main Valley Visitor Center after you dump your car in a day-use lot (if you're staying outside the park) or at your accommodations. The center is open daily from 8:30 a.m. to 5 p.m.

✔ On the west side, north of Arch Rock, is the **Big Oak Flat Entrance,** on Highway 120, which takes you through Groveland first. It's also valley-convenient, but you can pass by the congested valley and head straight for the High Country. If you're going to bypass the valley, be sure to stop by the **Big Oak Flat Information Station** (☎ 209-379-1899), just inside the park gate, for information and maps; open daily from 9 a.m. to 6 p.m.

✔ You can also arrive via the **South Entrance,** on Highway 41, about 35 miles south of Yosemite Valley. It's the most convenient entrance for those coming from points south, and it boasts some of the most wonderful vistas in the park. You'll also use it if you stay at **Tenaya Lodge** or at one of the accommodations options in Oakhurst (see the "Where to Stay and Dine outside the Park" section later in this chapter). The **Wawona Information Station** (☎ 209-375-9501) is open only in summer from 8:30 a.m. to 4:30 p.m. daily. Turn off Highway 41 at Chilnualna Falls Road and take the first right after the stables.

✔ The **Tioga Pass Entrance,** the eastern High Country gateway on Highway 120, is open only in summer. Use this entrance if you come from Lake Tahoe (see Chapter 15), or from **Death Valley National Park** (see Chapter 26). The **Tuolumne Meadows Visitor Center** (☎ 209-372-0263) is open daily in summer from 9 a.m. to 7 p.m.

Getting there by car

From Lake Tahoe, you can take U.S. 50 west out of Tahoe to I-395 south to Highway 120, which leads you into the park's High Country via the summer-only Tioga Pass Entrance. The three-and-a-half-hour drive is doable between late June and the first snowfall (usually early Nov). Otherwise, you have a five- or six-hour drive down winding Highway 49, which can be extra-slow-going in bad weather.

From San Francisco, the drive is about three and a half hours. Take I-580 west to I-205 to Highway 120, and then plan the rest of your route along highways 120, 99, or 140, depending on where you're staying.

Yosemite National Park

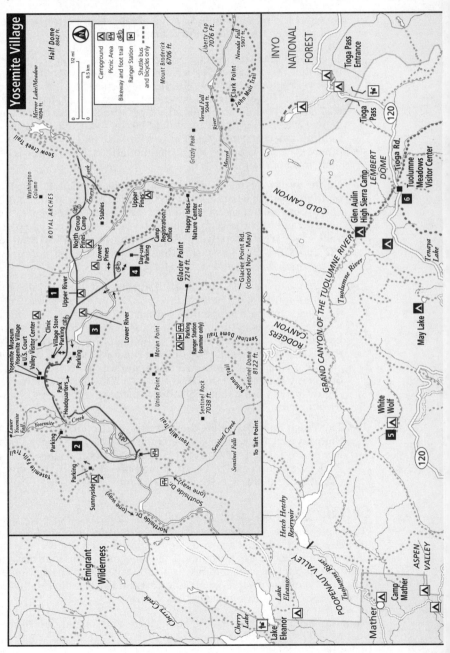

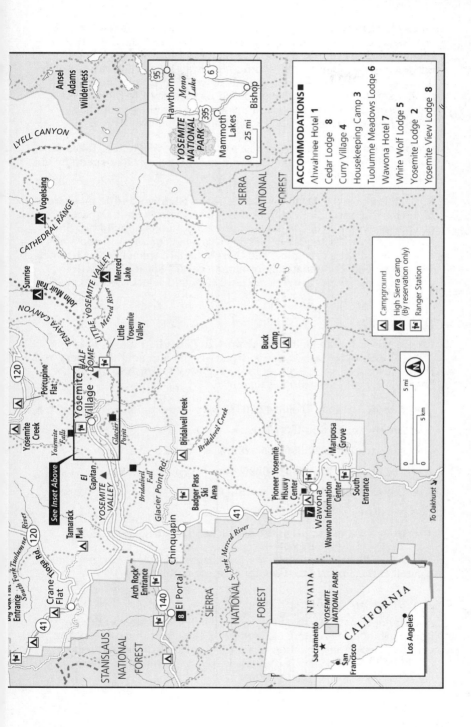

From the Central Coast, you have a couple of options, depending on your departure point. From the Monterey Peninsula, take U.S. 101 to Highway 152 to Highway 99 north to Highway 140 to the Arch Rock Entrance or take Highway 99 south to Highway 145 to Highway 41 north to the South Entrance — each roughly a five-hour drive. If you're starting farther south on the coast, take U.S. 101 or Highway 1 to Highway 41 (near Morro Bay) and follow it all the way to Yosemite's south gate. Expect to spend about five and a half hours on Highway 41.

From Los Angeles, the drive lasts about six and a half hours. Take I-5 north to Highway 99 to either Highway 41 or Highway 140, depending on where you're staying.

Rock slides closed a 600-foot-wide section of **Highway 140** 12 miles west of the park in April 2006. At press time, the California State Department of Transportation's (CalTrans) temporary solution is to build two one-lane bridges across the Merced River. This 7-mile detour will add a minimum of 30 minutes drive time and there's no date announced as to when 140 will reopen. For updated information, call ☎ **800-427-7623,** or log on to http://inciweb.org/incident/236 and select "Ferguson Rockslide."

Winging it

Fresno Yosemite International Airport, 5175 E. Clinton Ave., Fresno (☎ **559-498-4095;** www.flyfresno.org), is 90 miles south of Yosemite. From the airport, take Highway 180 to Highway 41 north to the park's South Entrance. These airlines fly in:

- ✔ **Alaska Airlines:** ☎ **800-426-0333;** www.alaskaair.com

- ✔ **American:** ☎ **800-433-7300;** www.aa.com

- ✔ **America West:** ☎ **800-235-9292;** www.americawest.com

- ✔ **Continental:** ☎ **800-525-0280;** www.flycontinental.com

- ✔ **Delta:** ☎ **800-221-1212;** www.delta.com

- ✔ **Northwest:** ☎ **800-225-2525;** www.nwa.com

- ✔ **United/United Express:** ☎ **800-241-6522;** www.united.com

You can rent a car from one of the major national car-rental companies located at the airport (see Chapter 7 for car-rental details).

Arriving by train

Another option is to arrive in Merced, 73 miles southwest of the Arch Rock Entrance, via **Amtrak** (☎ **800-872-7245;** www.amtrak.com). You can then book transportation or a park tour with **VIA Adventures** (☎ **800-842-5463;** www.via-adventures.com), which also offers packages that include accommodations.

Entering and navigating the park

Admission to the park is $20 per car, or $10 per person if you arrive by bus, by bike, or on foot. Your ticket is good for seven days, so keep it handy. Reservations are not required, and you're free to drive around the park as you please, but these policies can change; call ☎ 209-372-0200, or visit www.nps.gov/yose to check the latest info before you go.

Do everybody a favor while you're in Yosemite Valley: Park your car once (you'll be directed to a day-use lot if you're not staying within park bounds) and use the shuttle system, bikes, or your own tootsies to move around the valley floor. Free shuttle buses loop the valley daily year-round, as frequently as every ten minutes in high season. Park management is so eager for you to take advantage of this alternative that they make it a breeze to use. If you'd rather two-wheel it, bike rentals are available for the entire family at **Curry Village** (☎ 209-372-8319) year-round, and from April through November at **Yosemite Lodge** (☎ 209-372-1208). Use your car only to reach other, far-flung areas of the park, such as Glacier Point or the High Country.

The Yosemite Area Regional Transportation System (YARTS) offers bus service from some of the gateway communities, allowing you to leave your car behind at the motel. For example, both **Cedar Lodge** and **Yosemite View Lodge** just outside the Arch Rock Entrance have on-site pickups; you can also meet the bus if you're staying farther west on Highway 140 in Mariposa. For schedule and fare information, call ☎ 877-989-2787 or 209-372-4487, or visit www.yarts.com.

Preparing for Your Visit

Here are a few tips to help you get your visit off on the right foot:

- ✔ **Wear appropriately sturdy shoes.** Hiking boots are best, but at least bring sneakers. Platform slides aren't going to cut it here.

- ✔ **Always bring a jacket.** Even if the valley floor is hot, the air can really cool off in the High Country. Rain is most common in the colder months, but thunderstorms can happen at any time.

- ✔ **In summer, bring a swimsuit.** A hot day may tempt you to take a dip in the Merced River. An excellent swimming hole exists at Stoneman Bridge, near Curry Village in the valley.

- ✔ **In winter, come with the appropriate snow gear.** Bring snow boots, winter coats — the works. Don't leave home without tire chains in the trunk if you're driving your own car, or inquire about them when you book your rental vehicle.

- ✔ **In the High Country, opt for an easier hiking trail than you might normally choose.** The thinness of the air at these elevations can really tax your system and sap your energy.

✔ **Heed all warnings about the bear problem.** Terribly spoiled by years of human leftovers, black bears have decided that they prefer Big Macs, Cheetos, and PB&J sandwiches to Mother Nature's eats. As a result, they've become a real menace to personal property (and to themselves — Yosemite's bears are in danger of losing their natural hunting-and-gathering instincts).

✔ **Don't leave food in your car.** Don't even leave a stray french fry in the trunk. Bears have become experts at ripping open cars as if they were tin cans (most often, they wiggle their claws into the gap above the door and bend down). Trust us, you don't want to have to explain this to Avis. Statistics prove that they're particularly fond of white minivans — why, nobody knows. If you camp or stay in a tent cabin, diligently use the metal food-storage boxes.

Where to Stay and Dine inside the Park

If you're not thrilled with your lodging or campground reservation, call back one month before your arrival date to inquire about an upgrade. The majority of cancellations occur either 3 days or 30 days before arrival; in fact, rooms often turn over two and three times.

Mariposa County room tax adds an extra 10 percent to your bill.

DNC Parks and Resorts manages all in-park accommodations. You can make reservations up to one year and a day in advance. Call central reservations at ☎ 559-253-5635 to reserve, ideally 366 days before your intended arrival, especially if you hope to visit between Memorial and Labor days. The phone lines are open Monday through Friday from 7 a.m. to 6 p.m., Saturday and Sunday from 8 a.m. to 5 p.m., and the service accepts all major credit cards. You also can make real-time online reservations (and find a few more details about the in-park facilities discussed in this section) at www.yosemitepark.com. Park hotels book up further in advance than you may expect, so make reservations as early as possible.

All rates are based on double occupancy. Expect to pay between $3 and $11 for each extra person ($21 at the Ahwahnee). Kids can sometimes stay free, so ask. Call the special-offer hot line at ☎ 559-454-0555 for discounted prices on winter stays (mid-Nov through Mar).

Ahwahnee Hotel
$$$$$ Yosemite Valley

The park's most elegant place to sleep is this baronial, ultraromantic landmark lodge, handsomely decorated in Native American style. Despite the elegance, it's right at home in the valley — it has the same grand scale. Afternoon tea is served in the great lounge, and breakfast, lunch, and dinner are served in the stunning dining room. Feel free to come for lunch in your shorts and sneakers, but dinner is a jacket- or sweater-required affair.

See map p. 212. ☎ *559-253-5635.* www.yosemitepark.com. *Free parking. Rack rates: $394–$865 double. AE, DC, DISC, MC, V.*

Curry Village
$–$$ Yosemite Valley

Sitting in the shadow of Glacier Point is Curry Village, whose accommodations include a few standard motel rooms, rustic wood-frame cabins (some with private bathrooms, some without), and canvas-covered tent cabins that are halfway to camping but still have wood floors, electricity, and maid service; they share a couple of central bathhouses. The whole place has a summer-camp-gone-to-heck vibe about it, but it's convenient and fun if privacy isn't a big concern. The village includes a cafeteria, a burger shack, a coffee and ice-cream counter, and a pizza parlor, plus an outdoor swimming pool and an activities desk with bike rentals (cross-country skis, snowshoes, and skates in winter). Fifty heated tent cabins are available in the winter, when you can also make use of the outdoor ice rink.

If you book a tent cabin at Curry Village, ask when you arrive whether any cancellations have cleared the way for an upgrade. If it's available, chances are good they'll give it away for free. It never hurts to ask, especially outside the summer season.

See map p. 212. ☎ *559-253-5635.* www.yosemitepark.com. *Free parking. Rack rates: $74–$123 double. AE, DC, DISC, MC, V*

Housekeeping Camp
$ Yosemite Valley

This arrangement is the closest you can get to roughing it without toting your own tent. The camp basically consists of a collection of semi-furnished concrete-and-canvas lean-to's on the banks of the Merced River. Each unit has a fire pit and grill; this is the only accommodation in the area that allows guests to cook meals. The experience is like camping at a KOA, with shared bathhouse, laundry, and a small grocery store.

See map p. 212. ☎ *559-253-5635.* www.yosemitepark.com. *Free parking. Rack rates: $72 up to four persons in one unit. AE, DC, DISC, MC, V.*

Tuolumne Meadows Lodge and White Wolf Lodge
$–$$ High Country (North Yosemite)

Both of these lodges have the same metal-frame canvas tent cabins that Curry Village has, but without the chaotic squatters' vibe. They are clean and neat, and most cabins sleep four and have wood-burning stoves. (White Wolf also has four cute wood cabins with private bathrooms.) White Wolf is a bit more out of the way and has fewer facilities; breakfast and dinner are served in the restaurant/general store. Tuolumne Meadows is larger and has a burger stand, a grocery store, stables, a mountaineering school, a gas station, and a dining tent for breakfast and dinner.

See map p. 212. ☎ *559-253-5635.* www.yosemitepark.com. *Free parking. Rack rates: $78–$105 double. Open summer only. AE, DC, DISC, MC, V.*

Wawona Hotel
$$–$$$ **South** Yosemite

The Wawona isn't as spectacular or luxurious as the Ahwahnee, but this national historic landmark lies in the much quieter southern section of the park (providing great relief from the valley crowds in summer) and boasts great Roaring '20s charm. The rooms contain no TVs or telephones, and only about half offer private bathrooms. Facilities include a nice restaurant that serves three meals; a pool; a tennis court; and 9 holes of golf.

See map p. 212. ☎ *559-253-5635.* www.yosemitepark.com. *Free parking. Rack rates: $126–$183 double. AE, DC, DISC, MC, V.*

Yosemite Lodge at the Falls
$$–$$$ **Yosemite** Valley

At press time, Yosemite Lodge at the Falls was about to embark on major construction, scheduled for a 2008 debut. The plan includes new buildings with more of a lodge feel (as opposed to motel-like) and rerouting Northside Drive, which will separate the auto traffic from all the people walking to the falls. Park management does not intend to shutter the lodge during construction — the idea is that new rooms will open before existing ones are demolished. If you're determined to stay in the heart of the valley bustle during these works, the standard rooms are okay, but lodge rooms with a bit more space and a view of Yosemite Falls are much preferable. None has air-conditioning or TV. The lodge includes a food court, a lovely restaurant, and a snack shack by the pool, all of which will stay open.

The dinner menu at Yosemite Lodge's Mountain View restaurant and at the Ahwahnee are nearly identical, as is the quality of the food, but the prices are lower at the lodge.

See map p. 212. ☎ *559-253-5635.* www.yosemitepark.com. *Free parking. Rack rates: $98–$178 double. AE, DC, DISC, MC, V.*

In addition, Yosemite has so many campsites that managing them is its own cottage industry. Still, they book up very quickly, so call as early as possible, especially for stays from May through September. Park Services accepts campsite reservations up to five months in advance, starting on the 15th of each month. (In other words, on Feb 15 you can begin to make reservations for June 15–July 14.) Calling on the first day is wise if you want your first choice.

You can find a complete rundown of the camping options, including fee information and locations, at www.nps.gov/yose/trip/camping.htm. You can also get the information you need by calling the reservations line at ☎ **800-436-7275** or 301-722-1257 daily between 7 a.m. and 7 p.m.

You can make online reservations at http://reservations.nps.gov. If Yosemite campgrounds are full, the reservations agents will gladly refer you to the National Forest campgrounds just outside the park.

Where to Stay and Dine outside the Park

Each of the hotels in this section is near one of the park's main gates. In addition to the two motels closest to the park, **Cedar Lodge** and **Yosemite View Lodge** (see the listings in this section), **Yosemite Motels** (☎ 888-742-4371; www.yosemite-motels.com) also runs the just-fine **Comfort Inn Oakhurst** ($80–$100 double), 15 miles south of the South Entrance, as well as two motels in Mariposa the **Best Western Yosemite Way Station** ($87–$97 double) and **Comfort Inn Mariposa** ($50–$90 double). The Mariposa motels are fine choices if everything else is booked, but you're better off first trying to stay closer to the park.

If you stay at **Cedar Lodge** or **Yosemite View Lodge,** or at any of the Mariposa choices discussed previously, you can leave your car behind and use the YARTS shuttle to reach the park if you choose (see the "Entering and navigating the park" section earlier in this chapter).

The area can get booked up in the busy season, so if our favorites are full, contact the **Yosemite Sierra Visitors Bureau** (☎ 559-683-4636; www.go2yosemite.net) for additional options.

Expect to eat at your hotel restaurant: Only if you stay in Oakhurst or Mariposa will you have other restaurants to choose from. Even there, pickings are slim — limited largely to pizza and fast food — so don't let dining dictate your choice of base. The exception: **Erna's Elderberry House** at the sumptuous **Château du Sureau** in Oakhurst.

Best Western Yosemite Gateway Inn
$-$$ Oakhurst

This perfectly nice motel, 15 miles due south of the park, offers pleasant rooms that are big enough for families. All rooms have coffeemakers, many have microwaves and fridges, and some have kitchens. Facilities include an indoor pool area with a spa, sauna, and exercise equipment; an outdoor pool and spa; and a coin-op laundry.

40530 Hwy. 41. ☎ *800-528-1234 or 559-683-2378. Fax: 559-683-3813.* www.best western.com. *Free parking. Rack rates: $79–$109 double, $99–$144 suite. Rates include continental breakfast. AE, DC, DISC, MC, V*

Cedar Lodge
$$ El Portal

Another nice motel, this one is located 8 miles outside of the Arch Rock entrance in a hilly setting along the Merced River. Rooms are motel-standard but quite comfortable. On-site are two pools (one indoor, one outdoor), a spa, a grocery store, and two restaurants — one a nice dining room and the other a casual pizza parlor.

See map p. 212. 9966 Hwy. 140. ☎ 888-742-4371 or 209-379-2612. Fax: 209-379-2712. www.yosemite-motels.com. *Free parking. Rack rates: $99–$135 double, $159 suite. AE, MC, V.*

Château du Sureau
$$$$$ Oakhurst

Finding one of America's finest inns in the rinky-dink town of Oakhurst, just a 20-minute drive from Yosemite's South Entrance, is wild. Staying at this gated Relais & Châteaux villa is like being entertained by European royalty, complete with maids to bring you tea and cookies and butlers to press your dinner clothes. The inn is supremely gorgeous and comfy — and the staff won't bat an eye when you stumble in dusty after a day in the park. Even if you're accustomed to luxury travel, you'll never forget this place. One of California's most celebrated restaurants, **Erna's Elderberry House,** is on the premises. The French Provençal–style cuisine is well worth a special-occasion splurge, even if you don't stay here ($92 prix-fixe).

48688 Victoria Lane (just off Highway 41, 15 miles south of Yosemite's South Entrance). ☎ 559-683-6860, or 559-683-6800 for restaurant reservations. Fax: 559-683-0800. www. chateaudusureau.com. *Free parking. Rack rates: $375–$575 double. Rates include an elegant two-course breakfast. AE, MC, V.*

Groveland Hotel
$$–$$$ Groveland

The charm of this sweet historic inn and the Wild West–style one-horse town makes up for the drive (23 miles west from the Big Oak Flat Entrance). The hotel houses the finest restaurant in town, plus a groovy gold-rush-era saloon. Rooms are furnished with antiques and have private bathrooms. A great in-between base if you'd also like to do a bit of Gold Country exploring along Highway 49.

18767 Main St. (Highway 120, east of Highway 49). ☎ 800-273-3314 or 209-962-4000. Fax: 209-962-6674. www.groveland.com. *Free parking. Rack rates: $135–$175 double, $225–275 suite. Rates include continental breakfast and evening wine. AE, DISC, MC, V.*

Tenaya Lodge
$$$–$$$$$ Fish Camp

This just-remodeled, gorgeous destination lodge draws in parkgoers as well as conference groups with its stone's-throw proximity to the park, terrific facilities, on-site activities, and rustic-glamorous wilderness-lodge-goes-modern ambience. The ultracomfy rooms are done in area-appropriate style and boast all the latest comforts. The facilities include two pools, three restaurants, game room, gym, spa services, and a terrific kids' program.

1122 Hwy. 41 (2 miles south of the South Entrance). ☎ 888-514-2167 or 559-683-6555. Fax: 559-683-8684. www.tenayalodge.com. *Free parking. Rack rates: $225–$375 double, $259 and up suite. AE, DC, DISC, MC, V.*

Yosemite View Lodge
S$$ El Portal

Just 2 miles outside the Arch Rock Entrance, this large motel complex is the closest you can get to Yosemite without actually staying within park bounds. Rooms are large and very comfy; all have kitchenettes, and many have Jacuzzi tubs, gas fireplaces, and balconies overlooking the rushing Merced River (we recommend spending a little extra for one of these). On-site are three pools (two outdoor, one indoor) and five spas, a decent restaurant, a bar, a pizza parlor, and a well-stocked general store.

See map p. 212. 11136 Hwy. 140. ☎ 888-742-4371 or 209-379-2681. Fax: 209-379-2704. www.yosemite-motels.com. *Free parking. Rack rates: $149–$239 double, $209–$439 suite. MC, V.*

Exploring Yosemite

We highly recommend launching your visit with the two-hour guided **Valley Floor Tour,** conducted aboard an open-air tram in warm weather, a cozy bus in winter. The tour is an absolute must if your visit is limited to one day, because it's the only way you can see all the park's major features. You can see the valley highlights by tour in the morning, and then spend your afternoon exploring the High Country or heading south to Wawona. Tours run daily, year-round, at regular intervals throughout the day. Tickets are $22 adults, $17 children; you can buy them at a booth just outside the Valley Store in Yosemite Village, or at any park accommodations tour desk. For more information, call the **Yosemite Lodge Tour Desk** (☎ 209-372-1240). Also ask about similar seasonal tours of other regions of the park.

If you're driving into Yosemite Valley from the South Entrance along Highway 41, stop at **Tunnel View** for one of the park's most stunning vistas. Pull over along with everybody else after you pass through the Wawona Tunnel on Route 41 for a bird's-eye overview of the valley. You can also catch this view on the drive south from the valley to Glacier Point Road or the Wawona section of the park.

Yosemite Valley highlights

The mile-wide, 7-mile-long **Yosemite Valley** is the attraction-laden heart of the mammoth park. Most park services are located in **Yosemite Village,** which even has a post office and a sizable store.

Make the Valley Visitor Center your first stop in Yosemite Village. You can pick up all the maps and information you need here, watch a short introductory movie, check the schedule of orientation programs and ranger-led activities, and get enough information about glacial geology and the local flora and fauna to give you a basic understanding of the park.

Next to the visitor center sits the **Yosemite Museum,** where you can find out about life in the valley before the Europeans showed up, and the **Ansel Adams Gallery,** which is wonderful for both browsing and buying the works of the master photographer as well as contemporary photographers who have a special talent for training their lens on the natural world. Shuttle service takes you to all corners of the valley from here (see the "Entering and navigating the park" section earlier in this chapter).

You won't want to miss the following Yosemite Valley highlights:

✔ Even before you reach the valley, you'll see beautiful **Bridalveil Fall** on your drive in; just look to the right. It's one of the prettiest falls in the park. You can pull into the parking lot and follow an easy, short trail to the base of the falls. (Both Bridalveil and Yosemite falls are usually dry in the summer.)

✔ To your left as you drive in, past Bridalveil, is **El Capitan,** the largest piece of solid granite in the world. Pull in to the turnout at El Capitan meadow to scour the immense face of this 3,593-foot-tall monolith for rock climbers. (Climbers are a cinch to spot after dark, when they turn their headlamps on.)

✔ From shuttle stop no. 7, just west of the visitor center, take an easy half-mile round-trip walk to the base of **Lower Yosemite Fall.** As you stand on the bridge facing the spray, you'll really feel the impressive force of the continent's tallest waterfall.

✔ From the valley floor, look to the northeast and you can't miss **Half Dome,** Yosemite's most famous feature — 4,733 extraordinary feet of 87-million-year-old brawny rock.

✔ The **Nature Center at Happy Isles,** on the easternmost shuttle loop (stop no. 16), has great hands-on nature exhibits for kids, plus wheelchair-accessible paths that run along the banks of the Merced River. Stop here early in your visit for information on the Valley Junior Ranger Program, which gives kids the opportunity to earn rewards for completing special park projects.

Glacier Point

In summer, you can drive the 32 miles from the valley floor to 3,200-foot **Glacier Point,** which offers the park's most stunning panoramic views. Not only can you see all the valley's highlights, but you catch views of the High Sierras to the north and west that are beyond breathtaking. From the valley, take Highway 41 to the Chinquapin junction and turn left onto Glacier Point Road (turn right if you're coming up from the South Entrance); allow about an hour each way for the drive. Sunrise from Glacier Point is spectacular.

If you're visiting in winter, bring your cross-country ski gear (or rent it at Badger Pass). You can drive as far as Badger Pass Ski Area (less than halfway), and ski your way to Glacier Point from there. Call ahead to inquire about overnight cross-country ski excursions to the point.

Wawona/South Yosemite

Mariposa Grove, at the quieter, woodsy southern section of the park (about 35 miles south of the valley via Highway 41), is the most impressive of the park's three groves of giant sequoias, the world's largest trees. Giant sequoias are shorter but more massive than their lanky cousins, the coastal redwoods (see Chapter 14), with distinctive bell-bottom bases as large as 35 feet in diameter. That is one big tree — and you'll find a whole stand of them here! Grizzly Giant, the oldest tree in the grove, is one of the largest sequoias in the world.

From the parking area, an easy interpretive trail leads through the grove, with placards offering a self-guided tour. The grove also has a small museum. From the valley, follow Highway 41 south and take the signed turnoff; the drive takes about 75 minutes. You can also hop on a shuttle bus to reach the grove, but the long distance from the valley makes driving more efficient for time-challenged visitors. The grove is open year-round, but heavy snow occasionally closes the access road.

The High Country

At an 8,600-foot elevation, stunning **Tuolumne Meadows** bursts with wildflowers in summer (this high up, where the snow sticks around through June, summer seems more like spring). The 55-mile drive from the valley takes one and a half hours along the gorgeous Tioga Road (Highway 120; open in summer only). The magnificent drive alone is half the fun, so allow more time to stop at the myriad overlooks. You'll pass lush meadows, thickly wooded forests, granite domes, and ice-blue glacial lakes — the most notable being **Tenaya Lake,** a popular spot for windsurfing, fishing, and canoeing.

Consider buying a copy of *The Yosemite Road Guide* at the visitor center before you set out. This publication contains a good self-guided driving tour of the route. After you arrive, stop at the Tuolumne Meadows Visitor Center for orientation, trail, and program information.

Walking the walk: Hiking and nature trails

With 860 miles of trails, Yosemite has a hike for you, no matter what your level of stamina and experience. Nature writers dedicate whole volumes to hiking the park, so you're better off referring to a more complete source for the full range of options.

In addition to the walks to **Yosemite Falls** and **Bridalveil Fall** (see the "Yosemite Valley highlights" section earlier in this chapter), here are some of the best day hikes. Check the *Yosemite Guide* newspaper for additional day-hiking options. A very useful "Yosemite Valley Day Hikes" single-sheet handout is also generally available. Be smart and remember to check conditions at the visitor center before you set out.

✔ The easy mile-long round-trip walk to **Mirror Lake** will reward you with remarkable views. The trailhead leaves from shuttle stop no. 17 (behind the stables). You can then follow the lovely 5-mile loop around the lake if you choose.

✔ The **John Muir/Mist Trail** is the park's most popular hike, so set out early or save it for later in the day. The trail leaves from **Happy Isles** (shuttle stop no. 16) and climbs alongside the Merced River (whose rushing whitewater naturalist and park godfather John Muir called "the symphony of the Sierras") to **Vernal Fall.** The initial .75-mile portion of the trail is moderately difficult and follows a paved but steep trail that leads to a bridge with terrific views of the falls.

If you consider yourself to be hardy, you can continue along the strenuous .75-mile "Mist" portion, which sharply ascends 600 more feet (for a total elevation gain of 1,000 ft.) directly alongside the fall (expect spray) and includes countless granite steps (that StairMaster experience will really come in handy here) before you reach the pool at the top. Allow two to four hours.

✔ Up at Tuolumne Meadows, try the easy 1.5-mile round-trip walk to **Soda Springs.** The trailhead leaves from just east of the visitor center and follows a gurgling river through a peaceful section of meadow to a bubbling carbonated spring.

✔ Hardcore hikers may want to tackle the 17-mile cable-hike ascent to the top of **Half Dome,** a full-day affair that's only for the hardiest. You need leather gloves and hiking boots with serious traction. Call the **information line** at ☎ 209-372-0200 for details or consult a ranger before you go.

To tour the park with a knowledgeable guide — an excellent idea, especially if you want to venture off the busiest trails — go with **Yosemite Guides** (☎ 209-379-9111; www.yosemiteguides.com). They'll lead you on natural-history walks and birding tours, take you fly-fishing, and even rent you a mountain bike. They have a desk at the **Yosemite View Lodge** (see the "Where to Stay and Dine outside the Park" section earlier in this chapter), but we highly recommend booking before you arrive.

Talking the talk: Ranger-led programs

In addition to guided tram and bus tours (see the "Exploring Yosemite" section earlier in this chapter), park rangers offer a phenomenal number of guided walks and interpretive programs. The calendar is chockfull from morning until night with morning-light photo walks, birding walks, bear talks, Discover Yosemite family programs, brown-bag lunch lectures, fireside discussions . . . you get the picture. A number of children's programs are offered, and the Junior Ranger program is excellent. Some activities carry a fee, but many are free. Check the *Yosemite Guide* newspaper or inquire at the visitor center for the complete schedule.

The artist in you may want to check the schedule of free, informal, outdoor art classes offered in various media throughout the summer by the **Art Activity Center,** located in Yosemite Village next to the Village Store. You can find the schedule on the Yosemite Valley Activities page at www.yosemitepark.com, under "Recreation."

The highly respected **Yosemite Theater** (behind the Valley Visitor's Center) stages dramatic interpretive programs (actorly portrayals of *Spirit of John Muir,* for example, or *Conversations with a Tramp*), as well as occasional concerts in the evenings. Tickets are usually less than $10 for adults and less than $5 for kids. These events are hugely popular, so buy your tickets early in the day to avoid disappointment.

Gathering More Information

Whether traveling to Yosemite, Mammoth Mountain, or both, contact these visitor organizations for more details about your destination.

Yosemite National Park

Call the park's 24-hour **information line** at ☎ **209-372-0200,** or go online to www.yosemitepark.com. You can also use this number to check road conditions (always a good idea). Request a copy of the official *Yosemite Guide* when you call. You can find this seasonal newspaper in the park, but it has invaluable trip-planning information — including the latest on road construction and policy changes to mitigate traffic congestion — that can come in handy before you go.

The Yosemite Association maintains a useful site at www.yosemite.org, complete with an online bookstore where you can order materials to read up on the park before you go.

For information on the surrounding area, your best source is the **Yosemite Sierra Visitors Bureau,** 40637 Hwy. 41, Oakhurst (☎ **559-683-4636;** www.yosemite-sierra.org). In addition to providing general visitor information, they're happy to help with just-outside-the-park lodging reservations. Another good site is www.yosemite.com.

Part IV
The Central Coast

"Since we lost the dolphins, business hasn't been quite the same.

In this part . . .

This part covers California's Central Coast, which includes such wonderful destinations as the Monterey Peninsula, Big Sur, Hearst Castle, and our personal favorite (and hometown), Santa Barbara.

Where the San Francisco Bay Area meets the Monterey Peninsula sits Santa Cruz, California's kinda wacky surf town. If you ask us (and apparently you did), the Central Coast — that stretch between San Francisco and Los Angeles — represents California at its very best. The drive along coastal Highway 1 is breathtaking in more ways than one. The Monterey Peninsula Cradles Monterey Bay, one of the richest and most diverse marine habitats on Earth, plus a collection of the state's most delightful communities, from family-friendly Monterey itself to world-class golf mecca Pebble Beach to cozy Carmel-by-the-Sea. Be sure to dedicate a full day to the natural splendor of Big Sur; trust us, you won't regret it, even if you don't want to stay in one of the region's funky hotels. Hearst Castle, Cambria, fairy-tale Solvang, gorgeous Santa Barbara, and the peaceful Ojai Valley complete this thoroughly charming part of the state.

Chapter 17

Beach Blanket Babylon: Santa Cruz

Santa Cruz, the quintessential college town, beach town, and surf mecca, sits just a stone's throw from the Bay Area at the northwestern end of Monterey Bay. Monterey is the prime destination along the coast (see Chapter 18), but Santa Cruz is within easy reach of San Francisco — perfect for Northern California vacationers who want a taste of genuine Golden State beach life or for anyone who wants to avoid the tourist throngs that can overwhelm Monterey in summer.

Families with kids in tow will especially enjoy the **Santa Cruz Beach Boardwalk** (☎ 831-423-5590; www.beachboardwalk.com), the West Coast's only seaside amusement park. If you hail from the East Coast, push those visions of the gritty Jersey boardwalk from your mind — Santa Cruz's version is everything a seaside boardwalk was meant to be. It's clean, family-friendly, and filled with amusements, from arcade games ("Getcha stuffed Elmo right he-ah! Three plays for a dol-lah!") to cotton-candy and funnel-cake vendors to thrill rides — even an old-fashioned wooden roller coaster that's rickety good fun. And, in summer, the beach scene out front is straight out of the movie *Gidget*.

Inland from the beach lies a charming downtown whose hippie element has been minimized, but not eliminated, by necessary post-earthquake gentrification. (Santa Cruz was seriously damaged in the 1989 Loma Prieta earthquake.) As a result, you'll find a nice blend of affordable but high-quality restaurants and boutiques, along with a genuine and appealing laid-back California coast vibration.

Timing Your Visit

California's middle coastline enjoys mild weather all the time, with highs in the mid-70s in summer and the mid-50s in winter. Late summer — from mid-July through September, and often into October — is usually best for sunny beachgoing and boardwalk fun. Crowds do not present a huge problem; in fact, we like Santa Cruz best on summer weekends, when it's at its liveliest.

 Boardwalk operation is limited to weekends in spring and fall and restricted to holidays in winter, so be sure to check the schedule before you head here with the kids in the off-season.

If you want to stay in Santa Cruz, plan on one or two nights and a couple of days to enjoy it all, with maybe a third full day to book a fishing charter or kayak trip. If you're driving between Monterey and the Bay Area, allot at least a few hours to stop and enjoy the boardwalk and downtown a bit before continuing on your journey.

Getting There

Santa Cruz is 76 miles southeast of San Francisco. You can choose the quick route or the scenic route:

✓ **The quick route:** Take I-280 to Highway 85 to Highway 17, which deposits you onto Ocean Street, leading right to the beach. At its best, this route takes about 90 minutes, but could be much longer if you hit traffic.

✓ **The scenic route:** Take Highway 1 the entire way, which takes about twice as long. One stretch of Highway 1, called Devil's Slide, isn't for the faint of heart — as you may have guessed from the name — but the rest is pretty easy driving.

 If you're heading to Santa Cruz on a weekend morning, skip the quick route in favor of Highway 1, because Highway 17 tends to logjam with Bay Area beachgoers.

If you're coming from Monterey, 45 miles away, take Highway 1 north. The drive takes about an hour.

Orienting Yourself and Getting Around

Santa Cruz is small and easy to navigate. Both Highway 17 and Highway 1 take you straight into the heart of town (see the "Santa Cruz" map on p. 231). Exit Highway 1 from River Street and follow it to Front Street to reach the shopping and dining district in the heart of downtown (Pacific Avenue is the main drag).

Santa Cruz

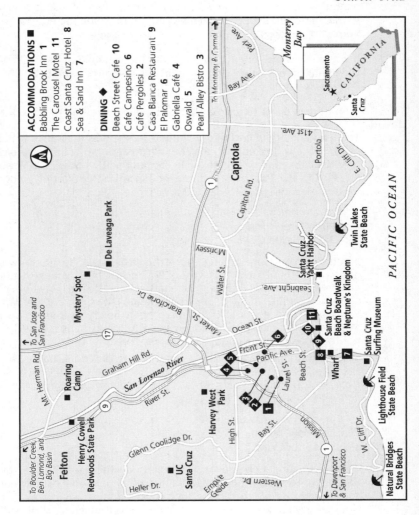

ACCOMMODATIONS ■
Babbling Brook Inn **1**
The Carousel Motel **11**
Coast Santa Cruz Hotel **8**
Sea & Sand Inn **7**

DINING ◆
Beach Street Cafe **10**
Cafe Campesino **6**
Cafe Pergolesi **2**
Casa Blanca Restaurant **9**
El Palomar **6**
Gabriella Café **4**
Oswald **5**
Pearl Alley Bistro **3**

Proceed down Front Street to oceanfront Beach Street to reach the
beach. Head west along Beach Street until it becomes West Cliff Drive,
whose beachfront path offers gorgeous ocean views and an excellent
look at the local surfing action (and probably a few clusters of fuzzy sea
lions sunning themselves on the rocks below).

Where to Stay in Santa Cruz

To be blunt, the choices around here are mediocre, with a few exceptions, and low expectations would be a sensible idea. Because Santa

Cruz is a beach destination, summer rates are significantly higher than winter rates. You'll also pay more for the privilege of visiting over the weekend — and expect a two-night minimum if you include Saturday in your stay.

If you'd like more lodging options than those included here, check with the **Santa Cruz County Conference and Visitors Council** (☎ 800-833-3494; www.santacruzca.org).

Count on an extra 12 percent in taxes being tacked on to your hotel bill.

 You'll find plenty of inexpensive motels by the beach, none of which sport much in the way of curb appeal, but we do approve of the **Carousel Motel** (see the listing in this section). The **Ocean Pacific Lodge,** 120 Washington St. (☎ 831-457-1234), is another economical choice offering great value for money; rates go as low as $59.

Babbling Brook Inn
$$$–$$$$ **Santa Cruz**

If you're looking for romance, book this little oasis. It's just a two-minute drive (or a ten-minute walk) west of downtown, but, because it sits among an acre of gorgeous gardens, you'd hardly know it. You can choose from 13 charming rooms, all based on an art theme (the Cezanne, the Monet, the Van Gogh, and so on). Baths have been newly renovated to include whirlpool tubs, and fireplaces have been added to many rooms. Lovely but not too cutesy, thank goodness — a real romantic treat.

See map p. 231. 1025 Laurel St. (at California Street). ☎ *800-866-1131 or 831-427-2437. Fax: 831-427-2457.* www.innsbythesea.com/babbling-brook. *Free parking. Rack rates: $142–$244 double. Rates include full breakfast and afternoon wine and hors d'oeuvres. AE, DC, DISC, MC, V.*

The Carousel Motel
$–$$$ **Santa Cruz**

 This is the budget choice for vacationers destined for the boardwalk and the beach. You enter the main building by way of a room card-key-accessed gate, a security feature that either strikes you the right way or has you wondering what all the fuss is about. Rooms are spacious, neat, and plainly furnished with pine pieces, microwaves, refrigerators, and TVs. Views encompass more building than ocean, but the price is right. Vacation packages that include boardwalk tickets make it an even better value.

See map p. 231. 110 Riverside Ave. ☎ *831-425-7090 or 800-214-7400.* www.santacruzmotels.com. *Free parking. Rack rates: $49–$169 double, $79–$179 double with spa. Rates include continental breakfast. AE, DISC, MC, V.*

Coast Santa Cruz Hotel
$$$–$$$$ Santa Cruz

This nice but architecturally bland hotel is the only lodging in town with direct beach access. The rooms are unremarkable but comfy; all have balconies with mesmerizing ocean views. In-room extras such as Sony PlayStations, minifridges, and coffeemakers mean they're family-friendly, too. The beachfront pool area is well furnished and leads right to Santa Cruz's prime stretch of sand. If it suits your budget, the location can't be beat and that's what you'll be paying for.

See map p. 231. 175 W. Cliff Dr. (adjacent to the Santa Cruz Wharf). ☎ **800-716-6199** *or 831-426-4330. Fax: 831-427-2025.* www.coasthotels.com. *Free parking. Rack rates: $169–$273 double, $225–$450 suite. AE, DISC, MC, V.*

Sea & Sand Inn
$$–$$$ Santa Cruz

This friendly and fabulously situated oceanfront motel is a true gem. It lies clifftop above the surf, a short walk from the beach and boardwalk. The motel rooms are really nice, all with good-quality furnishings and panoramic ocean views. The lovely garden, with a furnished terrace overlooking the water, is a wonderful place to relax. With a kitchen and a private patio with Jacuzzi, the suite is well worth a splurge or if you have the kids in tow. This is a terrific choice that would be perfect if it had a pool. Make reservations three months in advance for summer weekends.

See map p. 231. 201 W. Cliff Dr. ☎ **831-427-3400.** *Fax: 831-466-9882.* www.santa cruzmotels.com. *Free parking. Rack rates: $99–$209 double, $149–$279 double with spa, $199–$359 studio or suite. Rates include continental breakfast, plus afternoon refreshments in most seasons. AE, MC, V.*

Where to Dine in Santa Cruz

Santa Cruz boasts a thriving restaurant scene, so you can expect to eat well here. The following are our local favorites.

Beach Street Cafe
$ Santa Cruz   AMERICAN

You may be tempted to eat on the wharf, but take a nice walk out on the pier, admire the ocean, then turn around and breakfast at this friendly little cafe where the eggs are fine, the bacon isn't greasy, and the homemade muffins are quite yummy.

See map p. 231. 399 Beach St. ☎ **831-426-7621.** www.beachstreetcafe.com. *No reservations. Main courses: $5–$12. MC, V. Open: Daily 8 a.m.–3 p.m.*

Casa Blanca Restaurant
$$$–$$$$ Santa Cruz   CONTINENTAL/SEAFOOD

This wonderful restaurant is one of the most romantic in town. The white-linen-covered tables are terraced so that every diner has an ocean view, and twinkling white lights add to the ambience. The old-school, seafood-heavy menu more than lives up to the stellar setting. Look for such winning dishes as ruby-red ahi crowned with fresh mango and roasted green chili sauce, and New York steak in a bourbon-peppercorn demi-glace. The Casa Blanca has excellent service and a great wine list, too.

See map p. 231. In the Casa Blanca Inn, 101 Main St. (at Beach Street). ☎ *831-423-1570.* www.casablanca-santacruz.com. *Reservations recommended. Main courses: $19–$32. AE, DC, DISC, MC, V. Open: Daily 5–9:30 p.m.*

El Palomar
$$–$$$ Santa Cruz   MEXICAN

Airy and cheerful, this Mexican restaurant in the heart of downtown is a great place to enjoy an affordable meal. It doesn't have the best Mexican grub in California, but the generous plates are well prepared and quite pleasing. Expect all your favorites, from saucy enchiladas to sizzling fajitas. Seafood lovers shouldn't miss the excellent seviches, freshly prepared and perfectly seasoned with lime (the octopus is particularly good).

See map p. 231. 1336 Pacific Ave. ☎ *831-425-7575. Reservations recommended for dinner. Main courses and combo plates: $8–$20. AE, DISC, MC, V. Open: Mon–Fri 11 a.m.–3 p.m. and 5–10 p.m., Sat 11 a.m.–10:30 p.m., Sun 11 a.m.–10 p.m.*

Gabriella Café
$$–$$$ Santa Cruz   CALIFORNIA

Charming and romantic, Gabriella is a terrific bet if you want a touch of sophistication for a reasonable price. Expect fresh, organic veggies; perhaps a pan-roasted local halibut or mushroom and leek bread pudding;

Finding a hidden gem of a taco

For a quick bite, an alfresco lunch, or an über-casual dinner on a warm night, head for the 1100 block of Pacific Avenue and look for two permanent kiosks with seating in between. You'll discover some of the best Mexican food in town at **Cafe Campesino,** 1130 Pacific Ave. (☎ 831-425-5979), nothing fancy to say the least, but fresh and real. Customers choose from a handful of fillings and sauces to create a customized taco or quesadilla, using thick, chewy, handmade corn tortillas. Large plates are also offered, and we're anxious to get back to try the mole. Prices are more than reasonable; three enchiladas verde with rice and beans at $9.95 is the most expensive item on the menu. Another bonus: The street scene is vastly entertaining.

Finding a hidden gem of a cappuccino

Full of students, artists, writers, and intellectuals — both pseudo and actual, we're guessing — **Café Pergolesi,** 418A Cedar St. at Maple Street (☎ **831-426-1775**), gets our vote for coolest coffeehouse within 50 miles. The quintessential Santa Cruz hangout, a seat on the patio is the best place to study the locals in all their retro-hippie, granola-crunching, unselfconscious glory. Plus, the coffee is so good, we're tempted to tout it as the most delicious on the coast.

and *pan amore,* homemade focaccia with delectable roast garlic, basil pesto, and heirloom tomato spreads If you arrive during strawberry season, hope for the starter featuring local berries, fresh ricotta, and cress, with a splash of balsamic vinegar. Heavenly. The restaurant also offers al fresco seating in the cute alley garden.

See map p. 231. 910 Cedar St. (between Locust Street and Walnut Avenue, 1 block over from Pacific Avenue). ☎ 831-457-1677. www.gabriellacafe.com. Reservations recommended. Main courses: $15–$25. AE, DISC, MC, V. Open: Mon–Thurs 11:30 a.m.–9 p.m., Fri 11:30 a.m–10 p.m., Sat 10:30 a.m.–2:30 p.m. and 5–10 p.m., and Sun 10:30 a.m.–2:30 p.m. and 5–9 p.m.

Oswald
$$$–$$$$ Santa Cruz   CALIFORNIA/FRENCH

Located in a little courtyard, this intimate cottage is considered by many to be the best restaurant in town. The menu is seasonal but you may find pan-roasted skirt steak or seared scallops and toothsome sides such as creamy polenta and mushrooms on the list. Service is smart; wine drinkers will be pleased with the selection and advice. Chocolate lovers: Don't pass up the dessert soufflé.

See map p. 231. 1547 Pacific Ave. ☎ 831-423-7427. Reservations recommended. Main courses: $18–$26. AE, DISC, MC, V. Open: Tues–Sun 5:30–10 p.m.

Pearl Alley Bistro
$$–$$$ Santa Cruz   CALIFORNIA/FRENCH

Locals praise this attractive, slightly funky bistro for it's warm ambience, and it is also an excellent spot to enjoy an innovative meal. Expect French classics such as bouillabaisse and bacon-wrapped sweetbreads, but don't be surprised when the chef takes California-style liberties in preparation, offering such dishes as giant sea scallops served on artichoke bottoms and aromatically seasoned with lavender and thyme. An oddity is the do-it-yourself Mongolian barbecue, which you cook at your table on a sizzling rock. The restaurant offers friendly service and a decent wine selection, too.

See map p. 231. 110 Pearl Alley (between Lincoln and Walnut avenues). ☎ *831-429-8070.* www.pearlalley.com. *Reservations recommended. Main courses: $17–$26. AE, MC, V. Open: Sun–Thurs 5:30–9 p.m., Fri–Sat 5:30–10 p.m.*

Hitting the Boardwalk

All the good-time boardwalk fun detailed in this section faces **Cowell Beach,** a vast stretch of sand that really comes alive in summer. So grab your beach towel and catch some rays alongside the bevy of beach-goers, which range from vacationing Bay Area families to bikini-clad coeds to volleyball-playing surfer dudes.

The Santa Cruz Beach Boardwalk

This landmark oceanfront boardwalk — the only beach amusement park on the West Coast — is a retro jewel. The well-kept, beautifully maintained wooden boardwalk (here in one form or another since 1907) offers nearly 30 rides, plus dozens of skill games, tacky souvenir shops, and food vendors (hot dogs, cotton candy, funnel cake) — more than enough to entertain kids of all ages well into the evening, when a rainbow of bright lights heightens the appeal. The boardwalk boasts two national landmarks: the wooden **Giant Dipper** roller coaster, a 1924 original and still a marvelous thrill ride; and the 1911 **Looff Carousel,** a work of art with hand-carved wooden horses and a magnificent pipe organ. The boardwalk also includes a good kiddie area with nine rides. You'll pay for rides with tickets you buy at booths strategically placed along the boardwalk; the booths also offer unlimited-ride passes for committed thrill-seekers. The boardwalk is hugely popular, especially in summer, but the crowds are all part of the fun. Buy unlimited-ride passes online and save $5; also check for online coupons.

Along Beach Street, between Pacific and Riverside avenues. ☎ *831-426-7433 or 831-423-5590.* www.beachboardwalk.com. *Admission: Free; rides $1.95–$3.90; all-day unlimited-ride pass $26. Open: Memorial Day to Labor Day, daily 11 a.m.–late; hours for the rest of the year vary widely, with limited holiday operation in winter, so call or check the Web site for the schedule.*

Neptune's Kingdom and Casino Fun Center/Supercade

Think the boardwalk is limited to nostalgic entertainment? Not hardly! These enormous, indoor, family-fun centers feature loads of millennium-worthy fun, including the **MaxFlight CyberCoaster,** the world's only rider-programmable virtual roller coaster; laser tag; a two-story miniature-golf course with a pirate theme; and enough classic and cutting-edge arcade games to exhaust the National Mint's supply of quarters.

Adjacent to the boardwalk at 400 Beach St. ☎ *831-426-7433 or 831-423-5590.* www.beachboardwalk.com. *Admission: Free; charges vary for individual games and attractions. Open: Daily from 10 a.m.; closing hours vary; limited hours in winter.*

Santa Cruz Municipal Wharf

This old-time pier isn't as grimy or commercial as Monterey's; it has a nice maritime vibe, but it's still a shade on the tacky side. Locals cast and crab from the wooden pier, which is lined with cheesy shops, sportfishing charters, and the to-be-expected mediocre seafood restaurants. **Santa Cruz Boat Rentals** (☎ 831-423-1739) offers equipment rentals as well as bait and tackle. **Stagnaro's Fishing Trips** (☎ 831-427-2334) can take you deep-sea fishing as well as on whale- and sea-lion-watching cruises. The wharf also offers an excellent photo-op of the boardwalk. You can park here, too, for a minimal charge, but be aware that traffic can really back up; you may be better off putting your wheels in a street lot.

On Beach Street, just west of the boardwalk. ☎ *831-420-5270.* www.santacruz wharf.com. *Admission: Free. Open: Daily 5 a.m.–2 a.m. (most shops open daily 7 a.m.–9 p.m.).*

Surfing and Other Cool Stuff to See and Do

Follow Beach Street west from the boardwalk and it quickly turns into West Cliff Drive, a gorgeous clifftop road lined with fine old houses on one side and spectacular ocean views on the other.

At Lighthouse Point (within walking distance of the wharf) sits the petite **Santa Cruz Surfing Museum** (☎ 831-420-6289; www.santacruzsurfing museum.org), which traces surfing history from both local and broader points of view (with a nice accent on oft-neglected female surfers). You can easily see the collection of surfboards and other memorabilia in an hour or less. It's open Thursday through Monday from noon to 4 p.m. The suggested donation is $1.

Lighthouse Point also serves as the perfect vantage for **Steamer Lane,** Santa Cruz's infamous surfing spot. If you're lucky and the surf's up, you'll see some daredevil pros riding the waves.

Kayaking the bay

Monterey Bay is a fabulous place to kayak in summer, even for beginners. You'll glide right by sunbathing sea lions and snacking sea otters as shorebirds swoop through the air around you. **Venture Quest Kayaking** (www.kayaksantacruz.com) rents kayaks to experienced paddlers at their wharf location (☎ 831-425-8445). You can schedule a guided bay adventure ($45 per person) by calling the Beach Street location (☎ 831-427-2267). Venture Quest also offers a guided tour of Elkhorn Slough, a calm-as-can-be, wildlife-rich estuary of Monterey Bay ($65 per person).

Browsing Pacific Avenue

One of the best things about Santa Cruz is its charming downtown, which boasts an authentic laid-back California coast charm — not to mention a fair amount of shopping, most of it unique and affordable. The main drag for browsers is Pacific Avenue, which is chock-a-block with boutiques, bookstores, and record shops from Mission to Laurel streets. You'll find some gems on the side streets just off Pacific, too, such as **Annieglass,** 110 Cooper St. (☎ **831-427-4260**), an outlet store for locally made art-glass jewelry and housewares — a real find if you're looking for gifts.

Need a restroom downtown? The nice folks at **Bookshop Santa Cruz,** 1520 Pacific Ave. (☎ **831-423-0900;** www.bookshopsantacruz.com), allow access to theirs. According to one local we know, these are the only toilets on the street open to the public. (A fantastic selection of books is available as well.)

Marveling at the Mystery Spot

Okay, so you won't exactly marvel at the **Mystery Spot,** 465 Mystery Spot Rd. (☎ **831-423-8897;** www.mysteryspot.com), but lovers of kitsch will enjoy this funhouse in the woods. Ads tout it as a natural phenomenon where the accepted rules of gravity, perspective, compass, velocity, and height no longer exist (phooey on you, Newton!). It's a real hoot if you like silly stuff, and it's open daily from 9 a.m. to 7 p.m. in the summer and 9 a.m. to 5 p.m. in the winter. The tour lasts only 35 minutes, but expect an hour-long wait in summer. Admission is $5. Just *finding* the Mystery Spot can be a mystery: From Pacific Avenue, turn right on Water Street and left on Market Street, which turns into Branciforte Drive; follow the signs.

Taking a ride through the redwoods

Want a glimpse of California's majestic redwoods and pioneering past, but don't have time to visit the North Coast or the Gold Country? Catch a ride on the **Roaring Camp Narrow Gauge Railroad** (☎ **831-335-4484;** www.roaringcamprr.com), which takes riders aboard the nation's last steam-powered passenger railroad through the Santa Cruz Mountains on a 75-minute round-trip. Trips leave from Roaring Camp, a half-hour's drive from Santa Cruz, daily during the warmer months (weekends only in winter). Rates are $18 adults, $12 kids 3 to 12. They also offer a beach-to-redwoods round-trip for $20 adults, $15 kids.

A parsimonious friend of ours suggests parking on Highway 9 near the entrance to Henry Cowell Redwoods State Park, then walking into the park and through the little gate into Roaring Camp. You'll save on parking fees twice!

Adding some drama to the proceedings

The University of California at Santa Cruz has been home to a well-regarded and popular summer **Shakespeare Festival** since 1975. The season begins the second week of July and runs through the end of August with weekend matinees and evening performances. Much of the festival takes place outdoors, and regulars bring blankets or cushions to sit on, plus picnics to enjoy before the show. This isn't a student-run program — actors from all around the country vie for roles, and the direction is often edgy and provocative. For information on the summer season, ticket prices, and dates, check online at www.shakespeare santacruz.org or call the box office Tuesday through Saturday afternoons at ☎ 831-459-2159.

Gathering More Information

Call the **Santa Cruz County Conference and Visitors Council** (☎ 800-833-3494 or 831-425-1234) or point your Web browser to www.santa cruzca.crg. After you arrive, stop in at the friendly and helpful visitor center at 1211 Ocean St., at Kennan Street.

Chapter 18

The Monterey Peninsula

● ●

In This Chapter

▶ Deciding when to visit — and where to stay, eat, and play

▶ Visiting maritime Monterey's aquarium and other top attractions

▶ Hitting the links and seeing the sights in elite Pebble Beach

▶ Cozying up in romantic Carmel-by-the-Sea and the Carmel Valley

● ●

*P*repare yourself for some of the most spectacular real estate you'll ever see when you visit this rocky, cypress-dotted stretch of California coast. A mystical, foggy shoreline rich with natural beauty and steeped in maritime history, it's home to the largest marine sanctuary in the continental United States, as well as some of the state's most charming communities.

The Monterey Peninsula juts out into the ocean at the south end of Monterey Bay. The bay is the deepest part of the ocean just off the North American coast, twice as deep as the Grand Canyon. As a result, it houses one of the most diverse collections of marine animals on the planet. Sea lions, otters, pelicans, gulls, even whales are a major presence and set the tone for life here. (More than one hotel manager reports that guests in ocean-facing rooms frequently call to complain about the barking dogs that wake them in the predawn hours — to which the manager explains that you can't tell a sea lion to quiet down.)

The biggest draw on the peninsula is the town of **Monterey,** home to the justifiably world-famous **Monterey Bay Aquarium,** one of the premier attractions in the Golden State, and **Cannery Row,** the sardine-canning center immortalized by John Steinbeck and since transformed into a family-friendly tourist zone. The aquarium actually lies half in Monterey and half in neighboring **Pacific Grove,** which we discuss in conjunction with Monterey because the dividing line is unnecessary for our purposes. From a base in either town, you can easily enjoy the charms and attractions of both.

Sculpted out of the midsection of the peninsula is **Pebble Beach,** home to some of the most beautiful woodlands, some of the priciest residential real estate, and the best championship golf resorts in the country. If you're looking for world-class greens, this is the place to be — but pack that platinum card, because it doesn't come cheap. You even have to pay to tour this territory — $8.75 to be exact — along **17-Mile Drive,** a gorgeous private road that traverses hill and dale along a meandering loop.

At the south end of the peninsula is **Carmel-by-the-Sea,** one of the sweetest little towns around, and home to one of California's most stunning beaches. This upscale haven exists to delight you even if you want to do nothing more than eat, shop, and amble about the village. In fact, that's pretty much all there is to do here, but it's a pleasant way to while away the hours.

Timing Your Visit

The weather on the Monterey Peninsula is moderate year-round — the average daily temperature along the coast varies only by about 12 degrees throughout the calendar year, with average highs in the mid-60s and average lows in the low 50s. Fog can be a factor, consistently keeping the summers misty and gray, especially in the morning hours; in fact, you could see more sunshine in January than in July. Don't let fog-bound days keep you away, however — the misty haze only adds to the Monterey mystique. Still, the best time to visit is Indian summer, from August through October, when days are sunniest and warmest. Jazz fans may want to plan their trip around the **Monterey Jazz Festival** (☎ **831-373-3366;** www.monterey jazzfest.com), which takes over the town for a three-day weekend every September.

Temperatures are appreciably warmer and days are sunnier inland. Although most of the area's prime destinations lie along the coast, if it's sun that you're after, consider making Carmel Valley your headquarters. You have to drive inland only 15 minutes or so for temps to climb well into the 80s or 90s in July or August.

Expect hotel rates to peak in summer and on weekends. The good news for off-season travelers: You just may end up with the best weather at the lowest prices. The exception is late January and early February during the celebrity pro/am golf tournament in Pebble Beach: Even the pigeons have trouble finding accommodations at that time.

Take along a jacket, a sweater, and long pants, even if you're visiting in the height of summer. Shorts and T-shirts just won't do. For the current local forecast for the Monterey Peninsula, call ☎ **831-656-1725.**

Less than 5 miles separate Monterey on the north end from Carmel on the south end, but this action-packed peninsula boasts lots of attractions. Exploring the area can easily fill five or six days. If your time is limited, two days is enough to examine Monterey thoroughly, but set aside at least a half-day for the aquarium. Plan to spend a third day in Carmel (you can enjoy a lovely stretch of the 17-Mile Drive on your way there), lounging by the hotel pool or driving your way around a golf course.

Getting There

The Monterey Peninsula is just off Highway 1 (see the "The Monterey Peninsula" map on p. 244), about 46 miles south of Santa Cruz, 122 miles south of San Francisco, and 86 miles north of Hearst Castle.

✔ **To get there from Santa Cruz:** Take Highway 1 south for about an hour; follow the exit signs into Monterey, or go another 3 miles south to the Ocean Avenue exit to get to Carmel. (Watch for the Ocean Avenue exit, because it doesn't explicitly say "Carmel.")

✔ **To get there from San Francisco:** Follow the route suggested in Chapter 17 to Santa Cruz and pick up Highway 1 as described in the preceding bullet.

✔ **To get there from Cambria:** Follow Highway 1 through Big Sur. This spectacular drive is slow-going and can easily take a full day with stops (see Chapter 19 for details).

You can fly into Monterey Peninsula Airport, located on Olmsted Road 4 miles east of Monterey off Highway 68 (☎ **831-648-7000;** www. montereyairport.com). Serving the airport are

✔ **American/American Eagle:** ☎ **800-433-7300;** www.aa.com

✔ **America West Express:** ☎ **800-235-9292;** www.americawest.com

✔ **Delta:** ☎ **800-221-1212;** www.delta.com

✔ **United:** ☎ **800-241-6522;** www.ual.com

You can rent a car from one of the major national car-rental companies located at the airport (see Chapter 7 for car-rental details).

You can also catch a ride with **Yellow Cab/Carmel Taxi** (☎ **831-646-8294**), which usually has cabs circling the airport; expect the fare into Monterey to cost about $13.

Before you pay for a taxi, check with your hotel to find out whether it offers a complimentary shuttle service.

Monterey and Pacific Grove

As the first capital of California (when the state was under Spanish rule) and the hub of West Coast nautical life, Monterey has a rich history. The **Monterey State Historic Park** and the nicely preserved downtown boast beautifully restored Spanish adobes. Despite the dissolution of the sardine-canning industry, the town still thrives on its maritime past. Barely a day goes by without someone making a reference to the city's favorite literary light, novelist John Steinbeck.

Don't come expecting some bastion of historic high-mindedness, however — Monterey is quite comfortable maintaining its mass-market appeal, thank you very much. In fact, some feel that the town fathers have gone too far, succumbing to the worst impulses of tourism — witness campy **Cannery Row** and ultratacky **Fisherman's Wharf,** they say. It's true — you have to wade through some touristy schlock in these areas. But you can't argue with the appeal of the wonderful aquarium and that one-of-a-kind bay (be sure to get out on it if you can). And even Cannery Row and the wharf are good for a brief bit of fun, as long as you take them with a grain of salt (or an ibuprofen). Beyond the prime tourist zones, you'll discover a genuine ocean community with beautifully preserved architecture, stunning panoramic vistas, top-quality restaurants, and more.

Gorgeous and peaceful **Pacific Grove** makes a better base if you'd rather revel in the area's natural wonders and don't mind the short drive, bike ride, or walk it takes to reach the main attractions. If convenience is more important to you, or you want a more urban feel, book a room in Monterey proper. But even if you stay in Pacific Grove, the distances won't be that much of a factor. The Pacific Grove lodgings and restaurants may seem out of the way, but the drive into Monterey along Ocean View Boulevard is only around five minutes without traffic.

Orienting yourself and getting around

Monterey is divided into two main sightseeing areas:

▸ **Downtown** (centered on Alvarado Street) and adjacent **Fisherman's Wharf,** where you'll also find Monterey State Historic Park

▸ The **Cannery Row** area (sometimes referred to as "New Monterey"), where the aquarium is located

Cannery Row is roughly to the west/northwest of downtown and the wharf; beyond Cannery Row is Pacific Grove, which is easily reachable by bicycle and perfect for exploring on two wheels. The downtown–Fisherman's Wharf area and Cannery Row are both pedestrian-friendly, but visitors will most likely need to drive, bike, or take public transport between the two.

Parking can be somewhat difficult in Monterey's tourist areas, so you may want to park your car at your hotel when you arrive and leave it there for the duration of your stay. (All the recommended hotels are centrally located, making it easy to do just that.) If you do drive between sites, your best bet is to park in one of the paid lots — there's a big one near the aquarium. If you choose to rely on metered spots, be sure to have quarters on hand and pay attention to time.

If you visit between Memorial Day and Labor Day, use the **Waterfront Area Visitor Express (WAVE) shuttle** to get around. The WAVE operates buses between all the major tourist sites and hotel areas in Monterey

The Monterey Peninsula

ACCOMMODATIONS ■

Asilomar Conference Grounds **26**
Best Western Victorian Inn **9**
Casa Palmero **21**
Cobblestone Inn **31**
Colonial Terrace Inn **34**
Cypress Inn **33**
Grand View Inn/Seven Gables Inn **1**
The Inn at Spanish Bay **22**
The Lodge at Pebble Beach **20**
Los Laureles Lodge **18**
Mission Ranch **19**
The Monterey Hotel **15**
Monterey Plaza Hotel & Spa **10**
The Olympia Lodge **26**
Quail Lodge Resort and Golf Club **18**
Rosedale Inn **25**
Spindrift Inn **8**
Village Inn **30**

DINING ◆

Casanova **28**
The Fishwife at Asilomar Beach **23**
Flying Fish Grill **32**
The Forge in the Forest **29**
Isabella's **11**
Jack London's Bar & Grill **27**
Little Napoli **33**
Montrio **13**
Passionfish **2**
Robert's White House **2**
Rosine's **15**
Sea Harvest Fish Market
　& Restaurants **7**
Stokes Restaurant & Bar **14**
Zócalo **3**

ATTRACTIONS ●

Cannery Row **6**
Carmel Mission **19**
Culinary Center of Monterey **8**
Dennis the Menace Playground **16**
Fisherman's Wharf **12**
Maritime Museum of Monterey **12**
Monarch Grove Sanctuary **24**
Monterey Bay Aquarium **5**
Monterey State Historic Park **12**
National Steinbeck Center **17**
Pacific Grove Museum of Natural
　History **4**

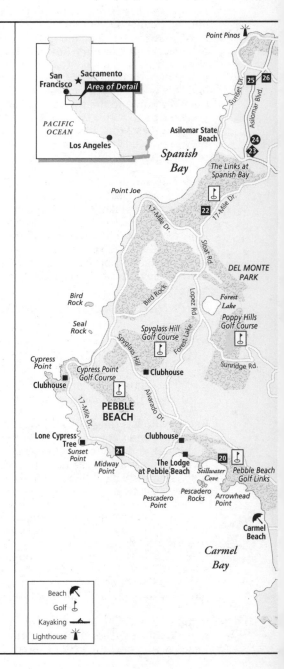

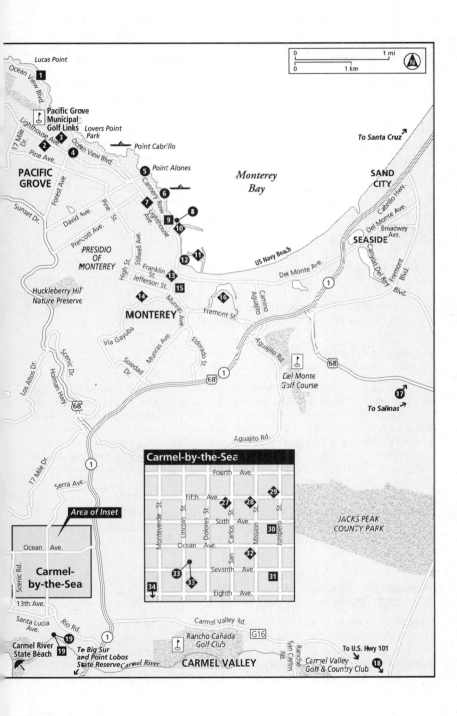

Lucas Point

Ocean View Blvd.

1

Pacific Grove
Municipal
Golf Links

Lighthouse Ave.

17 Mile Dr.

2

3

Lovers Point
Park

Ocean View Blvd.

Pine Ave.

4

Point Cabrillo

Point Alones

5

PACIFIC
GROVE

Forest Ave.

Sunset Dr.

David Ave.

Pine St.

Prescott Ave.

Cannery Row

6

7

Lighthouse
Ave.

8

9

10

PRESIDIO
OF
MONTEREY

Stillwell Ave.

High St.

Franklin
St.

Jefferson St.

11

12

13

15

Huckleberry Hill
Nature Preserve

14

Munras Ave.

MONTEREY

Fremont St.

16

Via Gayuba

Munras Ave.

Eldorado St.

Soledad
Dr.

Los Altos Dr.

Scenic Dr.

Holman Hwy.

68

Monterey
Bay

To Santa Cruz ↗

SAND
CITY

Cabrillo Hwy.

Del Monte Ave.

Broadway
Ave.

SEASIDE

Canyon Del Rey

Fremont
Blvd.

US Navy Beach

Del Monte Ave.

1

Camino
Aguajito

Aguajito Rd.

Del Monte
Golf Course

68

17

To Salinas ↗

68

1

1

Aguajito Rd.

17 Mile Dr.

Serra Ave.

Area of Inset

Ocean Ave.

Scenic Rd.

**Carmel-
by-the-Sea**

13th Ave.

Santa Lucia
Ave.

Rio Rd.

19

19

Carmel River
State Beach

1

To Big Sur
and Point Lobos
State Reserve

Carmel River

Carmel Valley Rd.

Rancho Cañada
Golf Club

G16

CARMEL VALLEY

Rancho
San Carlos Rd.

To U.S. Hwy 101 ↘

Carmel Valley
Golf & Country Club

18

0   1 mi
0   1 km

Carmel-by-the-Sea

Fourth   Ave.

Fifth   Ave.

27

28

29

Monteverde St.

Lincoln   St.

Dolores   St.

Sixth   Ave.

San Carlos   St.

Mission   St.

Junipero   St.

30

Ocean   Ave.

32

33

Seventh   Ave.

31

33

34

Eighth   Ave.

JACKS PEAK
COUNTY PARK

and Pacific Grove daily from 9 a.m. to 7:30 p.m. in season. Rides are absolutely free — a particularly good bargain, considering what you save on parking fees and headaches. For the latest information, contact **Monterey-Salinas Transit** (☎ **831-899-2555**), or visit www.mst.org.

For the lowdown on renting bikes — a very popular pastime — see the "More cool stuff to see and do" section later in this chapter.

Where to stay

You may want to try booking your room through a free reservations service such as **MontereyVisitorsGuide.com** (☎ **888-655-3424**; www.monterey-reservations.com) or **Resort 2 Me** (☎ **800-757-5646**; www.resort2me.com). Because they've established relationships with local hotels and inns, they may be able to negotiate a better rate for you than if you call the hotel directly; your best bet is to compare. They can also refer you to other reliable properties in the area if the choices in the sections that follow are full.

Most hotels require a two-night minimum on summer and holiday weekends. Count on an extra 10 percent in taxes added to your final hotel bill.

Always inquire about packages — which may include aquarium tickets or other incentives — even at the cheapest motel.

Asilomar Conference Grounds
$$–$$$ Pacific Grove

Situated on 105 gorgeous oceanfront acres of pines and dunes, this Julia Morgan–designed woodland conference center is open to individual bookings, and it's a great bargain for families on a budget. Rustic but immaculately kept stone-and-log lodges house plain guest rooms (private bathrooms, but no phones or TVs), plus a great room for lounging. Facilities include a heated pool, ping-pong, and billiards; a boardwalk leads to the beach and tide pools. This is a wonderful outdoorsy, summer-camp-like retreat, with Monterey's attractions just minutes away. Cafeteria-style dining halls (prix-fixe lunch $8.75, dinner $14) mean you save on meals, too.

See map p. 244. 800 Asilomar Blvd. ☎ *831-372-8016 or 831-642-4222. Fax: 831-372-7227.* www.visitasilomar.com. *Reservations accepted up to 90 days in advance. Free parking. Rack rates: $138 double, from $188 cottage or suite. Rates include full breakfast. MC, V.*

Best Western Victorian Inn
$$$–$$$$$ Monterey

This nice motel is just 2 blocks from Cannery Row. Don't let the Victorian theme fool you; the office is housed in a period home, but guest rooms are in a modern annex. Still, they're pleasant and feature such extras as marble fireplaces, minibars, coffeemakers, and VCRs, but no air-conditioning. Rack rates are *way* too high, but snagging a better rate through Best Western is pretty easy. Book a concierge-level room if you can, which adds cathedral ceilings, featherbeds, a whirlpool tub, CD player, and robes to the mix.

See map p. 244. 487 Foam St. ☎ *800-232-4141 or 831-373-8000. Fax: 831-373-4815.* www.victorianinn.com. *Parking: $12. Rack rates: $179–$349 double. Rates include continental breakfast and afternoon wine and cheese. AE, DC, DISC, MC, V.*

Grand View Inn/Seven Gables Inn
$$$–$$$$$ Pacific Grove

These gorgeous sister inns are two of the most spectacular we've ever seen — and they're ideally located to boot, along the stunning coast road and situated so that just about every room has an ocean view. The Edwardian style of the 1910 Grand View is somewhat subtler than the Seven Gables's more elaborate 1886 Victorian, but it's really a matter of taste. Everything is impeccable, from the marble baths to the faultless service. Romance-seeking couples simply can't do better. Book well ahead, especially for weekends.

See map p. 244. 555–557 Ocean View Blvd. ☎ *831-372-4341.* www.pginns.com. *Free parking. Rack rates: $175–$395 double. Rates include full breakfast and afternoon wine and cheese. MC, V.*

The Monterey Hotel
$$–$$$ Monterey

This charming Victorian hotel is beautifully located in the retail heart of downtown Monterey, an easy walk to Fisherman's Wharf. Opened in 1904, it has been impeccably restored, with beveled-glass details and mahogany polished to a high sheen. The smallish but lovely period rooms are elegantly and comfortably furnished, and have posh marble-tiled bathrooms. For the most space, book a *double-double* (two double beds or two queen beds) or a junior suite, which could serve a small family nicely. The staff is attentive and helpful. *Note:* The hotel has no working elevator (although that is supposed to change), but valet service is available. Plans are underway (but no firm dates yet) to add a few rooms, so inquire about any construction work when you phone to book.

See map p. 244. 406 Alvarado St. ☎ *800-966-6490 or 831-375-3184. Fax: 831-375-2899.* www.montereyhotel.com. *Valet parking: $15. Rack rates: $139–$189 double, $259–$299 suite. Rates include continental breakfast and afternoon and evening refreshments. AE, DC, DISC, MC, V.*

Monterey Plaza Hotel & Spa
$$$–$$$$$ Monterey

Monterey's finest waterfront hotel is dramatically situated to maximize the lovely bay views, and although it's next door to Cannery Row, it feels worlds away. Elegant teak-paneled public areas lead to spacious, extremely comfy guest rooms with big marble bathrooms and all the little luxuries. Go oceanview if you can, but even guests in the cheapest inland-view rooms can relax on the bayfront terrace. Service is top-notch, and facilities include a gym, a full-service spa, and a terrific restaurant, the Duck Club. Check the Web site for room specials.

See map p. 244. 400 Cannery Row. ☎ *800-368-2468 or 831-646-1700. Fax: 831-646-5937.* www.woodsidehotels.com. *Valet parking: $18. Rack rates: $355–$635 double, $550–$1,322 suite. AE, DC, DISC, MC, V.*

The Olympia Lodge
$–$$$ Pacific Grove

A low-budget fixture since the 1960s, this humble two-story motel is under new management and in the middle of a serious renovation. The rooms have been modernized with wonderfully comfortable beds, plantation shutters, coffeemakers, and sizable TVs; although the bathrooms are in decent shape, they, too, are being updated with new tile and whirlpool tubs. Sometime in 2007, the lodge may even have a larger swimming pool, a new deck, and a hot tub. The improvements will bring an increase in the rates (although you can get a good deal in the off season), but until then this is a hidden gem.

See map p. 244. 1140 Lighthouse Ave. ☎ *888-745-6343 or 831-373-2777. Fax: 831-375-8741.* www.theolympialodge.com. *Free parking. Rack rates: $80–$275 double. Rates include continental breakfast. AE, DISC, MC, V.*

Rosedale Inn
$$–$$$ Pacific Grove

Here's our favorite among Pacific Grove's sweet cottage-style motels. The lodgelike complex is actually much nicer than a motel. All the large rooms are beautifully done in a comfy country style and feature cathedral ceilings (with ceiling fans), VCRs, fireplaces, kitchenettes with microwaves and minifridges, and whirlpool tubs and hair dryers in the nice bathrooms. About half are two-room suites, each of which also has a sleeper sofa in the living room — perfect for families. Management is super-friendly, too. This place is a winner.

See map p. 244. 775 Asilomar Blvd. ☎ *800-822-5606 or 831-655-1000. Fax: 831-655-0691.* www.rosedaleinn.com. *Free parking. Rack rates: $135–$165 double, $170–$245 two-room suite. Rates include continental breakfast. AE, DISC, MC, V.*

Spindrift Inn
$$$–$$$$$ Monterey

If the Monterey Plaza Hotel is too swanked-out for your tastes, but you'd like a bay view with your breakfast, this smaller boutique property in the center of Cannery Row is another choice. Charming, well-appointed, and spacious rooms with fireplaces, hardwood floors, feather beds, marble bathrooms, and stunning ocean vistas provide a cushy shelter, but pony up for a bayview room — with a disco on the street side, nights can be noisy.

See map p. 244. 652 Cannery Row. ☎ 800-841-1879 or 831-646-8900. Fax: 831-646-5342. www.spindriftinn.com. *Free parking. Rack rates: $269–$499 double. Rates include continental breakfast and afternoon wine and cheese. AE, DISC, MC, V.*

Where to dine

Despite the kitsch that Monterey offers as an attraction destination, the area serves up some fine fixin's in its kitchens, some renowned even in the restaurant-sophisticated Bay Area.

The Fishwife at Asilomar Beach
$$ Pacific Grove SEAFOOD

This hugely popular fish house serves up affordable, filling meals in a simple, oceanview room that bustles with a chatty mix of tourists and locals. The seafood — which can be fresh but is often frozen — comes grilled or golden-fried, with black beans, rice, and a choice of salsas. The lunch menu features sandwiches, too, as well as steak and nonseafood pastas. Make reservations, but be prepared to wait a few minutes nonetheless. The Fishwife is a busy place.

See map p. 244. 1996½ Sunset Dr. (Highway 68), at Asilomar Boulevard. ☎ 831-375-7107. www.fishwife.com. *Reservations recommended. Main courses: Lunch $6–$10, dinner $10–$18. AE, DISC, MC, V. Open: Daily 11 a.m.–10 p.m.*

Isabella's
$$$–$$$$ Monterey ITALIAN/SEAFOOD

We had to be pushed into this Wharf fish house by a hungry companion who didn't share our disdain for the gentleman at the door, who was heartily attempting to convince passersby that this was the place to eat. Much to our surprise, we ended up agreeing with the guy. The fresh fish was sustainably caught and simply prepared as requested; the calamari and coconut shrimp appetizer was filling enough to serve as a main. The harbor views in the early evening added ambience. Most beasts, fish, and fowl show up on the huge menu in addition to lots of pasta, so the fussiest eater will find something to his liking. Service is attentive, but don't plan on lingering at your table after you finish your coffee.

See map p. 244. 60 Fisherman's Wharf. ☎ 831-375-3656. www.isabellasonthe wharf.com. *Reservations accepted. Main courses: Lunch $9.50–$23, dinner $16–$39. AE, DISC, MC, V. Open: Daily 11 a.m.–10 p.m.*

Montrio
$$–$$$ Downtown Monterey CALIFORNIA

One of the more stylish restaurants in town, Montrio is actually a blend of sizzle and substance that works for couples as well as for families seeking a good meal in grown-up surroundings. The menu, incorporating organic produce when available, includes a hamburger and a turkey sandwich for casual eaters, and raises the bar with crab cakes, rare steaks, or oven-roasted portobello mushrooms for more serious diners. Our paper-topped table included crayons, always a nice touch for busy hands.

See map p. 244. 414 Calle Principal, at Franklin Street. ☎ *831-648-8880.* www. montrio.com. *Reservations recommended for dinner. Main courses: $9–$32. MC, V. Open: Sun–Thurs 5–10 p.m., Fri–Sat 5–11 p.m.*

Passionfish
$$–$$$ Pacific Grove   CREATIVE AMERICAN

Easily one of the best restaurants in the area, dinner here is worth the short drive if you're bunking in Monterey. The daily changing menu is innovative yet accessible; seafood lovers should investigate the grilled shrimp or the Passionfish stew, which may feature mussels, swordfish, salmon, and bright green spinach gnocchi in a butternut squash broth — beautiful to behold and a joy to eat. The wine list cuts a swath through California and beyond, service is subtle, and the crowd enjoys every bite.

See map p. 244. 701 Lighthouse Ave., at Congress Street. ☎ *831-655-3311.* www. passionfish.net. *Reservations recommended. Main courses: $16–$22. AE, DISC, MC, V. Open: Sun–Thurs 5–9 p.m., Fri–Sat 5–10 p.m.*

Robert's The White House
$$$ Pacific Grove   CALIFORNIA/FRENCH

Set inside a historic Victorian mansion on Pacific Grove's main drag, Chef Robert Kincaid provides diners with delicious food in a pretty and quaint setting. We don't know how he does it, but $37 buys a three-course meal suitable for a special occasion. We skipped the appetizers (because we prefer dessert) and chose the baked onion soup and organic field greens gussied up with roasted beets, candied pecans, and blue cheese, both satisfying. Mains were especially superb. Herb-encrusted slices of rare ahi tuna had us talking to ourselves for days; the duck confit was crisp and tender. A chocolate "bag" filled with a chocolate-cream milkshake sent us away in a haze of caloric contentment. Service is a bit spotty, but the overall experience is a delight.

See map p. 244. 649 Lighthouse Ave., at 17th Street. ☎ *831-375-9626.* www.roberts whitehouse.com. *Main courses: $23, three-course menu $37. Open: Tues–Sun 5:30–9:30 p.m.*

Rosine's
$–$$ Monterey   WHOLESOME AMERICAN

If dessert is your downfall, you can't fall much farther than a slice from the triple-layer cakes in the glass counter near the entrance of this cheery downtown restaurant. Rosine's is the place to satisfy morning and midday cravings, with dishes to keep the entire family chewing happily. Breakfast is straightforward and filling with eggs, bacon, pancakes, and oatmeal; lunch consists of sandwiches and salads and, of course, slices of cake.

See map p. 244. 434 Alvarado St., at Bonifacio Street. ☎ *831-375-1400.* www.rosines monterey.com. *Main courses: Breakfast $5–$9, lunch $6–$11, dinner $10–$20. AE, DISC, MC, V. Open: Sun–Thurs 8 a.m.–9 p.m., Fri–Sat 8 a.m.–10 p.m.*

Sea Harvest Fish Market & Restaurants
$–$$ Monterey   SEAFOOD

This friendly place, where the chef from the Post Ranch Inn (see Chapter 19) does his shopping, is a fish market first and a restaurant second — which means that you can pick your filet right out of the case. It's grilled or fried on the spot, and served along with soup or salad at one of the casual tables. Fish simply doesn't come more off-the-boat fresh. The kitchen prepares delicious homemade Louis dressing and stellar chowder, too. Perfect if you'd rather avoid the Cannery Row tourist traps in favor of an authentic local meal.

See map p. 244. 598 Foam St., 2 blocks inland from Cannery Row, at Hoffman Street. ☎ *831-646-0547. Full meals: $8–$19. MC, V. Open: Daily 11 a.m.–8 p.m. (until 9 p.m. in summer).*

Stokes Restaurant & Bar
$$–$$$ Monterey   CALIFORNIA/MEDITERRANEAN

This attractive historic adobe gets major points for its Southwest-style charm and constant raves for its contemporary fare. The main dining room buzzes with energy and flair, while Chef Brandon Miller makes the most of the local bounty in his innovative but unfussy cuisine. The *San Francisco Chronicle* calls it "possibly the best food on the Monterey Peninsula." The restaurant is simply wonderful in every way.

See map p. 244. 500 Hartnell St., at Madison Street, just east of Pacific Street. ☎ *831-373-1110.* www.stokesrestaurant.com. *Reservations recommended. Main courses: Lunch $10–$14, dinner $14–$23. AE, MC, V. Open: Mon–Fri 11:30 a.m.–2 p.m., daily 5:30–10 p.m.*

Zócalo
$ Pacific Grove   MEXICAN

We ate some pedestrian Mexican food in a well-known downtown Monterey *taqueria* and were so peeved that we made it our mission to find the real thing. On a tip from a cute chef whom we chatted up at Sea Harvest Market, we ended up in a little storefront cafe off the main drag in Pacific Grove. Zócalo offers every favorite — tostados, tacos, burritos, enchiladas — as well as *pozole* (pork and hominy stew), which perks us up whenever we see it on a menu. They also serve beer, wine, and a refreshing *horchata*, a sweet rice drink that goes deliciously well with spicy food. Every meal out of that kitchen is composed of really fresh ingredients, far and away superior to what's sold in downtown Monterey. After you eat, walk around the center of Pacific Grove, an old-fashioned downtown with a patina of sophistication.

See map p. 244. 162 Fountain Ave., between Central and Lighthouse streets. ☎ 831-373-7911. Main courses: Lunch $6–$7, dinner $8–$15. No credit cards. Open: Tues–Thurs 11:30 a.m.–8 p.m., Fri–Sat 11:30 a.m.–9 p.m.

Monterey's top attractions

Well, as long as you're here anyway, you have no reason not to find out what all the fuss is about. If you're a connoisseur of the tacky and the tasteless, more power to you and enjoy your visit. If you're not, you can at least enjoy a good chuckle at the schlock on public display.

Cannery Row

Immortalized on the page by John Steinbeck, this former aromatic row of working sardine canneries is now a temple to the tourist dollar, rife with mass-appeal shopping, dining, and nightlife. The fish that fed the local sardine-canning industry — the largest in the world, processing 250,000 tons in 1945, the year Steinbeck's *Cannery Row* hit bookshelves — disappeared in the late 1940s from overfishing of the bay. Complaining about what replaced the canneries is easy (and believe us, locals do), but even Steinbeck found it to be an improvement over what was. In the '60s he wrote, "The beaches are clean where they once festered with fish guts and flies. The canneries that once put up a sickening stench are gone, their places filled with restaurants, antique[s] shops, and the like."

Stay away if you're averse to this kind of commercialism. But if you're not, you'll find that the T-shirt shops and theme restaurants haven't entirely quashed the row's maritime character. It's a nice renovation, and recent years have brought in a better quality of merchant to supplant some of the cheesier businesses. Highlights include **A Taste of Monterey Wine Tasting Center** (see the "Tasting the local grape" section later in the chapter), and the **Ghirardelli Chocolate Shop and Soda Fountain,** in Steinbeck Plaza, 660 Cannery Row (☎ 831-373-0997), where you can indulge your sweet tooth San Francisco–style.

Just off the Pacific Grove end of the row, on Ocean View Boulevard, is the **American Tin Cannery Premium Outlets** (☎ 831-372-1442), which boasts such big names as Reebok and Nine West among its 40 or so stores. Just off the other (Monterey) end is the **Cannery Row Antique Mall,** 471 Wave St. (☎ 831-655-0264), housing two levels of antiques and collectibles dealers.

What's probably the world's finest walking/biking path parallels the row, connecting up with it at a couple of points; for details, see the "More cool stuff to see and do" section later in this chapter.

See map p. 244. Bay front west of downtown Monterey, between David and Reeside avenues (the heart of the action is between David and Drake avenues). ☎ 831-373-1902. www.cannery-row.com.

Fisherman's Wharf

Cannery Row not cheesy enough for you? Don't worry — Fisherman's Wharf will be. Larger and more commercial than Santa Cruz's wharf and just as touristy as San Francisco's, this wooden pier is packed with T-shirt shops, seafood restaurants, and bay-cruise and sport-fishing operations out to snare a tourist buck or two. That said, it's still worth a look, primarily because the bay views are to die for, and this is one of the best perches for watching the frolicking seals and barking sea lions that populate the bay.

If the weather's good, buy a chowder-filled sourdough-bread bowl and park yourself along the pier to watch the offshore action. If it's not, find a bay-front seat at one of the pier's seafood restaurants; the best of the bunch is Italian-accented **Isabella's** (see the "Where to dine" section earlier in this chapter).

If you're the plan-ahead type who'd like to hit the water for some sport-fishing or whale-watching, contact the following operators.

Monterey Bay Whale Watch, 84 Fisherman's Wharf (☎ 831-375-4658; www.montereybaywhalecruise.com), offers daily year-round whale-watching cruises. Be aware, however, that you'll spot only the big'uns — California gray whales — from December through March. Trips run $34 to $43 for adults and $23 to $33 for children 4 to 12.

Chris' Fishing Trips, 48 Fisherman's Wharf (☎ 831-375-5951; www.chrissfishing.com), has four large (51- to 70-ft.) boats leaving on daily deep-sea hunts; cod and salmon are the main catches. Full-day trips run $55 for adults and $25 (weekdays) or $30 (weekends) for children.

If you'd rather watch the pros haul in their daily catches, head over to **wharf no. 2** (just next door to Chris', at the end of Figueroa Street), which is today's working commercial pier. To wiggle your toes in the chilly surf, head a bit farther east to **Monterey Bay Park,** where the big white-sand beach gradually slopes into sandy shallows that are just warm enough.

See map p. 244. Waterfront at the end of Alvarado Street. www.montereywharf.com. *Admission: Free.*

Monterey Bay Aquarium

One of the best, largest, and most enjoyable aquariums on the planet, the Monterey Bay Aquarium sits on the shore of one of the most spectacular marine habitats in the world. It's terrific for all ages, with gliding bat rays and other sea creatures to touch, instructive shows throughout the day (some featuring friendly, spotlight-savvy sea lions), interactive exhibits, and well-written placards at every display that even younger children can understand and enjoy. Exhibits tie in closely to the immediate surroundings, bringing home the reality of the marine environment and the message of conservation.

Have we mentioned how jaw-droppingly awesome this aquarium is? It displays more than 300,000 sea plants and animals representing 570 different species. At the heart of the loftlike, indoor/outdoor complex is a three-story tank replicating a kelp forest, which you can walk around up a spiral ramp, viewing the leopard sharks and bay fish from all sides.

Better yet is the **Outer Bay** exhibit, featuring inhabitants of the open ocean in a phenomenal million-gallon tank with the *largest window on Earth.* Almost cooler than the giant green sea turtles, schools of sharp-toothed

Aquarium timesavers

The ticket lines just to get into the **Monterey Bay Aquarium** can be a nightmare, especially in summer. Even on a Tuesday people may wait 15 to 30 minutes throughout the day. Do yourself a favor: Avoid the lines at the gate by arranging for admission tickets in advance.

Many of Monterey's hotels offer packages that include aquarium tickets. Even if you just book a straight daily rate, call ahead and ask the front desk if they sell advance tickets; most do. If your hotel doesn't sell aquarium tickets, you can order them directly from the aquarium by calling ☎ **800-756-3737** or 831-648-4937; the flat $3-per-order service charge is well worth the time saved. Don't worry about mailing time; the tickets can be left at will-call, where you'll never encounter a wait.

Here are some tips to help you make the most of your aquarium visit:

✔ Allow a minimum of three hours to see the aquarium; budget four or five if you want to see everything.

✔ You're allowed to leave and come back in the same day, as long as you get your hand stamped. We highly suggest leaving for lunch or a rest, which will give you a break from the ever-present crowds and rejuvenate you for more looking.

✔ Review the "Today at the Aquarium" schedule as soon as you arrive, so that you can budget your touring around any live programs you'd like to see (they usually last 15–30 minutes).

✔ If time is limited, head straight for the Outer Bay, followed by a visit to the two-story Sea Otter exhibit, and then a walk along the Habitats Path to the Touch Pool for maximum satisfaction.

barracuda, and the threatening-looking sharks are the jellyfish, which move in slo-mo, translucent unison like a modern-art exhibit come to life.

The aquarium regularly mounts new exhibits, but, unlike art shows, they stay a while. Opening in April 2007 is a special exhibit on river otters of the world, featuring live Asian and African small- and short-clawed otters communing with tree frogs, vine snakes, and other species from their natural habitat. Little kids will be irresistibly drawn into the **Splash Zone,** a permanent hands-on exhibition that combines live-animal displays (including tuxedoed penguins) with staff-led learning programs and good old-fashioned play areas.

See map p. 244. 886 Cannery Row. ☎ 831-648-4888 for 24-hour information. www. mbayaq.org. *Admission: $22 adults, $20 students (13–17 or with college ID) and seniors 65 and over, $13 disabled visitors and children 3–12. Open: Daily 10 a.m.– 6 p.m. (from 9:30 a.m. on holidays and in summer); check for extended hours in summer.*

Monterey State Historic Park

At the gateway to Fisherman's Wharf sit a dozen or so beautifully restored historic adobes that served as California's capitol under Spanish, Mexican, and initial U.S. rule. The state now collectively protects these buildings as Monterey State Historic Park. Even if you're not a big history buff, check out this area simply for the beauty of the buildings and the setting. You can tour it in a number of ways.

Do-it-yourselfers who just want to explore a bit can stop into the **Visitor Center** at the Maritime Museum and pick up the free Path of History map. The map will lead you through the historic park and adjacent Old Monterey (the beautifully restored downtown area), highlighting buildings of note along the way. You won't be able to enter the buildings, but the exteriors alone are worth a look.

If you'd like a little more background, go the **guided-tour** route. A number of tours are offered daily; call ☎ 831-657-6348 for a schedule. We recommend starting with the introductory walking tour, which provides a general exterior overview. Follow that with a house tour or two (or a garden tour, if you're visiting between May and Sept) of the buildings that caught your fancy in the course of your initial tour. Highlights include the **Cooper-Molera Adobe,** which depicts family life in the mid-1800s with living-history demonstrations throughout the 3-acre complex, and the **Larkin House,** generally considered to be the finest example of Monterey Colonial architecture still standing.

You can also explore the nearby **Maritime Museum of Monterey,** 5 Custom House Plaza, at the end of Alvarado Street (☎ 831-372-2608; www. montereyhistory.org/maritime_museum.htm), which tells the story of Monterey's seafaring past, from the Spanish conquistadors through the sardine fishers. Admission is $8 adults, $5 seniors, $2.50 teens 12 to 18, free for kids 12 and younger.

See map p. 244. ☎ *831-649-7118.* www.parks.ca.gov. *Admission: Free. Open: Most buildings daily 10 a.m.–5 p.m. Call for our schedules.*

More cool stuff to see and do

Don't miss the **Monterey Peninsula Recreation Trail,** one of the most scenic walking paths in the country. And the good news is that you don't have to hoof it; bikers and in-line skaters are welcome, too. You can pick up the paved path anywhere along Monterey's coastline and follow it into Pacific Grove all the way to Asilomar Beach.

Past the aquarium, in Pacific Grove, you'll ride along the beach side of Ocean View Boulevard. If you look inland, you can admire the gorgeous ocean-facing homes (including some stunning Victorians); on the bay side, gorgeous purple heather and the occasional gnarled cypress separates you from the frolicking sea lions and colorful kayaks gliding along the water.

Go at least as far as **Lovers Point Park** (where Ocean View meets Pacific Avenue in Pacific Grove), a gorgeous grassy point that juts out to sea. With a sheltered beach and tables for picnickers, it's the perfect place to take a load off and relax. From here, push on around the curve, where the road becomes Sunset Drive, and take it past picturesque **Point Pinos Lighthouse** (the oldest continually operating lighthouse in the West, since 1854) to undeveloped **Asilomar State Beach,** where you can spend a quiet day among the dunes, tidal pools, and barking sea lions. Hardy folks can continue along the **17-Mile Drive;** you'll find a gate on Sunset Drive just past Asilomar Avenue, and bicyclists can enter for free. (For more on the 17-Mile Drive, see the "Cruising the 17-Mile Drive," section, later in this chapter.)

Rent your bike or skates from **Adventures by the Sea** (www.adventures bythesea.com), which has a few convenient locations: 299 Cannery Row, across from the Monterey Plaza Hotel (☎ **831-372-1807**); 201 Alvarado Mall, next to the Maritime Museum (☎ **831-372-1807** or 831-648-7236); and at Lovers Point Park in Pacific Grove (summer only; no phone). Bikes cost $6 an hour, $18 for four hours, or $24 per day; locks and helmets are provided. Skates are $12 for two hours or $24 for the day, with all safety equipment included. Service is very friendly, and gear is in good condition. Advance reservations are gladly accepted.

Kayaking the bay

Monterey Bay is a great place to kayak in summer, even for beginners. You'll glide right by sunbathing sea lions and snacking sea otters as shorebirds swoop through the air and schools of jellyfish skirt just below the surface of the water. (A kayaking companion once called it "a horror movie in the making," but the gooey creatures are simply mesmerizing.)

Again, contact **Adventures by the Sea** (see the preceding section for locations and contact information). Kayaks cost $30 per person for the day, including waterproof gear and instruction to get you started. The bay is glassy enough for fearless novices to set out on their own in summer, but we highly recommend booking a tour if you're the least bit nervous, or if the surf is kicking up. The cost is $50 per person for a two-hour tour, and you should reserve ahead.

Exploring the underwater world

If you're an experienced scuba diver, pack your certification card — this national marine sanctuary is a dive you shouldn't miss. Contact **Monterey Bay Dive Center,** 225 Cannery Row (☎ **800-60-SCUBA** or 831-656-0454; www.montereyscubadiving.com), a PADI dive center that can arrange guided dives with pro dive masters. Call at least 48 hours in advance to schedule your dive, sooner if possible. The office is closed on Wednesdays.

Cooking by the bay

The **Culinary Center of Monterey,** 625 Cannery Row (☎ 831-333-2133; www.culinarycenterofmonterey.com), encompasses nearly everything food lovers could wish for, including weekend hands-on cooking classes for adults and kids, a wine bar, retail kitchenware and cookbooks, a restaurant and gourmet take-out, all located in a bay-front building with those stunning only-in-Monterey views from the patio. The lengthy roster of classes covers everything from sauces to desserts including an intriguing offering called "Cooking with Beer." Classes run about four hours and include copious tastings so that you don't faint from exertion. Even if you don't cook on vacation, it's fun to browse the retail area and then sit at the bar with a glass of wine and a snack. Closed Mondays.

Tasting the local grape

Monterey's Wine Country has really grown up in recent years, becoming California's third most prominent wine-growing region, behind Napa and Sonoma (even the *New York Times* has called it "The Next Napa"). Go ahead, review the shelves at your local wine store or the next wine list you're handed. The number of Monterey labels there may surprise you, as will the number of Monterey County winery names you know: Morgan, Estancia, Jekel, Talbott, J. Lohr, Smith & Hook, Chalone, and many others. Local vintners tend to specialize in chardonnay, pinot noir, and cabernet sauvignon — all popular grapes that are suited to the region's A-1 soil and growing conditions — and they're making some of the best wines that the California Wine Country has to offer.

For a free map to the region's wineries, the *Monterey Wine Country Wine-Tasting Guide,* stop by **A Taste of Monterey,** the Monterey County Wine and Produce Visitors Center, upstairs at 700 Cannery Row, next to the Bubba Gump Shrimp Co. (☎ 888-646-5446 or 831-646-5446; www.tastemonterey.com; open daily 11 a.m.–6 p.m.). This bayfront tasting room is a serious wine-tasting center and a great place to learn about, try, and buy local wines — ideal for one-stop shoppers. If you want to wend your way through the local vineyards and tasting rooms in person, ask the friendly staff for tips on where to go.

The map is also available at local visitor centers (see the "Gathering More Information" section at the end of this chapter).

You can arrange your Wine Country tour in advance by going online to the useful Web site run by the Monterey County Vintners & Growers Association at www.montereywines.org. Here you can preview the wineries you'd like to visit and order a free copy of the aforementioned wine-tasting guide (or order an advance copy by calling ☎ 831-375-9400).

Side-tripping to the National Steinbeck Center

The **National Steinbeck Center** is an easy 20-mile drive northeast from Monterey, at 1 Main St. in Salinas (☎ **831-796-3833;** www.steinbeck. org). The state-of-the-art museum is well worth a visit if you're a fan of the county's most beloved author, John Steinbeck (author of *Cannery Row, East of Eden, Of Mice and Men,* and *The Grapes of Wrath,* among others).

Even if you're not a literary buff but you're simply interested in the history of the region, you'll find the tour engaging, because many of Steinbeck's works were rooted in the local culture. The tour also appeals to film fans, because the multimedia approach makes prime use of the many first-rate, star-studded films that were crafted from Steinbeck's stories.

The museum is deliberately designed to be multisensory, and it largely succeeds. In the Agricultural Wing, which almost too playfully lays out how your artichokes get from field to kitchen, kids may scorn voting for their favorite vegetable, but taken as a whole, there's much to be learned on the subject. You can easily make your way through the museum in an hour or two; the kids will have enough to keep them busy. The center is open daily (except for major holidays) from 10 a.m. to 5 p.m. Admission is $11 adults, $8.95 students and seniors, $7.95 kids 13 to 17, $6.95 kids 6 to 12. To get there from Monterey, take Highway 68 east, which will lead you right through Old Town Salinas to the center (the biggest, brightest building in town — you can't miss it).

Strolling and shopping Old Monterey

Monterey's charmingly restored downtown, inland from Fisherman's Wharf and centered on Alvarado Street, is well worth exploring. History and architecture fans should pick up the **Path of History Walking Tour** (see the section on the Monterey State Historic Park earlier in this chapter), while shoppers should just hit the streets.

Tuesdays, Alvarado Street is blocked off from about 2 to 8 p.m. for the weekly farmers' market. The local fruits and vegetables are desirable, if somewhat impractical to pack, but vendors also hawk tie-dyed T's, handmade soaps, candles, olive oil, and such. Delicious-smelling barbecued ribs, chicken, and other snacking opportunities also tempt the senses.

Wintering with the monarch butterflies in Pacific Grove

Pacific Grove is also known as "Butterfly Town, USA." Why, you ask? Because monarch butterflies, it seems, know a good thing when they see it. Thousands of brilliant black-and-orange monarch butterflies converge on the town annually in October or early November, and stay until February or March. The best place to see them is in the **Monarch Grove Sanctuary,** between Grove Acre Avenue, Ridge Road, and Lighthouse Avenue (☎ **888-PG-MONARCH** or 831-375-0982; www.ci.pg.ca.us/ monarchs/default.htm), where they alight in the eucalyptus trees.

Tour guides are usually on hand on the weekends in season to answer questions about the fluttering beauties.

You can also peruse a detailed display on the winged winter visitors at the **Pacific Grove Museum of Natural History,** 165 Forest Ave., at Central Avenue (☎ 831-648-3116; www.pgmuseum.org). It's open Tuesday through Saturday from 10 a.m. to 5 p.m., and admission is free.

Leave your nets at home, collectors — the fine for harassing a butterfly in Pacific Grove is $1,000.

Playing with Dennis the Menace

Families with kids should definitely budget a couple of hours to run and jump at the **Dennis the Menace Playground** (☎ 831-646-3866), at Camino El Estero and Fremont Street, just east of downtown Monterey. Designed by Dennis creator (and Pacific Grove homeboy) Hank Ketcham, the way-cool playground boasts an old steam train to climb on, more colorful jungle gyms than we could count, rope-and-plank suspension bridges, a giant swing ride, and lots more low-tech, old-fashioned fun. It's open daily 10 a.m. to dusk (closed nonholiday Mondays in the winter); admission is free.

Pebble Beach: Nirvana for Golfers

Carved out of the middle of the peninsula is a whole different kind of world, Pebble Beach, where platinum cards and nine-irons rule the day. Rolling championship fairways, lush woodlands, and magnificent vistas are broken only by million-dollar homes and a few ultraluxury resorts that cater to a big-money, high-profile crowd. In golf terms, this is the big time — Pebble Beach is home to some of the most famous golf courses in the world. It hosts the star-studded annual **AT&T Pebble Beach National Pro-Am,** which has paired club-swinging celebs with PGA Tour stars annually (late Jan or early Feb) since 1937, and has played host to multiple U.S. Open Championships throughout the years (including 2000).

If you need to chat with your banker before making reservations in Pebble Beach, you probably can't afford to stay here. Even if you can, but you're the jeans-and-T-shirt type, Pebble Beach may not be for you. But you don't have to sleep over — or buy into the big-budget golf life — to enjoy the marvelous scenery. Everybody can — for a nominal fee — tour this spectacular territory along the **17-Mile Drive** (see the "Cruising the 17-Mile Drive" section later in this chapter), a gorgeous private loop road.

If you don't want to stay but do want to play a round of unparalleled golf, you can do that, too — with a little effort and luck.

Where to stay and play at the resorts

The **Pebble Beach Company** (☎ 800-654-9300; www.pebblebeach.com) runs all the Pebble Beach resorts, making price-shopping and comparing amenities easy. Always ask about packages that may include greens fees in the price. And always check with a travel agent, who may be able to get a better package price at these superluxury resorts than you can get on your own.

Guests at any of the Pebble Beach resorts get preferred service at all of Pebble Beach's facilities; facilities are accessible to nonguests on a more limited basis. (Read: The high-paying resort guests get first dibs.) See the "Hitting the links" section, later in this chapter, for details on the world-class golf courses, with information on greens fees and tee-time availability for resort guests and nonguests.

Book your tee times at the same time that you reserve your room, about a year ahead of schedule.

Of course, you'll be needing a nice body scrub after all that golf, and you can get one at the 22,000-square-foot Mediterranean-style **Spa,** next to Casa Palmero; call ☎ **888-565-7615** or 831-649-7615.

Casa Palmero
$$$$$ Pebble Beach

Pebble Beach's newest resort is ultra-exclusive — just 24 super-luxurious suites housed in a magnificent Mediterranean villa right on the fairway. It feels like a private estate, complete with a fireplace-lit living room, cozy library, and clubby billiards room. You'll want for nothing here — and if you do, your personal concierge will be happy to get it for you in a snap. Shockingly priced, but stunning.

See map p. 244. 1518 Cypress Beach Dr. ☎ 800-654-9300 or 831-647-7500. Fax: 831-644-7960. www.pebblebeach.com. *Free parking (at these prices, it should be). Rack rates: $745–$2,425 cottage or suite, plus $20 gratuity per night. Rates include continental breakfast. AE, DC, DISC, MC, V.*

The Inn at Spanish Bay
$$$$$ Pebble Beach

One of the few resorts to hold Mobil's highly coveted five stars — and a winner of the *Travel + Leisure*'s 2006 Top 500 Hotels in the World poll — Spanish Bay is a wonderful choice if you like big resorts. Rooms are large and done in a super-luxurious contemporary style. We'd choose this one over the Lodge at Pebble Beach (see the following listing) for its winning facilities and its location in the heart of the gorgeous Scottish-style Links at Spanish Bay. Still, it's hard to go wrong at either property.

See map p. 244. 2700 17-Mile Dr. ☎ 800-654-9300 or 831-647-7500. Fax: 831-644-7960. www.pebblebeach.com. *Free parking. Rack rates: From $535 double to $2,275 for the two-bedroom Presidential Suite, plus $20 gratuity per night. AE, DC, DISC, MC, V.*

The Lodge at Pebble Beach
$$$$$ **Pebble Beach**

The Lodge is somewhat more stately and formal than its sister resort at Spanish Bay, but it's equally elegant, service-oriented, and satisfying. The amenity-laden, utterly luxurious guest rooms are scattered throughout the glorious oceanfront property — most convenient for golfers set on teeing off on the legendary Pebble Beach Golf Links.

See map p. 244. 1700 17-Mile Dr. ☎ 800-654-9300 or 831-647-7500. Fax: 831-644-7960. www.pebblebeach.com. Free parking. Rack rates: From $610 double, $1,875 suite, plus $15 gratuity per night. AE, DC, DISC, MC, V.

Cruising the 17-Mile Drive

The only private toll road west of the Mississippi, the stunning 17-Mile Drive is well worth the $8.75 per auto price of admission.

Bicyclists can enter for free; see the "More cool stuff to see and do" section earlier in the chapter, for details on renting bikes. The ride is easy — mainly downhill — toward Carmel, but average folks may find it a real chore to make the uphill climb back. If you're not a long-distance biker, either stick to the Pacific Grove portion of the drive or arrange for a pickup at the **Lodge at Pebble Beach** or in Carmel.

The spectacular loop wends through the Monterey Peninsula, linking Pacific Grove to the outskirts of Carmel along the coast, turns inland, hitching up with the main highway for a moment, and then heads back toward Pacific Grove through the **Del Monte Forest.** It takes you along the stunning rocky coastline, past the most beautiful cypress trees on the peninsula, and through unspoiled woodlands. (The gnarled, wind-bent cypress trees that lend the peninsula such a distinct beauty are

---

Leisurely dining along the 17-Mile Drive

If you're not staying in Pebble Beach but you'd like to enjoy an elegant breakfast, lunch, or dinner here (and maybe a glimpse of a luxe resort in the process), book a table at **Roy's at Pebble Beach** ($23–$38 entrees), at the Inn at Spanish Bay (☎ 831-647-7423). Roy's is the best of Hawaii celebrity Chef Roy Yamaguchi's mainland restaurants. Expect well-prepared Euro-Asian cuisine with inspired sauces and pleasing California and island twists. Entrees are pricey, but keeping the bill down is easy if you make a meal of Roy's signature wood-fired pizzas or choose from the extensive appetizers list; don't miss those killer short ribs (better than dessert!).

If you'd rather put together a picnic to enjoy along the drive, stop into the **Pebble Beach Market** (☎ 831-622-8770), a gourmet deli at the Lodge at Pebble Beach, which has a lawn where you can spread out and enjoy your ready-to-eat meats, veggies, cheeses, and other gourmet goodies.

native to this region only; they can live to be 4,000 years old.) You'll see championship golfers and native deer cohabiting on some of the most scenic golf greens in the world, and watch sea lions and harbor seals bark and cavort in the whitecaps just offshore. The only buildings you'll see are massive — and we do mean massive — luxury homes tucked discreetly among the trees, and three world-class resorts, should you wish to seek them out (see the preceding section).

You can enter the drive through five different gates, paying your fee in exchange for a handy-dandy full-color map and brochure of the highlights along the route. You're likely to use one of these three gates:

✔ From Monterey or Pacific Grove, the most convenient gate is the **Pacific Grove Gate.** Follow Ocean View Boulevard from Monterey to Sunset Drive; after the road turns inland, you'll soon see 17-Mile Drive on your right.

✔ From Carmel, enter at the **Carmel Gate;** from downtown, turn right off Ocean Avenue onto San Antonio Avenue (1 block before the beach).

✔ If you're just passing by the peninsula and want to take a gander at this remarkable real estate, enter at the **Highway 1 Gate,** just off the main road at the Holman Highway exit.

Allot a leisurely afternoon for the drive. If you don't have a few hours to spare, you can see part of the route by using it to travel between Monterey and Carmel (or vice-versa). The disadvantage of this plan is that you have to choose between coastal and inland portions; we say go coastal, but it all depends on your aesthetic sensibilities.

The map features about 20 points of interest, and you can use pullouts at scenic points all along the drive. If you'd rather avoid a lot of stop and go, focus on these natural highlights:

✔ **Point Joe,** on the northern end of the coast, which offers a gorgeous vantage for spotting migrating whales between December and March.

✔ About midway down the coast are **Seal Rock** and **Bird Rock,** where you can spot countless gulls, cormorants, and other offshore birds, plus harbor seals and sea lions, gathering just offshore.

✔ **Fanshell Overlook** offers awesome views of Fanshell Beach, where harbor seals gather to birth their pups each spring.

✔ **Cypress Point Lookout** offers the drive's most spectacular coastal view and is ideal for sunset collectors.

✔ A little farther down the coast is the famous **Lone Cypress,** one of the peninsula's most distinctive and mesmerizing images. The magnificently gnarled, windblown tree looks as if it's growing right out of bare rock, but its insistent roots have actually burrowed deep through the rock's crevices. You're not allowed up close, but the view from the deck beside the parking area is magnificent.

You can see the best forest-and-ocean panorama from **Huckleberry Hill,** along the inland curve a little bit north of the Highway 1 Gate, which is the highest point along the drive.

Hitting the links

We won't lie to you — getting a tee time on one of the prime Pebble Beach courses without booking a room at one of the resorts is nearly impossible, even in the off-season (Nov–Mar). But try if you must.

Pebble Beach Golf Links, the **Links at Spanish Bay, Spyglass Hill Golf Course,** all on the 17-Mile Drive, and **Del Monte Golf Course,** in Monterey, are all administered by the **Pebble Beach Company** (☎ 800-654-9300; www.pebblebeach.com). If you'd like to book a lesson, call the **Pebble Beach Golf Academy** (☎ 831-622-8650), home to Laird Small, one of *Golf Digest's* Top 50 Teachers in America for 2003/04 and 2005/06.

✔ **Pebble Beach Golf Links,** at the Lodge at Pebble Beach, is the Big Kahuna of Pebble Beach golf courses. A links legend since 1919, this par-72, 6,719-yard rolling oceanfront beauty regularly ranks among the top five courses in the world, and many of golf's biggest names have called it the finest course they've ever played. This is a mature course with old-root trees and massive bunkers, at one with the land like few courses on Earth.

Unless you're willing to foot the bill for a Pebble Beach hotel room, don't get your heart set on playing here — though nonguests can book tee times just a day in advance, which means you have to get very lucky and catch a last-minute cancellation (nearly impossible). And expect to pay to play, big time: Greens fees are $450 for resort guests including a cart; they're the same for nonguests, but nonguests have to pay extra ($25) for a cart.

✔ **Spyglass Hill Golf Course,** at Stevenson Drive and Spyglass Hill Road in Pebble Beach, Robert Trent Jones, Sr.'s, par-72, 6,862-yard legend is one of the toughest golf courses in the world. Expect to test your skills — and every club in your bag — if you get to play here. Greens fees are $300 for guests including cart and the same for nonguests not including cart (an extra $25). Nonguests can book tee times up to a month in advance for this course — easier to get on than Pebble Beach, but still tough. (Even winter tee times book up a month in advance.)

Your best bets for garnering available tee times are the **Del Monte Golf Course** and the **Links at Spanish Bay,** where nonguests can book up to two months in advance. You should call as early as possible, even marking your calendar to dial at the two-month and one-month mark. If that fails, just call back and try to snag a cancellation.

✔ **Del Monte Golf Course,** at the Hyatt on Sylvan Road and Highway 1 in Monterey, is the oldest course west of the Mississippi. This par-72, 6,339-yard inland course has been challenging golfers since 1897, as well as wowing them with its tree-lined charm. And by Pebble Beach terms, greens fees are reasonable: $105 plus $20 per player for the cart.

✔ Designed by Robert Trent Jones, Jr., Tom Watson, and Frank Tatum, the **Links at Spanish Bay,** at the Inn at Spanish Bay, is the foremost Scottish linksland-style course in the United States; Tom Watson has said, "It's so much like Scotland, you can almost hear the bagpipes." Greens fees are $240 for guests and nonguests alike, but guests get the cart for free.

It's an even playing field for tee times at the public **Poppy Hills Golf Course,** just off 17-Mile Drive on Lopez Road (☎ 831-625-2035; www.poppyhillsgolf.com), where everybody has an equal shot. Robert Trent Jones, Jr., designed this par-72, 6,861-yard course, which is a favorite among duffers. The course accepts reservations up to 30 days in advance. Call as early as possible within that time frame for your choice of tee times, but you can usually snare a slot a week in advance. Greens fees are lower, too: $130 Monday through Thursday and $160 Friday through Sunday and holidays, with carts running an extra $32.

Carmel-by-the-Sea and Carmel Valley

If Monterey sounds too touristy, Pebble Beach too chi-chi, and Big Sur too woodsy or rustic (see Chapter 19), Carmel is the place for you. This high-end haven is among the stars of the California coast, and one of the loveliest towns in all of America. It's more like an elite artists' colony than a mass-market tourist town, with galleries and boutiques galore, quaint views or sweeping vistas at every turn, and a relaxed vibe that whispers "away from it all" like sweet nothings in your ear.

Carmel exudes charisma by the bucketload. This village displays its assets like a starlet in Cannes, with picture-perfect, cypress-dotted streets gradually leading downhill to one of the most spectacular beaches on the California coast. And 15 minutes away up Carmel Valley Road, the ocean gives way to mountains, ranches, and resorts.

Not everyone adores Carmel, however. For one, complaints of commercialism abound from those who knew it when — before Saks Fifth Avenue and all those cute inns set up shop. And like its most famous resident, Clint Eastwood (who served a high-profile stint as mayor a few years back), virtually all the residents are seven-figure types. As a result, prices are high across the board, restaurants are more upscale than casual, and an air of elitism prevails.

Carmel isn't really suited for children; romance-seeking couples rule the day here. If you have the kids in tow, you'll probably be happier basing yourself in the Carmel Valley, Monterey, or Pacific Grove, instead. You will find, however, that no one's more welcome in Carmel than the family pet; this is West Coast nirvana for those who travel with Fido.

Carmel is rather quiet and not overloaded with sightseeing "attractions" per se. Visiting is more about slowing down a bit — browsing the boutiques, ambling the back streets to admire the fabulous homes, and strolling that breathtaking beach. If you're looking for relaxation, stay a while. All you need is a day or so to explore the village itself, but Carmel also makes a good base for tooling around the entire peninsula, and even the stupendous Big Sur Coast (see Chapter 19).

Orienting yourself and getting around

Carmel-by-the-Sea is petite and easy to navigate. The town is laid out on a basic grid pattern, with Ocean Avenue running due west from Highway 1 to Carmel Beach and serving as the village's main drag.

Parallel to Ocean Avenue run numbered avenues: Fourth, Fifth, and Sixth avenues to the north, and Seventh and Eighth avenues to the south. (The town extends farther in each direction, but these streets shape downtown.)

Perpendicular to Ocean and the numbered avenues run a number of name streets: Mission Street, San Carlos, Dolores, Lincoln, and so on. You can get an easy-to-follow, cartoony map of downtown labeling most major businesses almost everywhere about town; for a preview (complete with links to business Web sites), point your Web browser to www. carmelfun.com. **Carmel Valley** is reached via Carmel Valley Road, just south of Carmel-by-the-Sea on Highway 1.

This quaint village has no need for such big-city affectations as street addresses. Thus, all addresses are given in general terms: San Carlos Street at Seventh, Sixth between Lincoln and Monte Verde, and so on.

Everything in town is within walking distance. Most likely, you'll be able to park your car at your inn or motel and leave it there for the duration of your stay. Parking has strict 30- to 90-minute time limits in the downtown area, but moving a few blocks off Ocean Avenue into more residential territory usually yields less restricted space. A free lot sits at Third Avenue and Torres Street, and another at the beach; a convenient pay lot is at Eighth Avenue and San Carlos Street.

Where to stay

Carmel is so completely adorable that it's a hugely popular weekend destination. Book well in advance if you're planning a visit over a Friday or Saturday night. And be aware that most places require a two-night minimum stay on weekends. Accommodations upvalley are a little easier to reserve, but you'll still want advance reservations in the summer.

You may want to try booking your room through a free reservations service such as **MontereyVisitorsGuide.com** (☎ 888-655-3424; www. monterey-reservations.com) or **Resort 2 Me** (☎ 800-757-5646; www. lodgingreservations.net), or the **Carmel Area Reservation Service** (☎ 888-434-3891 or 831-659-7061; www.carmel-california.com). You can sometimes get a better rate through these services than you can by calling direct, and they'll make alternative suggestions if the suggestions in this section are full.

Count on 10 percent in taxes being tacked on to your final hotel bill.

Cobblestone Inn
$$–$$$$ Carmel-by-the-Sea

This charming B&B offers flowery, romantic accommodations at moderate prices. The 24 rooms encircle a lovely courtyard. Each room features a fireplace, TV (not a given in B&Bs), and minifridge. The staff serves afternoon goodies in a warm and lovely living room. On the down side, the cheapest rooms are very small, and only two of the rooms with private baths have tub/shower combos. But the sacrifices are minimal considering the charms. Bikes are available for exploring.

See map p. 244. Junipero Street between Seventh and Eighth avenues. ☎ *800-833-8836 or 831-625-5222. Fax: 831-625-0478.* www.foursisters.com. *Free parking. Rack rates: $125–$260 double. Rates include full breakfast and afternoon wine and hors d'oeuvres. AE, DC, MC, V.*

Colonial Terrace Inn
$$–$$$$ Carmel-by-the-Sea

Set in a residential neighborhood a mere block from the beach, you'll trade convenience to Ocean Avenue (about 10 blocks away) for a tranquil garden and the sounds of the waves. Rooms, located in seven buildings around the lovely grounds, are a bit of a mixed bag, so have an in-depth conversation with reservations about your needs. Oceanview rooms, including no. 26 and no. 28, are your best bet. The inn is nonsmoking and surprisingly — for Carmel — doesn't allow pets.

See map p. 244. San Antonio Street and 13th Avenue. ☎ *800-345-8220 or 831-624-2741. Fax: 831-626-2715.* www.thecolonialterrace.com. *Free parking. Rack rates: $159–$259 double, $249–349 suite. Rates include continental breakfast. AE, MC, V.*

Cypress Inn
$$–$$$$$ Carmel-by-the-Sea

Carmel's pet-friendliest hotel is famous for being co-owned by screen legend Doris Day, whose movie posters grace the bar. This 1929 Moorish-Mediterranean inn is beautifully styled, but the building is old — we were dismayed to see space heaters in the guest rooms. Some of the standard doubles are quite small and on the spare side as well (and no. 111 is dark). However, a 12-room addition was completed in 2005, so request one of the new rooms or a corner king to get some space between you and your luggage. You can enjoy breakfast in the lovely courtyard on nice days, and the comfy fireplace-lit living room is a guest magnet in the evenings. The service is accommodating, especially to dogs. You might not want to book here without one.

See map p. 244. Lincoln Street and Seventh Avenue. ☎ *800-443-7443 or 831-624-3871. Fax: 831-624-8216.* www.cypress-inn.com. *Free parking. Rack rates: $195–$425 double. Rates include a generous continental breakfast spread. AE, DISC, MC, V.*

Los Laureles Lodge
$$–$$$ Carmel Valley

Carmel Valley has a number of expensive resorts, but us regular folks are quite fond of this historic ranch dating from 1830. Courtyard doubles, converted from former stables that once housed the Vanderbilt thoroughbreds, are comfortable and simply decorated around warm knotty-pine walls. Families with young children can cozy up in a Surrey Lane room, large enough for a queen bed and pull out sofa. There's a swimming pool, an outdoor bar so you don't have to supply your own piña coladas, and an extremely good restaurant. If you bring the kids, this is an especially pleasant place to stay.

See map p. 244. 313 West Carmel Valley Rd. ☎ *800-533-4404 or 831-659-2233. Fax: 831-659-0481.* www.loslaureles.com. *Free parking. Rack rates: $99–$160 double, $155–$595 suite. Rates include continental breakfast. Ask about golf, horseback riding, bicycling, and fly-fishing packages. AE, MC, V.*

Mission Ranch
$$–$$$$ Carmel-by-the-Sea

With the kindly assistance of Dirty Harry himself, Clint Eastwood, this 1850s farmhouse and its outlying buildings have been transformed into an elegant complex worthy of Ralph Lauren. The ranch lies on the outskirts of town, a good walk away from the village, but sheep-filled pastures and ocean views make it almost picture-perfect. Rooms vary depending on price and location, but all have an appealingly cozy ranchland feel. On-site is an excellent restaurant, plus a fitness room and tennis courts. No pool, however; it's too cold.

See map p. 244. 26270 Dolores St. (near the Carmel Mission). ☎ *800-538-8221 or 831-624-6436. Fax: 831-626-4163.* www.missionranchcarmel.com. *Free parking. Rack rates: $110–$265 double. Rates include continental breakfast. AE, MC, V.*

Quail Lodge Resort and Golf Club
$$$$–$$$$$ Carmel Valley

Owned by the Peninsula Group — one of the world's finest hotel chains — this magical destination resort spreads across 850 pastoral acres with gorgeous gardens, sparkling lakes, wildlife-dotted woodlands, and championship fairways. Luxuries abound in the spacious French-country rooms, and the extensive facilities — tennis courts, pools, hiking paths, and more — will keep you happy for days on end.

See map p. 244. 8205 Valley Greens Dr. ☎ 888-828-8787 or 831-624-2888. Fax: 831-624-3726. www.quaillodge.com. *Free parking. Rack rates: $225–$435 double, $325–$825 suite, $20 service charge per night. Ask about golf, romance, and holiday packages. AE, DC, MC, V.*

Village Inn
$$–$$$$ Carmel-by-the-Sea

If you're traveling on a budget, this superbly located motel is your best bet. The cute rooms have a bit more charm than you usually find at such bargain rates, as well as fridges and nice, newish bathrooms. The attractive property is spic-and-span, and management is conscientious and friendly. The double queens are a good bet for families.

See map p. 244. Junipero and Ocean avenues. ☎ 800-346-3864 or 831-624-3864. Fax: 831-626-6763. www.carmelvillageinn.com. *Free parking. Rack rates: $85–$195 double, $125–$245 suite. Rates include continental breakfast. AE, MC, V.*

Where to dine

It's really hard to go wrong dining out in Carmel. The locals have loads of discretionary income, so they can afford to demand the best. Of the more than 60 restaurants in this tiny town, most are better than average. This section describes our favorites — but if you pass something else that strikes your fancy, chances are good that it won't disappoint you. Reservations are a must on weekends.

Little Napoli
$$–$$$ Carmel-by-the-Sea   ITALIAN

Between the charming décor (think red gingham, braids of garlic), the excellent country-style cooking, the extensive all-Italian wine list, and the low prices, it's no wonder that Little Napoli inspires such local loyalty. Expect hearty favorites such as crispy-crust pizzas, hand-stuffed cannelloni, and Neapolitan-style seafood. Everything's fresh from the field or the bay. This restaurant is terrific — and a grade-A value to boot.

See map p. 244. In the El Paseo Building, Dolores Street between Ocean and Seventh avenues. ☎ 831-626-6335. www.littlenapoli.com. *Reservations highly recommended for dinner. Main courses: $12–$25. MC, V. Open: Mon–Thurs 11:30 a.m.–9:30 p.m., Fri–Sun 11:30 a.m.–10 p.m. (hours vary seasonally, so call ahead).*

Casanova
$$$–$$$$ Carmel-by-the-Sea   FRENCH/ITALIAN

In a town full of dreamy restaurants, this is far and away the most romantic. The Mediterranean-style house (former home of Charlie Chaplin's cook) spills over with candlelit old-world charm. But don't let all this talk of ambience fool you: The French-Italian menu is top-notch, the service is excellent, and the 30,000-bottle wine cellar is an award-winner. Considering that the meals include antipasto and dessert, prices aren't bad, either.

See map p. 244. Fifth Street between San Carlos and Mission streets. ☎ *831-625-0501.* www.casanovarestaurant.com. *Reservations recommended. Three-course prix-fixe: $22–$40. MC, V. Open: Daily 11:30 a.m.–3 p.m. and 5–10 p.m.*

Flying Fish Grill
$$$–$$$$ Carmel-by-the-Sea PACIFIC RIM/SEAFOOD

Chef/owner Kenny Fukumoto's dark and intimate pan-Asian seafood house is one of our favorite restaurants on the Monterey Peninsula. Expect creative, beautifully prepared seafood dishes with Japanese accents — rare peppered ahi and *yosenabe* (clay-pot seafood) are shining stars on the universally pleasing menu — plus specialties like rib-eye shabu-shabu for nonseafood eaters.

See map p. 244. In Carmel Plaza, Mission Street between Ocean and Seventh avenues. ☎ *831-625-1962. Reservations highly recommended. Main courses: $17–$26. AE, DISC, MC, V. Open: Sun–Thurs 5–9 p.m., Fri and Sat until 9:30 p.m.*

The Forge in the Forest
$–$$$ Carmel-by-the-Sea AMERICAN

For outdoor dining, this is the local favorite especially among dog lovers (there's even a menu for Barkley), but even when it's cold enough to defeat the patio heaters, the Forge is a fun place for lunch or dinner. The inside dining room couldn't be more casual, featuring a communal table and a well-attended bar. There's nothing sophisticated about the food either — burgers, hot pastrami or corned beef sandwiches, delectable baby-back pork ribs, steak, pizza, chicken, big salads, and so on — but it's straight-forward and tasty. Sometimes you just want to eat where the food doesn't require an explanation.

See map p. 244. Junipero Street at Fifth Avenue. ☎ *831-624-2233.* www.forgein theforest.com. *Main courses: $13–$28. MC, V. Open: Sun–Thurs 4–10 p.m. (until 11 p.m. Fri–Sat in summer); Sun 11 a.m.–2:30 p.m.*

Jack London's Bar & Grill
$$–$$$ Carmel-by-the-Sea AMERICAN

Come here when you tire of Carmel's high prices and pretentious airs. This 30-year-old bar and restaurant is a completely regular hangout that has never-theless been lauded by the *New York Times* for its charms. The huge menu ranges from burgers and chicken-breast sandwiches to pizzas, Tex-Mex spe-cialties, and Black Angus steaks. It offers great bathtub-size margaritas, too.

See map p. 244. San Carlos Street at Fifth Avenue. ☎ *831-624-2336.* www.jack londons.com. *Main courses: $10–$22. AE, DISC, MC, V. Open: Daily 11 a.m.–midnight (bar open until 2 a.m.), Sunday from 10 a.m.*

Exploring Carmel-by-the-Sea

At the foot of Ocean Avenue sits **Carmel Beach,** one of the most heavenly beaches in the United States, if not the world. A wide crescent of white sand skirts gorgeous, tide-pool-dotted Carmel Bay. A screen of gnarled cypresses separates street from sand, and the emerald-green cliffs of Pebble Beach rise in the distance. Swimming is a no-no because the waves are too rough (and the water's too cold year-round), but the beach is great for strolling, picnicking, and playing fetch with Fido, who's allowed to run off-leash here (you'll see lots of happy dogs cavorting in the sand). Take time to walk along this stretch of beach no matter what season you're visiting; walk north for the best views.

 The small parking lot at the end of Ocean gets crowded year-round, but you can often find additional spots along Scenic Road, from which wooden staircases lead down to the beach at various points along the road. (Note, however, that the only restrooms are at the parking lot on Ocean Avenue.)

If you want a little sand space to yourself, follow Scenic Road south around the promontory to **Carmel River State Beach,** a more remote, white-sand-dune-dotted stretch that's a paradise for birders.

Shopping and strolling

Shopping is tops among Carmel activities. Pricey apparel and home-furnishing boutiques, jewelry stores, and art galleries line the streets of downtown. Don't expect to find anything too funky; still, you can do lots of one-of-a-kind browsing. If you're a gallery hound, pick up the free **"Carmel Gallery Guide,"** available throughout town. Be sure to peek into Carmel's various courtyards, which often hide some of the best finds. The alfresco **Carmel Plaza,** at Ocean Avenue and Mission Street (☎ 831-624-0137; www.carmelplaza.com), houses about 50 shops, including familiar names such as Saks Fifth Avenue and Banana Republic.

Stepping into the past

Mission San Carlos Borromeo del Rio Carmelo, more commonly known as the **Carmel Mission,** 3080 Rio Rd. (☎ 831-624-3600; www.carmel mission.org), is one of the largest and most beautiful of the 21 Spanish missions established by Father Junípero Serra, Spanish founder of California's mission chain. Built in a baroque style with a towering Moorish bell tower, it has been in continuous operation since 1771. The burnished terra-cotta facade and soaring, romantic curves make it worth strolling by even if you don't go inside. Still, if you're a history buff, make the effort, because Serra is buried here and his cell contains some of the original furnishings.

It's open for self-guided tours Monday through Saturday from 9:30 a.m. to 5 p.m. (Sun from 10:30 a.m.), with extended hours in summer. Admission is $5 for adults, $4 for seniors, and $1 for kids 6 to 17. To reach the mission, take San Carlos Street south from town and follow the signs, or take Rio Road west off Highway 1 and follow it for a half-mile.

If you'd like to find out more about local history and color, take a two-hour guided walk with **Carmel Walks** (☎ 831-642-2700; www.carmel walks.com). The walks take place Tuesday through Friday at 10 a.m., Saturday at 10 a.m. and 2 p.m., for $20 per person. Tours leave from the Pine Inn at Lincoln Street and Ocean Avenue; call ahead to reserve your spot.

Sampling Big Sur's natural beauty

The spectacular beauty of the Big Sur Coast (see Chapter 19) begins just 3 miles south of Carmel-by-the-Sea at **Point Lobos State Reserve** (☎ 831-624-4909; www.pointlobos.org). A cypress-dotted headland, the Big Sur Coast has been variously called "the greatest meeting of land and water in the world" and "the crown jewel of the state parks system." It's a natural wonderland, all right, with sea lions, otters, harbor seals, and seabirds populating the ocean coves; spectacular coastal vistas (perfect for whale-watching in winter); picnic areas; and miles of hiking trails. The entrance fee is $8 per car, which includes a trail map. Open from 9 a.m. to 4 p.m. Arrive early, especially on weekends; if the lot is full, you have to wait for someone to leave before you can enter.

Gathering More Information

For peninsula-wide information before you arrive, point your Web browser to www.monterey.com, or contact the **Monterey Peninsula Visitors and Convention Bureau** on their 24-hour information hotline (☎ 831-649-1770). Another useful source of information is the **Monterey County Convention and Visitors Bureau** (☎ 888-221-1010; www.montereyinfo.org). For Carmel-specific information, you can call ☎ 888-434-3891, visit www.carmel-california.com (an advertiser-driven site), or you can check out the official city Web site at www.carmelcalifornia.com.

In Monterey

Stop in at the well-staffed and well-stocked **Monterey Visitors Center,** near downtown at Camino El Estero and Franklin Street (1 block inland from Del Monte Avenue). It's open Monday through Saturday from 9 a.m. to 6 p.m. (to 5 p.m. Nov–Mar), Sunday from 9 a.m. to 5 p.m. (to 4 p.m. Nov–Mar).

In Carmel

You can pick up information from the **Carmel Business Association,** upstairs next to the Eastwood Building on San Carlos Street between Fifth and Sixth avenues in Carmel-by-the-Sea (☎ 831-624-2522). You can also call ahead to have a visitor's guide sent to you. The office is open Monday through Friday from 9 a.m. to 5 p.m. and Saturday from 11 a.m. to 3 p.m. (check for Sun hours in summer).

Chapter 19

The Spectacular Big Sur Coast

*F*ew shorelines in the world are as breathtaking as the Big Sur Coast. Skirted by rugged shores and crescent-shaped bays, this pristine wilderness of towering redwoods and rolling hills is tranquil, unspoiled, romantic, dramatic, and overwhelmingly beautiful — and, as you may assume, perfect for a true getaway. If you want quiet, this is the place.

Although, technically, a Big Sur Village exists (29 miles south of the Monterey Peninsula on Highway 1), it's not much more than a post office and the Big Sur Bazaar/Deli, which sells sundries, gifts, and good take-away Mexican food (and has the best prices on sandwiches, in case you need a picnic). *Big Sur* actually refers to the gorgeous 90-mile stretch of land between Carmel-by-the-Sea and San Simeon. The main thoroughfare and scenic byway is Highway 1, blessed on one side by the 167,000-acre Ventana Wilderness, with the splendid Santa Lucia mountain range rising just beyond, and on the other by the wild, spectacular coast (see the "The Big Sur Coast" map on p. 274). The region is at its most woodsy and breathtaking in the northern half, but the entire coastline drive is stunning.

Development is minimal, and you'll find little more to do here than commune with nature — but oh, what nature it is! Make time to enjoy it. Hike the state parks, walk the beaches, stop along the drive to watch windsurfers pirouette among the waves and sea lions sun on the rocks, or perch yourself atop the cliffs and take in the sea breeze. You won't believe the effect Big Sur can have on your soul: Modern life fades into the background as you become absorbed in Mother Nature's world.

The flip side to all this poetic waxing, however, is that Big Sur requires some effort to enjoy. With just one winding, hairpin-plagued lane in each direction, Highway 1 is slow going and can be tummy turning. Tourist facilities along the route are limited, so don't expect a gas station every few miles or any chain motels or fast-food joints at all. The region's remoteness has fostered a special breed of local, quiet types who fiercely protect their privacy, their rustic lifestyle, and the unspoiled nature around them. A hippie vibe prevails — most residents came here to get away from it all, and they mean to keep it that way. Stay off private property and unmarked driveways, and stick to clearly marked pullouts, public areas, and parks. Take a cue from the locals: Appreciate Big Sur for what it is — glorious and unspoiled. Enjoy it, respect it, and leave no mark. Pack out everything you bring in.

Timing Your Visit

Like much of California's central and northern coast, Big Sur is at its clearest, warmest, and sunniest best during early fall — September and October. Summer is the busiest season traffic-wise and hotel-wise, so plan ahead and expect to pay top dollar.

What's the tradeoff for cooler weather in winter and spring? Clear skies, little fog, no crowds, lower hotel rates, and fabulous offshore views of the mammoth gray whales that migrate from Alaska to Mexico and back again between November and April. For a breakdown of the seasons and events, go to www.bigsurcalifornia.org and click on "Calendar."

Leave yourself plenty of time to mosey along the Big Sur Coast. Even though the distance is only about 110 miles from Carmel to San Simeon, you can't really drive the twisty-turny road in less than three hours. And trust us — you don't want to. Allow a whole day for the drive. New and exciting views present themselves at every turn, with plenty of vista points for stopping. An entire day gives you time to go hiking at one of the parks along the way, plus time for a picnic or a leisurely lunch.

If you want to stay overnight to spend more hours among the trees, be aware that the accommodations in this funky neck of the woods fall into two categories: big-money luxurious or comfort-challenged rustic. You won't find any affordable country inns or reliable chain motels in between, and TVs are not a common amenity no matter which budget level you choose. (Cellphone reception isn't too great, either.) If the choices in the "Where to Stay in Big Sur" section don't suit you, but you still want more than a day to explore Mother Nature's handiwork, base yourself just to the north on the Monterey Peninsula (Carmel is particularly convenient) or near Hearst Castle to the south.

The Big Sur Coast

ACCOMMODATIONS ■
Big Sur Lodge **4**
Deetjen's Big Sur Inn **7**
Post Ranch Inn **5**
Treebones Ragged Point Inn
  & Resort **9**
Ventana Inn & Spa **6**

DINING ◆
Big Sur Bakery & Restaurant **1**
Big Sur River Inn **3**
Big Sur Roadhouse **2**
Cielo **6**
Deetjen's Big Sur Inn **7**
Nepenthe/Cafe Kevah **8**

Getting There

You can access all the main attractions via Highway 1. If you're dedicating a day to the drive, set out early to take full advantage of daylight.
The slow, curving drive is a drag at night, and you can't see the great
scenery. Leaving early is especially important if you're heading north,
because the region's finest parks, Pfeiffer Big Sur and Julia Pfeiffer Burns
state parks, are about two-thirds of the way up the coast.

Where to Stay in Big Sur

Camping is certainly the truest way to experience this unspoiled region.
If camping's your thing, visit www.bigsurcalifornia.org for a complete list of campground options. If camping's not your thing, expect
10.5 percent in taxes to be tacked on to your hotel bill.

Big Sur Lodge
$$–$$$ **Big Sur**

Tucked among the redwoods of Pfeiffer Big Sur State Park are these 62 rustic cabins, many large enough to house families. Well-kept, spacious, and newly remodeled, all have private bathrooms and patios with lovely views, but no TV, telephone, or even an alarm clock to interrupt as you meditate on nature. Spend a bit more for a fireplace and/or kitchenette; nights get cool, and who wants to run out for coffee in the morning? A so-so restaurant, country store, and heated pool, plus all park amenities, are on-site.

See map p. 274. 47225 Hwy. 1, in Pfeiffer Big Sur State Park (26 miles south of Carmel). ☎ ***800-424-4787*** *or 831-667-3100. Fax: 831-667-3110.* www.bigsurlodge.com. *Free parking. Rack rates: $99–$249 one-bedroom cottage, $129–$259 two-bedroom cottage. Rates include day-use fees for four Big Sur–area parks. AE, MC, V.*

Deetjen's Big Sur Inn
$$–$$$ **Big Sur**

Built by a Norwegian homesteader and his missus in the 1930s and now a national historic site, Deetjen's is quintessential Big Sur: lovely, rustic, and funky to a fault. If you don't mind sacrificing creature comforts for rustic-cozy, you'll love the oddball collection of hand-hewn cabins. The cabins do not include phones, TVs, or central heating. Walls are single-board thin, so don't pass on a fire-heated room — even in summer — and don't expect privacy or quiet (families with kids younger than 12 must book two adjoining rooms). The restaurant is one of the local bests and a must if you love breakfast. Book well ahead, because the inn fills up months in advance.

See map p. 274. Highway 1 (4 miles south of Pfeiffer Big Sur State Park and 30 miles south of Carmel). ☎ ***831-667-2377.*** www.deetjens.com. *Free parking. Rack rates: $75–$180 double with shared bathroom, $110–$195 double with private bathroom. MC, V.*

Post Ranch Inn
$$$$$ **Big Sur**

Wide expanses of glass bring the outside in to 30 gorgeous, amenity-filled oceanfront cottages, spread out over 98 unspoiled, five-star acres at this environmentally friendly, ultraexclusive resort. No TVs, but you'll have a CD player and everything else you could want — even your own private slice of Big Sur to explore. A full menu of spa treatments is available in your room or outdoors — you decide. The restaurant is excellent, too — probably the best place around for a blowout meal. This place is ridiculously expensive (not to mention a tad pretentious), but it's worth every penny. Kids younger than 18 are not invited to stay here.

See map p. 274. Highway 1 (28 miles south of Carmel). ☎ ***800-527-2200*** *or 831-667-2200. Fax: 831-667-2824.* www.postranchinn.com. *Rack rates: $525–$2,000 double. Rates include continental breakfast. AE, MC, V.*

Ragged Point Inn & Resort
$$–$$$$ Ragged Point

This rustic motel at the southern gateway to Big Sur serves its purpose for travelers ready for a break, either from civilization or the road. Rooms are clean, and the upstairs "Tier 2" models feature newer furnishings, comfy beds, TVs, and balconies for enjoying the glorious oceanfront views. "Tier 4" rooms are even pricier, but you'll have better coastal vistas, a fireplace, kitchenette, and private patio. The resort includes a gorgeous stone-pillared restaurant with decent but expensive food and an ocean-facing patio. The grounds are fab — stop by for the sightlines even if you don't stay the night.

See map p. 274. 19019 Hwy. 1 (14 miles north of Hearst Castle). ☎ *805-927-4502. Fax: 805-927-8862.* www.raggedpointinn.com. *Free parking. Rack rates: $129–$289 double. AE, DISC, MC, V.*

Treebones Resort
$$–$$$ Big Sur

The newest lodging on the Big Sur coast features 16 *yurts* (round, canvas-covered structures akin to those favored by Turkish nomads). These spacious yurts, however, are furnished with sinks, space heaters, and double beds covered in fancy quilted bedspreads, and yurt no. 1 sports its own ping-pong table! It's camping taken up quite a number of notches. The remainder of the resort, which is on a cliff overlooking the ocean, consists of a swimming pool and a handsome lodge where guests can prepare their own complimentary waffle breakfast, partake in a not-inexpensive barbeque dinner, relax, or shop for snack foods and drinks. Treebones became immediately popular upon opening so make your reservations three months in advance. And bring flip-flops for the bathhouse.

See map p. 274. Highway 1 just above Gorda (25 miles north of San Simeon, 65 miles south of Monterey). ☎ *877-424-4787.* www.treebonesresort.com. *Free parking. Rack rates: $129–$189 double. MC, V.*

Ventana Inn & Spa
$$$$$ Big Sur

Across the highway from Post Ranch is Big Sur's original luxury oasis, spread over a whopping 243 meadowy, ocean-facing acres. The gorgeous rooms are more high-country cozy than contemporary, and TVs, VCRs, and CD players are among the in-room luxuries. You can't argue with the fabulousness of the grounds, and the 2,100-square-foot spa has amenities ranging from massages and mud treatments to aromatherapy sessions and astrology readings. We loved the complimentary afternoon yoga class followed by wine and cheese in the lobby where you can also sign up for a ten-minute chair massage. Dinner is served in the first-rate **Cielo** (see the following section). If you're with the kids on this trip, stay elsewhere.

See map p. 274. Highway 1 (2 miles south of Pfeiffer Big Sur State Park and 28 miles south of Carmel). ☎ **800-628-6500** or 831-667-2331. Fax: 831-667-0573. www.ventana inn.com. Free parking. Rack rates: $485–$1,155 double or suite. Rates include continental breakfast and afternoon wine and cheese. AE, DC, DISC, MC, V.

Where to Dine in Big Sur

In addition to the options listed in this section, consider these excellent choices at Big Sur's top places to stay (reservations are recommended):

- ✔ **Cielo,** at the Ventana Inn & Spa (☎ **831-667-2331**), is tops for a sophisticated lunch stop or a special dinner. Grab a midday table on the outdoor patio in nice weather — the views are incredible. The California cuisine doesn't disappoint, either. Main courses run $11 to $17 at lunch, $24 to $30 at dinner.

- ✔ The lovely restaurant at **Deetjen's Big Sur Inn** (☎ **831-667-2377**) is regaled for its hearty cooking and intimate ambience. Breakfast ($7–$10) includes all your farmhouse favorites, while dinner ($17–$29) features such sophisticated but unfussy dishes as New York steak with twice-baked potato and herb-crusted New Zealand rack of lamb. A country delight.

Big Sur Bakery & Restaurant
$–$$$ Big Sur AMERICAN

High-quality ingredients and loving hands in the kitchen are part of the ethos at this casual cafe. Come for coffee and pastries in the morning, or arrive later for wood-fired pizzas, grilled line-caught sea bass (*line-caught* means you can eat it guilt-free), caramelized onion tarts with candied walnuts and a dab of blue cheese, or just some homemade cookies to take on the road. It's all good.

See map p. 274. Highway 1 (26 miles south of Carmel, just past the post office). ☎ **831-667-0520.** www.bigsurbakery.com. Reservations recommended for dinner in season. Main courses: $6–$9.50 at lunch, $14–$36 at dinner. MC, V. Open: Tues–Sun 8 a.m.–9 p.m., Sat–Sun 10:30 a.m.–3 p.m.

Big Sur River Inn
$–$$ Big Sur AMERICAN

This popular stop is ideal for any time of day. Cozy up to the huge stone fireplace in cold weather or snag a table on the deck when the sun shines. Expect American classics ranging from hearty breakfasts to burgers and sandwiches to fresh fish, pastas, and ribs. Service is friendly, and the crowd is a nice mix of locals and visitors. Live entertainment on Sunday afternoons is usually of the foot-stomping variety.

See map p. 274. Highway 1 (2 miles north of Pfeiffer Big Sur State Park). ☎ **831-667-2700.** www.bigsurriverinn.com. Reservations recommended for dinner in *season. Main courses: $10–$18 at lunch, $11–$32 at dinner. AE, DC, DISC, MC, V. Open: daily 8 a.m.–8:30 p.m.*

The Big Sur Roadhouse
$$ Big Sur CALIFORNIA/LATIN AMERICAN

Considered by locals to be *the* place to eat (and drink), this charming diner is beyond terrific and a bargain by Big Sur standards. The Latino-inspired menu is delectable, featuring soft tacos du jour, a goat-cheese quesadilla sparked up with mango-basil salsa, a selection of enchiladas, yummy tortilla soup, and a glazed breast of chicken that was so tender and juicy, any bird with foresight would gladly sacrifice herself to this kitchen. For a fancy gourmet meal, head to the Post Ranch Inn or Cielo; for a stellar but easygoing dinner, the Roadhouse can't be beat.

See map p. 274. Highway 1 (across from Glen Oaks Motel). ☎ **831-667-2264.** *Reservations highly recommended for dinner. Main courses: $13–$20. MC, V. Open: Wed–Mon 5:30–9 p.m.*

Nepenthe
$$–$$$ Big Sur AMERICAN

Nepenthe's prices are too high if you consider only the strictly average American fare — steaks, broiled fish, burgers, quiche — but if you're choosing a restaurant based on the view, look no farther. The panorama is awe-inspiring, and starlit nights are pure magic. The redwood-beamed indoor/outdoor restaurant has a wonderful lodgelike atmosphere, and a casual party vibe prevails. Come by for a drink if you don't want to pay for the food. Or, better yet, on nice days, head a level down to the alfresco **Café Kevah.** Kevah's amazing patio boasts the same stellar views, and its casual healthy-gourmet daytime fare is a fraction of the dough.

See map p. 274. Highway 1 (2 miles south of Pfeiffer Big Sur State Park, just south of the Ventana Inn). ☎ **831-667-2345.** www.nepenthebigsur.com. *Reservations accepted for five or more. Main courses: $13–$35 at Nepenthe, $13–$19 at Café Kevah. AE, MC, V. Open: Nepenthe, daily 11:30 a.m.–10 p.m.; Café Kevah, Mar–Jan 5 daily 9 a.m.–4 p.m.*

Exploring the Big Sur Coast

We discuss the highlights in this section as you proceed along Highway 1 southbound, strictly to match the structure of this book. However, making the drive southbound brings no particular advantage, scenic or otherwise.

In addition to these stops, a number of smaller parks and scenic vistas with pullouts exist along the way.

✔ Just 3 miles south of Carmel lies **Point Lobos State Reserve** (☎ 831-624-4909; http://pt-lobos.parks.state.ca.us), a cypress-dotted headland that has been variously called "the greatest meeting of land and water in the world" and "the crown jewel of the state parks system." It's a natural wonderland, all right, with sea lions, otters, harbor seals, and seabirds populating the sea coves; superb coastal vistas (perfect for whale-watching in winter); picnic areas; and miles of hiking trails. The entrance fee is $8 per car ($4 if you have a senior citizen on board) and includes a trail map. If you have time for only a single stop, this is the one. But arrive early, especially on weekends. If the lot is full, you have to wait for someone to leave before you can enter.

✔ About 13 miles south of Carmel is the **Bixby Bridge,** which you may recognize, even if you've never been to Big Sur. Rising 260 feet over **Bixby Creek Canyon,** the much-photographed overpass is one of the world's highest single-span concrete bridges, and one of Big Sur's most iconic images. Park your car in the lot on the north side and walk across the span to take in the magnificent views.

✔ South of Bixby Bridge is **Point Sur Lightstation,** in Point Sur State Historic Park (☎ 831-625-4419 or 831-667-2315; www.parks.ca.gov). Built 361 feet above the surf and first lit in 1889 — and in continuous operation ever since — Point Sur is the only working 19th-century lighthouse on the California coast that's open to the public. Three-hour tours are scheduled on weekends (Sat 10 a.m. and 2 p.m., Sun 10 a.m. only), with some weekday and moonlight tours added in summer. The fee is $5 for adults, $3 for teens 13 to 18, $2 for kids 5 to 12, free for children younger than 5.

The lighthouse tour includes a steep half-mile hike each way, including stairs, so wear sturdy shoes and a (preferably waterproof) windbreaker to guard against the elements.

✔ About 20 miles south of Carmel is **Andrew Molera State Park** (☎ 831-667-2315; www.parks.ca.gov), the largest park on the Big Sur Coast, and the least crowded. Miles of trails meander through meadows and along bluffs. The 2½-mile-long beach is accessible via a lovely mile-long path flanked by wildflowers in spring. At low tide, you can walk the entire length of the beach; otherwise, stick to the bluff. No swimming, of course — the water's way too cold. Between April and October you can ride horseback on the sand with **Molera Horseback Tours** (☎ 800-942-5486 or 831-625-5486; www.molerahorsebacktours.com). Prices are $25 to $59 for one- to two-and-a-half-hour guided rides.

✔ Across from Molera State Park, you can pick up the **Old Coast Road,** the original 1880s thoroughfare, when only wagons traversed these parts. If you're heading south, you can follow it as a rough scenic alternative for about 8 miles by turning left before crossing the Bixby Bridge, but if you just backtrack about a mile north from this entrance, you get a spectacular view of the Big Sur Valley, Point Sur Lighthouse, and the Pacific beyond. Don't try the road in wet weather, though; you'll get stuck.

✔ Another 5 miles or so down the road (26 miles south of Carmel) is **Big Sur Station** (☎ 831-667-2315), a terrific source for maps, ranger advice, and other Big Sur information.

✔ Big Sur Station is just past the entrance to **Pfeiffer Big Sur State Park,** 800 acres of wildlife-rich parkland with excellent hiking opportunities for all levels of ability; maps are at the park entrance.

One excellent moderate walk is the 40- to 60-minute route to 60-foot-high **Pfeiffer Falls;** the walk takes you through one of Big Sur's most impressive redwood groves. If you're feeling energetic, add another hour to follow the trail to the **Valley View Overlook** (a half-mile from the falls) for panoramic views.

✔ About a mile south of the Pfeiffer Big Sur park entrance is Sycamore Canyon Road, which leads to beautiful **Pfeiffer Beach.** An arch-shaped rock formation offshore offers a distinctive view. Sycamore Canyon Road is an unmarked route that is the only paved, ungated road west of Highway 1 between the Pfeiffer Big Sur State Park and the Big Sur Post Office (you should see a "Narrow Road" sign as an additional clue). Take the sharp turn toward the coast and slowly follow the road for about 2 winding miles to a parking lot; parking is $5. A short path leads to the beach. Skip this trip if you're pulling a trailer or driving a motor home.

Although the sunsets are spectacular, locals advise that you come to Pfeiffer Beach in the morning hours to avoid windblown sand (the winds can kick up in the later hours).

✔ The **Henry Miller Memorial Library** (☎ 831-667-2574; www.henry miller.org) is on the mountain side of Highway 1, a quarter-mile south of Nepenthe. It is dedicated to the life and work of Miller, who lived in Big Sur from 1944 to 1962 and wrote such classics as *Tropic of Cancer.* First editions of his writings, as well as some of his artwork, are on display. The library makes a pleasant place for a short stop, especially for Miller fans. Admission is free. Open Wednesday through Monday from 11 a.m. to 6 p.m.

✔ Twelve miles south of Pfeiffer Big Sur is **Julia Pfeiffer Burns State Park,** a gem of a park and our absolute favorite spot for glorious ocean views.

Everyone can follow the **Overlook Waterfall Trail** — it's even wheelchair-accessible. The flat and easy .3-mile (each way) trail leads to a cliff top with views of **McWay Falls** plunging into a gorgeous cove where seals and sea otters play in the white-crested blue-green water. Cypress trees stepping down the rocky coast in the background create an only-in-Big-Sur mystique. In winter, park yourself on one of the benches to look for migrating whales. The view is particularly magnificent at sunset.

Above the parking lot is a small picnic area and trailheads to two more of the park's hiking trails. The .3-mile **Canyon Trail** is steeper and ungraded but still not difficult, and the payoff is a lovely forest waterfall and a bench from which to contemplate it (and rest your weary toes). The day-use fee is $6 per car; ask the park attendant to sell you a trail map for an additional buck.

The big attractions end after Julia Pfeiffer Burns State Park, but the drive is still stunning, and scenic turnoffs around. About 59 miles south of Carmel, just south of the U.S. Forest Service Station in Pacific Valley, is **Sand Dollar Beach,** which features a pleasant picnic area. Take the stairs to reach the beach, which may be devoid of sand if you visit in winter (it usually washes back in summer).

Farther south — just north of **San Simeon,** where the landscape opens up to rolling, golden hills — you'll see elephant seals sunning themselves on rocks and maybe a few colorful windsurfers dancing on the waves beyond. That's when you know you've almost reached the outrageous, infamous, legendary **Hearst Castle,** which is just around the bend. We discuss the Hearst Castle in Chapter 20.

TIP

Walking Big Sur

The single best thing we've done in Big Sur is to take a walking tour with **Big Sur Guides** (☎ 831-658-0199 or 831-594-1742; www.bigsurguides.com). Steve Copeland, who started his business decades ago, knows the secrets of the area, and his guides show you things that you're likely to miss if you head out on your own. You may even discover how to tame a banana slug — or at least develop some empathy for the ugly creatures. Rates for the two-and-a-half-hour walks are around $50 per person and include a picnic lunch.

Big Sur Guides also runs a free, one-hour guided discovery walk that leaves from the Ventana Inn lobby daily at 10 a.m. The walk is open to anyone in the neighborhood — you don't have to be a guest at the hotel. You'll likely catch a look at the inn's overly friendly turkey and perhaps the deer that hang about; you'll certainly hear some extraordinary stories about the surroundings.

Gathering More Information

Your best source for Big Sur information is the **Big Sur Chamber of Commerce** Web site (www.bigsurcalifornia.org); you can also call the chamber at ☎ 831-677-2100. Additionally, the **Monterey Peninsula Visitors and Convention Bureau** (☎ 888-221-1010; www.montereyinfo.org) can provide you with information on Big Sur.

For more information on Big Sur's state parks, call **California State Parks' Big Sur Station** at ☎ 831-667-2315, or point your Web browser to www.parks.ca.gov. Located 26 miles south of Carmel, a half-mile south of the entrance to Pfeiffer Big Sur State Park, Big Sur Station is the prime information stop for the region after you've arrived.

Chapter 20

Hearst Castle and Cambria

*P*ublishing baron and film mogul William Randolph Hearst was one of the most influential men of the 20th century. His extensive travels throughout Europe as a child fueled a dream to build a house as grand as the castles he admired. In 1919, he inherited 250,000 acres of ranchland, which had been originally known as "Camp Hill." He instructed his architect to "build a little something" where he could escape the stress of work and public scrutiny. It was to be his country estate, a relaxing and enjoyable environment for family and friends. He renamed his marvelous ranch 'La Cuesta Encantada" — The Enchanted Hill. In its heyday — the '30s and '40s, the so-called Golden Age of Hollywood — this real-life Xanadu was the playground for the silver screen's elite, among them Carole Lombard, Clark Gable, Charlie Chaplin, Cary Grant, and Harpo Marx.

The 165-room Mediterranean Revival–style estate — including its three guesthouses, Italian- and Spanish-inspired gardens, and two fabulous oversized swimming pools — has never been completely finished. It houses one of the world's finest collections of priceless antiques and museum-quality art — a collection that millions of people may never have seen if Hearst did not have the vision (and money) to buy countless pieces of European art offered for sale by governments after World War II. A recent earthquake, with an epicenter dangerously close to nearby San Simeon, nonetheless caused no structural damage, and luckily, only a few artifacts went tumbling (and then off to the repair shop).

From its beautiful gardens and striking architecture to its glorious art and history, Hearst Castle is impressive. Plus, it's a monument to the seemingly limitless powers of money and hubris and what happens to the American Dream when left unchecked. And, lest we forget, it inspired the greatest movie of all time (wanna fight about it?), *Citizen Kane*. This is a must-see stop in your exploration of California's Central Coast, and it has something for everyone. However, children younger than 6 may find walking and climbing hundreds of steps for almost two hours a bit overwhelming.

Hearst's sprawling compound sits high above San Simeon, which isn't really much of a town. But 6 miles to the south is Cambria (pronounced *cam*-bree-uh), which makes an excellent base of operations. Not quite Northern Californian and not quite Southern California, not quite coastal and not quite inland, this charming village has a distinct and winning personality and offers terrific opportunities for dining and strolling.

Because of its proximity, most people use Cambria as the jumping-off point for a visit to San Simeon. We can't argue with the convenience, but a case can be made for staying overnight in either Paso Robles or San Luis Obispo, interesting small towns located to the south in the Central Coast Wine Country (see Chapter 21). The access to wineries and better dining alone make both attractive alternatives.

Timing Your Visit

Hearst Castle and Cambria are enjoyable in any season. The biggest considerations are money and crowds.

You'll snare the lowest hotel rates in winter, and the castle is quiet enough that you needn't make advance tour reservations. Spring and fall are pleasant — you'll have the opportunity to take the evening tour (only offered in these seasons), and you'll still beat the crowds if you visit midweek.

You pay the highest hotel rates and wrestle with the biggest crowds in summer. You should make weekend hotel reservations, in particular, as far in advance as possible, and we highly recommend purchasing advance tickets for castle tours (more on this subject in the "Visiting the Castle" section later in this chapter).

Set aside two days to enjoy the castle and the charms of Cambria. If you're just coming to see the castle, one day will do, but expect it to be a longish one and sandwich it between a two-night stay.

Getting There

Cambria is right off Highway 1, smack dab in the middle of the coast. It's located 223 miles south of San Francisco, 105 miles south of Monterey, 130 miles north of Santa Barbara, and 230 miles north of Los Angeles. San Simeon, home to the Hearst Castle Visitor Center, is on Highway 1, 6 miles north of Cambria. See the "The Cambria and San Simeon Area" map on p. 286.

 ✔ **Driving from points north:** If you're following the scenic route through Big Sur, just keep going — stay on Highway 1 until you see signs for Hearst Castle, and for Cambria a few minutes beyond.

If you're coming directly from San Francisco or Monterey, take U.S. 101 south to Paso Robles, then Highway 46 west to Highway 1, and Highway 1 north to Cambria and the castle.

✔ **Driving from points south:** Take U.S. 101 north to San Luis Obispo, where you'll pick up Highway 1 north to Cambria and the castle.

Orienting Yourself

San Simeon is less a town than a stretch of Highway 1 lined with motels and services catering to castle visitors. The entrance to Hearst Castle rests just north of San Simeon on the inland side of the road.

Cambria lies 6 miles south of the Hearst Castle Visitor Center. The town's Main Street runs roughly parallel to Highway 1 inland, connecting up with the highway at each end of town.

Tiny Cambria actually has three distinct parts. Along Main Street is "the Village," which is divided into two sections: the **West Village** and the **East Village.** The West Village is the newer, somewhat more touristy end of town where you'll find the visitor information center. The more historic East Village is a bit quieter, more locals-oriented, and a tad more sophisticated than the West Village.

If you cross Highway 1 to the coastal side at the far west end of town (or the north end, if you're considering how the freeway runs), you'll reach Cambria's third part, **Moonstone Beach.** Lined with motels, inns, and a few restaurants on the inland side of the street, ocean-facing Moonstone Beach Drive is our favorite place to stay in Cambria.

Where to Stay near the Castle

If you're planning to explore both Hearst Castle and the Big Sur coast from one perch, consider staying at the **Ragged Point Inn & Resort,** just 14 miles north of Hearst Castle near the southern gateway to Big Sur (discussed in Chapter 19).

If Hearst Castle is your only destination, there is only one reason to choose lodging in San Simeon instead of Cambria — money. Standard, run-of-the-mill motels line both sides of Highway 1, which runs through this town. But if you're a little flexible with the time of year you plan to visit the area, you can find some comparable bargains in a couple of the inns in Cambria, such as the Creekside Inn or the Bluebird Inn.

In general, hotel rates are usually lowest in the winter season and at their highest during the summer; so plan accordingly. Expect an extra 9 percent in taxes to be tacked on to your Cambria or San Simeon hotel bill.

The Cambria and San Simeon Area

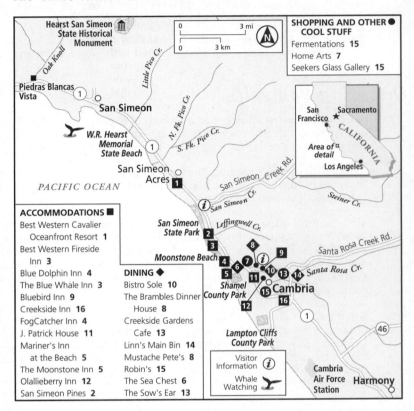

Hearst San Simeon State Historical Monument

0 — 3 mi
0 — 3 km

SHOPPING AND OTHER ● COOL STUFF
Fermentations **15**
Home Arts **7**
Seekers Glass Gallery **15**

Piedras Blancas Vista **1**

San Simeon

W.R. Hearst Memorial State Beach **1**

San Simeon Acres **1**

PACIFIC OCEAN

San Francisco ★
Sacramento
Area of detail
Los Angeles
CALIFORNIA

San Simeon Creek Rd.
Steiner Cr.
Santa Rosa Creek Rd.

ACCOMMODATIONS ■
Best Western Cavalier
  Oceanfront Resort **1**
Best Western Fireside
  Inn **3**
Blue Dolphin Inn **4**
The Blue Whale Inn **3**
Bluebird Inn **9**
Creekside Inn **16**
FogCatcher Inn **4**
J. Patrick House **11**
Mariner's Inn
  at the Beach **5**
The Moonstone Inn **5**
Olallieberry Inn **12**
San Simeon Pines **2**

San Simeon State Park **2**

Moonstone Beach **4**

DINING ◆
Bistro Sole **10**
The Brambles Dinner
  House **8**
Creekside Gardens
  Cafe **13**
Linn's Main Bin **14**
Mustache Pete's **8**
Robin's **15**
The Sea Chest **6**
The Sow's Ear **13**

Shamel County Park

Cambria **15 16**

Lampton Cliffs County Park

Santa Rosa Cr.

46

Visitor Information ⓘ
Whale Watching

Cambria Air Force Station

Harmony

 You can't go wrong with almost any inn on Moonstone Beach Drive. However, White Water Inn is the only inn that fails to deliver on its promised ambience and charm in comparison to the other comparably priced inns. If atmosphere, charm, and beautiful décor are not necessities, **Mariner's Inn at the Beach,** at 6180 Moonstone Beach Dr. (☎ 805-927-4624; www.marinersinncambria.com), is your best option for price and locale.

 If you want a super-cheap choice, try the **Creekside Inn,** 2618 Main St. (☎ 800-269-5212; www.cambriacreeksideinn.com). It's more basic than the motels that follow and doesn't boast the same oceanfront perch, but the village location is extremely convenient and the rates are considerably lower — $39 to $169 double, year-round.

Best Western Cavalier Oceanfront Resort
$$–$$$ San Simeon

This upscale oceanfront motel is a real gem, for a chain hotel. It's well situated along the coast, with lots of oceanview rooms. Every room is very comfortable (cozy bedding!) and outfitted with a VCR, minibar, and hair dryer. Coastal evenings can be chilly year-round, so book a room with a fireplace if you can. On-site extras include two heated pools, a Jacuzzi, an exercise room, two restaurants, and a coin-op laundry, plus video rentals next door. The motel welcomes kids and pets, too.

See map p. 286. 9415 Hearst Dr. (3 miles south of Hearst Castle on Highway 1). ☎ 800-826-8168, 800-780-7234, or 805-927-4688. Fax: 805-927-6472. www.best western.com. *Free parking. Rack rates: $139–$299 double; $109–$149 family room (two queen-size beds). AE, DC, DISC, MC, V.*

Best Western Fireside Inn
$$–$$$$ Cambria

Nicely done in a charming country style with new sprucings such as fresh paint, headboards, and the like, the spacious rooms are a few steps above motel standard. Each has a coffeemaker and minifridge, most have gas fireplaces, and some have Jacuzzi tubs. Extras include a nice heated pool and spa, and a friendly staff.

See map p. 286. 6700 Moonstone Beach Dr. ☎ 888-910-7100, 800-780-7234, or 805-927-8661. Fax: 805-927-8584. www.bestwesternfiresideinn.com. *Free parking. Rack rates: $139–$349 double. Rates include continental breakfast. AE, DC, DISC, MC, V.*

Bluebird Inn
$–$$$ Cambria

This simple, modern motel built around a local landmark is centrally located in the East Village. Standard rooms are comfortably furnished, but it's the deluxe rooms that offer the country charm you want, including a fireplace and a private patio or balcony. Family suites and connecting rooms are also available. This is the best bargain around in terms of price, locale, and décor.

See map p. 286. 1880 Main St. ☎ 800-552-5434 or 805-927-4634. Fax: 805-927-5215. www.bluebirdmotel.com. *Free parking. Rack rates: $50–$220 double. Children under 12 are free. AE, DC, DISC, MC, V.*

Blue Dolphin Inn
$$–$$$$ Cambria

Part country inn, part upscale motel, the Blue Dolphin is an excellent choice if you don't mind paying a bit more for high-quality accommodations. The romantic rooms have nice amenities — gas fireplaces, big TVs with VCRs, hair dryers, and minifridges — and cozy, frilly, chintzy English-country décor. The inn also offers a complimentary, expanded continental breakfast and afternoon tea served in a cozy tearoom. The best rooms (and most expensive, of course) have private garden patios with ocean views. The inn is very attractive and professionally run, but it has no pool.

See map p. 286. 6470 Moonstone Beach Dr. ☎ *800-222-9157 or 805-927-3300. Fax: 805-927-7311.* www.bluedolphininn.com. *Free parking. Rack rates: $99–$319 double. AE, DC, DISC, MC, V.*

The Blue Whale Inn
$$$–$$$$ **Cambria**

Nearly perfect. This is the ultimate seaside getaway — a bed-and-breakfast masquerading as an inn. The incredibly charming white cottage-style building features six oceanview minisuites, each with its own outdoor entrance, canopy bed, marble and granite bathroom (with whirlpool tub), fireplace, TV, and French/English country décor. This is the only bed-and-breakfast between Carmel and Santa Barbara with a AAA four-diamond rating.

See map p. 286. 6736 Moonstone Beach Dr. ☎ *800-753-9000 or 805-927-4647. Fax: 805-927-0202.* www.bluewhaleinn.com. *Free parking. Rack rates: $295–$350 single or double. Rates include gourmet breakfast, afternoon tea, and happy hour, including local wines. Three-night minimum on most holidays and weekends. AE, MC, V.*

FogCatcher Inn
$$$–$$$$$ **Cambria**

This is one of our favorite Moonstone Beach inns (we know families who return here year after year); it also has an outdoor heated pool and spa. The English Tudor architecture, with thatched roofs and garden pathways, makes it a standout among the seaside inns. Each room features a stone fireplace, a refrigerator, a microwave, a coffeemaker, a TV, and an honor bar. You feel as if you're actually in an English seaside village.

See map p. 286. 6400 Moonstone Beach Dr. ☎ *800-425-4121 or 805-927-1400. Fax: 805-927-0204.* www.moonstonehotels.com. *Free parking. Rack rates: $149–$329 single or double. Rates include a deluxe full buffet breakfast. Two-night minimum on most holidays and weekends. AE, MC, V.*

J. Patrick House
$$$ **Cambria**

Tucked away on a woodsy hill just minutes above the East Village is this utterly lovely B&B, Cambria's best. The main house is an elegant log cabin; the nearby carriage house contains seven of the eight impeccable, unfussy rooms. Named for the counties of Ireland and brimming with country warmth, each room boasts beautifully chosen antiques, a wood-burning fireplace, and a private bathroom. The innkeepers couldn't be more agreeable or attentive.

See map p. 286. 2990 Burton Dr. ☎ *800-341-5258 or 805-927-3812. Fax: 805-927-6759.* www.jpatrickhouse.com. *Free parking. Rack rates: $165–$215 double. Rates* *include full breakfast, early evening wine and hors d'oeuvres, and bedtime cookies and milk. Two-night minimum; three-night minimum holidays. AE, DISC, MC, V.*

The Moonstone Inn
$$-$$$$ Cambria

If you're economically challenged but you still want English-country-style décor and comfort with a personal touch, this is your best bet (on the lower end of the rate scale, that is). The folks at this family-owned and -run operation are committed to giving each guest personal service. Amenities include a complimentary breakfast served on china, silver, and crystal in your room; a TV and VCR with free video choices; and a coffeemaker and refrigerator. Select rooms offer fireplaces and Jacuzzi tubs. All guests are welcome to indulge in a Jacuzzi on the oceanfront patio. It's not the most attractive inn externally, and the rooms have a slight musty odor, but it's a good deal for the locale and price.

See map p. 286. 5860 Moonstone Beach Dr. ☎ 800-821-3764 or 805-927-4815. Fax: 805-927-5790. www.moonstoneinn.com. Free parking. Rack rates: $119–$239 single or double. Rates include continental breakfast. Two-night minimum on most holidays and weekends. MC, V.

Olallieberry Inn
$$-$$$$ Cambria

Step back in time and indulge yourself in this 19th-century historical house. This bed-and-breakfast has nine guest rooms, six in the main house and three in the Innkeeper's Cottage, and each room is individually named after one of the local towns or a feature unique to the room. All rooms have fireplaces, and all are charmingly decorated with antiques and floral fabrics. For the same money that you might spend on, say, the White Water Inn on the beachfront (which we tell you to avoid), you can stay here. No contest.

See map p. 286. 2476 Main St. ☎ 888-927-3222 or 805-927-3222. Fax: 805-927-0202. www.olallieberry.com. Free parking. Rack rates: $130–$220 single or double. Rates include full breakfast and early evening wine and hors d'oeuvres. Two-night minimum on weekends between Memorial Day and Labor Day. AE, MC, V.

San Simeon Pines
$$-$$$ San Simeon

This camplike resort is nothing fancy, but it's a great alternative to a family motel and a good choice if you're looking for a top-notch value. To meet everyone's needs, the resort divides units between family and adult areas. The well-kept grounds feature a solar-heated pool, a playground, and a 9-hole, par-3 golf course. The grounds have no view, but they do feature private beach access. Ask for a room away from the highway for total quiet.

See map p. 286. 7200 Moonstone Beach Dr. (at the north end of Moonstone Beach, just off Highway 1). ☎ 866-927-4648 or 805-927-4648. www.sspines.com. Free parking. Rack rates: $100–$150 double. AE, MC, V.

Where to Dine

As with your lodging options, stay in Cambria to sample the region's most attractive dining choices.

The Brambles Dinner House
$$$–$$$$ Cambria   CONTEMPORARY/MEDITERRANEAN

This 132-year-old house has been a restaurant for nearly 50 years; it's currently under the proprietorship of a Greek family and features an eclectic assortment of food, including some Greek specialties. We've tried the calamari fritti (like buttah!), the *saganaki* (fried cheese, in this case feta — not as greasy or as heavy as it sounds), and a Cajun halibut (blackened and served with an avocado relish that cut the spiciness nicely). Desserts are terrific. This is one of the most expensive dinner options in town, but it also has the most extensive menu, and the food is good.

See map p. 286. 4005 Burton Dr. ☎ *805-927-4716.* www.bramblesdinnerhouse. com. *Reservations recommended. Main courses: $18–$34. AE, MC, V. Open: Daily 5–10 p.m.; Sun champagne brunch 9:30 a.m.–2 p.m.*

Creekside Gardens Cafe
$ Cambria   AMERICAN/MEXICAN

This unpretentious local favorite is the place for breakfast. The pancakes are to die for. If you're feeling adventurous, don't miss the Danish *ableskiver,* ball-shaped pancakes served with Solvang sausage. Lunchtime brings tasty sandwiches, salads, and Tex-Mex specialties, while dinner is strictly dedicated to the head chef's Jalisco roots. The results are authentic Mexican specialties accompanied by fresh-from-the-oven corn tortillas.

See map p. 286. 2114 Main St. ☎ *805-927-8646. No reservations. Main courses: $6–$8 breakfast and lunch. No credit cards. Open: Mon–Sat 7 a.m.–2 p.m. and 5–9 p.m.; Sun 7 a.m.–1 p.m.*

Linn's Main Bin Restaurant & Gift Shop
$–$$ Cambria   AMERICAN HOME COOKING

Sadly, this comfortable and charming farmhouse restaurant/bakery/gift shop suffered a devastating fire in April 2006. Lucky for us, not only are the owners committed to reopening — and should have succeeded in doing so by the time you read this — but they've supplemented their mainstay business with not one, but *two* options. **Easy As Pie,** 4251 Bridge St., is a smaller cafe version of the original, while **Linn's Gourmet Gifts,** 4241 Bridge St. (☎ 805-924-1064), sells frozen pies, baked goods, and other gift items. Meanwhile, the original, when it's back up and running, is a great place to bring the family and relax over a hearty home-style meal morning, noon, or night. Or simply come to enjoy a midday cappuccino and a generous slice of olallieberry pie (a local specialty; the berries taste some-what like blackberries). Order anything with a crust and you can't go wrong. The homemade potpies are pure comfort in a pastry dish.

See map p. 286. 2277 Main St. ☎ 805-927-0371. www.linnsfruitbin.com. *Reservations not required. Main courses: Breakfast $4.50–$7.50, lunch and dinner $6–$13. AE, DISC, MC, V. Open: Mon–Sun 7:30 a.m.–9 p.m.*

Mustache Pete's
S–$$ Cambria   CONTEMPORARY ITALIAN

The friendly, casual atmosphere makes this a very good place for families. The main menu attraction is its gourmet pizzas, a staple that seems indig-enous to California/Italian eateries. You won't be disappointed by the vari-ety, however. Also on the menu are traditional pasta dishes that come in big portions and are served with soup or salad.

See map p. 286. 4090 Burton Dr. ☎ 805-927-8589. www.mustachepetes.com. *Main courses: $7.95–$32. AE, DISC, MC, V. Open: Mon–Sat 11 a.m.–10 p.m.; Sun 10 a.m.–10 p.m.*

Robin's
$$ Cambria   INTERNATIONAL

Hugely popular Robin's comes through on all counts: It offers cozy ambi-ence, dedicated service, and satisfying cooking from around the globe. Well-prepared with fresh ingredients and a healthy bent, dishes range from house-specialty pastas and bouillabaisse to Indian-spiced lamb and Asian curries. A bit schizophrenic for comfort, perhaps, but you can't argue with success. The menu features lots of good choices for vegetarians, too. Don't miss dessert if you respect your sweet tooth.

See map p. 286. 4095 Burton Dr. ☎ 805-927-5007. www.robinsrestaurant.com. *Reservations recommended. Main courses: Lunch $8.50–$15, dinner $14–$25. DISC, MC, V. Open: Sun–Thurs 11 a.m.–9 p.m.; Fri–Sat 11 a.m.–9:30 p.m.*

The Sea Chest
$$–$$$ Cambria   SEAFOOD

This place is everything a good seafood house should be: casual, bustling, and dedicated to serving the freshest seafood in preparations that let the quality of the fish shine through. Start with bluepoints on the half shell, follow with a fresh green salad, follow that with one of the day's catches (usually lightly grilled with just a little lemon and butter), and the world is your oyster. You may have to wait for a table, but the wait will be well worth it. Skip the lackluster chowder.

See map p. 286. 6216 Moonstone Beach Dr. ☎ 805-927-4514. No reservations. Main courses: $14–$19. No credit cards. Open: Wed–Mon 5:30–10 p.m.; hours vary seasonally.

The Sow's Ear
$$-$$$ Cambria CONTEMPORARY AMERICAN

The kid's menu makes the Sow's Ear good for families, but the relaxing and intimate ambience makes it the place to go for casual romance as well. You'll know that it's special from the moment you're presented with the addictive signature marbled bread, baked and served in a terra-cotta flowerpot. The beautifully prepared gourmet comfort food includes such favorites as fried brie, shrimp scampi, barbecued baby-back ribs, and chicken and dumplings. Don't miss the sow's ear grilled chicken breast with a honey-lemon sauce and served with wild rice and julienne vegetables or the warm cinnamon bread pudding with cinnamon frosting oozing down the sides. This restaurant could easily become one of our Cambria favorites.

See map p. 286. 2248 Main St. ☎ *805-927-4865.* www.thesowsear.com. *Reservations recommended. Main courses: $15–$29; early-bird specials (5–6 p.m.) $12–$20. DISC, MC, V. Open: Daily 5–9 p.m.*

Visiting the Castle

The only way to see Hearst Castle (which is now run by the California State Parks system and is officially known as **Hearst San Simeon State Historical Monument**) is via guided tour. The castle is open daily except on Thanksgiving, Christmas, and New Year's Day.

Getting on the bus

Four different 1¾-hour tours depart regularly throughout the day. Each one includes the outdoor Greco-Roman-style Neptune Pool (which you'll likely recognize from photos) and the stunning indoor Roman Pool, decorated from floor to ceiling with clear and colored glass tiles.

Each tour departs from the visitor center by bus and is led by a well-trained guide. Before you board the bus, a mandatory photograph will be taken of you for security purposes (thanks to the September 11, 2001, terrorist attacks). The first tour leaves the visitor center at 8:20 a.m.; the last one leaves at 3:20 p.m. in winter, later at other times of the year. The Evening Tour start times are dictated by the time of sunset.

> ✔ **Tour 1 (The Experience Tour)** is the introductory tour and is recommended for first-time visitors. It is also the least strenuous tour, but a sign at the boarding entrance to the bus warns that there are 150 steps to climb on this tour. It focuses on the opulent ground-floor rooms in **Casa Grande,** as the main house is called, including the **movie theater,** where you'll see a few minutes of Hearst's home movies (starring more than a few famous faces). Speaking of movies, the giant iWERKS film in the National Geographic Theater is included in this tour (see the "Keeping busy between trips to the top" section later in this chapter). You'll also see the art-filled **gardens** and some of the luxurious guest quarters in the 18-room **Casa del Sol guesthouse.**

✔ **Tour 2** should be called the Kitchens and Bathrooms Tour. It concentrates on the private and less formal spaces on **Casa Grande's
upper floors.** These rooms include the impressive **library** (one of
the most memorable rooms in the house), **Hearst's private suite,**
the massive and surprisingly modern **kitchen and pantry,** and
guest rooms with lots of fabulous bathrooms. The stories are great
on this one.

✔ **Tour 3** focuses on the construction of Hearst Castle, which never
really ended. You'll see a portion of the estate that wasn't completed, all of the ten-room **Casa del Monte guesthouse,** and a **wing
of guest suites** in Casa Grande that were completed in Hearst's final
years and show the castle's most modern face. Great for anybody
interested in the story behind the design and construction of the
house.

✔ **Tour 4** runs only between April and October, and it's a good one. At
the heart of this tour is a detailed overview of the **gardens and
grounds,** including a hidden terrace that was never completed and
only recovered during restoration. You'll also see more of the
Neptune Pool building; Casa del Mar, the largest and most eye-
popping of the guesthouses; and the **wine cellar.** Be aware that this
tour does not visit any of the interiors of the main house.

For each tour, a bus takes you on the 15-minute ride up the hill from the
visitor center to the castle and back. You cannot linger at the castle on
your own or wait for your next tour there. No matter how many tours
you take in a day, you must return to the visitor center each time and
ride the bus back to the top of the hill with your tour group, so allow at
least two hours between tours when you buy your tickets. All tours
involve a good deal of walking, including climbing between 150 and 400
steps, so be sure to wear comfortable shoes.

Specialty tours worth considering

Evening Tours are held most Friday and Saturday nights in spring and
fall, and usually nightly around Christmas. This 2¼-hour tour is a real
gem, and worth the extra money (see the "Getting tour tickets" section
later in the chapter) and the extra stars. The illuminated tour offers all
the castle highlights from Tours 1, 2, and 4, and features docents in
1930s period costume who wander the grounds and occupy the rooms.
These living-history players, plus the stories told during the tours about
the famous visitors to the castle, provide the closest glimpse of what life
may have been like in Hearst's day. In December, when the house is
decked out for Christmas, it's pure magic. Don't miss this tour if it's
offered.

Accessibly Designed Tours for persons with limited mobility are offered
at least three times a day and cover the ground floor of the main house
as well as the castle gardens and grounds. Book at least ten days in
advance by calling ☎ 800-444-4445.

Selecting the tour that's right for you

We recommend that you take two of the four standard one-and-three-quarter-hour tours; this way, you can see a few different views of the estate without being overwhelmed. You can easily suffer from museum overload here, however — all the over-the-top excesses can really start looking the same after a while. Taking in two tours and the other castle attractions makes for quite a full day.

Because you pay for each tour individually, you may want to spread your castle visit over two half-days, especially if you quickly tire of walking, crowds, or theme-park-like bureaucracy. We strongly suggest this approach if you decide to take more than two tours.

Getting tour tickets

Tickets for the daytime tours are $24 for adults and $12 for kids 6 to 17. The Evening Tour is $30 for adults and $15 for kids. Children younger than 6 are free. Prices are a few bucks cheaper during the off-season.

Booking your tour tickets in advance is always a good idea. You can buy tickets right at the visitor center, but you have no guarantee that they'll be available — a day's slate of tours can easily sell out. You pay no fee for advance reservations, and you can make them from one hour to eight weeks in advance. Call the **California State Parks reservations line** at ☎ **800-444-4445,** where a knowledgeable operator can assist you. Ask about packages that include big-screen movies at the new National Geographic Theater (see the following section). You can also order tickets via the Internet at www.hearstcastle.org. If you're ordering tickets from outside the United States, call ☎ **916-414-8400, ext. 4100.** If you need more information, call ☎ **805-927-2020.**

Keeping busy between trips to the top

You'll find plenty to keep you busy at the visitor center before, after, and in between tours. In addition to an **observation deck** offering a good view of the Enchanted Hill, **two gift shops,** and **food vendors** (think ballpark variety and you'll get the picture), the center also includes a surprisingly good small **museum.** In addition, visitors can learn more about the castle's history, art, and architecture, and even touch examples of the materials used in the construction of the estate at the permanent **William Randolph Hearst Exhibit.**

The center's newest attraction is **Hearst Castle Experience National Geographic Theater** (☎ 805-927-6811; www.ngtheater.com). In this theater, you can watch larger-than-life films, including the 40-minute *Hearst Castle: Building the Dream* and other films in five-story-high iWERKS format (just like IMAX) with seven-channel surround sound. Shows begin every 45 minutes throughout the day. The movie is included in the price of Tour 1, but if you want to take one of the other tours and still see the movie separately, it's going to cost you $8 for adults, $6 for kids 6 to 17.

Hitting the Central Coast Beaches

Just across Highway 1 from the entrance to the Hearst Castle Visitor Center is **W. R. Hearst Memorial State Beach.** This pleasant day-use beach is generally too cold for swimming, but picnic tables, barbecues, and bathrooms make it perfect for in-between- or after-tour picnicking. You can even do some fishing. Look for whales offshore in winter.

 Just north of San Simeon is a wonderful vista point called **Piedras Blancas** where you can watch elephant seals doing their natural thing up close and personal, frolicking and sunning themselves on the rocks year-round. If you have questions about these creatures, don't hesitate to ask the docents on hand. Finding this beach is easy — just stop at the packed parking lot 4½ miles north of the castle and follow the crowds along the short, sandy walk for a good vantage. Keep your distance from these giant mammals, and don't go beyond the marked areas — not only is it unhealthy for them but it can be dangerous for you.

In Cambria, Moonstone Beach is great for strolling and whale-watching in season. Keep your eye on the sand for the semiprecious jasper stones that give the beach its name.

Exploring Cambria

Strolling the streets of laid-back Cambria is a pleasant change of pace after a day of lines and hectic sightseeing at Hearst Castle. This charming artists' colony has little more than 4 or 5 blocks to explore, but if you're tired of theme-park madness, it's worth checking out. You'll find the area's best restaurants (see the "Where to Dine" section earlier in this chapter) and shops, less of the tacky touristy variety and more that are focused on good-quality crafts.

Before you set out, pick up the Cambria Historical Society's "Welcome to Cambria" brochure at your hotel, and take a simple but fun **self-guided tour** of the historical buildings in the East Village. You'll not only get a history lesson about this quaint village, but you'll also discover a few places you may have overlooked otherwise, such as the **blacksmith shop** at 4121 Burton Dr., or the **Santa Rosa Chapel and Cemetery** at 2353 Main St.

The shopping highlight of the West Village is **Home Arts,** 727 Main St. (☎ 805-927-ART1; www.home-arts.com), which boasts an appealingly eclectic mix of country and contemporary home fashions and gifts.

The East Village has lots of worthwhile stops. Tops among them is **Seekers Glass Gallery,** 4090 Burton Dr. (☎ 800-841-5250 or 805-927-4352; www.seekersglass.com), a museum-quality art-glass gallery. We also love **Fermentations,** 4056 Burton Dr. (☎ 800-446-7505; www. fermentations.com), which serves as a great introduction to the Central Coast Wine Country through tastings, wine sales, and wine-themed gifts.

Gathering More Information

For Hearst Castle information, call ☎ 800-444-4445, or visit the comprehensive Web site at www.hearstcastle.org.

For information on Cambria, contact the **Cambria Chamber of Commerce,** which operates a visitor center at 767 Main St. (☎ 805-927-3624; www. cambriachamber.org).

Chapter 21

Central Coast Wine Country

C alifornia wine. It's not *all* about Napa Valley, although those pesky Northern California–centrics may make you think so. The Central Coast Wine Country is at once the oldest and the newest of California's wine-growing areas. The old Franciscan missions strung along the coast, and just inland by it, attest to the area's heritage when early Spanish settlers planted grapevines and olive trees. But the area's wine production went into decline during Prohibition. After Prohibition was repealed, Napa and Sonoma valleys shot ahead as the leading and best-known producers. But in the last 25 years, the Central Coast has experienced a boom in grape production and winemaking. Not to mention PR galore in the form of that little indie movie, the Oscar-nominated *Sideways,* which bypassed higher-profile Napa for the setting of its idyllic and socially complicated wine-tasting weekend.

With the new growth in winemaking has come general growth, much of it geared to visitors. A wide range of hotels and spas, golf courses, restaurants, art galleries, museums, antiques stores, and even a Vegas-style casino means an array of recreational options. We have to say that we hope the boom slows down now, because this region is one of the few unspoiled parts of California; far be it from us to deny anyone their creature comforts, but it would be a shame to see the area go down the high-end development road to Gener cville. Little of this area — except perhaps for the bakeries in Solvang — will thrill your kids, but adults will be pleased by the pace and beauty of the region, and understand why California has become such a mythic place in the collective cultural mind.

The principal parts of the Central Coast Wine Country are **Paso Robles** (the town of this name and the surrounding countryside), **San Luis Obispo** (again, the town of the same name plus the nearby areas of Edna Valley and Arroyo Grande), and **northern Santa Barbara County** (the Santa Maria and Santa Ynez valleys). The great news for visitors is that the areas, while distinctly different, are sufficiently close enough together to make visiting all, or parts of all, practical on even a short timetable. And staying in Paso Robles or San Luis Obispo is also a convenient option for visiting Hearst Castle (see Chapter 20), offering more to do (or, at least, more to drink) than quaint Cambria.

Timing Your Visit

Like the rest of the Southern California coast, there is no bad time to visit in terms of weather. It's almost always sunny, but not too hot. Some summer days are toasty in Paso Robles or Santa Ynez as you go farther inland, but you can always escape to the coast.

The real issue in timing is crowds. Summers and weekends are popular with visitors. Numerous festivals and other events also attract large numbers. Room rates go up during high-volume periods, and two-night minimums are common on summer weekends. The various local tourist centers and winegrowers associations will supply information on calendars of events.

Although crowded, one of the various local wine festivals may be the perfect option for you. These festivals offer the opportunity to sample a lot of different wines in a short time with a good chance of meeting the winemaker or vineyard owner. Plus you'll often find related music and food activities that just add to the fun.

The Santa Ynez Valley is geared for tourism, and certain times are busier than others. Definitely call in advance if you plan to stay on weekends. The towns get very crowded from June to October, when the **Pacific Conservancy of the Performing Arts** (PCPA; ☎ 805-922-8313; www. pcpa.org) presents outdoor theater, including comedies, dramas, and musicals, at the **Solvang Festival Theatre.**

The festivities go on year-round, but things really pick up when the apples are ready for picking from August to October. Come for **Solvang Danish Days** (late Sept), the annual **Celebration of Harvest** (mid-Oct), **Winterfest Celebration** (month of Dec), and other minifests that the visitor bureaus will be happy to tell you about. Contact the **Santa Ynez Valley Visitors Association** (☎ 800-742-2843; www.santaynezvalleyvisit.com) or the **Solvang Conference & Visitors Bureau** (☎ 800-468-6765; www.solvang usa.com) for more festival information.

Getting There

Paso Robles, San Luis Obispo, and northern Santa Barbara County, in this order from north to south, lie along Highway 101, a major thoroughfare between San Francisco and Los Angeles. Paso Robles is almost at the exact midpoint between San Francisco (210 miles north) and Los Angeles

The Central Coast

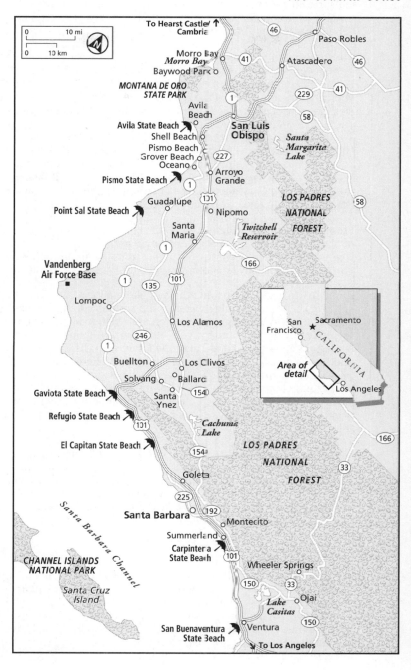

(230 miles south). It's about 30 miles from Paso Robles to San Luis Obispo and about 100 miles to Santa Ynez in northern Santa Barbara County. Another 35 miles farther south is the city of Santa Barbara. (See "The Central Coast" map on p. 299.)

The only convenient way to tour in this area is by car. No public-transit system connects all the localities, and many of the more interesting wineries are inaccessible except by car. If you don't want to drink and drive, you can take advantage of the readily available group tours and car services. Local winegrowers associations can offer recommendations.

To reach the Santa Ynez Valley from the north, take Highway 101 to Highway 154 at the artist colony of Los Olivos. Tiny Ballard lies 3 miles south off Baseline Road. The turnoff for Solvang is just beyond, west on Highway 246, while a straight jaunt on Highway 154 will take you through the spectacular **San Marcos Pass** and on to Highway 101 toward Santa Barbara, Los Angeles, and Hollywood.

From the south, take Highway 154 off Highway 101 at Goleta (just north of Santa Barbara), up through the San Marcos Pass. A turn west on Highway 246 takes you into Solvang; continuing along Highway 154 takes you through Los Olivos and onto Highway 101 toward Cambria.

And why do we keep pushing the San Marcos Pass? Because it offers some of the most stunning vistas in the southern half of the state. Of course, if a two-lane highway with an arch bridge makes you nervous, this may not be the route for you, but then you'd miss the **Los Padres National Forest;** sparkling **Cachuma Lake,** with the chance to see eagles and hawks soaring overhead; and the **varied views** (the road changes from 2,200 ft., dropping down to sea level) of sun-dappled fields, grazing herds, and craggy hills on this 15-minute detour. Plus, in the spring, **wildflowers,** especially the golden California poppy and purple lupine, erupt in startling displays of bold, clashing colors (don't pick them, there's a stiff fine!).

But if you'd prefer a more sedate route, simply bypass the pass from the north by taking Highway 154 to Highway 246 through Solvang, then on to Highway 101; and from the south by doing the reverse. You'll have missed some of the most glorious, glowing scenery in the state, so we definitely recommend that you take the pass; you'll be glad you did.

Paso Robles

Arriving in downtown Paso Robles (*Pass*-o *Ro*-bulls) is like taking a step back in time and right into a movie set. The main town square is surrounded by blocks of Victorian-era commercial buildings, so it looks like every single idyllic small town in every Hollywood movie ever. The city park is home to the public library, a neoclassical building from 1907 and a good place to start your visit before heading out into the rolling hills and broad valleys covered with vineyards.

Orienting yourself

Central Paso Robles sits adjacent to Highway 101 with clearly marked exit signs. Leading out of the central area on the east side of Highway 101 is Highway 46 East. South down Highway 101, you'll find Highway 46 West. Along these two roads are numerous wineries and lots of wonderful scenery. Highway 46 West also leads to Hearst Castle some 40 miles away.

Where to stay

Paso Robles Inn
$$–$$$ Paso Robles

This historic inn is within walking distance of downtown shopping and dining. Lush gardens (complete with oaks, brooks, and waterfalls) surround the low Monterey-style buildings. Many rooms (some larger and more recently renovated than others) have fireplaces, and some offer "hot springs therapy" in the form of a Jacuzzi tub outside the room that pumps in the (slightly sulfur-smelling) mineral water that runs beneath the inn (excellent for your skin). Grounds include a regular pool, a salon, and a fitness room. They also have a nifty restored vintage 1940s coffee shop.

1103 Spring St. (at 11th Street). ☎ *800-676-1713 or 805-238-2660. Fax: 805-238-4707.* www.pasoroblesinn.com. *Rack rates: $129–$175 double. AE, DISC, MC, V.*

Villa Toscana
$$$$$ Paso Robles

This new all-suites hotel (Spanish-style, down to the colonnade-rimmed courtyard) is nestled in the vineyards at the Martin & Weyrich vineyard just east of downtown. Suites are large, with beds set into recessed alcoves and decorated with plenty of elegant frills of various colors (we like the suites done in blue best), and have a DVD and VCR, satellite dish, high-speed Internet access, Jacuzzi tubs (in most), wood-beamed ceilings, the occasional fireplace, and kitchenettes. They also offer in-room spa treatments. Despite the beauty, what's offered may not be worth the rack rates, but special deals are frequently offered on the Internet.

4230 Buena Vista (½ mile north of Circle B Road). ☎ *805-238-5600. Fax: 805-238-5605.* www.myvillatoscana.com. *Rack rates: $375–$425 double, $525–$575 Innkeeper Residence (Casa Dolcetto), $1,875–$2,200 Winemaker's Residence. AE, DISC, MC, V.*

Where to dine

Bistro Laurent
$$–$$$ Paso Robles   FRENCH

This is an elegant French restaurant in an historic building just off the city center. The excellent wine list complements the wonderful fare. The bistro serves dinner only, but sister restaurant Le Petit Marcel, next door, offers lunch fare in an open patio setting.

1202 Pine Street (at 12th Street). ☎ *805-226-8191. Fax: 805-227-4128. Reservations recommended. Main courses: $18–$35. MC, V. Open: Mon–Sat 11:30 a.m.–2 p.m. and 5:30–10 p.m.*

Odyssey World Café
$$ Paso Robles   CONTINENTAL

Odyssey offers an eclectic range of foods reflecting world influences in a cozy, casual atmosphere at affordable prices. Lunch choices include salads, pizzas, pastas, sandwiches, and roast chicken, with full dinners available in the evening.

1212 Pine St. (at 12th Street). ☎ *805-237-7516.* www.odysseyworldcafe.com. *Reservations accepted. Main courses: $7–$15. AE, MC, V. Open: Mon–Thurs 11 a.m.– 8:30 p.m., Fri–Sun 11 a.m.–9 p.m.*

Vinoteca Wine Bar
$$ Paso Robles   WINE BAR

In case you need more wine-tasting opportunities or just dislike touring wineries, the proprietor offers a wide array of local and global wines by the bottle or glass plus an outstanding array of cheeses and appetizers.

835 12th St. (between Park and Pine streets). ☎ *805-227-7154.* www.vinoteca winebar.com. *No reservations. Appetizers and cheese selections: $3–$21. AE, DISC, MC, V. Open: Tues–Thurs 4–10 p.m., Fri–Sat 4–11 p.m., Sun 4–8 p.m.*

Exploring Paso Robles

Downtown Paso Robles is fully accessible on foot, and street parking is easy except during major events. Cute shops abound, especially those specializing in antiques. Wine tasting is readily reached by car on Highway 46 East and Highway 46 West, which lead off Highway 101. For another taste experience, try the Pasolivo olive oil at **Pasolivo Olive Oil Tasting Room,** a family-owned and -operated olive ranch and press just west of town (☎ **805-227-0186;** Fri–Sun 11 a.m.–5 p.m., or call for an appointment).

San Luis Obispo

The locals call this lively, artsy, small city "SLO." At the intersection of Highway 101 and State Highway 1, the town has a young and vibrant atmosphere thanks in part to the presence of California Polytechnic University–SLO (Cal Poly, for short), not to mention the unrepentant (and we mean that in the best of ways) hippie culture. The central section of town features restored historic buildings now converted to retail and restaurants, many of which back up to a park with a slow-flowing stream.

Orienting yourself

Central SLO is well marked with exits from Highway 101. Ample parking is available on the streets and in city lots. The area is easy to explore on foot. National chain stores sit side-by-side with local shops.

To head for the Wine Country, take Broad Street or follow the signs to the airport. Broad becomes Edna Road, which leads into Edna Valley and Arroyo Grande. Wineries are well marked.

Where to stay

Madonna Inn
$$–$$$$$ San Luis Obispo

A beloved Central Coast landmark for nearly 50 years, this engaging and fall-down-laughing inn offers 108 rooms, each with its own theme and color scheme. The Caveman room is the height of ludicrous kitsch, the walls and ceiling done to look like, well, a cave, with fur bedspread and so forth. Don't get us started on the room with a waterfall and the ones that look like bordellos. We can't talk about any of it with a straight face. It's the ultimate in (and perhaps the first) fantasy hotel, and it's every bit as hilarious as you can hope. The best rooms (the ones where the themes are laid on the heaviest) are the most expensive, and usually booked up far in advance. It's an experience you must have once, but come with the right attitude and don't expect the Four Seasons (even though the place is quite pretty and service very friendly). Spa services and golf are available.

100 Madonna Rd. (at Highway 101). ☎ *800-543-9666 or 805-543-3000. Fax: 805-543-1800.* www.madonnainn.com. *Rack rates: $168–$380, weekend rates $195–$625. AE, DISC, MC, V.*

Petit Soleil Bed & Breakfast
$$–$$$ San Luis Obispo

Evoking the charms and colors of Provence (they overdo the theme a bit), this B&B is so fresh and clean and sweet that we're total suckers for it all. From the cobblestone courtyard to the 16 distinct rooms (queens smaller than kings, but none are huge), it's just adorable. We like the style of the Van Gogh room and the celery green of the Herbs de Provence room. They discourage bringing children younger than 12.

1473 Monterey St. (at California Boulevard). ☎ *800-676-1588 or 805-549-0321. Fax: 805-549-0383.* www.petitsoleilslo.com. *Rack rates: $139–$199, including fancy full breakfast and afternoon wine tasting with appetizers. AE, MC, V.*

Where to dine

Big Sky Café
$$–$$$ San Luis Obispo CALIFORNIA

This local institution features local organic produce and fresh seafood used in innovative dishes. Its casual, funky décor makes dining a fun experience. Local wines are available by the glass or bottle. And it's *the* place for a great breakfast.

1121 Broad St. (at Higuera Street). ☎ *805-545-5401.* www.bigskycafe.com. *Reservations not necessary. Main courses: $12–$22. AE, DISC, MC, V. Open: Mon–Sat 7 a.m.–10 p.m., Sun 8 a.m.–9 p.m.*

Café Roma
$$$ San Luis Obispo ITALIAN

Rustic Italian cuisine served in a warmly clean and streamlined cafe. Expect homemade pasta and desserts plus fresh seafood, not to mention an excellent wine list.

1020 Railroad Ave. (at Santa Rosa Street). ☎ *805-541-6800.* www.caferomaslo. com. *Reservations recommended for dinner. Main courses: $14–$25. AE, DC, DISC, MC, V. Open: Mon–Fri 11:30 a.m.–2:30 p.m. (closed for lunch during the summer), Fri–Sun 5–9 p.m.*

North Santa Barbara County

North Santa Barbara County presents a picturesque blend of Arabian horses standing beside pristine vineyards, rolling pastures dotted with spreading oaks, graceful Victorian farmhouses and barns beside cutting-edge wineries, all surrounded by imposing mountains. The results are soothing and intriguing.

Orienting yourself

Highway 101 runs down the region roughly from north to south. In the north is the Santa Maria Valley, which spreads out around the town of the same name. To the south is the Santa Ynez Valley, which is further divided into the Los Alamos Valley and the Santa Rita Hills. The towns and farms don't really have visually distinct boundaries: It all blurs together gracefully. Fortunately for the visitor, the pace of traffic is slow, and the friendly residents are always handy with directions. Six towns make up the urban side of the Santa Ynez Valley, and they lie within a 10-mile radius.

Buellton, on Highway 246 is the southernmost. **Solvang,** just 3 miles northeast from Buellton, is the largest tourist draw; Highway 246 becomes Mission Drive, the town's main thoroughfare. To get to **Ballard** from Solvang, take Highway 246 (Mission Drive) to Highway 154 and turn west on Baseline. Or follow Alisal Road out of town, where it meets

Alamo Pintado Road; Ballard lies east on Baseline off of Alamo Pintado. Staying on Alamo Pintado takes you past many wineries and drops you in the heart of **Los Olivos,** on Grand Avenue.

Los Alamos, tied with Ballard for the teensiest-town award, is reached by taking Highway 154 north to Highway 101; you'll pass through the town if you're coming in from the north on Highway 101. Eponymous **Santa Ynez** lies east of Solvang on Highway 246.

Where to stay

The Ballard Inn
$$$$–$$$$$ **Ballard**

A 15-room inn right in the center of Wine Country action. It's a little too dully decorated for our tastes — oh, t's nicely done, don't get us wrong, but it doesn't feel especially imaginative or inspired. But it is pretty, so we should probably hush up. Breakfast and afternoon wine and appetizers are included and winery and golf packages are available. Its restaurant is also well regarded and known for creative country cuisine and a wide selection of wines.

2436 Baseline Ave. (just east of Alamo Pintado Road). ☎ *800-638-2466 or 305-688-7770. Fax: 805-688-9650.* www.ballardinn.com. *Rack rates: $225–$305 double. AE, MC, V.*

Best Western King Fredrick Inn
$$–$$$ **Solvang**

This very nice chain motel is located in the heart of Solvang. The rooms have a bit of charm, and some come with refrigerators. The pool is large, and the rates are reasonable, so book early; this popular spot often sells out and always requires a two-night stay on weekends. Theater packages are available.

1617 Copenhagen Dr., facing Mission Drive. ☎ *800-549-9955 or 805-688-5515. Fax: 305-688-1600.* www.bestwestern.com. *Rack rates: $89–$159 double (higher on weekends and in the summer). AE, DISC, MC, V.*

Fess Parker's Wine Country Inn & Spa
$$$$–$$$$$ **Los Olivos**

Yes, *that* Fess Parker — Daniel Boone and Davy Crockett, both. But when he's not playing pioneer legends, he's a big developer in these here parts. This inn is a deep lap of luxury, with each room decorated by "Mrs. Marcy Parker." The rooms certainly are spiffy, and we love the fireplaces, the turn-down with lavender, the cushy comforters, and other touches such as complimentary American breakfast, a gratis bottle of wine in each room, and a free wine tasting for two at the adjoining winery. The inn also boasts a full spa and a pool. The staff is attentive and devoted.

2860 Grand Ave. (at Hollister Street). ☎ *800-446-2455 or 805-688-7788. Fax: 805-688-1942.* www.fessparker.com. *Rack rates: $280–$450. AE, DISC, MC, V.*

Solvang Gardens Lodge
$–$$ **Solvang**

Solvang's oldest motel is also one of the best values in the entire Santa Ynez Valley. The rooms are all nonsmoking and comfortably sized, with floral prints and marble bathrooms. Nine rooms have full kitchens and seating areas, and the lodge offers weekly and monthly rates, as well as dinner, golf, and theater packages. Rates vary depending on the season.

293 Alisal Rd. ☎ *805-688-4404. Fax: 805-688-9975.* www.solvanggardens.com. *Rack rates: $149–$219 double, $169–$209 suite. DISC, MC, V.*

Solvang Inn & Cottages
$–$$$ **Solvang**

It's clean, it's convenient, it's inexpensive. Plus you get a complimentary continental breakfast at delicious Olsen's Bakery across the street! It's certainly not the fanciest hotel in town, but it does quite nicely, and the staff is very friendly.

1518 Mission Dr. ☎ *800-848-8484 or 805-688-4702. Fax: 805-688-6907.* www.solvang inn.com. *Rack rates: $72–$250 double. AE, DISC, MC, V.*

Storybook Inn
$$–$$$ **Solvang**

One of the most expensive lodgings in town, this hotel captures the essence of Solvang and distills it for your sleeptime. Each of the nine rooms has a romantic theme based on Hans Christian Andersen's fairy tales, which, after a day spent ogling dirndl skirts and statues of the Little Mermaid, can be a mite overwhelming. It's very, very cute, with antiques and marble fireplaces and that bedtime-story vibe. Some rooms have Jacuzzi tubs; all have queen-size feather beds and down comforters.

409 First St. ☎ *800-786-7925 or 805-688-1703. Fax: 805-688-0953.* www.solvang storybook.com. *Rack rates: $180–$295 double, including full breakfast and wine and cheese each evening. DISC, MC, V.*

Where to dine

For a quick sandwich or burger on its deck, or to select prepared salads, breads, and cheeses for a picnic to go, try the **Los Olivos Grocery,** 2621 W. Hwy. 154 (☎ **805-688-5115**). Everything's less than $10, and it's open daily from 7 a.m. to 9 p.m.

Brothers Restaurant at Mattei's Tavern
$$–$$$$ Los Olivos   CONTINENTAL

Located in a restored stagecoach stop, this popular restaurant features the contemporary cuisine of Matt and Jeff Nichols. The brothers have built a reputation over the years for innovative updates to classic dishes using the finest and freshest local ingredients.

2350 Railway Ave. (east of Grand Avenue). ☎ *805-688-4820. Reservations recommended. Main courses: $16–$32. AE, MC, V. Open. Daily 5–9 p.m., bar open from 4 p.m.*

Hitching Post II
$$–$$$$ Buellton   BARBECUE

A significant stop on any *Sideways* fan's pilgrimage, because this is where the hapless cast members dine a couple of times. Don't expect it to be romantic — it's more of a family-style restaurant. A meat-eater's dream, featuring the best local beef and other fresh items barbecued over open flames. So why did *Sideways* come here? Probably the excellent selection of local wines, including their own famous pinot noirs.

406 E. Hwy. 246 (at Thumbelina Drive). ☎ *805-688-0676. Fax 805-686-1346. Reservations recommended. Main courses: $15–$35. AE, MC, V. Open: Daily 5–9 p.m., bar open from 4 p.m.*

Los Olivos Cafe
$$–$$$ Los Olivos   CALIFORNIA/MEDITERRANEAN

Mediterranean-style food, including gourmet sandwiches, salads, and pastas — think grilled eggplant and ham on hearth bread, pesto ravioli, and raspberry walnut salad. The sunny patio is perfect for lunch, the inside is warm and beckoning, and the place is comfortable enough that locals eat here. Plus, you can sample some amazing wines with your meal, and do pick up their signature olive oil. Along with lunch and dinner, they serve light afternoon snacks and pizza from 3 to 5 p.m.

2879 Grand Ave. ☎ *805-688-7265. Fax: 805-688-5953. Reservations recommended.* www.losolivoscafe.com. *Main courses: $10–$12 lunch, $10–$12 afternoon snack, $17–$28 dinner. AE, DISC, MC, V. Open: Daily 11 a.m.–9 p.m.*

Meadows
$–$$$ Solvang   CALIFORNIA

Meadows is located in the Royal Scandinavian Inn. Their menu is ambitious and adult oriented. with most of the food served with wine-based sauces. Vegetarian dishes are available at lunch and dinner; the lunch sandwiches are a bit too fussy for children. Breakfast is available daily, with a prime-rib dinner served on Fridays and Saturdays. Don't expect Solvang's ubiquitous culinary tourist attraction; the smorgasbord only appears when specially arranged for a large tour group.

Stalking the Solvang smorgasbords

While in Solvang, you can always try the smorgasbords, which are, um, interesting, to say the least (who knew ravioli was a Danish specialty?). In their desire to please everyone (read: tourists), the Danish restaurateurs of Solvang have resorted to some odd smorgasbord choices (such as ravioli and fried chicken) along with the traditional *frikadeller* (meatballs), *medisterpolse* (sausages), and *rodkaal* (warm pickled red cabbage). And herring. Pickled herring to go with the pickled cabbage and pickled beets. Herring in mustard sauce, herring in a scary, sweetish red sauce. And then more pickled foodstuffs (which are all very traditional, given the long winters in Denmark), sandwich meats, creamed cold peas, pasta salad, green salad, fruit salad, cheese — sort of a potluck that nonplussed us. But if you can't say no to a buffet, then go for it at **Bit O'Denmark**, 473 Alisal Rd. (☎ 805-688-5426; lunch $11, dinner $14, children 10 and younger $6.95; open daily 11 a.m.–9 p.m.), the **New Danish Inn**, 1547 Mission Dr. (☎ 805-688-4311; lunch $9.50, dinner $15; open 11 a.m.–9 p.m.), or the **Red Viking**, 1684 Copenhagen Dr. (☎ 805-688-6610; lunch $11, dinner $13; open Mon–Sun 8 a.m.–8 p.m.), owned by the Olsens of bakery fame. All restaurants serve sandwiches and regular food as well as the Danish all-you-can-eat specialty; most post their menus outside to help with your choice. And ask to look at the smorgasbords; you may see something you can't resist!

420 Alisal Rd. ☎ 805-688-9003. Reservations recommended. Main courses: $7–$10 breakfast, $7–$12 lunch, $17–$28 dinner, $15 smorgasbord. AE, DC, DISC, MC, V. Open: Mon–Sat 7 a.m.–3 p.m., Sun 7 a.m.–2 p.m., daily 5–9 p.m.

Pea Soup Andersen's
$ Buellton DINER

If you're a gourmand you're shuddering now, but darn it, we have to include this local legend family restaurant. Anyone who grew up in California knows the sign for this family restaurant, with a big chef (H-Pea) endeavoring to split a tiny little pea (held by tiny Chef Pea Wee) with a chisel. They've been in business for over 75 years. We hate split pea soup. We still eat here. And we're never sorry.

376 Avenue of the Flags. ☎ 805-688-5581. www.peasoupandersen.net. *No reservations. Main courses: Everything less than $15. AE, DISC, MC, V. Open: Daily 7 a.m.–10 p.m.*

Exploring Solvang and the valley environs

There's really not much to do in **Ballard** after you see the old schoolhouse and Edie Sedgwick's grave. Itty-bitty **Los Alamos** — population 1,200 at last count — is notable for the **Depot Mall**, 515 Leslie St. (☎ 805-344-3315), the largest antiques store on the Central Coast, housed in a huge railroad station. With 50 dealers, there's a lot to pick through here, including Budweiser collectibles, Victorian glass, wrought iron, Indonesian imports, and, well, stuff.

It's really up to **Los Olivos** (pop. 3,800) and the quaint town of **Solvang** ("more Danish than Denmark" is the oft-heard local mantra) to provide most of the entertainment during your trip to the valley. And they do make an effort, and for the most part succeed. A good thing, too: Solvang alone sees over a million tourists a year.

Founded in 1911 by Danish immigrants longing for sunny weather, the tourist town of Solvang boasts plenty of tourist attractions of the most leisurely sort, centered on eating and shopping. Free parking! A bakery on every block! Thatched roofs! Windmills! Cozy shops bursting with needlework, clogs, trolls, and quaint handicrafts! Plus plenty of pickled foods and butter cookies! Flying flags! Hans Christian Andersen! Antiques! Blooming flowers! Woodcarvings of storks! No litter! The whole town looks like a Thomas Kinkade painting, so it's no wonder that America's most populist painter has an outlet located on the main drag (**Thomas Kinkade Places in the Heart Gallery**, 1576 Mission Dr.; ☎ 805-693-8337). Does all this sound tourist-tacky kitschy? You betcha! But we direct you to plenty of classy towns elsewhere in this book, so consider this a change of taste.

Speaking of taste, one of the biggest attractions in Solvang is the conspicuous abundance of baked goods. Oh yes, delectable pastries abound — not only Danishes (duh) but Sarah Bernhardts, kringles, kransekage, and their equally salubrious cousins beckon from shop windows, making incredibly visitor-friendly Solvang a great place to stop for a leg stretch and a sugar rush between Hearst Castle and Santa Barbara. **Olsen's Danish Village Bakery**, 1529 Mission Dr. (☎ 800-621-8238 or 805-688-6314; www.olsens danishbakery.com), is our favorite and justly the most famous. All of Solvang's bakeries offer tubs of butter cookies for sale — an excellent road snack indeed. Go ahead, sample a little from every bakery you can spot, and see if you concur with our suspicions that they all come from the same central oven.

Solvang is also full of Danish import shops stuffed with Royal Copenhagen collectibles, lace, and carvings. **Gerda's Iron Art Gift Shop**, 1676 Copenhagen Dr. (☎ 805-688-3750); the **Royal Copenhagen Shop**, 1683 Copenhagen Dr. (☎ 805-688-6660); and **Gaveaesken**, 433 Alisal Rd. (☎ 805-686-5699), all offer a large selection of china, cookware, potholders, and cute Danish gift items. **Lemos Feed and Pet Supply**, 1511-C Mission Dr. (☎ 805-693-8180), has the best-ever selection of gifts for pets and the humans who love them. Antiques fiends will find plenty to admire and buy at the **Solvang Antique Center**, 486 First St. (☎ 805-686-2322), where over 50 dealers display their collections.

If you're a thrill-seeker, almost nothing beats a hang glider ride over the gorgeous valley (**Windhaven Glider Rides** at Santa Ynez Airport; ☎ 805-688-2517; www.gliderrides.com). Or for a different kind of frisson, try your luck at the **Chumash Casino**, a fully equipped Las Vegas–style casino on Highway 246 in Santa Ynez (☎ 877-248-6274; www.chumash casino.com). We have a certain father who recently gambled there and loved it.

If you have a passion for cemeteries, you may enjoy browsing through **Oak Hill Cemetery,** 2560 Baseline Ave., Ballard, where Andy Warhol's troubled muse, Edie Sedgwick, is buried, and vintage tombstones abound.

Sampling the local wines

Santa Barbara County, and the Santa Ynez Valley in particular, have an excellent reputation for producing estate-bottled wines and for providing tourists — especially first-timers — with a nonintimidating wine-tasting experience. **Los Olivos Cafe and Wine Merchant,** 2879 Grand Ave. (☎ 805-688-7265; www.losolivoscafe.com), offers more than 300 local and international wines, with tastings until 8 p.m. Sample your way through the many fine vintages at the **Los Olivos Tasting Room & Wine Shop,** 2905 Grand Ave. (☎ 805-688-7406; www.losolivostastingroom.com), which bills itself as "consumable art in Los Olivos."

If you'd prefer to visit wineries, there are more than 80 vineyards in the area, most with tasting rooms, and all are within a half hour's drive of each other. Try **Firestone Vineyard,** 5000 Zaca Station Rd., Los Olivos (☎ 805-688-3940; www.firestone wine.com), the oldest estate vineyard (built by heirs to the Firestone tire fortune) in Santa Barbara County, with two gold-medal wins for their sauvignon blanc wine. And yes, hunky "The Bachelor" contestant Andrew is still the sales manager and, apparently, still single.

Sanford, 7250 Santa Rosa Rd., Buellton (☎ 805-688-3300; www.sanfordwinery. com), was featured in *Sideways* when Miles attempts to teach Jack the basics of wine tasting. The winery has become popular since the movie, so crowds can be a problem, but the wines are reasonably priced and as overflowing as the crowds with flavor.

Rancho Sisquoc, 6600 Foxen Canyon Rd., Santa Maria (☎ 805-934-4332; www.rancho sisquoc.com), offers a cozy wine-tasting experience. The pour list is extensive (most wineries pour from four to six, but they pour over ten for the same price). The tasting room is nothing more than a small shack in the middle of a hillside, though with plenty of picnic tables. The smashing views make this the perfect stop for an after-noon picnic.

Wildheart Winery, 2933-C Grand Ave., Los Olivos (☎ 805-688-7386; www.wildheart winery.com), has a very nice zinfandel. The **Vintner's Festival** occurs in late April; mid-October is the **Celebration of Harvest.** For information, contact the **Santa Barbara County Vintners' Association** (☎ 800-218-0881; www.sbcountywines.com).

Fans of *Sideways* have all sorts of options available to help re-create personal favorite moments. You can take the self-guided tour (www.santabarbaraca.com) or stay at the **Wine Valley Inn,** which offers a *Sideways* vacation package (☎ 800-824-6444 or 805-688-8824; www.winevalleyinn.com; $145 Sun–Thurs, $440 Fri–Sat), including a winery tour map, dinner at a Solvang restaurant, movie tickets, wineglasses and a bottle of wine from the Firestone Winery. The inn also offers a variety of other tour packages, while Personal Tours LTD can chauffeur you around in style (or in a minivan) as you visit locations from the movie (☎ 805-685-0552; www.personaltoursltd.com).

The mission and museums

If you feel the need to wedge some history and culture between bites of pastries and sips of wine, the valley is the home of the historic, tragic **Mission Santa Ines,** 1760 Mission Dr. (☎ 805-688-4815; www.mission santaines.org; open: Mon–Fri 9 a.m.–5:30 p.m.), with its interpretive display of Chumash, religious, and Spanish artifacts, paintings, and documents. Built in 1804, the mission fell into disuse and disrepair after a series of natural and man-made disasters, but near-divine intervention — in the form of Capuchin monks — helped resurrect the mission, which now serves Mass and hosts an annual fiesta in midsummer.

Dedicated to documenting and preserving America's flora and fauna, the small and utterly wonderful **Wildling Museum,** 2329 Jonata St., Los Olivos (☎ 805-688-1082; www.wildlingmuseum.org; open: Wed–Sun 11 a.m.– 5 p.m.; $2 donation requested for admission), is solely supported by donations. Its three rooms offer a changing display of photographs and paintings that depict the history of our vanishing lands and wildlife, and it's truly a labor of love.

Both the **Hans Christian Andersen Museum,** 1680 Mission Dr. (upstairs), Solvang (☎ 805-688-2052; open: daily 10 a.m.–5 p.m.), and the **Elverhoj Museum,** 1624 Elverhoj Way, Solvang (☎ 805-686-1211; www.elverhoj. org; open: Wed–Sun 1–4 p.m.), have displays made to delight children, especially the Elverhoj, which is designed to stimulate children to celebrate the life of Denmark's most famous citizen. Downstairs is the Bookloft and Kaffe Hus, with a reading area for children.

Adventures with (really cute) animals

Miniature horses supposedly make great house pets, but you may not want to mention that to your kids until you're far, far away from **Quicksilver Miniature Horse Ranch,** 1555 Alamo Pintado Rd., Solvang (☎ 800-370-4002 or 805-686-4002; open: daily 10 a.m.–3 p.m.), because the things are so darn cute! No more than 34 inches high, these four-legged Lilliputians can be petted and played with during visiting hours. If you're enthralled with full-sized equines, visit **Day Dream Arabians,** 2065 Refugio Rd., Solvang (☎ 805-688-9106), for a presentation, tour, and the opportunity to stroll with and feed the mares and foals.

If you'd rather visit more-exotic animals, call in advance and book a tour at the **Flying V Llama Ranch and Llama Memories Gift Shop,** 6615 E. Hwy. 246, Lompoc (☎ 805-735-3577; $5 per person, children under 6 free), 6½ miles west of Buellton, and technically just outside of the Santa Ynez Valley — for a chance to see and pet the gentle, graceful llamas, a South American relative of the camel. If birds are more your bag, **Ostrich Land,** 610 E. Hwy. 246, Buellton (☎ 805-686-9696), lets you view the 8½-foot-tall, 350-pound bipeds from a safe distance, and then buy some low-fat ostrich meat, which surprisingly tastes like — no, not chicken! — beef.

Off the beaten track: Discovering the dunes

California was once rich in dramatic, windswept sand dunes, replete with sheltered valleys of wildflowers and willows, and lakes full of pond turtles, red-legged frogs, muskrats, and nesting birds. San Francisco's dunes are now covered in part by Golden Gate Park, while Los Angeles's dunes were leveled to create beach towns and the airport. But travelers cruising the coast north of Solvang have a unique opportunity to visit what's now a rare sight, by stopping at the **Guadalupe-Nipomo Dunes Preserve** just north of the tiny agricultural hamlet of Guadalupe.

The preserve comprises 18 miles of the largest, most biodiverse coastal dune-lagoon ecosystem on the planet. They have been the subject of photographers including Ansel Adams and Brett Weston; home to the Dunites, a utopian group of artists founded in 1931; and the setting for Cecil B. DeMille's spectacular 1923 film, *The Ten Commandments*. Designated by the Nature Conservancy as number one in its "Last Great Places on Earth" campaign, these dunes are now permanently protected for wildlife and passive recreation.

The **Dunes Center interpretative facility,** 1055 Guadalupe St., Highway 1, Guadalupe (☎ 805-343-2455; www.dunescenter.org), located in a restored 1910 Craftsman-style home, is open Tuesdays through Sundays from 10 a.m. to 4 p.m. A schedule of guided walks is available on the Web site.

The Dunes are accessible at the southern end by driving on West Main Street (Highway 166) to a parking lot just below Mussel Rock Dunes, the highest coastal dunes in the world. The middle of the dunes are accessible off Highway 1, 3 miles north of Guadalupe. Turn west onto Oso Flaco Lake Road, pay a small parking fee, and walk along a rare riparian corridor to a bridge that crosses Oso Flaco Lake. A 1-mile boardwalk leads you to the ocean through one of the best examples of coastal dune scrub in the country.

Gathering More Information

The **Paso Robles Chamber of Commerce,** 1225 Park St. (☎ 800-406-4040 or 805-238-0506), maintains a visitor center downtown and publishes a helpful directory for visitors. The **Paso Robles Vintners & Growers Association** (☎ 805-239-8463; www.pasowine.com) is happy to provide extensive information on its members and their activities. Annual wine events include the Zinfandel Festival (third weekend in Mar), the Wine Festival (third weekend in May), and the Harvest Wine Tour (third weekend in Oct).

The **San Luis Obispo Chamber of Commerce,** 1039 Chorro St. (☎ 805-781-2777; www.slochamber.org), lists local events and other useful information. The **San Luis Obispo Vintners & Growers Association,** 5828 Orcutt Rd. (☎ 805-541-5868; www.slowines.com), happily provides extensive information on its members, their activities, and events and resources in the community. Annual events include the "Roll Out the Barrels" spring event (first weekend of May) and the "Harvest

Celebration" fall event (usually held either the last weekend in Oct or the first weekend in Nov).

For Santa Ynez Valley information, contact the **Santa Ynez Valley Visitors Association** (☎ 800-742-2843; www.santaynezvalleyvisit. com). The local and comprehensive Web site www.solvangca.com also carries information about the entire valley, as well as Santa Barbara, Lompoc, and Santa Maria. The **Solvang Conference and Visitors Bureau** (☎ 800-468-6765 or 805-688-6144; www.solvangusa.com), with two offices (1511 Mission Dr. and 1639 Copenhagen Dr.), can provide maps and brochures. For information on wineries, contact the **Santa Barbara County Vintners' Association** (☎ 800-218-0881; www.sbcountywines. com), always the definitive authority for activity in the Santa Maria and Santa Ynez valleys.

Chapter 22

Santa Barbara and the Ojai Valley

*L*ooking for the perfect realization of the Southern California dream? Stop reading now — you've found it. If Carmel is the gold standard of up-coast Golden State beauty (and it is), gorgeous **Santa Barbara** is the Southland version. It's a sleepy, sunny berg, as pretty and sweet as it can be. And it's only miles away from another California archetype, the mystical New Age Shangri-La, **Ojai** (pronounced *oh*-high) **Valley.**

The Jewel of the Coast: Santa Barbara

Santa Barbara has natural assets galore, starting with a unique stretch of coast: Santa Barbara lies at the foot of the Santa Ynez Mountains on a narrow strip of coastline that has the singular, jaunty confidence to run east-west rather than north-south. So even when it's cool, cloudy, rainy, or smoggy all over the rest of the region, this Spanish-Mediterranean beauty tends to sparkle in the sun like the rare jewel it is. (But forgive us if it's overcast or foggy when you arrive!) Offshore islands and tide breaks even keep the Pacific waves calm and under control.

What's more, this picture-perfect beach hamlet remains unspoiled thanks to its distance from Los Angeles. Located about 100 miles to the northwest, it's a smidgen too far outside the city's reach to be absorbed into the megalopolis, even by L.A.'s otherworldly commuting standards.

These idyllic, sun-drenched environs don't exactly inspire a bustling business world or low real-estate prices — so don't quit your job to move here just yet. Santa Barbara is the self-proclaimed domain of the "almost wed and almost dead" — mainly college students (at UC Santa

Barbara) and rich retirees who can afford to kick back and go with the mellow flow. So come join these well-rehearsed relaxees for a little down-time. You couldn't pick a better place to do it.

Timing your visit

Any time is a good time to visit Santa Barbara; the climate is mild and sunny year-round. With temperatures generally hovering between the low 60s and mid-70s, Santa Barbara has little in the way of an off-season, and the strolling and sightseeing are great anytime. Still, come before mid-October for guaranteed beach time and perpetual sunshine, avoiding weekends in summer and fall to miss the capacity crowds.

Plan on staying two nights to enjoy Santa Barbara at the pace that it warrants — slow. Give yourself the two-days/three-nights combo if you're planning to park yourself on the beach for an extended period or venture into the surrounding Wine Country. Unless you really need some serious relaxation time, the town can get a bit stale after a few days.

If you're traveling with kids, Santa Barbara is family-friendly enough, but teens may well be bored, while the little ones would prefer plenty of beach time.

Getting there

Santa Barbara is 134 miles southeast of Hearst Castle, 35 miles southeast of Solvang, and 102 miles northwest of Los Angeles. U.S. 101 is the fastest and most direct route to Santa Barbara from points north or south. The highway runs right through town.

Attention, southbound travelers: For a scenic detour that will add no more than a few minutes to your drive, pick up the **San Marcos Pass (Highway 154)** near Los Olivos, about 35 miles northwest of Santa Barbara. Highway 154 offers a gorgeous peek at ranchlands and forests before depositing you back onto U.S. 101 just north of Santa Barbara. Chapter 21 has a few more details on this route.

Winging it

You can fly into **Santa Barbara Municipal Airport** (☎ 805-967-7111; www.flysba.com), located 8 miles west of downtown in Goleta. The following airlines fly into Santa Barbara:

- ✔ **Alaska Air:** ☎ 800-252-7522; www.alaskaair.com
- ✔ **American Airlines:** ☎ 800-433-7300; www.aa.com
- ✔ **America West Express:** ☎ 800-235-9292; www.americawest.com
- ✔ **Delta Connection:** ☎ 800-221-1212; www.delta.com
- ✔ **Horizon Air:** ☎ 800-547-9308; www.horizonair.com
- ✔ **United Airlines:** ☎ 800-241-6522; www.united.com

Santa Barbara

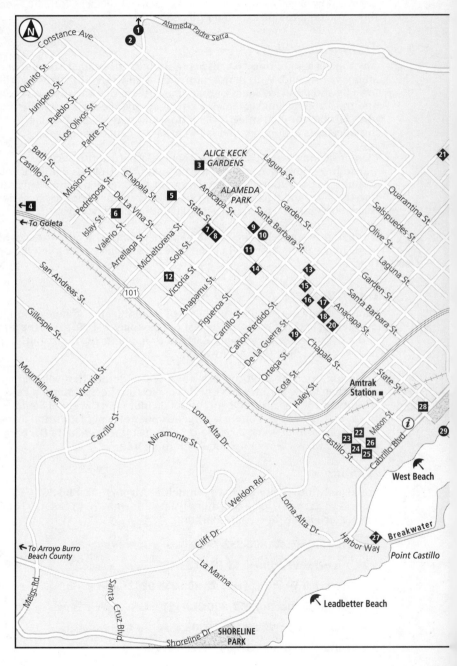

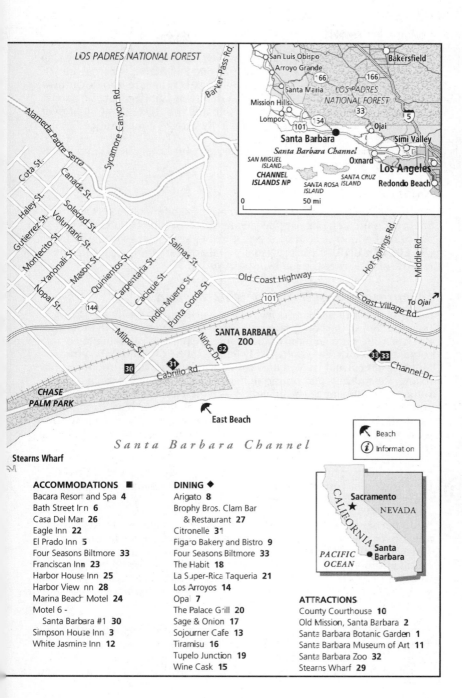

LOS PADRES NATIONAL FOREST

San Luis Obispo
Bakersfield
Arroyo Grande
66
166
Santa Maria   LOS PADRES
Mission Hills   NATIONAL FOREST
Lompoc   33
101   154   Ojai   5
Santa Barbara   Simi Valley
Santa Barbara Channel
SAN MIGUEL   Oxnard
ISLAND
CHANNEL   **Los Angeles**
ISLANDS NP   SANTA CRUZ
SANTA ROSA ISLAND   Redondo Beach
ISLAND
0   50 mi

Barker Pass Rd.
Sycamore Canyon Rd.
Alameda-Padre Serra
Cota St.
Canada St.
Haley St.
Soledad St.
Voluntario St.
Gutierrez St.
Montecito St.
Yanonali St.
Mason St.
Nopal St.
Quinientos St.
Carpenteria St.
Salinas St.
Cacique St.
Indio Muerto St.
Punta Gorda St.
Old Coast Highway
Hot Springs Rd.
Middle Rd.
101
Coast Village Rd.   To Ojai
144
Milpas St.
Ninos Dr.
**SANTA BARBARA
ZOO**
32
30   31
33 33   Channel Dr.
Cabrillo Rd.

**CHASE
PALM PARK**

East Beach

S a n t a   B a r b a r a   C h a n n e l

Beach
Information

Stearns Wharf

Sacramento
NEVADA
CALIFORNIA
Santa
PACIFIC   Barbara
OCEAN

Most of the major car-rental companies have an airport location in Santa Barbara. See Chapter 7 for help with renting a car.

You can also catch a ride with **Yellow Cab** (☎ 805-965-5111), **Rose Cab** (☎ 805-564-2600), or **Checker Cab** (☎ 805-560-8284), which usually have cabs lined up outside the terminal. Expect the fare into downtown Santa Barbara to cost $20 to $25, plus tip. If, for some reason, no cab is on hand, call Yellow Cab or Checker Cab and they'll send one right over. Rose Cab schedules advance pickups only with 24 hours' notice.

Before you pay for a taxi, find out whether your hotel offers complimentary shuttle service.

Riding the rails

Amtrak (☎ 800-USA-RAIL; www.amtrak.com) offers daily service to Santa Barbara along its San Diegan and Coast Starlight routes. Trains arrive at the Amtrak station at 209 State St., just 2 blocks from the beach (☎ 805-963-1015). Taxis are usually available, or you can pick up the electric shuttle (see the following section).

Orienting yourself and getting around

Downtown Santa Barbara is laid out in a grid and is easily navigable (see the "Santa Barbara" map on p. 316) — although keep in mind that the coastline here generally faces south. When you're taking in a romantic ocean view, you're likely gazing in the direction of Santa Monica, not Hawaii, as you may think, which can make directions confusing. Restaurant- and boutique-lined State Street is the main drag. It runs perpendicular to the coastline — which means it goes north-south — and serves as the east-west dividing line: Ortega Street, for example, is East Ortega to the east of State Street, West Ortega to the west. Cabrillo Boulevard runs along the ocean and separates the city's beaches from the rest of the town.

Even if you drive into town, you may want to leave your car parked for the duration of your stay, because parking can be tough to find downtown, and weekend traffic can be a nightmare.

Santa Barbara is a joy for strollers, and most attractions are easily reachable on foot. A popular method for exploring the coast is by bike or surrey (see the "Hitting the beaches" section, later in this chapter, for rental information). Taxi companies such as Yellow Cab, Rose Cab, or Checker Cab (see the "Getting there" section earlier in this chapter) can get you from your hotel to dinner and back again, or wherever else you'd like to go.

Another option is to hop aboard the **Downtown-Waterfront Shuttle.** These electric shuttles run along State Street every ten minutes and Cabrillo Boulevard every half-hour daily from 10:15 a.m. to 6 p.m. The visitor-friendly shuttles are foolproof; you can pick them up at designated stops every block or two along each route. The fare is 25¢ (free for kids younger than 5); if you'd like to transfer to the other line at the junction of State and Cabrillo, ask the driver for a free transfer. For more information, call the **Metropolitan Transit District (MTD)** at ☎ **805-MTD-3702** or the **visitor center** at ☎ **805-965-3021,** or go online to www.sbmtd.gov.

A valuable reference source is www.santabarbaracarfree.org with information about every way to access Santa Barbara without driving. Walking tours, information about bicycle rentals, links to all sorts of tours, bus maps and schedules, and more are all here.

Where to stay

Santa Barbara isn't a big city by any means, but you may want to decide where your emphasis will be — shopping and strolling or beach-going? If the former, you want a hotel or B&B (and there are many adorable ones to choose from, in addition to the ones listed in this section) near State Street. If it's the latter, we list a number of hotels on Bath Street, each within 2 blocks of the sand. If you've just turned up in town without a reservation (generally not a good idea), walk those 2 blocks and go from hotel to hotel — with one exception noted in this section, which we love, and the Coast Beach Inn, which we do not recommend and have not listed, the hotels along this street are interchangeable enough that the place that gives you the best price is where you should stay.

Santa Barbara is so hugely popular as a weekend destination that every lodging in town can be fully booked, so make your arrangements well in advance if your visit includes Friday and Saturday. If you're coming between May and October, book even a midweek stay as far in advance as possible. You pay the highest rates during the summer season (mid-May through mid-Sept at most hotels). If you can't get a room on short notice, consider nearby Solvang (see Chapter 21).

Two free reservations services, **Hot Spots** (☎ **800-793-7666;** www.hot spotsusa.com) and **Coastal Escapes** (☎ **800-292-2222;** www.coastal escapes.com), can refer you to other reliable properties in the area if the accommodations listed in this section are full. Hot Spots also maintains a walk-in center at 36 State St., between Cabrillo Boulevard and Mason Street, but we strongly recommend having reservations before you come to town.

Be aware that most places require a two-night minimum stay on weekends. And expect an extra 12 percent in taxes to be tacked on to your hotel bill at checkout time.

Bacara Resort and Spa
$$$$$ Santa Barbara

The poshest and ritziest resort around, the Bacara is too high profile not to discuss here, but approach it with caution. Certainly, it's a jewel — at least, on the surface. Located a good 20 minutes outside of Santa Barbara proper, on its own isolated 78 acres (nice employees are available around the clock to drive you about in golf carts if the distances are too great for you), situated so that it has a drop-dead-gorgeous view of the ocean, this Spanish-style resort is a knockout. The resort offers three infinity-style pools, the grounds are landscaped to a fare-thee-well, and a beach is just a short hop down a dirt path. Rooms (some with fireplaces, some with extraordinary beach or grounds views, and some stuck at ground level that seem all too cavelike) are a fresh and clean combo of Provençal, Spanish, and beach styles, all blues and whites and gleaming wood, while wood shutters separate the sunken tub and the rest of the bathroom, so you may choose to lounge in bubbles and watch TV. In spite of these amenities, we noticed a great deal of plaster chipped from outside walls and scuff marks on room walls. And visitors are hit with plenty of extra charges (at this rate, can't they at least make the DVDs free?); the isolation may mean romance and privacy but also a reliance on the resort's pricey restaurants or else a bit of a drive into Santa Barbara.

See map p. 316. 8301 Hollister Ave. ☎ *877-422-4245 or 805-968-0100. Fax: 805-968-1800.* www.bacararesort.com. *Valet parking: $20. Rack rates: $450 and up. AE, DISC, MC, V.*

Bath Street Inn
$$–$$$$ Santa Barbara

Bath Street Inn is a top choice if you're a value-minded B&B lover, which means none of the 12 immaculate rooms in this Queen Anne–style Victorian (and not-as-old annex) is as fancy or as tasteful as the higher-priced B&Bs around. But each room has its own charms, be it a claw-foot tub, a gas Franklin stove, or a sliver of an ocean view in the distance. Even the smallest room has more space than other "cozy" accommodations. The main house has three stories, so if you have mobility challenges, choose the annex, which comes with more modern amenities, such as gas-burning fireplaces and Jacuzzi jet tubs. Some kind of snack (such as wine and cheese or homemade cakes and cookies) is available around the clock, the kind of attention to detail that 30 years in the inn business (the current owners worked for the original owner) produces.

See map p. 316. 1720 Bath St. (just north of Valerio Street). ☎ *800-341-2284, 800-549-2284, or 805-682-9680. Fax: 805-569-1281.* www.bathstreetinn.com. *Free parking and easy street parking. Rack rates: $150–$270 double, $270 suite. Rates include generous breakfast, afternoon tea, and evening wine and cheese. MC, V.*

Casa Del Mar
$$–$$$$ Santa Barbara

This establishment calls itself a bed-and-breakfast, but the breakfast is just a well-stocked continental affair. Overall, it's smaller than some of the other hotels in these couple of beach blocks, with rooms that suffer from "attack of the motel-room furniture." Otherwise, rooms are livened up with tile fireplaces and floors, some also have balconies, and many have separate sitting areas. You can find free copies of the *Los Angeles Times* and

Saveur magazine in the lobby, plus afternoon wine-and-cheese receptions. The inn accepts pets with some restrictions.

See map p. 316. 18 Bath St. ☎ 800-433-3097 or 805-963-4418. Fax: 805-966-4240. www.casadelmar.com. *Free parking. Rack rates: $154–$289 double. Rates include continental breakfast. AE, MC, V.*

Eagle Inn
$$–$$$$ Santa Barbara

This inn is friendly, full of vivid murals, and with an overall spiffy Spanish remodel, which of course doesn't extend to the rooms, but here the color scheme and the hotel generic furniture do not clash. All rooms are generously sized, except for the ones with queen beds, and most have either a balcony, a gas fireplace, a kitchen, or a whirlpool tub. Bathrooms are also prettier than at many others in the area.

See map p. 316. 232 Natoma Ave. (at Bath Street). ☎ 805-965-3586. Fax: 805-966-1218. www.theeagleinn.com. *Free parking. Rack rates: $110–$299 double. AE, DC, DISC, MC, V.*

El Prado Inn
$$–$$$ Santa Barbara

Full disclosure: Author Herczog is married to the family who owns this hotel, and author Tevis has been friends with that same family since infancy. Nepotism aside, there is much to recommend the El Prado. Start with a basic hotel (one regularly upgraded and renovated for additional guest comfort, earning a AAA three-diamond rating), albeit one that is family owned and operated — which translates to friendly and personal service — and add nice touches like a good continental breakfast, afternoon cookies, and even lobby mascots (one cat, one dog). Then there's the location, which is hard to beat for downtown accessibility: 3 blocks from the Arlington Theater and the start of the main State Street action, 8 blocks from the bustling Paseo Nuevo, and 15 blocks from the beach. Rooms are clean and large, and the pool area is most pleasant (we love that the hills loom as a backdrop). *Insider tip:* Ask for manager specials for even lower prices.

See map p. 316. 1601 State St. ☎ 800-669-8979 or 805-966-0807. Fax: 805-966-6502. www.elprado.com. *Free parking. Rack rates: $90–$210 double. AE, DC, DISC, MC, V.*

Four Seasons Biltmore
$$$$$ Montecito

Built in 1927 and spread over 19 luxuriant acres, this Spanish Revival resort is the place to stay if you're looking to experience the American Riviera in its full, four-star glory. You won't want for anything here. The hotel includes 213 sumptuous rooms (including 12 cottages), amenities galore, and resort dining at its best. On the downside, the beach is not for swimming, and downtown is a ten-minute drive away. But at a resort as fab as this one, who wants to leave? Beginning in July 2007, guest will be able to enjoy the newly renovated beachside pool at the Coral Casino Club, and a full-service salon with spa treatments provides nonstop pampering. Kids are pampered, too, with bedtime milk and cookies, video-game units, and a "Kids for All Seasons" program, which offers organized activities, such as swimming, arts and crafts, and a painting jamboree.

See map p. 316. 1260 Channel Dr. (use the Olive Mill Road exit off U.S. 101 and turn toward the ocean). ☎ *800-819-5053 or 805-969-2261. Fax: 805-565-8323.* www.four seasons.com/santabarbara. *Parking: Free self-parking, $22 valet parking. Rack rates: $500–$900 double, $1,130–$4,400 suite. AE, DC, DISC, MC, V.*

Franciscan Inn
$$–$$$ Santa Barbara

This lightly Spanish-styled upscale motel has a light teal-and-mauve lobby color scheme that unfortunately extends to the slightly musty rooms, where it clashes like crazy with the wood furniture. Nevertheless, it's way better than you'd expect for the money. All rooms have VCRs and free HBO. Spend a slight amount more for one of the spacious suites, some of which have full kitchens and thus are terrific for families. The grounds have a nice heated pool and Jacuzzi, plus a coin-op laundry. Movie rentals are free. The staff is terrific, and West Beach is a block away. Book well ahead.

See map p. 316. 109 Bath St. (at Mason Street). ☎ *805-963-8845. Fax: 805-564-3295.* www.franciscaninn.com. *Free parking. Rack rates: Sept 15–May 15 $99–$150 double, $135–$180 suite; May 16–Sept 14 $125–$180 double, $195–$225 suite. Rates include continental breakfast and afternoon cookies and drinks. AE, DC, MC, V.*

Harbor House Inn
$$–$$$ Santa Barbara

By far the best option on the hotel-heavy blocks of Bath Street, this hotel has only ten rooms, but new owners stripped the rooms of icky wallpaper and repainted in soft colors, and then filled the rooms with all sorts of refurbished and gorgeous antiques (many of which belonged to their grandmother). The results are striking, such a change from the cookie-cutter hotel rooms around town, and in very good taste. We absolutely love the charming and tasteful Room 4, which includes some particularly lovely antiques. Most rooms have small kitchens. Free wireless Internet access throughout the property makes up a bit for the lack of a pool. Add in a welcome breakfast basket full of unusual goodies, plus the best prices in the nearby couple of blocks, and no wonder locals who put up their own families here begged us not to reveal their secret. We're sorry. We only hope that if business here gets overwhelming, some of the other hotels will follow their lead and rethink their looks.

See map p. 316. 104 Bath St. ☎ *888-474-6789 or 805-962-9745.* www.harborhouse inn.com. *Free parking. Rack rates: $109–$255 double. AE, MC, V.*

Harbor View Inn
$$$$–$$$$$ **Santa Barbara**

It's pricey, but it's worth the splurge if you're looking for something special by the sea. The hotel is built hacienda-style, like a mini Biltmore in the heart of town (and facing a better beach, no less). The gorgeous, contemporary-styled rooms are big enough to host a cocktail party; and all boast granite bathrooms (some with oversize tubs) and patios or balconies. Ocean views are expensive, but you won't need one to be happy here. On-site are a restaurant, a gym, and a lovely pool.

See map p. 316. 28 W. Cabrillo Blvd. (at State Street). ☎ ***800-755-0222*** *or 805-963-0780. Fax: 805-963-7967.* www.harborviewinnsb.com. *Free parking. Rack rates: $250–$800 double, $350–$800 suite. AE, DC, MC, V.*

Marina Beach Motel
$$ **Santa Barbara**

It's a mere 37 steps to the beach from this button-cute motel — just ask the friendly owners, who've turned the step-count into their biggest selling point. This is another very good Santa Barbara motel bet. Rooms are spotless, and country/beachy touches save them from the budget doldrums. More than half have full-size kitchens at no extra charge, so ask for one when you book. Amenities include lovely tropical gardens, but no pool. Bicycles are on hand for your use. Children stay free, and cribs are available.

See map p. 316. 21 Bath St. (at Mason Street). ☎ ***877-627-4621*** *or 805-963-9311. Fax: 805-564-4102.* www.marinabeachmotel.com. *Free parking. Rack rates: $89–$259 double. Rates include continental breakfast. AE, DC, DISC, MC, V.*

Motel 6 — Santa Barbara #1
$–$$ **Santa Barbara**

The first Motel 6 ever is the best super-cheap sleep in town — and it's less than a block from fab East Beach, no less. The rooms are what you'd expect, but they're well kept, management is friendly, and there's a petite pool. Book as far ahead as possible, because this place fills up way in advance.

See map p. 316. 443 Corona del Mar (less than a block from Cabrillo Boulevard). ☎ ***800-4-MOTEL-6*** *or 805-564-1392. Fax: 805-963-4687.* www.motel6.com. *Free parking. Rack rates: $106–$136 double. AE, DC, DISC, MC, V.*

Simpson House Inn
$$$$–$$$$$ **Santa Barbara**

AAA's only five-diamond B&B (in all of North America!) is simply spectacular. Hidden behind towering hedges on dazzlingly manicured grounds, this 1874 Victorian oasis feels like a world into itself. Rooms are decorated to perfection and overflowing with luxuries, including the homemade cake that greets your arrival. Some of the main-house rooms have space issues (what with being converted maids' quarters, complete with closets turned into bathrooms). We adore the Greenwich, Abbywood, and Plumstead cottages (the latter is two stories) with their river-stone wood-burning fireplaces, soft beds, and big oval Jacuzzi tubs — utterly romantic. The Tack room (in the former barn — note the grooves left behind by horses chewing on the walls) is somewhat manly, perfect if you prefer a more spare style with plenty of space. The staff provides concierge-style service, and an evening hors d'oeuvres spread makes dinner redundant. Spa services are available, as are complimentary bikes for tooling around town. Very expensive, but it's money well spent if you're celebrating.

See map p. 316. 121 E. Arrellaga St. (between Santa Barbara and Anacapa streets). ☎ *800-676-1280 or 805-963-7067. Fax: 805-564-4811.* www.simpsonhouseinn.com. *Free parking. Rack rates: $235–$605 double, $585–$615 suites and cottages. Rates include full gourmet breakfast, afternoon tea, evening hors d'oeuvres, and wine. AE, DISC, MC, V.*

White Jasmine Inn
$$–$$$$ Santa Barbara

Formerly known as the Glenborough Inn, this charming inn is precisely what you want in a B&B (well, maybe you want lower prices, and we can't blame you): sweet rooms (each with its own personality — and they vary in size), with perhaps a fireplace, Jacuzzi, or patio; a full breakfast (brought right to your room for breakfast in bed!); a welcoming atmosphere (including evening snacks such as homemade cookies); and a hot tub in the garden, for private use if you want. It's a real romantic getaway.

See map p. 316. 1327 Bath St. ☎ *888-966-0589 or 805-966-0589. Fax: 805-564-8610.* www.glenboroughinn.com. *Rack rates: $137–$289 double (some suites/cottages are higher). Rates include full breakfast. AE, DC, DISC, MC, V.*

Where to dine

Reservations are *always* a good idea on weekends, year-round, and weeknights in summer.

If you're in town for the weekend, consider the all-you-can-eat Sunday brunch ($55 per person) at the **Four Seasons Biltmore** (see the "Where to stay" section earlier in the chapter). This feast is the ultimate in elegant pig-outs; trust us, you won't have to eat for the rest of the day. Reservations are recommended.

Arigato
$$$ Santa Barbara   SUSHI

This chic sushi bar serves top-notch sushi to a hip crowd that appreciates the excellent quality and super-freshness of the fish, much of it flown in daily from Hawaii and Japan. The young servers are friendly and attentive, and the dimly lit room has a dash of romance about it.

See map p. 316. In Victoria Court, 1225 State St. (at Victoria Street). ☎ 805-965-6074. No reservations. Sushi: Two-piece sushi orders and rolls $4–$14; other dishes $14–$25. AE, MC, V. Open: Daily 5:30–10 p.m

Brophy Bros. Clam Bar & Restaurant
$–$$$ Santa Barbara   SEAFOOD

Serving fresh-off-the-boat seafood in a casual, boisterous maritime setting, Brophy Bros. is everything a good seafood house should be. Belly up to the bar for fresh-shucked clams, oysters on the half shell, or a bowl of killer chowder. Or take a table and choose from the day's catches, which can range from local thresher shark to flown-in Alaskan king salmon. Outdoor seating on two sides, but the bar also boasts great harbor views. The only downside? Everybody loves this place — locals and visitors alike — so the wait can be unbearable on weekend nights.

See map p. 316. In the Santa Barbara Marina. 119 Harbor Way (at Cabrillo Boulevard), second floor. ☎ 805-966-4418. No reservations. Main courses: $6.95–$22. AE, MC, V. Open: Sun–Thurs 11 a.m.–10 p.m., Fri–Sat 11 a.m.–11 p.m.

The Habit
$ Santa Barbara   HAMBURGERS

Don't miss this walk-up window, part of a family-owned business that goes back 30 years, where you can get a fat, juicy well-dressed charbroiled burger of such perfection that, well, let's just say the last one we ate was during a day that included a dinner at one of the nicest restaurants in town. And guess which meal we most want to repeat? The Habit also serves thick shakes, real fries, and even an ahi tuna burger if you're of that sort of mind. A great deal on State Street. which can be a bit pricey. Another branch a couple of blocks from Cabrillo, at 216 S. Milpas St. (☎ 805-962-7472), is a convenient stop for anyone staying at East Beach hotels.

See map p. 316. 628 State St. ☎ 805-892-5400. No reservations. Main courses: Everything under $6. No credit cards. Open: Daily 10:30 a.m.–8 p.m.

La Super-Rica Taqueria
$ Santa Barbara   MEXICAN

This legend reaches well beyond the confines of this small beach town. People drive just to eat here, which explains why this unassuming taco shack has earned a whopping 25 (out of a possible 30) rating from the restaurant bible Zagat — no mean feat for a place where nothing costs over $6.95. It also explains why the lines are so long — and deceptive. Even a short line can mean about an hour between you and the delivery of your food. Portions are small, so order generously — but at these prices, you can afford to. The prices also make this a good family-friendly choice. The soft tacos are divine, and the weekend brings freshly made tamales. A few casual tables allow for instant satisfaction. Expect lines.

See map p. 316. 622 Milpas St. (just north of Cota Street). ☎ *805-963-4940. No reservations. Main courses: $1.30–$6.95. No credit cards. Open: Mon–Sun 11 a.m.–9 p.m.*

Los Arryos
$–$$ **Santa Barbara**   MEXICAN

It's hard to find cheap food in downtown Santa Barbara, so it's no wonder this excellent Mexican café is always packed, given the prices. (Locals are grousing that said prices have gone up too much lately, making it not quite the same bargain it was.) Tacos (on house-made tortillas) come either soft or hard, with steak filling the former only. In addition to excellent guacamole and house-made chips, look for Mexican cheese soup (thick and hearty), beef and chicken alambre, daily specials, and fresh hortas drinks.

See map p. 316. 14 W. Figueroa St. ☎ *805-962-5541. Reservations not necessary. Main courses: $8–$20. AE, MC, V. Open: Mon–Fri 11 a.m.–9 p.m., Sat 9 a.m.–9 p.m., Sun 9 a.m.–8 p.m.*

Opal
$$ **Santa Barbara**   CALIFORNIA/MEDITERRANEAN

This pretty, pretension-free bistro, very popular at lunch, has such friendly service that you may not mind that it can be slowish to keep up with the demand. The kitchen specializes in an eclectic California cuisine that makes the most of such ingredients as fresh mozzarella, sun-dried tomatoes, roasted garlic, and mellow chiles. Salads are clever and include prettily arranged combinations such as grilled eggplant accompanied by rounds of pizzalike crostini topped with goat cheese. Pizzas are plump with toppings such as shrimp, pesto, and roasted peppers. Entrees include lemongrass-crusted salmon in a Thai curry sauce or honey-glazed duck with a chambord blackberry compote. It's located little above the main State Street action, but is worth the walk.

See map p. 316. 1325 State St. (at Sola Street). ☎ *805-966-9676. Reservations recommended. Main courses: $12–$20. AE, DISC, MC, V. Open: Mon–Sat 11:30 a.m.–2:30 p.m., Sun–Thurs 5–10 p.m., Fri–Sat 5–11 p.m.*

The Palace Grill
$$$ **Santa Barbara**   CAJUN-CREOLE

This rollicking Cajun-Creole restaurant is a nice antidote to Santa Barbara's wealth of romantic bistros, and one of our perennial favorites in town. Come for big portions of bold and fiery N'awlins favorites, such as jambalaya, étouffée, house-smoked andouille sausage, our favorite chicken Tchoupitoulas (chicken cooked in a Cajun hollandaise sauce), and even Bananas Foster for dessert (though we prefer the pastry swan filled with ice cream, floating on a lake of warm chocolate). Saturdays bring a sax player and a singalong rendition, complete with toasting of Louis's "What a Wonderful World." Free valet parking is a nice plus, as are baskets of warm muffins. *Note:* The owners also own the Palace Express, which offers a simpler, cheaper version of the menu, in the Paseo Nuevo.

See map p. 316. 8 E. Cota St. (between State and Anacapa streets). ☎ *805-963-5000.* www.palacegrill.com. *Reservations accepted Sun–Thurs (Fri–Sat for 5:30 p.m. seating only). Main courses: Lunch: $5.50–$25, dinner $12–$25. AE, MC, V. Open: Daily 11:30 a.m.–3 p.m., Sun–Thurs 5:30–10 p.m., Fri–Sat 5:30–11 p.m.*

Sage & Onion
$$$$ Santa Barbara CALIFORNIA

A lovely, utterly marvelous establishment, perhaps the best restaurant in town, so good even the most snooty of foodie cities would be glad to have it. The menu changes seasonally (check out the archived menus on its Web site), but among the entrees from the past that have thrilled us are an English cheddar soufflé, silky Hudson Valley foie gras, venison with maple-glazed garnet yams, and roast pork with potato-apple-onion purée. We like writing about this food so much, we have to mention a few recent offerings, such as sautéed local farmed abalone; roasted arctic char with cauliflower griddle cake and citrus champagne butter; filet of beef, potato hash with white cheddar sweet corn and bacon cabernet reduction; and a trio of appealing desserts; liquid center chocolate cake with pistachio ice cream, and rhubarb trifle. It's a natty place but not stuffy, and it would be a mistake to miss it.

See map p. 316. 34 E. Ortega St. ☎ *805-963-1012.* www.sageandonion.com. *Reservations suggested. Main courses: $25–$32. AE, MC, V. Open: Mon–Thurs 5:30–10 p.m., Fri–Sat 5:30–10:30 p.m., Sun 5:30–9:30 p.m.*

Sojourner Cafe
$ Santa Barbara HEALTH FOOD

This health-food restaurant has been a local tradition since 1978, but don't let that scare you off. The cafe serves meat (just not red meat), and the food prep has that vital component so often missing from similar places — namely, flavor (probably because the stuff isn't low-fat, thank heavens). One complaint is that menu descriptions do not always accurately depict what you receive. For example, the Tofu Buddha Salad ("marinated sesame tofu over rice and greens") is minced tofu mixed with red cabbage, and the Greek salad looks different from the usual representatives of that dish. If your Dijon chicken salad or pan-fried catfish with eggs and papaya-kiwi salsa arrives in an unexpected form, it will nevertheless be as gorgeous as you could want. Which, by the way, also describes the adorable staff.

See map p. 316. 134 E. Canon Perdido St. ☎ *805-965-7922.* www.sojournercafe. com. *Reservations not necessary. Main courses: Everything under $11. MC, V. Open: Mon–Sat 11 a.m.–11 p.m., Sun 11 a.m.–10 p.m.*

Tiramisu
$$–$$$ Santa Barbara ITALIAN

A fairly authentic (folks with accents run the joint) take on Northern Italian food, complete with homemade noodles and cannoli. (Short pasta, such as rigatoni, is not made in-house.) An unusual option is the pappadelle noodles in a lemon and white saffron broth. Look for daily specials featuring local fresh fish such as sea bass, halibut and ahi tuna, as well as regular secondi features such as lamb loin. Given the location (right in the prominent shopping center), and the prices, Tiramisu is a fine choice for a better-than-average lunch or dinner.

See map p. 316. 12 W. De La Guerra St. ☎ 805-962-3805. Reservations not necessary. Main courses: $9–$15. AE, MC, V. Open: Sun–Thurs 11:30 a.m.–9 p.m., Fri–Sat 11:30 a.m.–10 p.m.

Tupelo Junction
$$–$$$ Santa Barbara   SOUTHERN

This restaurant may be the best restaurant in the price range in town, with whimsical dishes rooted in the South. Plus, it's convenient — right on State Street. Try the messy BBQ pulled pork, with a splash of Jack Daniels in the sauce, and Gouda sloppy Joe; the hush puppies, with shrimp and more Gouda; the fried green tomatoes; or the lobster and sweet corn chowder. Try anything, really, as long as you save room for dessert. Though the menu no longer includes a couple of our favorite desserts, we've tried all the rest (just to maintain quality control) and we have a hard time choosing a new favorite — probably a tie between the chocolate caramel beignets and the Bananas Foster over the thick house-made biscuit. Breakfast is served through lunchtime. The place is small, so you may want to book ahead.

See map p. 316. 1212 State St. ☎ 805-899-3100. www.tupelojunction.com. Reservations recommended. Main courses: $11–$17 breakfast and lunch; $16–$28 dinner. AE, MC, V. Open: Daily 8 a.m.–2 p.m. and 5:30–9 p.m.

Wine Cask
$$–$$$$ Santa Barbara   CALIFORNIA/ITALIAN

Choose between the gorgeous dining room (request a table by the fireplace for maximum romance) or the wonderful terra-cotta-tiled courtyard, complete with bubbling fountain. The menu features consistently terrific California fare with an Italian flair, and the award-winning wine list is an oenophile's dream come true. And, even with genuine special-occasion appeal, it's not overly pricey. They recently opened a branch in Los Olivos.

See map p. 316. In El Paseo, 813 Anacapa St. (between Canon Perdido and De La Guerra streets). ☎ 805-966-9463. www.winecask.com. Reservations recommended. Main courses: $13–$16 at lunch, $23–$38 at dinner. AE, DC, DISC, MC, V. Open: Mon–Fri 11:30 a.m.–2:30 p.m., Sun–Thurs 5:30–9 p.m., Fri–Sat 5:30–10 p.m.

Exploring Santa Barbara

For the best and most efficient overview, catch a ride on the **Santa Barbara Old Town Trolley** (☎ 805-965-0353; www.sbtrolley.com). These motorized red trolleys offer narrated 90-minute tours of the city's main sightseeing areas, including State Street, the beachfront, and Santa Barbara's mission. It's a particularly good bet if you're short on time and long on curiosity. The fee is $16 for adults, $9 for kids 12 and younger if you order online; buying them at the trolley stop will run you an extra two bucks per adults only. The trolley runs daily, and you can pick it up anywhere along the route. Your ticket allows for on-and-off privileges all day. **Santa Barbara Car Free** (www.santabarbaracarfree.org) has information about other tour companies offering tours around town, sea and shore nature excursions (whale-watching, kayaking, scuba, hiking, and more), and trips into the Wine Country and beyond.

Hitting the beaches

Santa Barbara has a terrific collection of beaches. Most are flat and wide, with calm waters, gorgeous white sands, and lots of blanket space, even on busy summer days.

✔ **East Beach/West Beach:** These sister beaches run as a 2-mile unbroken strip along Cabrillo Boulevard. **Stearns Wharf,** at the end of State Street, is the dividing line: The wide white sands to the east of the pier are **East Beach,** and those to the west are (you guessed it) **West Beach.** West Beach is fine, but East Beach is the real beaut. A grassy median and a palm-lined bike path separate it from the busy boulevard. On Sundays, a local artists' mart pops up along here. On the sand are volleyball courts, a picnic area with barbecue grills, good facilities, and a landmark bathhouse from the 1920s. An excellent choice, and the best one for families — and free parking is nearby.

Rent bikes, in-line skates, tandems for couples, and four-wheeled surreys to accommodate the whole family at **Wheelfun Rentals,** just up from the beach at 22 State St. (☎ 805-966-6733). Rates are $7 to $35 for the first hour ($12–$60 for three to five hours), depending on the kind of wheels you want. Beach toys are available for rental, too.

✔ **Leadbetter Beach:** On Cabrillo Boulevard just west of the harbor (turn left past La Playa School), this pretty beach runs to Santa Barbara Point. Less protected than other beaches, Leadbetter is popular with local surfers when the waves kick up; fortunately, the waters generally stay calm for swimmers in summer. A great vantage point for watching boats cruise in and out of the harbor, the facilities include a sit-down cafe and limited free 90-minute parking. Stay longer and parking is $6 and up for the day.

✔ **Shoreline Park:** Long, grassy Shoreline Park sits atop the cliffs just past Leadbetter Beach. Spectacular panoramic ocean views make it a marvelous spot for a picnic. A lovely, bench-lined strolling path leads to neatly kept facilities and a small playground. Parking is free.

✔ **Arroyo Burro Beach County Park (Hendry's Beach):** Arroyo Burro Beach County Park is well worth the 2-mile drive from downtown. This narrow but long crescent-shaped beach nestled below the cliffs feels secluded thanks to its distance from the main road — and its status as a wetlands sanctuary for shorebirds adds an appealing natural element. The sands are dark but still lovely, and locals love 'em for sunbathing, shelling, and swimming. This beach makes a great choice for sunset strolling, too. The Brown Pelican restaurant is here, plus restrooms, showers, and free parking. To get there, follow Cabrillo Boulevard west as it turns into Shoreline Drive. Turn right on Meigs Road, then left onto Cliff Drive; go 1 mile and turn left into the signed lot.

Seeing the county courthouse and other highlights

The county courthouse serves as a great starting point for the **Red Tile Tour,** a self-guided walk covering a 12-square-block area of historic downtown. Pick up the map and brochure at the visitor center (see the "Gathering More Information" section at the end of this chapter). Allow one and a half to three hours to see everything along the route.

County Courthouse

In a city of stunning Spanish Colonial Revival architecture, the courthouse serves as the finest example of the vernacular. Completed in 1929 and taking up an entire downtown block, the building is utterly magnificent and well worth a look. You can explore on your own. If the clock tower is open, you'll be rewarded for the climb to the observation deck with great views of the surrounding red-tile roofs and the ocean and mountains beyond. Don't miss the courtyard garden. Free guided tours are offered Monday, Tuesday, and Friday at 10:30 a.m. and Monday through Saturday at 2 p.m. — but times can vary, so call ahead.

See map p. 316. 1100 Anacapa St., between Anapamu and Figueroa streets (enter mid-block from the Anacapa Street entrance to reach the information desk). ☎ *805-962-6464. Admission: Free. Open: Mon–Fri 8:30 a.m.–4:30 p.m., Sat–Sun 10 a.m.– 4:30 p.m.*

Old Mission, Santa Barbara

Founded in 1786, this majestic hilltop complex is considered the queen of the California mission chain. Even if you're not interested in the Spanish Colonial and/or Native American history of California, it's well worth a look — it is, probably, the top photo-op in town! The mission set the architectural tone for the rest of Santa Barbara and offers spectacular views all the way out to the Channel Islands. The self-guided tour includes a cool cemetery.

2201 Laguna St. (at Los Olivos Street, at the north end of town). ☎ *805-682-4149.* www.sbmission.org. *Admission: $4 adults, $1 children 6–11, children under 5 free. Open: Daily 9 a.m.–5 p.m. Closed Easter, Thanksgiving, and Christmas.*

Santa Barbara Botanic Garden

Situated in the foothills above town, this lovely garden is great for walkers, as 5.5 miles of trails wind through indigenous California greenery. Guided tours are offered daily at 2 p.m., plus Thursday, Saturday, and Sunday at 10:30 a.m.

See map p. 316. 1212 Mission Canyon Rd. (1½ miles north of the mission). ☎ *805-682-4726.* www.sbbg.org. *To get there: From the mission, go north and turn right on Foothill Road, then left on Mission Canyon; the garden is ½ mile up on the left. Admission: $7 adults, $5 seniors, $4 teens and students and military with ID, $1 kids 5–12. Open: Daily Mar–Oct Mon–Fri 9 a.m.–5 p.m., Nov–Feb until 5 p.m.*

Santa Barbara Museum of Art

This little gem feels like a private gallery — one with works by Monet, Picasso, Braque, Chagall, Rodin, and other masters. It contains some good 20th-century Californian and Asian art, too, and is well worth an hour. If you don't go inside, stop by to examine the mural recently mounted in a special display along State Street. Be sure to read the thrilling story of its discovery (the artist, David Alfaro Siquieros, was a very important Mexican muralist) as part of a Pacific Palisades pool house, and the absurdly cautious and executed journey to get it to its current display position. (Here's a preview: They had to move the entire pool house.)

See map p. 316. 1130 State St. (at Anapamu Street). ☎ *805-963-4364.* www.sbmuseart.org. *Admission: $9 adults, $6 seniors, $6 students with ID and kids 6–17, free for the under-6 set; free for all on Sun. Open: Tues–Sun 11 a.m.–5 p.m.*

Santa Barbara Zoo

You've probably been told that size doesn't matter, so consider taking in this charming, pint-size zoo. one of the best small zoos in the country. Having undergone some renovations, including the transformation of the old sea-lion exhibit into a perky penguin party palace, plus lions, elephants and gazelles, it is ideal stop for little ones. It also is a zoo with a view — the smashing vista goes on for days. Exploring the attractions here should take only a couple hours.

See map p. 316. 500 Niños Dr. (east of Milpas Street; turn up Niños from Cabrillo Boulevard). ☎ *805-962-5339.* www.santabarbarazoo.org. *Admission: $10 adults, $8 seniors and kids 2–12. Parking: $3. Open: Daily 10 a.m.–5 p.m. (arrive before 4 p.m.). Closed Thanksgiving and Christmas.*

Experiencing the harbor life

At the end of State Street is **Stearns Wharf,** a 19th-century vintage pier that offers great views but is otherwise pretty touristy. Head, instead, to **Santa Barbara Harbor** for a genuine look at local maritime life. To get there, follow Boulevard west past Castillo Street, and turn left on Harbor Way.

> ✔ **Brophy Bros. Clam Bar & Restaurant** is a great place to soak in the atmosphere, not to mention some divine chowder and oysters on the half shell (see the "Where to dine" section earlier in this chapter).

> ✔ If you want to hit the water, **Stardust Sportfishing** (☎ 805-963-3564; www.stardustsportfishing.com) offers half- and full-day sportfishing trips. The **Santa Barbara Sailing Center** (☎ 800-350-9090 or

805-962-2826; www.sbsail.com) has a wide array of excursions, including dinner cruises, afternoon sailing, and whale-watching (Feb–May).

✔ If you'd like to cruise over to **Channel Islands National Park,** the fleet at **Truth Aquatics** (☎ 805-962-1127; www.truthaquatics.com) offers hiking, camping, and natural history trips as well as fishing, diving, and whale-watching.

Shopping 'til you drop

The main shopping area is the Paseo Nuevo, a new mall that was nicely built to copy the classic State Street Spanish architecture (located on State Street between Canon Perdido and Ortega streets). You won't find many nonchain stores here, but it's so pretty (splashing fountains, carts with jewelry, and such) that even usual mall haters don't mind.

Boutiques abound along State Street and in the offshoot blocks, where you'll find such local treats as the **Book Den,** 15 E. Anapamu St. (☎ 805-962-3321; www.bookden.com), a used bookstore.

If you're an antiques hound, seek out **Brinkerhoff Avenue,** a block-long passage 1½ blocks west of State between Cota and Haley streets that brims with vintage goodies. Most shops along Brinkerhoff are closed Monday, and they close as early as 5 or 6 p.m. on weekdays.

Also worth seeking out is **El Paseo,** at 814 State St. (between Cañon Perdido and De La Guerra Street), a charming arcade lined with boutiques and galleries that's reminiscent of an old Spanish street. It also happens to be the oldest shopping street in Southern California — and is across the street from the Paseo Nuevo (hence the name).

Touring the local Wine Country

In the past few years, Santa Barbara's Wine Country has really come into its own, with local labels achieving national prominence and wineries attracting visitors from around the world. To explore the local tasting rooms — which include such familiar labels as Cambria, Firestone, Meridian, and Au Bon Climat — stop into the local visitor center here or in nearby Solvang (see Chapter 21) and pick up the brochure and map called **Santa Barbara County Wineries.** You can also order a copy by contacting the Santa Barbara County Vintners Association (☎ 800-218-0881 or 805-688-0881; www.sbcountywines.com).

Serene Shangri-La: The Ojai Valley

The Ojai Valley has been known as Shangri-La ever since director Frank Capra chose the area as the background for his 1947 movie *Lost Horizon.* To local Native Americans, the valley had long been a sacred holy place, but it was Capra who put it on the international map. One look around this landscape, handsomely tucked into the mountains between Santa Barbara and Los Angeles, and you'll understand why everyone who visits finds it so special. For visitors to Southern California who think the state consists of nothing but bright lights and big cities, Ojai is the perfect soul-soothing antidote.

In the late 19th century, settlers from the East Coast began to arrive in Ojai in search of a healthful climate — believed to be beneficial for sufferers of everything from allergies to tuberculosis — and spiritual enlightenment. Just as the Native Americans believed that the area possessed sacred qualities, later visitors found the valley (with its unusual east-west orientation) conducive to certain loftier pursuits.

Those lofty pursuits really took off in 1923 with the arrival of J. Krishnamurti, an Indian prophet whose work in combining eastern and western philosophies marks him as the founder of what would become the **New Age movement.** He was later joined by such luminaries as Aldous Huxley in developing institutions of higher understanding in Ojai. Those institutions still operate, and you can visit them.

With folks such as Krishnamurti and Huxley in residence, Ojai became a logical choice for **artists and musicians.** The famed sculptor Beatrice Wood, known as the Mama of Dada, moved here in the 1940s, followed by many other artists. Her studio remains open to the public, as are those of many other working artists (Wood died in 1998, at age 105). The annual **Ojai Festival,** in May of every year, brings together performers and scholars from all over the world for a series of concerts and symposia celebrating both classical and modern orchestral music.

If you love the outdoors, Ojai offers an unparalleled set of opportunities for **camping, hiking,** and **mountain biking** in Los Padres National Forest, which borders the northern edge of town. The forest is the largest in the national forest system and presents countless options for recreational fun. For a less-active outdoor experience, the scenic beauty of the Ojai Valley is alone worth the trip. Rising up to 6,000 feet above sea level at the east end of the valley is the magnificent **Topa Topa Bluff.** Every evening as the sun sets, the bluff takes on a remarkable shade of coral, creating the "pink moment" for which Ojai is famous.

Timing your visit

Ojai is a wonderful place to visit all year long. The summer months of July, August, and September can be hot (but not as hot as Palm Springs). The rest of the year is quite pleasant. The city of Ojai is only 16 miles from the ocean, and sea breezes rising up the valley and cool things off nicely, especially in the evenings. Weekends are the busiest time, especially in spring and fall.

Getting there

The best way to get to Ojai is by car. Ojai is located 85 miles northeast of Los Angeles and 35 miles southeast of Santa Barbara, about 15 miles inland from the city of Ventura.

- ✔ **From Los Angeles:** Take I-5 north to Castaic, then go west on Highway 126 to Santa Paula, then north on Highway 150 to Ojai; or go north on U.S. 101 to Ventura, then go east on Highway 33 to Ojai.

- ✔ **From Santa Barbara:** Take U.S. 101 south to Highway 150, which leads to Ojai.

Orienting yourself and getting around

Ojai is compact and laid out simply along one main road, Highway 150, also known as **Ojai Avenue.** In the center of town, the principal shopping district is clearly distinguishable by the **Arcade,** a block-long row of shops with a Spanish Colonial–style colonnade of arches. Ample parking is located behind the shops. Across the street is **Libbey Park,** with a great play area for kids, tennis courts, and the Libbey Bowl, home of concerts and plays. Directions to everything else in the valley are generally given in relationship to the Arcade.

The **Ojai Trolley** makes a circuit around town (the full ride is about an hour) and stops at shops, schools, hotels, and more. The service operates Monday through Friday from 7:15 a.m. to 5:40 p.m. and Saturday and Sunday from 9 a.m. to 5 p.m. Riding the trolley costs 25¢.

Where to stay

Ojai offers a wide range of accommodations, from the most luxurious to charming and funky to basic and affordable.

 Ojai is an extremely popular destination for weekend visitors from all over Southern California, so make reservations before your arrival if your visit involves a Friday- or Saturday-night stay. Many of the top establishments have two-night minimums on weekends, and minimums or higher rates during important events or festivals. Many offer lower rates during the week. Ojai is also popular with business travelers, with substantial facilities for conferences and corporate meetings.

Blue Iguana Inn
$$–$$$$ Ojai

The Southwest-style buildings of the Blue Iguana surround a courtyard with beautiful gardens and a pool and Jacuzzi. The small inn features studio and one- and two-bedroom units with fully equipped kitchens. Continental breakfast is included on the weekends. A sister property nearby, the **Emerald Iguana Inn,** offers similar rooms with fireplaces or wood-burning stoves, in California Craftsman–style buildings.

Highway 33, 11794 N. Ventura Rd. ☎ *805-646-5277.* Fax: 805-640-9512. www.blue iguanainn.com. *Rack rates: $99–$249 double. Free parking. Weekly rates available. AE, DISC, MC, V.*

The Lavender Inn
S$–$$$ Ojai

Located in a historic Victorian house in the heart of town, this charming nonsmoking inn offers seven rooms (five with private bathroom), most with a private balcony overlooking the exquisite gardens or with a view of the mountains. (The grounds also include a 1,000-sq.-ft. cottage with a kitchenette and private patio.) Breakfast and the complimentary afternoon wine-and-cheese hour are served on the deck overlooking the landscaped grounds and pond.

210 E. Matilija St. ☎ *805-646-6635.* Fax: 805-646-4995. www.lavenderinn.com. *Rack rates: $140–$210 double, $275 cottage. Free parking. AE, DISC MC, V.*

The Oaks at Ojai
S$–$$$$ Ojai

One of Ojai's highlights, this relatively affordable inclusive health-spa experience offers guests three (decent-quality) meals totaling a mere 1,000 calories per day (!!) and a slate of daily exercise classes, from pool aerobics to yoga. Spa treatments are available for an additional fee, and it's all served up in a bucolic mountain setting. Morning walks through the sweet town of Ojai and amid surrounding mountains make exercise far more enjoyable than it ought to be. Rooms vary in size and quality; the ones in the main house can be quite tiny, while the cottages are plenty large but have frumpy furnishings. The newer suites are smashing — good furniture, lovely tile, private patios, Jacuzzi tubs — well worth it if you want the whole spa pampering experience. Sure, it's less posh than pricier places, but it's also less terrifyingly chic. Real people with real-people thighs are among the loyal clientele.

122 E. Ojai Ave. ☎ *800-753-6257* or 805-646-5573. Fax: 805-640-1504. www.oaksspa.com. *Rack rates: $175–$299 per person. Free parking. AE, DISC, MC, V.*

Ojai Valley Inn & Spa
S$$$–$$$$$ Ojai

Consistently ranked by major travel magazines as one of America's top resorts, the Ojai Valley Inn is a destination in itself. Start with stunningly beautiful grounds, add luxury rooms and a staggering array of activities, including a championship 18-hole golf course, swimming pools, horse ranch and stables, tennis courts, banquet and meeting facilities, casual and fine dining, plus the elegant **Spa Ojai,** which offers complete spa services and a state-of-the-art fitness center. The inn also has a variety of children's programs. All this comes at a price, of course.

905 Country Club Rd. ☎ *888-697-8780 or 805-646-1111. Fax: 805-646-7969.* www.ojai resort.com. *Rack rates: $400–$650 double, $800 and up suites. Free parking. AE, DISC, MC, V.*

Ojai Rancho Inn
$–$$$ Ojai

Formerly the Rose Garden Inn, this low-slung ranch-style building surrounds (what else?) an immaculate rose garden, which always seems to be in bloom. (Thank that California weather, which produces roses from Mar–Dec!) Simply decorated rooms include kitchen units. The inn has a pool, a spa, a sauna, and other outdoor amenities and serves a complimentary continental breakfast.

615 W. Ojai Ave. ☎ *800-799-1881. Fax: 805-640-8455.* www.ojairanchoinn.com *or* www.ojairanchoinni.com. *Rack rates: $85–$205 double. Free parking. AE, DC, DISC, MC, V.*

Theodore Woolsey House
$$–$$$ Ojai

One of Ojai's oldest homes, this seven-room inn sits on 7 lush acres with mountain views, and offers elegant-yet-casual sophistication in a peaceful, secluded setting. A pool, hot tub, croquet court, and putting green are on-site, and rooms have private bathrooms, balconies, and fireplaces. The property is nonsmoking.

1484 E. Ojai Ave. ☎ *805-646-9779.* www.theodorewoolseyhouse.com. *Rates: $95–$185 double. Free parking. MC, V.*

Where to dine
The dining choices in Ojai are remarkably diverse, from high-end California cuisine to basic American or Mexican fare. There's a general emphasis here on local ingredients and healthy food.

Azu
$$–$$$ Ojai   SPANISH

A relative newcomer, Azu offers a wide array of tapas, the traditional small plates of Spain, plus a selection of large salads and entrees inspired by Mediterranean cuisine. The restaurant also offers a full bar and an excellent wine list with Spanish and Central Coast California selections. The atmosphere is lively, and the décor is bright and cheerful. Desserts are made on-site.

457 E. Ojai Ave. ☎ *805-640-7987. Reservations recommended. Main courses: $16–$28; tapas $7–$13. AE, DISC, MC, V. Open: Tues–Sat 11 a.m.–3 p.m., Mon–Sun 5–9 p.m. in winter (opens an hour later in summer); tapas bar Tues–Sun 11 a.m.– 9 p.m.; Sun brunch 11 a.m.–2 p.m.*

Bonnie Lu's
$ Ojai BREAKFAST/LUNCH

Another Ojai institution, located in the Arcade, Bonnie Lu's is the place to come for traditional American breakfasts and lunch-counter fare. Beware of the morning crowds on weekends.

328 E. Ojai Ave. ☎ 805-646-0207. No reservations. Main courses: Nothing more than $10. MC, V. Open: Sun –Tues and Thurs–Sat 7 a.m.–2:30 p.m.

Deer Lodge
$$–$$$ Ojai HEARTY AMERICAN

An Ojai institution since 1932, the Deer Lodge offers hearty fare in a rustic but comfortable environment. The main feature on the menu is venison, but other choices range from coconut shrimp to vegetarian fettuccine Provençal. The restaurant hosts live music and dancing on weekends, plus an oak barbecue and blues music. The hamburgers at lunch are big and tasty, and breakfasts are hearty.

2261 Maricopa Hwy. ☎ 805-646-4256. Reservations recommended. Main courses: $12–$27. AE, MC, V. Open: Mon and Wed–Thurs 11 a.m.–10 p.m., Fri 11 a.m.–2 a.m., Sat 8 a.m.–2 a.m., Sun 8 a.m.–10 p.m.

Pangea
$$–$$$ Ojai FUSION

The menu draws from the cuisines of the world with clearly apparent ties to Asian, Mediterranean, and American sources. The finest local ingredients are combined with imagination and flair. The ambience is casual, with seating in the bar or on the covered terrace. The chef offers daily seafood and pasta specials as well as a superior hamburger. Although the kitchen stops serving food at the times below, the bar serves drinks until 10 p.m. Tuesday through Thursday and 11 p.m. the rest of the week.

139 E. Ojai Ave. ☎ 805-640-8001. Reservations recommended. Main courses: $12–$32. AE, MC, V. Open: Tues–Thurs 4–9 p.m., Fri–Sat 4–10 p.m., Sun 4–8 p.m.

Rainbow Bridge
$ Ojai HEALTH-FOOD/DELI

Strictly speaking, Rainbow Bridge is a health-food grocery store, but it also has a full deli serving takeout and extra items presented at lunch and dinner to eat in. It's the perfect place to acquire provisions for a picnic or a hike, and it's the top choice in town for vegetarians and health-conscious diners.

211 E. Matalija St. ☎ 805-646-4017 or 805-646-6623. No reservations. Main courses: Nothing more than $6. Open: 8 a.m.–9 p.m. daily. DISC, MC, V.

The Ranch House
$$–$$$ Ojai   CALIFORNIA CUISINE

One of the pioneers of California cuisine, this garden restaurant presents creative interpretations of classic dishes using regional produce. The setting is an intimate wooded glen with meandering streams. Service is top-notch, and an on-premises bakery supplies fresh breads. The wine list is nationally recognized.

South Lomita Avenue. ☎ *805-646-2360.* www.theranchhouse.com. *Reservations required. Main courses: $23–$33. AE, MC, V. Open: Tues–Fri 5:30 –8:30 p.m., Sat seatings 5:30–6:30 p.m. and 8–8:30 p.m., Sun 11 a.m.–7:30 p.m.*

Ruben's Burritos
$ Ojai   MEXICAN

This is real Mexican food, with a heart-healthy choice of ingredients. Ruben's doesn't have a lot of atmosphere, but it does offer plenty of good choices in the burrito category, ranging from *carne asada* (pan-seared steak) to chicken en mole to vegetarian options, plus daily specials of traditional soups and stews. It also has dinner plates of chile relleno or pollo pico, sturdy breakfasts of huevos rancheros, and a children's menu.

104 N. Signal St. (behind the Arcade). ☎ *805-646-6111. No reservations. Main courses: Nothing more than $10. AE, MC, V. Open: Daily 8 a.m.–9 p.m.*

Sea Fresh
$$ Ojai   SEAFOOD

A restaurant with its own boat can't help but serve great seafood. Using fresh-caught fish from local waters with the best seafood from other sources, Sea Fresh presents an array of classic dishes, such as fish and chips, fried calamari, and charbroiled red snapper, plus fish tacos and a full-service sushi bar. There's also a market for fresh fish to take home.

533 E. Ojai Ave. ☎ *805-646-7747. Reservations not necessary. Fried combos or tacos: $7.45–$12; main courses$9.95–$18 at dinner; sushi $3.50–$12. Open: Sun–Thurs 11 a.m.–9 p.m., Fri–Sat 11 a.m.–10 p.m.*

Suzanne's
$$$–$$$$ Ojai   SOUTHWESTERN/CALIFORNIA

Suzanne's serves a California-based, sophisticated, Southwest-leaning menu featuring lots of fresh fish, pastas, hearty salads, and an ancho chile chimichurri-marinated grilled rib eye, perfect for meat lovers and anyone suffering from anemia. Many of the ingredients are sourced locally; some are from Suzanne's own garden. Although we enjoyed a casual meal at the bar, the intimate dining room is perfect for a romantic dinner and the pretty covered patio is popular with parties of locals celebrating upcoming nuptials and birthdays. Very friendly and accommodating, not in the least bit stuffy, and did we mention how pretty it is?

502 W. Ojai Ave. ☎ *805-640-1961.* www.suzannescuisine.com. *Reservations not necessary. Main courses: $15–$32. AE, MC, V. Open: Wed–Mon 11:30 a.m.–3 p.m. and 5:30–9 p.m.*

Exploring the Ojai Valley

Ojai is home to a number of annual events that draw visitors from all over the country and the world. Among them are the **Ojai Tennis Tournament** (every Apr; featuring the Pacific 10 anc National Juniors championships); the **Ojai Music Festival** (the first weekend after Memorial Day; presenting the latest in adventurous classical music); the **Ojai Wine Festival** (every June; presenting wines from 40 Central Coast makers in the Lake Casitas Park); the **Ojai Shakespeare Festival** (every July); **Bowlful of Blues** (every Oct; blues and jazz on the shores of Lake Casitas); and the **Ojai Studio Artists Tour and the Detour** (every Oct; for self-guided tours through 70 artists' studios).

The arts in Ojai

If art is your interest, you'll find plenty of year-round opportunities to appreciate the local talent. The Arcade is filled with interesting galleries and shops offering works from local and other artists. Among the best are **Human Arts Gallery and Home,** 310 and 246 E. Ojai Ave. (☎ **805-646-1525** and 805-646-8245; open Mon–Sat 11 a.m.–5 p.m., Sun noon–5 p.m.), featuring art, crafts, and jewelry from more than 206 artists; and **Primavera Gallery,** 214 E. Ojai Ave. (☎ **805-646-7133;** www.primaveraart.com; open daily 10 a.m.–5 p.m.), offering contemporary American art.

For the intellectually inclined

Ojai is a destination for book lovers who come for its outstanding independent bookstores. In the Arcade, **Table of Contents,** 208 E. Ojai Ave. (☎ **805-640-9250;** open daily 10 a.m.–5 p.m.), has a great children's section along with books for adults. True book lovers beat a path to the rumble-tumble treasures at **Bart's Bocks,** 302 W. Matilija St. (☎ **805-646-3755;** open daily 9:30 a.m.–sunset), with 100,000 used books shelved on tree-shaded patios; books remain on the street after hours, sold by an honor system.

Outdoor adventures

The first stop for the outdoor adventurer is the Ojai Ranger Station of the **Los Padres National Forest,** 1190 E. Ojai Ave. (☎ **805-646-4348;** call for hours). The rangers provide trail maps, parking permits, and information for camping. For campsite reservations, call ☎ **800-280-CAMP.**

If you prefer less-strenuous outdoor exercise, try the **Ojai Valley Trail,** a 16.5-mile paved track running from Ojai to the beach at Ventura. The trail is perfect for walking, biking, or horseback riding. To rent a bicycle, contact **Bicycles of Ojai,** 108 Canada St. (☎ **805-646-7736**). For horses, call the **Ojai Valley Inn Ranch & Stables** (☎ **805-649-5552**).

If you'd prefer to see the outdoors without working up a sweat, contact **Pink Moment Jeep Tours** (☎ 805-653-2502). This company offers guided tours of area sites in open-air Jeeps, including excursions to the best spots to witness the famous "pink moment."

Gathering More Information

The **Santa Barbara Conference and Visitors Bureau** (☎ 800-549-5133 or 805-966-9222) has a wealth of information, much of it in easily printable form, at www.santabarbaraca.com. The **Santa Barbara Tourist Information Center** is just across from the beach at 1 Garden St., at Cabrillo Boulevard (☎ 805-965-3021). This center offers good maps and other literature, and the friendly staff can answer specific questions. Open Monday through Saturday from 9 a.m. to 5 p.m. and Sunday from 10 a.m. to 5 p.m.

You may also want to pick up a copy of the *Independent,* a free weekly paper with comprehensive events listings. It's available from sidewalk racks and in shops and restaurants around town.

The **Ojai Valley Chamber of Commerce and Visitors Center,** 150 W. Ojai Ave. (☎ 805-646-8126; fax 805-646-9762; www.ojaichamber.org), publishes an excellent visitor guide and other brochures and can answer any questions you have about Ojai. Walk-ins are welcome Monday through Friday from 9 a.m. to noon and from 1 to 4 p.m.

Part V
The Southland Cities and the Desert

The 5th Wave   By Rich Tennant

In this part . . .

This part focuses on Southern California — Los Angeles, San Diego, and the Disneyland Resort — along with California's *real* hot spots: Palm Springs and the desert. In addition to being rich in glitz and gloriously fun, Los Angeles is the state's finest museum town — no kidding. The Disneyland Resort is the original theme park, an unadulterated blast for kids of all ages. San Diego is a sunny, laidback city with lots of kid-friendly attractions and golden beaches galore.

Unlike other destinations in this book — which are generally popular in summer and largely pleasant to visit year-round — Southern California is fun to visit in any season *but* summer, when scorching heat can be a bit much to bear. Still, even on the most simmering days, you can find respite from the heat. The Palm Springs area is the place to go for desert cool by a sparkling swimming pool, and if you're looking for the perfect day at the beach, head to easy-going Laguna. The fabled mission at San Juan Capistrano has lush gardens that burst forth with color, celebrated by a flower and garden festival in June.

And if really hot isn't hot enough for you, head for the otherworldly beauty of the state's desert parks, Joshua Tree National Park and Death Valley National Park.

Chapter 23

Los Angeles

● ●

In This Chapter

▶ Knowing when to go, how to get there, and how long to stay
▶ Getting to know the lay of La-La Land
▶ Choosing your neighborhood and finding the best places to stay and eat
▶ Seeing the sights, shopping, and living it up after the sun goes down

● ●

*W*e love L.A. — we really, really do, but that's because we know how to best find and experience its admittedly subtle charms. Yes, it's got smog (although increasingly less); yes, it has traffic (alas, more than ever); and yes, much of the distinctive architecture has been torn down thanks to an utter disinterest in preservation. And yes, it's far-flung and public transportation stinks, so you absolutely have to buck that afore-mentioned heavy traffic to get anywhere to enjoy anything.

But. Here's a place where you can surf and ski on the same day. Here's a place where your sightseeing will only be enhanced by one of the 350 cloudless days a year. Here's a place where movie-star footprints are enshrined, and Gettys give a great deal of money to amass one of the finest art collections in the world. Here's a place where you can enjoy the L.A. Philharmonic (and other internationally known artists) for just a few dollars (of course, for that price, way up high) out in the fragrant night air, at the gorgeous Hollywood Bowl. Here's a place where just a 1-mile stretch of Hollywood Boulevard peacefully holds Thai, Mexican, Romanian, Armenian, Vietnamese, and Persian restaurants, all of them with some of the most wonderful food you've ever tasted, for a bargain price. Here's a place where weirdness and eccentricity are embraced — and of course, if you can turn it into a sitcom, so much the better. Here's a place where you can grocery-shop right next to the actors who star in those very sitcoms, just like they were regular folks.

El Pueblo de la Señora, la Reina de Los Angeles ("the city of Our Lady, Queen of the Angels") was founded by the Spanish in 1781, but truth be told, it wasn't really on the map until the movie folks came out here in search of outdoor locations that didn't suffer from snow. By World War I, the movie business had a hold on the town, and in the 1920s and '30s, people came here in droves seeking their fortunes. Very few of them were discovered sipping sodas in malt shops, a la Lana Turner, but that didn't stop anyone from trying.

That crush of people came with cars, and as early as 1940, the Arroyo Seco Parkway, the first freeway, was opened. The automobile business solidified L.A.'s total dependence on cars by crushing the then-quite-handy public transport (the Little Red Cars trolley system). More freeways followed, and more people came to work in the thriving aerospace industry (led by McDonnell Douglas) and the new television industry. It didn't help that every year, Pasadena put on the glorious Rose Parade under inevitably clear blue skies, causing snowbound Midwesterners and others to throw everything in the car and go to permanently join the balmy fun. In no time at all, L.A. became an urban sprawl of impossible dimensions.

And they keep on a'comin', although a few events have quenched migration enthusiasm, at least briefly. In 1971, an earthquake measuring 6.2 on the Richter scale rocked nearby Sylmar, but although it loomed in legend for more than 20 years, it was nothing compared with the Biggish One, the Northridge quake (6.8 on the Richter scale) that left nearly 60 people dead and a portion of the freeway collapsed. Riots in the wake of the Rodney King verdict shut down the city for several days as homes and businesses burned and the National Guard came out to restore order. And then there was O.J.

But thanks to its blessedly short memory, floods, fires, and football players haven't stopped this town. And on one of those clear days — after the Santa Ana winds have blown away the smog — when the sky is a memorable blue, the mountains stand out so sharply they seem cut out of glass, the impossibly blooming bougainvillea flaunts a floozy pink, the air smells of gardenia, and you're in your shirt sleeves, enjoying the sun on your face as you sip some coffee, you think to yourself "It's January?" . . . and, well, you may find yourself loving L.A., too.

Timing Your Visit

People are fond of complaining that Los Angeles has no seasons. Sure, certain flowers bloom all year long, but the seasonal changes are there — they're just subtle, that's all. In the winter, trees are bare (well, not the palm trees), and spring here looks like spring most anywhere.

If it's going to rain — and odds are, it won't, unless another *El Niño* snakes its way out of the tropics — it's most likely going to happen in spring. Even then, heavy rainstorms are unusual. It can get nippy — oh, not Minnesota, 40-below nippy — but it can get down in the 20s at night in winter, so bring a coat. Actually, a light wrap is always a good idea, thanks to temperatures that can annoyingly flit from 80°F during the day to 50°F at night. Autumn can bring the Santa Anas, the surprisingly strong, warm winds that are a bane to firefighters. Note also that the Westside neighborhoods (Santa Monica, Brentwood, Pacific Palisades, and even Westwood) can be 20°F (or more) cooler than Hollywood, Pasadena, and the Valley (the latter two are the hottest places in the city area). Go figure. Thank the ocean breezes.

Most visitors come in summer, but Los Angeles is pleasant year-round. Year-round, daytime temperatures seldom drop below the mid-60s, and nighttime lows waffle between the 40s and 50s (bring a jacket anytime you come), except during the height of summer, when it stays more balmy.

Summer comes late to L.A. June is often on the cool side and plagued by *June gloom* — morning fog that doesn't burn off until early afternoon (and June gloom can actually last into August, especially around the beach, which doesn't seem fair at all) On the upside, low humidity and ocean breezes keep the climate relatively dry and comfortable, even 20 miles inland, in the heat of summer (July, Aug, and well into Sept). The valleys can get smoggy and miserable on the hottest days — which means you could end up broiling at Universal Studios — but are otherwise comfortable.

Winter is a great time for avoiding crowds and escaping the bitter cold back home. Though the weather will likely be too cool for the beach, the occasional 80°F day will pop up, and hotel bargains are common (except at holiday time). And the rain and winds blow away smog and haze, leaving a landscape of such beauty that you suddenly understand why people live here — and you may even want to join them.

L.A.'s attractions are spread out, and traffic can be horrendous, which means one of two things:

- ✔ You need three full days to get a good overview of the city.

- ✔ If you're not a city person and you know that L.A. is going to get under your skin quickly (or you just don't have three full days to give), you should zero in on where your interests lie, see those attractions in a day or two, and skedaddle outta town.

Getting There

Los Angeles International Airport, commonly called **LAX** (☎ 310-646-5252; www.lawa.org/lax), is the city's major gateway, and most likely where you'll fly in. LAX is on the ocean south of Marina del Rey at the intersection of the 405 and 105 freeways, 9½ miles from Santa Monica and 16 miles from Hollywood. From the airport, it's approximately a 30-minute drive to downtown, and a 40-minute drive to West Hollywood, depending on the traffic.

Burbank-Glendale-Pasadena Airport (☎ 818-840-8840; www.burbank airport.com) is usually just referred to as "Burbank." It's officially **Bob Hope Airport,** but call it the "Bob Hope Airport," and people will look puzzled. Whatever you call it, it's 8 miles northeast of Hollywood within a rough square bounded by the 5, 134 and 170 freeways. Burbank is far smaller and more manageable than LAX and is definitely the most convenient gateway if you're basing yourself in Hollywood. Most flights coming into Burbank arrive from other California cities or nearby cities like Phoenix and Vegas. From the airport, it's approximately a 25-minute drive to downtown and a 20-minute drive to West Hollywood, depending on the traffic.

Long Beach Airport (☎ 562-570-2619; www.longbeach.gov/airport) is a sweet, old-fashioned landing strip with a gorgeous Art Deco terminal out of which only two domestic airlines fly. It's tiny and, if there's no traffic, conveniently close — only half an hour away from downtown. Otherwise, the trip can be stressful and interminable.

All major car-rental companies have branches at these three airports, and each provides shuttle service between the terminals and its off-site lot.

Getting to your hotel from LAX

If you're staying in Santa Monica, take Sepulveda Boulevard north and follow the signs to Lincoln Boulevard/Highway 1 (Pacific Coast Highway, or PCH) north. To reach West L.A., Beverly Hills, or Hollywood, take Century Boulevard to I-405 north; Santa Monica Boulevard east is the likeliest exit, but check with your hotel to be sure.

If you won't be renting a car at the airport, **SuperShuttle** (☎ 310-782-6600 or 323-775-6600; www.supershuttle.com) offers door-to-door shuttle service. Expect to pay between $15 and $45 (plus tip) for the first person in your party and $10 to $15 for each additional person, depending on your drop-off point. Although you don't need reservations for your arrival, you must make them at least a day in advance for your return trip to the airport. Note that you won't be the only passenger on board, and that the journey to your destination can take as much as a couple of hours, depending on how many stops the van has to make along the way.

Taxis line up curbside at each terminal. Expect to pay between $31 and $40 (plus tip), depending on your destination. All LAX pickups include a $2.50 surcharge. Taxis can accommodate up to five riders.

Getting to your hotel from Burbank

Follow the signs to U.S. 101 south (the Hollywood Freeway), and exit at Vine Street for Hollywood hotels; continue south on the 110 to the 10 west if you're staying on the Westside or at the beach.

SuperShuttle (☎ 818-556-6600; www.supershuttle.com) offers door-to-door shuttle service from Burbank; expect to pay $15 plus tip to Hollywood for the first person in your party and $10 to $15 for each additional person. Reserve airport pickups and returns in advance. If you forget, taxis wait outside the terminal. Taxi fare will depend on your final destination, but expect to pay between $20 and $30 to Hollywood.

Getting to your hotel from Long Beach

Follow the signs to the 405 north, exit on Sunset Boulevard eastbound for Hollywood. For beach and Westside hotels, take the 405 north to the 10 west.

If you won't be renting a car at the airport, **SuperShuttle** (☎ 310-782-6600 or 323-775-6600; www.supershuttle.com) offers door-to-door shuttle service. Expect to pay $40 (plus tip) for the first person and $10 to $15 for each additional person, depending on your drop-off point. Although you don't need reservations for your arrival, you must make them at least a day in advance for your return trip to the airport.

Taxis line up curbside at each terminal. Expect to pay at least $50 (plus tip) to downtown, $70 to Hollywood, more if there's traffic. Taxis can accommodate up to five riders.

Arriving by car

If you're driving from Santa Barbara and coastal points north, follow U.S. 101 south to I-405:

- ✔ For **West L.A., Beverly Hills,** or **West Hollywood,** exit at Santa Monica Boulevard.

- ✔ **For Santa Monica,** pick up I-10 west, which will drop you right at the ocean.

- ✔ **If you're heading to Hollywood** stay on U.S. 101 until it becomes the Hollywood Freeway (be sure to take the Hollywood Freeway/U.S. 101 turnoff, or you'll end up in Pasadena before you know it). Exit the Hollywood Freeway at Vine or Gower street.

If you're driving from San Francisco or Monterey and prefer to bypass the scenic coastal route, follow I-5 through the middle of the state. Heading south on I-5, you'll pass a small town called Grapevine, which marks the start of the Grapevine Pass a mountain pass that leads you into the San Fernando Valley and L.A. Take I-405 south to Santa Monica, West L.A. Beverly Hills, and West Hollywood; for Hollywood, follow I-5 past I-405 to Highway 170 south to U.S. 101 south (this route is called the Hollywood Freeway the entire way).

From points east, including Palm Springs or Phoenix, take I-10 west, which dead-ends in Santa Monica. For Hollywood, take I-110 (the Harbor Freeway) to U.S. 101 (the Hollywood Freeway) north; for West L.A. and Beverly Hills, follow I-10 to I-405 north.

From Disneyland or San Diego, head north on I-5 (the Santa Ana Freeway). If you've been following along, you'll know to pick up I-405 north to Santa Monica, West Los Angeles, and Beverly Hills, and continue on to U.S. 101 for Hollywood.

Arriving by train

Amtrak (☎ **800-872-7245;** www.amtrak.com) trains arrive at Union Station, 800 N. Alameda St. (☎ **213-624-0171**), on the northern edge of downtown just north of U.S. 101. From there, you can take one of the taxis that line up outside.

Orienting Yourself and Getting Around

Los Angeles resides on the flatlands of a huge basin, sandwiched by mountains and ocean, with downtown L.A. as its midpoint 12 miles east of the Pacific. The sprawling city includes dozens of neighborhoods and municipalities that are so complex that even a city planner would need some serious time to sort it all out. A web of freeways knits everything together, with the major ones forming a rough box around the area where you'll spend your time (see the "Los Angeles's Neighborhoods" map on p. 350):

- ✔ **I-10 (the Santa Monica Freeway)** runs east-west from Palm Springs (actually from Georgia) all the way to within a few miles of the ocean in Santa Monica.

- ✔ **Highway 1 (the Pacific Coast Highway, or just PCH),** is a standard four-lane avenue called Lincoln Boulevard from just north of the airport to Santa Monica, where it turns into a surface highway and cuts west to hug the coast all the way to Malibu.

- ✔ **I-405 (the San Diego Freeway)** runs north–south through L.A.'s Westside, roughly parallel to PCH and about 3½ miles inland from the coast.

- ✔ **U.S. 101** is the **Ventura Freeway** as it runs east–west through the San Fernando Valley (on the north side of L.A.), becoming the **Hollywood Freeway** after U.S. 101 takes a sharp turn right, running northwest–southeast to connect the Valley with downtown L.A. (The Ventura Freeway continues directly east on California 134.)

- ✔ **I-110 (the Harbor Freeway)** starts in Pasadena (as the Pasadena Freeway) and runs directly south. You'll likely use the section that runs along the western edge of downtown, connecting the Hollywood Freeway to I-10.

- ✔ **I-5 (the Golden State Freeway)** runs along the eastern edge of downtown on its way from San Francisco to San Diego.

An underlying grid of surface streets complements the freeways. The major east–west boulevards connecting downtown to the beaches are, from north to south, Sunset, Santa Monica, Wilshire, Olympic, Pico, and Venice boulevards.

Locals refer to L.A. freeways both by their numbers and their names. For example, I-10 is both "the 10" and "the Santa Monica Freeway."

A good city map is a must; even born-and-raised Angelenos carry one in their cars. AAA publishes the best maps of L.A., bar none. Members can stop in at one of the local offices (see the "Fast Facts" section at the end of this chapter). If you're not a member, any good foldout map will do, as long as all streets and freeways are clearly marked and the map has address number notations.

L.A.'s neighborhoods

In L.A.'s neighborhoods, the wheat is separated from the chaff in a really big way, boiling down the city to the neighborhoods where most visitors (and most locals) head for sightseeing, entertainment, and general fun in the sun. Who really wants to go to Van Nuys, anyway?

Unlike in most cities, urban life in L.A. doesn't focus on downtown. You'll likely spend the bulk of your time in the beach communities, on the city's Westside, and in Hollywood. For a visual aid to this section, see the "Los Angeles's Neighborhoods" map on p. 350.

Santa Monica

Santa Monica is L.A.'s premier beach community. It's fun, festive, and pretty, with a deserved left-of-center reputation. It extends for 3 miles along the coast, starting out artsy-funky around Ocean Park Boulevard and getting ritzier as you go north. Ocean Avenue runs blufftop along the coast, meeting Colorado Boulevard at the **Santa Monica Pier,** famous for its amusements. Dining and shopping north of Colorado centers on the **Third Street Promenade** and along Main Street south of Colorado. The 10 freeway drops you into the heart of the action.

Venice and Marina del Rey

South of Santa Monica is Venice, an early-20th-century planned community with its very own canals. But the real draw is wild, wacky, funky boho **Venice Beach,** which just may be the ultimate human carnival. Main Street leads you into Venice from the north — you'll know you've arrived when it becomes Pacific Avenue — and Venice Boulevard and Washington Avenue are the main routes from points east.

Malibu

Malibu is the ultimate symbol of beachy super-celebrity. Its vast network of rugged canyons leads from Santa Monica north all the way to the northern border of L.A. County. Only the Pacific Coast Highway (and an almost-unbroken row of ocean-facing houses that are *much* larger — and pricier — than they look from PCH) separates Malibu's canyons from its gorgeous wide beaches. Malibu is extremely remote (one of its great appeals for the rich and famous) and without freeway access. Consequently, the drive to Malibu from just about anywhere else in the city takes around an hour.

Los Angeles's Neighborhoods

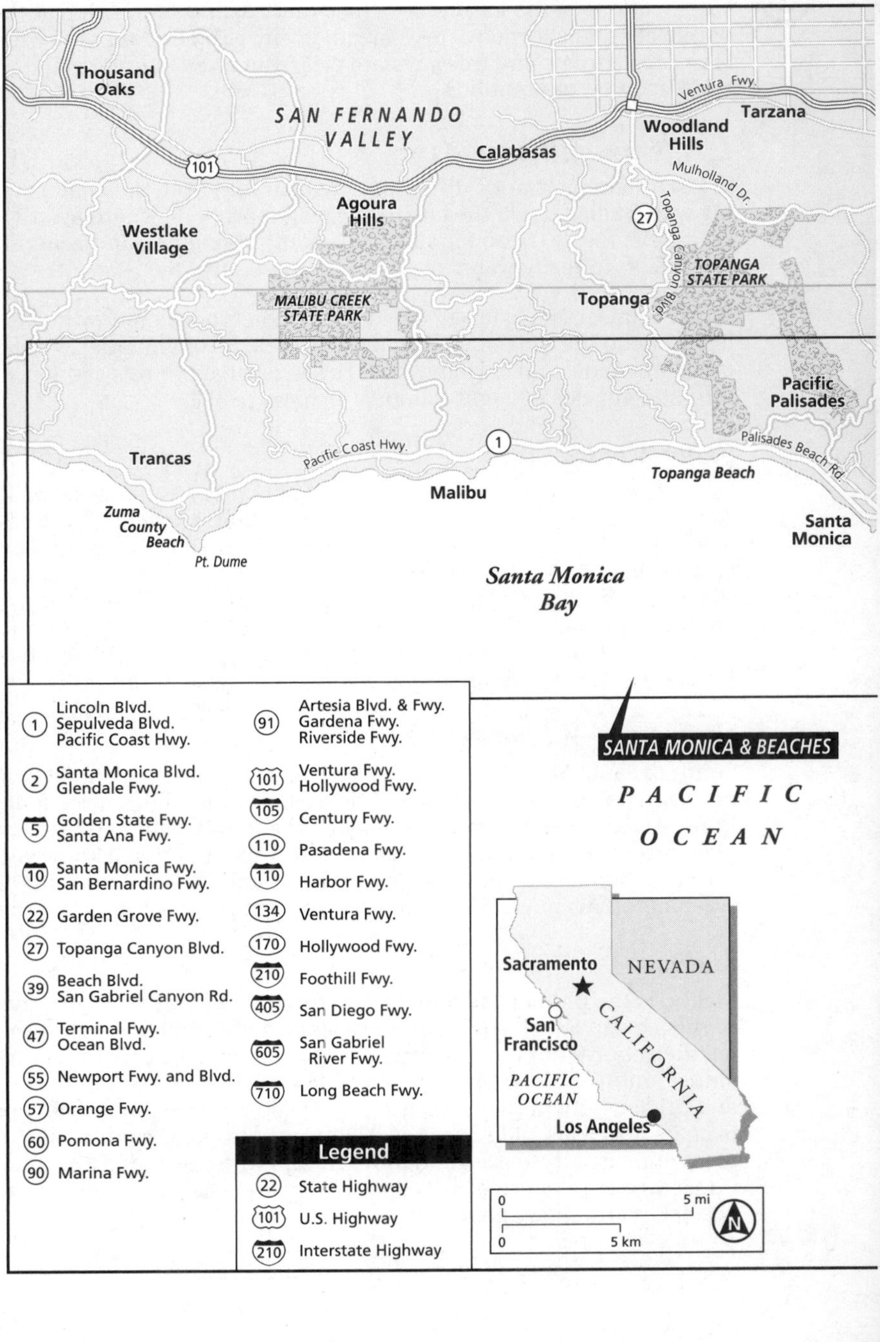
Thousand Oaks
SAN FERNANDO VALLEY
Ventura Fwy.
Tarzana
Woodland Hills
Calabasas
101
Mulholland Dr.
Agoura Hills
27
Topanga Canyon Blvd.
Westlake Village
TOPANGA STATE PARK
MALIBU CREEK STATE PARK
Topanga
Pacific Palisades
1
Pacific Coast Hwy.
Palisades Beach Rd.
Trancas
Topanga Beach
Malibu
Zuma County Beach
Pt. Dume
Santa Monica
Santa Monica Bay
1 Lincoln Blvd. Sepulveda Blvd. Pacific Coast Hwy.
2 Santa Monica Blvd. Glendale Fwy.
5 Golden State Fwy. Santa Ana Fwy.
10 Santa Monica Fwy. San Bernardino Fwy.
22 Garden Grove Fwy.
27 Topanga Canyon Blvd.
39 Beach Blvd. San Gabriel Canyon Rd.
47 Terminal Fwy. Ocean Blvd.
55 Newport Fwy. and Blvd.
57 Orange Fwy.
60 Pomona Fwy.
90 Marina Fwy.
91 Artesia Blvd. & Fwy. Gardena Fwy. Riverside Fwy.
101 Ventura Fwy. Hollywood Fwy.
105 Century Fwy.
110 Pasadena Fwy.
110 Harbor Fwy.
134 Ventura Fwy.
170 Hollywood Fwy.
210 Foothill Fwy.
405 San Diego Fwy.
605 San Gabriel River Fwy.
710 Long Beach Fwy.
Legend
22 State Highway
101 U.S. Highway
210 Interstate Highway
SANTA MONICA & BEACHES
PACIFIC OCEAN
Sacramento
NEVADA
CALIFORNIA
San Francisco
PACIFIC OCEAN
Los Angeles
0
5 mi
0
5 km
N

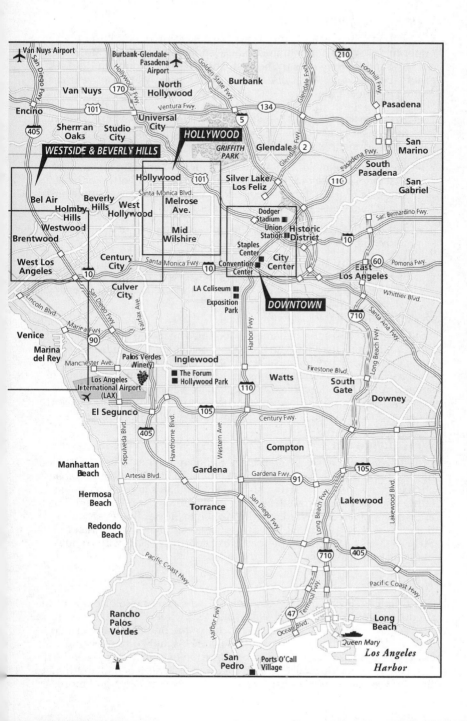

West Los Angeles

West L.A. is basically an umbrella for the collection of middle- and upper-middle-class communities sandwiched between Santa Monica to the west and Beverly Hills to the east. Some of these communities lack exact labels beyond "West L.A.," but they're perfectly nice nonetheless. Among the most notable are

- ✔ **Brentwood,** the upscale residential area north of Wilshire Boulevard and west of the 405 that O.J. Simpson made famous (to the chagrin of his former neighbors).

- ✔ **Westwood,** home to UCLA and a restaurant- and shop-laden village that caters largely to the college kids. It's the area between the 405 and Beverly Hills, bounded by Santa Monica and Sunset boulevards; the village is just north of Wilshire Boulevard.

- ✔ **Bel-Air,** the gated domain of the rich and famous north of UCLA above Sunset Boulevard.

- ✔ **Century City,** the pocket of high-rises just west of Beverly Hills, between Santa Monica and Pico boulevards. It has the Westside's only real city skyline, but is otherwise sanitized and uninteresting.

Beverly Hills

You know; it's where the swimming pools and the movie stars are. Aren't they? Well, some, for sure. The traditional bastion of L.A.'s ultrarich and -famous is a glitzy but easily enjoyable community. The area south of Wilshire Boulevard is largely upper-middle-class residential and home to some surprisingly affordable hotels. North of Wilshire is the **Golden Triangle,** Beverly Hills's downtown, where you find the ritzy shops. North of Santa Monica Boulevard is the hilly, star-studded residential area.

West Hollywood

Ground zero for L.A.'s gay and rock-'n'-roll communities, West Hollywood houses some of L.A.'s best (or liveliest, anyway) hotels, restaurants, bars, and clubs. It's long and narrow, shaped kind of like a house key, and feels either upscale or lowbrow, depending on where you are. The main drags are Santa Monica Boulevard and the stretch of Sunset Boulevard between Doheny Drive and Crescent Heights Boulevard known as the **Sunset Strip** — L.A.'s tattooed-and-pierced party central, packed with trendy bars and rocking clubs.

Hollywood

The original epicenter of movie glamour had degenerated into one of the seediest parts of town by the 1980s, but it's a whole different story of late. A major urban revitalization (much like the one that transformed New York's Times Square) began in the late '90s and continues apace. **Hollywood Boulevard** will never be a bastion of high culture — in fact, L.A. hardly gets more touristy than this, and it never has had anything to do with the actual movie business — but it's cleaner, safer, and more attractive than it has been in decades. The boulevard's **Walk of Fame** and the shopping/entertainment center **Hollywood & Highland Center** are the main attractions, but the neighborhood extends from Beverly Boulevard north into the Hollywood Hills, encompassing the famously funky alterna-shopping strip **Melrose Avenue.**

Mid-Wilshire District/Miracle Mile

This corridor flanks Wilshire Boulevard east from Beverly Hills to (roughly) Western Avenue. The highlight is the stretch of Wilshire between Fairfax and La Brea avenues, which serves as the city's impressive **Museum Row.**

Los Feliz and Silver Lake

This hip haven between Hollywood and downtown is further notable as a gateway to **Griffith Park,** the massive urban park that's home to the Griffith Observatory (remember *Rebel without a Cause?*).

Universal City and Burbank

These San Fernando Valley communities are the joint capitals of TV Land, and all you need to know about the Valley. Universal City, west of Griffith Park between the Hollywood and Ventura freeways (U.S. 101 and California 134), houses **Universal Studios Hollywood** and **Universal CityWalk,** the adjoining shopping-and-dining spread.

Just north of Universal City and the 134, Burbank hosts L.A.'s secondary airport and the **NBC** and **Warner Bros.** studios, open to the masses for TV tapings and tours.

Downtown

Boxed in by the 101, the 110, the 10, and the 5 freeways, downtown is the business center of the city — and totally entertainment-industry-free. After a scruffy period, the area cleaned up nicely in recent years, even drawing some hip restaurants. As more old office buildings are bought up and turned into living spaces (either apartments or more hotels), developers hope more culture and urban life will follow. Right now, **MOCA,** the new **Disney Hall, Olvera Street,** the new **Cathedral,** and the **Music Center** ought to be enough to lure you down for at least a quick peek.

Pasadena

Pasadena, blissfully free of Hollywood glam, is the premier draw of the San Gabriel Valley (a network of pretty, upscale bedroom communities east of the San Fernando Valley). The biggest day of the year here is January 1, when the **Tournament of Roses Parade** draws national attention to the attractive 'burb. You can also find a few year-round attractions here, such as the **Norton Simon Museum of Art.**

Drive, she said: Getting around

Yes, driving around L.A. is a hassle. Yes, you pretty much have to do it. There may be the brave tourist who will dare to use the public-transportation system, and if you are he (or she), we say, Godspeed and drop us a note to tell us how it went.

The complex web of freeways and surface streets may be intimidating at first. After you get the hang of it, however, it's not bad; driving in New York City, or even the daunting hills of San Francisco, is worlds more difficult. Just think of L.A. as one big, bad suburb and you'll be fine.

Do yourself a favor and keep these tips in mind as you drive — and park — around the city:

- ✔ **Allow more time than you think it will actually take to get where you're going.** You need to make time for traffic and parking. Double your margin in weekday rush hours, from 7 to 9 a.m. and again from 3 to 7 p.m. We've often found the freeways to be much more crowded than we expect all day on Saturdays, too, especially heading toward the ocean on a warm sunny day.

- ✔ **Plan your exact route before you set out.** Know where you need to exit the freeway and/or make turns — especially lefts — and merge in plenty of time. Otherwise, you're likely to find yourself waving at your freeway exit from an inside lane or your turnoff from an outside one. Pulling over and whipping out your map if you screw up is never easy, and it's darn near impossible on the freeways.

- ✔ **Those kids you brought can come in handy.** Most freeways have a High Occupancy Vehicle (HOV) — carpool — lane, which lets you speed past some of the congestion if you have three people in the car (sometimes two; read the signs). Don't flout the rules; if you do, expect to shell out close to 300 bucks for the ticket.

- ✔ **Watch turning right on red.** You can turn right on red as long as a posted sign doesn't tell you otherwise. Come to a full stop first — no rolling.

- ✔ **Beware of left turns.** Many major intersections don't have a left-turn arrow, and most people run yellow lights, so it's pretty common for left-turners to have to do so just after the light turns red. Conversely, if you're going straight through an intersection, you want to make sure there aren't any left turners in the middle of the intersection in front of you when the light first turns green.

- ✔ **Accept the fact that you will sometimes have to pay for parking.** Your hotel will offer parking, either for free or for a charge. Many other establishments (in some areas, most) don't have their own self-park lots, so free street parking is the holy grail. It's sometimes available, but not always. Side streets are often a good bet, but beware of residential neighborhoods; an increasing number allow only permit parking, and you will be towed or ticketed. Metered street parking is much easier to find, but can still be tough to locate in the most popular areas of Santa Monica, Beverly Hills, and Hollywood. Otherwise, expect to valet or garage it and to pay between $5 and $25 for the privilege. Many restaurants, nightclubs, and even some shopping centers offer curbside valet parking.

✔ **Have plenty of quarters on hand.** Angelenos scrounge for parking-meter quarters like New Yorkers do for laundry quarters: They are the equivalent of pure gold. Save yourself some hassle and just buy a roll or two at your bank before you leave home.

✔ **Always read the street-parking signs, because they often limit your parking time.** You will be ticketed if you overstay your welcome. Read the meters as well as street signs. On the upside, meter fares are often waived in the evenings.

✔ **Don't lose your car in a parking garage.** Take it from two reasonably intelligent, well-educated people who have done it more than once — *it happens.* You know how you feel when you forget where you parked your car at the mall? Multiply that by ten levels. Most garage levels and subsections are letter-, number-, and color-coded. Always make a mental note or a physical one, if need be.

If you must: By bus and metro

Sigh. We really want to encourage visitors to travel by bus or subway, but we can't, not in good conscience. This city is too large, for one, to be covered by a good public-transportation system, and what is here is a wildly inefficient one.

The award-winning **Blue Buses** in Santa Monica do actually work quite well, and a case could be made for getting around via subway if all you plan to do is go around Hollywood, Universal City, and downtown. Try it if you dare; an all-day pass costs just $3. The Metropolitan Transit Authority (MTA) runs the bus network in addition to the limited four-line **Metro Rail system,** really conceived as a park-and-ride system for suburban commuters. The "subway" (it still makes us snicker to call it that) does work pretty well, provided you want to go to the eight (okay, there are more than that) places it stops. For information, call ☎ **800-COMMUTE** (800-266-6883), or go online to www.mta.net, where you'll find a custom online trip planner (have the exact addresses of your start and endpoint on hand).

By taxi

Taxis don't cruise the streets, so call well ahead for pickup. Keep in mind that distances are long, so the meter adds up quickly. If you need a cab, call **L.A. Taxi Co-op** (☎ **310-715-1968**) or **Independent Taxi** (☎ **323-666-0045**).

Where to Stay in Los Angeles

In choosing Los Angeles's best hotels, we've concentrated on those neighborhoods that are the most visitor-friendly and offer the easiest access to L.A.'s main attractions. Still, consider your major sightseeing goals before you decide where to stay. That beach hotel that's just right for some may be all wrong for avid shoppers or club-hoppers.

Count on an extra 12 to 18 percent in taxes being tacked on to your hotel bill, depending on where you're staying. Ask what the local percentage is when you book.

For hotels with locations in Westside and Beverly Hills, see the "Westside and Beverly Hills Accommodations, Dining, and Attractions" map. For hotels with locations in Hollywood, flip to the "Hollywood Accommodations, Dining, and Attractions" map. For hotels with locations in Santa Monica and the beaches, go to the "Santa Monica and the Malibu Beaches" map in the "Hitting the beaches" section later in this chapter.

Avalon Hotel
$$$–$$$$ Beverly Hills

Mae West and Marilyn Monroe once lived here, when it was an apartment building, and Lucy and Ricky Ricardo stayed here when they went to Hollywood in *I Love Lucy*. Now, it's a small, chic hotel, aggressively styled and inadvertently harkening back to the 1950s/Jetsons futurism — look for all the green polished concrete and atom-age emblems. Rooms are spare but oh so comfortable — think high-end Italian linens! Moulton Brown–brand bathroom amenities! CD and DVD players! The bathrooms are smallish, with inexplicable bamboo poles (for stripper practice?). The pool demands a good bathing suit and a figure to match. Ask about rooms 240 through 244, which include furnished terraces.

See map p. 358. 9400 W. Olympic Blvd. (at Cañon Drive). ☎ *800-670-6183 or 310-277-5221. Fax: 310-277-4928.* www.avalonbeverlyhills.com. *Parking: $26. Rack rates: $250–$505 double. AE, DC, DISC, MC, V.*

Best Western Hollywood Hills Hotel
$$–$$$ Hollywood

Famous for the huge sign declaring this to be the "Last Cappuccino before the 101" and with a coffee shop (now under new ownership and design and renamed the **101 Coffee Shop** — see the "Where to Dine in Los Angeles" section later in this chapter) that was featured in the movie *Swingers,* this motel is usually crowded with local musicians, actors, and lounge-abouts digging into the hearty, reasonably priced food. The rooms are large, the large pool is tiled and heated, and the location is good for public transportation and excellent for driving. Star-spotting spots are within walking distance (Victor's Deli and Café, Gelson's/Mayfair Market, Bourgeois Pig, and Cosmopolitan Books and Music), Universal Studios is five minutes away on the freeway, and Hollywood is just down the hill. And for the kids, Dodger Stadium and the Los Angeles Zoo are not too far. *See map p. 362. 6141 Franklin Ave. (between Vine and Gower streets).* ☎ *800-287-1700 or 323-464-5181. Fax: 323-962-0536.* www.bestwestern.com/hollywood hillshotel. *Free parking. Rack rates: $99–$210 double. AE, DC, DISC, MC, V.*

Best Western Ocean View Hotel
$$–$$$$ Santa Monica

A Best Western, but a top-of-the-line one, so if you're looking for a standard modern hotel with a slippery marble foyer/lobby, look no further. Rooms are medium-sized, comfortable, heavy on the pinky-goldy color scheme, and instantly forgettable (although some rooms do have ocean views, and some are handicapped accessible, which isn't always the case in the older Santa Monica hotels — call for availability). Palisades Park is across the street, and the Pier and the Third Street Promenade are just a block or so away.

See map p. 397. 1447 Ocean Ave. (across from Palisades Park). ☎ *800-452-4888 or 310-458-4888. Fax: 310-458-0848.* www.bestwestern.com/oceanviewhotel. *Parking: $15. Rack rates: $149–$279 double. AE, DC, DISC, MC, V.*

Beverly Hills Reeves Hotel
$–$$ Beverly Hills

Wow, talk about facelifts! This used to be a cheap place to stay in Beverly Hills; now it's a *nice* and cheap place to stay while vacationing in the 90210. Bought by a caring corporation, the Reeves has a fresh coat of paint, new carpeting, an attractive lobby, and cleaner rooms, thanks to the new owners. Yet the shockingly low room rates remain shockingly low. There's no room service, but a decent continental breakfast is included, and each room has a small TV with cable; for daily and weekly guests, maid service and private bathrooms are included, although it's possible to rent rooms with shared bathrooms (and that means sharing everything). At the Reeves, you're within walking distance of the glitz and glitter of Rodeo Drive and points adjacent. Instead of spending all your vacation cash on rooms, you can shop and dine and still say you stayed in Beverly Hills. Caveat: Parking is limited to street parking, so observe posted hours; the front desk closes at 11:30 p.m., making this a bad choice for late-night arrivals.

See map p. 358. 120 S. Reeves Dr. (half a block from Wilshire Boulevard). ☎ *310-271-3006. Fax: 310-271-2276. Free parking on street 6 p.m.–8 a.m. only. Rack rates: $89–$109 double per day, $638–$730 double per week. AE, DC, DISC, MC, V.*

Beverly Terrace Hotel
$$ Beverly Hills

This is the best hotel value in Beverly Hills. It's located six (long) blocks from the heart of Beverly Hills and a steep quarter-mile hike from Sunset Strip. The exterior is fabulous 1950s glamour mirrored by the interior's midcentury, modern-beach-house feel. A pair of chatty cockatiels in the

Westside and Beverly Hills Accommodations, Dining, and Attractions

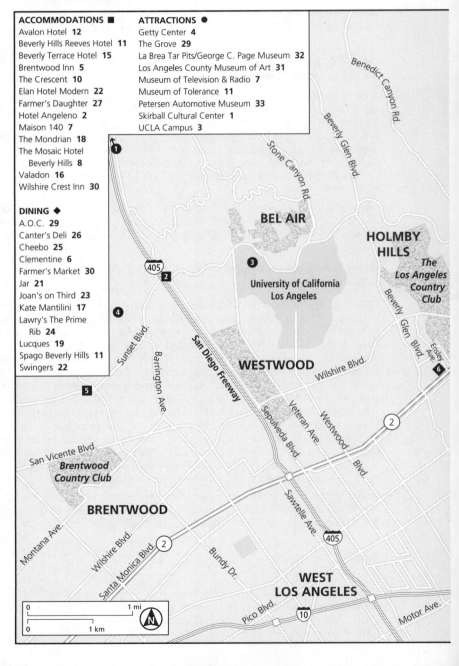

ACCOMMODATIONS ■
Avalon Hotel **12**
Beverly Hills Reeves Hotel **11**
Beverly Terrace Hotel **15**
Brentwood Inn **5**
The Crescent **10**
Elan Hotel Modern **22**
Farmer's Daughter **27**
Hotel Angeleno **2**
Maison 140 **7**
The Mondrian **18**
The Mosaic Hotel
   Beverly Hills **8**
Valadon **16**
Wilshire Crest Inn **30**

DINING ◆
A.O.C. **29**
Canter's Deli **26**
Cheebo **25**
Clementine **6**
Farmer's Market **30**
Jar **21**
Joan's on Third **23**
Kate Mantilini **17**
Lawry's The Prime
   Rib **24**
Lucques **19**
Spago Beverly Hills **11**
Swingers **22**

ATTRACTIONS ●
Getty Center **4**
The Grove **29**
La Brea Tar Pits/George C. Page Museum **32**
Los Angeles County Museum of Art **31**
Museum of Television & Radio **7**
Museum of Tolerance **11**
Petersen Automotive Museum **33**
Skirball Cultural Center **1**
UCLA Campus **3**

BEL AIR

HOLMBY HILLS

The Los Angeles Country Club

University of California
Los Angeles

WESTWOOD

Wilshire Blvd.

Brentwood Country Club

BRENTWOOD

WEST LOS ANGELES

0   1 mi
0   1 km

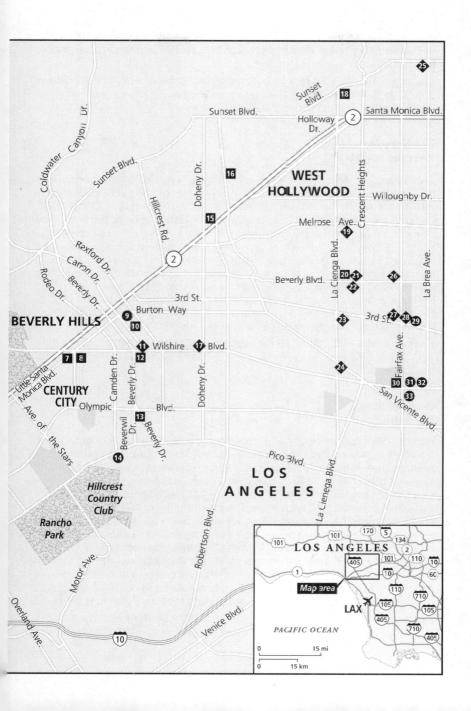

Sunset Blvd.

Sunset Blvd.

Holloway Dr.

2

Santa Monica Blvd.

25

18

Coldwater Canyon Dr.

Sunset Blvd.

Hillcrest Rd.

Doheny Dr.

16

15

WEST HOLLYWOOD

Crescent Heights

Willoughby Dr.

Melrose Ave.

19

La Cienega Blvd.

La Brea Ave.

Rexford Dr.

Canon Dr.

Beverly Dr.

Rodeo Dr.

2

Beverly Blvd.

20 21
22

26

3rd St.

Burton Way

BEVERLY HILLS

9
10

23

3rd St.

27 28
29

Fairfax Ave.

11
12

Wilshire

17

Blvd.

24

Little Santa Monica Blvd.

7 8

Camden Dr.

Beverly Dr.

30 31 32
33

San Vicente Blvd.

CENTURY CITY

Olympic

Blvd.

Doheny Dr.

13

Pico Blvd.

Ave. of the Stars

Beverwil Dr.

Beverly Dr.

14

LOS ANGELES

La Cienega Blvd.

Hillcrest Country Club

Rancho Park

Robertson Blvd.

Motor Ave.

Overland Ave.

10

Venice Blvd.

LOS ANGELES

101
101
170
5
134
101
2
110
10
60
110
710
105
105
710
405
405
405

1

Map area

LAX

PACIFIC OCEAN

0   15 mi

0   15 km

lobby add to the inviting atmosphere. The entire hotel is nonsmoking, although you can puff poolside. The rooms, all of which come with refrigerators, are not large, and that's being kind. Most rooms feature showers only, although you can request a tub room. A complimentary continental breakfast is served poolside daily, and the **Trattoria Amici** restaurant is located on-site.

See map p. 358. 469 N. Doheny Dr. (at Santa Monica Boulevard). ☎ *800-842-6401 or 310-274-8141. Fax: 310-385-1998.* www.beverlyterracehotel.com. *Free parking. Rack rates: $135–$200 double. AE, DISC, MC, V.*

The Brentwood Inn
West Los Angeles

This charming, sophisticated-yet-cozy, 20-unit cottage-style motel billowing with roses is an unexpected business venture, and yet fits perfectly into the wealthy yet relaxed section of Los Angeles called Brentwood. Located just minutes from UCLA to the east and the beach to the west (and scandal lovers will be pleased to learn, smack dab in the middle of the route O.J. may have taken that fateful night), the Brentwood Inn has long been a place where families put up out-of-town visitors. Cool turquoise and soothing browns predominate in the rooms, which feature complimentary wireless and flat-screen TVs, though no tubs; there are showers only. The bedding is hypoallergenic and all rooms are nonsmoking and pet free. In the morning, muffins and pastries are served in the lobby by the fireplace, while a fountain bubbles on the enclosed patio.

See map p. 358. 12200 Sunset (at Kenter Avenue). ☎ *800-840-3808 or 310-476-9981. Fax: 310-471-0768.* www.thebrentwood.com. *Free parking. Rack rates: $179–$229 double. AE, DISC, MC, V.*

Cadillac Hotel
$$ Venice

Built in 1905 as Charlie Chaplin's residence, this hotel is funky but cheap, a sort of Southern California version of the classic European *pensione*. A multimillion-dollar renovation, a top-to-bottom redo, was just beginning at press time. (Well, so they say. It was also "just beginning" a couple of years ago. They've raised their prices in what one hopes is anticipation of the actual remodel!) All rooms are being redesigned in "complete Art Deco style," with slightly different décor for each. It is a nice old building, with a fun, grand old lobby. There's wireless Internet access throughout the building. The two-room suite with beach views at the top may be the best bargain in town (around $199 a night). The rooftop has a sweeping view of the bay, and you can see up to four different fireworks shows from here on July 4th. The hotel is also just a couple blocks from the happening part of Venice's Main Street — and did we mention that it's right on the beach?

See map p. 397. 8 Dudley Ave. (at Speedway). ☎ *310-399-8876. Fax: 310-399-4536.* www.thecadillachotel.com. *Free parking. Rack rates: $179–$199 double. AE, MC, V.*

Cal-Mar Hotel Suites
$$ Santa Monica

Neatly situated just 2 blocks from Montana Avenue, 2 blocks from the ocean and 1 block from the Third Street Promenade, this all-suite hotel in an otherwise residential neighborhood features reasonable rates considering the location and the amenities: heated pool, full kitchens and dining room in each suite, queen-size sofa beds in the living room, cribs on request, and self-service laundry room, making it just about perfect for families. Plus, as a guest, you have access to nearby Eaton's gym. It's not super-fancy (think basic, serviceable hotel décor) but it's very clean, convenient and friendly.

See map p. 397. 220 California Ave. (at Second Street). ☎ *800-776-6007 or 310-395-5555. Fax: 310-451-1114.* www.calmarhotel.com. *Parking: $9.90. Rack rates: $149–$214 double. AE, MC, V.*

Channel Road Inn
$$$–$$$$$ Santa Monica

Nestled in Santa Monica Canyon and less than 2 blocks from the beach, this three-story Colonial Revival Craftsman has been lovingly restored by owner Susan Zolla. Transformed into a period-perfect bed-and-breakfast (with modern conveniences such as in-room VCRs and a business center), the inn features 14 unique, circa-1920 rooms where fresh-baked cookies and handwritten notes greet guests. Each room has a private bathroom, and each suite includes a Jacuzzi tub. Homemade lemonade sits on the sideboard in the relaxed wicker-filled breakfast room where award-winning egg soufflés are served. Although the canyon section of Santa Monica is not loaded with shops, downtown Santa Monica and Montana Avenue shopping districts are minutes away by car, and the inn provides free bicycles if you want to pedal around the area.

See map p. 397. 219 W. Channel Rd. (off Pacific Coast Highway). ☎ *310-459-1920. Fax: 310-454-9920.* www.channelroadinn.com. *Free parking. Rack rates: $225–$425 double. AE, MC, V.*

Chateau Marmont
$$$$–$$$$$ Hollywood/West Hollywood

Although its most notorious fame comes from John Belushi's overdose death (in Bungalow 2 in 1982), this fabulously romantic, slightly spooky old hotel is much favored by celebs who value naturally acquired style and quirk. The whole thing looks like a setting for a Raymond Chandler–style mystery, to say nothing of discreet assignations, which is probably why legendary studio boss Harry Cohn famously said, "If you must get into trouble, do it at the Chateau Marmont." Once a residence hotel (and there remain many a long-time occupant), the rooms can often be ridiculously large, especially the suites (to say nothing of the cottages and bungalows), which were originally intended as apartments. The furnishings and style in said rooms may put you in mind of the slightly faded Art Deco grandeur of the Coen Brothers' movie *Barton Fink* (although beds are modern and

Hollywood Accommodations, Dining, and Attractions

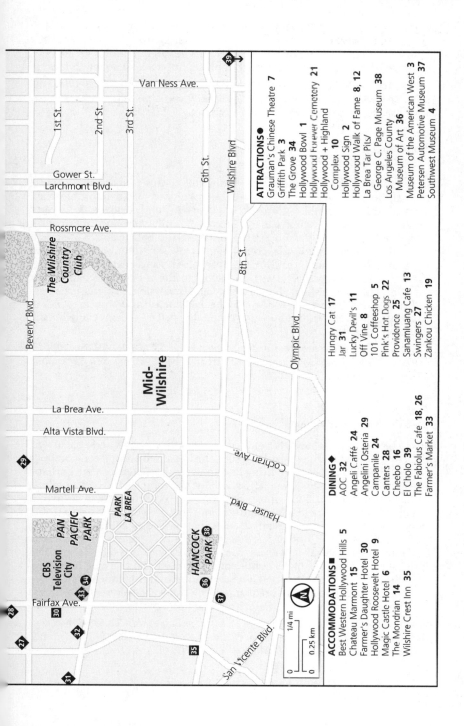

Van Ness Ave.

1st St.
2nd St.
3rd St.

Gower St.
Larchmont Blvd.

Rossmere Ave.

Wilshire Blvd

6th St.

ATTRACTIONS●
Grauman's Chinese Theatre **7**
Griffith Park **3**
The Grove **34**
Hollywood Bowl **1**
Hollywood Forever Cemetery **21**
Hollywood + Highland
 Complex **10**
Hollywood Sign **2**
Hollywood Walk of Fame **8, 12**
La Brea Tar Pits/
 George C. Page Museum **38**
Los Angeles County
 Museum of Art **36**
Museum of the American West **3**
Petersen Automotive Museum **37**
Southwest Museum **4**

The Wilshire
Country
Club

Beverly Blvd.

8th St.

Mid-
Wilshire

Olympic Blvd.

Hungry Cat **17**
Jar **31**
Lucky Devil's **11**
Off Vine **8**
101 Coffeeshop **5**
Pink's Hot Dogs **22**
Providence **25**
Sanamluang Cafe **13**
Swingers **27**
Zankou Chicken **19**

La Brea Ave.

Alta Vista Blvd.

Cochran Ave.

DINING◆
AOC **32**
Angeli Caffé **24**
Angelini Osteria **29**
Campanile **24**
Canters **28**
Cheebo **16**
El Cholo **39**
The Fabiolus Cafe **18, 26**
Farmer's Market **33**

Martell Ave.

PARK
LA BREA

Hauser Blvd.

PAN
PACIFIC
PARK

HANCOCK
PARK **38**

ACCOMMODATIONS■
Best Western Hollywood Hills **5**
Chateau Marmont **15**
Farmer's Daughter Hotel **30**
Hollywood Roosevelt Hotel **9**
Magic Castle Hotel **6**
The Mondrian **14**
Wilshire Crest Inn **35**

CBS
Television
City

Fairfax Ave.

San Vicente Blvd.

1/4 mi
0.25 km
0

comfortable). The tree-rimmed pool area is gorgeous, and, along with the '20s Spanish Mission lobby, is a hot spot for star spotting. As we write this, Lindsay Lohan is in the middle of a lengthy residence full of all sorts of gossip-column antics. It is that sort of place, but it's also so much more.

See map p. 362. 8221 Sunset Blvd. (near Laurel Canyon Boulevard). ☎ *800-CHATEAU (800-242-8328) or 323-656-1010. Fax: 323-655-5311.* www.chateaumarmont.com. *Valet parking: $25. Rack rates: $320 and up double. AE, DC, MC, V.*

The Crescent
$$$–$$$$ Beverly Hills

Originally an auxiliary building for Paramount Pictures (in the 1920s, when the studio was located in this area, actors used it for naps between scenes), this chic hotel — formerly the charming and serviceable Beverly Crescent — has undergone a major facelift. It's still charming, but now it's also hip and sleek. Think concrete vanities in the bathrooms, flat-screen TVs, DVD players and iPods, complimentary Wi-Fi, fluffy bathrobes, and custom Italian linens in each room. **Boe,** the hotel's restaurant/lounge, draws the arty and powerful with its haute-cuisine version of Asian "street food" and fusiony dishes, and serves up an Oscar-themed signature cocktail, the Mystic River. Yet despite the fabulosity and upscale accoutrements, the Crescent is still very reasonably priced — especially for the neighborhood.

See map p. 358. 403 N. Crescent Dr. (at Brighton Way). ☎ *800-451-1566 or 310-247-0505. Fax: 310-247-9053.* www.crescentbh.com. *Valet parking: $24. Rack rates: $175–$245 double. AE, DC, DISC, MC, V.*

Elan Hotel Modern
$$–$$$ West Hollywood

Just a block from the Beverly Center, this strives for a sleek and chic image, difficult to do when the lobby looks out at a Taco Bell and a (well-combed) Goodwill. Still, they seem to bring in a lot of hip-hop business, so perhaps the image is successful enough. Essentially, the rooms have nice versions of classic hotel/motel furniture, although the bathrooms are stylish, if small, with fruity-smelling amenities. Note that you can get some traffic noise if your room faces Beverly Boulevard. Instead of calling room service, order from Jan's Coffee Shop across the street from 6 a.m. to 2 a.m. and have them jaywalk it over for you (the crosswalk is too far away). The hotel serves complimentary continental breakfast and has a nightly wine-and-cheese reception. We wish a generic hotel had this much style (note the splashes of colored tile breaking up the otherwise all-white showers) or at least that this hotel had more generic hotel prices.

See map p. 358. 8435 Beverly Blvd. (at La Cienega Boulevard). ☎ *888-661-0398 or 323-658-6663. Fax: 323-658-6640.* www.elanhotel.com. *Parking: $15. Rack rates: $169–$225 double. AE, DC, DISC, MC, V.*

Farmer's Daughter Hotel
$$ West Hollywood

For a long time, this was a rather notcrious hot-sheets hotel, but a facelift made it a hip kind of dive in the right way. It's as if someone stuck a motel, an old family hotel, and a B&B into a blender and let 'er rip. It seems to be working; right now, it's at the epicenter of fashionable action. The building still betrays its motel origins, although now it's tarted up in shades of bright blues and teals. Rooms, cute but not plush, are done in "His" and "Hers" styles (just a change in color scheme, plus rooster wallpaper for the boys) and include rocking chairs and slightly dingy gingham curtains (to evoke that farmhouse the daughter would have lived in), CD players, and high-speed Internet access. Many have balconies that overlook either busy Fairfax Avenue or the parking lot and concrete public spaces. The location, across from the Farmers Market and Grove, and down the street from the Jewish Fairfax district, is optimum, full of shopping and eating opportunities for all budgets. All rooms are nonsmoking.

See map p. 358. 115 S. Fairfax Ave. (at Beverly). ☎ *800-334-1658 or 323-937-3930. Fax: 323-932-1608.* www.farmersdaughterhotel.com. *Valet parking: $12. Rack rates: $149–$219 double. AE, DC, DISC, MC, V.*

Hilton Checkers
$$–$$$ Downtown

A gorgeous limestone-facade 1927 building (the renovated Mayflower), in a corner of L.A. that has a surprising Manhattan/San Francisco vibe, this is as well situated as a hotel in downtown can be, right next to the Central Library, across from the plush Biltmore, and an easy stroll to the Music Center and Walt Disney Concert Hall, MOCA, and the fashion and jewelry districts. Nicely styled, still fresh rooms feature great bedside lighting (a rarity), dark wood built-in Chippendale-style cabinetry, comfortable mattresses, silky duvets, and lovely cove molding. The windows actually open; even the rooms fronting Grand Avenue are quiet (not much street life in these parts in the midnight hours, and if you're out and about, you'd be well advised to drive or take cabs). Note that rooms ending in 02 are big enough to swing a cat, but only just, while 07s are the largest. You get high-speed Internet access in your room and 24-hour room service; plus, the lovely restaurant serves one of the nicest afternoon teas in town. Service is personable, well-informed, and friendly. Rates can be much, much cheaper than the rack rates suggest, especially on the weekends, so it's worth making the call, but do note that difference in the size of the rooms, if you care about that sort of thing.

535 S. Grand Ave. (between Fifth and Sixth streets). ☎ *800-423-5798 or 213-624-0000. Fax: 213-626-9906.* www.hiltoncheckers.com. *Valet parking: $26. Rack rates: $350 double weekdays, $289 double weekends. AE, DC, DISC, MC, V.*

Hollywood Roosevelt Hotel
$$$–$$$$ **Hollywood**

This fabulous old Roaring '20s Deco/Mission wonder keeps getting new leases on life. Thanks to the latest beautiful restoration, with its focus on appealing to the current crop of celebrities and beautiful people, it's once again a first choice A-list hangout. Somehow, it manages to walk the line that makes it popular with both Paris Hilton and Marilyn Monroe's ghost (who reportedly haunts the place). It doesn't hurt that that line lies smack in the middle of Hollywood Upgrade Central (across the street from Grauman's and down the street from the Hollywood & Highland Center; the Walk of Fame runs right in front of it), and you won't get more style and a better Hollywood location at a cheaper price. The rooms in the main hotel are decorated with an elegant 1950s feel — dark wood, chocolate brown, and cream predominate, and like the more expensive, more rock-'n-roll-styled cabana accommodations, feature down duvets, and wireless Internet, though the latter for a daily fee. There are views of mountains and the Hollywood sign from one side of the hotel, and the rest of the city from the other side. The very first Academy Awards banquet was held here, and David Hockney just repainted the inside of the palm-tree-ringed swimming pool, restoring his original mural. You may spot a big name or two here, especially if you rent a cabana room which guarantees you entrance into the very hip, celeb-packed Tropicana bar.

See map p. 362. 7000 Hollywood Blvd. (between La Brea and Highland avenues). ☎ *800-950-7667 or 323-466-7000. Fax: 323-469-7006.* www.hollywoodroosevelt. com. *Valet parking: $23. Rack rates: $238–$1,500 double, $400–$2,000 cabana. AE, DC, DISC, MC, V.*

Hotel Angeleno
$$$–$$$$ West Los Angeles

Ooooh, who knew West L.A. could be so sexy? Once a Holiday Inn, the Hotel Angeleno retained the building's famously phallic exterior while turning the interior in a chic, svelte collection of rooms with Italian bed linens, flat-screen TVs, natural-fiber wallpaper and luxuriously tiled bathrooms (the suites feature showers that convert to steam rooms). The modern seductive atmosphere is carried through at **West,** the top-floor lounge/Italian steakhouse with a 360-degree view of the city, a white marble bar, blown-glass chandeliers, and black-leather banquettes. The entire hotel is non-smoking, though each room has a tiny, postage-stamp balcony for nicotine fiends. The Television Academy of Arts and Science (the folks who put on the Emmys) think the place glamorous enough to hold parties and receptions poolside, while its prices are reasonable enough to lure travelers off the freeway (yes, this is hardly in a glamorous location, right at the intersection of the 405 and Sunset). The hotel is well situated for a winding drive up to Hollywood or down to the beach, and the Getty is right up the hill behind you. Check the Web site for special packages for families and business travelers.

See map p. 358. 170 N. Church Lane (at Sunset Boulevard and the 405 freeway). ☎ *866-ANGELENO or 310-476-6411. Fax: 310-472-1157. Parking: $18. Rack rates: $179–$229 double, $329 suite. AE, DISC, MC, V.*

Hotel California
$$$ Santa Monica

Cute, clean, and friendly, the Hotel California is just a stone's throw from the pier. Only the suites have ocean views, but everybody has direct beach access down a courtyard path, plus loveseats, VCRs, minifridges, pretty florals, and freshly tiled bathrooms. The rooms facing Ocean Avenue, which tend to cost less, are noisier than the courtyard rooms.

See map p. 397. 1670 Ocean Ave. (south of Colorado Avenue). ☎ *866-571-0000 or 310-393-2363. Fax: 310-393-1063. www.hotelca.com. Parking: $15. Rack rates: $169–$309 double. AE, DISC, MC, V.*

Hotel Figueroa
$$ Downtown

Someone is taking great care with a lovely old hotel. The Figueroa has, hands-down, the most gorgeous public spaces of any downtown hotel: décor in a Moorish theme (think Moroccan meets Spanish), exotic fabrics, wrought-iron and wood furniture, tiles and other decorative bits of fancy, and soaring ceilings — how the heck did this place land here? Rooms are not quite as splashy, but boy, did somebody try; they have successfully tarted up what was probably a dumpy old hotel by painting the walls with bold faux-finish paint and adding more exotic furniture and fabric. Recently, they replaced old TVs and removed the acoustic tile, exposing some wonderful beamed ceilings. Wireless Internet access is also available for a reasonable daily rate. Given that you can get similarly priced (at least, on weekends), more up-to-date rooms at the Hilton Checkers, this may not be the place for you, but note that a former top executive with a national hotel chain volunteered that this is the only place he stays when he's in town.

939 S. Figueroa St. (at Olympic Boulevard) ☎ *800-421-9092 or 213-627-8971. Fax: 213-689-0305. www.figueroahotel.com. Parking: $8. Rack rates: $124–$174 double. AE, MC, V.*

Magic Castle Hotel
$$–$$$ Hollywood

The Magic Castle is a long-time clubhouse hangout for magicians and is impossible to get into unless you're a member (or invited by one) or unless you stay at this former dump now transformed into a nice bit of lodging. (There is a $20 door charge, but trust us: It's worth it.) The gray-and-green, spanking-clean, new rooms (embellished with magician showbills) with free wireless Internet have plenty of elbow room; many rooms even have kitchenettes (grocery-shopping services are available). The on-site pool is square and situated in the middle of the courtyard, but you also have access to the curvy number up the street at the hotel's sister establishment, the all-suites

Hollywood Hills Hotel, 1999 N. Sycamore (☎ 323-874-5089; www.hollywood hillshotel.com; same rates and also worth checking out). The immediate surroundings are pulpy — as opposed to seedy — but it does have secured parking, which is good, because you'll need a car; this hotel isn't precisely walking distance to anything, although the Hollywood & Highland Center (with shops, movie theaters, and cafes, and the Janice Dickenson Modeling Agency) and the Metro station are not too many blocks (depending on your perspective) away — take advantage of the complimentary continental breakfast before you start out. It's not the most pleasant block; however, this area is ripe for transition, so take advantage of the charm and prices while you can still afford them.

See map p. 362. 7025 Franklin Ave. (between La Brea and Highland avenues). ☎ *800-741-4915 or 323-851-0800. Fax: 323-581-4926.* www.magiccastlehotel. com. *Parking: $8. Rack rates: $160–$369 double. AE, DC, DISC, MC, V.*

Maison 140
$$$ Beverly Hills

Once a boardinghouse owned by silent-screen star Lillian Gish, Maison 140 is now the sexiest, most decadently decorated hotel in the greater Los Angeles area. From the all-black lobby with the most minimal touches of white and red to the smallish but luxe rooms stocked with Frette linens, chinoiserie furnishings, and Philosophy bath products (most rooms have showers only, but you can request one with a tub), this boutique hotel swathes you in glamorous, sybaritic elegance. The hotel's sitting area is home to continental breakfast in the morning and then shifts into a full bar at cocktail hour. An off-site kitchen cooks up 24-hour room service, a small fitness center features clean new machines, and you're within walking distance of all Beverly Hills. Oh, this place is gorgeous!

See map p. 358. 140 S. Lasky Dr. (just south of Wilshire Boulevard). ☎ *800-432-5444 or 310-281-4000. Fax: 310-281-4001.* www.maison140.com. *Parking: $18. Rack rates: $149–$229 double. AE, DC, MC, V.*

The Mondrian
$$$$–$$$$$ West Hollywood

If you want creature comforts and a high hip factor, skip the equally hip Standard and stay here. It's as pretentious as can be and not quite cozy enough for the price, but celeb-heavy **Skybar** is still L.A.'s hottest watering hole; book a room to guarantee admission. If you're an early-to-bed type, be aware that shutting out the din is difficult.

See maps p. 358 and p. 362. 8440 Sunset Blvd. ☎ *800-606-6090 or 323-650-8999. Fax: 323-650-5215.* www.mondrianhotel.com. *Valet parking: $26. Rack rates: $395–$565 double. AE, DC, DISC, MC, V.*

The Mosaic Hotel
$$$–$$$$$ Beverly Hills

What was once a nice, moderately priced 49-room inn suddenly became very aware of its perfect location on a quiet street in Beverly Hills and turned itself into a very likeable boutique hotel. Think nouveau-Byzantine glass mosaic tiling meets European-*moderne* for the public areas and small but handsome and comfortable rooms with sleek black furniture upholstered in neutrals and mossy greens plus squooshy beds and sparkling bathrooms (be careful about which amenities are free and which are added to your bill, though). A sleek bar is just off the lobby and a pan-Asian restaurant in the same décor features global cuisine. The small pool is lushly landscaped and heated year-round. Despite the chic presence, the staff is most friendly. Be discrete in the elevator; more than one well-heeled and famous name uses this as a post-cosmetic-surgery retreat. Again, rack rates may not be indicative of real pricing, so make some calls. It's a lovely stay.

See map p. 358. 125 S. Spalding Dr. (south of Wilshire Boulevard). ☎ *800-463-4466 or 310-278-0303. Fax: 310-278-1728.* www.mosaichotel.com. *Parking: $25. Rack rates: $350–$700 double. AE, DC, DISC, MC, V.*

Sea Shore Motel
$$ Santa Monica

Located more or less at the beginning of the interesting bits of Main Street, this family-owned and -operated establishment admittedly looks a little dumpy on the outside, but rooms are better than that, although inexplicably Southwestern in theme (inspired, possibly, by the California Heritage Museum across the street), some with tile floors and most with oddly roomy, immaculate bathrooms. Suites feature full kitchens and separate bedrooms. No room service is offered but laundry facilities are next door, delis and restaurants are close by, the beach is just another couple of blocks west, and free parking is provided in an area where spots are otherwise impossible to come by. Unless you absolutely need a posh place to rest your head, this is a fine bargain.

See map p. 397. 2637 Main St. (just south of Ocean Park Boulevard). ☎ *310-392-2787. Fax: 310-392-5167.* www.seashoremotel.com. *Free parking. Rack rates: $105–$110 double, $180–$210 suite. AE, DISC, MC, V.*

Sheraton Delfina
$$$$–$$$$$ Santa Monica

The Sheraton Delfina is a not-always-successful hybrid between the new, hip, branded hotels and the name-brand business-style comfort expected from the Sheraton label. Nonetheless, if you frequent Sheratons, and thus might be in a position to get a discount or more, the location and the wannabe-hip vibe, particularly blatant in the public areas, make this worth considering. Rooms are snazzy, although sometimes the temperature control is a bit wonky. Bathrooms, oddly, have not been redone and as such can come as a shock. Much more stylish than a regular Sheraton, and though not exactly *immediate* walking distance to the beach and other Santa Monica locations, it's only a matter of blocks to all of it. *See map p. 397. 530 W. Pico Blvd.* ☎ *888-627-8532 or 310-399-9344. Fax: 310-399-2504.* www.thesheraton.com. *Parking: $22. Rack rates: $399–$500 double. AE, DC, DISC, MC, V.*

Shutters on the Beach
$$$$$ Santa Monica

Staying at Shutters is like staying at a really rich friend's L.A. beach house. In fact, you might well spot some folks who used to be on *Friends* or, at least, seem oddly familiar, until you realize you recognize them from CD and magazine covers. Facing Santa Monica Beach in all its gray-clapboarded glory, this oceanfront gem is a stunner. Rooms are airy and gorgeous, with such playful touches as rubber duckies in the whirlpool tubs and nighttime storybooks on the Frette-made beds. The food is terrific, and the casually elegant service is excellent.

See map p. 397. 1 Pico Blvd. (at the beach!). ☎ *800-334-9000 or 310-458-0030. Fax: 310-458-4589.* www.shuttersonthebeach.com. *Valet parking: $27. Rack rates: $480–$775 double. AE, DC, DISC, MC, V.*

The Standard–Downtown
$$–$$$$$ Downtown

Downtown's first hipster hotel and one that is long overdue, the Standard offers style on top of style, and is self-consciously playful if a little chilly, although the staff is friendly enough. This is where the happening downtown nightly scene finds a place to kick it, complete with a live DJ spinning in the lobby at night. Rooms are design conscious, with platform beds and "desks" that are really a wide shelf running under the entire 14-foot length of the windows. In the smallest rooms (not that small — 300 sq. ft., which is why room categories are called Huge, Gigantic, Enormous, and Wow!, and can go up to $1,000 a night), a shower-only bathroom has said shower separated from the sleeping area by a glass wall. Peekaboo! (You can request rooms without this feature, if modesty demands it.) The sexy pool area has a wonderful view of downtown, plus cabanas with round water beds and a bar. You can imagine the scene up here at night.

550 South Flower St. (at Sixth Street). ☎ *213-892-8080. Fax: 213-892-8686.* www.standardhotel.com. *Valet parking: $25. Rack rates: $99–$1,000 double. AE, MC, V.*

Valadon
$$$–$$$$ West Hollywood

Located in a quiet residential neighborhood, a short walk up a steep hill from the Sunset Strip, this is a definite budget bargain, but only if you don't have serious aesthetic needs. Not that there is anything wrong with this hotel, but its '80s-era décor is not going to wow you. But here's the thing: The smallest room has a decent amount of space, including a kitchenette or, at least, a breakfast nook, while the next level up, the junior suite, has a sunken living/sitting area. And all accommodations have gas fireplaces (with remote controls, naturally), which just adds to the hilarity factor. The small rooftop pool has near-360-degree city views. When you see how these prices compare to some of the fancier, and smaller, digs around, the dated style probably won't bother you a bit.

See map p. 358. 8822 Cynthia St. (off San Vicente Boulevard). ☎ *800-835-7997 or 310-854-1114. Fax: 310-657-2623. Parking: $18. Rack rates: $285–$376 double. AE, DC, DISC, MC, V.*

Venice Beach House
$$–$$$ Venice

If you were to take the best of what L.A. has to offer, what makes this city its own and not some other random large city, and shrink it down and then make it a B&B, it might look something like this. An archetypal Craftsman home, steps away from the beach (the sandy part, anyway), surrounded by lawn (the front gate leading right to the walk to the beach). with bougainvillea and other blooms, it's the dream of L.A., for sure. (The nightmare of L.A. being the hideous modern apartment buildings that block the home's formerly perfect ocean views.) Each room has its own theme — from the tiny Tramp's Quarters (the smallest room) to the spacious Pier Suite (with a fireplace and sitting room) — and delights (such as the wool-plaid-upholstered walls in Abbot Kinney's room and the fireplace in the James Peasgood room), as well as its own drawbacks (size varies, and four rooms share two bathrooms between them). The good parts of Main Street, not to mention the delights of Santa Monica, are a good hike away, so plan on having a car (although restaurants are within walking distance).

See map p. 397. 15 30th Ave. (at Speedway). ☎ *310-823-1966. Fax: 310-823-1842* www.venicebeachhouse.com. *Parking: $12. Rack rates: $144–$235 double. AE, MC, V.*

Wilshire Crest Inn
$$ Near Beverly Hills

Wilshire Boulevard is a major artery for L.A., moving from downtown to the beach, past museums and shopping areas with regular, swift public transportation along its busy lanes. And the freshly painted and updated owner-operated Wilshire Crest Inn (which is actually right off Wilshire on a side street), a reasonably priced, attractive hotel, is perfectly situated to take advantage of all that the boulevard offers. Rooms are good-sized and the dining room off the lobby has complimentary pastries, bagels, coffee, and tea in the morning, which draws visiting staff from the nearby consulates plus guest speakers and curators from the many museums down the road.

See maps p. 358 and p. 362. 6301 Orange St. (off Crescent Heights, north of Wilshire Boulevard). ☎ *800-654-9951 or 323-936-5131. Fax: 323-936-2013.* www.wilshirecrestinn.com. *Free parking. Rack rates: $89–$109 double. AE, DC, DISC, MC, V.*

Where to Dine in Los Angeles

You can eat very well in Los Angeles, whether you're feasting at gold-plated institutions, innovative up-and-comers, or, in particular, at one of the innumerable hole-in-the-wall ethnic joints that serve up delicious creations for a pittance. We try to give you a cross-section of all that, mostly in the areas of town in which you're most likely to find yourself.

For restaurants in the Westside and Beverly Hills, see the "Westside and Beverly Hills Accommodations, Dining, and Attractions" map earlier in this chapter. For restaurants in Hollywood, go to the "Hollywood Accommodations, Dining, and Attractions" map earlier in this chapter. For restaurants in Santa Monica and the beaches, go to the "Santa Monica and the Malibu Beaches" map in the "Hitting the beaches" section later in this chapter.

Angeli Caffé
$$ West Hollywood   RUSTIC REGIONAL ITALIAN

Evan Kleiman, the chef/owner of this much-beloved near-institution, is known for her dedication to the local farmers' markets, ensuring that her menu always reflects the seasons. (She also hosts the local public radio station's food show on Saturdays.) Curious experiments with produce aside, you can expect dedicatedly authentic Italian. This may seem like a chic cafe, but it's quite child friendly; kids who come in are given a ball of dough to mash and shape as they please. The dough is then cooked in the oven and presented to them when it's done, a process that can keep the most wriggly kid entertained enough for the parents to enjoy a nice meal.

See map p. 362. 7274 Melrose Ave. (near Alta Vista Boulevard). ☎ *323-936-9086.* www.angelicaffe.com. *Reservations highly recommended. Main courses: $10–$25. AE, DISC, MC, V. Open: Tues–Fri 11:30 a.m.–2:30 p.m., Tues–Sun 5–11 p.m.*

Angelini Osteria
$$–$$$ West Hollywood   HOME-STYLE ITALIAN

The operators of this instantly likable restaurant (everyone seems so darned pleased when you come in) are long-time fixtures on the L.A. dining scene (Chef Gino Angelini cooked for the now-defunct Rex in downtown L.A.); consequently, this establishment was an almost instant hit. Of course, that success is also due to the quality of the food — genuine Italian cooking, lovingly and thoughtfully prepared. All the pastas are heavenly, but only at lunch will you find Nonna Elvira's (that's Gino's mom) green lasagna, light and airy, topped with flash-fried spinach, a former favorite at Rex. A children's menu has a few simple dishes for the less curious of palate.

See map p. 362. 7313 Beverly Blvd. (near Martell Avenue). ☎ *323-297-0070.* www.angeliniosteria.com. *Reservations recommended. Main courses: $12–$24 lunch, $20–$38 dinner. AE, MC, V. Open: Tues–Fri noon–2:30 p.m., Tues–Sun 5:30–10:30 p.m.*

A.O.C.
$$$ West Hollywood   MEDITERRANEAN/TAPAS

From the people who brought Lucques (see the listing later in this section) to L.A., this brick-lined place (a little too noisy to be romantic) specializes in "small plates." Think tapas — not necessarily just Spanish or just appetizers, but necessarily divine ones — or even sampling the wares at the best French or Tuscan countryside grocer you can imagine. The wine list (the establishment's name is an abbreviation for the Appellation d'Origine Contrôlée laws of France, which govern all wine) is a finely tuned standout, because this is really a wine bar that serves interesting food, and all these small plates are meant to enhance that experience.

See map p. 358. 8022 W. Third St. ☎ *323-653-6359.* www.aocwinebar.com. *Reservations strongly suggested. Small plates under $15 (but adds up to around $30–$40 a person). AE, MC, V. Open: Mon–Fri 6–11 p.m., Sat 5:30–11 p.m., Sun 5:30–10 p.m.*

Border Grill
$$–$$$ Santa Monica   MEXICAN

This modern cantina from Mary Sue Milliken and Susan Feniger, the Food Network's "Too Hot Tamales" (and the authors of *Mexican Cooking For Dummies,* published by Wiley), is a brash, bold, colorful space serving up inspired South-of-the-Border cuisine. The ladies' creative cooking is firmly rooted in the traditional Mexican canon, so if you're looking for gloopy Southern California Mexican (and there is nothing wrong with that), you may be disappointed, until, of course, you find out what real Mexican home cooking is like. Despite the overall quality, we'd suggest avoiding basic meat entrees, because they can be dry.

See map p. 397. 1445 Fourth St. (between Broadway and Santa Monica Boulevard). ☎ *310-451-1655.* www.bordergrill.com. *Reservations recommended. Main courses: $8–$20 lunch, $15–$30 dinner. AE, DC, DISC, MC, V. Open: Sun–Thurs 11:30 a.m.–10 p.m., Fri–Sat 11:30 a.m.–11 p.m.*

Bread & Porridge
$ Santa Monica   AMERICAN

This adorable little cafe is most notable for breakfast, although lunch is worthwhile as well. Omelets are huge affairs (the vegetarian: three eggs, spinach, mushroom, tomato, cheddar cheese, and onion, garnished with red potatoes and fruit), and the fluffy, well-constructed pancakes aren't much smaller (we admit to having a great fondness for the kid-pleasing chocolate-chip ones, oozing melted chocolatey goodness) — in short, all of it portioned to share. *Note:* It's a popular place, and on the small side, so you may want to time your meal for off-hours.

See map p. 397. 2315 Wilshire Blvd. (near 26th Street). ☎ *310-453-4941. Reservations not necessary. Main courses: $5–$10 breakfast, $8–$12 lunch. AE, DISC, MC, V. Open: Daily 7 a.m.–2 p.m.*

Campanile

$$$–$$$$ West Hollywood   CALIFORNIA/MEDITERRANEAN

Campanile is one of two restaurants most likely to be the answer to the question, "What's the best restaurant in L.A.?" We won't say for sure that Campanile can live up to the hype (but to be fair, what could?), but we will say it's someplace special. Chef/owner Mark Peel is a great talent, and his ex-wife, Nancy Silverton, is the genius behind La Brea Bakery (their bread is served all over the city), the original of which is next door. Come for dinner, where you may eat the likes of a beautifully simple bibb lettuce and herb salad with lemon vinaigrette and *fleur de sel* (one of the finest salads we've ever tried), rosemary-charred baby lamb, cedar-smoked Tasmanian salmon, pulled-pork ravioli, or even precious Persian mulberries (only during a very short July season); or for brunch, considered the best in town; or for Thursday night, when they try gourmet twists on the humble grilled-cheese sandwich. And always save room for dessert; the pastry chef is renowned.

See map p. 362. 624 S. La Brea Ave. (north of Wilshire Boulevard). ☎ *323-938-1447.* www.campanilerestaurant.com. *Reservations recommended. Main courses: $15–$24 lunch, 22–$38 dinner. AE, DC, DISC, MC, V. Open: Mon–Fri 11:30 a.m.–2:30 p.m., Sat–Sun 9:30 a.m.–1:30 p.m., Mon–Thurs 6–10 p.m., Fri–Sat 5:30–11 p.m.*

Canter's Deli

$$ West Hollywood   DELICATESSEN

We just love Canter's. It's the whole package: a classic old deli, open 24 hours, full of both elderly Jewish couples and young hipsters, all drawn to the large menu and solidly good food. (Okay, the hipsters come because they can get soup at 3 a.m., and because two good clubs are across the street; plus, Canter's own **Kibitz Room** hosts its own music shows — for years, before he was anyone other than his father's son, Jacob Dylan played there regularly.) We've eaten more than our share of Canter's brisket (the Brooklyn: brisket, Russian dressing, and slaw on a roll) when we weren't eating a bagel liberally covered with lox. But that's just us.

See maps p. 358 and p. 362. 419 N. Fairfax Ave. (just north of Beverly Boulevard). ☎ *323-651-2030.* www.cantersdeli.com. *No reservations. Main courses: $4.95–$13 sandwiches, $8.95–$15 entrees. DISC, MC, V. Open: Daily 24 hours.*

Cheebo

$–$$ West Hollywood   ITALIAN

A playful spot with a kid's menu that works for families (although don't expect a kiddie-place — the Tangiers style makes it quirky and grown-up) and if you're on a budget, Cheebo also attracts a decent number of Bright Young Things (or at least, those wishing to become BYT by scoring a TV series). It's best known for its long (up to a yard, although that's for take-out only), narrow, sourdough-bready pizzas, with a variety of toppings ranging from the traditional (maybe not pepperoni, but certainly homemade sausage with fennel or pesto and mushrooms) to the sort of ingredients we here in California liberally throw on pizza dough (goat cheese, smoked salmon). Sandwiches, especially the popular pressed pork, are also a good choice, as are hearty pastas.

See maps p. 358 and p. 362. 7533 Sunset Blvd. (at Sierra Bonita). ☎ *323-850-7070.* www. cheebo.com. *Reservations suggested. Main courses: Under $15 breakfast, $8.75–$25 lunch, $9–$25 dinner. AE, MC, V. Open: Mon–Sat 8 a.m.–11 p.m., Sun 8 a.m.–10 p.m.*

Ciudad
S$–$$$ Downtown   LATIN

The two "Too Hot Tamales," Mary Sue Milliken and Susan Feniger, the hard-working chefs behind Border Grill, branched out a bit with this downtown

The cupcake revolution

The current rage in Los Angeles is the cupcake elevated from its days as the humble dessert your mom used to bring to your grade-school class on your birthday. Monster sizes, gourmet flavors — they're so simple and yet sublime. You can find fancy-pants cupcakes at Joan's and Lucky Devil's, listed elsewhere, but why not try a place dedicated to the art of all things cupcake?

Sprinkles, 9635 Little Santa Monica Blvd., Beverly Hills (☎ 310-274-8765; www. sprinklescupcakes.com), boldly started out steps from Rodeo Drive and was rewarded when all sorts of Beverly Hills patrons forgot their diets and stood in lines around the block. After receiving a box from none other than Barbra Streisand, Oprah declared these her favorite cupcakes. In just two short years, they already plan to spread Sprinkles around the country, with upcoming branches in a number of other cities. Their assortment changes daily (we're partial to the red velvet and the Callebaut dark chocolate), so check their Web site to place orders in advance in case you don't want to miss out on a favorite flavor.

Well-situated for tourists needing a sugar rush post–Universal Studios, **Yummy Cupcakes,** 2918 W. Magnolia, Burbank (☎ 818-558-1080; www.yummycupcakes. com), has even fancier, ridiculous confections (including flavors like pink lemonade and rocky road), some of which feature cream in the center. And if that's not enough, try their cupcake bar, where they will frost to order.

Nearby, and thus allowing for compare-and-contrast possibilities, is the brand-new **Big Sugar Bakeshop,** 12182 Ventura Blvd., Studio City (so new it doesn't have a phone yet; www.bigsugarbakeshop.com), whose owners have spent years thrilling the sweet teeth of a number of TV and movie types. In addition to cupcakes of wonder, they offer other fantastic baked goods, including gold-rush brownies and cakes of all description. Don't be surprised to see various TV shows, which shoot nearby on the CBS Radford lot, filling large orders for a hungry cast and crew. It's open early seven days a week, which means that, unlike other cupcake-exclusive stores, it can offer morning-appropriate treats such as doughnuts and muffins. Look for special flavors each day, including lemon buttercream with fresh lemon and the Dalmatian, which is studded with mini chocolate chips.

location. (Check out their book *Mexican Cooking For Dummies,* published by Wiley.) Hearty, world-wise dishes such as Argentine wild-mushroom empanadas, short ribs glazed with South American barbecue sauce, super-moist chicken bathed in sweet garlic, and traditional Cuban pressed sandwiches are served in a sophisticated space that's a playful blend of contemporary art and Austin Powers mod. Ciudad is perfect for pretheater dining — or as a special trip on its own.

445 S. Figueroa St., Suite 100 (at Fifth Street). ☎ *213-486-5171.* www.ciudad-la. com. *Reservations recommended. Main courses: $12–$18 lunch, $16–$29 dinner. AE, DC, DISC, MC, V. Open: Mon–Tues 11:30 a.m.–9 p.m., Wed–Thurs 11:30 a.m.–10 p.m., Fri 11:30 a.m.–11 p.m., Sat 5–11 p.m., Sun 5–9 p.m.*

Clementine
$ West Los Angeles   HOMEMADE SEASONAL FOOD

A small, charming cafe on a side street near Century City, Clementine has quickly become a local favorite. The menu changes seasonally, so only the most current, fresh ingredients are used in its sandwiches and salads. But here are some things you can get anytime: tiny ham biscuits; hot chocolate with homemade marshmallows; perfect deviled eggs; bacon and cheddar flat bread; sweet cream-filled cupcakes; and many, many cookies and tarts. We've had more marvelous sandwiches here than we can possibly list, especially during Grilled Cheese Month (that's April to you) when they have a different creation every day (from salami, fontina, and cherry tomatoes to cheddar, applewood-smoked bacon, and apples). Parking is a pain and tables are hard to find at the peak of lunch and weekend breakfast, so try to come at an off hour.

See map p. 358. 1751 Ensley Ave. (near Santa Monica Boulevard). ☎ *310-552-1080.* www.clementineonline.com. *Reservations not necessary. Main courses: Everything under $10. AE, DISC, MC, V. Open: Mon–Fri 7 a.m.–7:30 p.m., Sat 8 a.m.– 5 p.m.*

Cora's Coffee Shop
$–$$ Santa Monica   DINER

The coffee-shop concept somewhat L.A.-ized, which is to say that the menu at this restored 1920s classic greasy spoon looks awfully familiar until you realize the enormous, drippy burgers are made of fancy beef, the plate-sized pancakes are orange-flavored, and there is *buratta* (fresh mozzarella with a heart of pure cream — a sublime cheese) on the salad. (Heck, there's a salad! What self-respecting diner has that?) Devotees won't eat anywhere else; critics complain it's too costly. Well, for a diner, maybe. But otherwise? It's tiny, it's crowded, it's easy to miss, but don't, because it's got so much packed into it. Okay, maybe give it a miss on Sundays when the wait is ridiculous.

See map p. 397. 1802 Ocean Ave. ☎ *310-451-9562. No reservations. Main courses: Everything under $15. AE, MC, V. Open: Tues–Sat 7 a.m.–2 p.m.*

El Cholo
$–$$ Hollywood/Santa Monica   MEXICAN

L.A.'s oldest Mexican restaurant — since 1927 — is as popular as ever, thanks to legendary frosty margaritas; marvelous green corn tamales; classic monster combo plates; and fresh, chunky guacamole that sets the standard. Nothing ground-breaking, but that's the whole, satisfying idea. For best results, bypass the newer beach location (on Wilshire Boulevard) for the original pink hacienda on Hollywood's outskirts.

See maps p. 362 and p. 397. 1121 S. Western Ave. (south of Olympic Boulevard). ☎ 323-734-2773. 1025 Wilshire Blvd. ☎ 310-899-1106. www.elcholo.com. *Reservations recommended at dinner. Main courses: $10–$17. AE, DC, DISC, MC, V. Open: Mon–Thurs 11 a.m.–10 p.m., Fri–Sat 11 a.m.–11 p.m., Sun 11 a.m.–9 p.m.*

The Fabiolus Cafe
$–$$ Hollywood   ITALIAN

Sure, this often-overlooked Italian restaurant may not be as innovative as some, but it ain't all spaghetti and meatballs. Portions are generous (we've rarely finished one), prices are reasonable, and everything is cooked fresh. In addition, bowls of olive oil dipping sauce accompany the bread. They have two locations, and both are colorful and pleasant. What more could you want? (Avoid the Melrose location at lunchtime; it's located near Paramount and tends to fill up with studio folks.)

See map p. 362. 6270 W. Sunset Blvd. (near Argyle Avenue). ☎ 323-467-2882. 5255 Melrose Ave. ☎ 323-464-5857. www.fabiolus.org. *Reservations always recommended. Main courses: $8.95–$20 lunch; $9.95–$21 dinner. AE, DC, DISC, MC, V. Open: Daily 11:30 a.m.–10 p.m.*

Farmers Market
$ Hollywood   GLOBAL

Can't agree on what to eat? No problem! Head to this L.A. landmark, the original food court. The 65-year-old indoor-outdoor bazaar is a global bonanza of good eats, from French crepes and Chinese combo plates to home-baked cakes and pies to gumbo and beignets, traditional Indonesia and Mexican food, and pizza and panini . . . you get the picture. You can choose from two sit-down diners (one trendy, one traditional), plus an oyster bar and a couple of beer-and-wine bars. The atmosphere is pleasingly festive, especially at weekend brunchtime, and the vendors are budget-friendly across the board.

See maps p. 358 and p. 362. 6333 W. Third St. ☎ 323-933-9211. www.farmers marketla.com. *No reservations. Prices vary by vendor. No credit cards. Open: Mon–Fri 9 a.m–9 p.m., Sat 9 a.m.–8 p.m., Sun 9 a.m.–7 p.m.*

Grand Central Market
$ Downtown VARIOUS

Operating since 1914, the Grand Central Market is precisely the sort of chaotic marketplace (open sides, but with a roof overhead) you'd find in, say, Turkey or Malaysia, but not in Los Angeles. Stall after stall offers fresh produce, spices, meats (check out those cow tongues!), and junky toys and kitsch, and in between all that is stall after stall selling some of the best and most affordable Mexican food in town — when they aren't hawking Thai, Chinese, or deli fare.

317 S. Broadway (near Third Street). ☎ *213-624-2378.* www.grandcentralsquare. com. *No reservations. Prices vary by vendor. No credit cards. Open: Daily 9 a.m.–6 p.m.*

Hungry Cat
$$$ Hollywood DINER/SEAFOOD

A casual spot from the culinary star behind Lucques and A.O.C., this charmingly named bistro is meant to evoke a seafood bar in San Francisco, or a beach shack in New England, where patrons order up a dozen oysters, and then a lobster roll, and then maybe another half-dozen oysters. Oddly, though, its most popular item is its burger, possibly the best of the double-digit-priced ones around, and all the better for being topped with blue cheese and served on a La Brea bakery roll. The lobster roll (butter style, rather than mayo) has its frenetic fans, though anyone who has been to Maine won't be impressed with the size and price. If you're in the area for a movie at the ArcLight, or shopping at Amoeba records, or just sightseeing in Hollywood, it is a quality spot for a light meal, particularly because of the commendable wine list.

See map p. 362. 1535 N. Vine St. ☎ *323-462-2155.* www.thehungrycat.com. *Reservations not necessary. Main courses: $8–$22. AE, MC, V. Open: Tues–Fri 11:30 a.m.–2:30 p.m., Mon–Sat 5:30 p.m.–midnight, Sun 5:30–11 p.m.*

Jar
$$$$ West Hollywood STEAKHOUSE

This instantly likable space (modern, clean, just a step or two above cozy) was co-created by Mark Peel of Campanile and — thanks to a recent makeover — is even better than ever. Most days, it's a steakhouse, and though hardly burger-stand cheap, it's certainly more affordable than its peers around town. Even so, who could have predicted the single most popular dish would be pot roast? Braised with care and cooked for hours until it falls apart at a touch, it's what Mom would make if she were a gourmet cook. The steaks are just fine, and the sides heavenly, but oh, that pot roast. Meanwhile, think about coming here on Monday nights, when Nancy Silverton (late of Campanile) presides over Mozzarella Mondays, creating all sorts of divine nibbles with a certain creamy fresh Italian cheese. Be warned, though: Most of L.A. finds that night a good one to drop by, too.

See maps p. 358 and p. 362. 8225 Beverly Blvd. (corner of Harper Avenue, between La Cienega and Fairfax boulevards). ☎ 323-655-6566. www.thejar.com. Reservations recommended. Main courses: $13–$45. AE, DC, MC, V. Open: Tues–Sat 5:30–10:30 p.m., Sun 10 a.m.– 2 p.m. and 5:30–10 p.m.

Joan's on Third

$ West Hollywood   TUSCAN/MEDITERRANEAN

It's just a tiny little cafe, better known for takeout (although they do have a few tables), but it's an absolute treasure. From the lovely sandwiches (ham and brie with mustard caper sauce or turkey meatloaf) on fresh, terrific bread (the baguettes, especially) to daily specials (pesto-crusted salmon or grilled maple-rosemary chicken breast), salads of all sorts, and finally, but most importantly, the desserts, everything is a delight. They also have a small but well-chosen cheese counter. Skip some fancy place for dinner and get Joan's for takeout to eat in your hotel room or at a nearby park.

See map p. 358. 8350 W. Third St. (near Beverly Boulevard). ☎ 323-655-2285. www.joansonthird.com. No reservations. Main courses: Everything under $12. AE, MC, V. Open: Mon–Sat 10 a.m.–8 p.m., Sun 11 a.m.–6 p.m.

Kate Mantilini
$$$ Beverly Hills   AMERICAN

This perennial favorite is still stylish and popular, especially among the late-night crowd. The mammoth menu offers something for everyone, including upscale takes on traditional American diner fare. The restaurant features a full bar, excellent meatloaf, and valet parking.

See map p. 358. 9101 Wilshire Blvd. (at Doheny Drive). ☎ 310-278-3699. Reservations accepted for six or more. Main courses: $14–$38. AE, MC, V. Open: Mon–Thurs 7:30 a.m.–1 a.m., Fri 7:30 a.m.–2 a.m., Sat 11 a.m.–2 a.m., Sun 10 a.m.–midnight.

Lawry's The Prime Rib
$$$$$ Beverly Hills   PRIME RIB

Okay, it has been around a long, long time. But darn it, Lawry's is good — as long as you like prime rib. Otherwise, it's not so good. Time was when Lawry's had only one dish — the prime rib — but now they've added chicken and fish. Don't bother with those. Come, instead, for a ritual shared by generations of Angelenos, one unchanged by time. You eat one heck of a good cut of prime rib, possibly as good as you've ever had. You may want to have dessert. That's all. And that's enough.

See map p. 358. 100 N. La Cienega Blvd. (just north of Wilshire Boulevard). ☎ 310-652-2827. www.lawrysonline.com. Reservations recommended. Main courses: $28–$41. AE, DC, DISC, MC, V. Open: Mon–Fri 5–10 p.m., Sat 4:30–11 p.m., Sun 4–9:30 p.m.

Lucky Devils
$–$$ Hollywood   DINER

Only in Los Angeles can a guy who had his 15 minutes of fame playing an oh-so-shirtless construction worker in a Diet Coke commercial open up a popular diner, and get people to pay $14 for a burger — and a good one, at that. The place also serves up all-beef hot dogs, gourmet cupcakes made with Scharffenberger chocolate, and thick shakes made with toasted pecan and bourbon vanilla. Also, Lucky (Vanous, that is), often presides over the joint. Hmm. Come to think of it, we are glad this place is here.

See map p. 362. 6613 Hollywood Blvd. (at Cherokee). ☎ *323-465-8259.* www.lucky devilshollywood.com. *Sun–Wed 11 a.m.–midnight, Fri–Sat 11a.m.–3a.m. AE, DISC, MC, V.*

Lucques
$$$–$$$$ West Hollywood   CALIFORNIA

A star in the L.A. foodie firmament, Lucques (say "Luke" — it's a kind of olive, and one that is placed on your table, along with salt, sweet butter, and wonderful bread) features California cuisine with French and Mediterranean influences. The menu changes seasonally; a recent lunch menu offered duck confit with celery root remoulade and a grilled pork burger with chipotle aioli. Dinner features items such as grilled snapper with winter vegetables, Portuguese pork and clams with chorizo, and Lucques's (quickly growing famous) braised short ribs. Desserts may feature bittersweet chocolate pot de crème. (A.O.C., a "small plates" restaurant listed earlier in this section, is from the same chef-owner.)

See map p. 358. 8474 Melrose Ave. (east of La Cienega Boulevard). ☎ *323-655-6277.* www.lucques.com. *Reservations recommended. Main courses: $20–$44, Sun three-course prix-fixe dinner $40. AE, DC, MC, V. Open: Tues–Sat noon–2:30 p.m., Mon–Sat 6–11 p.m., Sun 5:30–10 p.m.*

Off Vine
$$–$$$ Hollywood   AMERICAN

A charming restaurant in an old Craftsman house, Off Vine doesn't have the high profile it used to, and that's a shame, because we've never *not* enjoyed a meal here, both for taste and ambience. There's nothing, truth be told, shockingly innovative at Off Vine, but you aren't going to feel cheated, because the food is interesting enough and done well, and the prices are reasonable. The room is pretty, as is the plant-filled courtyard. It's romantic but not intimidating, and nicely situated for the Hollywood area.

See map p. 362. 6263 Leland Way (off Vine Street). ☎ *323-962-1900.* www.offvine. com. *Reservations accepted. Main courses: $10–$18 lunch, $12–$28 dinner. AE, DC, DISC, MC, V. Open: Mon–Thurs 11:30 a.m.–2:30 p.m., Fri 11:30 a.m.–3 p.m., Sat–Sun 10:30 a.m.–2:30 p.m., Mon–Thurs 5:30–10:30 p.m., Fri 5:30–11:30 p.m., Sat 5–11:30 p.m., Sun 5–10 p.m.*

101 Coffee Shop
$–$$ Hollywood DINER

A landmark restaurant, kinda, in that it's housed in the Best Western Hollywood Hills Hotel, the side of which carries a large sign informing the freeway-bound that it is the "Last Cappuccino until the 101," a sign that has turned up in various movies, including *The Brady Bunch*. The original coffee shop the sign used to signal, featured in the movie *Swingers*, has since closed; however the 101 has taken its place nicely. Check out the hours ("Why even close at all?" wonders one loyal patron), check out the patrons in the booth next to you (you've probably seen them in some movie, TV show, rock video, or commercial), and check out the menu, featuring thick, hearty soups; honest tuna melts; more-exotic salmon and grilled skirt steak; plus Mexican-style specialties; wonderful banana shakes; and honest-to-gosh breakfasts (served all day). It's an essential, you bet.

See map p. 362. 6145 Franklin Ave. (in the Best Western Hollywood Hills Hotel). ☎ 323-467-1175. No reservations. Main courses: $6.50–$14. AE, DISC, MC, V. Open: Daily 7 a.m.–3 a.m.

Patina
$$$$$ Hollywood FRENCH-CALIFORNIAN

The Patina is the other restaurant (besides Campanile and newcomer Providence) justly considered by most to be L.A.'s finest, and the first by Joachim Splichal, whose name (and restaurant conglomerate, the Patina Group) pops up a great deal more here. Originally based in Melrose, Patina moved into a corner of the newly opened Disney Hall in 2003; the Patina Group had previously had good luck with restaurants in both the Music Center and MOCA. The result, visually, is the very model of a modern restaurant. The menu will change, but here's what we ate recently, and see if this doesn't read like food pornography: a "Quartet of the Sea" (components change nightly, but we ate butter-soft hamachi with a confit of grapefruit, miso-glazed smoked eel on marinated shitake mushrooms, Spanish anchovies with fried capers and olive tapenade, and bluefin tuna tartar); hand-rolled pasta alla Chitarra, with wild mushrooms and porcini espuma (that's foam); a large piece of plump, superb sautéed foie gras with black pepper rhubarb compote, green pepper emulsion, and pink peppercorn ice cream; 1¼ pounds of lobster placed in a hollowed-out artichoke heart, lightly touched with butter and artichoke foam. Note that the restaurant often is less in demand while a show is in progress, but quite full right before and right after.

141 Grand Ave. (between First and Second). ☎ 213-972-3331. www.patinagroup.com. *Reservations strongly recommended. Main courses: $17–$24 lunch, $34–$40 dinner (tasting menus higher). AE, DC, DISC, MC, V. Open: Mon–Fri 11:30 a.m.–1:30 p.m., daily 5–10:45 p.m.*

Philippe the Original
$ Downtown AMERICAN/SANDWICHES

Believe it or not, some people in L.A. have never heard of Philippe's, which completely bemuses those who consider it an essential component of life in this city. Founded in 1918 — which, right there, is reason enough to come — Philippe's claims that one day its owner dropped part of a sandwich roll in the juices of a roast beef and gave it to a customer who raved. Voila! — the French dip was invented. Throw in a 10¢ cup of coffee and a clientele that ranges from punks to opera goers, and you have a true L.A. experience. And the sandwiches are darn good.

1001 N. Alameda St. (at Ord Street). ☎ *213-628-3781.* www.philippes.com. *Reservations not necessary. Main courses: Everything under $10. No credit cards. Open: Daily 6 a.m.–10 p.m.*

Pink's
$ West Hollywood HOT DOG STAND

A dumpy little hot dog stand, you may think, except there *is* that line of people standing outside at all hours of the day or night. Hmmm. Do they know something you don't? You bet — except, of course, we're letting you in on the secret: Pink's has divine hot dogs, juicy, with a casing that has the right amount of snap, available with chili or Chicago-dog style, or just plain.

See map p. 362. 709 N. La Brea Ave. (at Melrose Avenue). ☎ *323-931-4223.* www. pinkshollywood.com. *No reservations. Main courses: Everything under $10. No credit cards. Open: Sun–Thurs 9:30 a.m.–2 a.m., Fri–Sat 9:30 a.m.–3 a.m.*

Providence
$$$$$ Hollywood FRENCH/SEAFOOD

It's nervy, taking over the space formerly occupied by what many considered the best restaurant in L.A. but Providence has proved itself a sublime successor to Patina (now near the Disney Hall downtown). Scoring a James Beard nomination for Best New Restaurant in 2006, the place hit the ground running and is one of the finest dining options in the city right now. Because of a deep commitment to seasonal ingredients, the menu changes frequently, but the emphasis is on innovative, French-inspired preparations of seafood. (There may well be some obscure Asian fish you have never encountered among the evening's offerings. Try it.) Having said that, its foie gras preparations can make foodies weep, and we were ridiculously happy over a crispy-skinned pork belly appetizer. Not so much a place for romantic dining (it's sexy, but a little noisy), but it is a place for grown-up considerations of the possibilities of food.

See map p. 362. 5955 Melrose Ave. ☎ *323-460-4170. Reservations not necessary. Main courses: $17–$35, tasting menu $95. AE, D, MC, V. Open: Mon–Fri 6–10 p.m., Sat 5:30–10 p.m., Sun 5:30–9 p.m.*

Sanamluang Cafe
$ Hollywood THAI

We call it "Samalangadingdong," because we can never remember how to pronounce it, but this carelessness does not reflect our real feelings for this utterly unprepossessing cafe. It's the first place we think of when we want to eat Thai food. Sanamluang is famous for its noodle dishes (General's Noodles are full of garlic, pork, duck, and spices; a bowlful feeds several and can cure the common cold), and you won't believe how good and cheap the food is. (We've brought a group of 7, ordered 11 dishes, and ended up paying about $7 each.) Open way late, it's situated in a tacky minimall.

See map p. 362. 5170 Hollywood Blvd. (near Winona Boulevard). ☎ *323-660-8006. Reservations not necessary. Main courses: Everything under $9. MC, V. Open: Daily 10:30 a.m.–4 a.m.*

Spago Beverly Hills
$$$$$ Beverly Hills CALIFORNIA

America's first celebrity chef, Wolfgang Puck, has created a fitting temple to California cuisine in his high-style signature restaurant. Is the one that started it all everything it's cracked up to be? Oddly enough, apparently so. Local foodies continue to rave. Certainly, it's an experience. Expect accents from Puck's native Austria on the Cal-French menu, and a high glam factor in the crowd. Book a table on the twinkle-lit patio if the weather's nice, and be sure to ask for the not-on-the-menu favorite, the Jewish Pizza (smoked salmon and crème fraiche).

See map p 358. 176 N. Cañon Dr. (just north of Wilshire Boulevard). ☎ *310-385-0880. www.wolfgangpuck.com. Reservations a must. Main courses: $17–$49 lunch, $31–$76 dinner, tasting menu $120, $160 with wine pairing. AE, DC, DISC, MC, V. Open: Mon–Fri 11:30 a.m.–2:30 p.m., Sat noon–2:30 p.m., Sun–Thurs 5:30–10:30 p.m., Fri–Sat 5:30–11 p.m.*

Sushi Gen
$$ Downtown JAPANESE

Although, to a certain extent, an argument can be made that all sushi places are created equal, that argument is made only by someone who has never experienced truly good sushi. And then there are those who say that you can have that kind of experience only in pricey locales, such as Los Angeles's Matsuhisa, and perhaps they're right — but you can come darn close for considerably less money at Sushi Gen. When you've had Sushi Gen's lovely, ultrafresh cuts of yellowtail or *toro* (fatty tuna), it's hard to go back. Plus, the appetizer menu features "original salted squid guts."

422 E. Second St. (near South Central Avenue). ☎ *213-617-0552. Reservations not necessary. Sushi: $4 and up. AE, MC, V. Open: Mon–Fri 11:15 a.m.–2 p.m. and 5:30–10 p.m., Sat 5:30–10 p.m.*

Swingers
$ West Hollywood   COFFEE SHOP

The best way to describe this place is classic-coffee-shop-meets-Kid-Rock, with a dash of *Love, American Style* retro-hip thrown in for good measure. The neo-diner grub is actually terrific, and nobody in town can beat the super-thick milkshakes. The restaurant is hugely popular with L.A.'s tattooed-and-pierced crowd — don't be surprised if you see a rock star roll in for breakfast (around 1 p.m., of course).

See maps p. 358, p. 362, and p. 397. In the Beverly Laurel Motor Hotel, 8020 Beverly Blvd. (between Fairfax Avenue and La Cienega Boulevard). ☎ *323-653-5858. 802 Broadway, Santa Monica.* ☎ *310-393-9793. No reservations. Main courses: Everything under $13. AE, DC, DISC, MC, V. Open: Wed–Mon 6:30 a.m.–4 a.m., Tues 6:30 a.m.–1:45 a.m.*

Yang Chow
$$ Downtown   CHINESE

Okay, if you're a foodie, we admit there are better Chinese restaurants in town, but most of those require a drive to the San Gabriel Valley, and you don't have time for that. This downtown Chinese restaurant is awfully good, and nowhere else can you eat Yang Chow's Slippery Shrimp, a dish that inspires devotion in countless customers and that's not at all slippery but rather features shrimp battered and deep-fried and then doused in a sweet, garlicky sauce of indefinite origin (but it came from somewhere good). They make platters and platters of this stuff daily; hardly a table is without one.

819 N. Broadway (at Alpine Street). ☎ *213-625-0811. 3777 E. Colorado Blvd., Pasadena.* ☎ *626-432-6868.* www.yangchow.com. *Reservations not necessary. Main courses: $7–$15. AE, MC, V. Open: Sun 11:30 a.m.–9:45 p.m., Fri–Sat 11:30 a.m.–10:45 p.m.*

Zankou Chicken
$ Hollywood/Van Nuys/Other Locations   ARMENIAN/CHICKEN

The day we accidentally stepped into this unprepossessing strip-mall hole-in-the-wall joint, with its dull Formica tables and utter lack of décor, is a day that will forever live in our hearts. It's not just because, when you place an order, you barely have time to read one of the many reviews on the wall (nearly every foodie in town ranks this place on their top-ten list), praising the place, before the order is ready. It's not just because the roast chicken is, well, perfect — juicy and flavorful, with a crispy seasoned skin that has you forgetting all the health warnings about fat and instead battling your loved ones for that last piece. It's all that, and then there's the garlic sauce. Trust us when we say that when we die, the food served to us in heaven will have Zankou garlic sauce accompanying it. Trust us also when we say that every time we bring a first-timer here, he or she tries to go back the very next day to do it all over again.

See map p. 362. 5065 W. Sunset Blvd. (near North Mariposa Avenue). ☎ *323-665-7842. 5658 Sepulveda Blvd. # 103, Van Nuys.* ☎ *818-781-0615. (Check Web site for other locations.)* www.zankouchicken.com. *No reservations. Main courses: Everything under $9. AE, MC, V. Open: Daily 10 a.m.–midnight.*

Exploring L.A.'s Top Attractions

You won't lack for exciting things to do in the City of Angels, whether it's seeing top museums, taking a back-stage studio tour, visiting an old movie palace, or riding the rides at Universal Studios and Anaheim's Disneyland Resort. Heck, you may just come for the beaches and the year-round welcoming weather. This section gives you the highlights from which you can pick and choose.

You can save a few bucks on admission fees to some major attractions by investigating the CityPass. $50 for adults, $40 for kids 3 to 11, gets you a Starline Tour, a Red Line Tour, and the Hollywood Wax Museum, plus a choice of either the a guided tour of the Kodak Theatre (frequently closed for events) or the Hollywood Museum based in the old Max Factor building. Better still, for those families intending to hit all the area theme parks, the Southern California Pass. For $199 adults, $139 kids 3 to 11, you get a three-day Park Hopper Pass — unlimited admission to Disneyland and California Adventure — plus early admission to both parks, plus SeaWorld and San Diego Zoo admissions, and front-of-the-line upgrades and admission to Universal Studios. Given that a regular Park Hopper Pass is $169, and Universal starts at $49, this is practically a steal. You can purchase CityPass at any of the aforementioned attractions, as well as from the CityPass Web site at www.citypass.com.

For attractions in the Westside and Beverly Hills, see the "Westside and Beverly Hills Accommodations, Dining, and Attractions" map. For attractions in Hollywood, go to the "Hollywood Accommodations, Dining, and Attractions" map. Both are located earlier in this chapter.

Universal Studios Hollywood

Situated on the real Universal lot, the one-time studio tour has grown into a sizable theme park that can absorb an entire day. The hour-long **Backlot Tram Tour** is still the heart of the matter, taking in such classic movie sites as the **Bates Motel,** plus a few silly-but-fun staged "disasters," including a not-so-secret one starring Jaws the shark. Silliness aside, this is an actual working studio, so you could see filming in action — although it's not likely.

Here are just a few of the thrills and chills to choose from at Universal:

✔ The world's fastest indoor rollercoaster **Revenge of the Mummy . . . The Ride,** loaded with special effects, takes those with strong stomachs on a high-speed journey through curse-ridden ancient Egypt as depicted in the popular series of movies.

✔ Another attraction is **Van Helsing: Fortress Dracula,** a haunted-house-style walking tour of sets from the movie that's supposed to be scary, but isn't.

✔ You get very, very wet on **Jurassic Park . . . The Ride,** a glorified log flume with a "small world" full of robotic dinosaurs and one very steep drop. Pay the extra buck for the poncho — or maybe even splurge for two.

✔ Expect the most jostling from **Back to the Future . . . The Ride,** which left us longing for a massage, or at least a vibrating chair. The ride's concept is that some evil guy in an ugly Hawaiian shirt has stolen a time-traveling DeLorean (wasn't this funnier in the '80s?), and you're along for the ride.

✔ **Shrek 4-D** bridges the gap between the first and second movies with a fun 15-minute animated 3-D short featuring the original voice actors (Mike Myers, Eddie Murphy, and so on). It's screened in a theater with motion-coordinated seats (they move in time with stuff happening on-screen) and water and wind special effects that make the show entertaining without being too intense for people who usually can't handle true motion-simulator rides.

✔ **Terminator 2: 3-D** is a live-action show mixed with 3-D filmmaking effects. It is based on plot points of the first two *Terminator* movies that seem dated after the third *Terminator* movie and that whole California gubernatorial thing.

✔ **Backdraft** and the **Special Effects Stages** take you behind the scenes to show how fire effects, green screens, robotics, and sound engineering turn dull moments into movie magic. Both are interesting, but if the line is long, come back later.

✔ **Animal Planet Live!, WaterWorld, The Blues Brothers,** and **Spider-Man Rocks** are live-action shows featuring animals, stunts, music, and other assorted "entertainment." The only one really worth your time is the Animal Planet show, but it's too short to justify the long lines getting in and out of the stadium. And the only reason you should see the 20-minute musical version of "Spider-Man" is to giggle as they try to work "Holding Out for a Hero," "She Bangs," and "Lady Marmalade" into the story.

Come midweek if you can, preferably not in summer, to avoid long lines. Little ones will be plenty entertained, but the park really targets kids 7 and up. Adjoining the park is Universal's cartoony shopping-and-dining complex **CityWalk** (in case you haven't spent enough dough already), which boasts good after-park dinner options.

Universal Studios Hollywood, 100 Universal City Plaza, Universal City. ☎ *800-864-8377.* www.universalstudioshollywood.com. *Admission: $50 adults, $40 children under 48 inches tall; front-of-line passes and VIP packages also available. Open: Hours can vary, so call ahead. At times, special savings coupons are passed out upon admission to the park. Check Web site for updates, changes, and additional specials, as well as changes in shows and attractions.*

Hooray for Hollywood!

Right off the bat, we must explain that "Hollywood" is both a neighborhood in Los Angeles and a catchall term for the motion-picture industry that is not, contrary to popular belief, based in Hollywood. Or anywhere near Hollywood. Nor was it ever. Well, okay, that's not strictly true. Columbia had studios at Sunset and Gower and still shoots TV shows there, and many silent-movie studios were in the eastern part of Hollywood (Los Feliz and Silver Lake). But no studio was ever on Hollywood Boulevard, much less at the legendary Hollywood and Vine.

Of course, the reality doesn't explain the mythos that has arisen around that name, term, and locale. And though locals may rarely be caught dead on **Hollywood Boulevard,** sniffing that it's either full of clueless tourists or tourist traps, or that it's rundown (true, but expensive efforts are seeking to change that) or kitschy (ditto), we stand firm that all tourists, especially first-time tourists, need to visit, puzzle over some of the unrecognizable names in the boulevard's **Walk of Fame,** and compare their own footprints with those enshrined in cement outside **Grauman's Chinese Theatre.**

Enormous amounts of money are being thrown at the Hollywood area, in the hopes of cleaning up the boulevard and giving it a whole new legitimate personality. Right now, the results are mixed. Sure, the fabulous **Hollywood & Highland Center,** home to the Kodak Theatre (which hosts the Oscars; when it's not hosting the Oscars, plays, concerts, and other live entertainment — the finale of *American Idol,* for example — fill the seats), along with many generic shopping-mall stores, not to mention several fine glamorous **old theaters.** But the neighborhood still lacks good, affordable restaurants. Instead, it remains an excess of tacky souvenir and T-shirt stores and a number of shops selling naughty lingerie and high heels clearly meant for strippers. Sparkly glitter in the asphalt goes only so far, you know.

The following are the most obvious and prominent Hollywood locales. Don't be snooty; it's your job as a visitor to see these places at least once (and frankly, we rather delight in having out-of-town guests, because then we have a legitimate opportunity to make return visits ourselves). If you hit each site listed and spend a certain amount of time at each listed site (but don't linger), it will take about half a day to see them all. If you want to tour the *real* Hollywood (studios and scandals), get yourself a copy of Ken Schessler's *This Is Hollywood* (Ken Schessler Publishing; $5.95), a comprehensive guide to the history of Hollywood, from landmarks to murders and suicides. Updated regularly, it offers tours of the significant local sites of renown and infamy.

Grauman's Chinese Theatre

Normally, this is when we haul out phrases like "newly restored to its former glory." Although it's true that Sid Grauman's fabulous movie palace, built in 1927 and designed to look like a Chinese temple, has been given a massive facelift, the restoration removed some of the 1950s glitz — usually a good thing, but in this case it turned what was a riot of Oriental stylings into a rather dull-gray concrete structure. Authentic is not always best, we note. Heck, even the neon dragons are gone! But at least the Mann chain (which bought the theater some years ago) officially returned the name Grauman (locals never did cave and call it *Mann's* Chinese Theater), and the interior remains a classic example of glorious movie-theater pomp, all deep reds and gilt and fanciful curlicues, along with one giant screen. And of course, there are the footprints immortalized in concrete outside the theater. It began as a publicity stunt — oh, heck, it's *still* a publicity stunt, but thank heavens for it, because how else could we see that Mary Pickford had such itty-bitty feet? How else could there have been one of the best *I Love Lucy* shows of all time, when Lucy "borrowed" John Wayne's bootprints as a souvenir? (The Duke's bootprints are still here. And they are surprisingly small.) Yes, the stars of yesteryear, and some of today, have enshrined their shoeprints, hand prints, and in some cases nose prints (Jimmy Durante) and leg prints (Betty Grable) in concrete, to last beyond their ruin. Go ahead, compare your appendages to theirs — you know you want to. And when you're done, see *any* movie at the theater (as long as it's on the big screen), even if it's terrible, because it's what the movie-going experience ought to be.

See map p. 362. 6925 Hollywood Blvd. ☎ *323-464-6266 or 323-461-3331.* www.mann theatres.com/chinese. *Showtimes vary. Call for movie-ticket prices.*

Hollywood & Highland Center

The Hollywood & Highland Center is a little bit nightlife, a little bit attraction, and a whole lot shopping — but we're sticking it here because it's in Hollywood, right in the middle of everything else you're seeing and doing. Plus, it is the spiffy centerpiece of what the city still desperately hopes will be a major rejuvenation of Hollywood Boulevard. But basically, when you get right down to it, it's a shopping mall. A grand shopping mall, to be sure. We glory in the detailing that includes quotes in mosaic from anonymous actors and others about their epic struggles to "Make It," the way the staircase entrance is designed to frame the Hollywood sign, the courtyard full of stands and umbrellas and cafe tables, and, best of all, the **Babylon Court,** which pays homage to D.W. Griffith's fantastic Babylon set for his movie *Intolerance.* The **Kodak Theatre** was built specifically as a permanent home for the Academy Awards show, although it also hosts concerts and theater road companies throughout the year. Hollywood & Highland is also the home to *Jimmy Kimmel Live* (which airs late-night on ABC), and bands often play live right there in the complex. You can also find two nightclubs, a bowling alley, access to nearby movie theaters, restaurants, and a self-guided audio tour of the Walk of Fame. They did a fine job with the design, we have to admit — for a shopping mall.

See map p. 362. Northwest corner of Hollywood and Highland. www.hollywood andhighland.com. *Hours: Mon–Sat 10 a.m.–10 p.m., Sun 10 a.m.–7 p.m. (some establishments may be open later).*

The Hollywood Sign

Iconic. We so rarely get to use this word properly, so savor the moment. What else would you call those nine 50-foot-tall white letters, perched high up in the Hollywood Hills? They constitute one of the most instantly recognizable sights in the world. The sign dates back to 1923, and it originally read "Hollywoodland," the name of the development it was drawing attention to. (The last four letters came down in the '40s.) Struggling actors, despairing of ever getting their big break, were rumored to have made it a favorite suicide spot, but the only person confirmed to have actually done so was actress Peg Entwhistle, who jumped off the letter *H* in 1932, poor despondent dear. You can't drive to the sign, nor can you walk right up to it, but you can hike up from Durand Avenue off of Beachwood Canyon. You can get a good picture from Sunset Boulevard at Gower and also at Bronson; otherwise, drive up Beachwood 'til it gets closer and closer and you get the shot you want.

See map p. 362. At the top of Beachwood Canyon.

Hollywood Walk of Fame

Granite stars rimmed in brass are implanted in the sidewalk on Hollywood Boulevard (and down Vine Street toward Sunset Boulevard), with the names of the Greats and the once Greats (and those who had really good publicists and some pocket change) of film, radio, television, and the recording arts. We hate to shatter any illusions, but the stars *pay* for their stars; pretty much anyone, of a rather minimal level of success, can get nominated. The Hollywood Chamber of Commerce, after making sure he or she can cough up the money, gives out a star. But so what? Walk along Hollywood Boulevard and see how many names you still recognize (to say nothing of seeing what strange accidental neighbors the juxtaposition of names creates). It's something you should do at least once.

See map p. 362. Hollywood Boulevard, between Gower Street and La Brea Avenue, and Vine Street between Hollywood Boulevard and Sunset. ☎ *323-469-8311.* www. hollywoodchamber.net. *Call or check online to find out who is where and who may be getting a star while you're in town.*

Museum Row

Along Wilshire Boulevard in the Miracle Mile area lies L.A.'s greatest concentration of museums, including three standouts. To get there, take the 10 to Fairfax Avenue and head north.

La Brea Tar Pits/George C. Page Museum
Los Angeles

It's goopy, it's smelly, it's oozing, and it's wonderful . . . it's the La Brea Tar Pits. It's a gruesome story, so let's repeat it. Millions of years ago (okay, 40,000 — *whatever*), unsuspecting prehistoric critters (wooly mammoths, saber-toothed tigers) would wander over to an attractive pool of water and wade out in it, only to discover that the water was floating on top of tar, in which they would then be permanently stuck. Death would follow (starvation or suffocation), their bodies would sink down into the muck (sometimes thus additionally condemning a predator, who had hopped on thinking it was getting an easy meal by preying on a trapped beastie — sucker!), and there they stayed, until the world discovered archaeologists. The archaeologists found that if you dredge those pits (and a messy business that is), you can find whole, beautifully preserved skeletons. And so they dig, or exhume, or whatever you call it when you have to grope around in tar pits, and they put what they find on display. And amazingly, all this is located along Wilshire Boulevard, one of the busiest streets in L.A. In fact, all the buildings in this complex (including the Los Angeles County Museum of Art next door) are built to float, more or less, on the tar, which remains in full forceful presence. (And it's still sticky, even if you're just picking up a little bit to give to someone as a souvenir — not that we know from personal experience or anything.) Kids love it. During the late summer, the pits are open to the viewing public, so you can see the scientists at work as they try to excavate more bones.

See maps p. 358 and p. 362. 5801 Wilshire Blvd. ☎ *323-934-7243.* www.tarpits. org. *Admission: $7 adults, $4.50 students and seniors, $2 children 5–10, children under 5 free. Open: Mon–Fri 9:30 a.m.–5 p.m., Sat–Sun 10 a.m.–5 p.m.*

Los Angeles County Museum of Art
Los Angeles

The Getty Center (see the "More terrific museums" section later in this chapter) is worth seeing for the house, but this museum complex (itself a wacko marriage of architectural styles) is the place to go if you want to see first-rate art collections. Indeed, this museum contains the finest encyclopedic art collection west of the Mississippi, perhaps second only to the Met in NYC. Most impressive is the Japanese Pavilion (the only building outside of Japan dedicated to Japanese art), which has shoji-like exterior walls that let in soft natural light, allowing you to see the magnificent collection as it was meant to be seen. The museum also excels at modern and contemporary works, includes a mind-blowing Dada collection, and has a terrific costumes and textiles collection. Because LACMA usually draws in the high-profile traveling collections (Van Gogh, the recent King Tut exhibit, and so on), the special exhibitions are standouts more often than not.

LACMA can easily occupy an entire day, but we suggest not trying to see the whole place. Instead, pick up a map upon arrival, dedicate three hours to the areas that most interest you, and then move on to another museum along Museum Row for something completely different.

See maps p. 358 and p. 362. 5905 Wilshire Blvd. ☎ *323-857-6000.* www.lacma.org. *Admission: $9 adults, $5 seniors and adult students with ID, children under 17 free. Open: Mon, Tues, Thurs noon–8 p.m., Fri noon–9 p.m., Sat–Sun 11 a.m.–8 p.m., closed Wed.*

Petersen Automotive Museum
Los Angeles

This quintessential Southern California museum is dedicated to — what else? — car culture. Four floors creatively display more than 200 sets of wheels, from the first Ford Model Ts to groovy hot rods, one-of-a-kind movie rides, and cars of the future. This terrific museum is a real blast — and so mythically, marvelously L.A. It is well worth a couple of hours; put it high on your sightseeing list.

See maps p. 358 and p. 362. 6060 Wilshire Blvd. (at Fairfax Avenue). ☎ *323-930-2277.* www.petersen.org. *Admission: $10 adults, $3 children 5–12, $5 seniors and students with valid ID, children under 5 free. Open: Tues–Sun 10 a.m.–6 p.m., closed Mon (but open regular hours on Mon holiday-observance days, such as Martin Luther King Day, Labor Day, and Memorial Day), closed on other major holidays.*

More terrific museums

California ScienCenter
Downtown

This highly enjoyable institution, a long-term L.A. staple, formerly known as the Museum of Science and Industry, got a complete makeover, which helped bring it as up to date as a museum that focuses on the wonders of science and industry ought to be (it's so hard to keep pace, isn't it?). Learn about the human body thanks to Tess the 50-foot woman (she's like a giant version of that fabled model toy), build miniature structures and find out how earthquake-proof they are (and sample some quake-shaking yourself), learn about physical development (from how a single cell turns into that complex system known as a human being to the timeless fun of watching chicks hatch), or ride a bike on a cable three stories above ground (it's safe, but it costs extra). There is plenty of hands-on, interactive fun, again of the sort that probably thrills adults for its cleverness more than kids, who are often more interested in the bright lights and loud noises than learning. But that's okay, you're on vacation, and a little education is bound to sink in anyway, even by accident. Naturally, it's hugely popular with school field trips, so take that into consideration when you plan your own visit. An IMAX theater generally shows features tied to either permanent or traveling exhibits.

700 State Dr. (in Exposition Park). ☎ *323-724-3623.* www.casciencectr.org. *Admission: Free. Open: Daily 10 a.m.–5 p.m.; closed Thanksgiving. Christmas, and New Year's Day.*

Getty Center
Brentwood

If you're not the Universal Studios type, chances are good that you're visiting L.A. to see this high-profile arts center, which opened to great acclaim in late 1997 and houses 20th-century millionaire (sounds so quaint now, doesn't it?) J. Paul Getty's enormous collection of art. The collection includes not only the antiquities that were at the old Getty Museum, but also early Renaissance and Impressionist paintings (including van Gogh's *Irises*), French decorative arts, illuminated manuscripts, and contemporary photography and graphic arts. The galleries are state of the art and the collections extensive, but, as a whole, not nearly as impressive as what you can see at LACMA (which also mounts the best traveling exhibitions) or, even better, the Norton Simon (detailed later in this section). In fact, if it weren't for fear of art majors everywhere gunning for us, we'd say it's a bit underwhelming. Then again, recent high-profile scandals over forged or looted art have made everyone a bit wary. Ultimately, Richard Meier's ultramodern complex is the real draw. It presides over the landscape with appropriate grandeur, and the views are stunning. The alfresco spaces are as impressive as the interior ones, particularly the circular gardens.

Don't bother coming unless you have at least three or four hours to spare. A great way to avoid the crowds is to visit later in the afternoon, especially on Fridays, when the center is open until 9 p.m. The sunset and after-dark panoramic views are lovely, and the Westside and Santa Monica are convenient for a late dinner.

You can also make your way up PCH to the Getty's original home, built in the manner of a classical Roman villa, which currently houses the institute's ancient Greek, Roman, and Etruscan collections. Beautifully renovated in a process that took years, and already in a striking setting overlooking the Pacific, it is a charming and special museum visit unlike anything else in Los Angeles. Though the scandals touch here, too, this collection is certainly superb.

You may want to pair your visit to the main Getty Center with a stop at the relatively new (and also strikingly modern) **Skirball Cultural Center,** 2701 N. Sepulveda Blvd., at Mulholland Drive (☎ **310-440-4500;** www. skirball.org), whose galleries focus on the marriage of Jewish life and the American Dream. It's quickly establishing a reputation for top-flight temporary exhibits, too. Admission is $8 adults, $6 seniors and students, and free for kids younger than 12. Open Tuesday, Wednesday, Friday, and Saturday noon to 5 p.m., Thursday noon to 9 p.m., and Sunday 11 a.m. to 5 p.m.

See map p. 358. 1200 Getty Center Dr. ☎ 310-440-7330. (Villa: 17985 Pacific Coast Hwy.) www.getty.edu. *Admission: Free for Center and Villa, but latter requires advance, timed tickets. Open: Center Tues–Thurs and Sun 10 a.m.–6 p.m., Fri–Sat 10 a.m.–9 p.m.; Villa Thurs–Mon 10 a.m.–5 p.m. Closed major holidays.*

Museum of Contemporary Art/MOCA at the Geffen Contemporary Downtown

See, first they decided to build L.A. a contemporary art museum, but they needed to start the museum up before the real building was in place, so they used a warehouse-like building near Little Tokyo. It was dubbed the Temporary Contemporary. Then the real building (a geometric structure that promptly won architectural awards) opened, on Grand Street, near the Music Center, but by then everyone loved the Temporary Contemporary so much (for one thing, it's fun to say!) that it was made permanent. Then David Geffen gave a great deal of money, as he is wont to do, to the institution and the Temporary became the Geffen Contemporary, except many locals still don't call it that (because it's not as euphonious). Anyway, the upshot is that L.A. has one museum in two locations. All mediums are represented, from abstract to pop art to emerging new artists. Both locations offer permanent collections (Lichtenstein, de Kooning, Warhol, Rauschenberg, Rothko, Schnabel, Stella, Pollock, and Arbus) and special exhibits. The Geffen is more likely to have conceptual or installation art, simply because the shape of the facility is conducive to such exhibits. Free gallery tours, offered by most-knowledgeable docents, are regularly offered several times most days — we highly encourage you to plan a visit around these, because they're among the best deals in L.A. Admission covers both buildings, and a shuttle runs regularly between the two buildings; plan to spend at least an hour at each, probably a bit more. Recently, MOCA opened a small branch at the Pacific Design Center in West Hollywood to satisfy those unwilling or unable to make the trek from WeHo to downtown.

250 S. Grand Ave. and 152 N. Central Ave. ☎ *213-626-6222.* www.moca.org. *Admission: $8 adults, $5 seniors and students with ID, children under 12 free; free admission for all on Thurs. Open: Mon 11 a.m.–5 p.m., Thurs 11 a.m.–8 p.m., Fri 11 a.m.– 5 p.m., Sat–Sun 11 a.m.–6 p.m.. Also 8687 Melrose Ave.* ☎ *310-289-5223. Admission: Free. Open: Tues–Wed and Fri 11 a.m.–5 p.m., Thurs 11 a.m.–8p.m., Sat–Sun 11 a.m.– 6 p.m.*

Museum of Television & Radio
Beverly Hills

Ah, the timeless family-vacation dilemma: Junior is whining about having to visit some dusty old art exhibit because he feels that it would really be a lot more fun to watch TV. Voilà — the solution: a contemporary museum (a branch of the institution located in New York City) where the idiot box is enshrined and treated like the cultural touchstone it really is. This museum has a few galleries to see, but the real heart of the matter are the private consoles, which allow you to conjure up your favorite moments of broadcast history, from the Beatles's first appearance on the *Ed Sullivan Show* to the crumbling of the Berlin Wall. Open screenings can range from "Laurence Olivier: Four Crowning Achievements" to "The World of Hanna-Barbara" — call or check the Web site for the current calendar. There's a two-hour limit on the consoles — but if no one is waiting, getting a second library pass for a second two hours is easy.

See map p. 358. 465 N. Beverly Dr. (at Santa Monica Boulevard). ☎ *310-786-1000.* www.mtr.org. *Admission: $10 adults, $8 students and seniors, $5 children under 14. Open: Wed–Sun noon–5 p.m.*

Museum of the American West
Los Angeles

The Singing Cowboy, Gene Autry, loved the Wild West and the money it made him. This museum was his gift to Southern California. It's mostly a romanticized view of the Old West, with emphasis on the romance of the cowboy. The uninformed could easily come away from a visit believing that nothing really bad happened during the country's relentless pursuit of Manifest Destiny, it was all for the Good of America. (You know, as in, it's kind of too bad we killed the buffalo, but wasn't it fun to shoot them from trains?) Still, although the museum is rather Hollywood pop culture, it is most entertaining, and popular with the kids (and, alas, school groups). Seven galleries feature all aspects of the West, including the Gallery of Western Expansion. Combine it with other Griffith Park sightseeing (see the "Playing in Griffith Park" section later in this chapter) for a solid half-day of fun.

See map p. 362. 4700 Western Heritage Way (at Curson Avenue). ☎ *323-667-2000.* www.museumoftheamericanwest.org. *Admission: $7.50 adults, $5 seniors over 60 and students, $3 children 2–12; free for all after 4 p.m. Thurs. Open: Tues–Sun 10 a.m.–5 p.m. (until 8 p.m. Thurs).*

Museum of Tolerance
West Los Angeles

One can make the argument that tolerance or, rather, lack thereof, is at the base of many of the most pressing issues of our day. Note that this isn't to say everyone has to like each other; we just have to *tolerate* each other by learning to understand each other and allow for differences in appearance, religious worship, and cultural mores. We ignore this to our peril. The Holocaust is the most obvious example of the tragedies and horrors that occur when this sort of understanding and acceptance fails to manifest, and this excellent facility naturally focuses much attention on that horrific event. The exhibits include many interactive and video displays. Located in the Simon Wiesenthal Center, the museum covers many more related areas — in other words, this isn't just a Holocaust museum. It's designed to topple many of your preconceived notions from the very beginning, when you have a choice of starting your tour through one of two doors — "prejudiced" and "not prejudiced." Guess which one simply doesn't open at all? Note that the museum is laid out so that you follow a mandatory route, which can take up to three hours to complete.

See map p. 358. 9786 W. Pico Blvd. (at Roxbury Drive). ☎ *310-553-8403.* www.museum oftolerance.com. *Admission: $10 adults, $8 seniors, $7 children 2–18 and students with ID. Open: Mon–Thurs 11:30 a.m.–6:30 p.m., Fri 11:30 a.m.–5 p.m. Sun 11 a.m.–7:30 p.m. Last entrance two hours before closing. Closed Sat, Jewish holidays, Thanksgiving, and Christmas.*

Norton Simon Museum of Art
Pasadena

Packaged-foods mogul Norton Simon gathered a mind-blowing art collection, now housed on the Rose Parade route (and under the direction of his widow, actress Jennifer Jones). It's a stunning — and undisputedly excellent — assemblage of European painting and sculpture spanning the 14th through 20th centuries, with the masters extremely well represented. The museum is well worth an afternoon excursion for serious art lovers, although the rest of us may find it a little less than enthralling.

411 W. Colorado Blvd. ☎ *626-449-6840.* www.nortonsimon.org. *Admission: $8 adults, $4 seniors, free for children under 18 and students with valid ID. Open: Wed–Thurs and Sat–Mon noon–6 p.m., Fri noon–9 p.m.*

Southwest Museum
Highland Park

Opened in 1907, this was the first museum in Southern California; it is now part of the Autry Center, which includes the Museum of the American West and the Institute for the Study of the American West. Exhibits focus on the grim flip side of the Old West myth presented by the Museum of the American West (see the earlier listing). This fine, serious museum outlines different aspects of Native American life, from clothing to religion, by covering the western tribes. There are three ways to enter this Mission-style building: You can journey through a tunnel lined with very good dioramas of Native Americans; you can walk up the Hopi Trail, which is very steep and landscaped; or you can bypass it all and drive up to the tippy-top. Local educators prefer the Southwest Museum (politically correct, sensitive, and enlightened, not to mention educational) to the Museum of the American West (rip-roaring cowboy fun), and we certainly understand and don't disagree. Of course, all of this got quite a shake-up when the Autry people essentially bought the always financially struggling Southwest Museum Both are now under one blanket foundation umbrella. It's too early in the relationship to judge how this will affect either — more flash for this one? More cred for the other? Stay tuned.

See map p. 362. 234 Museum Dr. (in the Highland Park District). ☎ *323-221-2164. www.southwestmuseum.org. Admission: Free. Open: Sat–Sun noon–5 p.m. and on Mon holiday-observance days such as Martin Luther King Day, Labor Day, and Memorial Day; closed on other major holidays.*

Hitting the beaches

The following sections describe L.A.'s best beaches as they run along PCH (Highway 1) from south to north (see the "Santa Monica and the Malibu Beaches" map on p. 397).

Venice Beach and Ocean Front Walk

Starting at Venice Boulevard and running north to Rose Avenue is L.A.'s beach scene at its wackiest, wildest, and sleaziest. The sand is less the draw than the continuous carnival on the paved promenade known as **Ocean Front Walk** that runs along the beach, where vendors sell dirt-cheap merchandise, from sunglasses to silly tchotchkes, and busking entertainers run the gamut from talking-parrot wranglers to chainsaw jugglers. The constant crowd is the city's most eye-popping and includes plenty of muscle-bound pretty boys, buxom beach bunnies on in-line skates, and tattooed biker types and their chicks.

Head elsewhere if you want to relax on the sand; come here for the local color. Look in the blocks east of Pacific Avenue for a street parking space or west of Pacific Avenue for a pay lot.

Santa Monica Beach and Pier

As you move north on Ocean Front Walk and cross into Santa Monica, the scene gets appreciably prettier and more subdued. The walk opens up for bikers and skaters, the beach is more suitable for playing and sunbathing, the bay waters are calm, and the food options and facilities improve.

The best beach access is along Bernard Way, which runs parallel to Ocean Avenue (called Neilson Way here) along the ocean from Marine Street (2 blocks north of Rose Avenue) to Pico Boulevard. The scene is very relaxed; this is where locals come to kick back. The sands are wide, white, flat, and gorgeous, with grassy areas great for picnicking, good facilities, a playground, and lots of parking.

If you're looking for a livelier scene and more facilities, you may prefer gathering midbeach on either side of the **Santa Monica Pier** (☎ 310-458-8900; www.santamonicapier.org), at the end of Colorado Avenue. After years of neglect, the landmark wooden amusement pier is back in top form. It boasts a number of snack shacks and attractions, including a turn-of-the-century carousel (☎ 310-458-8867) that had a featured role in the movie *The Sting*. **Pacific Park** (☎ 310-260-8744; www.pacpark.com) is a fun zone with a roller coaster, a dozen other rides, and old-fashioned midway games. You can also stop in **Playland Arcade** (☎ 310-451-5133) for high-tech arcade games. Below the carousel, at beach level, is the **Santa Monica Pier Aquarium,** 1600 Ocean Front Walk (☎ 310-393-6149; www.healthebay.org/smpa), where you can learn a thing or two about the Santa Monica Bay marine environment (admission $5; free for children younger than 12).

Weekends and summer daytimes are best for experiencing all that the pier has to offer. If you're visiting at another time, call the specific attractions that catch your interest before you go to avoid disappointment. The pier is about a mile up Ocean Front Walk from Venice; it makes a great round-trip stroll.

North of the pier along Ocean Avenue is **Palisades Park,** a lovely, grassy bluff-top park with benches. Anyplace along here is a good place to stop and take in the stunning ocean views; you'll find lots of metered parking (getting a spot is generally easier as you go north).

Rent bikes, in-line skates, boogie boards, baby joggers, beach chairs, and umbrellas from **Perry's Beach Cafe** (www.perryscafe.com), south of the pier at 2400 and 2600 Ocean Front Walk, at Ocean Park Boulevard (☎ 310-372-3138); and north of the pier at 930 and 1200 Pacific Coast Hwy. (☎ 310-458-3975 and 310-260-1114). Bike and skate rentals run $8 to $14 per hour or $23 to $38 per day ($6 per hour for kids). Call for info on skating lessons if you're a newbie.

The Malibu beaches

An alternative to coming up through Santa Monica to reach these beaches is to head west on Sunset Boulevard for a gorgeous, winding drive. Turn left on Temescal Canyon Road (follow the "to PCH" signs) to reach Will Rogers Beach; continue on Sunset all the way to PCH and turn right to reach the others.

Santa Monica and the Malibu Beaches

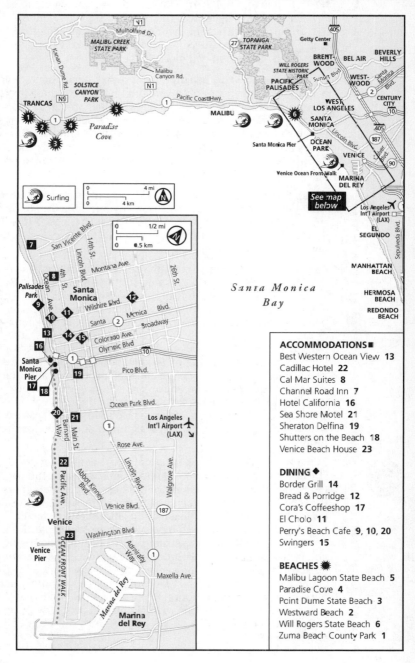

ACCOMMODATIONS ■
Best Western Ocean View **13**
Cadillac Hotel **22**
Cal Mar Suites **8**
Channel Road Inn **7**
Hotel California **16**
Sea Shore Motel **21**
Sheraton Delfina **19**
Shutters on the Beach **18**
Venice Beach House **23**

DINING ◆
Border Grill **14**
Bread & Porridge **12**
Cora's Coffeeshop **17**
El Cholo **11**
Perry's Beach Cafe **9, 10, 20**
Swingers **15**

BEACHES ☀
Malibu Lagoon State Beach **5**
Paradise Cove **4**
Point Dume State Beach **3**
Westward Beach **2**
Will Rogers State Beach **6**
Zuma Beach County Park **1**

✔ **Will Rogers State Beach,** which runs from Temescal Canyon Road north to Sunset Boulevard, is where the Malibu vibe begins. The Temescal (south) section of the beach is especially nice — wide, flat, and pretty, with calm, swimmer-friendly surf, lifeguards, a snack bar, restrooms, beach-toy rentals, and easy parking. Surfers hang out at the north end, near Sunset.

✔ **Malibu Lagoon State Beach,** the curvaceous dark-sand beach and natural wetlands north of the Malibu Pier, is extremely popular with surfers. Swimming is allowed only in a small area near the pier, where the waters are protected by rocky shallows. Come instead to watch the locals hang-ten on the waves; weekends or after-work hours are best. The entrance is just south of Cross Creek Road. Parking will cost you a few bucks; do as the locals do and park along the PCH to save the dough.

If you want to rent a surfboard — smart only if you already know what you're doing — head to **Zuma Jay Surfboards,** about ¼-mile south of Malibu Pier at 22775 Pacific Coast Hwy. (☎ 310-456-8044). Surfboards are $20 for the day, wetsuits $10. You can also rent bodyboards and kayaks.

✔ **Paradise Cove** is nestled well off the highway at the base of a cliff at 28128 Pacific Coast Hwy., a mile south of Kanan-Dume Road. This lovely private cove beach is pricey to visit but well worth the dough if you're looking for a pretty place to spend the day. The beach is just a narrow curve, but a small parking lot keeps the crowds at bay. Come early (before noon on weekends); the $25 parking charge ($5 for walk-ins) keeps out the riff-raff, but plenty of families are more than happy to shell out for such a private haven. The waters are especially calm and well-protected, and therefore great for little ones. Claim your blanket space at the south end if you plan to spend the whole day, because the north end becomes shaded by mid-afternoon. On-site is **Bob Morris's Paradise Cove Beach Cafe,** plus picnic tables, restrooms, and nice changing rooms with showers.

✔ **Zuma Beach County Park** is L.A.'s largest beach playground. Zuma starts a mile north of Kanan-Dume Road (watch for the turnoff on the right, which takes you under the highway). Beach-goers pack the more than 2 miles of sand on warm summer weekends. They're drawn by the wide sand beach and comprehensive facilities, including lifeguards, volleyball courts, swing sets, snack bars, and beach-toy rentals. Restrooms are strategically placed along the beach, so you're never far from a bathroom. The wide expanse of sand (and even wider parking lot) means that street noise isn't a big problem, especially when the revelers kick into high gear. Come midweek to have plenty of sand for yourself or on the weekend to catch the scene. Parking is $2 (at this writing, but will probably go up); bring exact change in the off-season, because the fee is collected automatically.

✔ You can separate yourself from the masses and the highway noise by heading to **Westward Beach,** hidden by sandstone cliffs at the south end of Zuma. To get there, turn left at Westward Beach Road (at the Malibu Country Inn), two minutes after the Heathercliff Road light (just before the right-hand turnoff for Zuma). At the end of Westward Beach Road is a $6 parking lot for **Point Dume State Beach,** another wonderful stretch of sand below the cliffs.

Playing in Griffith Park

Hilly, 4,000-acre **Griffith Park** (☎ 323-913-4688; www.laparks.org/dos/parks/griffithPK/griffith.htm) is the nation's largest public municipal park and urban wilderness (five times as large as New York's Central Park). It was a donation of the double-barreled-named Colonel Griffith J. Griffith, who was trying to 1) get on the city's good side after a messy courtroom drama involving the attempted murder of his wife, 2) seek tax relief, and 3) remove a curse from his first wife (bad luck with women), a Spanish land-grant heiress from whom he stole much of this property. It's popular with a strong cross-section of Angelenos, from families at play to picnicking bohos to the healthy and health-seeking, marching up and down trails that range from easy to challenging. It has a number of attractions worth seeking out, and makes a good place to unwind or let the kids run off steam if you tire of the urban madness. The park is open daily from 5 a.m. to 10 p.m.

In addition to the **Museum of the American West** (see the "More terrific museums" section earlier in this chapter), the park's other biggest attraction is the **Griffith Observatory,** 2800 E. Observatory Rd., at the end of Vermont Avenue (☎ 323-664-1191; www.griffithobs.org). The observatory reopened in 2006 after a years-long, $93-million makeover that should make this white jewel on the hillside above the park gleam more brightly than ever. When it's reopened, you can look for most of the innovations and upgrades inside. The gorgeous interiors, complete with historic murals, will be restored and the planetarium will be state of the art. The bust to James Dean will remain (the climatic fight scene from *Rebel without a Cause* was staged outside). Don't miss the Leonard Nimoy Event Horizon Theater, a gift from an actor who knows he owes a debt or two to space. A trip up here, on a clear day, offers one of the finest views of the city, and now the inside will match.

At the **Travel Town Transportation Museum,** 5200 Zoo Dr. (☎ 323-662-5874; www.cityofla.org/RAP/grifmet/tt), kids can climb aboard vintage trains. The adjacent **Los Angeles Live Steamers** (☎ 323-661-8958; www.lals.org) can take you choo-chooing on a scale-model steam train. Travel Town also rents bikes for two-wheel exploring (☎ 323-662-6573). Also in the park is the **Los Angeles Zoo** (☎ 323-644-4200; www.lazoo.org), which has experienced ups and downs in its career but is always a hit with kids, and always has some extremely rare animals on display.

Hiking the trails

L.A.'s other favorite outdoor activity — no, it's not that — it's hiking! There are some lovely trails, but figure you'll never be alone, which can be good — look carefully, movie stars may be hiding under those baseball caps. **Will Rogers State Historic Park,** 1501 Will Rogers State Park Rd. (☎ 310-454-8212), off of Sunset Boulevard in Pacific Palisades, is the former home of the man who never met a man he didn't like. It's a sweet little respite area and has easy trails through the Santa Monica Mountains.

In Los Feliz, **Griffith Park** (see the "Playing in Griffith Park" section, earlier in this chapter) has a 53-mile network of trails, including the Bronson Canyon Trail, on the west side of Griffith Park, which goes past the Bat Cave entrance from the old *Batman* TV series; the canyon itself starred in many a TV Western. Trails close at dusk.

Runyon Canyon (Franklin Avenue at Fuller Boulevard in the Hollywood Hills) is part of the old Errol Flynn estate, and the easy trails offer astounding views. But they are crowded, and if you don't like dogs (many of which are off-leash), avoid this place, especially on weekends and after 4 p.m. daily. But keep in mind that anytime you go you may run into famous faces catching fresh air alone or with their dogs or trainers.

Always bring a nice big bottle of water on your hikes and wear sunblock. If you're hiking in the spring and summer, be aware that there are snakes, specifically rattlesnakes, and they can be very cranky when disturbed. Wear light-colored clothes and appropriate shoes, stay on the trails, and don't try to pick up anything that looks like a stick.

Studio tours and TV tapings

This is Tinseltown; of course you want to see Hollywood in action! We recommend that visitors call the studios before visiting to ensure that they are keeping the hours listed below.

Studio tours

In addition to the backlot tour at Universal Studios Hollywood (see the "Exploring L.A.'s Top Attractions" section earlier in this chapter), here are a few other studio tours worth considering.

NBC Studios
Burbank

This 70-minute, behind-the-scenes walking tour includes sets of the *Tonight Show with Jay Leno;* wardrobe, makeup, and set construction demonstrations; and special-effects and sound-effects sets. You should call at least two weeks in advance for tickets.

3000 W. Alameda, Burbank. ☎ *818-840-3538. Admission: $8.50 adults, $7.50 seniors, $5.50 children 5–12, and children under 5 free. Open: Mon–Fri 9 a.m.–3 p.m. on first-come basis.*

Paramount Studios
Hollywood

Two-hour walking tour through the landmark gates, behind the scenes and history, includes prop room, Foley studio, and the chance to see a star, or at least a few extras in costume. Reservations required for the twice daily tours.

5555 Melrose Ave. ☎ *323-956-1777. Admission: $35. Tours: Mon–Fri 10 a.m. and 2 p.m.*

Sony Pictures Studios
Culver City

Home to Columbia Pictures and Columbia TriStar Television, this two-hour walking tour guides visitors through the facets of a real working studio. Visit the archival museum, watch movie clips in a private screening room, sneak a peek at artists painting scenic backdrops, and visit the stage set of current television shows. Reservations are required during the summer.

10202 W. Washington Blvd. ☎ *323-520-TOUR. Admission: $25 adults and children 12 and older, no one younger than 12 admitted. Open: Mon–Fri (call for hours).*

Warner Bros. Studio Tour
Burbank

Visitors to this working movie and TV studio observe filming whenever possible. The two-hour tour includes a film collage (Errol Flynn to Denzel Washington), the Warner Bros. Museum, historic back lots, cavernous soundstages, and the "world's most extensive costume department." Reservations are available for the first three tours of the day; all others are on a first-come-first-served basis.

Gate 4, Hollywood Way and Olive Avenue. ☎ *818-972-TOUR. Admission: $39. Open: Mon–Fri 8:30 a.m.–3 p.m.*

TV tapings

For tickets to live tapings of TV shows, contact **Audiences Unlimited** (☎ 818-753-3470; www.tvtickets.com), which provides audiences for over two dozen shows. The schedule is updated daily, listing available shows up to 30 days in advance. Your best chance to ensure getting tickets is to request shows that are new or not big hits. The highest-rated comedies are sold out months in advance, so don't plan a special trip on the off chance that you'll get tickets to your fave show.

Audiences Unlimited also has a booth inside Universal Studios, near the tour departure area, that provides tickets for shows taping that day. Often, it provides bus transportation from Universal Studios to the set of the show. For details on show requirements (some talk shows include shots of the audience, for example, and may require a dress code for some tapings), go to Audiences Unlimited's Web site or call its voice mailbox.

You also can take advantage of the opportunity to be an audience member at shows taped on the Paramount Lot. Call ☎ 323-956-1777. Tickets are released five business days prior to a taping; however, you can call and ask what shows have seats available.

Seeing L.A. by Guided Tour

We pretty much sniff at guided tours for Los Angeles; they just load you on a bus or some other vehicle and show you the cheesiest sights. You can easily do that on your own. But one we recommend is **Architecture Tours L.A.** (☎ 323-464-7868; www.architecturetoursla.com), which offers several two-hour tours, ranging from overviews and highlights of L.A. architecture to specific programs designed around various neighborhoods and their own special look (the Pasadena tour might specialize in Greene and Greene, for example, and the Silver Lake tour gives you plenty of Neutra and Schindler). Customized tours are also available. The owner has a master's degree in architecture history, and tours are conducted in a luxurious van with two sunroofs for maximum visibility.

Shopping 'til You Drop

Ardent shoppers won't lack for diversions in Los Angeles. What follows are L.A.'s finest hunting grounds. For a visual reference, see the "Los Angeles's Shopping Neighborhoods" map on p. 404.

Santa Monica

For the average tourist, this charming beach town offers the best shopping possibilities, with a range from affordable to movie-star wealthy, and all of it in pleasant walkable settings.

Third Street Promenade

This sunny pedestrian-only walk is a real crowd-pleaser, with something for everyone: record shops, bookstores (mostly chains), and familiar clothing chains and one-off boutiques. It's a browser's delight, and most stores stay open for after-dinner shopping. Take the 10 freeway to Fourth Street and park in a structure between Fourth and Second streets.

Main Street

This hip, casual strip is the place to find the beach vibe in Santa Monica shopping. The nice mix of national favorites, one-of-a-kind boutiques, and sidewalk cafes between Rose Avenue and Strand (north of Ocean Park Boulevard) makes for a lovely stroll. Check out the Web site at www.mainstreetsm.com.

Bergamot Station

Bergamot Station, 2525 Michigan Ave. (☎ 310-829-5854), is the city's top stop for contemporary art, with 20 beautifully browsable galleries running the gamut from Japanese paper to jewelry, painting, and sculpture. Take the 405 to Cloverfield/26th Street, turn right on Cloverfield Boulevard, and right on Michigan; parking is free and plentiful.

Montana Avenue

This grown-up shopping strip at the upscale north end of town is wonderful for one-of-a-kind browsing. The best boutiquing is just east of Ninth Street, where you'll find lots of casually elegant clothing boutiques for women. Visit www.montanaave.com for a rundown.

Beverly Hills's Golden Triangle

This world-famous corner of couture is more accessible than you may think. You may not be able to afford it, but good for you if you can! Anchoring the retail area north of Wilshire Boulevard between Santa Monica Boulevard and Rexford Drive are three high-fashion department stores, NYC's **Barneys New York** and **Saks Fifth Avenue,** plus Texas couturier **Neiman Marcus,** sitting like ducks in a row between 9500 and 9700 Wilshire.

Rodeo Drive is the most famous — and most exclusive — of the shopping streets, with two Euro-style, piazza-like couture malls (**2 Rodeo** and the **Rodeo Collection**), plus top designer boutiques such as Chanel, Van Cleef and Arpels, and many more. But you'll find plenty of reasonably priced booty throughout the easily walkable area, too. For a list, see www.beverlyhillsbehere.com. Though the city of Beverly Hills offers two hours free parking in their underground lots, those can fill up quickly, so expect to pay for a parking-lot space — bring quarters!

West Third Street

Right in the shadow of the famous **Beverly Center** mall (☎ 310-854-0071; www.beverlycenter.com), which sits like a prison at Beverly and La Cienega boulevards, is one of the city's most appealing shopping streets. Running east from La Cienega, West Third's shops are whimsical, accessible, and just upscale enough, such as **Traveler's Bookcase,** no. 8375 (☎ 323-655-0575), and the **Cook's Library,** no. 8373 (☎ 323-655-3141), two of the best specialty bookstores around; and **Freehand,** no. 8413 (☎ 323-655-2607), a first-rate crafts gallery. You should find meter parking, although perhaps a couple blocks or more from precisely where you want to be. Mall rats will enjoy the **Grove** (☎ 888-315-8883 or 323-900-8080; www.grovela.com), with its dancing water show, 14-screen theater designed to look like an Art Deco movie palace, and plenty of upscale chain stores and eateries located at Third and Fairfax, just east of the Farmers Market.

Los Angeles's Shopping Neighborhoods

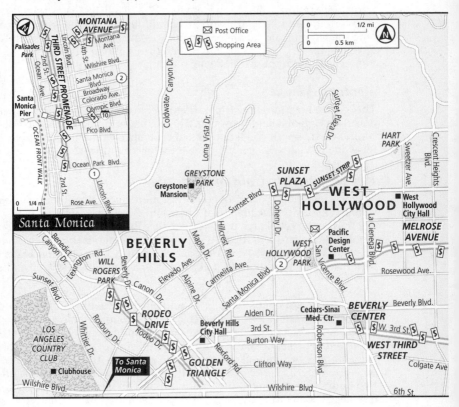

West Hollywood

Sunset Plaza is one of the oldest and poshest shopping districts in Los Angeles. It lines both sides of Sunset Boulevard, from 8720 Sunset to 8589 Sunset, anchored on the southwest by the former **Le Dome,** home away from home for many a now-bereft celebrity, and the celebrity caffeination spot **Coffee Bean & Tea Leaf** on the northeast (Britney Spears, Mark Wahlberg). There you'll find superstar retailer **Tracey Ross,** 8595 Sunset Blvd. (☎ 310-854-1996), whose clients include some of the brightest stars in Hollywood. Jeweler **Philip Press,** 8601 Sunset Blvd. (☎ 310-360-1180), offers fine platinum, colored stones, and diamonds, while **Armani Exchange,** 8700 Sunset Blvd. (☎ 310-659-0171), and other boutiques beckon. With over a half-dozen restaurants offering sidewalk brunching, lunching, and dining (expect smokers on the patios), Sunset Plaza provides a wealth of people-watching and a cosmopolitan flair. But don't park here unless you're shopping here; guards are vigilant and they will tow.

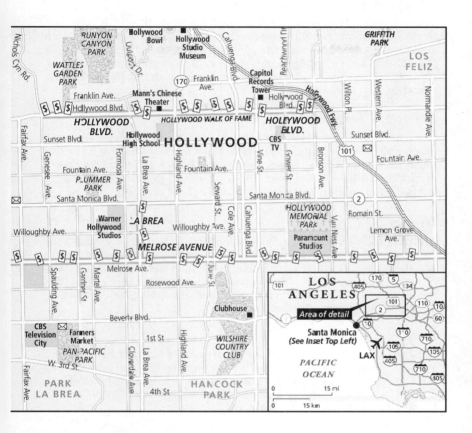

Hollywood

The hip, moneyed, and otherwise find the most righteous duds and trends here.

Melrose Avenue

L.A.'s wildest shopping strip starts out sophisticated at La Cienega Boulevard with **Marc Jacobs** (☎ 323-653-5100) and gets progressively more rock-'n'-roll as you move east. This area is great for star sightings, and the first place you should start is the **Fred Segal** boutique minimall, at Crescent Heights (☎ 323-651-1800), where the famous faces come and go at a fast and furious pace. East of Fairfax is where the Angelina Jolie/Courtney Love skanky/cool style kicks in with an emphasis on faddish shoes, cheap styles, and funky toys.

La Brea Avenue

The unsung stretch between Wilshire and Santa Monica boulevards is terrific for fashionable and retro-fascinated shoppers. Best is mammoth, eternally hip **American Rag, Cie.,** 150 S. La Brea, north of Second Street (☎ 323-935-3154), for high-end vintage wearables and vintage-like new wear. Antiques shops and other curious furniture stores are thick along this strip.

Hollywood Boulevard

Come here for dusty memorabilia shops full of vintage movie posters, autographed lobby cards, dog-eared scripts, and the like. You'll pay top dollar for top quality at **Hollywood Book & Poster,** 6562 Hollywood Blvd. (☎ 323-465-8764). Ignore the silly T-shirt and souvenir stores, unless you absolutely promised someone a piece of kitsch.

Universal City

Just over the Cahuenga Pass from Hollywood, Universal City is both the name of a sporadically interesting neighborhood (a section of Burbank) and the complex that includes Universal Studios and Universal CityWalk. Although there are a few older restaurants worth seeking out, the bulk of your time will be spent at the theme park and shopping mall, leaving little time for such explorations.

Universal CityWalk

Adjacent to Universal Studios is a kid's dream of a mall (☎ 818-622-4455; www.citywalkhollywood.com). It's a fake version of a real urban setting, but kids love it. CityWalk also offers some good dining and nightlife options — but, at $8, the parking fee is inexcusable. Take the 101 to Universal Center Drive or Lankershim Boulevard.

Living It Up after Dark

To see what's on, get the Sunday *Los Angeles Times* for its "Calendar" section, or the free *L.A. Weekly* and *New Times L.A.* Also check "The Guide" at the back of the glossy monthly mag *Los Angeles.* Use the Web resources (see the "Gathering More Information" section, later in this chapter) if you want to plan from home.

The major and the minor: Theater

One of the great surprises about L.A. is the high quality of its live-theater scene. All those wannabes have to do something before they get their big break on the CW, right? Actually, movie and TV actors often feel the urge to conquer the stage after their celluloid successes — or to exercise their atrophied live-acting chops.

The **Los Angeles Stage Alliance** (☎ 213-614-0556; www.lastage alliance.com) offers half-price Web tix to many major and minor shows, some the same day and others a few days in advance. Here's how it works: Go online and choose the show you want, enter your credit-card number, and the tickets will be waiting for you at the box office. Full-price tickets for major stagings generally vary from $25 to $75, but smaller productions can be as cheap as $10; you pay half, plus a service charge between $2 and $5.

The major

Of course, Los Angeles has theater on a larger level, and that brings us to downtown's venerable **Music Center** (the Performing Arts Center of Los Angeles County; www.musiccenter.org). Actually, it's four separate theaters: the gleaming **Disney Concert Hall,** 111 S. Grand Ave. (☎ 323-850-2000), the new home for the Los Angeles Philharmonic, a Frank Gehry–designed wonder of a building complete with state-of-the-art acoustics, which you should drive or walk past even if you don't attend a concert; the **Dorothy Chandler Pavilion,** 135 N. Grand Ave. (☎ 213-972-0711), which usually hosts classical music and opera; the **Ahmanson,** 135 N. Grand Ave. (☎ 213-628-2772; www.taperahmanson.com), the mid-size theater that runs about four plays a year; and the smaller **Mark Taper Forum,** 135 N. Grand Ave. (☎ 213-628-2772; www.taperahmanson.com), with nearly in-the-round-seating. Along with the new **Kirk Douglas Theatre** in Culver City, they are known as the Center Theater Group.

Another terrific stage is the **Geffen Playhouse,** 10886 Le Conte Ave., Westwood (☎ 310-208-5454; www.geffenplayhouse.com).

The minor

This town contains so many small theaters that your best bet is to start with **Los Angeles Stage Alliance** (☎ 213-614-0556; www.lastage alliance.com), which has all the current listings. You can also find ads for plays in the *L.A. Weekly.* Companies worth seeking out include the **Colony Studio Theatre** (☎ 818-558-7000; www.colonytheatre.org), generally considered to be L.A.'s finest small company; the scrappy and irreverent **Actors' Gang Theater** (☎ 310-838-GANG; www.theactors gang.com), which counts Tim Robbins among its founders; the **West Coast Ensemble Theater** (☎ 323-525-0022; www.wcensemble.org), known for smart stagings of familiar but well-chosen musicals and dramas; and **L.A. Theatre Works** (☎ 310-827-0889; www.latw.org), more often than not showcasing big-name actors in productions at the Skirball Cultural Center.

A little night music at the Hollywood Bowl

If you seek out one special venue before all others, make it this legendary alfresco bandshell at 2301 N. Highland Ave., at Odin Street (☎ 323-850-2000; www.hollywoodbowl.org). Recently entirely renovated — this is the fourth version of its iconic shell form — the Bowl is set in the hills above Hollywood in a natural amphitheater. It's a magical place to see a show under the stars, including the Los Angeles Philharmonic Orchestra (in residence all summer). The season runs from June through September and always includes a jazz series, summer fireworks galas, and other events.

Box seats are usually sold to season subscription holders, so single-ticket buyers generally end up in the bleacher seats or on the lawn. The bleachers are packed tight for sold-out events, and the setup is not overly comfortable. The magic of the evening more than compensates, but if you prefer more space, opt for the lawn. (That extra blanket in the closet of your hotel room will finally come in handy.)

One of the great Bowl traditions is picnicking before or during the show. Most concertgoers bring their own gourmet spread and wine. If you'd rather not bother, order a portable feast (with or without wine) from the Bowl's Food Services Department, now under the ownership of Patina, one of L.A.'s best restaurants (see the "Where to Dine in Los Angeles" section earlier in this chapter). It's expensive — around $17 for the cheapest cold entrée all the way up to around $50 for a three-course meal — but the Patina Group's reputation for fine food and the convenience of picking it up right there make it worth considering. Order by phone (☎ 323-850-1885) at least a day prior.

To get there, take the 101 to the Highland Avenue exit. Parking is extremely limited, so your best bet is to reserve a parking space in advance, or use one of the Park-and-Ride or shuttle services, for which you can purchase advance tickets. If you're feeling hearty, note that the Hollywood & Highland Center is about a mile and a half away, downhill. You can park there for a $2 validation (buy a cookie or something at a local shop, just to be fair) and hoof it up, thus avoiding the often ghastly lines that form trying to exit the over-crowded Bowl parking lots. Call the Bowl at ☎ 323-850-2000, Ticketmaster at ☎ 213-480-3232, or go online to www.hollywoodbowl.org and click on "Getting to the Bowl" for details.

The symphony in Los Angeles

We won't say there's just one game in town, but that's sort of true (certainly, it's hard to get anyone other than the critics to recall any other options), and its name is the **Los Angeles Philharmonic,** 135 N. Grand Ave. (☎ 213-850-2000; www.laphil.com), led by Finnish poster-boy Esa-Pekka Salonen and offering an annual slate of regular performances, celebrity-artist recitals, chamber music, and visiting artists-in-residence. Prices vary according to the kind of performance but can be as cheap as $12 (up in the heavens) and as expensive as $80.

The Philharmonic is now ensconced in its magnificent new home, the **Walt Disney Concert Hall.** Designed by Frank Gehry, this is L.A.'s first real landmark building, a sinuous, sensuous, gleaming-silver, curvy marvel that evokes a galleon ship, sails a' billowing. You must see it, even if you don't attend a concert — but you should: The interior is nearly as breathtaking as the outside, while the acoustics are so state of the art that local music critics are running out of adjectives to describe and praise it.

Opera in Los Angeles

It may not be La Scala (but then, what is?), but the **Los Angeles Opera, Dorothy Chandler Pavilion, 135 N. Grand Ave. (☎ 213-972-8001;** www. losangelesopera.com), regularly stages some extraordinary shows, generally earning across-the-board raves. No wonder; besides the depth of musical talent, the company has regular access to superb visual artists, always creating sets and staging that sparks serious talk (even if that talk runs to controversy, as with a recent stark, modern staging of Bach's *Mass in B Minor*). One complaint may be that the company relies too heavily on tried-and-true classics, but then again, they also stage and perform said classics magnificently. Placido Domingo is the opera's Artistic Director, and has been known to turn up as guest conductor, and none other than Hollywood director Billy Friedkin (yes, *The Exorcist* guy) recently directed Bartok's *Bluebeard's Castle*, so you can see the company does have a curious range.

Play it big and play it loud

For the less sedate, from rock to world and all points between, you'll likely find it playing at the **Gibson Amphitheatre** (formerly Universal Amphitheatre — nostalgic locals still call it that) or the **Greek Theatre.** The difference between them more or less, is that the former is indoors, and the latter outdoors. Note that parking for the Gibson means parking at Universal CityWalk, and often a long walk it is from your lot to your seat, so forego the high heels unless you're really skilled at strolling in stilettos.

Given our druthers, we like the **Greek, 2700 N. Vermont Ave. (☎ 323-665-1927;** www.greektheatrela.com); built in the '20s, it's graceful and pretty and set in the middle of Griffith Park, although its parking lot is a nightmare. (We've taken to parking around Los Feliz Boulevard and walking the ¾-mile up to the Greek. You'll have company, so it's safe enough.) Bring a sweater, in case it gets chilly.

For those about to rock

Ah, yes, L.A. rocks. The city is thriving with new and veteran rock clubs, and the music scene is hotter than Riverside asphalt (ouch!). The area with the highest concentration of good rock clubs is the Sunset Strip in West Hollywood. It's well lit at night, and most venues have valet parking as well as a variety of cover charges (call for details).

Avalon
Hollywood

This Art Deco ex-vaudeville theater on Vine across from the famed Capitol Tower recently underwent a multimillion-dollar renovation that removed some of the nostalgic charm but added some creature comforts. Once known as the Hollywood Palace (as such, the site of a '60s TV variety show) and later just the Palace (primarily used for music events, with Nirvana, Prince, and many other major acts having played there), it now offers rock events, and on Fridays and Saturdays hosts popular dance-club events into the wee hours, along with dining, several full bars, and a private club-within-a-club called the Spider Room.

1735 N. Vine St. ☎ *323-462-8900.* www.avalonhollywood.com.

Key Club
West Hollywood

At the west end of the Sunset Strip is the ultrasnappy Key Club. This postmodern rock club was built at the site of a legendary L.A. rock club called Gazzarri's (think the early Doors but later Van Halen), and in a few short years has become a very popular destination for live music and late-night dancing.

9039 Sunset Blvd. ☎ *310-274-5800.*

Largo
Hollywood

People are so devoted to this live-music supper club that if you duck out of the show early, you may get the stink-eye. It's understandable — musical mad-hatter Jon Brion, who produced the *Magnolia* soundtrack, and such artists as Fiona Apple perform quirky sets each Friday to a star-studded audience. Monday nights is comedy with name performers (Sarah Silverman shows up regularly as well as Patton Oswald), and a variety of musical and comedy acts, ranging from unknowns to the likes of Margaret Cho fill out the rest of the week. You may want to make dinner reservations to assure seating, though standing room is an option even when the tables are full.

432 N. Fairfax Ave. ☎ *323-852-1073.* www.largo-la.com.

The Roxy
West Hollywood

Since the early '70s, this Sunset Strip club has been part of the celebrated Hollywood rock triumvirate that included the Whisky a Go-Go and the Troubadour. Although its history includes storied shows by Neil Young, Bruce Springsteen, David Bowie, and many others, these days the Roxy tends to host unknown local acts trying to break into the business.

9009 Sunset Blvd. ☎ *310-278-9457.* www.theroxyonsunset.com.

Safari Sam's
Hollywood

The reincarnation of a mid-'80s local live-music staple, this 465-person venue features local and touring acts ranging from punk rock and New Wave progenitors such as Agent Orange and the Plimsouls to touring up-and-comers, along with theme clubs such as the retro-fashioned Dandy where attendees sport garb from the 1820s to the 1930s. The space also features a restaurant and art gallery. A fine addition to the L.A. club scene — welcome back!

5241 Sunset Blvd. (between Western and Normandie). ☎ *323-666-7267.* www.safari sams.com.

Spaceland
Silver Lake

The Silver Lake nightclub that started it all still rocks. The live-music venue born out of an old discothèque is permanently art-damaged and not terribly fancy, but that's part of its charm. Surprise guests show up often during the week, and artists such as Beck, Daniel Lanois, and Fiona Apple have performed spontaneous sets.

1717 Silver Lake Blvd. ☎ *323-661-4380.* www.clubspaceland.com.

The Troubadour
West Hollywood

Just down the hill from the Sunset Strip is this veteran nightclub offering cutting-edge live music. The wood-grain interior is a relic from the days when this cozy Hollywood club showcased the Byrds and the Eagles in the '60s and '70s. It was also a key stop for such quintessential L.A. acts as Van Halen in the '70s and Motley Crüe in the '80s. In recent years, the booking has been something of a hodgepodge, but it's a good bet that some local, national, and international alt-rock acts on their way up will stop here, as well as some surprises: The Red Hot Chili Peppers played here under an assumed name to show off the *Stadium Arcadium* album to their friends before leaving on their 2006–2007 world tour.

9081 Santa Monica Blvd. ☎ *310-276-6168.* www.troubadour.com.

The Viper Room
West Hollywood

The music legacy of the Viper Room is unparalleled. Since its '93 debut, this black-hot nightclub formerly owned by that red-hot actor Johnny Depp has featured world-class talent on a weekly basis. You never know who's going to show up on stage — or in the audience.

8852 Sunset Blvd. ☎ *310-358-1881.* www.viperroom.com.

Snazzy bars

There's nothing like a night on the town at one of Hollywood's gorgeous bars. We handpicked some of our favorites, narrowing the list from many choices based on style, comfort, and easy access.

One of Hollywood's hottest bars is **Beauty Bar,** 1638 Cahuenga Blvd. (☎ 323-464-7676; www.beautybar.com), a luscious pink confection with DJs nightly. The bar, designed to look like an old-school beauty parlor (the original in New York *was* an actual beauty parlor), serves real martinis and real manicures (on weekends by appointment).

The **Velvet Margarita Cantina,** 1612 Cahuenga (☎ 323-469-2000; www.velvetmargarita.com) — a huge, campy, sexy, semi-Goth-themed Mexican bar/restaurant with black-light paintings, velvet Elvis portraits, a ceiling made of silver mariachi hats, and purple velvet booths — features (what else) tequilas and margaritas. It also serves food and has thoughtfully single-priced the appetizers and entrees to make splitting the bill easier on its lubricated patrons.

If you're going to either of these, parking is directly across the street, but you run the risk of a jaywalking ticket or, worse, getting creamed by a speeding car. Use the crosswalks 200 feet to the north or the valet parking in front of the venues!

What if you could shop for shoes while sipping on a cocktail? Well, **Star Shoes,** 6364 Hollywood Blvd., Hollywood (☎ 323-462-7827), can grant you your wish. The beautiful bar doubles as a shoe store, with eye-popping displays of vintage shoes enticing customers in off the street. There's a dance floor for late-night frolicking and an easy-breezy attitudeless atmosphere. Open nightly.

As much a club as it is a bar, **Ivan Kane's Forty Deuce,** 5574 Melrose Ave. (☎ 323-465-42424), was the flashpoint for the revival of burlesque, the classy bump and grind that put the tease back in striptease, and made it safe for the whole family. Okay, maybe not, but the gals here put on such a good show that any number of celebs (and we mean high-level names such as Brad and Justin) can be found gathered around the runway, shamelessly urging them on. Particularly skilled DJs keep the beat going when the girls are offstage. Expect a cover charge and bad sightlines, unless you reserve a table, which will set you back even more.

During the warm-weather months, the **Cat & Fiddle,** 6530 Sunset Blvd., Hollywood (☎ 323-468-3800), is a favorite watering hole for the beer-drinking set. The British pub features a large outdoor patio, with live music on weekends. The staff is particularly nice, and the authentic fish and chips lure people back year after year. It's a good place for a large party. Open nightly; 21 and older at night, all ages during the day.

The legendary **Lava Lounge,** 1533 N. La Brea Ave., Hollywood (☎ 323-876-6612; www.lavahollywood.com), opened its doors a month before the great quake of January '94, and it's still shaking. The tiki-themed bar, which erupts with live music Wednesday through Saturday nights, once called Quentin Tarantino and Jon Favreau (of *Swingers* fame) regulars, and now it's serving up a whole new breed. The exotic drinks are adorned with plastic monkeys and mermaids, and you can't beat that with a swizzle stick. Open nightly; 21 and older.

Stop by the **Dresden Lounge,** 1760 Vermont Ave., Los Feliz (☎ 323-665-4294; www.thedresden.com), and give a thumbs up to Marty and Elayne, the jazz combo popularized in the movie *Swingers.* We've known that lovely couple for a long time now, and frankly, they're tired of being asked to play "Stayin' Alive." Do us a favor: Ask Elayne to play "Autumn in New York"; she'll blow you a kiss. Marty and Elayne perform Monday through Saturday; 21 and older in lounge.

At ten years old, the **Three Clubs,** 1123 N. Vine St., Hollywood (☎ 324-462-6441), was among the first of the new wave of hipster bars that took Hollywood by storm in the late '80s and '90s. It still has that sizzle, with its dark interior, friendly bartenders, and casual-cool clientele. Some nights you may find a DJ lurking in the back room, where it's *really* fun to lurk. Twenty-one and older.

At this writing, the latest steaming hot hangout was tiny **Hyde Lounge,** 8029 Sunset Blvd. (☎ 323-656-4933), which means that by the time you read this, it will either be a must-stop for any serious partying visitor, or it will have cooled into nonexistence. If it's still as sizzling as when we wrote this, expect supreme difficulty gaining entrance (all the more to whet your appetite), including valets who might not even take your car until they're assured you're in the door. Feeling inferior? Frankly, because we don't have names like Nichole Richie, Lindsay Lohan, Paris Hilton, and others who have acted up and out during this club's early days, so do we. If you get in, enjoy the floor show they'll likely provide.

The **Tropicana** at the Hollywood Roosevelt, 7000 Hollywood Blvd. (☎ 323-466-7000), was the hottest bar until Hyde opened, but it's probably likely to stick around longer, thanks to the oh-so-L.A. poolside den vibe. As always, it can be a hard bar to crack if you aren't super famous, though renting a cabana room at the hotel guarantees entree. If watching the likes of Jeremy Piven, Owen Wilson, Kirsten Dunst, the Hilton sisters, and assorted sordid Hollywood types gives you the thrills, we suggest you get there early — and avoid Thursday nights when the velvet rope is notoriously solid.

Drinks with a view

There are any number of reasons to visit the **Highlands,** 6801 Hollywood Blvd., Hollywood (☎ 323-461-9800), a grand nightclub and restaurant at the new Hollywood & Highland Center, home to the Academy Awards and the Kodak Theatre. First, the bilevel club is located on the fourth floor of Hollywood & Highland and offers a terrific view of Hollywood Boulevard. Second, its Friday- and Saturday-night dance parties are fueled by top local and touring DJs. The club includes three outdoor decks and plentiful parking at the complex. And when you get tired of boogieing, you can window-shop at swanky and trendy Hollywood & Highland boutiques. Cover varies ($15–$20 on weekends); 21 and older.

One of the legendary L.A. haunts, **Yamashiro,** 1999 Sycamore Ave., Hollywood (☎ 323-466-5125; www.yamashirorestaurant.com), still has our favorite view. The classic Japanese restaurant overlooks Hollywood in all its glory, and if you arrive in time for sunset, you can settle in for the night and watch the colors of the sky fade from pink to ink. It's terribly romantic and worth the long, winding drive up the hill. No cover; open nightly.

Gay faves

Just a couple of blocks from the hard-rocking hetero nightlife of the Sunset Strip lies the heart of gay Los Angeles, Santa Monica Boulevard and what is affectionately (most of the time) known as Boys' Town. Most of West Hollywood is gay-friendly, but the area near San Vicente Boulevard boasts the hottest of the hot meeting places, stores, restaurants, and of course nightclubs.

No matter what year or what day of the week, **Rage,** 8911 Santa Monica Blvd., West Hollywood (☎ 310-652-7055; www.ragewesthollywood. com), rages. The long-running gay dance club is a scorcher of a scene, although it's aggressively young, pretty, and trendy, so you may want to stop at the gym and do a few thousand ab crunches before you go. Rage books a wide variety of DJs, who spin everything from progressive house to alternative rock. Cover varies; 21 and older.

Micky's, 8857 Santa Monica Blvd., West Hollywood (☎ 310-657-1176; www.mickys.com), is sort of "Rage Lite," with all the big crowds, packed dance floor, and pretty men, but a little less stand-and-pose attitude. Cover varies; 21 and older most nights.

Other notable Boys' Town bars include the **Abbey,** 692 N. Robertson Blvd., West Hollywood (☎ 310-289-8410; www.abbeyfoodandbar.com), a trendy java joint and restaurant by day and a busy indoor/outdoor cruise bar at night, growing all the more popular thanks to its new owner, a local club impresario; **Revolver,** 8851 Santa Monica Blvd., West Hollywood (☎ 310-659-8851), a video bar hosting very popular karaoke events several nights a week; and just to prove it's not all about the boys, there's **Girl Bar** at the **Factory,** 652 La Peer Dr., West Hollywood (☎ 310-659-4551), L.A.'s hottest lesbian nightclub. The spacious dance party boasts women DJs, go-go dancers, and promoters. It's a weekly girl-power powwow (although Fridays only and with a $10 cover).

One of the most popular West Hollywood bars is actually located a couple of miles up the street from the Boys' Town epicenter, but it's worth the trek. **Fubar,** 7994 Santa Monica Blvd., West Hollywood (☎ 323-654-0396; www.fubarla.com), somehow managed to turn a narrow, hole-in-the-wall neighborhood bar into a hip, happening lounge with hot DJs (despite the lack of dance floor), wild entertainment that verges on performance art (we once saw a drag queen attack a Christmas tree — you had to be there), and a fun crowd of all types.

Fast Facts

AAA

Multiple Tinseltown offices include 1900 S. Sepulveda Blvd., south of Santa Monica Boulevard in West L.A. (☎ 310-914-8500); 5550 Wilshire Blvd., between Fairfax and La Brea avenues, Hollywood (☎ 323-525-0018); and 2601 S. Figueroa St., at Adams Boulevard, downtown (☎ 213-741-3686).

American Express

You'll find L.A. offices at 8493 W. Third St., at La Cienega Boulevard, across from the Beverly Center (☎ 310-659-1682); and 327 N. Beverly Dr., between Brighton and Dayton ways, Beverly Hills (☎ 310-274-8277).

Baby Sitters

Hotels can usually recommend reliable baby sitters. If yours can't, contact the Baby-Sitters Guild (☎ 323-938-8372 or 818-552-2229), L.A.'s only bonded baby-sitting agency and recently named best in the city by *Los Angeles* magazine. Book a Saturday-night sit no later than Thursday morning.

Emergencies

For police, fire, or other emergencies, dial ☎ 911.

Hospitals

Cedars Sinai Medical Center, 8700 Beverly Blvd., at San Vicente Boulevard, a block west of La Cienega Boulevard (☎ 310-423-3277), has a 24-hour emergency room.

Internet Centers

Fed-Ex Kinko's, 7630 Sunset Blvd., between Fairfax and La Brea avenues in Hollywood (☎ 323-845-4501), offers Internet access 24 hours a day for 20¢ per minute.

Newspapers and Magazines

The daily is the *Los Angeles Times;* the "Calendar" section in the Sunday edition is the source for arts-and-entertainment listings. The *L.A. Weekly* is L.A.'s answer to New York's *Village Voice;* this free alternapaper is easily available around town; *City Beat* and *L.A. Alternative Press* provide the same service with differing editorial slants. *Los Angeles* magazine is a glossy monthly with good coverage of L.A.'s dining and arts scenes.

Police

Dial ☎ 911 in an emergency. For nonemergency matters, call ☎ 877-ASK-LAPD (877-275-5273) or 213-485-2121. In Beverly Hills, call ☎ 310-550-4951 for nonemergencies.

Post Office

Call ☎ 800-ASK-USPS (800-275-8777) to find the nearest post office.

Taxes

Sales tax is 8.25 percent. Hotel taxes range from 12 to 17 percent, depending on the municipality you're in.

Taxis

Call L.A. Taxi Co-op (☎ 310-715-1968) or Independent Taxi (☎ 323-666-0045).

Weather

Call ☎ 213-554-1212 for the daily forecast.

Gathering More Information

Contact the **Los Angeles Convention and Visitors Bureau** (☎ 800-366-6116 or 213-689-8822; www.lacvb.com) to request a free visitor's kit, find out about upcoming events, or ask specific questions.

After you're in town, you'll find an excellent walk-in **Visitor Information Center,** downtown at 685 S. Figueroa St., between Wilshire Boulevard and Seventh Street; it's open Monday through Friday from 8 a.m. to 5 p.m. and Saturday from 8:30 a.m. to 5 p.m. You may also want to stop by the staffed **Hollywood Visitor Information Center,** at 6541 Hollywood Blvd., just west of Cahuenga Boulevard, which is open Monday through Saturday from 9 a.m. to 5 p.m. You can find Hollywood information at www.hollywoodcoc.org.

In addition, many municipalities maintain their own visitor centers:

- ✔ The **Beverly Hills Conference and Visitors Bureau** is at 239 S. Beverly Dr., south of Wilshire Boulevard between Charleville and Gregory Way (☎ 800-345-2210 or 310-248-1015). Official Beverly Hills information is online at www.beverlyhillsbehere.com.

- ✔ The **Santa Monica Convention and Visitors Bureau** has a walk-up center in Palisades Park, 1400 Ocean Ave., near Santa Monica Boulevard (☎ 310-393-7593). Santa Monica information is at www.santamonica.com.

- ✔ The **West Hollywood Convention and Visitors Bureau** is in the Pacific Design Center, 8687 Melrose Ave., Suite M25, at San Vicente Boulevard (☎ 800-368-6020 or 310-289-2525; www.visitwesthollywood.com).

Your best source for the latest arts, entertainment, dining, nightlife, and event listings is the *Los Angeles Times*'s www.calendarlive.com. Other good sources for the latest on what's happening in the city are the *L.A. Weekly* site at www.laweekly.com and www.digitalcity.com/losangeles. The online version of *Los Angeles* magazine at www.lamag.com is another good source, especially if you're looking for more good restaurants to choose from.

Chapter 24

The Happiest Place on Earth: The Disneyland Resort!

In This Chapter

▶ Planning your visit
▶ Getting there
▶ Finding the perfect places to stay and eat
▶ Practicing proven tips for touring the legendary park
▶ Exploring the resort's newest attractions

1 s it really the "Happiest Place on Earth?" Who can say (there are places in Bali that are very happy, indeed), but we have to admit, we get happy just writing the word *Disneyland.*

Sure, the one in Florida may be bigger, and the one in France may have Pirates singing in French (*quelle* hoot!), but this is the original. "Walt's Folly," the naysayers called it, because they predicted an embarrassing, costly failure, bless them. It didn't fail, naturally. And decades after its conception, it remains *the* top sight of Southern California. With or without a kid, we recommend visiting at least once.

Disneyland is no longer just Disneyland; it is now the **Disneyland Resort,** which encompasses Walt's original amusement park, the ambitious theme park **California Adventure,** three hotels, and the big dining/entertaining/shopping complex known as **Downtown Disney.** Downtown Disney is actually located outside the park (although it's considered part of it), but you may find yourself walking through it to get to Disneyland (on the left) or California Adventure (on the right), depending on your arrival point. Downtown Disney has no entrance fee and no gate, but you have to pay for parking if you drive in. Anyone who wants to leave the resort to visit Downtown Disney can have a hand stamped for re-admittance to the parks. To lure teens and the college crowd, Downtown Disney offers clubs and other late-night attractions; to lure moms and dads, there are fancy restaurants and shopping.

It would be easy to dismiss the park as commerce over fantasy, because Disneyland has always been about product tie-ins (although really slick about it — a spoonful of sugar helps the medicine go down, don't you know). But in every inch of the place, a tremendous amount of thought, detail, research, and, yes, imagination is still given. No matter how it evolves, Disneyland remains a place of delight, a place where even in the midst of souvenir stands and overpriced snacks, a kid can burst into giggles of pure joy because a mouse waved at him. And every time we go, we still play the game of who can spot the Matterhorn first, and shiver with pleasure when it appears, because that means we're almost there.

Choosing When to Visit

The best time to visit may be when you have vacation and the kids are off from school. If you're flexible with your schedule, though, a number of factors can influence your decision, because the Disneyland Resort has seasons of its very own.

- ✔ **Busiest times:** Disneyland is busiest in summer (between Memorial Day and Labor Day), but it can also be crowded on holidays (Thanksgiving week, Christmas week, President's Day weekend, Easter week, and Japan's Golden Week in early May) and weekends year-round. All other times make up the off-season.

  During the busy summertime, Tuesday through Thursday is the best time to come; Friday and Saturday are the most crowded days.

- ✔ **Fireworks, shows, and parades:** If you want to see all the shows and parades, you have to visit during the high season, because scheduling is sporadic on off-season weekdays. Disneyland's famed fireworks displays happen mostly in summer with, occasional exceptions. Christmas also brings its own special magic to Disneyland, when the park is dressed up for the holidays, complete with giant decorated trees, wreaths everywhere, and visits with Santa and the Candlelight Parade, wherein carolers from all over the Southland lead visitors in a special recital of "The Christmas Story." Special celebrity guests have included James Earl Jones and Dick Van Dyke.

  Currently, **Fantasmic,** a nighttime musical stage show, which incorporates fireworks, projected water screens, moving water crafts and other special effects as it chronicles Mickey Mouse's battle of good against evil, takes place over Rivers of America. This mystical and magical extravaganza is awesome but can be scary for the more timid tykes.

  Also, for the time being, the favorite old-school **Electrical Parade** (it used to run along Main Street many, many years ago and was, at the time, the ultimate spectacular) has returned to **California Adventure** after a short stint in Tokyo.

- ✔ **Summer scorchers:** Consider the summer heat when deciding when to go. Scorching days in July, August, and September can make waiting to board a ride feel like a death march, with everyone crowding into available shady spots, and super-long lines to buy cold drinks. Visiting during these months can be fine; just plan to take advantage of the indoor attractions during the midday heat. Your reward later on will be a pleasantly balmy evening, when being outdoors becomes a delight.

- ✔ **Crowd-free days:** If you want to avoid crowds, visit on a weekday, preferably in November, December, or January (excluding Thanksgiving and Christmas weeks). You run the risk that some rides may be closed for maintenance (never more than three or four at a time), but visiting during this low, low season is the best way to maximize a single day. Going for a Sunday/Monday combination at this time of year almost guarantees that you'll hit everything you want while also getting to enjoy the shows and parades.

- ✔ **First-quarter rains:** Southern California gets most of its precipitation between January and April, but only a sustained downpour should affect your Disney plans. If the forecast predicts rain, bring both a collapsible umbrella and a waterproof rain poncho (or splurge on the cute Mickey Mouse ponchos that suddenly appear when the first raindrop falls). Even if you get wet, you'll enjoy the lightest crowds of the year! (The locals know the truth: The very best time to visit Disneyland is a drizzly, slightly cold winter day midweek — provided you're not with kids younger than 4.)

Deciding How Long to Stay

You want to devote at least one (very) full day to the original park. If you're planning to visit during one of the peak periods, crowds and wait times will limit the attractions you're able to enjoy in a single day, so plan to spend the night and re-enter Disneyland fresh the following morning. If California Adventure holds any interest for you, set aside two days to experience both parks.

Park Hopper passes (see the following section) are a great deal for the money, and the passes don't require you to visit on consecutive days (if you want to break up your Disney stay with a day at the beach, for example). If you're traveling with small children, you want the multiday option, regardless of the season. Although surviving a marathon Disney day is a badge of honor for older kids, you know that naptime crankiness will eventually rear its ugly head with the young ones.

All in all, we suggest allotting two or three full days for the Disney attractions, which gives you enough time to immerse yourself in the fantasy before moving on to the next leg of your California visit. (If you're staying elsewhere in Southern California but would like two days at the park, plan on spending the night at the park rather than driving back again the next day. You'll be glad you did.)

Getting the Lowdown on Admission

At press time, admission to either Disneyland or California Adventure — including unlimited rides and all festivities and entertainment — was $59 for adults and kids ages 10 and older and $49 for kids ages 3 to 9 (kids younger than 3 enter free). Keep in mind, though, that these prices can go up at any time.

Disney currently offers multiday **Park Hopper passes,** which allow unlimited access to both Disneyland and California Adventure. A three-day pass is $160 for adults and $130 for kids ages 3 to 9. Five-day passes cost $210 and $180, respectively. (Two- and four-day passes are also available.) Though the passes must be used within 13 days of the first day of use, the days spent at the park need not be consecutive, so the Park Hopper route is the most practical way to go. We go into further detail in the "Exploring the Resort" section later in this chapter, but there are good reasons to have access to both parks, provided you don't pay full price for California Adventure.

Disney offers regular deals on ticket prices, especially during the slow winter months (when Park Hopper passes go for less money), so make sure you check their Web site or call in advance.

Expect to pay a parking charge of between $8 and $10, which may be included in some admission packages. Always ask whether parking is part of any package you buy from Disney.

Opening the starting gate

The Disneyland Resort is open every day of the year, but operating hours vary widely. Call for the information that applies to the time frame of your visit (☎ 714-781-4565). You can also find exact open hours, ride closures, and show schedules online at www.disneyland.com.

Generally speaking, the park is open from 9 or 10 a.m. to 8 p.m. on weekdays, fall to spring; and from 8 or 9 a.m. to midnight or 1 a.m. on weekends, holidays, and during summer vacation periods. California Adventure tends to close two to four hours earlier than Disneyland. If you'd like to receive a copy of the park's "Vacation Planner" brochure to orient yourself before you go, call ☎ 800-225-2024.

Buying in advance can be an enormous time, and sometimes money, saver. If you plan to arrive during a busy time (either when the gates open in the morning or between 11 a.m. and 2 p.m.), purchasing your tickets in advance and getting a jump on the crowds at the ticket counters is your best bet. You can buy your tickets through the Web site, at Disney stores throughout the United States, or by calling the mail-order line (☎ 714-781-4043). Many area hotels also sell tickets at regular cost (including whatever special deal is being offered at the time).

Discovering the art of the (package) deal

If you intend to spend two or more nights in Disney territory, investigating the available package options can pay off. Start by contacting your hotel (even those in Los Angeles or San Diego) to find out whether they offer Disneyland Resort admission packages. Some of the airline vacation packagers include admission to Disneyland in their inclusive packages (see Chapter 6 for more information).

In addition, check with the official Disney agency, **Walt Disney Travel Co.** (☎ **800-225-2024** or 714-520-5060; www.disneyland.com), whose packages are value-packed time and money savers with lots of built-in flexibility. As this book went to press, they were offering a free child's Park Hopper pass with every paid adult Park Hopper Pass, so you can see that bargains are to be found there. You can request a glossy catalog by mail or log onto the Web site and search for "Vacation Packages" to peruse package details, take a virtual tour of participating hotel properties, and get online price quotes for customized, date-specific packages.

Hotel choices range from the official Disney hotels to one of 35 neighboring hotels in every price range. A wide range of available extras includes admission to other Southern California attractions and guided tours (such as **Universal Studios** or a **Tijuana** shopping trip) and behind-the-scenes Disneyland tours, all in limitless combinations. Rates are highly competitive, especially considering that each package includes multiday admission, early park entry, and free parking (if you choose a Disney hotel), plus keepsake souvenirs and coupon books. If you want to add air transportation or car rental, the Walt Disney Travel Co. can make those arrangements, too.

Getting to the Disneyland Resort

The Disneyland Resort is located in the heart of Anaheim in Orange County, about 30 miles south of Los Angeles and 98 miles north of San Diego. To get there from either city, follow I-5 until you see signs for Disneyland; dedicated off-ramps from both directions lead directly to the park's parking lots and surrounding streets.

From the Palm Springs area, follow I-10 westbound to Highway 60 west. In Riverside, pick up Highway 91 west to Anaheim, and then take Highway 57 south. Exit at the Ball Road off-ramp and turn right (west), proceeding 2½ miles to Disneyland. The drive totals 110 miles.

If you'd rather wing it, **Los Angeles International Airport (LAX)** is the region's major airport, about 30 miles away. You can rent a car at the airport and drive to Anaheim, or you can take advantage of the many public-transportation services at LAX (see Chapter 23 for details).

If you'd rather fly directly into Anaheim from another state or another California city, the nearest airport is **John Wayne International Airport** in Santa Ana, 15 miles from Disneyland at the intersection of I-405 and Highway 55 (☎ 949-252-5200; www.ocair.com). Most national airlines and major rental-car agencies serve the airport. To reach Anaheim from the airport, rent a car and take Highway 55 east, then follow I-5 north to the Disneyland exit.

An entire family can also catch a ride with **Yellow Cab** (☎ 800-535-2211), whose cabs queue up at the Ground Transportation Center on the lower level; reservations are not necessary. Expect the fare to Disneyland to run about $30. If only two of you are making the trip, however, consider using Super Shuttle (☎ 800-BLUE-VAN; www.supershuttle.com), which charges $10 per person to the Disneyland area. Advance reservations are recommended.

Before you pay for a taxi or shuttle service, ask when you make your reservation whether your Anaheim hotel offers airport transportation.

Deciding Where to Stay

The official Disney hotels are our favorites, both for convenience and ambience. But lots of reasons exist to stay at one of the many other hotels and motels that line the surrounding blocks, not the least of which is that sometimes all 2,200-plus Disney guest rooms are full.

Staying in official Disney digs

Can't decide whether to stay off-campus or splurge on one of the official Disney hotels? The main advantages of going 100 percent Disney are

- ✔ **The Disney monorail:** Circumnavigating the theme park, the monorail also stops at each official hotel (and soon at California Adventure as well). So when you get weary of hoofing it, simply hop aboard and zip straight to your room. Dedicated ticket booths and entry turnstiles at the monorail stations mean you can also avoid the main-entrance crush.

- ✔ **Just plain fun:** The official properties are just plain fun to stay at. Each gets the patented Disney treatment, with fantasy settings and imagination-stimulating diversions. Rooms, too, bear the Disney touch: bathroom amenities, for example, are plastered with Disney characters — and simply scream "free souvenir"!

Disneyland Hotel
$$$$ Disneyland

The Disneyland Hotel is the original Disney hotel, bless its heart, and for a while, it was the only Disney hotel. It was once so very, very grand and fun to stay at, but now that we've seen the Grand Californian, it's hard to go back. The hotel had a recent, and overdue, renovation, so rooms are fresh once again. Rooms have a vague Fantasyland theme, with Cinderella's castle on the headboards, glow-in-the-dark Tinkerbells around the tops of the walls, armoires with sketches of the original Disneyland on them, and Mickey hands supporting the bathroom sconces. Although whimsical, the hotel is just a bit more grown-up than a hotel that ought to be geared for kids should be. (They have weekday newspaper delivery, for pity's sake. Good for adults, but where's the kiddie love? A video arcade isn't enough.) But that's okay: There is still a Peter Pan–themed pool area, complete with water slide and pirate ship, as well as Goofy's Kitchen, an "all-you-care-to-eat" buffet hosted by all the traditional Disney characters (many experienced Disney-goers say this is *the* best place for the up-close-and-personal experience). Note that rooms in the Bonita tower are the largest and quietest.

1150 Magic Way. ☎ *714-956-6425. Fax: 714-956-6597.* www.disneyland.com. *Parking: Free self-parking, valet parking $26. Rack rates: $245–$300 double. AE, DISC, MC, V.*

Disney's Grand Californian
$$$$–$$$$$ **Disneyland**

It's a thing of lavish and loving beauty, a drop-dead gorgeous hotel that has been painstakingly researched and designed. The curmudgeonly might snark that it has the potential to give one an Arts and Crafts–overload headache. To heck with them. Styled to evoke Yosemite's landmark Ahwahnee Hotel (it's the Mock-wahnee, if you will), it has incredible period detail, from the cavernous, multistoried lobby with the giant roaring fireplace right down to the door fixtures and even the trash cans in each room. Several times a day, a storyteller thrills kids with campfire tales geared toward California; it's a charming free service parents must take advantage of. The rooms are Arts and Crafts smashes, with pocket doors, nature themes (branches and leaves), lush amenities, and even a lack of maid carts in the hallways (baskets deliver the fresh linens in the morning). Suites are even better, but all rooms have robes, cribs, irons and boards, dual vanities, and coffee pots. The beds are comfy and firm, although the towels could be a bit softer and the bathrooms a bit bigger, to tell the truth. Aren't we ungrateful? We just love this place to pieces — Disney should be justly proud of themselves. Even the locals tend to venture here for a night or two. Come take a look at it even if you don't stay over, and feel free to use its very own entrance into California Adventure.

1600 S. Disneyland Dr. ☎ *714-956-6425. Fax: 714-300-7300.* www.disneyland.com. *Parking: Free self-parking, valet parking $26. Rack rates: $300–$375 double. AE, DISC, MC, V.*

Disney's Paradise Pier
$$–$$$$ **Disneyland**

This hotel, the second of the Disneyland hotels — and the smallest of the three (500 rooms) — has the lowest profile. Basically, the only reason to stay here is, well, because the other Disney hotels are full. There's nothing *wrong* with it; it even has a theme, finally, if you can call something as vague as "ocean fun" a theme. Recently renovated rooms (which seem larger than some at the Grand Californian) have a sort of beachy vibe with nautical fittings, bleached wood, striped fabrics, and a disturbing bubble-print carpet. The lobby has a (deliberate) ocean smell, and a kiddie TV room is decorated to evoke the beach with beige carpet, beach chairs, and a TV monitor (that runs nonstop cartoons) encased in a giant painting of a sandcastle. The third-floor pool is rooftop, which can be kind of cool, but it pales to its sibling hotels, although there is a water slide.

1717 S. Disneyland Dr. ☎ *714-956-6425. Fax: 714-776-5763.* www.disneyland.com. *Parking: Free self-parking, valet parking $26. Rack rates: $215–$275 double. AE, DISC, MC, V.*

Bunking beyond the resort

You can usually find more economical rooms at the many hotels lining the streets surrounding the park than at those within the park. Naturally, they're not as lavish and entertaining as the Disney hotels; but if saving money is your prime concern, the off-campus hotels offer such advantages as free shuttles, free parking, and free breakfast. Depending on the season and on availability, the rack rates can be deeply discounted. Be sure to check online and/or by telephone to get the best deal possible.

Disney has an arrangement with a number of hotels in the area called the "Good Neighbor Package." You can purchase Disneyland tickets from the participating hotel at the regular price, thus saving a wait in a potentially very long line at the parks. If Disney is offering any special ticket discounts at that time, the hotels offer the same discount.

Some hotels offer free shuttles to the park, while others are on the **Anaheim Resort Transit** line (☎ **888-364-ARTS;** www.atnetwork.org/art_routes.html), a shuttle service that picks up at clearly marked stops near or at hotels and goes to Disneyland, returning regularly from the Disneyland main shuttle drop-off area. The shuttles run every 20 minutes along Ball Road, Katella Avenue, and Harbor Boulevard. Rates are $3 for unlimited rides all day, $1 for children 3 to 9 (kids younger than 3 ride free). Tickets are available at hotels along the routes and at the shuttle drop-off in Disneyland.

Anaheim Plaza Hotel & Suites
$–$$ Anaheim

Don't be put off by the initial appearance; from the outside, this hotel complex looks like an unappealing strip mall. But there's a lot going on among its 9 acres, which provide plenty of lawn space for playing, not to mention an Olympic-sized swimming pool. Inside, a surprisingly large marble lobby has a small business center, a bar, and a Mexican-themed grill where kids younger than 9 eat free, plus a pool table which children can use. Making it even more family-friendly is a laundry room — with glass doors and windows so families can keep an eye on each other. The ample rooms are in two-story garden-style bungalows, which make the place feel more like

Hawaii than Orange County. Rooms come with microwaves, coffeemakers, and wet bars; ground-floor accommodations have enclosed patios, while second-floor rooms have balconies. And it's just across the street from the Disneyland Resort.

1700 S. Harbor Blvd. ☎ **800-631-4144** or 714-772-5900. Fax: 714-772-8386. www. anaheimplazahotel.com. *Free parking. Rack rates: $69–$139 double. AE, DC, DISC, MC, V.*

Camelot Inn & Suites
$$ Anaheim

Of all the many hotels on Harbor Boulevard, this is the only one with any kind of interesting architecture, sort of old-world Tudor (okay, prefab, but still) rather than typical concrete block. All rooms are being upgraded, and the new color scheme should make them look lighter and fresher. The rooms are adequately sized and come complete with microwaves and a small fridge, which makes this a fine choice for families looking to save some money on dining. A terrace-level pool and Jacuzzi are on the fourth floor, more or less facing Disneyland. It's an extremely friendly place (winner of the 2002 President's Award for commitment to customer service), with a fireplace going in the lobby and a decent continental breakfast. And it's right at the corner of Disney Way, so you can't beat the location. Millie's, the coffee shop next door (good home cooking; see the review in the following section), offers 24-hour room service.

1520 S. Harbor Blvd. ☎ **800-670-7275** or 714-635-7275. Fax: 714-635-7276. www. parkinn-anaheim.com. *Free parking. Rack rates: $125–$169 double. AE, DISC, MC, V.*

Candy Cane Inn
$–$$ Anaheim

This is more or less the heir to those fairy-tale-themed motor courts that sprung up outside the Disneyland gates after the park opened in 1955. There is something to be said for staying in a place that tries to look like an old cartoon village (complete with cobblestones, balconies, flowers, and vines), and certainly it's a sweet, fun, and family-friendly place. Recent upgrades include new carpeting and tile in the rooms, grind-and-brew coffeemakers, and a complimentary in-room breakfast (as opposed to nearby competitors who have continental breakfasts in the lobby); a small workout room and Internet access were recently added. Two premium rooms offer a queen-size bed instead of doubles elsewhere in the establishment. With a little pool (and a kiddie wading pool), it feels more like a retreat than one would expect smack dab on a major boulevard. Because it's independent, you have to pay a bit more than you would for a room at its chain-hotel neighbors.

1747 S. Harbor Blvd. ☎ **800-345-7057** or 714-774-5284. Fax: 714-772-1305. www.candy caneinn.net. *Free parking. Rack rates: $99–$169 double. AE, DISC, MC, V.*

Holiday Inn Anaheim at the Park
$$ Anaheim

The most upscale non-Disney hotel on our list is a couple of minutes from the park, but it does offer a shuttle. Rooms are large, with a separate living area, and although the hotel is generic, the furniture offers better-quality wood (not veneer pasteboard, let's say). Bathrooms are also bigger than those found in the more moderately priced hotels listed. Basically, you're paying for more space and somewhat better amenities. This is more a hotel for grown-ups visiting the park who want only a certain amount of childhood fun — a resort hotel but without the theme or any kind of Disney stamp. Special deals (senior discounts, lower rates during slow times) pop up all the time, so ask. Dataports and cable are free here, whereas at other places, they're nonexistent or cost extra. A limited spa offers workouts, massages, and the like; the workout room is open 24 hours. KidSuites feature bunk beds and a queen bed, and kids younger than 12 eat for free in the cafe as long as their accompanying adult has paid for their own meal.

1221 S. Harbor Blvd. ☎ *800-545-7275 or 714-758-0900. Fax: 714-553-1804.* www.holiday-inn.com. *Free parking. Rack rates: $110–$150 double. AE, DC, DISC, MC, V.*

Howard Johnson Hotel
$$–$$$ Anaheim

Comfortable, reliable, unsurprising except that it's a bit nicer than you may expect from the orange-roofed conglomerate. It's actually pretty attractive-looking — that orange roof isn't even visible in the courtyard pool area. This hotel is directly across the street from Disneyland and has a regular cable-car-looking trolley that shuttles guests to and from the park. The recently renovated rooms are spacious, light, and airy. Each has a small fridge. Two garden pools (one especially for kids) top it off. They have room service with Mimi's Café (open 7 a.m. to 11 p.m.), a French/New Orleans family-style restaurant offering American cuisine. There's also a Laundromat on the premises.

1380 S. Harbor Blvd. ☎ *800-446-4656 or 714-776-6120. Fax: 714-533-3578.* www.hojoanaheim.com. *Free parking. Rack rates: $99–$199 double. AE, DC, DISC, MC, V.*

Tropicana Inn & Suites
$$ Anaheim

This is the Park Inn's sister hotel. It's been newly and nicely renovated in warm Mediterranean colors, with nearby Millie's providing room service. A pretty pool has wood-beamed huts for shade, and an oversized Jacuzzi can seat up to 12. Two gift shops can supply you with everything you may need, including extra T-shirts for messy kids, toys, snacks, and light reading materials. Like its sibling, it's clean and pleasant, with friendly helpful staff. It's walking distance to the ART public transport stop and resort entrance.

1540 S. Harbor Blvd. ☎ *800-828-4898 or 714-635-4082. Fax: 714-635-1535.* www. tropicanainn-anaheim.com. *Free parking. Rack rates: $139 double. AE, DISC, MC, V.*

Dining Out

You'll go broke before you go hungry at the Disneyland Resort. You can find food everywhere: a dozen sit-down restaurants and cafeterias inside the park, and seven more full-service restaurants between the **Disneyland** and **Paradise Pier** hotels (with two more in the works at the **Grand Californian Hotel**). And that doesn't count snack carts, casual walk-up stands, and packaged-food shops. As you would expect, you can also find a number of good restaurants conveniently located outside the park and near your hotel.

Dining at the resort

Most dining facilities inside Disneyland are overrated, overcrowded, and overpriced, redeeming themselves only by convenience. The exceptions are the offerings at **California Adventure,** described in the following section, and the dining/entertainment complex known as **Downtown Disney,** described in the "Downtown Disney" section. All park restaurants accept American Express, Discover, MasterCard, and Visa. Your options aren't as bad as the day when Twinkies and space punch (and not much else) were served in Tomorrowland, but hamburgers and carbs still rule the day, and although it all works as fuel, it hardly works as haute cuisine (and don't get us started on those fake beignets offered in New Orleans Square). On the other hand, it tickles us that those giant dill pickles are still inexplicably offered as snacks at stands in Adventureland and in the Bountiful Valley Farm section of California Adventure. Here are some exceptions worth seeking out:

- ✔ Disney has made an effort to accommodate guests who want to eat more healthily. Several fresh-fruit-and-vegetable carts (albeit not cheap) are scattered throughout Disneyland (we spotted them on Main Street and in Adventureland and Critter Country), offering melon, pineapple, grapes, and assorted raw veggies and dip, along with kosher pickles, bottled water, and that healthy beverage, Coca-Cola. For other healthy snack options, head to Adventureland for refreshments at the **Tiki Juice Bar** and **Indy Fruit Cart,** which offer tropical juices and unembellished fresh fruit for a natural sugar boost and healthier options.

- ✔ If you're a low-carb eater, you'll appreciate the Bengal Barbeque with a choice of fish, chicken, beef, or veggie kabobs served with (salty/sugary) sauces. Hardcore anti-carbists can forgo the basting or order the bacon-wrapped asparagus: quick, cheap (by Disneyland standards) protein pick-me-ups. Giant turkey legs a la carte (so Henry VIII, isn't it?) can also be found at a couple of carts — usually one on Main Street near Sleeping Beauty's Castle and one between the Matterhorn and Small World.

✔ Located throughout Disneyland — and (thank goodness!) plotted on the official park map — are **churro carts,** which dispense these absolutely addictive cylindrical Mexican donuts (rolled in sugar) beginning at 11 a.m.

✔ The food itself may be unremarkable (or even pretty bad, although there are great fans of the authentic Monte Cristo sandwich), but the **Blue Bayou Restaurant,** the only restaurant in the park that requires reservations (stop by early in the day to make yours), is worth a look. It meticulously re-creates a classic New Orleans verandah, complete with lush, vine-wrapped ironwork, lazily chirping crickets, and (nonalcoholic) mint juleps. Its misty, sunless atmosphere comes from being literally inside the Pirates of the Caribbean ride, so boatloads of pirate-seeking parkgoers drift by during your meal.

✔ The **Royal Street Veranda** in New Orleans Square offers those same faux-beignets, but also some decent (if hardly authentic) gumbo in a sourdough bowl.

Breakfast places fill up as soon as the park opens. Because these are expensive and uninspired, we say skip it; have some cereal before you arrive and get right to the rides. In fact, try to avoid prime eating hours as much as you can, because everyone else will be noshing at that time as well.

California Adventure

Do the bulk of your eating, if possible, at **California Adventure,** where the options are better in terms of quality and crowds. If you have the Park Hopper pass, head on over to California Adventure, especially if you're an adult who doesn't want hot dogs. Even the fast food seems a bit more inventive and interesting over there. Among the highlights is **Golden Vine Winery,** which offers two dining options: a more casual trattoria downstairs, and a formal dining room upstairs that offers prix-fixe tasting menus. Both are surprising entries in an amusement park (actual mature dining options), and both serve excellent, grown-up food. Patronize them, please, so there's a chance that more such ventures will open in the future. **Pacific Wharf Café** is modeled after restaurants found in San Francisco — tourist traps, of course, but at Disneyland, what the heck? It sits on the edge of the mock harbor (full of hungry ducks), and you can get real sourdough bread and clam chowder, maybe in a sourdough bowl (made on park premises; after, you can go over to the Boudin Bakery and watch loaves bake). **Cocina Mexican Grill** offers decent Mexican food made with fresh tortillas on the premises. A visit to the tortilla press is riveting fun for small children. The prix-fixe menu and need for reservations may keep you from wanting to commit to **Ariel's Grotto,** but if any members of your party are princess-obsessed, this is the place to take them, because everyone from — you guessed it — Ariel to Alice mills around this wharf-top venue ready to sign autographs and pose for pics.

Downtown Disney

The big dining/entertaining/shopping complex known as **Downtown Disney** is another part of the Disneyland Resort, but it has no entrance fee and no gate, so it's considered to be "outside the park." If you want to leave the resort to visit Downtown Disney, you can have your hand stamped for re-admittance to the parks. You really can't go wrong dining at one of the restaurants in Downtown Disney, unless, of course, you're on a strict budget. In that case, you may want to resort to fast food or chain restaurants.

In addition to the restaurants listed in this section, you can try the theme restaurants **(ESPN Zone, House of Blues, Rainforest Café)**. All the restaurants have outdoor balcony or patio seating facing the Downtown Disney traffic, so the people-watching potential is very high.

Catal
$$–$$$ Downtown Disney   MEDITERRANEAN RIM

One of three Pinot Group restaurants (the Pinot Group was founded by the creator of L.A.'s Patina — see Chapter 23) in Downtown Disney, this one specializes in more coastal Mediterranean dishes, such as bouillabaisse, cassoulet, braised lamb, lots of rotisserie items, and light pastas. It's set in a lovely two-story space, with a Deco facade and a strong wood décor throughout that emphasizes a wine-and-harvest theme. Casual dining is on the first floor, more formal on the second.

1510 Disneyland Dr. ☎ *714-774-4442. Reservations recommended. Main courses: $8.50–$31. AE, DISC, MC, V. Open: Daily 8 a.m.–10 p.m.*

La Brea Bakery
$–$$ Downtown Disney   CAFE

The original La Brea Bakery is just that — a bakery, in Los Angeles, on La Brea. There, Nancy Silverton nearly single-handedly brought about a revolution of sorts, bringing the concept of artisan bread to the masses. Or so it became when she turned her bakery into a conglomerate and household name. The bread here is indeed amazing, as are the pastries and the grilled sandwiches with ham or turkey and cheese or the (breadless) salads, which fare far better. There's also a walk-up window with a full range of coffee drinks, sandwiches, pastries, and salads, all of which cost a bit less than the sit-down service.

1556 Disneyland Dr. ☎ *714-490-0233. Reservations recommended. Main courses: $3.50–$30. AE, DISC MC, V. Open: Full-service dining Mon–Fri 11 a.m.–9 p.m., Sat–Sun 8 a.m.–11 p.m.; express-service dining Sun–Fri 8 a.m.–10 p.m., Sat 8 a.m.–11 p.m.*

Napa Rose
$$$$ Downtown Disney   CALIFORNIA CUISINE

Located in the Grand Californian Hotel, Napa Rose is elegant, but not stuffy (the architect John MacIntosh designed it); all you want to do is sit and look at the detailing, the floor-to-ceiling stained glass, the storytelling mural that lines the ceiling, the fireplace, and on it goes. This is Very Important Dining, with a price tag to match, but what a treat. Clearly, you're meant to think you're in the heart of California Wine Country, where they take dining (to say nothing of wine) very seriously, indeed. Menus change seasonally, but here are some highlights from a recent list: scallops with a sauce of lemon, lobster, and vanilla; pheasant with merlot-date essence; truffled risotto cake stuffed with fontina with rock shrimp Bolognese. Wasted on kids, you say? Perhaps, but note that they have a children's menu, with things such as simple buttered noodles, quesadillas, and pizzas — so Mom and Dad can have gourmet fun and won't have to fret about Junior's finicky eating habits. Oh, and they have 22 sommeliers, so, naturally, you can guess what that wine list looks like.

1600 S. Disneyland Dr. ☎ *714-MICKEY-1. Reservations recommended. Main courses: $27–$38. AE, DISC, MC, V. Open: Daily 5:30–10 p.m.*

Ralph Brennan's Jazz Kitchen
$$–$$$ **Downtown Disney   CREOLE/CAJUN**

New Orleans comes to Disney — well, it already did, over at the park in the New Orleans Square — in the form of a building that looks as though it was lifted straight off Royal Street in the French Quarter (in fact, they copied the iron grillwork on the outside from the Royal Street Café). The "Brennan" in the name is that of the finest New Orleans restaurant family — the same ones who bring you Commander's Palace (perhaps the best restaurant in that food-mad city). Fittingly, this is the best restaurant in Downtown Disney. Start with a minisampler of soup, with perfect gumbo, and then move on to the fried soft-shell crabs, if in season, or the filet mignon Rockefeller, if not. The latter floats on a sauce of butter and pernod, with sautéed spinach flecked with bacon, and buttermilk mashed potatoes piped into oyster shells. If it's lunchtime, get the *couchon de lait* (Cajun roast pork) po' boy sandwich, or better still, the BBQ shrimp, which is actually done in a peppery butter sauce and demands to be soaked up with French bread. The jambalaya, gumbo, and seafood are all heavenly. All in all, this is our first choice for Downtown Disney dining.

1590 S. Disneyland Dr. ☎ *714-776-5200. Reservations recommended. Main courses: $13–$24. AE, DISC, MC, V. Open: Main dining room Sun–Thurs 11 a.m.–10 p.m., Fri–Sat 10 a.m.–11 p.m.; no seating 4–4:30 p.m. daily. The lower-priced Jazz Kitchen Express starts serving coffee and beignets to go at 8 a.m. with all other Express options available daily 10 a.m.–10 p.m.*

Dining outside the parks
Even with (or perhaps in spite of) all the choices inside the parks, you can find a decent meal to appeal to the whole family at locations outside the Disneyland Resort. Here are a few of our favorites.

Casa Garcia
$–$$ Anaheim   MEXICAN

Mexican food, family-style and family-friendly — and authentic (well, in that Southern Californian Mexican way). Located about a half mile from Disneyland (in a strip mall), it has nothing on the menu over $14, and that's for the paella (rice with all kinds of meats and seafood in it). The award-winning menu (with the occasional charming mistake: "Barbacoa — oven cooked in a red chile sauce"; doesn't that sound like the oven itself is cooked in red chile sauce?) covers the ground from shrimp *al mojo de ajo* (in garlic sauce) to taco combo platters to Texas BBQ pork ribs. It's a local favorite (always a good sign), with a casual cafe style. Come early because there will be a line for dinner, or come for breakfast!

531 W. Chapman Ave. ☎ 714-740-1108. Reservations not necessary. Main courses $5.95–$14. AE, MC, V. Open: Daily 8 a.m.–10 p.m.

Chu's Wok Inn
$–$$ Anaheim   CHINESE

With an attractive Chinese décor, this restaurant is slightly more upscale than you may think from the name. It's not daring Chinese food — more like Chinese food for timid tourists — but it's tasty, well prepared, and generously portioned.

3053 Chapman Ave. ☎ 714-750-3511. Reservations not necessary. AE, MC, V. Open: Sun–Fri 11:30 a.m.–10 p.m., Sat noon–10 p.m.

Millie's
$–$$ Anaheim   HOME COOKING

Miss home cooking? Sure you do. We won't say this is like your mom used to make (or your grandma, more likely — moms don't often cook like this anymore) because we don't know her, but we hope it is, because it's that good. For breakfast, we seriously recommend the "world-famous" cinnamon rolls. Omelets are fresh and fluffy and come with fresh biscuits and buttermilk gravy, the sort we just don't get often enough here in Southern California. For dinner, try the pot roast — at $10, you get a huge portion of falling-apart meat (no knives required!) served over carrots and potatoes (both mashed and otherwise) with soup or salad and cornbread. That one portion may serve an entire family, unless you're with a lot of teenagers. Force yourself to eat dessert; they have an Oreo fudge berry sundae. Skip the nearby Denny's and IHOP and come here.

1480 S. Harbor Blvd. (next to the Park Vu Inn, which uses the restaurant for room service). ☎ 714-535-6892. Reservations not necessary. Main courses: $5–$8 for breakfast, $8–$15 for lunch and dinner. AE, DC, DISC, MC, V. Open: 24 hours.

Exploring the Resort

You've done your homework, you've packed the right park-going clothes, and you've got a game plan in order. Now it's time to hit the parks. See the "The Disneyland Resort" map on p. 433 to get started.

Plan to get to the gates of either park a few minutes, at least, before opening. This means, if you're driving down, get an early start, because you need to take into account early-morning rush-hour traffic, plus the drive itself, and the parking, and the getting to the gate from the parking lot, all before 9 a.m. That alone may be reason enough to stay in the Anaheim area.

The **ticket booths** are located precisely between the entrances to Disneyland and California Adventure (one on the left, the other on the right). You can expect to go through security and have your bags searched, which adds still more time to the entering process.

 Get off the tram at Downtown Disney and walk away from the park toward the Disneyland Hotel (or self-park in the Downtown Disneyland lot instead of the theme-park lots). On your right is the Monorail Station and booth where you can buy tickets to Disneyland. The Monorail drops you off in Tomorrowland. By using this entrance to Disneyland, you can beat the crowds and avoid the long lines — though your bags will still be searched.

If you have limited time, here is a suggested game plan:

> ✔ **If you have only one day:** Get to the park early and start by riding the most popular rides (described throughout this section) first — or obtaining FASTPASS tickets early (see the following paragraph) — so that you don't waste precious time in line.

> ✔ **If you have two or more days:** You have the luxury of enjoying some Disney extras not essential enough to pack into a single day. Avoid the midday-rides crush by strolling along **Main Street U.S.A.,** shopping for **Disney souvenirs,** and ducking into **Great Moments with Mr. Lincoln,** the patriotic look at America's 16th president, Walt Disney's first foray into audio-animatronics.

 One of the finer innovations in recent Disney history, the automated **FASTPASS** system allows visitors to buy advance tickets to certain rides, permitting them to return in, say, one to two hours (having gone on some other rides or eating a snack in the meantime), bypass the regular line, and more or less hop right on. Not all rides have this option, but the most popular ones in both Disneyland and California Adventure do, and although it doesn't eliminate lines entirely — after all, other people have the same return time as you — it does help you do the park more efficiently; Disney allows only a limited number of people to be in the FASTPASS queue at the same time. Get your FASTPASS tickets at the FASTPASS machines located at or near the entrances to the attractions where the pass is offered. You will be assigned a one-hour window of

The Disneyland Resort

time during which you can board the attraction. Look for the signs directing you to the FASTPASS queue (not the Standby queue); it can be a bit confusing, so read the signs carefully or just ask. Note that you're allowed to use only one FASTPASS at a time — for example, you have to use the Haunted Mansion pass before you can get a pass for another ride. There is absolutely no reason not to take advantage of this option as often as you can. And by the way, it's *free*.

The 2005 50th anniversary of Disneyland brought all kinds of celebrations, from special parades to new attractions (or renovations of old favorites, such as Space Mountain), and more, some of which have stayed longer than had initially been scheduled. We don't know how long they'll remain, but perhaps you'll still get to experience a couple.

Tips from the pros

Avoid common pitfalls by avoiding the mistakes of others:

✔ **Wear your most comfortable walking shoes.** You'll spend many hours walking, standing, and putting lots of strain on your legs and feet. Running or tennis shoes are best. Open-toed shoes are fine, especially on hot days; just make sure they have impact-cushioning soles and support your feet.

✔ **Expect a dramatic temperature drop after dark, even in summer.** Bring a sweatshirt or jacket, perhaps even long pants; you can store them in a locker, leave them in the car, or tote them in a backpack. Too many visitors have shown up in shorts and tank tops, only to discover that by 10 p.m. they're freezing their buns off!

✔ **Don't forget such bare necessities** as sunscreen (the park gets a lot of direct sun); camera film (more than you think you'll want; film costs more in the park) and spare batteries; extra baby supplies; bottled water or a sports bottle you can refill at drinking fountains; and snacks (if the kids get hungry in line, or you just balk at the concession prices). Although anything you may forget is available for purchase inside Disneyland, you'll cringe at the marked-up prices.

✔ **Purchase tickets in advance** (over the Internet or phone, or through your hotel). Not only do Disney Resort hotels sell tickets, but so do many area hotels, through an arrangement with Disney, as a service to their guests. This saves you from standing in what can be slow and long ticket lines. Visit the Web site at www.disneyland.com.

✔ **Make sure your child is ready to play.** It is certainly not a given that all children love, or will love, Disneyland. Some rides may simply be too intense (fast, dark, subtle) for certain ages or personalities. We strongly urge you to seriously consider your own child's tolerance level and individual tastes, phobias, and neuroses before bringing him to this fabulous, but pricey, destination.

✔ **Ask about ride restrictions before you come.** Some rides have age and height restrictions; check in advance so that your kids aren't crestfallen to find that they can't ride a particular ride when they get to the park. For most attractions, you have to be 7 years or older to ride alone, for example. On the bright side, Bjorn-restricted bundles of joy are welcome on most of the rides. For the more active, high-speed rides, such as Space Mountain, Splash Mountain, and Big Thunder Mountain Railroad, kids are required to be at least 40 inches high and 3 years old. Ask Disney employees about a Switch Pass if one or more of your kids aren't tall enough for the adventure that you want to go on. (This pass allows one or two group members to watch a child who cannot ride an attraction while the rest of the group waits in line and rides the ride. Once the majority of the group is done the one or two group members who watched the child can take the Child Switch Pass and walk up the exit to get on the attraction without any wait!)

Disneyland

As the clock strikes 9 a.m., the gates open, and the crowd floods in. You start on **Main Street,** the famous replica of an ideal American small town — Mark Twain's mid-19th century with a little Beaver Cleaver thrown in. (Actually, all buildings in the park are two-thirds size, the better to make kids feel at ease, and adults sentimental.) We urge you, even if you've never been here before, not to linger — everyone else is bolting to their favorite rides, and every minute you dally, the lines are getting longer.

Main Street feeds into the central area of Disneyland, from which several main "lands" branch off, like the fingers on a hand: **Fantasyland, Tomorrowland, Frontierland, Adventureland, New Orleans Square, Critter Country,** and **Mickey's Toontown.** Where you go at this point depends on your preferences. We detail each area in this section, highlighting the most popular rides, to help you decide which you should target first. From experience, however, we can say that among the most perennially popular rides, park-wide, are the **Pirates of the Caribbean, Haunted Mansion, Indiana Jones, Space Mountain, Buzz Lightyear,** and **Roger Rabbit.**

Although many visitors tackle Disneyland systematically, beginning at the entrance and working their way clockwise around the park, the most effective method historically has been to arrive early and run to the most popular rides first, where midday lines can last an hour or more.

Adventures with kids

If you have small kids with you, concentrate on **Fantasyland** (behind Sleeping Beauty's Castle), a kids' paradise with fairy-tale-derived rides such as **King Arthur Carousel, Dumbo the Flying Elephant, Mr. Toad's Wild Ride, Peter Pan's Flight** (be prepared; though this is a pretty neat ride, for some inexplicable reason, this seems to be one of the slowest queues in the park), **Alice in Wonderland, Pinocchio's Daring Journey,** and the Disney signature ride, **It's A Small World.**

Elsewhere in the park, little ones will enjoy clambering through **Tarzan's Treehouse,** experiencing the **Many Adventures of Winnie the Pooh and Friends,** and doing space wheelies on **Astro Orbitor,** which is tamer than the name implies (not worth a long wait for grown-ups). **Mickey's Toontown** is a wacky, gag-filled world inspired by the *Roger Rabbit* films, featuring endless amusement for young imaginations. The interactive **Buzz Lightyear Astro Blasters** gives kids and grown-ups the opportunity to best each other's scores as they blast targets with ray guns.

Look ma — no lines!

That's what *you* think. Nearly every Disney ride is fiendishly designed to look as if there's no line in front of it — either by having the line snake in such a way that its true length is obscured, or by having most of it hidden inside the ride structure itself. You walk up and think, "Hey, there's no line — let's try this ride!" only to get inside and find out that quite a few people and a lengthy wait are ahead of you. It's a clever psychological trick we fall for *each and every time.* The upside is that many of the newer rides have some kind of visual device, little sights, details, or other amusements (talking cars before Autopia, say, or a "set" that makes you think you're "backstage" at Roger Rabbit) that can help while away the time. It's a good idea to bring a book or a magazine, though, and if you have kids in tow, make sure they have a book or comic to keep themselves occupied during the wait.

Adventures for thrill-seekers

If high-speed thrills are your style, follow the **Indiana Jones Adventure** into the Temple of the Forbidden Eye, with hair-raising perils that include the familiar cinematic tumbling boulder — very realistic in the front seats!

Most of Disneyland's best action roller coasters are "mountain" themed. Perennial favorite **Space Mountain** is a pitch-black indoor roller coaster that assaults your ears and equilibrium. **Splash Mountain** is a water flume with a big, wet splash at the end (be prepared!). The **Matterhorn Bobsleds** offer a zippy coaster ride through faux-alpine caverns and fog banks, while runaway train cars careen through a deserted 1870s gold mine on **Big Thunder Mountain Railroad.**

Diverging from the mountain theme, stationary **Star Tours** encounters a space-load of misadventures on the way to the Moon of Endor. This *Star Wars*–inspired Tomorrowland virtual ride manages to achieve real queasiness with motion seats and video effects.

Longtime faves

Some of Disneyland's highlights are long-time favorites that have stood the test of time. Two all-time best bets are in New Orleans Square: The intriguingly spooky **Haunted Mansion** showcases the brilliance of Disney Imagineers and boggles your mind with too many details to absorb in just one visit. Keeping even regular Disney attendees on their toes is the fact that the ride changes depending on time of year. From somewhere around the first week or two of October until perhaps mid-January the Mansion undergoes a nifty transformation that incorporates Tim Burton's *Nightmare Before Christmas.* We love it both ways!

The recently renovated **Pirates of the Caribbean** presents an enchanted world of swashbuckling and rum-running as you glide through via a realistic southern bayou. Coming full circle, the ride that inspired the movie now incorporates its spawn, so expect to see a few animatronic Captain Jack Sparrows along the way as well as an awfully cool misty waterfall effect. Though some Disney purists were up in arms about the new changes, we feel that they're innocuous enough to not interfere with the original intent and long-time charm of the ride.

Parade and show-going tips

The park's parades and shows draw huge crowds into relatively small areas. Parades usually run twice a day, in the afternoon and mid-evening. If a parade doesn't interest you, make a point to steer clear of these areas during and immediately after the parade; use this time to take advantage of shorter ride lines in Frontierland **(Big Thunder Mountain Railroad)**, Tomorrowland **(Space Mountain)**, and New Orleans Square **(Haunted Mansion** and **Pirates of the Caribbean)**.

California Adventure

Ah, this is the "new" park, which opened to great fanfare in 2001. The first major new development at Disneyland since, hmm, maybe Toontown — except this is so much bigger. Toontown was just a new land; this is a whole new *park*.

After going on — and on and on and on — about the general overall perfection of Disney, we now have to say that California Adventure may have been a major misstep. And unless you get one of those multiday Park Hopper passes, you can safely save your money and skip the new park altogether. (Although there are constant efforts to add newer and better attractions to California Adventure to make it a more worthy relative of the original Disneyland.)

Don't get us wrong; the park is gorgeous. Disney design would produce no less. Every detail, as always, is extensively researched and exquisite — heck, we can think of few sights that are as visually appealing as Paradise Pier at dusk. But did you notice the name? Do you know what the theme is? That's right: California. It's a miniversion of California in (need we point out?) *California*. It boasts a mock version of Yosemite, a highly stylized version of San Francisco, and a wishful-thinking version of Hollywood Boulevard. We cannot stress how weird and wrong this idea is, but we can illustrate it by observing that you, the visitor, may well go from the real Hollywood Boulevard, to the cartoon version here in the same day. And though this may be terrific for prompting discussions of the Platonic ideal and archetypes, it just doesn't sit well as an amusement park, at least one that is based in, we'll just mention it again, *California*.

But never mind that. A more egregious sin (one that could easily be a by-product of the overall failure to meld design and place) is that the entire park lacks the same magic of Disneyland — which is, after all, based on mythologies or faraway lands and times, rather than a re-creation of something that lies right outside the gates. Consequently, it's artificial in a Vegas way, not a Disney dazzle way. Plus, it's a much more generic amusement park; there aren't many rides for the space, and those that are here often disappoint or are completely ordinary, lacking the special Disney touch. Also, the park seems less efficiently laid out; after a couple of waits in line and a walk from one section to another, you've used up a couple of hours with little to show for it.

Which is not to say that there isn't plenty to enjoy (and increasingly more as they work on it), but California Adventure is much more a stroll-around-and-admire park than an amusement park, much better for adults weary of lines or rides in general. And if the place didn't cost a whole separate expensive admission, we would probably think more kindly of it than we do. Which is where that Park Hopper pass comes in; it pays for itself in just a couple days of Disneyland admission alone. With it, families can readily take advantage of the admittedly better food options here and the smaller crowds.

California Adventure for kids

Grizzly River Run is a thoroughly enjoyable water ride; expect to get either somewhat damp or soaked through. The **Redwood Creek Challenge Trail,** given a new slightly New Age/spiritual theme to tie in with the animated flick *Brother Bear,* is part of a kids' playground area, allowing them to run around, climb on ropes or on rock-climbing walls, and just generally get their ya-yas out in an area designed to look like Yosemite ("oh, it's *faux*-semite," observed one attendee). Also featured is the **Soarin' Over California** ride; riders pile into rows of seats that are then lifted up so that they may sway and tilt, hang-glider style, while watching an IMAX-type film. It's one of the better rides, although prone to long lines and a tad disappointing if you thought you were going to do more of an actual hang-gliding-type activity.

Paradise Pier is essentially Disney's version of a traditional amusement park. It's Carnie Central, with the sort of rides that fly around on chains or whiz into the air and generally make you sick to your stomach. Except for the super-fun roller coaster **California Screamin',** it's nothing you haven't ridden before and, as such, hardly a must-do. Then again, how lovely that in this manic, high-tech, short-attention-span world, there are still kids who get a thrill riding a merry-go-round or Ferris wheel that alternates stationary and swinging buckets.

Addressing the many concerns about the lack of old-fashioned Disney magic, the newish **A Bug's Land** caters mostly to the smaller set (note how everything is scaled to make each visitor feel bug-sized; good perspective for adults), but it's so darn sweet, and more to the point, so Disney-clever (which is very clever indeed) that all but the most jaded teens will get a kick out of it. Ride **Heimlich's Chew-Chew Train,** as the Teutonic caterpillar from *A Bug's Life* chomps his way through various foliage (smell the watermelon as he plows through it), and enjoy other

:nsect-themed activities. If the line isn't too long, the brand-new **Monsters, Inc. Mike & Sulley to the Rescue** ride will be thoroughly enjoyed by the young'uns, though not so interesting to anyone else.

California Adventure for adults

For adults, there is honest-to-gosh wine tasting at the **Golden Vine Winery,** where you can learn about wine-making (right out of Napa Valley) and even taste the juice of the grape. There is also a replica of the **rotunda of San Francisco's Palace of Fine Arts** (like Cinderella's Castle, it makes a great meeting spot), and a copy of the **Pacific Wharf,** where you can watch bread being made or, better still, a tortilla-making machine in action (and you get a free tortilla, fresh off the machine, just for coming in).

California Adventure for superstar wannabes

The **Hollywood Pictures Backlot** is possibly the most dubious portion of the park. We've already mentioned how very odd it is to see this highly stylized, cartoon version of Hollywood Boulevard (which, as we mention in Chapter 23, has no real association with the motion-picture industry). The **Tower of Terror** is part of a (so-far successful) effort to rehabilitate California Adventure's image — in other words, here's another clever ride (the best in this park), in this case, a trip through a crumbling hotel-like structure, complete with a movie about the hotel's murky and horrible past. And then, well, hang on tight when you get into that elevator — it's a hard, fast drop down. Otherwise, this side still doesn't have much to do, although the **Muppet 3D Adventure** is sweetly enjoyable and **Turtle Talk with Crush** invites interactive chat with the animated turtle from *Finding Nemo* — how do they do that, anyway?

Gathering More Information

For the latest **Disneyland** and **California Adventure** developments, call the parks' information line at ☎ 714-781-4565 or 714-781-7290 to talk to a real person who, oddly enough, seems genuinely happy to answer any and all of your questions. You can find online information at www.disneyland.com.

To get more information on the surrounding area, check with the **Anaheim/Orange County Visitor and Convention Bureau,** 800 W. Katella Ave. (☎ 714-765-8888; www.anaheimoc.org). The bureau is just inside the Convention Center (across the street from Disneyland) and welcomes visitors Monday through Friday from 8 a.m. to 5 p.m.

Chapter 25

San Juan Capistrano and Laguna Beach

*T*wo favorite getaway destinations for Los Angelenos are San Juan Capistrano and Laguna Beach, both close to the city in distance but far away in feel. San Juan Capistrano is located 15 minutes southwest of Laguna Beach, so you can hit both in the course of a short trip. We suggest that you visit the historic sights of San Juan Capistrano during the day, have lunch at one of the restaurants described in this chapter, and stay in one of Laguna's fine lodgings at night. You can spend a most enjoyable few hours getting to know the area.

San Juan Capistrano

It's easy to understand why San Juan Capistrano's famed swallows return to the town's 10-acre mission every March 19, but the real question is why would they ever want to leave in the first place? Although spectacular unto itself, this "Jewel of the Missions," as it has become known, with its botanical courtyards and narrative displays, was founded November 1, 1776, and is only a tiny portion of what makes San Juan Capistrano special.

Getting there by car

San Juan Capistrano marks the halfway point between Los Angeles and San Diego, about 70 minutes from the heart of each city. Exit I-5 at Camino Capistrano and head due west about 3 blocks to break up the monotony of the San Diego to Los Angeles (or vice versa) drive.

What to see and do

This diverse community offers glimpses into the past, present, and future, with architecture ranging from the 18th-century **Montanez Adobe** (31781 Los Rios St.) to renowned architect Michael Graves's postmodern **Regional Library** (31495 El Camino Real).

The **Mission San Juan Capistrano** (Ortega Highway/California 74; ☎ 949-234-1300; www.missionsjc.com; admission: $6 adults, $5 seniors, $4 children 3–12, free for children younger than 3; open: daily 8:30 a.m.– 5 p.m.) is the seventh of the 21 California coastal missions. Centuries-old adobe walls shelter gardens and fountains. The ruins of the Great Stone Church (begun in 1796, completed in 1806, collapsed by an earthquake in 1812), with its 125-foot native-stone bell tower, are undergoing preservation to stem the structure's decay. The mission is best known for its swallows, which, according to legend return to nest here each year on March 19, St. Joseph's Day. Legend aside, swallows can be seen here year-round.

Adjacent to the Mission, off of Verdugo and just across the railroad tracks, is **Los Rios Street,** the oldest remaining residential street in all of California. If you brought the young'uns with you for your San Juan Cap adventure, reward their good behavior with a trip to the quaint **Zoomars Petting Zoo and Bird Park,** 31791 Los Rios St. (☎ 949-831-6550). Zoomars is open daily from 10 a.m. to 5 p.m., rain or shine. The admission price of $2 will give your child access to over 100 friendly animals (ranging from guinea pigs and bunnies to emus and llamas) to pet. Adults 13 and older pay $3 and there are pony rides, train rides, and snacks (for humans as well as the animals) available at an additional charge. Not the most exciting stop, but kids love it and the place always provides that perfect photo-op.

Nestled between a couple of distinctive gift stores lies the **Ramos House Cafe,** 31752 Los Rios St. (☎ 949-443-1342; open Tues–Sun 8:30 a.m.– 3 p.m.; weekends have a prix-fixe brunch), undoubtedly one of the yummiest breakfast and lunch spots in Southern California. The owner lives in the 1881 house with a converted commercial kitchen and treats his guests to contemporary American cuisine (with Southern influence) underneath the mulberry tree on the rustic open patio.

One former U.S. president (the reliable rumor is it was Richard Nixon) so loved the local flavor served up in the Mexican kitchen of the National Historical Landmark **El Adobe,** 31891 Camino Capistrano (☎ 949-493-1163; open: daily 11 a.m.–9 p.m.), they actually named the President's Choice combination dinner after his favorite trio of dishes. If you simply don't have time for a leisurely meal, **Pedro's Tacos,** 31721 Camino Capistrano (☎ 949-489-7752; open: daily 10 a.m.–8 p.m.), across the street from the mission, serves delicious, authentic, not to mention wonderfully inexpensive, Mexican fare.

Sushi fans, jump back on the I-5 North, exit a few miles up at Crown Valley where you'll make a right, and then an immediate left into a peach and green stucco center called the Kaleidoscope. **Riptide,** 27741 Crown Valley Pkwy. (☎ **949-282-0182;** www.rockinrestaurants.com), with its "Rockin" theme — kinda like Benihana on steroids and sugar — seems like it would be all image, but the substance is surprisingly outstanding. Fresh sushi, including a host of exotic rolls, stellar teppan performances, a well-rounded dinner menu, and a gluttonous Polynesian Sunday brunch make this destination a bright light in suburbia. Reservations are a must on the weekend.

Laguna Beach

In spite of all of the attention it has received courtesy of Kristin, LC, and the rest of the cast of MTV's Orange County–based reality series, Laguna Beach has long been a quiet and romantic getaway for Southern Californians, and for many a good reason. Number one, with its clean beaches, beautiful homes, and terrific landscape, the place is simply gorgeous. Number two, though it's pretty much a sleepy little town, the artists' community here ensures that you're never at a loss for things to do. And finally, it's just a short road trip from most Southern California metropolises.

When to go

The height of tourist season is between Memorial Day and Labor Day, because everyone yearns to engage in Laguna's magnificent summer events as well as frolic on the sand in the warm sun. Room rates go up (not tremendously, but enough to notice if your stay is longer than a night or two), and the village becomes a wee bit more congested than in the winter. Keep in mind, however, that Southern California usually gets hit with what we call *June gloom* — overcast mornings that tend to burn off by mid- to late afternoon. Does this detract from the town's beauty? Heck no! And if you're a tanning fiend, you can still get good color because UV rays are intensified through the clouds. On the other hand, although California's mild winter may not be necessarily conducive to bathing trunks and bikinis, it can be inviting to beachcombers who enjoy taking long walks in cool, fresh air.

Getting there by car

Laguna Beach is about a 20-minute drive from **John Wayne Airport** in Orange County. Simply exit the airport (take the soft left) and merge (right) onto the 405 (San Diego) freeway south. Continue down the 405. Veer onto the 133 south toward Laguna Beach. This highway becomes Laguna Canyon, which then becomes Broadway and takes you directly to Coast Highway.

If you're driving from **Los Angeles,** the directions remain the same, except you'll spend about 40 minutes longer on the 405 south.

Coming from **San Diego,** take I-5 north until you reach the CA-1 exit toward Beach Cities. This exit takes you under the freeway and onto Coast Highway (CA-1). Continue north on CA-1 through Dana Point. After a scenic 15-minute drive, you'll be in South Laguna Beach.

Getting around

As is true in much of California, relying solely on your feet may not be in your best interest. If you're staying in the village, you'll be fine, but if you like to explore, you'll want to have a car. Be forewarned: Although most hotels are kind enough to provide complimentary parking, if you park at a meter, be sure to pay attention to the signs and feed the meters as posted, usually a quarter for ten minutes.

Where to stay

Seclusion is the name of the game for lodging in the Laguna Beach area, and these accommodations offer plenty of it.

The Blue Lantern Inn
$$$–$$$$$ Dana Point

If you're in the mood for a more secluded territory than Laguna Beach, you needn't head more than a few miles south. This charming bed-and-breakfast in the quaint beach town of Dana Point may suit you perfectly. Located atop a bluff overlooking Dana Point Harbor this is one of the Four Sisters Inns' elegant collection of California and Pacific Northwest properties, and it easily lives up to their standard of service, beauty, and comfort. Each of the 29 romantic rooms features a fireplace, Jacuzzi tub, coffeemaker, and a refrigerator stocked with soft drinks. A gourmet breakfast is available free of charge every morning, and wine and hors d'oeuvres are offered each afternoon. Other features include a fitness room and bicycles for sightseeing. As you take in the surroundings stop by **J.C. Beans** (34114 Pacific Coast Hwy.) for the best latte in Orange County in a friendly, nonfranchise environment.

34343 Street of the Blue Lantern. ☎ *800-950-1236 or 949-661-1304. Fax: 949-496-1483.* www.bluelanterninn.com. *Rack rates $170–$500 double; AAA discounts available. AE, DC, DISC, MC, V.*

Casa Laguna Inn
$$$–$$$$$ South Laguna Beach

Incorporating the enchanting spirit of Laguna Beach, this former artists' colony turned bed-and-breakfast features 22 romantic rooms laden with luxurious linens and antiques. Most of the rooms boast incredible ocean views amid traditional early-20th-century Spanish-California architecture. The warm and friendly staff prepare afternoon refreshments while their chef prepares the full gourmet breakfast. For an extra fee, your pets are welcome to enjoy the accommodations as well.

2510 S. Coast Hwy. ☎ *800-233-0449* or 949-494-2996. Fax: 949-494-5009. www.casa laguna.com. *Rack rates: $200–$550 double; AAA discounts available. AE, DISC, MC, V.*

Hotel Laguna
$$–$$$$ **Laguna Beach**

Slightly south of Main Beach, in the heart of the village, this Laguna Beach classic boasts the best rates for an oceanfront hotel. The view and food from the Terrace and Claes restaurants attract diners from all over, while the Lounge is a great spot to enjoy a cocktail or two.

425 S. Coast Hwy. ☎ *800-524-2927* or *949-494-1151. Fax: 949-497-2163.* www.hotel laguna.com. *Rack rates: $130–$335. AE, DC, DISC, MC, V.*

Inn at Laguna Beach
$$–$$$$$ **Laguna Beach**

On the ocean side of Pacific Coast Highway stands this family-friendly, comfortably appointed hotel. Not only are CD players and VCRs standard in each room, but the hotel has an extensive video library. Adjacent to Main Beach and overlooking the town's infamous volleyball and basket-ball courts (where, if you're lucky, you may very well see a Clipper or Laker on his day off), it features a heated pool, a spa, and a sun terrace. Complimentary continental breakfast is served in your room.

211 N. Coast Hwy. ☎ *800-544-4479* or *949-497-9722. Fax: 949-497-9972.* www.innat lagunabeach.com. *Rack rates: $129–$599 double. AE, DC, DISC, MC, V.*

La Casa del Camino
$$–$$$$$ **South Laguna Beach**

Built in 1927 as a romantic seaside retreat for Hollywood movie stars, this Mediterranean Revival–style hotel houses European-style rooms ranging from cozy to grand, some with ocean views and some without. Although the smaller rooms are not recommended for claustrophobes, all of the rooms are lovely and dressed in one-of-a-kind, mostly antique, furnishings. Guests are welcome to enjoy their complimentary continental breakfast up at the Roof Lounge (a great place *any* time of day, truth be told — sunset anyone?), and we love dinner at lobby level Savoury's.

1289 S. Coast Hwy. ☎ *888-367-5232* or *949-497-2446 Fax: 949-494-5581.* www.casa camino.com. *Rack rates: $129–$429, depending on size, season, day of the week, and occupancy. AE, DC, DISC, MC, V.*

Montage Resort & Spa
$$$$$ **South Laguna Beach**

Situated on a coastal bluff, this place offers the amenities and conveniences of an ultraluxury hotel, coupled with the warmth and appeal of a cozy

Craftsman-style inn. Perfectly manicured lush gardens, a stunning collection of California Impressionism, elegant accommodations, a beachfront spa, and three gorgeous swimming pools are merely a few aspects of the exquisite attention to detail for which this place is known. Even if you can't afford to sleep here (and quite frankly, who can?), you'll want to peek in or even try the resort's award-winning restaurants — Studio, the Loft (can you say French Laundry's chef from Napa?), and Mosaic Bar & Grill — but only with a reservation. Could this place be any more beautiful? We think not. Could it be any pricier? Again, we think not.

30801 S. Coast Hwy. ☎ *866-271-6953 or 949-715-6000. Fax: 949-715-6100.* www. nontagelagunabeach.com. *Rack rates: $645 and up for doubles in the off season (after Labor Day through the beginning of June); higher in summer. AE, DC, DISC, MC, V.*

Where to dine

Laguna Beach does a pretty good restaurant business, given its proximity to the southernmost regions of the Los Angeles area, and you can find quite a variety. The following are our local favorites.

Cedar Creek Inn
$–$$$ Laguna Beach   AMERICAN

For nearly 20 years this warm and inviting restaurant, situated in a historic building in the Lumberyard Mall, has been serving Laguna residents lunch, dinner, and Sunday brunch. One of the many likeable points about this place is that you have the freedom to make it as casual or as formal as you like depending upon with whom and how you dine. The wonderfully potent Jalapeño-Jack Pasta can be enjoyed at the same table as the market-price swordfish, or the Monte Cristo sandwich either indoors or on the tree-covered brick patio. We have yet to try anything here that hasn't made our tummies happy. The bar side includes an award-winning grill menu, as well as live music Wednesday through Sunday evenings with late-night and light dining daily until 11 p.m.

384 Forest Ave. ☎ *949-497-8696. Reservations recommended. Main courses $10–$28. AE, MC, V. Open: Sun–Thurs 11 a.m.–9 p.m., Fri–Sat 11 a.m.–10 p.m. (Also at 27321 La Paz Rd. Laguna Niguel,* ☎ *949-389-1800; and 26860 Ortega Hwy., San Juan Capistrano,* ☎ *949-240-2229).*

Dizz's As Is
$$–$$$ South Laguna Beach   INTERNATIONAL

Located a few miles south of the village, this local favorite since 1977 serves up an eclectic mix of mouth-watering international cuisine with French-Belgian flair. Upon being seated at one of the cozy tables, you and your party will be given a stack of pages describing the special entrees of the evening. The generous portions will leave you wondering how you can possibly fit in a bite of one of the delectable desserts, but to leave without trying the chocolate crème brûlée is just not right.

2794 S. Coast Hwy. at Nyes Place. ☎ *949-494-5250. Reservations accepted only for large parties. Dinners (including appetizers and soup or salad): $19–$35. AE, MC, V. Open: Tues–Sun 5:30 p.m.–1 a.m.*

Eva's Caribbean Cafe
$$ **South Laguna Beach   CARIBBEAN**

Kick back, get yourself a rum-infused libation, and enjoy an evening in a friendly, festive, and fun island atmosphere. Savory aubergine choka (a Trinidadian grilled-vegetable dish); spicy Cajun prawns sweetened by a pineapple, mango, pepper, and passion-fruit salsa; or any of the other appetizing treats segue deliciously into the authentic Caribbean entrees. And the desserts, well, chocolate bread pudding freshly concocted by Eva herself — need we say more?

31732 Pacific Coast Hwy. ☎ *949-499-6311. Reservations recommended on the weekends. Main courses: $17–$21. AE, DISC, MC, V. Open: Tues–Thurs and Sun 5–9 p.m., Fri–Sat 5–10 p.m.*

La Sirena Grill
$ **Laguna Beach   MEXICAN**

This order-at-the-counter-and-try-to-find-yourself-a-seat spot has the freshest Mexican tasties in Laguna (with two locations). Whether you try a carne asada burrito, an avocado-lime salad with chicken, or any one of their vegetarian specialties, your taste buds will dance with glee. Perfect to take with you on a picnic.

Downtown Laguna: 347 Mermaid St. ☎ *949-497-8226. No reservations. Main courses: Everything less than $10. DISC, MC, V. Open: Mon–Sat 11 a.m.–9 p.m. Second location at 30862 S. Coast Hwy.* ☎ *949-499-2301. Open: Daily 11 a.m.–9 p.m.*

K'ya
$$–$$$ **Laguna Beach   ASIAN FUSION**

In the spirit of the hotel in which it resides, even if K'ya weren't home to a gamut of superb Asian-infused seafood and other delights, its warm and wonderful atmosphere with a staff to match would make it worth a visit.

1287 S. Coast Hwy., lobby level of La Casa del Camino. ☎ *949-376-9718. Reservations recommended for dinner. Main courses: $14–$36. AE, MC, V. Open: Daily 5:30–10:30 p.m.*

Splashes
$$–$$$ **Laguna Beach   CALIFORNIA CUISINE**

A restaurant in such a prime locale with such a beautiful view doesn't have to be this good — but lucky for us, it is. On the lower level of the Surf & Sand Resort & Spa, practically on top of the ocean, this ridiculously romantic nook is devoted to the art of fine cuisine. Their filet is so tender you question why they even bothered bringing you the steak knife when, truly, a butter knife would do. Oh, and their seafood, well, it's the beach, baby. Enjoy, 'cause like we said, it's that good.

1555 S. Pacific Coast Hwy, just north of Bluebird Canyon. ☎ 949-497-4477. Reservations recommended. Main courses: $8–$21 breakfast, $12–$29 lunch, $25–$40 dinner, $8–$22 Sunday brunch. AE, MC, V. Open: Daily 7–11 a.m. and 11:30 a.m.–3:30 p.m., Sun 11:30 a.m.–3:30 p.m., Sun–Thurs 5–10 p.m., Fri–Sat 5–11 p.m.

The Sundried Tomato
$–$$$ Laguna Beach CALIFORNIA CUISINE

The truly delicious California cuisine is reason enough to embrace this lunch and dinner spot. Lunch features an array of creative salads, pastas, and sandwiches; dinner incorporates more entrees and specials. The cream of sun-dried tomato soup is a must! The dog-friendly patio allows you and your pooch to dine in tandem amidst the sun-drenched courtyard complete with waterfall.

361 Forest Ave., 2 blocks east of Coast Highway. ☎ 949-494-3312. Reservations recommended for dinner and can be handy for lunch. Main courses: $9–$13 lunch, $16–$28 dinner. AE, MC, V. Open: Sun–Thurs 11:30 a.m–10 p.m., Fri–Sat 11:30 a.m.– 10:30 p.m. (Also at 31781 Camino Capistrano, ☎ 949-661-1167, where they also serve breakfast Sat–Sun.)

Ti Amo
$$–$$$ South Laguna Beach ITALIAN

This is South Laguna Beach's quintessential restaurant of romance. Modeled after an Italian villa, it offers a cozy, charming atmosphere with a fireplace and ocean views. The extensive wine list and divine Italian-Mediterranean menu embrace Ti Amo's philosophy that the marriage of food and wine is the key to good health and living. Who are we to argue with that kind of logic? And the Chocolate Sin dessert is even more wonderfully wicked than it sounds.

31327 S. Coast Hwy. ☎ 949-499-5350. Fax: 949-499-9760. Reservations recommended. Main courses: $16–$32. AE, DC, DISC, MC, V. Open: 5:30–10:30 p.m daily.

Zinc Café & Market
$ Laguna Beach VEGETARIAN

Although it's far from shocking that the artsy community's vegetarians would flock to Zinc for breakfast and lunch as often as possible, the tasty, surprisingly healthy food is what inspires the carnivores to visit just as often. Beachgoers, get food to go from the counter or their market.

344 Ocean Ave. ☎ 949-494-2791. No reservations. Main courses: Everything under $10. Open: Cafe daily 7 a.m.–4 p.m.; Market: Sun–Mon 7 a.m.–5 p.m., Tues–Sat 7 a.m.–6 p.m.

Lookin' for a tequila sunset?

Whether you're with that special someone, with a group of great friends, or just taking in the sights solo, there's something to be said for relaxing in a perfect setting as the sun meanders down past the edge of the earth. **Las Brisas**, 361 Cliff Dr. (☎ 949-497-5434), has outdoor seating, fantastic drinks, a mediocre bar menu, and worse dining, but the view is magnificent. Tasty Mexican food accompanied by great margaritas can be found in South Laguna Beach at **Coyote Grill**, 31621 S. Pacific Coast Hwy. (☎ 949-499-4033). Watch the sunset and hang out for hours with the locals while enjoying drinks and appetizers at La Casa del Camino's casual yet sublime **Roof Lounge**, 1289 S. Pacific Coast Hwy. (☎ 949-497-2446), or class it up at Surf & Sand Resort & Spa's **Splashes Bar,** 1555 S. Pacific Coast Hwy. (☎ 949-497-4477), and then stroll along the beach — you'll be literally steps away from it as you sip your chardonnay.

Laguna events

Laguna residents love to take advantage of their weather-type amenities and celebrate their festivals. Here are a few of the more interesting options to consider in the area.

Laguna Beach Art Walk

On the first Thursday of every month, locals and visitors alike converge upon the eclectic group of galleries that line Laguna's Pacific Coast Highway for the **Laguna Beach Art Walk.** Although some proprietorships rely solely on the merit of the artists' work to bring in a crowd, others resort to bribery in the form of a light snack and beverages ranging from Evian to chardonnay. Adding to the festival feel is music, sometimes live and sometimes canned. With all the inviting restaurants, a beautiful stretch of beach, and a dose of culture in such close proximity, your vacation should start on the first Thursday night of a month. Admission is free. Free trolley service from approximately 6 to 9 p.m. starts at the Laguna Art Museum. For more information, call ☎ 949-497-0716 or go to www.firstthursdaysartwalk.com.

The Festival of Arts and Pageant of the Masters

Presented in July and August since 1932, California's oldest annual art show, the **Festival of Arts,** is held in a scenic 6-acre Laguna Canyon park, at 650 Laguna Canyon Rd. For a nominal entrance fee ($7 general, $4 students and seniors), this celebration of the area's most esteemed artists offers an introduction to their work, as well as the opportunity to purchase original artworks to add to your personal collection.

Running concurrently with the festival since 1935 is the renowned **Pageant of the Masters.** Set in an outdoor amphitheater accompanied by live narration and a professional orchestra, this nightly show features real people in elaborate costumes and settings re-creating classical and contemporary works of art. It sounds hokey, we know, but it's not — it's actually quite remarkable, and we bet it elicits a wow from even of the most jaded. The highly coveted tickets to these events go on sale in December, many months prior to the July opening. They range in price from $15 to $65, if you're able to get them from the box office (☎ 949-497-6582), and believe the ticket agents when they tell you that there are no bad seats. Binoculars are a must regardless of where you're seated, because they're the only way to home in on the fine details. If you're unable to get tickets the old-fashioned way, fret not — you have a few alternatives. The box office generally releases a limited number of tickets each show date, so plan to line up early and cross your fingers. A reliable way is to try a hotel concierge desk. The most foolproof — though expensive — way to get tickets is to use a ticket broker: **Good Times** (☎ 714-432-7383) may be able to help you.

To confirm dates and times for both the pageant and the festival — they change annually — go the Web site at www.foapom.com or call ☎ 949-494-1145. You can reach the box office at ☎ 800-487-3378 or 949-497-6582.

Sawdust Art Festival

Over 150 local artists, artisans, and craftspeople exhibit and sell their wares at the annual summer **Sawdust Art Festival.** Each booth or display has a personality of its own — and it's a fine way to dispense with the year's Christmas shopping as you wander across, yes, the sawdust (you were expecting gold dust?) from wooden booth to wooden booth, checking out pottery, jewelry, painting, and sculpture. Be sure to seek out the entertainment, craft displays, and cafes. The festival also returns for a brief stint for four winter weekends — perfect for more holiday shopping! The Sawdust Art Festival is located at 935 Laguna Canyon Rd. For information, call ☎ 949-494-3030 or go to www.sawdustartfestival.org.

Vistas, views, and adventure

Whether you're a mountain biker, a couple in search of the ideal sunset, a walking enthusiast trying to burn off what you've been indulging in, or part of a family with children, the **Alta Laguna Park** will intrigue you. Begin by heading east on Park Avenue (the first light south of Forest at Coast Highway). You'll drive up a steep hill and pass many architectural delights until you can no longer drive forward at Alta Laguna; at that point, make a left. Continue over two speed bumps, and then pull into the parking lot on your right-hand side. After parking, exit the lot the way you came, only this time by foot, and make a right. On a clear day, as you reach the picnic tables, you'll be able to see the coastline extending all the way from Palos Verdes to the north down to southernmost San Diego. Offshore, Catalina Island will seem much, much closer than 26 miles across the sea. If you're yearning for exercise, head in the other direction through the toddler-friendly playground to the miles of trails overlooking the expansive canyons and parks of South Orange County. The park closes at dusk.

Theater

Founded in 1920 by some of Hollywood's most prestigious elite, including Bette Davis, Charlie Chaplin, and Mary Pickford, the **Laguna Playhouse,** 606 Laguna Canyon Rd., is the oldest continuously operating theater on the West Coast. Offering a year-round performance schedule, this renowned venue always has something wonderful to be seen. It's adjacent to the Festival of Arts. Call ☎ **949-497-2787** or go to www.laguna playhouse.com for information and ticketing.

Gathering More Information

For a complete listing of shops, events, restaurants, and accommodations in San Juan Capistrano, contact the **San Juan Capistrano Chamber of Commerce** at ☎ **949-493-4700** or simply log on to www.sanjuan capistrano.org.

For more information about Laguna Beach, contact the **Laguna Beach Visitors Bureau,** 252 Broadway, just east of Coast Highway (☎ **800-877-1115** or 949-497-9229; www.lagunabeachinfo.org).

Chapter 26

Ring-a-Ding-Ding: Palm Springs

. . . .

In This Chapter

▶ Deciding when to go to Palm Springs — and how to get there

▶ Choosing the best places to stay and eat

▶ Checking out the gay and lesbian scene in Palm Springs

▶ Exploring the top desert attractions

▶ Hitting the links in the heat

▶ Living it up after the sun goes down

▶ Making a trip to the desert parks

. . . .

*V*isitors have a love-hate relationship with Palm Springs. If you love desert landscapes, bikinis, bronzed complexions, and an easygoing vibe, you'll likely fall into the former category. If you want more culture and less hot sun, you'll probably fall in the latter.

Long a place for the rich and the elderly to while away their time, Palm Springs has a new ring-a-ding-ding hipness for Gen X, lured by the spa-and-sun lifestyle, while golfers have always loved it. And it has become one of the top tourist destinations for gay and lesbian travelers, with more than 40 resorts catering exclusively to the clientele.

The majesty of the surrounding landscape is undeniable: soaring palms and flowering cacti, the surprising natural lushness and vivid hues of the landscape, the brilliant blue of the daytime sky and the pink-purple glow that dusk ushers in, and jagged mountains that rise from the flat desert floor not too far in the distance. The scale alone is enough to impress.

But the main drag of Palm Springs is frozen in time in a '50s-meets-modern-day-strip-mall boredom. And although there are plenty of ways to sit back and relax, if you're looking for more stimulation than can be found by a pool with a frothy drink, look elsewhere.

On the other hand, in this fast-paced, hectic world, what could be better than a little peace and quiet? Palm Springs is the place to experience the kind of renewal that only comes from getting away from it all. Whether you draw inner peace from communing with spectacular nature or renewing your acquaintance with a gleaming set of irons, Palm Springs has the answer for you. And bring the kids: Virtually all the big resorts, and a few smaller ones, welcome them with open arms — and who's happier than a kid frolicking the day away in a sun-splashed pool?

Timing Your Visit

Unlike most of the rest of California, the Palm Springs off season is summer. From mid- or late May through September, daytime highs soar into the 100s. We're talking 110°F or more during July and August. And one memorable, apocalyptic day, it was 135°F. Those kinds of numbers can keep away all but the most faithful of sun worshipers — or those looking for serious hotel deals.

"In-season" is everything else: From October through April, average highs range between 69°F and 92°F. Keep in mind, however, that you can't always count on pool weather during these months; anyone who knows the desert will tell you that 70°F doesn't really feel like summer with virtually no humidity in the air and a sprinkling of clouds in the sky. The coolest months are usually December through February, when highs seldom get past the low 70s and nighttime temps dip into the 40s (perfect weather if you're a golfer who doesn't relish the notion of a broiling midday sun). Fall and spring are best — that's when it feels like a regular summer, with highs generally in the 80s and nights in the 50s or 60s. Spring and early summer can bring serious winds, gusting about like nobody's business.

With the "season" comes the crowd, especially urban-escaping weekenders and *snowbirds* (annual refugees from colder climes, often retirees, who head back home — just like their feathered friends — 'round about Apr). Luckily, the area seldom feels overcrowded. Still, if you have your heart set on a certain hotel, or you want prime tee times, plan ahead, especially if your visit falls over a weekend. Spring break — usually sometime before or around Easter — is worth avoiding if you can help it.

If you're not averse to packing an economy-size bottle of sunscreen and dealing with a little sizzling heat, off-season — summer — can be a bargain-hunter's bonanza. Nothing is very crowded, and hotel rooms go for a song: You can get terrific accommodations for as little as $49, and luxury resorts sell $300-a-night rooms for less than $150. Of course, it's not a great time to take full-day hikes in the desert, but if your plan is to lie under the umbrella poolside, taking a cooling dip every once in a while, summer is just fine. Even as a golfer, you can enjoy yourself in summers, as long as you book 6 or 7 a.m. tee times. After the sun goes down, summer evenings are lovely. Still, know what you're in for if you plan a July or August stay: The weather is going to be hot, hot, hot.

If you're treating this as a vacation from your vacation, a chance to unwind, you'll probably need at least three days — it takes a couple of days alone to really relax! But don't plan on staying more than two nights if you're easily bored.

If you want to work in a side trip to **Joshua Tree National Park** or **Death Valley National Park** (see the "Joshua Tree and Death Valley: A Trip to the Dry, Hot Desert Parks" section later in this chapter), you should set aside enough time in your schedule for it.

Getting There

The Palm Springs resorts are 108 miles east of Los Angeles and 141 miles north of San Diego.

✔ **From L.A.,** it's a straight shot east on I-10. Take the Highway 111 turnoff into Palm Springs, which drops you directly onto North Palm Canyon Drive, the main thoroughfare. The drive takes about two hours with normal traffic, but be warned that a Friday afternoon "getaway" can take four hours in bumper-to-bumper gridlock.

If you're heading to Palm Desert, stay on I-10 past the Highway 111 junction. Exit at Monterey Avenue and turn right. The distance is 122 miles from L.A. to Palm Desert.

✔ **From San Diego,** take I-15 north to I-215, then head east on Highway 60 until you connect to I-10 in Banning. From I-10, take the Highway 111 turnoff into Palm Springs, which drops you directly onto North Palm Canyon Drive, the main thoroughfare. The drive takes about two and a half hours.

If you're heading from San Diego to Palm Desert, the route changes a bit. Take I-15 north to Temecula, where you'll pick up Highway 79 to Highway 371 to Highway 74, which leads you into Palm Desert from the south. This nice 122-mile drive takes about two and a half hours. If you'd rather stick to the interstate, follow the directions to Palm Springs and allow three hours.

Flying right into Palm Springs is also easy. Pleasant **Palm Springs International Airport** is just a mile from the heart of downtown at 3400 E. Tahquitz Canyon Way, at El Cielo Road (☎ 760-318-3800; www.palm springsairport.com). The following airlines fly in year-round:

✔ **Alaska Airlines:** ☎ 800-426-0333; www.alaskaair.com

✔ **American:** ☎ 800-433-7300; www.aa.com

✔ **Continental:** ☎ 800-525-0280; www.continental.com

✔ **Delta/Skywest:** ☎ 800-453-9417; www.delta-air.com

✔ **Horizon:** ☎ 800-547-9308; www.horizonair.com

✔ **Northwest:** ☎ 800-225-2525; www.nwa.com

✔ **United Express:** ☎ 800-241-6522; www.united.com

✔ **US Airways:** ☎ 800-428-4322; www.usairways.com

Additional smaller carriers such as Harmony and Sun Country fly into Palm Springs on a seasonal basis. Check the airport Web site for more details. All the national car-rental companies have airport locations (see Chapter 7 for more about renting a car). You can also set up a ride with one of the desert's many taxi companies, such as **Palm Springs Taxi** (☎ 760-323-5100) or **Yellow Cab of the Desert** (☎ 760-345-8398). However, we strongly suggest renting a car, unless you plan on parking yourself at a destination resort or at one of the inns a walk away from Palm Springs's Palm Canyon Drive, and intend to do zero exploring.

Orienting Yourself

The desert resorts are a breeze to navigate after you get a handle on what's where. They cover a roughly 25-mile-long stretch of desert running parallel to I-10, from Desert Hot Springs in the northwest to Indio in the southeast. With the exception of Desert Hot Springs (only worth a visit if you're visiting Two Bunch Palms; see "Ahhh — the spa" later in the chapter), all the big resort communities lie on the south side of I-10, laid out in an angled grid pattern far enough away from the interstate that through traffic doesn't interfere (see the "The Palm Springs Desert Resorts" map on p. 455).

Palm Springs, the oldest community, is the heart of the desert resort action. North Palm Canyon Drive is downtown Palm Springs's main drag, where many — but not all — of the restaurants and mall and boutique shopping are. Tahquitz Canyon Way (say Tah-kwitz not Tah-keetz to avoid sounding like a tourist) meets North Palm Canyon at the town's primary intersection, tracking a straight line from the airport into the heart of town.

Most of the luxury resorts and championship golf courses are in newer communities to the east of Palm Springs, notably Rancho Mirage, Palm Desert, and La Quinta. The main connecting road between them is East Palm Canyon Drive, known as Highway 111 as soon as you leave Palm Springs. **Palm Desert** is the desert communities' other tourism-oriented commercial hub. Its central intersection is Highway 111 and Monterey Avenue, with El Paseo (often likened to Beverly Hills's Rodeo Drive), 1 block to the south, serving as the main dining-and-shopping drive.

Where to Stay in Palm Springs

We can't stress it enough: The off-season and other slow times offer tremendously discounted rates, so if you can plan your trip accordingly, you can get some great bargains. Be sure to check hotels' Web sites, when applicable, where some of these said bargains may be lurking.

The Palm Springs Desert Resorts

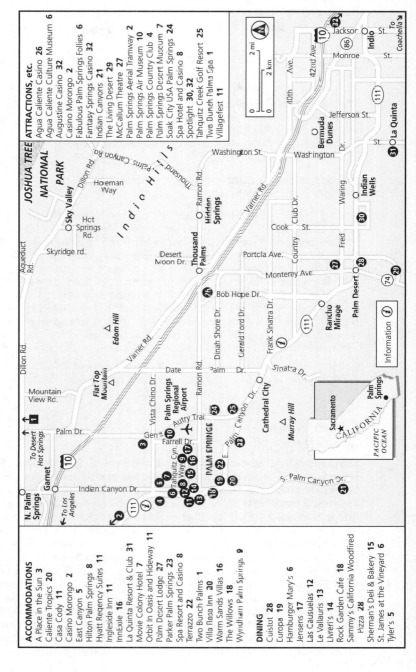

If our recommendations are full, try for one of the gazillion other places to stay through the free reservation services offered by the **Palm Springs Bureau of Tourism** (☎ 800-347-7746; www.palm-springs.org), which is particularly helpful for gay-oriented lodging.

An extra 10 to 11 percent in taxes will be tacked on to your hotel bill at checkout time.

Note that in fall 2006, the Colony Palms Hotel, 572 N. Indian Canyon Dr. (☎ 800-557-2187; www.colonypalmshotel.com), touted as a "more intimate" version of L.A.'s celebrity- and history-laden Chateau Marmont, will open. With just as rich a history, not to mention a serious makeover, expect it to be just as celebrity-friendly, and überhip.

A Place in the Sun Garden Hotel
$$–$$$ Palm Springs

Named because local legend has it that this classic 1950s motor-court hotel was built to house the crew of the Montgomery Clift/Liz Taylor/ Shelley Winters classic as it shot nearby, this is a kicky way to recapture old Palm Springs getaways. Sixteen separate bungalow and studios (including kitchenettes) are grouped around a saline pool (touted for its health benefits, a nice retro touch back to when Palm Springs was a weekend retreat for the well-heeled who needed a touch of health-spa rejuvenation), which, along with a pet-friendly policy, makes this a good family option. Rooms themselves are updated and comfortable, but sport too much of a motel décor to be truly chic. Breakfast (continental on weekdays, more extensive on the weekends) is served outside in the gazebo.

See map p. 455. 754 San Lorenzo Rd. ☎ *800-779-2254 or 760-325-0254. Fax 760-322-3479.* www.aplaceinthesun.com. *Rack rates: $79–$199 double. AE, DISC, MC, V.*

Caliente Tropics
$$$$ Palm Springs

Devotees of Tiki subculture will go mad for this Polynesian paradise, lovingly restored in 2001 to its original '60s-era thatched roof grandeur. Originally built by Ken Kimes, Sr. (husband and father to con artists and convicted murderers Sante and Kenny Kimes — we can't help it; we love our true-crime connections), the resort was a haven for famous faces including Elvis, Nancy Sinatra, and Victor Mature. After years of decline, the entire hotel has been revived, and now three wings of 90 rooms and suites surround a lush pool and garden area, anchored by a full-blown Tiki lounge (under which was once a nightclub frequented by the Rat Pack, now filled in with concrete due to earthquake code) and two restaurants. The rooms are bamboo wonders with comfy and colorful furnishings and all the amenities you'll need, including TV with pay-per-view, minifridges, coffeemakers, hair dryers, high-speed Internet, and more. The hotel hosts frequent Tiki events (who knew there were such things?) and are especially pet-friendly. The entire property is nonsmoking.

See map p. 455. 411 E. Palm Canyon Dr. (at Via Salida). ☎ **866-468-9595** or 760-327-1391. Fax: 760-318-1883. www.calientetropics.com. Rack rates: $225–$275. AE, DISC, MC, V.

Casa Cody
$–$$ Palm Springs

Founded by Buffalo Bill's cousin back in the '20s, Casa Cody is a charming and surprisingly modern place to stay. Two dozen lovely rooms, all decorated with Southwestern panache, are set hacienda-style around two pools and a Jacuzzi. Studios and suites have equipped kitchens, and some have fireplaces and/or private patios. This is a terrific value — and a great location, too, with Palm Canyon shopping and dining a mere stone's throw away.

See map p. 455. 175 S. Cahuilla Rd. (between Tahquitz Canyon Way and Arenas Road). ☎ **800-231-2639** or 760-320-9346. Fax: 760-325-8610. www.casacodypalm springs.com. Rack rates: $69–$169 room or studio, $109–$209 one-bedroom suite, $169–$379 two-bedroom suite. AE, DC, DISC, MC, V.

Casino Morongo
$$$–$$$$$ Cabazon

This hotel, the casino, and the resort were created by many of the same people responsible for the hip and happening Palms in Las Vegas. The $250-million property features a 23-story tower with over 300 large rooms, each done in luxurious but modern décor including flat-panel TVs, DVD players, coffee service, high-speed Internet, and much more. The top of the tower features a two-story glass penthouse with a restaurant and nightclub, while the base has a 150,000-square-foot casino, more restaurants and nightclubs (including Palms carry-overs N9NE and Raina, sister to the Sunset Strip's legendary Key Club), a luxury spa, and a resort-level pool deck. Oddly, Los Angeles's famed punk band X played a show here recently, which either says something about the band, or something about the kind of clientele (aging hipsters?) the resort wants to attract. If you want Vegas but don't want to actually go to Vegas, you have a great alternative here.

See map p. 455. 49500 Seminole Dr. ☎ **800-252-4499** or 909-849-3080. www.morongo casinoresort.com. Rack rates: $179–$399. AE, DISC, MC, V.

Hilton Palm Springs
$$–$$$ Palm Springs

Its location, 2 blocks from downtown and right next door to the Spa Casino, is the first reason you should notice this 260-room property, but the wealth of amenities and very upscale rooms could very well seal the deal. Every room has a patio or balcony, minibar (sorry, now known as a "snack center"), TV with pay-per-view and video games, wireless and high-speed Internet capability, and coffeemakers to name a few. There's an overwhelmingly well-equipped fitness center (aren't you supposed to be on vacation?), lush gardens surrounding a large pool and two Jacuzzis, an on-site restaurant, a lounge, and spa facilities. Pay the extra $7 or so for the

Resort Value Pack, which includes parking, unlimited fitness-center access, Internet, airport shuttle, tennis, phone calls, two-for-one meal coupon, and more, saving yourself a bunch of dough in the process.

See map p. 455. 400 E. Tahquitz Canyon Rd. (1 block east of Indian Canyon). ☎ *800-522-6900 or 760-320-6868. Fax: 760-320-2126.* www.hiltonpalmsprings.com. *Rack rates: $140 and up double. AE, DISC, MC, V.*

Hyatt Regency Suites
$$–$$$$$ Palm Springs

Located in the heart of downtown, the 193 suites are larger than most in town, with a small sitting area complementing the sleeping quarters. Each comes fully equipped with the expected bells and whistles, and though not exactly luxurious, they are tidy and nicely furnished. Everything is located off a soaring six-story marble atrium that also features a bar with limited food service and billiards tables, two full-service restaurants, a gift shop, a small exercise room, a small spa and salon, and even a putting green by the valet parking. A big pool deck looks out over a golf course and the mountains that the kids will love and a pool bar that you will. Rates can be surprisingly low, which, combined with the terrific location, makes this a first-rate choice.

See map p. 455. 285 N. Palm Canyon Dr. (at Amado Road). ☎ *800-55-HYATT or 760-322-9000. Fax: 760-322-6009.* www.palmsprings.hyatt.com. *Rack rates: $90–$375 one-bedroom suite, $425–$600 executive one-bedroom or VIP two-bedroom suite. AE, DC, DISC, MC, V.*

Ingleside Inn
$$–$$$ Palm Springs

If these walls could talk, you would know a lot more about your favorite movie star (the host-owner has rubbed shoulders with everyone from Sinatra to Travolta over the past 25 years). Old Hollywood is preserved in the heart of the desert — with rich fabrics, dark woods, antiques, art, and fireplaces. In a word, elegant. No two rooms are alike in this historic full-service inn, which has welcomed celebrities for more than 60 years. Enjoy cocktails by the pool (oddly located across the driveway) or watch the sun set on the wooden porch swing. Dine on Continental cuisine at **Melvyn's,** the hotel's sophisticated restaurant.

See map p. 455. 200 W. Ramon Rd. (at Belardo Road). ☎ *800-772-6655 or 760-325-0046. Fax: 760-325-0710.* www.inglesideinn.com. *Rack rates: $99–$165 double, $205–$295 minisuite, $165–$275 villa, $375–$600 one- or two-bedroom suite. AE, DC, DISC, MC, V.*

La Quinta Resort & Club
$$$–$$$$$ La Quinta

If you want to hit the links or courts — or simply surrender to the lap of luxury — come to La Quinta. Destination resorts don't come much finer than this Spanish-style spread. Set in single-story *casitas* (freestanding houses) on lush, oasis-like grounds, each room has an air of intimacy and privacy. Championship golf and tennis, first-rate dining and spa facilities, kids' programs — the works. It's a bit far removed from the rest of the Palm Springs area, but who cares? You won't want to leave.

See map p. 455. 49–499 Eisenhower Dr. ☎ *800-598-3828 or 760-564-4111. Fax: 760-564-5768.* www.laquintaresort.com. *Rack rates: $175–$635 double, $415–$3,800 suite or villa; $20 resort fee applied nightly. AE, DC, DISC, MC, V.*

Movie Colony Hotel
$$–$$$ Palm Springs

This fab resort hotel is in a renovated '50s motel, where the original style is chock-full of the sort of kitsch fun that appeals to retro-lovin' Gen-X types, or anyone with a sense of humor (unless midcentury modern, even served up with a wink, makes you break out in hives). Rooms take after the W model of sleek boutique hotel, but with a retro wink. It's a complete hoot, and a likely place to find self-aware young Hollywood types lounging by the pool.

See map p. 455. 726 N. Indian Canyon Dr. ☎ *888-953-5700 or 760-320-6340. Fax: 760-320-1640.* www.moviecolonyhotel.com. *Rack rates: $99–$225 (suites and villas higher). AE, DISC, MC, V.*

Orbit In Oasis
$$–$$$$ Palm Springs

This modern revival wonder would be too hip for its own good if the theme hadn't been executed so faithfully and spotlessly. Two mid-'50s gems a few hundred yards from each other had been left to decay in the merciless desert sun until they were rescued and restored using all the original fixtures and architecture from the period. The result is an eye-catching throwback to the era, complete with groovy furniture (we swear we had those nightstands in our living room in 1962), funky artwork (Rat Pack record covers, historical photos of the property), and cool music playing on the in-room sound systems. Even the bathrooms are period, with pink tile and ceramic fixtures in some rooms — fun to look at, but they are small. Rooms come in a variety of sizes and layouts, and each has high-speed Internet, robes, TV, VCR, and private patio. The Oasis has a saltwater pool, an outdoor bar/lounge, social area, a Jacuzzi, and complimentary just-about-everything, including bicycles. The Hideaway has a regular pool and no Jacuzzi but adds a gorgeous indoor lounge/meeting area with a giant stacked-slate fireplace. The hipsters would probably love this place, but the good news is you can, too.

See map p. 455. 562 W. Arenas Rd. (just west of Belardo Road). ☎ *877-996-7248 or 760-323-3585. Fax: 760-323-3599.* www.orbitin.com. *Rack rates: $169–$309. AE, MC, V.*

Palm Desert Lodge
$$–$$$ Palm Desert

This family-run motel is a great bet if you want to be near world-class golf or El Paseo shopping without paying resort prices. The rooms are clean, fresh, and attractive. Each has a minifridge, and most are double-doubles big enough to sleep four; some of the poolside units are even bigger and boast VCRs and/or fully equipped kitchens. A pool and Jacuzzi area is simply but pleasingly landscaped.

See map p. 455. 74–527 Hwy. 111 (at Deep Canyon Road). ☎ *760-346-3875. Fax: 760-773-0084.* www.palmdesertlodge.com. *Rack rates: $79–$179 double; as low as $59 in summer. AE, DC, DISC, MC, V.*

The Parker Palm Springs
$$$–$$$$$ Palm Springs

The former Merv Griffin resort reborn to follow the evolution of Hollywood royalty, this resort good-naturedly allowed itself (and its ilk) to be skewered on the Emmy-nominated HBO series *The Comeback*. Comfy but sometimes tiny rooms, hip but sometimes remote décor, and best of all, the jostling for the best position by the pool — it was all there. And yet, so is everyone else, drawn by all the resort opportunities (four pools, including two indoor separated by gender, tennis, spa, even croquet!) and the generally posh and pampering atmosphere. It's definitely grown-up playtime, and you never know what famous — or used-to-be-famous-and-looking-for-a-comeback — face might be reclining on the adjacent lounge chair.

See map p. 455. 4200 E. Palm Canyon Dr. ☎ *760-770-5000.* www.theparkerpalm springs.com. *Rack Rates: $185–$599. AE, DC, DISC, MC, V.*

Spa Resort and Casino
$$–$$$$$ Palm Springs

Because most of Palm Springs is on the Agua Caliente Indian reservation, this is probably the only town in California with a casino right in the center of it. Of course, the casino and all its attendant restaurants are just an amenity. The main attractions for a long time (and a long time to come) are the unique hot-water mineral wells that power the spa portion of the resort's name, with two huge pools (one mineral, one regular), two therapeutic Jacuzzis, and a state-of-the-art spa with every treatment known to man (including their signature Five Waters — wet sauna, dry sauna, eucalyptus aromatherapy, mineral-water tub, and cool-down relaxation room). Each of the 228 basic hotel rooms has a balcony or a patio, offering beautiful views of the surrounding mountains, and has all the comforts needed to make this a great getaway spot.

See map p. 455. 100 N. Indian Canyon Dr. (at Tahquitz Canyon). ☎ *888-999-1995 or 760-325-1461.* www.sparesortcasino.com. *Rack rates: $109–$399 double. AE, DISC, MC, V.*

Two Bunch Palms
$$$–$$$$$ Desert Hot Springs

If you're coming to the desert to do the spa thing, here's your heaven. Push thoughts of bouffanted ladies in designer sweat suits out of your mind — Two Bunch is intimate, easygoing, and understated, the kind of low-key oasis where multimillionaire movie execs and splurging suburban house-wives are at one in their quest to de-stress. Spread over 56 lush acres, this eclectic low-rise complex has been here since the 1930s (Al Capone used it as a hideout). Accommodations range from simple but comfortable guest rooms to full-on villas. Frankly, the accommodations are nothing spe-cial; the real draw is the phenomenal menu of spa treatments, the oh-so-soothing natural mineral grotto, and the unparalleled service. More than divine — sublime.

See map p. 455. 67425 Two Bunch Palms Trail (off Palm Drive/Gene Autry Trail). ☎ *800-472-4334 or 760-329-8791. Fax: 760-329-1874.* www.twobunchpalms.com. *Rack rates: $195–$345 double, $395–$725 suite or villa; summer rates as low as $129. Rates include continental breakfast buffet. AE, MC, V.*

Villa Rosa Inn
$$ Palm Springs

This hidden and charming gem is under new management, has undergone renovation, and is a terrific bargain. Built hacienda-style around a lovely courtyard pool landscaped with colorful potted flowers and plants, each of the six individually decorated units reflects a Southwestern theme. Amenities include a TV, refrigerator, pool towels, morning paper, and con-tinental breakfast with fruit plucked from the inn's fruit trees.

See map p. 455. 1577 S. Indian Trail (off East Palm Canyon Drive, between South Palm Canyon and Sunrise Way). ☎ *800-457-7605 or 760-327-5915. Fax: 760-416-9962.* www.villarosainn.com. *Rack rates: $99–$139 double, $129–$175 suite with full kitchen (two-night minimum stay required for all rooms in high season). AE, MC, V.*

The Willows
$$$$–$$$$$ Palm Springs

Hideaways don't get more romantic than this restored 1930s Mediterranean villa, which once played host to names such as Gable, Lombard, and Einstein. Set against the mountains just a stone's throw from Palm Canyon Drive, it's both conveniently located and deliciously private. Eight luxuri-ous rooms overflow with antiques, sumptuous textiles, and other impec-cable appointments, plus modern comforts including TVs and dataports. Gorgeous gardens and a fine pool complete the perfect picture. A stay here makes a worthy special-occasion splurge.

See map p. 455. 412 W. Tahquitz Canyon Way (just west of Palm Canyon Drive). ☎ *800-966-9597 or 760-320-0771. Fax: 760-320-0780.* www.thewillowspalmsprings.com. *Rack rates: $295–$575 in season, $225–$450 in summer; two-night minimum stay on weekends. Rates include three-course breakfast and afternoon hors d'oeuvres. AE, DISC, MC, V.*

Wyndham Palm Springs
$$–$$$$ Palm Springs

Its location next to the convention center is a great choice for business travelers, but take note of it if you're traveling with a family. The hotel has the biggest pool and recreation area in town (5,000 sq. ft. and 24,000 sq. ft., respectively), beautiful public areas that include an on-site restaurant (serving Tuscan cuisine), and a lounge with a pool table and other games. The 410 rooms in no way leave a long-lasting impression, with their vaguely Mediterranean décor, but they're big and comfortably furnished. All rooms have convertible sofas, minifridges, high-speed Internet, two TVs with pay-per-view movies, and more — and many have balconies or patios, allowing for some great views. Only about a half-mile farther from downtown than some of the other big-name resorts, the walk there should be a pleasant one — unless it's 110°F outside.

See map p. 455. 888 E. Tahquitz Canyon Way (at Avenida Cabelleros). ☎ *800-996-9486 or 760-322-6000. Fax: 760-325-0130.* www.wyndham-palmsprings.com. *Rack rates: $89–$229. AE, DC, DISC, MC, V.*

Where to Dine in Palm Springs

The Palm Springs area boasts lots of excellent restaurants, but don't expect much in the way of innovation. Strangely, the trend is toward traditional styles of cuisine, which may strike some as too formal or heavy for the desert. But desert dwellers really *love* classic French food served on white linen and bone china by tuxedoed waiters. That said, diversity abounds — it's just a matter of knowing where to look.

Cuistot
$$$–$$$$ Palm Desert   CALIFORNIA-FRENCH

Here's the desert's best restaurant — no small claim in an area that invites so much disposable income. Expect dazzling French cuisine with enough innovation and lightness of touch to give it a distinct California flair, with unpretentious, welcoming service, and the kind of perfectly calibrated lighting that makes diamonds sparkle just that much more. Inside seating is preferable to the patio thanks to the winning ambience of the contemporary room. A real star — perfect for celebrating.

See map p. 455. 72-595 El Paseo (at Highway 111). ☎ *760-340-1000.* www.cuistot restaurant.com. *Reservations highly recommended. Main courses: $14–$24 lunch, $26–$46 dinner. AE, MC, V. Open: Tues–Sat 11:30 a.m.–2:30 p.m., Tues–Sun 6–9:30 p.m. Closed during the summer.*

Europa
$$$–$$$$ Palm Springs   CALIFORNIA-CONTINENTAL

This longtime favorite is one of the desert's most romantic restaurants. Housed in what was once ice skater and B-movie actress Sonja Henie's house, the dining room shines with candlelight and old-world charm. Expect lots of modern accents on the Continental menu; the succulent rack of lamb is a standout. Everything is prepared with care and beautifully presented, including the divine desserts. The patio is pure magic on a lovely desert evening.

See map p. 455. At the Villa Royale, 1620 Indian Trail (off East Palm Canyon Drive, between South Palm Canyon Drive and Sunrise Way). ☎ *800-245-2314 or 760-327-2314. Reservations recommended. Main courses: $18–$38. AE, DC, DISC, MC, V. Open: Tues–Sun 5–10 p.m. (6–10 p.m. in summer).*

Hamburger Mary's
$$ Palm Springs   DINER

One of about a dozen locations nationwide, this sassy little joint is sort of a gay-friendly version of T.G.I. Friday's, with posters of Liberace, Debbie Reynolds and any movie with the word *Mary* in it decorating the walls. Tops on your list should be the burgers. How can you resist a half-pounder stabbed with garlic cloves and doused in red wine called Buffy the Hamburger Slayer? The chicken-ranch sandwich comes slathered in a tangy hot sauce along with cool ranch making a fun flavor combo, and is, like much of the offerings, bigger than your head. No human being should be able to consume this much food at one sitting, but it sure is fun trying. Soups, some inventive salads (steak and potato, crispy caramel chicken), wraps, hot and cold sandwiches, and a couple of entrees (fajitas, steak, chicken potpie) round out the menu, with most items less than $10. Oh, and even if you don't think it'll go with your meal, don't miss the aptly named Mary's Tasty Fries, coated in a zesty seasoning powder and piled higher than a drag queen's wig. Yum.

See map p. 455. 415 N. Palm Canyon Dr. (between Alejo and Amado roads). ☎ *760-778-6279.* www.hamburgermarysps.com. *No reservations. Main courses: $6–$15. AE, DISC, MC, V. Open: Daily 11 a.m.–10 p.m., bar open till midnight.*

Jensen's Fine Foods
$$ Palm Springs   DELI AND BAKERY

Generations of Southern Californians who journeyed to Lake Arrowhead know about Jensen's, the tiny local grocer and bakery made good. That they have a branch here is a marvelous addition to a Palm Springs getaway. A fine, small deli offers plenty of prepared and preparable picnic and other snacks (especially nice because so many local hotel rooms come with kitchenettes). Their sheepherder's bread, a crusty yet fluffy loaf, is a must-try, not to mention a frequent take-home, though we remain partial to the glazed donuts dipped in chocolate, a combination we wish more donut shops would consider. From cakes to beer, it's a useful stop.

See map p. 455. 102 Sunrise Way (at Tahquitz Canyon Way). ☎ *760-325-8282. No reservations. Main courses: Everything under $15. AE, DISC, MC, V. Open: Daily 7 a.m.–9 p.m.*

Las Casuelas Terraza
$–$$ **Palm Springs** MEXICAN

You'll enjoy the terrific Mexican cuisine, but it's the sidewalk patio — terrific for people-watching — that makes this place the choice for locals and tourists. Live music and an even livelier happy hour set the tone for the festivities.

See map p. 455. 222 S. Palm Canyon Dr. (between Baristo and Arenas roads). ☎ 760-325-2794. www.lascasuelas.com. *Reservations recommended for dinner. Main courses: $7.25–$14 lunch, $7.25–$19 dinner. AE, DC, DISC, MC, V. Open: Mon–Thurs 11 a.m.–11 p.m., Fri 11 a.m. to "when the last person leaves," Sat–Sun 10 a.m. to "when the last person leaves."*

Le Vallauris
$$$–$$$$ **Palm Springs** FRENCH

For more than 30 years, this elegant little restaurant, in a restored, historic home tucked up by the mountain, has widely been considered the best of the best in Palm Springs, and for good reason. The tuxedo-clad staff, the white tablecloths, the elegant dining rooms, the gorgeous outdoor dining patio (always pleasant thanks to the quietly humming swamp coolers), and even the piano player ("Strangers in the night, exchanging glances . . .") all act as a throwback to the days when going out for a good meal was an event not to be taken lightly. The menu changes often — in fact, it's presented on giant dry-erase boards brought to your table — but the French-influenced cuisine offers enough variety to delight all taste buds. The veal medallions smothered in an earthy truffle sauce with mushroom ravioli are stunning, a melt-in-your-mouth experience that made us want to cleanse our palates between forkfuls to get that first bite feeling over and over again. Wine connoisseurs take note: The phone-book-sized wine list covers every base from recognizable domestic to fascinating international varieties, including a ten-bottle course of such rare vintage that it costs a cool $25,000 for the privilege.

See map p. 455. 385 W. Tahquitz Canyon Way (just west of Palm Canyon). ☎ 760-325-5059. www.levallauris.com. *Reservations highly recommended. Main courses: $15–$26 lunch, $25–$43 dinner. AE, DISC, MC, V. Open: Daily 11:30 a.m.–2:30 p.m. and 5:30–10 p.m. Closed summers.*

Rock Garden Cafe
$–$$ **Palm Springs** CALIFORNIA

Think of it as a coffee shop gone mad with power: four dining rooms; three outdoor patios with misters, fountains, and rock gardens (and the occasional frog); and a menu that includes everything from biscuit-and-gravy breakfasts to steak-and-lobster dinners. In between, you'll find pasta, seafood, wood-fired pizza, vegetarian dishes, stir fry, more than a dozen burgers, sandwiches, salads, and a bunch of Greek dishes scattered about, owing to the owner's heritage. The owner heads to L.A. personally every week to stock up on the finest, freshest produce and meats, showing an obvious devotion to his customers. Try the souvlaki pita, stuffed with lamb, veggies, and an amazing dill sauce. And save room for dessert — specially made cakes, pies, and tarts from an in-house pastry chef.

See map p. 455. 777 S. Palm Canyon Dr. (just south of Sunny Dunes). ☎ *760-327-8840. Reservations recommended. Main courses: $4–$11 breakfast, $7–$12 lunch, $7–$30 dinner (but most under $15). AE, MC, V. Open: Daily 7 a.m.–10 p.m.*

Sammy's California Woodfired Pizza
S–$$ **Palm Desert** PIZZA

The menu at this bright, airy gourmet pizzeria also features entree-size salads, wraps, and pastas, but come for the pizza. Sammy's specializes in single-serving-size traditional pies, as well as more innovative versions with toppings such as smoked duck sausage and artichokes. The restaurant is friendly, well priced, and satisfying.

See map p. 455. 73-595 El Paseo (at Larkspur Drive). ☎ *760-836-0500.* www.sammys pizza.com. *Reservations not necessary. Main courses: $8–$17 (but most less than $13). AE, DISC, MC, V. Open: Sun–Thurs 11 a.m.–9 p.m., Fri–Sat 11 a.m.–9:30 p.m.*

Sherman's Deli & Bakery
S **Palm Springs** DELI

A kosher-style family restaurant that serves healthy portions of typical deli food in a casual and friendly atmosphere. Leave room for desserts such as the sugar-free chocolate cake (moist and tasty) or the coconut cream cake (light and sweet), which are baked daily on the premises.

See map p. 455. 401 Tahquitz Canyon Way (1 block east of Indian Canyon Drive). ☎ *760-325-1199. No reservations. Main courses: $3.25–$16 breakfast, $6.25–$13 sandwiches, $9.95 early-bird dinners (4–6 p.m.). AE, DC, MC, V. Open: Daily 7 a.m.–9 p.m.*

St. James at the Vineyard
$$$–$$$$$ **Palm Springs** ECLECTIC

A candlelit hacienda in the heart of the Palm Canyon action houses one of the desert's most thrilling restaurants. The kitchen excels at preparing innovative, globe-hopping cuisine, from coriander-steamed New Zealand mussels to rich curries with chutney and papadum to tequila-fired shrimp to homemade wild mushroom ravioli. The bold flavors, sophisticated ambience, gracious service, and top-flight wine list make for an exciting night on the town. The bar plays host to a lively weekend scene.

See map p. 455. 265 S. Palm Canyon Dr. (between Baristo and Arenas roads). ☎ *866-365-6500 or 760-320-8041.* www.stjamesrestaurant.com. *Reservations recommended. Main courses: $17–$39. AE, DC, DISC, MC, V. Open: Sun–Thurs 5:30–10 p.m., Fri–Sat 5:30–11 p.m.*

Tyler's
$ Palm Springs BURGERS

This cute and utterly casual indoor/outdoor burger shack serves up juicy burgers, crispy fries, and on-tap brew, plus hot dogs, turkey and egg-salad sandwiches, and yummy root beer floats and malts. The burgers come piled high with traditional fixin's, and portions are generous. The Friday-only clam chowder is a must for chowderheads.

See map p. 455. 149 S. Indian Canyon Dr. (at La Plaza). ☎ 760-325-2990. No reservations. Main courses: $5–$8. No credit cards. Open: Mon–Fri 11 a.m.–4 p.m., Sat 11 a.m.–5 p.m. Closed summers.

Gay Palm Springs

Palm Springs has become a major destination for gays and lesbians, with more than 40 hotels devoted exclusively to the community. What we include in this section is a small representation of some of the better and/or more interesting resorts (shown on the map earlier in this chapter), offering a wide variety of styles, prices, and atmospheres. Most are clothing optional and although some are traditional hotels in all aspects of the word, you may find things happening in the pool that you won't see at the Hyatt. If strict rest and relaxation is more important to you than being amongst "family," then check out one of the resorts listed earlier in this chapter.

Where to stay

For information on other resorts, visit the **Desert Gay Tourism Guild** at www.palmspringsgayinfo.com or check with the very gay-friendly **Palm Springs Bureau of Tourism** (☎ 800-347-7746; www.palm-springs.org).

East Canyon
$$$–$$$$$ Palm Springs

This former '50s-era apartment building was transformed a few years back into one of the most luxurious of the gay resorts, complete with 300-count linens, giant bathrooms, tastefully restrained décor, and an on-site day spa. With only 12 relatively expensive rooms (ranging from two-queen-bed standards to a suite with square footage and furnishings to rival big-name luxe resorts), the service is friendly and personal, and the clientele more intent on relaxing than partying. This is the only gay resort that is not clothing optional at the pool or Jacuzzi area, lending a quiet air of civility often missing from the rest of the pack. It's not really within walking distance to many of the other gay resorts or bars, so consider it an oasis in the gay desert, if that's what you're looking for.

See map p. 455. 288 E. Camino Monte Vista (just east of Indian Canyon). ☎ 877-324-6835 or 760-320-1928. Fax: 760-320-0599. www.eastcanyonps.com. Rack rates: $109–$359 double. AE, MC, V.

Inn Exile
$$ Palm Springs

This is one of the most popular resorts in the Warm Sands area, drawing a diverse crowd that trends a little younger than most places in the neighborhood. The sprawling modern Southwestern compound is mostly concrete, rock, and stucco — not a lot of greenery here — but it does feature four pools (including a long, shallow "promenade" pool), two Jacuzzis, a steam room, a lounge with snacks and a billiard table, a fully stocked exercise studio, and a small on-site cafe for pizza, salads, coffee, and more. The 31 guest rooms come in a variety of sizes and shapes, from simple studios to one-bedroom suites with fireplaces, but all have TVs, VCRs, fridges, and microwaves. Some rooms are modernized versions of old rooms, and, as such, the bathrooms in them are very small. Everything is well maintained, clean, and modern — a refreshing change next to some of the places in this market. The frisky-o-meter is off the charts here, but in a way that seems much more tasteful than some of the other more carnal hotels. Friendly staff and clientele make this a sure option if you're looking for a frolicking good time.

See map p. 455. 526 Warm Sands Dr. (at Ramon Road). ☎ *800-962-0186 or 760-327-6413. Fax: 760-320-5745.* www.innexile.com. *Rack rates: $94–$121. AE, MC, V.*

Terrazzo
$$–$$$ Palm Springs

You get more bang for your buck at this lovely 14-room clothing-optional gay hotel. Colorfully decorated rooms (think Southwest meets West Hollywood) come stocked with large TVs, VCRs, CD players, minifridges, microwaves, central air, ceiling fans, and big comfy beds. Rates include breakfast and lunch (special-ordered daily to your specifications) plus unlimited sodas, water, snacks, coffee, and tea; turndown service (with cookies!); a small but fully stocked gym; a large video library; weekend cocktail hours; and wireless Internet access throughout the property. They'll even help you configure your laptop! There's a giant pool, Jacuzzi, and barbecue area with complimentary flip-flops, sun-visors, suntan lotion, sarongs, and more to make the heat bearable. All of this, plus a social, demographically mixed crowd, makes this one a winner.

See map p. 455. 1600 E. Palm Canyon Dr. (just west of Sunrise). ☎ *866-837-7996 or 760-778-5883. Fax: 760-416-2200.* www.terrazzo-ps.com. *Rack rates: $119–$209. AE, MC, V.*

Warm Sands Villas
$$–$$$ Palm Springs

If you want to be in the heart of the gay resort area but don't want to deal with the noise and "activity" that most of those resorts bring with them, there is no better choice than Warm Sands Villas. Built in the '30s and '40s as a desert getaway for the rich and famous (Clark Gable and Shirley

Temple were said to be regulars here), the entire facility has been brought up to date with modern furnishings that are simple but functional, and comfortable to boot. Many rooms have kitchenettes and a few have fireplaces; all have TVs with built-in VCRs, free cable, and "educational channels." The only downside we see is that some units have bathrooms that should be measured in inches rather than feet. The rooms, the gorgeous lawns and lush landscaping, the charming Jacuzzi, the unique rooftop sun deck, and the giant pool are all lovingly cared for, and the clientele tends to the over-30 set, making this a quiet getaway in the midst of the madness.

See map p. 455. 555 Warm Sands Dr. (at Camino Parocela). ☎ *800-357-5695 or 760-323-3005. Fax: 760-323-4006.* www.warmsandsvillas.com. *Rack rates: $99–$239. AE, MC, V.*

Finding the nightlife

Because the gay resorts are the primary meeting grounds — many people BYOB and resort-hop — the gay bars in town are not as "must-see" as those in some other meccas. But you certainly have a lot to choose from if you feel the need to get away from the pool. Here are two of the best:

✔ **Hunter's,** 302 E. Arenas Rd. (☎ **760-323-0700;** www.huntersnight clubs.com), is probably the most popular, a big two-room space, with music videos and the like in one and a dance floor commanding the second. A nice outdoor patio with misters is perfect for a warm evening cocktail and cruise of the traffic on Arenas Road, where you'll find several bars and gay-themed businesses. Hunter's is event-heavy, with a Wednesday night underwear contest that is now legendary.

✔ **Tool Shed,** 600 E. Sunny Dunes Dr. (☎ **760-320-3299;** www.toolshed-ps.com), a dark dungeon of a leather bar packed tight with devotees and a few wide-eyed naves who choose it because it's within walking distance of the gay resorts.

Several other bars can be found in town, mostly of the neighborhood variety, but also more themed bars as well. You can get more information on most of them at the **Desert Gay Tourism Guild** (www.palm springsgayinfo.com).

Exploring Palm Springs and the Resorts

A surprising number of activities exist out here, but if you just want to hang around the pool or pamper yourself with a spa treatment, we won't blame you at all.

Touring the top attractions

You can locate these top attractions on the map earlier in this chapter.

Palm Springs Aerial Tramway

Probably Palm Springs's best-known traditional sightseeing attraction is this cool funicular, which takes you on a 10- to 12-minute ascent 2½ miles to near the top of Mount San Jacinto, the second highest point in Southern California. It's quite a remarkable ride, straight up the side of the mountain through five different climate zones — somewhat akin to moving from Mexico to Alaska inside of minutes. The ride is perfectly stable, and sleek new Swiss funicular cars rotate to give you 360-degree views along the way. Still, it's not for anyone who's afraid of heights, because the car ascends at a very steep angle — that cable looks mighty small, even to brave hearts, after you're far enough off the ground to notice. Otherwise, the entire family will love it.

At the top is the 14,000-acre Mount San Jacinto State Park and Wilderness Area, an alpine setting, complete with 54 miles of hiking trails, plus a three-story '60s-ski-lodge-style building housing a minimuseum, a fine dining restaurant called the **Peaks,** and an adequate cafeteria called the **Pines** (skip the Ride 'n' Dine package unless you're planning on spending the day). You can spend the whole day here or just come up for the panoramic views and head back down on the next tram out. Temperatures are typically 40 degrees cooler than on the desert floor, so bring a sweater in summer, a full-fledged coat in winter. Snow covers the ground in the cold months; locals bring the kids up for sledding and other snowy fun. An **adventure center (☎ 760-325-1449)** rents snowshoes and cross-country skis. Bring your AAA card or check for an online coupon to soften the blow.

See map p. 455. At the end of Tramway Road (turn toward the mountains off Highway 111/North Palm Canyon Drive), Palm Springs. ☎ 888-515-8726 or 760-325-1449. www. pstramway.com. Open: Cars depart every half-hour Mon–Fri 10 a.m.–8 p.m., Sat–Sun 8 a.m.–8 p.m. (daily to 9 p.m. Memorial Day through Labor Day). Admission: $22 adults, $20 seniors, $15 kids ages 3–12. Ride 'n' Dine combo (available after 3 p.m.) $34 adults, $22 kids.

Palm Springs Desert Museum

This small but well-endowed museum is Palm Springs's secret weapon in the culture wars, standing brave and tall against the schmaltz that tends to dominate the desert. Highlights include terrific Western and Native American art collections, as well as natural-science and history exhibits focusing on the local Coachella Valley desert and its first people, the Cahuilla tribe. The well-curated special exhibits stick to similar themes.

See map p. 455. 101 Museum Dr (at Tahquitz Canyon Way, just west of North Palm Canyon Drive), Palm Springs. ☎ 760-325-7186. www.psmuseum.org. Open: Tues–Wed and Fri–Sun 10 a.m.–5 p.m., Thurs noon–8 p.m. Admission: $13 adults, $11 seniors, $5 kids 6–17.

The Living Desert

Part museum, part zoo, and all learning center, this wildlife and botanical park is dedicated to introducing the wonders of the local ecosystem to those who consider the desert a flat, colorless, inhospitable wasteland.

You can walk or take a tram ride through re-creations of several distinct desert zones, seeing and learning about the local geology, plants, insects, and wildlife as you go. Critters run the gamut from tarantulas to mountain lions, with bighorn sheep, roadrunners, and golden eagles in the mix. Although you can't beat seeing the real desert with the help of an outfitter (see the "Desert excursions" section later in the chapter), this is a great alternative if you're not so inclined or if you have a family with little ones.

See map p. 455. 47–900 Portola Ave. (off Highway 111, between Monterey Avenue and Cook Street), Palm Desert. ☎ 760-346-5694. www.livingdesert.org. *Open: Sept through mid-June daily 9 a.m.–5 p.m. (last entrance 4 p.m.), mid-June through Aug daily 8 a.m.–1:30 p.m. Admission: Sept through mid-June $12 adults, $10 seniors, $7.50 kids 3–12; mid-June through Aug $8.75 adults and seniors, $4.75 kids 3–12; free for children under 3.*

Soak City

Your kids will be in water-hog heaven at this 16-acre playground, which boasts more than a dozen thrilling water slides (several dedicated to tots), a wave-action pool, an inner-tube ride, and lots more wet 'n' wild fun. Landlocked facilities include private beach cabanas, a video arcade, a 20,000-square-foot health club, and dressing rooms and lockers. You'll find height restrictions on some rides.

See map p. 455. 1500 S. Gene Autry Trail (between Ramon Road and East Palm Canyon Drive), Palm Springs. ☎ 760-327-0499. www.soakcityusa.com. *Open: Daily 10 a.m.–6 p.m. (varies; call ahead). Admission: $27 adults, $15 kids 3–11, free for children 2 and under.*

Palm Springs Air Museum

This museum holds one of the world's largest collections of WWII flyers. It's adjacent to the airport, so flying demonstrations are a regular part of the program. Many of the tour guides are veterans, so expect lots of good real-life stories, too.

See map p. 455. 745 N. Gene Autry Trail (between Ramon and Vista Chino roads). ☎ 760-778-6262. www.palmspringsairmuseum.org. *Open: Daily 10 a.m.–5 p.m. Admission: $10 adults, $8.50 seniors and military, $5 kids 6–12, free for children 5 and under.*

VillageFest

If you can time your visit to include a Thursday night, you can catch this once-weekly street fair and farmers' market. The main drag in Palm Springs is closed down for several blocks worth of food, music, art, entertainment, and a few delirious oddities ("Meet the Author!"; "Ask the Rabbi!"). The whole thing has the air of a Midwestern small-town celebration, where neighbors greet each other with a "hey" as they chow down on homemade creations. Okay, perhaps it's not as Mayberry as all that, but it's pretty darn fun, anyway.

See map p. 455. Palm Canyon Drive between Amado and Baristo, Palm Springs.
☎ *760-320-3781. Admission: Free. Open: Thurs only, Oct–May 6–10 p.m., June–Sept 7–10 p.m.*

Casino hopping, Palm Springs–style

Palm Springs seems designed to make you want to just sit down in the shade and relax for a while. But if you're like us, sitting is entertaining only for so long unless something exceptionally good is on TV or you have a really fabulous book. So what do you do in Palm Springs if you don't like to golf and you've already done the few attractions worth visiting in the city? Gamble, of course, silly!

California allows Las Vegas–style gambling on Native American reservations throughout the state. Because the bulk of the Palm Springs area is either on or near one of many tribal reservations, the city has been one of the hot spots for the multibillion-dollar state gaming market. Six major casinos are in the area, and we took a driving tour of all of them back to back. (There was nothing good on TV.)

✔ We started at the **Spa Resort and Casino,** 401 Amado Rd. (☎ **800-258-2WIN;** www.sparesortcasino.com), in the heart of downtown Palm Springs. The casino portion was co-developed by the folks at MGM Mirage (Bellagio, MGM Grand, and others), and although they don't have a hand in running it, their imprint is all over the place. Lovely, rambling Spanish Mission architecture on the outside and tastefully understated décor on the inside make the place a virtual replica of about half a dozen Vegas casinos we know and like. Gamblers can choose from 900 slots and video poker of varying denominations from 5¢ to $5, all with the handy ticket-in/ticket-out technology. Table games such as blackjack, roulette, and Let It Ride ring the center of the room, while a lounge with live entertainment, an upscale Asian restaurant, and a good and inexpensive buffet line the outside.

✔ Next we jumped on Highway 111 north out of town to I-10 and drove a few miles to Cabazon, the home of the **Casino Morongo Resort,** 49500 Seminole Dr. (☎ **800-252-4499;** www.morongocasino resort.com). Anyone who is familiar with Vegas, including us, will drive up to the place thinking, "This looks a lot like the Palms." There's a good reason for that: Many of the people involved in creating that Vegas hot spot worked on Casino Morongo. At more than 150,000 square feet, it's larger than most Vegas gambling halls but looks instantly familiar, with plenty of recognizable slots and all the typical table games presented in a tastefully sleek and modern package.

✔ Back in the car, we headed east on I-10 about 26 miles to the Ramon Road exit in Rancho Mirage, where we found the **Agua Caliente Casino,** 32–250 Bob Hope Dr. (☎ **760-321-2000;** www.hotwater casino.com), at the end of the off ramp. This is the sister casino to the Spa in Palm Springs, and although it's not quite as nice as its newer sibling, you still will probably never be able to tell you aren't in Vegas after you get inside the doors. Several restaurants, bars, and lounges keep you amused if all the slots, video poker, and blackjack tables aren't doing it for you.

✔ The next leg of the journey took us on another 20-mile-or-so drive east on I-10 to Indio — not a bad drive, especially if done at off-peak hours. Get off at Golf Center Parkway, cross over the freeway, and take a frontage road to find **Fantasy Springs Casino,** 84–245 Indio Springs Pkwy. (☎ 800-827-2946; www.fantasyspringsresort. com). Expanded from a relatively simple casino in 2006, Fantasy Springs now includes a 250-room hotel, several restaurants and lounges, a bowling center, and a larger casino with the latest slots and video poker plus the traditional table games.

✔ Once again to I-10, only this time we got off the freeway almost as soon as we got on, taking the 86S bypass route to the Dillon Road exit a couple of miles down the pike. Go under the freeway and you'll see **Spotlight 29,** 46–200 Harrison Place, Coachella (☎ 866-377-6829; www.spotlight29.com). It was called Trump — yes, that Trump — before reverting back to its original tribal given name. Fear not: The sleek, modernist revival building actually looks much more appealing up close than it does zooming by on the nearby interstate. Inside, the retro-chic design continues through the giant casino with tons of slots, table games, a huge poker room, several restaurants, a food court with a McDonald's, and a showroom featuring a rotating list of B- or even C-list entertainers.

✔ The final casino on the list is one you can feel free to skip if you've had enough — and really, who can blame you at this point? **Augustine Casino,** 84–001 Avenue 54 (☎ 888-PLAY2WIN; www. augustinecasino.com), is about 7 miles down a dark and desolate (at least at night) two-lane highway in Coachella. It's smaller than the others, unimaginatively designed with machines and tables crammed in too tightly, and it seemingly caters to mostly hard-core, stone-faced video-poker junkies. Unless you're one of them, there's no need to visit. Instead, get back on I-10 going west. Go back to the Ramon Road exit and take that west about 8 miles to the heart of downtown Palm Springs.

So, how did we do on our gambling junket? Well, California casinos are notoriously stingier than Vegas casinos (if you can believe it), and we now have evidence of it. On this particular tour, we did poorly everywhere, except for Spotlight 29, and only moderately so then. However, on subsequent visits we did quite well at both Casino Morongo and the Spa Casino, so perhaps it's not all bad news.

Hitting the links

If fairways and five-irons draw you to the desert, your best bet is to stay at one of the area golf resorts, such as **La Quinta** or **Rancho Las Palmas,** where you can play on some of the country's best championship golf courses without leaving the grounds (see the "Where to Stay in Palm Springs" section earlier in the chapter). La Quinta, in particular, is home to some of the finest fairways around; in fact, three of the four are ranked in *Golf* magazine's "Top 100 Courses You Can Play."

Other resorts you may want to consider include **Hyatt Grand Champions** (☎ 800-633-7313 or 760-341-1000; www.hyatt.com) and **Westin Mission Hills** (☎ 888-625-5144 or 760-328-5955; www.westinmissionhillsgolf. com). Westin's Resort Course is a stellar Pete Dye design that's more forgiving than most of his legendary courses. Expect greens fees to be between $80 and $175; twilight rates cut fees nearly in half.

If you want to experience desert golf but you're not up to splurging on one of the big boys, consider **Tahquitz Creek,** 1885 Golf Club Dr., off East Palm Canyon Drive between Gene Autry Trail and Cathedral Canyon Drive, Palm Springs (☎ 800-743-2211 or 760-328-2375; www.tahquitz creek.com), whose two diverse courses run by the Arnold Palmer Group appeal to mid-handicappers. Greens fees range from $45 to $70, and discounted twilight rates are available.

Another good bet is **Palm Springs Country Club,** 2500 Whitewater Club Dr., off Vista Chino Road (☎ 760-323-2626; www.palmsprings.com/golf/pscc.html), home to the oldest public course in Palm Springs, and especially popular with golfers on a budget. Greens fees start around $35 and go even lower for twilight hours.

Tee times at many courses can't be booked more than a few days in advance (a problem for hotel nonguests who want to play at the big resorts), but several companies can make advance arrangements for you, the best of which is **Golf à la Carte** (☎ 877-887-6900; www.palm springsgolf.com). **Palm Springs Tee Times** (☎ 760-324-5012; www.palmspringsteetimes.com) may be able to book you in at a discount as much as 60 days in advance.

Always ask about golf packages when you're making hotel reservations, because many area properties — even the most unassuming motels — offer packages that include tee times.

If you arrive in the desert without prebooked tee times, **Stand-By Golf** (☎ 760-321-2665) specializes in same-day and next-day tee times.

The visitor bureau is dedicated to making golfers happy and can provide you with tons of additional golf information (see the "Gathering More Information" section later in this chapter). Their great *Desert Golf Guide* is available to purchase online at www.desertgolfguide.ccm, which also offers a complete list of the many tournaments held in the area (mainly Nov–Apr), including celebrity pro-ams, if you're more the spectating type than a hands-on golfer. Another excellent source is Golfer's Guide (www.golfersguide.com).

Ol' Blue Eyes slept here

In the mood for some sanctioned gawking? Then hitch a ride on a nice air-conditioned bus for one of the **Palm Springs Celebrity Tours**, in the RimRock Plaza Center, at Gene Autry Trail and Highway 111 (☎ 760-770-2700). Some actual history is thrown into the mix, but most of the tour is dedicated to seeing the stars' homes. The company also offers a streamlined one-hour version for $25 adults, $23 seniors, and $12 kids 14 and under. But if you're gonna do it, go for the whole enchilada: The two-and-a-half-hour tour heads into Rancho Mirage and Palm Desert to take in the grandest estates of the biggest celebs — yep, including Sinatra — at a cost of $32 adults, $30 seniors, and $14 for kids. Make advance reservations.

Ahhhh — the spa

The desert is the perfect place to indulge in some serious pampering. Without a doubt, our top place to relax is at **Two Bunch Palms,** 67–425 Two Bunch Palms Trail, Desert Hot Springs (☎ **800-472-4334** or 760-329-8791; www.twobunchpalms.com). You can enjoy this place even if you don't stay over. Book one of the little-advertised Day Spa packages, which include two one-hour treatments, lunch or dinner, and full access to the grounds for six to nine hours, plus taxes and gratuities for (at press time, at least) $395 to $435 plus the cost of a taxi back to your hotel when it's all over, because human gelatin just can't drive. Call seven days in advance to make your reservations. For further information, see the "Where to Stay in Palm Springs" section earlier in the chapter.

For something a little more down to earth, book a treatment or two at the **Spa Hotel and Casino,** 100 N. Indian Canyon Dr., Palm Springs (☎ **888-293-0180** or 760-778-1772; www.sparesortcasino.com), run by the Aqua Caliente tribe on a square block of reservation land in the heart of town. The natural therapeutic hot-spring waters are the same that local Native Americans have been using for hundreds of years, but now they've built a sleekly modern, full-service spa around 'em.

Desert excursions

In addition to the following options, you may also consider a day trip to **Joshua Tree National Park** (see the "Joshua Tree and Death Valley: A Trip to the Dry, Hot Desert Parks" section later in this chapter).

Taking a guided tour

To the untrained eye, the desert can look like a lot of nothing. Put yourself in the hands of a knowledgeable and enthusiastic guide, however, and it's a whole different story — an entire, fascinating world you never knew existed will open up to you like a rare flower.

Hands down, the area's best tour operator is **Desert Adventures Jeep Eco-Tours** (☎ 888-440-5337 or 760-340-2345; www.red-jeep.com), whose off-road eco-tours, offered in signature seven-seater red Jeeps, are led by naturalist guides. The company is extremely reliable, and the experienced guides are great at communicating their vast knowledge of desert ecology, geology, history, and lore as well as earthquake science in a manner that's both smart and enjoyable. They're expert at giving meaning to what you see around you.

Still, the experience isn't for everyone. For one thing, the open Jeep is bouncy and dusty, and the weather can get really hot in summer. (Springtime, in particular, is a great time to go, because the weather is ideal and the wildflowers are in bloom.) If you have mobility issues, ask whether the tour can comfortably accommodate you. Kids, on the other hand, will love the rough-and-ready "on safari" feeling, although the tours don't accept children younger than 6.

Offerings change periodically, so call or check the Web site to see what's on while you're in town. Most tours include a visit to the legendary **San Andreas Fault,** with detailed explanations of how tectonic forces work and a look at evidence of recent and ongoing fault activity. If you have cultural interests, you can choose to tour an authentically re-created ancient Cahuilla village to find out how Native Americans carved a life out of the barren land. Tours that include desert walks are also offered for hikers. Tours last three or four hours and vary in price from $79 to $129 ($5 off for seniors and kids younger than 12). Reservations are required; call at least a day in advance.

Hiking

The reservation land that comprises **Indian Canyons** (☎ 800-790-3398 or 760-323-6018; www.palmsprings.com/points/canyon), at the end of South Palm Canyon Drive (3 miles south of the turnoff for East Palm Canyon/Highway 111), is terrific hiking territory. At press time, four stunning canyons were open to hikers of all levels; stop at the **Trading Post** for detailed trail maps. Admission is $8 adults, $6 seniors and students, and $4 for kids 6 to 12. Open daily from 8 a.m. to 5 p.m.; tours are offered daily at 10 a.m. and 1 p.m. Call ahead in summer; the canyons are closed from June through Labor Day.

A visit to the **Agua Caliente Cultural Museum,** in the Village Green Heritage Center, 219 S. Palm Canyon Dr., at Arenas Road (☎ 760-323-0151; www.accmuseum.org), pairs up well with a visit to Indian Canyons. Of particular note is the beautiful collection of basketry. Admission is free. From Labor Day through Memorial Day, the museum is open Wednesday through Saturday 10 a.m. to 5 p.m. and Sunday noon to 5 p.m.; during summer, hours are Friday and Saturday 10 a.m. to 5 p.m. and Sunday noon to 5 p.m.

Shopping

If you're looking to spend money, you'll have no trouble in Palm Springs. Boutiques are abundant along Palm Canyon Drive and the side streets in the heart of Palm Springs. If you're an antiques and collectibles hunter — especially if you have groovy midcentury-modern tastes — you'll enjoy the many '50s finds along North Palm Canyon, north of the downtown action.

Over in Palm Desert, you'll find Beverly Hills–style boutiquing along El Paseo, which curves south off Highway 111 between Fred Waring Drive and Cook Street and is lined with about 200 higher-end shops.

The **Gardens on El Paseo** is a lovely open-air mall at El Paseo and Larkspur Drive (☎ 760-862-1990; www.thegardensonelpaseo.com), with offerings that run the gamut from Ann Taylor to terrific one-of-a-kind shops and galleries. One of our favorites is the **Tommy Bahama's Emporium** (☎ 760-836-0288), a terrific source for island and desert resort wear.

Living It Up after Dark

For the latest bar and club happenings, pick up the free weekly *Desert Sun Weekend,* easily available around town. Also check out the *Desert Guide,* available at the visitor centers (see the "Gathering More Information" section, later in this chapter).

Nightlife revolves largely around North Palm Canyon Drive, at the heart of downtown Palm Springs. Restaurants and bars spill out onto the street until late, so your best bet is to just wander down the street and pop into whichever establishment pleases you.

The rollicking street festival known as **VillageFest** takes over Palm Canyon Drive, between Amado and Baristo roads, on Thursdays from 7 to 10 p.m. (6–10 p.m. Oct–Apr). The all-ages fun offers arts-and-crafts vendors, food booths, and street entertainers.

The **Fabulous Palm Springs Follies,** 128 S. Palm Canyon Dr. (☎ 760-327-0225; www.palmspringsfollies.com), is a Vegas-style extravaganza filled with show tunes from the '30s and '40s and lively production numbers complete with leggy showgirls. This silly show is so popular that it has run for over a decade; reserve in advance. Tickets run from $42 to $95 for the two-and-a-half-hour show; matinees are slightly lower.

For more highbrow entertainment, see what's on at the **McCallum Theatre,** at the **Bob Hope Cultural Center,** 73000 Fred Waring Dr., Palm Desert (☎ 760-340-ARTS; www.mccallum-theatre.org).

Joshua Tree and Death Valley: A Trip to the Dry, Hot Desert Parks

Sure, Palm Springs is hot and dry. But it's just steps away from a wet martini, served poolside under shady palms, and within crawling distance of a frosty air-conditioned hotel suite. If it's *really* dry and *really* hot you crave, however, you're in the right neighborhood. California's desert parks are great places to experience the wonders of the desert outside the carefully pruned environs of Palm Springs resort living. As national parks, they preserve refuges of rare beauty, where living things thrive in a seemingly hostile environment. Here are two wilderness areas where you can fully experience the desert's rough-edged grandeur.

Joshua Tree National Park

Joshua Tree National Park got its name from the oddball tree that's actually a yucca. The park encompasses two quite different desert environments: In the northwestern section — where you'll enter the park — is the **Mojave Desert**, the cragged, hilly land where rugged boulders set the tone and the Joshua tree lives. Head southeast through the park, and the elevation drops and the landscape morphs into the hotter, drier, **Colorado Desert,** which looks more like the desert you expect, dotted with cacti and creosote. Oases here point to natural water sources and serve as gathering spots for the park's wildlife — a range of critters, from roadrunners to golden eagles to bighorn sheep. The park was hit by two serious wildfires (started by lightning strikes) in July 2006, but though many acres were burned, from nature's viewpoint, fire can be as invigorating as it is devastating. Old growth is burned away, allowing the chance for newer plants and even species to emerge. It was hardly the first time the park has endured such a thing, and it was fairly small by comparison with the nearly 19,000-acre wildfire in 1999. The main concern is for the trees themselves; it takes about 100 years to replace a Joshua tree.

 ✔ **When to come:** Spring or fall.

 ✔ **How much time to set aside:** A full day's trip from Palm Springs. Leave early in the morning; the park entrance is a good hour from the resorts.

 ✔ **Getting there:** None of the three access points is close to Palm Springs. The **South (Cottonwood Spring) Entrance** is off I-10, about 53 miles east of Palm Springs, but we don't suggest you use it. Instead, use either the **West Entrance,** at the village of Joshua Tree, or the **North (Oasis of Mara) Entrance** in Twentynine Palms. To reach both entrances from Palm Springs, take Gene Autry Trail to I-10 west; after 6 miles, take the turnoff for Highway 62 (the Twentynine Palms Highway), which curves around the west and north sides of the park. The distance is about 44 miles to the West Entrance, 55 miles to Twentynine Palms and the main gate.

At the corner of National Park Drive and Utah Trail, a half-mile south of Highway 62 in the funky desert town of Twentynine Palms, is the **Oasis Visitor Center,** the park's official main visitor center, open daily from 8 a.m. to 5 p.m. The park has no restaurants or stores, so pick up any supplies you'll need in Twentynine Palms.

✔ **Where to stay:** The park offers no lodgings, but Twentynine Palms has a few basic options within 5 miles of the North Entrance. Or choose from nine basic campgrounds scattered throughout the park. Find further details, including fee information, online at www. nps.gov/jotr.

✔ **What to see:** The best bet if you're a day-tripper looking for the full Joshua Tree experience is to enter the park at either the West or North entrance and explore the northern loop (Park Boulevard) first. Then follow the **Pinto Basin Road** to the lush southeast Cottonwood section of the park where you can exit the park, go south to I-10, and be back in Palm Springs for dinner. This drive will take you past all the major highlights and through both desert climate zones. (The distance through the park from the North Entrance to the Cottonwood gate is 41 miles.)

✔ **Worth knowing:** Despite the optimism in the introductions, the series of major brush fires in 2006 may have affected some of the details listed earlier. Be sure to call ahead or visit the National Park Service Web site to find out if any areas of the park are closed before you visit.

✔ **For more information:** Contact the **Park Superintendent** (☎ 760-367-5500; www.nps.gov/jotr). The **Joshua Tree National Park Association**'s site at www.joshuatree.org is even more useful.

Death Valley National Park

Death Valley National Park may not be on your agenda on your first trip to California. No easy way exists to get there, it's not close to anything, and services are minimal. Still, plenty of people manage to work Death Valley into their vacation plans. You can't deny the draw of such extremes: The hottest, the highest, the largest, the lowest, the driest — you want it, Death Valley's got it. The landscape is both savage and spectacular.

✔ **When to come:** Most people prefer to visit the park in the temperate months, from October through April. Heat-seeking desert lovers come in the summer when the crowds thin out and daytime temperatures soar well past 100°F.

✔ **How much time to set aside:** Death Valley is the largest national park in the lower 48 states. Because you need to set aside two days for driving alone, a visit to Death Valley requires a minimum of three days. Four is smarter.

✔ **Getting there:** Even though Death Valley is basically due east of the Central Coast, some pesky mountains and a couple of national forests conspire to make you go south — way south — to get there. From Southern California, take I-15 (which connects with I-10 midway between L.A. and Palm Springs) to Baker, where you connect with Highway 127 north to Highway 190 east. The drive is 300 miles or six and a half hours. Or you can take I-14 north from the L.A. area (it connects with I-5) to Highway 178 to Highway 190, which takes roughly the same amount of time.

✔ **What to see:** Death Valley has been called a "windshield wilderness" because the best way to see the park is by car. Two-lane roads wind through a remote landscape devoid of commercial activity. Note that you should only tackle many of the park's backcountry roads in a four-wheel-drive vehicle or a light truck.

The place to start is **Death Valley Visitor Center,** in the middle of the park at **Furnace Creek,** 15 miles inside the eastern boundary at the junction of highways 190 and 178, open daily from 8 a.m. to 6 p.m. If you're traveling out of the Furnace Creek Visitor Center, take the 24-mile drive through Furnace Creek Walsh badlands to **Dante's View,** a scenic overlook with a park basin panorama amid enveloping mountain ranges. Or take **Artist's Drive,** which coils through colorful canyon terrain. In the northwest section of the park is **Scotty's Castle,** a 1920s mansion built in the desert as a vacation retreat. It's got a pool f t for a desert — all 270 feet of it. Reserve ahead for tours of the house and grounds.

✔ **Where to stay:** The valley holds four places to stay. Among them, the elegant **Furnace Creek Inn** ($260–$400 double) is a beautifully restored 1930s desert oasis with a formal dining room (☎ **760-786-2361;** www.furnacecreekresort.com). For camping information and reservations, call ☎ **800-365-2267** (http://reservations.nps.gov).

✔ **For more information:** Contact the **Death Valley National Park Service** (☎ **760-786-3200;** www.nps.gov/deva). Admission to the park is $20 per car and is good for seven days; keep your stub.

Gathering More Information

You can get excellent assistance at the **Palm Springs Visitors Information Center** (☎ **800-347-7746** or 760-778-8415; www.palm-springs.org), which concentrates on Palm Springs proper. The well-stocked and -staffed visitor center is at 2781 N. Palm Canyon Dr., just south of Tramway Road, an easy stop on your way into town.

If you're interested in Palm Desert, call the **Palm Desert Visitors Information Center** at ☎ **760-568-1441** or visit it online at www.palm-desert.com. The walk-in center is at Highway 111 and Monterey Avenue (pull into the Denny's parking lot).

Free publications with good maps are available at hotels, restaurants, shops, and visitor centers throughout the area. The best of the bunch is *Palm Springs Life* magazine's free monthly *Desert Guide.* Gay visitors will want to pick up the free *Palm Springs Gay Guide,* which is also easy to find. Other useful Web sites include www.palmsprings.com and www.thedesertsun.com; the latter is excellent for arts and entertainment coverage.

To check the local weather, dial ☎ 760-345-3711.

American Express has an official travel office in Palm Springs at Andersen Travel Service, 700 E. Tahquitz Canyon Way (☎ 760-325-2001).

Chapter 27

San Diego

. . . .

In This Chapter

▶ Determining the perfect time to visit

▶ Getting there and orienting yourself, neighborhood by neighborhood

▶ Sleeping and dining in the city

▶ Exploring the city's sights, on your own or by guided tour

▶ Discovering San Diego's top shopping sites

▶ Enjoying a night on the town

. . . .

San Diego is California's grown-up beach town. Year-round sunshine, postcard-perfect beaches, vibrant Spanish-Mexican heritage, and three fantastic family-oriented attractions (four, if you count LEGOLAND in nearby Carlsbad) make an appealing combination, especially for families and anyone with a kidlike sensibility and a need to kick back. In fact, count on one or more of the city's animal-themed fun spots — the San Diego Zoo, SeaWorld, and the Wild Animal Park — to be at the top of your sightseeing agenda.

Little more than an overgrown Navy base just a few decades ago, San Diego still feels more provincial than some might like, but that's part of its appeal. An influx of new residents has forced San Diego to start keeping up with culinary styles and cultural trends. Though some insist it's the next South Beach (with a much, much nicer climate, might we add), it's still not exactly bright lights/big city. The most radical changes thus far have taken place throughout the Gaslamp Quarter (heck, even the Hard Rock has a super-hip condo-hotel underway on Sixth) and are radiating north with Mission Beach and Pacific Beach glamming things up a wee bit.

The astonishing growth rate threatens to bring Los Angeles–style ills (traffic, noise, pollution) into the oasis best known for squeaky-clean fun. Still, the easygoing pace and sunny beach-town optimism here remains worlds apart from L.A.'s congestion and commitment to trends and appearance.

Deciding When to Visit — and How Long to Stay

San Diego has a reputation for reliably mild weather. Is it deserved? You bet. Average daytime highs range seasonally from 65°F to 78°F, with nighttime lows between 46°F and 66°F. The sun shines all year-round, except (believe it or not) in June and July, when ocean fog rolls in during the wee morning hours and burns off slowly, sometimes not until mid-afternoon. A puny 9½ inches of rain falls annually, primarily between mid-December and mid-April.

Summer means crowds of people on the sand, in the restaurants, at the major attractions, and occupying hotel rooms reserved months before. The best time to visit is in the fall — September through early December — when the crowds have vanished, winter snowbirds are still months away, and the possibility of rain is nearly nil. You can still comfortably bare it all at the beach through October. No matter when you visit, though, pack a swimsuit because "freak" warm weather (often in Nov or Jan) is common.

The few weeks between Thanksgiving and mid-January constitute the city's only bona fide low season, in time for lucky holiday travelers.

If you're a fan of music, food, and chaos, you may want to venture out early to mid-August for Street Scene (www.street-scene.com). This 20-plus-year-old tradition recently moved from the cordoned-off-for-the-event Gaslamp Quarter to just outside of Qualcomm Stadium and brings with it lots of stages showcasing a diverse array of just-emerging to well-known artists, the Taste of San Diego, and a number of minifestivals. Disappointingly, this has turned what was a charming street festival into something less distinguishable from any number of other outdoor rock-stadium festivals. If this seems like more of an irritant than a bonus, stay far, far away from Qualcomm during this time.

You'll likely want to spend two to four nights in town, depending on your sightseeing goals (which are governed, mainly, by how many animal parks you want to visit). You can get acquainted with the rest of the city in just a couple of days.

Getting There

As a top destination, San Diego is accessible by plane and train, as well as by automobile. So take your pick.

By plane

San Diego International Airport (☎ 619-231-7361; www.san.org), locally known as Lindbergh Field, is right on the water on Harbor Drive, just 3 miles from downtown. Most of the major domestic carriers fly into the airport, and all the major car-rental agencies maintain offices at the airport.

Chances are very good you'll want to have a rental car (for more on driving in San Diego, see the "Getting Around" section later in the chapter). If not, taxis line up outside the airport and charge around $12 (plus tip) to take you downtown.

> ✔ **To reach downtown** from the airport, take Harbor Drive south to Broadway, the main east–west thoroughfare, and turn left.
>
> ✔ **To reach Hillcrest or Balboa Park,** exit the airport toward I-5 and follow the signs for Laurel Street.
>
> ✔ **To reach Mission Bay** (home of SeaWorld), take I-5 north to I-8 west.
>
> ✔ **To reach La Jolla,** take I-5 north to the La Jolla Parkway exit, turning onto Torrey Pines Road.

If you're the plan-ahead type and would prefer to arrange for shuttle service, contact **Cloud 9** (☎ **800-9-SHUTTLE** or 858-9-SHUTTLE; www.cloud9shuttle.com). Expect to pay $11 to $13 for downtown and Hillcrest and $29 to La Jolla (quoted rates are for the first person; additional members of your party pay less).

San Diego hotels commonly offer airport shuttle service — usually free, sometimes for a nominal charge — so ask before you make other arrangements. Make sure the hotel knows when you're arriving and get precise directions on where they'll pick you up.

By car

I-5 is the route from Los Angeles, Anaheim, and coastal points north. The drive is about 120 miles, or two hours flat, from L.A., and 97 miles from Disneyland.

I-15 leads from inland destinations and the deserts to the north. As you enter San Diego, take I-8 west to reach the main parts of the city. From Palm Springs, take I-10 west to Highway 60, then I-215 south to I-15 south. The distance is 141 miles, about two and a half hours.

I-8 cuts across California from points east such as Phoenix, crossing I-5 and ending at Mission Bay.

By train

Amtrak (☎ **800-872-7245**; www.amtrak.com) trains arrive at Santa Fe Station, 1050 Kettner Blvd. (at Broadway), within walking distance of many downtown hotels and 1½ blocks from the Embarcadero (waterfront). Taxis line up out front, the trolley station is across the street, and a dozen local bus routes stop on Broadway or Pacific Highway, a block away.

Orienting Yourself

Thinking of San Diego without envisioning the water is impossible. You'll probably never be more than 5 miles from the bay while in San Diego, and you may never even lose sight of the blue Pacific.

The bay is San Diego Bay — not to be confused with Mission Bay, which is a protected body of water, fed by the sea but isolated from it by thin strips of land. Mission Bay is north of San Diego Bay. The airport lies between the bays, a stone's throw from most city neighborhoods.

The neighborhoods are well-defined by the undulating geography of foothills, shallow canyons, and coastline: Downtown grew up on the waterfront, wrapping around San Diego's huge natural bay, which brought in crucial shipping commerce and, later, the influential U.S. Navy presence. Downtown, the historic Gaslamp Quarter sits several blocks inland from the bayfront Embarcadero, and the uptown neighborhood of Hillcrest has prime bay views from about a mile away.

Almost — but not quite — an island, Coronado lies smack-dab in the middle of San Diego Bay. The communities of Ocean Beach, Mission Beach, and Pacific Beach — as their names imply — sit directly on the water, up the coast from the city proper, with La Jolla (la *hoy*-ya) occupying its own hilly peninsula at the northernmost edge.

You'll probably spend freeway drive time on I-5, which runs through San Diego north-south, jogging a bit around downtown before it leads straight to the border. East-west I-8 passes above Hillcrest and Old Town on its way to Mission Bay.

Here's a quick rundown of what you can expect in San Diego's main neighborhoods (see the "San Diego's Neighborhoods" map on p. 486).

Downtown

You'll probably be directed early on to the original downtown (see the map, "Downtown San Diego"), especially the commercial **Gaslamp Quarter.** With the spring 2004 introduction of retro Petco Park, home to Major League Baseball's San Diego Padres, this area is undergoing an extreme makeover of its own. Its new-and-improved personality is redefined every few months as more and more businesses open their doors. Once known as a raunchy red-light district, the Quarter — loosely bounded by Broadway, Island Avenue, and First and Fifth avenues — now boasts splendid late-19th- and early-20th-century buildings housing trendy restaurants and upscale nightspots. It really vibrates on weekends and game nights when folks come to hang out in the bars and cafes. (And, by the way, the gas lamps have been converted to electricity. Dang.)

Along Harbor Drive between Ash and Market streets is the **Embarcadero,** San Diego's waterfront, with hotels, attractions, and plenty of activity, from commercial fishing to a busy cruise-ship terminal, as well as home-port for the *Star of India,* the world's oldest seafaring ship.

North of the downtown core (between downtown and the airport), **Little Italy** is quickly gaining a reputation as the art and interior-design region recognized as TADD (The Art and Design District). It stretches along India and Columbia streets and Kettner Boulevard between Cedar and Kalmia streets. And yes, it still boasts the best pizza and cannoli in town!

Hillcrest

San Diego's early elite rode home in horse-drawn carriages to uptown neighborhoods with nicknames such as "Banker's Hill" and "Pill Hill" (the doctors' 'hood). Preservation-minded residents, including an active and fashionable gay community, have restored Hillcrest's charms after years of neglect. It's now our favorite part of the basic city of San Diego (see the "Hillcrest/Uptown" map on p. 490). Think of Hillcrest as the local equivalent of L.A.'s West Hollywood or New York's SoHo. Loosely bounded by Washington and Hawthorn streets to the north and south, deep, hilly ravines to the west, and Sixth Avenue at the east, Hillcrest stretches along the edge of San Diego's green jewel, Balboa Park (see the "Balboa Park" section later in the chapter).

Old Town

Its official name is **Old Town State Historic Park** and it's closed to ve-hicular traffic. Nestled into a wedge north of the airport where the I-5 and I-8 freeways intersect (see the "Old Town" map on p. 491), the com-pact, Spanish-era core of San Diego is a genuine historic area that has been bastardized by commercialism. It's the equivalent of L.A.'s Olvera Street, so you may appreciate the opportunity to experience the vestige of history that remains. The interactive and educational aspects have been steadily improving (making it a decent place to bring kids), and you may enjoy the history lesson and the notable 19th-century build-ings. The shopping is kitschy but fun and pretty much avoidable unless you're prowling for souvenirs, but even locals come here for Mexican food.

Coronado

Located in the middle of San Diego Bay west of downtown, the "island" of Coronado is actually a peninsula, best known for the landmark **Hotel Del Coronado,** the Victorian grand dame most famous for its costarring role — alongside Marilyn Monroe, Jack Lemmon, and Tony Curtis — in *Some Like It Hot.* Coronado is home to the U.S. Naval Air Station, a village of pretty cottages, charming shops along Orange Avenue, and a lovely duned beach. It's sleepy and completely adorable, and walking the gold-glitter beaches (it must be pyrite) is a pleasure. You can reach it from the "mainland" via the soaring Coronado Bay Bridge, a thrilling span to drive.

San Diego's Neighborhoods

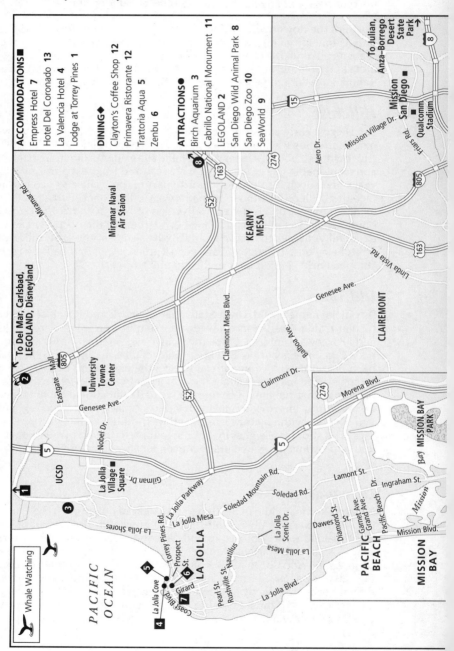

ACCOMMODATIONS■
Empress Hotel **7**
Hotel Del Coronado **13**
La Valencia Hotel **4**
Lodge at Torrey Pines **1**

DINING◆
Clayton's Coffee Shop **12**
Primavera Ristorante **12**
Trattoria Aqua **5**
Zenbu **6**

ATTRACTIONS●
Birch Aquarium **3**
Cabrillo National Monument **11**
LEGOLAND **2**
San Diego Wild Animal Park **8**
San Diego Zoo **10**
SeaWorld **9**

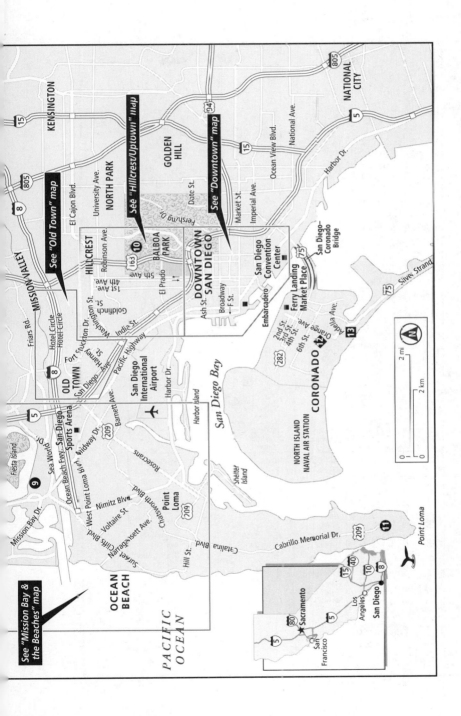

Downtown San Diego

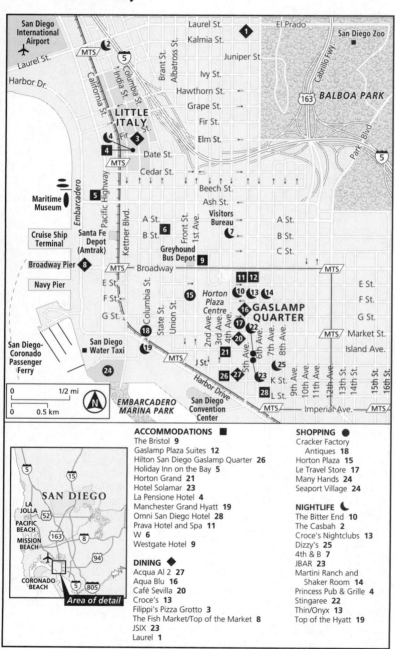

ACCOMMODATIONS ■
The Bristol **9**
Gaslamp Plaza Suites **12**
Hilton San Diego Gaslamp Quarter **26**
Holiday Inn on the Bay **5**
Horton Grand **21**
Hotel Solamar **23**
La Pensione Hotel **4**
Manchester Grand Hyatt **19**
Omni San Diego Hotel **28**
Prava Hotel and Spa **11**
W **6**
Westgate Hotel **9**

DINING ◆
Acqua Al 2 **27**
Aqua Blu **16**
Café Sevilla **20**
Croce's **13**
Filippi's Pizza Grotto **3**
The Fish Market/Top of the Market **8**
JSIX **23**
Laurel **1**

SHOPPING ●
Cracker Factory
 Antiques **18**
Horton Plaza **15**
Le Travel Store **17**
Many Hands **24**
Seaport Village **24**

NIGHTLIFE ☾
The Bitter End **10**
The Casbah **2**
Croce's Nightclubs **13**
Dizzy's **25**
4th & B **7**
JBAR **23**
Martini Ranch and
 Shaker Room **14**
Princess Pub & Grille **4**
Stingaree **22**
Thin/Onyx **13**
Top of the Hyatt **19**

The duchess from Coronado

From 1917 to 1921, a woman named Wallis Spencer lived in San Diego, primarily on the peninsula of Coronado, and was a well-known social figure about town. Eventually, Wallis divorced her husband, married a man named Simpson, and moved to England, where she once more became a well-known social figure around town and, eventually, the girlfriend of the then Prince of Wales. The prince later became King Edward VIII, but gave up his throne to marry her. Yes, the eventual Duchess of Windsor was a local, for a time (her friends placed a $75 transatlantic call to her when the royal scandal hit), and you can stay in her former house, which is now part of the Hotel Del Coronado property. Just imagine, if she had stayed put on Coronado, how different things may have been: no Diana, no Fergie, and, when the Queen Mum died, just a simple paragraph about the death of a long-lived, minor royal.

Mission Bay

This labyrinth of protected waterways may look artificial, but Mission Bay is really a natural saltwater bay that selective dredging has enhanced for use as an aquatic playground. Condos, cottages, and a few choice hotels line the shore, along with paved paths for joggers, in-line skaters, and bicyclists. **SeaWorld** is located on prime bayfront property.

The bay, bounded on the south and east by the San Diego River and I-5, is separated from the ocean by a narrow strip of land known as **Mission Beach,** a funky community of artists, free spirits, and surfers. This is a great place to stay if you want to be close to both the beach and downtown's attractions (see the map, "Mission Bay and the Beaches").

Pacific Beach

Looking for superlative dining or sophisticated culture? Then don't come to Pacific Beach. This water-hugging neighborhood north of Mission Bay is laid-back to the extreme, featuring acres of family-friendly beach and dozens of casual pub-style restaurants where, with a few exceptions, the cuisine takes a back seat to the sunset view (and happy-hour discounts). **Ocean Front Walk** is a paved promenade featuring an eye-popping human parade akin to L.A.'s Venice Ocean Front Walk. This is another great place to stay for easy access to both the beach and downtown.

La Jolla

Both chic and conservative, this wealthy Rodeo Drive–meets–the Mediterranean community is surrounded by beach and boasts outstanding restaurants and pricey shopping in "the village." The scenic spot that appears on most postcards is stunning **La Jolla Cove.** The cliffs above the cove hold grassy **Ellen Browning Scripps Park,** a perfect spot for picnicking.

Hillcrest/Uptown

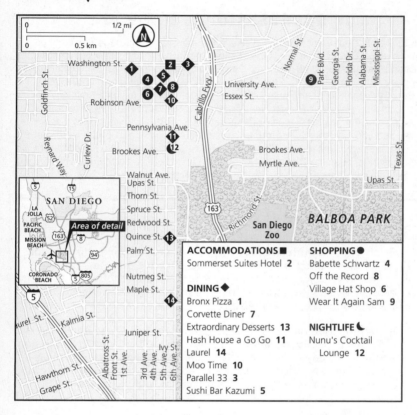

ACCOMMODATIONS ■
Sommerset Suites Hotel **2**

DINING ◆
Bronx Pizza **1**
Corvette Diner **7**
Extraordinary Desserts **13**
Hash House a Go Go **11**
Laurel **14**
Moo Time **10**
Parallel 33 **3**
Sushi Bar Kazumi **5**

SHOPPING ●
Babette Schwartz **4**
Off the Record **8**
Village Hat Shop **6**
Wear It Again Sam **9**

NIGHTLIFE ☾
Nunu's Cocktail
Lounge **12**

On the down side, La Jolla is insulated from most of San Diego, because it's at the northernmost edge of the city with no convenient freeway access. In rush hour, getting from the village to I-5 can take half an hour, plus a ten-minute drive to downtown. This makes La Jolla a poor base if you're planning to hop in the car every morning for far-flung sightseeing, but ideal for experiencing the "California Riviera" vibe that this jewel is known for. If you choose to stay elsewhere, La Jolla is worth an after-noon and evening for window-shopping and excellent dining. To reach Torrey Pines Road, La Jolla's main artery, take I-5 north to La Jolla Parkway, or I-5 south to La Jolla Village Drive.

Getting Around

Chances are good that you'll want to have a car in San Diego. The city is pretty spread out, but it's one of California's easiest cities to drive. Streets are clearly marked (and often in grids, but beware of the many

Old Town

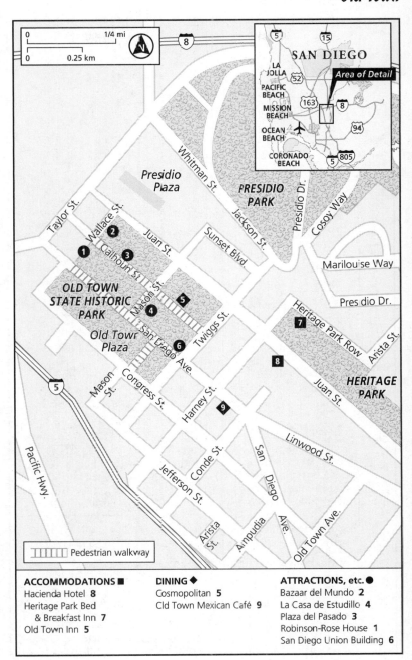

0 — 1/4 mi
0 — 0.25 km

SAN DIEGO
LA JOLLA
PACIFIC BEACH
MISSION BEACH
OCEAN BEACH
CORONADO BEACH
Area of Detail

Presidio Plaza

PRESIDIO PARK

Whitman St.
Taylor St.
Wallace St.
Calhoun St.
Juan St.
Jackson St.
Sunset Blvd.
Presidio Dr.
Cosoy Way

Marilouise Way

OLD TOWN STATE HISTORIC PARK

Old Town Plaza

Mason St.
San Diego Ave.
Twiggs St.
Congress St.
Harney St.

Pres dio Dr.
Heritage Park Row
Arista St.

HERITAGE PARK

Juan St.

Linwood St.

Pacific Hwy.
Jefferson St.
Conde St.
San Diego Ave.
Arista St.
Annpudia
Old Town Ave.

⬜⬜⬜⬜ Pedestrian walkway

ACCOMMODATIONS ■
Hacienda Hotel **8**
Heritage Park Bed
& Breakfast Inn **7**
Old Town Inn **5**

DINING ◆
Cosmopolitan **5**
Cld Town Mexican Café **9**

ATTRACTIONS, etc. ●
Bazaar del Mundo **2**
La Casa de Estudillo **4**
Plaza del Pasado **3**
Robinson-Rose House **1**
San Diego Union Building **6**

Mission Bay and the Beaches

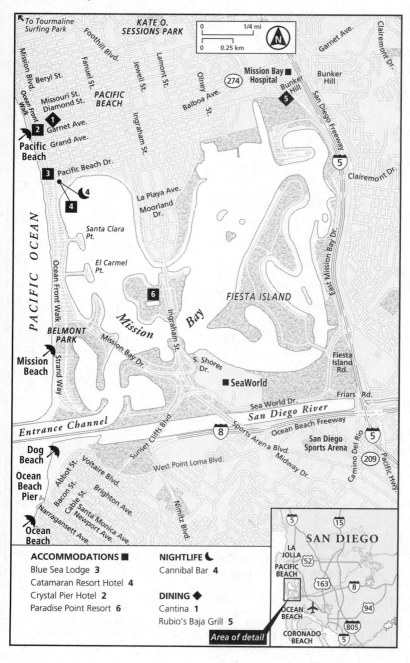

To Tourmaline Surfing Park

KATE O. SESSIONS PARK

0   1/4 mi
0   0.25 km

N

Mission Blvd.
Ocean Front Walk
Beryl St.
Missouri St.
Diamond St.

Fanuel St.
Foothill Blvd.

Jewel St.

Lamont St.

Olney St.

Balboa Ave.

274

Mission Bay Hospital

Bunker Hill

Bunker Hill

Garnet Ave.

Clairemont Dr.

5

San Diego Freeway

5

Clairemont Dr.

PACIFIC BEACH

1

Garnet Ave.

2

Grand Ave.

Pacific Beach

Ingraham St.

3

Pacific Beach Dr.

4

La Playa Ave.

4

Moorland Dr.

Santa Clara Pt.

El Carmel Pt.

6

Mission Bay

FIESTA ISLAND

East Mission Bay Dr.

PACIFIC OCEAN

Ocean Front Walk

BELMONT PARK

Mission Bay Dr.

Strand Way

Mission Beach

Ingraham St.

S. Shores Dr.

Fiesta Island Rd.

■ SeaWorld

Friars Rd.

Entrance Channel

Sea World Dr.

San Diego River

Sunset Cliffs Blvd.

8

Sports Arena Blvd.

Ocean Beach Freeway

San Diego Sports Arena

5

Camino Del Rio

209

Pacific Hwy.

Dog Beach

Ocean Beach Pier

Abbot St.
Voltaire Blvd.

Bacon St.

Brighton Ave.

Cable St.

Santa Monica Ave.

Newport Ave.

West Point Loma Blvd.

Midway Dr.

Nimitz Blvd.

Ocean Beach

Narragansett Ave.

ACCOMMODATIONS ■
Blue Sea Lodge **3**
Catamaran Resort Hotel **4**
Crystal Pier Hotel **2**
Paradise Point Resort **6**

NIGHTLIFE ☾
Cannibal Bar **4**

DINING ◆
Cantina **1**
Rubio's Baja Grill **5**

SAN DIEGO

5   15

LA JOLLA   52

PACIFIC BEACH   163

8

OCEAN BEACH

94

805

CORONADO BEACH   5

Area of detail

one-way streets), and traffic is relatively light except for brief morning and evening rush hours. Although the public-transit system isn't as worthless as L.A.'s, it's not as comprehensive as San Francisco's.

Driving is a nuisance in certain areas, most notably the Gaslamp Quarter, Pacific Beach, and La Jolla. When you visit these spots, park your car on the street or in a parking garage and walk, instead. If you stay in one of these neighborhoods and don't plan to venture much beyond it other than where public transportation can take you efficiently, you can easily make do without a car. But if you want to explore more of the city or visit the **Wild Animal Park** or **LEGOLAND,** mass transit will leave you in the lurch.

If you're planning to do without wheels, consult a map and pick your hotel carefully so that you won't feel stranded.

Tips for driving and parking

Pay careful attention to freeway exits, because the names can differ from one direction to the other. For example, to reach La Jolla, you take La Jolla Parkway from I-5 north, but La Jolla Village Drive from I-5 south.

Finding a place to stow a car is pretty easy in San Diego, but it may strain your supply of small change. Parking meters are plentiful in most areas: Posted signs indicate operating hours — generally between 8 a.m. and 6 p.m., even on weekends — and most meters accept only quarters.

In the Gaslamp Quarter, where parking is ridiculously scarce, consider parking in Horton Plaza's garage (G Street and Fourth Avenue), which is free to shoppers (with validation) for the first three hours.

Spaces are elusive in downtown La Jolla, because street parking is free and public lots are scarce.

By bus and by trolley

The **San Diego Metropolitan Transit System** or MTS (☎ 619-685-4900 or 619-233-3004; www.sdcommute.com) operates city buses and trolleys.

The terrific **San Diego Trolley** system runs bright-red trains south to the **Mexican border** (a 40-minute trip) and north to **Old Town** and **Mission Valley,** a sprawling slice of suburbia with mega shopping centers, and the trolleys can help you avoid the nasty parking situation at Petco Park. Within the city, trolleys stop at many popular locations, and the fare is $1.50 for one station, $1.75 for two, $2 for three stations, and $2.25 for four to ten stops; the fare to the Mexican border (the San Ysidro stop) is $2.50. Children younger than 5 ride free; seniors and riders with disabilities pay $1 for all rides.

Trolleys operate on a self-service fare-collection system; purchase your ticket from machines in the station before boarding. Trains run every

15 minutes during the day, every half-hour at night. Trolleys generally operate daily from 5 a.m. to about 12:30 a.m.

Unfortunately, the trolleys don't come close to covering the entire city. If they go where you're going, *hooray!* If not, take the bus.

Rectangular blue signs mark bus stops at every other block or so on local routes. Most fares range from $1.75 to $4, depending on the distance and type of service (local or express). Exact change is required ($1 bills are accepted). Get a transfer from the driver when boarding.

For recorded MTS information, call ☎ 619-685-4900. To talk to a real person, call ☎ 619-233-3004 daily between 5:30 a.m. and 8:30 p.m. Because the MTS controls both the buses and trolleys, they do a pretty good job of providing you with information on using them in conjunction. The **Transit Store,** 102 Broadway, at First Avenue (☎ 619-234-1060), is a complete information center, supplying passes, tokens, timetables, and maps. The store is open weekdays from 8:30 a.m. to 5:30 p.m., Saturday and Sunday from noon to 4 p.m.

The **Day-Tripper pass** allows unlimited rides on the public-transit system (buses and trolleys). Passes are good for one, two, three, and four consecutive days, and cost $5, $9, $12, and $15, respectively. You can get Day-Tripper passes from the Transit Store, online, and at all trolley-station ticket vending machines.

Some hotels offer complimentary shuttles to popular shopping and/or dining areas around town. Check to see whether yours does.

By taxi

Taxis don't cruise the streets, so call ahead for quick pickup. If you're at a hotel or restaurant, the front-desk attendant or maitre d' will call for you.

Among the local companies are **Orange Cab** (☎ 619-291-3333), **San Diego Cab** (☎ 619-226-TAXI), and **Yellow Cab** (☎ 619-234-6161).

Ferry on over to Coronado

The pedestrian-only **Coronado Ferry** (☎ 619-234-4111) is a charming way to get a quickie harbor cruise, and a boon if you're concerned about fighting street traffic on crowded summer weekends. It leaves from the Broadway Pier on the **Embarcadero** (at the foot of Broadway) every hour; the one-way fare is $3 per person. The ferry docks at **Coronado's Ferry Landing Marketplace.**

Where to Stay in San Diego

The San Diego lodging scene has multiple personalities. Downtown hotels cater to conventions and baseball games, so they tend to have reduced weekend rates when the Padres are on the road or during the off-season. Seaside hotels, on the other hand, sometimes offer deals mid-week, and always have lower prices after summer ends. We've noticed that many of the hotels in older buildings seem to have the sorts of problems you would encounter in similar places in Europe — they're often dark and creaky, and the plumbing can be unreliable. This holds true even for some very-high-end hotels in older buildings, so if you require brand-spanking-new, stay at a newer facility.

If you're planning to visit between Memorial Day and Labor Day, make your reservations several months in advance, especially if you want a hotel on the beach.

Some people worry about air-conditioning in hotels, but San Diego's cooling ocean breezes make that a minor concern. Still, if you're visiting between July and September and are particularly sensitive, ask about air-conditioning when booking. And just in case your trip involves a bit of business as well, almost all downtown and Gaslamp hotels feature complimentary high-speed Internet access.

Count on an extra 10.5 percent in taxes being tacked on to your hotel bill.

Blue Sea Lodge
$$–$$$$$ Pacific Beach

What it lacks in glamour, the Blue Sea Lodge more than makes up for in location and price. This active Best Western with center-stage pool is literally steps from the Pacific Beach sands. Most rooms sport at least a partial ocean view while the beachfront digs have full water views and LCD TVs. The in-room microwaves and minifridges in conjunction with the close proximity of a few little grocery stores also counts as a plus.

See map p. 492. 707 Pacific Beach Dr. (just west of Mission Boulevard). ☎ *800-258-3732 or 858-488-4700. Fax: 619-858-488-7276.* www.bestwestern-bluesea.com. *Self-parking: $8. Rack rates: $105–$355 double. AE, DC, DISC, MC, V.*

The Bristol
$$–$$$ Gaslamp Quarter

If you want to enjoy the contemporary ambience of the W but just don't have the dough, this is the perfect alternative. Fun and funky, with hallway carpets reminiscent of Alice and her travels through Wonderland, the recently remodeled, colorful rooms have the modern creature comforts you want, including mighty-plush robes and CD players for relaxed lounging.

See map p. 488. 1055 First Ave. (just north of Broadway). ☎ *800-662-4477 or 619-232-6141. Fax: 619-232-0118.* www.thebristolsandiego.com. *Valet parking: $19. Rack rates: $99–$200 double. AE, DC, DISC, MC, V.*

Catamaran Resort Hotel
$$$$–$$$$$ **Pacific Beach**

Lush palm groves and night-lit tiki torches amplify the Polynesian theme at this large, activity-oriented bayfront resort — imagine Gilligan's Island with in-room coffeemakers and poolside cocktails. Tower rooms offer the best views, while the low-rise rooms feel the most resortlike. In keeping up with the development that seems to have taken over San Diego, the Catamaran opened a shiny new spa that some insist is a marked improvement over the Cannibal Bar that used to reside in its space. After dark, the Pacific Beach party scene is just a couple of blocks away.

See map p. 492. 3999 Mission Blvd. ☎ *800-422-8386 or 858-488-1081. Fax: 858-488-1387.* www.catamaranresort.com. *To get there: Take I-5 to Grand/Garnet exit; go west on Grand Avenue, then 4 blocks south on Mission Boulevard. Parking: Self-parking $11, valet parking $14. Rack rates: $185–$595 double. Rates often drop based on occupancy; packages are also available, such as the B&B deal, which includes breakfast and room tax for as little as $139 per night. AE, DC, DISC, MC, V.*

Crystal Pier Hotel
$$$$–$$$$$ **Pacific Beach**

Built on an ocean pier, these 26 wooden cottages (circa 1936, but recently renovated) are San Diego's most unusual lodgings. Like tiny vacation homes, they're as darling as can be and book up fast for summer. Each has a private patio, living room, bedroom, full kitchen, and breathtaking sunset views. Beach gear is available for rent, but BYO beach towels — though plenty of boardwalk vendors carry pretty towels that are also relatively cheap.

See map p. 492. 4500 Ocean Blvd. ☎ *800-748-5894 or 858-483-6983. Fax: 858-483-6811.* www.crystalpier.com. *To get there: Take I-5 to Balboa/Garnet exit; follow Garnet Avenue to the pier. Free parking. Rack rates: Mid-June through late Sept $270–$320 (three-night minimum stay); early Oct through mid-June $225–$300 (two-night minimum stay). DISC, MC, V.*

Empress Hotel
$$–$$$ **La Jolla**

Located in La Jolla Village, this former residence hotel is a more affordable La Jolla alternative to La Valencia or Lodge at Torrey Pines. Although fairly standard, the recently renovated rooms are spacious and nicely appointed with snuggly bathrobes, in-room Starbucks, a couple of water bottles, and comfy beds. Fresh cookies welcome afternoon guests, and a continental breakfast is served daily on the terrace.

See map p. 486. 7766 Fay Ave. ☎ *888-369-9900 or 858-454-3001. Fax: 858-454-6387.* www.empress-hotel.com. *Valet parking: $10. Rack rates: $159–$349 double. AE, DC, DISC, MC, V.*

Gaslamp Plaza Suites
$$ Gaslamp Quarter

As San Diego's skyline keeps extending upward, don't forget that this former office building was San Diego's very first skyscraper. This 60-room boutique hotel is not without its quirks It's impeccably restored, complete with exquisite period detail (wood, marble, etched glass, brass) in the public areas, but the rooms are puzzlingly done in a mock-Regency style with Asian art prints — and to make things even more confusing, each is named after a prominent literary figure. Some standard rooms are better lit than the one-bedroom suites, although the higher-priced suites are better yet again. The cheapest rooms are too tiny for anyone with personal-space issues. The complimentary breakfast is surprisingly generous. All in all, if this were a Euro-pension-type hotel, we might cut it more slack.

See map p. 488. 520 E St. (at Fifth Avenue). ☎ *800-874-8770 or 619-232-9500. Fax: 619-238-9945.* www.gaslampplaza.com. *Valet parking: $21. Rack rates: $109–$269 double. Rates include continental breakfast AE, DC, DISC, MC, V.*

Hacienda Hotel
$$ Old Town

At this Best Western all-suite hotel perched above Old Town, walkways thread through attractive courtyards bearing a rustic Mexican Colonial ambience. This hotel is tops in its price range, with extensive in-room amenities, tons of on-site services including a pool and fitness area, and plenty of fun 'n' food within easy walking distance.

See map p. 491. 4041 Harney St. ☎ *800-888-1991 or 619-298-4707. Fax: 619-298-4771.* www.haciendahotel-oldtown.com. *To get there: Take I-5 to Old Town Avenue exit, turn left onto San Diego Avenue and right onto Harney Street. Free parking. Rack rates: $139–$225 double based on seasonal availability. AE, DC, DISC, MC, V.*

Heritage Park Bed & Breakfast Inn
$$–$$$$ Old Town

Surrender to the romance of utterly charming bedrooms, polished and pampering service from a friendly staff, and attention to every conceivable detail in this exquisite 1889 Queen Anne mansion, set on a hillside a short walk from Old Town dining and shopping.

See map p. 491. 2470 Heritage Park Row (off Harney Street). ☎ *800-995-2470 or 619-299-6832. Fax: 619-299-9465.* www.heritageparkinn.com. *To get there: I-5 to Old Town Avenue exit; turn left onto San Diego Avenue, then right on Harney Street. Free parking. Rack rates: $140–$280 double. Rates include an extravagant breakfast, an afternoon tea abundant with tea sandwiches, and in-room goodies. AE, DC, DISC, MC, V.*

Hilton San Diego Gaslamp Quarter
$$$–$$$$$ Gaslamp Quarter

The contemporary yet elegant lobby leads you to spacious, well-appointed rooms with down comforters atop snug pillow-topped beds, complimentary coffee bar, and high-speed Internet access, as well as a fitness center open 'round the clock. Room service provided by its New Leaf restaurant is surprisingly reasonable and good. For a few extra bucks, go for a loft or suite in the Enclave, their newest addition, which is housed in a redbrick building with blond hardwood walkways. Pretty snazzy, we must say.

See map p. 488. 401 K St. (at Fourth Avenue). ☎ *800-HILTONS or 619-231-4040. Fax: 619-231-6439.* www.sandiegogaslampquarter.hilton.com. *Valet parking: $26. Rack rates: Start at $199 double. AE, DC, DISC, MC, V.*

Holiday Inn on the Bay
$$$–$$$$ Downtown

Sprawling along the Embarcadero, this predictable but appealing and well-maintained chain hotel offers 600 rooms in a variety of buildings; choose the tower for cool bay or city views. Airport-convenient, the hotel boasts a bevy of on-site dining options and swimming pools, plus the restaurants and recreation of the bay boardwalk across the street, making families happy as clams.

See map p. 488. 1355 N. Harbor Dr. (at Ash Street). ☎ *800-465-4329 or 619-232-3861. Fax: 619-232-4924.* www.holiday-inn.com. *Parking: Self-parking $18, valet parking $22. Rack rates: $159–$249 double. AE, DC, DISC, MC, V.*

Horton Grand
$$$–$$$$ Gaslamp Quarter

Two historic hotels (one a former brothel) were linked to form this likable facility just steps from hot nightlife. Each of the Victorian rooms is individually decorated with period furniture and comes complete with a gas fireplace and pull-chain toilet, while the suites have full-fledged kitchenettes. We recommend going for a room with a courtyard balcony, because the view is lovely. If you have an affinity for the supernatural, you'll appreciate this: Rumor has it, the Horton Grand has friendly spirits roaming the grounds — most notably in room no. 309 (book really early if this is where you want to spend Halloween).

See map p. 488. 311 Island Ave. (at Fourth Avenue). ☎ *800-542-1886 or 619-544-1886. Fax: 619-544-0058.* www.hortongrand.com. *Valet parking: $24. Rack rates: $179–$299 double. AE, DC, MC, V.*

Hotel del Coronado
$$$$–$$$$$ Coronado

This grand old seaside Victorian is our favorite place to stay in San Diego. Opened in 1888, it's loaded with personality and storybook architecture. You can see the landmark red turrets from miles away — and you may recognize them when you do, because the hotel had a supporting role in the classic movie *Some Like It Hot* (it stood in for the Miami resort where most of the shenanigans took place). Rooms range from compact to extravagant.

Those in the original building overflow with antique charm and perfectly modern appointments (we prefer those), while Ocean Towers rooms sport a contemporary look. Views vary; ocean views go for more money, but parking-lot views are actually of a stretch of the island and not half bad. A pristine white-sand beach (glittering with pyrite gold dust) awaits, along with swimming pools, tennis courts, day-spa facilities, nice dining facilities, and a worthwhile guided tour. Service is superb, with staff catering to any need or whim. At Christmastime, the hotel is festooned with thousands of tiny white lights that can be seen from miles around. We love it and would stay here forever.

See map p. 486. 1500 Orange Ave. ☎ 800-468-3533 or 619-435-6611. Fax: 619-522-8262. www.hoteldel.com. To get there: From Coronado Bridge, turn left onto Orange Avenue. Parking: Self-parking $20, valet parking $26. Rack rates: $335 and up double (garden or city view), $600 and up double (ocean view). AE, DC, DISC, MC, V.

Hotel Solamar
$$$$–$$$$$ Gaslamp Quarter

An emphasis on nautical art and local artists, coupled with the perfect blend of style, warmth, and attitude, grants the Solamar everything it could possibly need to be *au courant* without resorting to pretense. Even the staff is helpful, attentive, and unassuming. Intriguing and inviting, the urban beach house aesthetics are permeated with an air of romance that manages to embrace the family travelers as well. Home to the Kimpton hotel's wine hour from 5 to 6 p.m. daily, the lobby's living room is divided into a library and a fireplace-centric conversation area, which take their warm glow from chandeliers comprised of platforms of softly lit candles. The airy guest rooms feature a chocolate and aqua palette, plush beds, animal-print robes, rich mahoganies, and the kind of spalike, Italian-glass-tiled bathroom you'd want in your own home (really, it looks like a Kohler ad). For extra luxury, go for a Spa King room with the Fuji-soak tub and separate shower. You must have a drink or two at Jbar — and lobby level dining at Jsix is a bonus!

See map p. 488. 435 Sixth Avenue (at J Street). ☎ 877-230-0300 or 619-531-8740. Fax: 619-531-8742. www.hotelsolamar.com. Parking: $24. Rack rates: $249–$379 standard, $400–$1100 suite. AE, DC, DISC, MC, V.

La Pensione Hotel
$ Little Italy

This remarkable value is conveniently located near downtown attractions and draws folks who seek out economy without compromise (that is, no youth hostels). Though not large, guest rooms make the most of their space and feature minimalist modern furniture that's durable without looking cheap. Extras include fridges and microwaves, plus Little Italy shopping and dining just outside. Ask for a city or bay view; the nearby train tracks may bother you if you're an extra-light sleeper, but most guests never even notice the noise.

See map p. 488. 606 West Date St. (at India Street). ☎ *800-232-4683 or 619-236-8000. Fax: 619-236-8088.* www.lapensionehotel.com. *To get there: From the airport, follow Harbor Drive south to A Street east; turn left on India. Free parking. Rack rates: $80 double. AE, DC, DISC, MC, V.*

La Valencia Hotel
$$$$$ La Jolla

Within its bougainvillea-draped walls and wrought-iron garden gates, this clifftop bastion of gentility has been La Jolla's crown jewel since it opened in 1926. Although the bathrooms can be smallish, every fabric and furnishing is of the finest quality, and the service is exceptional. The hotel overlooks La Jolla Cove and features the clubby **Whaling Bar,** heady with expensive Scotch. Long a hideaway for Hollywood celebs, its colorful dome was used as a civil-defense lookout during World War II.

See map p. 486. 1132 Prospect St. (at Herschel Avenue). ☎ *800-451-0772 or 858-454-0771. Fax: 858-456-3921.* www.lavalencia.com. *To get there: From Torrey Pines Road, turn right on Prospect Place, which becomes Prospect Street. Valet parking: $17. Rack rates: $305–$750 double. AE, DC, DISC, MC, V.*

Lodge at Torrey Pines
$$$$$ La Jolla

At the northernmost tip of La Jolla is this breathtaking (really, truly, no lie) escape from reality. What is it about Craftsman architecture that is just so dreamy? The rooms feature custom-designed furniture, 300-thread-count sheets, fabrics and carpets featuring William Morris–style designs, and bath products infused with local botanicals crafted specifically for the hotel. As if the five-diamond establishment isn't enough on its own, it overlooks the 18th hole of the famed Torrey Pines Golf Course (host of the 2008 U.S. Open) and the ocean. Also in the vicinity is the Torrey Pines State Reserve, which offers miles of trails for hikers, environmentalists, and anyone that simply wants to enjoy some serenity. And we haven't even mentioned the dining or spa. In a word, spectacular, and worth a peek even if you can't stay.

See map p. 486. 11480 N. Torrey Pines Rd. ☎ *858-453-4420. Fax: 858-453-0691.* www. lodgetorreypines.com. *Valet parking: $18. Rack rates: $350–$750 double, $950–$3,500 suites. AE, DC, DISC, MC, V.*

Manchester Grand Hyatt San Diego
$$$–$$$$$ Marina District (Gaslamp Adjacent)

The two towers of the Grand Manchester Hyatt, the largest hotel in Southern California, boast spectacular views of the bay, Coronado, Point Loma, and beyond, and are connected by a seriously fancy lobby. Along the Embarcadero and set apart from the downtown hustle and bustle, the traditional rooms more than meet comfort needs, while the luscious pool and spa setting can make even the most heinous business trip feel like a vacation. On the lobby level of the Harbor Tower, give in to your gluttonous side at Lael's lavish and delicious Sunday brunch (a spread that caters to low-carb hunters while embracing the pancake/crepe/dessert crowd as well). The Tower's 40th floor is home to renowned lounge, Top of the Hyatt.

See map p. 488. One Market Place. ☎ *800-233-1234 or 619-232-1234. Fax: 619-239-5678.* www.manchestergrand.hyatt.com. *Valet parking: $26. Rack rates: Start at $190 double. AE, DC, DISC, MC, V.*

Old Town Inn
$–$$ Old Town

This is a basic but sweet motel, so don't expect much from the rooms, although they are clean. The Spanish-style public areas are unexpectedly nice, however, and the pool will only get better as the landscaping matures. Grounds are well kept, TVs have HBO, and it's conveniently located across the street from access to the Old Town Historical District and the trolley to the rest of the city. Yes, it sits on a busy highway, surrounded by industrial blech, but with the low rates, plus AAA discounts galore, you're hard-pressed to do better if you're on a budget.

See map p. 491. 4444 Pacific Hwy. ☎ *800-643-3025 or 619-260-8024. Fax: 619-296-0524.* www.oldtown-inn.com. *Rack rates: $79–$250 double. Rates include continental breakfast. AE, DC, DISC, MC, V.*

Omni San Diego Hotel
$$$–$$$$$ Gaslamp Quarter

Although the contemporary Petco-friendly Omni couldn't be more welcoming of the business traveler with all its amenities and whatnot, the beautiful pool, Gaslamp location, and kid-welcoming features make it a rather alluring family and vacation destination as well. If you're a Padres ticket holder you must take advantage of the hotel's sky bridge that takes guests over Tony Gwynn Way (aka Seventh Street) and directly into the park — with in-and-out privileges. And for those without tickets, the awfully pretty and plush rooms, a number of which look directly into the park, come stocked with peanuts and Cracker Jacks.

See map p. 488. 675 L St. (at Sixth Avenue). ☎ *800-843-6664 or 619-231-6664. Fax: 619-231-6439.* www.omnisandiegohotel.com. *Valet parking: $24. Rack rates: Start at $199 double. AE, DC, DISC, MC, V.*

Paradise Point Resort
$$$–$$$$$ Mission Bay

Situated on its own island in Mission Bay, this complex is as much a theme park as is its closest neighbor, SeaWorld (a three-minute drive away). You can have so much fun at this resort that you may never want to leave. With so many activities for the younger set, even parents can enjoy their vacation. Single-story duplex bungalows dot 44 acres of tropical gardens and swim-friendly beaches. All have private patios (many facing duck-filled lagoons) and plenty of thoughtful conveniences. Recent renovations kept the low-tech '60s charm but lost the tacky holdovers; rooms now sport refreshingly colorful beach-cottage décor. Fire pits allow for that perfect Kumbaya kind of evening.

See map p. 492. 1404 W. Vacation Rd. ☎ *800-344-2626 or 858-274-4630. Fax: 858-581-5977.* www.paradisepoint.com. *To get there: I-8 west to Mission Bay Drive exit; take Ingraham Street north to Vacation Road. Self-parking: $20. Rack rates: $159–$495 double, $209–$5,000 suite depending on season and availability. AE, DC, DISC, MC, V.*

Sommerset Suites Hotel
$$–$$$ Hillcrest

This all-suite hotel on a busy street has an apartment-like ambience and unexpected amenities such as huge closets, medicine cabinets, and fully equipped kitchens in all rooms; executive suites even have dishwashers. Other terrific touches include a basket of welcome snacks, a courtesy van to shopping and attractions, a newly renovated pool and spa, and an afternoon wine reception. Several blocks of chic Hillcrest lie within easy walking distance.

See map p. 490. 606 Washington St. (at Fifth Avenue). ☎ *800-962-9665 or 619-692-5200. Fax: 619-692-5299.* www.sommersetsuites.com. *To get there: I-5 to Washington Street exit. Free parking. Rack rates: $129–$199 double. AE, DC, DISC, MC, V.*

W
$$$$$ Downtown

This place is downright cool, and yet, surprisingly friendly. Although the word *hip* is overused and sounds rather dated, its nuance perfectly coincides with these nifty digs. White down comforters and inviting robes mark the breezy blue rooms that are filled with a ton of creature comforts, not to mention fancy-label amenities. The second-floor Beach bar is named not for the ocean's proximity, but for the sand dunes in which your toes mingle, and the lobby's Living Room, featuring upscale beverages and house music, has the trendsetters (in San Diego, who'd'a thunk it?) flocking on weekend nights. Rice, the hotel's signature restaurant, serves up an eclectic mix of global contemporary cuisine and features a bourbon–brown sugar cured salmon appetizer. Yum!

See map p. 488. 421 West B St. ☎ *877-946-8357 or 619-231-8220. Fax: 619-231-5779.* www.whotels.com. *Valet parking: $26. Rack rates: $449 double. AE, DC, DISC, MC, V.*

Westgate Hotel
$$$–$$$$$ Gaslamp Quarter

A venerable history accompanies this grand hotel (San Diego's only *Leading Hotel of the World* member) in the heart of the Gaslamp Quarter, because dignitaries, celebrities, and the briefly famous have stayed here throughout the decades (from princesses to presidents to pop stars). It's elegant and frilly, gracious and dignified, all marble and chandeliers and

Convention-al accommodations

Many a traveler ventures to San Diego with one destination in mind: the Convention Center. Situated between the Embarcadero and the train tracks, the center is merely steps from great lodging and a few extra feet beyond that from the Gaslamp Quarter. Super-light sleepers take note: Though the disruptions are few and far between, every now and again sleeping quarters this close to the Convention Center are also privy to the rumbles and the whistles of passing trains.

antiques. Rooms are generously sized, with down comforters and robes, and decorated in a mock-Regency style that is veering towards rococo, and fast. It has a small, nice gym, an even smaller business center, and a restaurant that serves rich food at prices to match. The staff could not be better mannered or better trained. Rack rates are a bit high, but hidden discounts are there for the asking, so do.

See map p. 488. 1055 Second Ave. ☎ *619-238-1818. Fax: 619-557-3737* www. westgatehotel.com. *Valet parking: $22. Rack rates: $345 and up for double. AE, DC, MC, V.*

Where to Dine in San Diego

So far, San Diego doesn't compete with New York or San Francisco on the culinary playing field, but its growing sophistication has sparked a new spirit of experimentation and style. There are many little cafes in the Gaslamp and especially in the Hillcrest districts, and you may well consider taking a chance on any one of them.

Acqua Al 2
$$–$$$ Gaslamp Quarter TUSCAN

You've gotta love any eatery whose only sister restaurant is in Florence, Italy. Yes, that's right, you can dine at Acqua Al 2 in San Diego or Florence, whichever you prefer. That fun fact aside, the food here is wonderfully authentic and quite tasty, too. If you're a gnocchi person, you cannot miss the Topini al Radicchio Rosso, which combines potato dumplings with the restaurant's house tomato sauce, Italian red cabbage, mascarpone, and Parmesan. With an outdoor patio merely steps from Petco Park, it's definitely worth checking out before or after a game.

See map p. 488. 322 Fifth Ave. ☎ *619-230-0382.* www.acquaal2.com. *Reservations recommended. Main courses: $9–$15 lunch, $12–$25 dinner. AE, DC, DISC, MC, V. Open: Mon–Fri 11:30 a.m.–2 p.m., Sat 1–3 p.m., Sun–Thurs 5–10 p.m., Fri–Sat 5–11 p.m.; bar open till midnight.*

There's Mexican, Mexican, and also Mexican

Yep, those are pretty much your dining choices when you come to Old Town. What's more, we have to point out that it's all largely predictable Southern California Mexican. Which is fine — many a homesick expat Californian dreams of exactly the sort of meals offered here. It is said that each restaurant and shop within the Plaza del Pasado (formerly the Bazaar del Mundo) represents a particular period of time in history — the Mexican Period (1821–46), the Transitional Period (1846–56), or the American Period (1856–72). We can't quite say that we were able to distinguish the differences, however locals have favorites they swear by. We think you can pretty much just pick the one with the shortest line or the nicest courtyard. Most are open daily for lunch and dinner from 10 a.m. or so until closing. Among your options are **Casa De Reyes** representing the Mexican Period (☎ 619-220-5040), the Transitional Period **Jolly Boy** (☎ 619-291-3200), and **Cosmopolitan Hotel and Restaurant**, formerly Casa de Bandini, 2754 Calhoun St. (☎ 619-209-3525), defining the American Period with, amongst other things, a mighty delish carnitas salad. Outside of the Plaza, **Old Town Mexican Café**, 2489 San Diego Ave. (☎ 619-297-4330), tends to be rather popular.

Bronx Pizza
$ Hillcrest ITALIAN

Leave the cellphones off until you're done ordering at this terrific little pizza joint straight outta New York. They have attitude, they have plastic chairs, and, in addition to truly amazing pizza, they have calzones and soda. That's all they have, but quite frankly, it's all they need.

See map p. 490. 111 Washington St. ☎ 619-291-3341. No reservations. Main courses: Everything less than $10. No credit cards. Open: Sun–Thurs 11 a.m.–10 p.m., Fri–Sat 11 a.m.–midnight.

Café 222
$ Marina District BREAKFAST/LUNCH

From the street, this little breakfast and lunch spot looks like any other little spot within a cool, contemporary facade until you notice the people — lots of people — lining up to enjoy chef/owner Terryl Gavre's lusciously creative menu in which she has mastered the art of creating foods rich with subtle flavors. From the Pumpkin Waffle and Eggs Italia to the Posole (a rich, spicy chicken stew) and Caesar salad, every morsel is crafted in-house. And yes, that was Terryl on Food Nation with Bobby Flay demonstrating her peanut-butter-and-banana-stuffed French toast. By the way, the nifty coffee cup and spoon chandeliers were designed and built by Gavre because she ran out of money when she was building the restaurant 15 years ago and had to send back the light fixtures.

222 Island Ave. ☎ 619-236-9902. No reservations, but large parties can call in while en route to be put on the wait list. Dogs are welcome and are served a bowl of water and a treat when the food comes. Main courses: Almost everything is less than $10. MC, V. Open: Daily 7 a.m.–1:45 p.m.

Café Sevilla
$ Gaslamp Quarter SPANISH

It's a Spanish restaurant! It's a tapas bar! It's a nightclub! It's all of these and more! But somehow, instead of each aspect detracting from the other, they fuse together to form a fun space that feeds its guests with myriad wonderful flavors. To experience it all, order a bunch of different tapas, because a few of these tasty little Spanish appetizers can make a full meal. Don't forget the sangria! A lively atmosphere in the tapas bar makes for a good time, but if you're interested in hearing what your dinner companions have to say, try the dining room, then salsa the night away downstairs.

See map p. 488. 555 Fourth Ave. ☎ 619-233-5979. www.cafesevilla.com. Reservations recommended for dining room. Main courses: $17–$29, tapas $6–$11. AE, DC, DISC, MC, V. Open: Daily 5 p.m.–2 a.m.

Capriotti's
$ Hillcrest SANDWICHES

Capriotti's is an East Coast institution that took Las Vegas by storm, and is now even farther west, to our great delight. Capriotti's makes divine submarine sandwiches, overstuffed monsters that easily feed two (the 20-incher could feed three — unless those are three football players!), making this one of the best meal deals in town. They roast their own beef and turkey, and pile the cold cuts high in any combination you like. We suggest trying a house specialty, like the Slaw B. Joe (shredded roast beef, provolone, coleslaw, and Russian dressing) or the Bobby (turkey, stuffing, cranberry sauce — it's like Thanksgiving on a roll!). Perfect for a picnic or an end-of-the-day feast in your hotel room.

646 University Ave. ☎ 619-692-0100. Reservations not necessary. Main courses: Everything under $12. AE, MC, V. Open: Mon–Sat 11 a.m.–7 p.m., Sun 11 a.m.–6 p.m.

Cantina
$–$$ Pacific Beach LATIN/ASIAN FUSION

Health-conscious self-proclaimed "Foodgirl," Isabel Cruz, has fused two worlds to create an eclectic blend of dynamic flavors in a setting that's as deliciously colorful as the menu itself. The Bonsai Burrito (a hearty combination of brown rice, corn, black beans, shiitake mushrooms, and Asian ginger sauce) is merely one of the great treats served in this fabulous room abundant in autumnal reds, greens, and golds — sort of Far East meets West with a cameo appearance by the Greene Brothers. When it comes time (and yes, their motto is "We support the slow food movement" — however if you let them know you're in a rush, they'll do their darnedest to accommodate you) for flourless chocolate cake or coconut flan, justify it by noting how healthy the rest of your meal was. **Seaside Cantina,** a pared-down version offering breakfast and lunch, is on the PB Boardwalk, 4111 Ocean Blvd. (☎ 858-273-0775).

See map p. 492. 966 Felspar St. (just west of Cass). ☎ *858-272-8400.* www.cantina collective.com. *Reservations recommended for dinner. Main courses: $5–$10 breakfast, $6–$11 lunch, $10–$18 dinner. AE, MC, V. Open: Daily 8 a.m.–3 p.m., 5–10 p.m.*

Clayton's Coffee Shop
$ Coronado   COFFEE SHOP

A dying breed, this is your basic neighborhood coffee shop/diner — you know the sort, with the curved sit-down counter, soda fountain, and booths, plus righteous hamburgers, shakes (which taste wonderful after a day spent roaming the Coronado beach), hearty breakfasts (marvelous omelets) made to order, and daily specials such as meatloaf. Adorable local kids work here during the summer, but you should come any time of year.

See map p. 486. 979 Orange Ave. ☎ *619-435-5425. No reservations. Main courses: Nothing over $10. No credit cards. Open: Mon–Sat 6 a.m.–8 p.m., Sun 6 a.m.–2 p.m.*

Corvette Diner
$ Hillcrest   DINER

Corvette Diner is a faux-'50s diner, complete with loud sassy waitresses who sport hairsprayed wigs and poodle skirts yukking it up with the many customers who fill the place, while DJs add to the party. Okay, we're a tad cynical, because, too often, real old diners, without the embellished frills, get overlooked in favor of commercially created places like this. Then again, we're also the last to deny the pleasures of a great burger and shake, both of which are to be had here (along with vegetarian specials). Besides, it's a hoot for the kids.

See map p. 490. 3946 Fifth Ave. ☎ *619-542-1001. No reservations. Main courses: Most under $10. AE, MC, V. Open: Sun–Thurs 11 a.m.–10 p.m., Fri–Sat 11 a.m.–11 p.m.*

Croce's
$$$–$$$$ Gaslamp Quarter   AMERICAN/ECLECTIC

This restaurant was founded by Ingrid Croce, widow of singer-songwriter Jim, and she has turned this large (and beautifully restored) 1890 building into a semi-shrine to her late husband. Her efforts on one hand should be applauded, because it helped spark the resurgence of the Gaslamp Quarter. But the food is disappointing and overpriced, and the Croce soundtrack during lunch gets repetitive and almost a little creepy. But at night, it's a jumping spot, thanks to live jazz and R&B, so consider stopping by for a drink then.

See map p. 488. 802 Fifth Ave. (at F Street). ☎ *619-233-4355.* www.croces.com. *Call for same-day priority seating (before walk-ins). Main courses: $19–$33. AE, DC, DISC, MC, V. Open: Mon–Fri 5:30 p.m.–midnight, Sat–Sun 8:30 a.m.–midnight.*

Extraordinary Desserts
$ Hillcrest   PASTRIES/CAKES

If you're a dessert-lover, don't miss Chef Karen Krasne's shrine to all things sweet, which serves only the favorite course (plus gourmet coffees and teas). Among the dozens of divine creations that blend Parisian style with exotic ingredients and homespun favorites are raspberry Linzer torte layered with white-chocolate buttercream and Grand Marnier chocolate cheesecake on a brownie crust and sealed with bittersweet ganache. Definitely extraordinary!

See map p. 490. 2929 Fifth Ave. (between Palm and Quince streets). ☎ *619-294-2132. www.extraordinarydesserts.com. No reservations. Desserts: $2–$7. MC, V. Open: Mon–Thurs 8:30 a.m.–11 p.m., Fri 8:30 a.m.–midnight, Sat 11 a.m.–midnight, Sun 11 a.m.–11 p.m. A second location is in Little Italy at 1430 Union St. (*☎ *619-294-7001).*

Filippi's Pizza Grotto
$–$$ Little Italy   ITALIAN

Several reasons explain why Filippi's has been a Little Italy anchor since 1950: The food is *molto bueno*, the portions are enormous, and the staff welcomes everyone like family. Just follow the intoxicating aroma of traditional Sicilian pizza, lasagna, spaghetti, and antipasto through the Italian grocery/deli to the back dining room, traditionally outfitted with Chianti bottles and red-checkered tablecloths.

See map p. 488. 1747 India St. (between Fir and Date streets). ☎ *619-232-5094. No reservations. www.realcheesepizza.com. Main courses: $4.75–$13. AE, DC, DISC, MC, V. Open: Sun–Mon 11 a.m.–10 p.m., Tues–Thurs 11 a.m.–10:30 p.m., Fri–Sat 11 a.m.–11:30 p.m.; deli opens at 8 a.m. A second location is in Pacific Beach at 962 Garnet Ave. (*☎ *858-483-6222).*

The Fish Market/Top of the Market
$$–$$$$ The Embarcadero   SEAFOOD

Ask San Diegans where to go for the freshest fish, and they'll send you to the bustling Fish Market. Chalkboards announce the day's catches, available in a number of simple, classic preparations. Upstairs, Top of the Market offers similar fare at jacked-up prices; we recommend having a cocktail in the posh, clubby Top — which has stupendous bay views — then heading downstairs to the more cheery, casual restaurant for affordable eats, including treats from the sushi and oyster bars.

See map p. 488. On the Embarcadero, 750 N. Harbor Dr. ☎ *619-232-3474 downstairs, 619-234-4867 upstairs. www.thefishmarket.com. No reservations downstairs, recommended upstairs. Main courses: $8–$42. AE, DC, DISC, MC, V. Open: Daily 11 a.m.–10 p.m.*

George's at the Cove/George's Ocean Terrace
$$$–$$$$$ La Jolla   CALIFORNIA

These sibling restaurants — a fancy downstairs dining room and a breezy upstairs cafe — share an ahh-inspiring ocean view, attentive service, and tasty smoked chicken/broccoli/black bean soup. George's downstairs kitchen turns up the finesse factor for inventive and formal California cuisine, while the Ocean Terrace cafe offers crowd-pleasing versions. Both are great, so choose based on your mood and budget.

1250 Prospect St. ☎ *858-454-4244.* www.georgesatthecove.com. *Reservations recommended at George's at the Cove, not accepted at Ocean Terrace. To get there: From Torrey Pines Road, right on Prospect Place, which becomes Prospect Street. Main courses: George's at the Cove $26–$44 dinner; Ocean Terrace $10–$14 lunch, $14–$25 dinner. AE, DC, DISC, MC, V. Open: George's at the Cove Sun–Thurs 5:30– 10 p.m., Fri–Sat 5–10:30 p.m.; Ocean Terrace daily 11:30 a.m.–4 p.m. and 4:30–10 p.m.*

Hash House A Go Go
$–$$$ Hillcrest   BREAKFAST

We don't know whether to tell you to go early or go hungry. In a perfect world, we'd opt for going really hungry first thing or advise going during the week because they pack 'em in after 9 a.m. on Saturdays and Sundays. The beautifully presented creative offerings such as Indiana Sage Fried Chicken Eggs Benedict and Captain Crunch Flapjacks are not only out-of-this-world good but seriously huge. Why not box up half of your meal and share with your friends so that you don't have to worry about finding a spot for lunch? You can eat here all day, and it's all good, but the breakfast is its toast-and-butter.

See map p. 490. 3628 Fifth Ave. (between Pennsylvania and Brooks). ☎ *619-298-4646.* www.hashhouseagogo.com. *Reservations recommended for dinner. Main courses: $5.95–$16 breakfast, $5.95–$17 lunch, $14–$32 dinner. AE, DC, DISC, MC, V. Open: Mon–Sat 7:30 a.m.–2 p.m., Sun 7:30 a.m.–2:30 p.m., Sun–Thurs 5:30–9 p.m., Fri–Sat 5:30–10 p.m.*

Jsix
$–$$$ Gaslamp Quarter   COASTAL CUISINE

Situated on the bottom level of the mighty cool Hotel Solamar, there is nothing hotel-ish about this warm dining room adorned with dangling Italian light fixtures. San Francisco Chef Christian Graves brings his impressive CV and his penchant for seafood to create a destination unto itself. Heck, he even acts responsibly by choosing only the sustainable from the Monterey Bay Aquarium's Seafood Watch list. We were rather impressed with the grilled halibut special and the Kobe beef with the cilantro glaze. You may want to call in advance to see if he's made his signature caramel and balsamic gelato, because even if the dining is a little out of your price range, this is a dessert to be had.

See map p. 488. 616 J Street. (at Sixth). ☎ *619-531-8744.* www.jsixsandiego.com. *Reservations recommended. Main courses: $9–$17 breakfast/brunch, $8–$13 lunch, $16–$32 dinner. AE, DC, DISC, MC, V. Open: Daily 7 a.m.–10:30 a.m., Sat–Sun 11:30 a.m.–2:30 p.m., Mon–Fri 11:30 a.m.–2:30 p.m., Sun–Wed 5:30–10 p.m., Thurs–Sat 5:30–11 p.m.*

Laurel
$$$$ Downtown/Hillcrest MEDITERRANEAN

Here's a restaurant that takes itself seriously. It offers a swank room reminiscent of Paris and London in the '60s, featuring contemporary Mediterranean cuisine tempered with traditional French elements. This restaurant is solid evidence that the San Diego restaurant scene has gotten with it. Laurel is the best choice for pretheater dining, thanks to its shuttle service to and from the Old Globe Theatre, which allows you to leave your car at the restaurant and not bother with Balboa Park parking. The ride is pleasant, efficient, and free (for the price of dinner, of course).

See maps p. 488 and p. 490. 505 Laurel St. (at Fifth Avenue). ☎ *619-239-2222.* www.laurelrestaurant.com. *Reservations recommended. Main courses: $22–$34. A pretheater tasting menu offering three courses is available 5–6:30 p.m. daily for $35 per person (with wine pairing for $55). AE, DC, DISC, MC, V. Open: Sun–Thurs 5–10 p.m., Fri–Sat 5–11 p.m.*

Pacific Coast Grill
$$–$$$ Solana Beach ECLECTIC

An easy jump off the freeway on your way to or from San Diego, and probably worth the short drive from the city, this modern, gaily decorated establishment has a number of curious, clever dishes, but our favorite is the shrimp dumplings, served in a port-wine butter sauce that will have you calling for more of the good house bread to soak it up. Fresh fish dishes dominate the menu, from lobster tacos to grilled mahimahi, but carnivores will be happy to discover that the burger comes on a fluffy roll and is stuffed with herb butter. Note that lunchtime sandwiches can be ordered at dinner even though they aren't on the menu.

437 S. Hwy 101. ☎ *858-794-4632.* www.pacificcoastgrill.com. *Reservations recommended. Main courses: $8–$12 lunch, $14–$28 dinner. AE, DC, DISC, MC, V. Open: Sun–Thurs 11:30 a.m.–9:30 p.m., Fri–Sat 11:30 a.m.–10:30 p.m.*

Parallel 33
$$$ Mission Hills ECLECTIC

Named for the mythical line on which, geographically, you find Morocco, Japan, India, and yes, San Diego, this is a delightfully sophisticated but not intimidating little place just a few blocks away from the Hillcrest district. On a recent trip, we started with *b'stilla* (the Moroccan dish of chicken, sugar, and cinnamon wrapped in phyllo) and a wonderful salad dressed with preserved lemon vinaigrette. From there, we had pan-seared halibut with a yellow tomato coulis (perfect), salmon with a roasted-sesame crust on braised veggies (even better), and an Asian duck breast and five-spice sauce (the best of all). Desserts are made with style and care (do try the vanilla-rose ice cream, a special Middle Eastern treat).

See map p. 490. 741 W. Washington St. ☎ *619-260-0033. Reservations recommended. Main courses: $18–$25. AE, DISC, MC, V. Open: Mon–Thurs 5:30–10 p.m., Fri–Sat 5:30–11 p.m.*

Primavera Ristorante
$$–$$$ Coronado ITALIAN

This is one of a number of cute little cafes and restaurants on Coronado, especially along the main drag heading to and from the Hotel Del. It's a popular place for dinner, a cheaper nice-night-out option than some of the hotel dining rooms, with fresh fish and pasta entrees (we prefer the latter; simpler seems to be more successful here). It's classy, but not overwhelmingly so, and most friendly. Next door is its pastry cafe, which, despite the Italian name, emphasizes French pastries — come here to get your éclair fix.

See map p. 486. 932 Orange Ave. ☎ *619-435-0454. Reservations recommended.* www.primavera1st.com. *Main courses: $14–$33. AE, DC, DISC, MC, V. Open: Daily 5–10 p.m.*

Rubio's Baja Grill
$ Pacific Beach TACOS

Local-surfer-made-good Ralph Rubio brought home the simple recipe common to Mexican fishing villages — batter-dipped, deep-fried fish fillets folded in corn tortillas and garnished with shredded cabbage, salsa, and tangy white sauce — and launched the you-can't-eat-just-one Baja-fish tacos craze. Wash 'em down with an ice-cold something. Locations are all over San Diego, but the original area is the most fun.

See map p. 492. 910 Grand Ave. ☎ *858-270-4800.* www.rubios.com. *No reservations. Main courses: Most under $7. MC, V. Open: Mon–Thurs 10:30 a.m.–10 p.m., Fri–Sat 10 a.m.–11 p.m., Sun 10 a.m.–9 p.m.*

Sushi Bar Kazumi
$$–$$$ Hillcrest JAPANESE

If you don't come early to this tiny cafe, you may have to battle locals for a seat. The owner and his son oversee the sushi bar; the former is so dedicated that he gets visibly pained when asked to make some silly roll. Why put him through that when you can have this master sushi chef (who serves only fish that meets his exacting standards) or his lovely, knowledgeable son, choose your fish for you? You may end up trying Japanese snapper, sea urchin, or giant clam. If raw fish isn't your game, try one of their regular meals, reminiscent of what you would find in corner diners all over Japan.

See map p. 490. 3975 Fifth Ave. ☎ *619-682-4054. No reservations. Main courses: Sushi around $4; entrees $8–$18. AE, DISC, MC, V. Open: Tues–Fri 11:30 a.m.–2 p.m., Tues–Thurs 4:30–10 p.m., Fri–Sat 4:30–11 p.m., Sun 4:30–9 p.m.*

Trattoria Acqua
$$$ La Jolla ITALIAN/MEDITERRANEAN

Enjoy the Italian Mediterranean ambience of this romantic restaurant, where diners are encouraged to relax and linger over such rich dishes as the lobster pot pie, which features ½-pound Maine lobster tail, carrots,

Catch a wave — before you even hit the sand!

Fun with or without the family is easy to be had at the **Wave House** (www.wave house.com) in Mission Beach. Tom Lochtefeld, one of the masterminds behind Raging Waters (the water park made famous by Bill and Ted) has created something even more ingenious: A wave machine! Not one of those funky little desk jobbies — we're talking two grand-scale replicas of the real thing! Extreme-sports enthusiasts and novices alike enjoy taking their turns on the Bruticus Maximus (where 800 horse-power come together to create the perfect 10-foot barreling wave) and the (tamer) FlowRider, respectively. Beyond the technology there are also outdoor kava bars, yummy food, open-air barbeques, a fire ring, hammocks, tropical palms, and an adjacent fitness center. Bring the kids to the Wave House during the week, but you may want to leave them home on the weekends as the more adult kids roll in to party hearty. As if the Wave House isn't enough on its own, it's surrounded by the 7-acre **Belmont Park** (www.belmontpark.com), the historic amusement park complete with a big, ol' wooden roller coaster, carnival rides and games, cotton candy, an Olympic-size swimming pool, souvenir vendors, and everything else you'd expect at the boardwalk.

organic corn, asparagus, potatoes, and green beans all nestled together under a pastry puff crown. The menu always has plenty of *secondi* (second courses) of meat and fish, as well, and every pasta dish is available in an appetizer portion (how considerate!. The wine list is a perennial *Wine Spectator* award-winner.

See map p. 486. 1298 Prospect St. (on Coast Walk). ☎ *858-454-0709.* www.trattoria acqua.com. *Reservations recommended for dinner. To get there: From Torrey Pines Road, turn right on Prospect Place, which becomes Prospect Street. Main courses: $9.95–$22 lunch, $15–$31 dinner. AE, DC, MC, V. Open: Daily 11:30 a.m.–2:30 p.m., Mon–Thurs 5–9 p.m., Fri–Sat 5–10:30 p.m., Sun 5–9:30 p.m.*

Zenbu
$$–$$$$ La Jolla JAPANESE

Though it would seem to be simply a place for locals, with its minimall setting and all, Zenbu has San Diegans schlepping from all across the county. Why? Well, first and foremost the fish prepared to the nines in such silly-named rolls as the Johnny and the Jackie Chan, is amazingly fresh. In fact, the owner commissions the fish farming himself to get the freshest catch — and whatever doesn't come in from his own boats, he handpicks from the best purveyors. And it's not just the formerly finned that spawns greatness here as the mere thought of their Wasabi-Seared Tenderloin inspires a Pavlovian response. Somebody hand us a napkin — and another round of Saketinis, please. By the way, it also happens to be awfully hip and cool inside with its contemporary Japanese atmosphere.

See map p. 486. 7660 Fay Ave., Suite 1. ☎ 858-454-4540. www.zenbu.signonsan diego.com. *Reservations recommended. Main courses: $18–$36 for dinner. MC, V. Open: Mon–Fri 11:30 a.m.–2:30 p.m., Sun–Thurs 4:30–10 p.m., Fri–Sat 4:30–11 p.m.*

Exploring San Diego

What do San Diego and central Florida have in common? They both feature big-name family attractions, the spend-all-day kinds of places around which you're probably planning your stay. This section contains everything you need to know about them, plus suggestions for filling any free time after you're done.

The "Big Four" — the animal and theme parks

Each of these parks can eat up at least half a day — a lot more if you have kids.

San Diego's main family attractions have joined forces, offering **combo ticket deals** that reward you with big savings for taking on what we like to call the Vacation Endurance Challenge. Here's how it works: You get to visit both the **San Diego Zoo** and **Wild Animal Park** (deluxe zoo package, Wild Animal Park admission) for $54 adults and $34 for kids 3 to 11. The two-park ticket includes one visit to each attraction, which you must use within five days of purchase.

What's that? You say you want more? Add **SeaWorld** to your plans with a three-park ticket (deluxe zoo package, Wild Animal Park admission, and SeaWorld admission) for $100 adults, $77 kids 3 to 11. With this one, you get unlimited use at all three parks for five days from date of purchase — wow! If you're feeling really ambitious and want to hit LEGOLAND, too, the four-park ticket runs for $163 adults and $122 kids 3 to 11. Deals change often, so check with the parks.

Note also that many hotels in the area offer advance tickets for all the parks at a discount, as well as other deals that include trolley rides, harbor cruises, and the like.

SeaWorld

One of the best-promoted attractions in California, this 165-acre aquatic playground is a showplace for marine life, made politically correct with an only nominally "educational" atmosphere that we wish the park took further. At its heart, it's a (genuinely) fun-filled family entertainment center with performing dolphins, otters, sea lions, walruses, and seals. Several successive 4-ton black-and-white killer whales have functioned as the park's mascot, Shamu.

The hands-on area called **Shamu's Happy Harbor** encourages kids to play and get wet. One of the newer attractions is **Journey To Atlantis,** a "water" coaster with a six-story plunge and lots of special effects, as well as a

130,000-gallon Commerson's dolphin pool — the only public exhibit of these rare dolphins in the Western Hemisphere. Shows for short attention spans run continuously throughout the day, and you can rotate through the various theaters; best is the silly, plot-driven sea-lions-go-to-Gilligan's-Island show. Other draws include **Wild Arctic,** an extremely cool virtual-reality trip to the frozen North, complete with polar bears, beluga whales, walruses, and harbor seals, that's well worth making time for; and **Shamu Close Up,** where you can watch the whales in their off hours through underwater windows while keepers explain what you're seeing. If that's not close enough for you, see if you can make a reservation to dine with Shamu (a buffet meal served next to his enclosure where you can eye him and his trainers while you dine).

See map p. 486. 500 Sea World Dr., Mission Bay. ☎ 619-226-3901. www.sea world.com. *To get there: From I-5, take the Sea World Drive exit; from I-8, take the West Mission Bay Drive exit to Sea World Drive. Admission: $54 adults, $44 kids 3–9. Plenty of Web site and AAA deals are to be had so do your homework before you go. Open: Hours vary dramatically by season and by day — again, check the Web site.*

San Diego Zoo

More than 4,000 animals reside at this world-famous zoo, founded in 1916. Even if other zoos have caught up to it in terms of animal awareness in the intervening century, this granddaddy is still highly respected in the field. Every new exhibit features an even more high-tech method for simulating the climate, flora, and other conditions of the residents' natural habitat, and the preservation of endangered species is a primary concern. It also happens to be a whole lot of fun.

The 1996 loan of two magnificent giant pandas from the People's Republic of China brought the zoo more attention than ever, and in 1999, Bai Yun and Shi Shi became the parents of Hua Mei, an adorable baby panda who's quite an achievement of reproductive research (pandas rarely conceive in captivity). Shi Shi and Hua Mei have since returned to China, but in August 2003, Bai Yun gave birth to the lovable Mei Sheng who had been conceived naturally with the zoo's latest import, Gao Gao. Born in August 2005, Su Lin is the current big baby draw. The pandas are the big attention-getters — and deservedly so — but the zoo contains many other rare and exotic species, with the cuddly koalas drawing the next biggest crowds.

The zoo offers two types of **bus tours:** a 35-minute guided tour and an on/off bus ticket you can use throughout the day. Both provide a narrated overview and allow you to see 75 percent of the park. We strongly encourage first-timers, especially parents with young kids, to spend the extra few bucks on the bus, because the zoo covers a lot of acreage, much of it terraced and extremely hilly. You can then use your energy to revisit the creatures that you like best, and to see those not covered on the tour, such as the pandas. Even by starting with the bus tour, you'll have a hard time visiting everything in the course of a long day, so wear your most comfortable sneakers. Come extra-early or later in the afternoon and plan on spending the evening in summer, because the animals tend to hibernate in the heat of day. And don't miss the hippos — if you get lucky, you'll see them frolicking, which is a sight to behold.

See maps p. 486 and p. 516. 2920 Zoo Dr. (off Park Boulevard), Balboa Park. ☎ 619-234-3153. www.sandiegozoo.org. Admission: $22 adults, $15 kids 3–11. Deluxe package (admission, guided bus tour, round-trip Skyfari aerial tram) $32 adults, $20 children. Open: Daily 9 a.m.–4 p.m. (grounds close at 6 p.m.), summer 9 a.m.–9 p.m. (grounds close at 10 p.m.).

San Diego Wild Animal Park

Originally begun as a breeding facility for the **San Diego Zoo,** the **San Diego Wild Animal Park (WAP)** now holds around 3,200 animals — many endangered species — all roaming freely over the park's 1,800 acres. Approximately 650 baby animals are born every year in the park.

The real beauty of the park is that you, not the animals, are the caged ones. The park has a network of paths (with catchy but meaningless names like "Kilimanjaro Safari Walk" and "Heart of Africa") that skirt many of the enclosures. Only glass separates you from the cats in **Lion Camp,** the park's new naturalistic exhibit that immerses visitors within the lion pride's territory — you arrive in a Range Rover, and the lions are less than 20 feet away, just hanging out.

The best way to see the animals, however, is by riding the Wgasa Bush Line Railway (aka the tram), which is included in the admission price; for the best views, sit on the right-hand side. During the 50-minute ride, you'll pass through vast landscapes resembling Africa and Asia. Trains leave every 20 minutes from the station in **Nairobi Village,** the commercial hub of the park, which has souvenir stores and refreshment vendors. (The food is mediocre and overpriced, so think about smuggling in your own snacks.) Otherwise, Nairobi Village is not much more than a small, traditional zoo whose best feature is the nursery area, with irresistible young'uns frolicking, being bottle-fed, and sleeping.

If you really want to experience the vast landscape and large animals that make the WAP so special, take a **photo caravan tour** ($90–$130 per person, plus park admission). The photo-taking is secondary — for us, anyway — to the enjoyment of crossing the fence to meet rhinos, ostriches, zebras, deer, and giraffes on their home turf. You can even feed the giraffes along the way — an amazing experience. Advance reservations are recommended.

See map p. 486. 15500 San Pasqual Valley Rd., Escondido (30 miles northeast of San Diego). ☎ 760-747-8702. www.sandiegozoo.org/wap/index.html. To get there: I-15 north to Via Rancho Parkway; follow signs for about 3 miles. Admission: $29 adults 12 and over, $18 kids 3–11, free for kids under 3. Open: Daily 9 a.m.–4 p.m. (grounds close at 5 p.m.); extended hours in summer and Dec.

LEGOLAND

Opened in 1999, this Euro-infused theme park is the ultimate monument to the world's most famous plastic building blocks. Three other enormously successful LEGOLANDs exist, in Germany, Denmark, and England, but this is the only one in America.

The 2006 introduction of Pirate Shores — four new fun water-play attractions consisting of a pirate ride equipped with water cannons designed to drench your friends and family in battle, a miniflume log ride, and two water-play structures — invites guests to don sunscreen, bathing suits, flip-flops and a "heck with it all, let's have some fun" attitude. Little kids, big kids, and parents alike can be seen cavorting and running for cover in this awfully damp section of the park. Do yourself a favor and bring a change of clothes and towels for any member of your crew who'll be partaking — and if you want to stay dry, stay far, far away.

Although the majority of rides (short on duration and thrills) and other playgrounds are strictly for kiddies or older kids who actually get a kick out of hanging with their younger sibs, the addition of minicoasters such as the Dragon and the LEGO Technic Test Track as well as Pirate Shores have been major turning points in entertaining the over-10 set. Still, the admission price is hefty for what you get. Most rides average a height minimum of 34 to 36 inches — some go as high as 40 to 42 inches — and, boy, are they strict. One nifty touch is that many of the ride queues feature play areas where the younger set may indulge in Legomania while the parents wait in line — much, much better than restraining a squirmy 2-year-old!

The single best part, scale models of international landmarks (the Eiffel Tower, Sydney Opera House, and so on, all constructed out of real LEGO bricks), will appeal to grown-ups who don't mind just looking at stuff. Although the official guidelines imply that the park is geared toward children of all ages, if you're traveling with a bunch of 'tweens who pride themselves on their newfound coolness, be forewarned that they may very well find it a snooze. Still, with its fresh and yummy (although not inexpensive) food, LEGOLAND is a lovely place for parents to relax while the kiddies get tuckered out.

See map p. 486. 1 Lego Dr., Carlsbad (30 miles north of San Diego). ☎ *877-534-6526 or 760-918-5346.* www.legolandca.com. *To get there: I-5 north to Cannon Road exit east, following signs for Lego Drive. Admission: $57 adults, $44 kids 3–12 and seniors but check the Web site for AAA discounts and other specials. Preferred parking for Volvos. (We aren't kidding.) Open: Winter and off-season Mon, Thurs–Sun 10 a.m.–5 p.m.; summer and holidays daily with extended hours.*

Balboa Park

Balboa Park is one of San Diego's must-see attractions. Not only does it house the world-famous **San Diego Zoo** (see the preceding section), but this 1,200-acre verdant wonderland — which bills itself as the largest urban cultural park in the country — serves as the cultural and recreational heart of the city. Spanish-Moorish buildings originally built for the 1915 Panama-California Exposition house most of the city's museums, surrounded by a series of cultivated gardens, small forests, tropical oases, and shaded groves coaxed from a formerly scruffy brown canyon. Lest it all sound too refined for you, the park boasts ample places to play, as well (see the "Balboa Park Attractions" map, p. 516).

Balboa Park Attractions

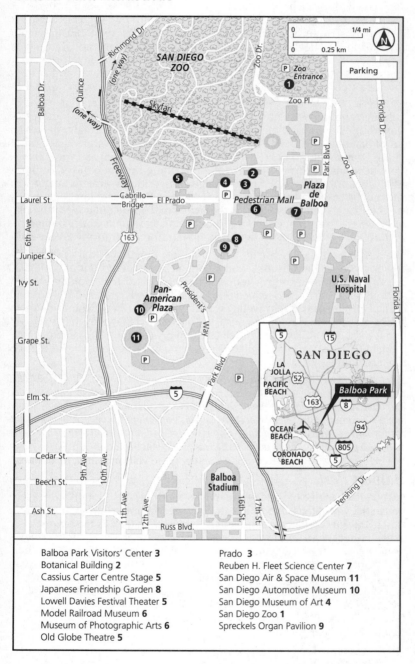

Balboa Park Visitors' Center **3**	Prado **3**
Botanical Building **2**	Reuben H. Fleet Science Center **7**
Cassius Carter Centre Stage **5**	San Diego Air & Space Museum **11**
Japanese Friendship Garden **8**	San Diego Automotive Museum **10**
Lowell Davies Festival Theater **5**	San Diego Museum of Art **4**
Model Railroad Museum **6**	San Diego Zoo **1**
Museum of Photographic Arts **6**	Spreckels Organ Pavilion **9**
Old Globe Theatre **5**	

Balboa Park lies at the northern edge of downtown, bordered on the west by Sixth Avenue. From downtown, 12th Avenue leads directly in, becoming Park Boulevard and passing the entrance to the zoo. From Sixth Avenue, Laurel Street becomes El Prado, the park's main thorough-fare; many of the park's major museums, along with the visitor center, are lined up along this avenue. The park contains plenty of parking lots, although you may not have your first choice on busy days. That's all right, though, because walking from place to place is part of the fun. Distances are easily manageable, but if the hills start to dog you, hop aboard the free trams that run regularly through the park. (The one exception to the distance rule is the zoo. It sits far enough away that you'll want to use its parking lot.)

Sure, San Diego has other museums in town, but because you have lim-ited time (not to mention limited patience), make sightseeing easy on everyone by choosing from among the park s 14-plus museums, which offer more museum fix than you'll need in the course of your visit. The best of the bunch are described in this section; for a complete list of park attractions, go to www.balboapark.org or, after you arrive, pick up a map at the well-staffed **Balboa Park Visitors Center,** 1549 El Prado (☎ 619-239-0512). Note, however, that many park attractions are closed on Mondays.

In the courtyard behind the center you'll find the **Prado** (☎ 619-557-9441), an upscale Nuevo Latino restaurant set within the historic walls of the House of Hospitality. If you'd prefer something lower on the food chain price-wise, snack bars and casual cafes are scattered throughout the park.

All the park's museums are free one Tuesday each month. The museums participate on a rotating schedule so that three or more waive their entrance fees every Tuesday. If you plan to visit more than three of the park's museums, buy the **Passport to Balboa Park,** a coupon booklet that allows one entrance to each of 11 museums that charge an entry fee (the others are always free) and is valid for one week. You can purchase the $30 passport at any participating museum, the visitor center, or online.

Museum of Photographic Arts

If names such as Ansel Adams, Margaret Bourke-White, Imogen Cunning-ham, Edward Weston, and Henri Cartier-Bresson pique your interest, don't miss this 3,600-plus image collection, one of the few in the United States devoted exclusively to photography. Set aside an hour or two.

See map p. 516. 1649 El Prado. ☎ 619-238-7559. www.mopa.org. Admission: $6 adults; $4 students, seniors, active military; free for kids under 12 (with adult). Free second Tues of the month. Open: Daily 10 a.m.–5 p.m. (until 9 p.m. on Thurs).

Reuben H. Fleet Science Center

A must-see for kids of any age — yep, including grown-up kids — this tantalizing collection of hands-on exhibits is designed to provoke the imagination while teaching scientific principles. Although we don't see the educational element in **Comet Impact,** a motion-simulation adventure that resembles Disneyland's Star Tours ride, it is quite fun. The Fleet also houses a 76-foot domed OMNIMAX theater, an excellent place to experience larger-than-life IMAX films. You'll need one and a half to three hours to explore all the exhibits, not counting IMAX movie time.

See map p. 516. 1875 El Prado. ☎ *619-238-1233.* www.rhfleet.org. *Admission (includes IMAX film, Deep Sea ride, and exhibit galleries): $15 adults, $13 seniors, $12 kids 3–12; free first Tues of the month. Open: Daily at 9:30 a.m.; closing varies by day and season.*

San Diego Air & Space Museum

The number-two kid-pleaser in town (after the Fleet Science Center — see the preceding entry), this enormously popular museum provides an overview of national and local aviation history, from hot-air balloons to the space age, with plenty of biplanes and fighters in between. In 1935, the Ford Motor Company built the stunning cylindrical hall, which houses an imaginative gift shop with goodies such as freeze-dried astronaut ice cream. Plan on spending one and a half to two and a half hours.

See map p. 516. 2001 Pan American Plaza. ☎ *619-234-8291.* www.aerospace museum.org. *Admission: $10 adults, $8 seniors, $5 juniors 6–17, free for those under 6 or for active duty members of the military. Open: Daily 10 a.m.–4:30 p.m., until 5:30 p.m. in the summer.*

San Diego Automotive Museum

Even if you don't know a distributor from a dipstick, you'll ooh and aah over the classic, antique, and exotic cars here. Every one is in such pristine condition you'd swear it just rolled off the line, from the 1886 Benz to the 1981 DeLorean. You can easily see the collection in a little over an hour.

See map p. 516. 2080 Pan American Plaza. ☎ *619-231-2886.* www.sdautomuseum. org. *Admission: $7 adults, $6 active military and seniors, $3 kids 6–15. Free fourth Tues of the month. Open: Daily 10 a.m.–5 p.m.*

San Diego Model Railroad Museum

It may not be high culture as we know it, but this museum is cool and cute, and well worth 30 to 60 minutes of your time, even if you don't consider yourself a train buff. Six permanent, scale-model railroads depict Southern California's transportation history and terrain with an astounding attention to detail. Kids will love the hands-on Lionel trains, and visitors of all ages will appreciate the interactive multimedia element.

See map p. 516. 1649 El Prado. ☎ *619-696-0199.* www.sdmodelrailroadm.com. *Admission: $5 adults, $4 seniors, $3 students with ID, $2.50 active military, free for kids under 15 (with adult). Free first Tues of the month. Open: Tues–Fri 11 a.m.–4 p.m., Sat–Sun 11 a.m.–5 p.m.*

Scanning the winter seas for whales

Whale-watching is a hugely popular pastime between mid-December and mid-March. California gray whales hug the shore on their annual migration from Alaskan feeding grounds to breeding lagoons in Mexico — and back again, with calves in tow. If you've ever been lucky enough to spot one of these gentle behemoths, you understand the thrill.

✔ Grab binoculars and head to **Cabrillo National Monument** (☎ 619-557-5450; www.nps.gov/cabr) on Point Loma, where an elevated, glassed-in observatory offers a prime vantage point. Take I-5 or I-8 to Highway 209/Rosecrans Street and follow signs to the monument; admission is $5 per car or $3 per person on foot. It's open from 9 a.m. to 5:15 p.m.

✔ On the UCSD campus in La Jolla, the outdoor plaza at the **Birch Aquarium** at Scripps Institution of Oceanography (☎ 858-534-3474; www.aquarium.ucsd.edu) offers an excellent whale-watching perch. Take I-5 to La Jolla Village Drive, go west for a mile (past Torrey Pines Road), and turn left at Expedition Way.

✔ If you want to get a closer look, head out to sea with **Classic Sailing Adventures** (☎ 800-659-0141 or 619-224-0800; www.classicsailingadventures.com). Four-hour expeditions (one each in morning and afternoon) cost $65.

San Diego Museum of Art

With one of the grandest entrances along El Prado, this museum also boasts outstanding collections of Italian Renaissance and Dutch and Spanish baroque art, along with an impressive collection of Toulouse-Lautrec's works. The museum often shows prestigious traveling exhibits, and the interactive computer image system allows you to locate highlights and custom-design a tour. Plan on spending one to three hours here.

See map p. 516. 1450 El Prado. ☎ *619-232-7931.* www.sdmart.com. *Admission: $10 adults, $8 seniors, $7 students with ID, $4 kids 6–17. Free third Tues of the month. Open: Tues–Sun 10 a.m.–6 p.m. (until 9 p.m. on Thurs).*

Other attractions to consider in Balboa Park include the following:

✔ Along El Prado, just beyond the Lily Pond, is the **Botanical Building,** a 250-foot-long wooden lath conservatory from the 1915 Exposition that looks like something out of a Victorian costume drama and houses about 1,200 tropical and flowering plants. Admission is free.

✔ The largest outdoor pipe organ in the world is at **Spreckels Organ Pavilion,** south of El Prado (☎ 619-702-8138; www.scsorgan.com), an ornate, curved amphitheater offering free Sunday concerts at 2 p.m. year-round and free evening concerts in July and August.

The sound is stupendous, and the whole experience serves to amplify (pun intended) the old-fashioned Sunday-in-the-park quality of your visit.

✔ The **Japanese Friendship Garden** (☎ 619-232-2721; www.niwa.org; open Mon–Fri 10 a.m.–5 p.m., Sat–Sun 10 a.m.–4 p.m), adjacent to the organ pavilion, is a serene, meticulous oasis. From the elaborately carved gate, a crooked path (to confound evil spirits, who move only in a straight line) threads its way past nearly 100 carefully arranged plantings, a stream with colorful koi, and a traditional zen garden. Admission is $3 for adults, $2.50 for seniors, $2 for students and military with ID, free for kids younger than 7.

Old Town State Historic Park

Whether you're a history buff looking for an authentic slice of early California or a hungry theme-park refugee in search of a Mexican combo plate and a cheesy souvenir, chances are very good that you'll end up in **Old Town** — and you should.

The birthplace of San Diego — indeed, of California — Old Town was founded by Spanish friars in 1769, along with Mission San Diego. The town of San Diego grew up around the mission and its military presidio, which thrived here until the early 1870s. After San Diego's commercial core moved closer to the harbor (to "New Town," now the **Gaslamp Quarter**), Old Town was abandoned. In 1968, the park was established to preserve the structures that remained and rebuild several atop their original foundations. As the years have gone by, sensitivity to historical accuracy has improved greatly, making the park a combination of Disneyesque attractions and eerily authentic sites.

If you can get past the touristy veneer and into the true spirit of this pedestrian-only 6-block historic district, you'll step back to a time of one-room schoolhouses and village greens, when the people who lived, worked, and played here spoke Spanish. Depending on your interest level — whether you want only to cover the main points of interest or see everything *and* have lunch — you can spend anywhere from one to five hours here.

Old Town is bounded by Congress, Juan, Wallace, and Twiggs streets. To get there: Take I-5 to Old Town Avenue exit; parking is free in the many lots scattered around the park's perimeter, and the large lot for Old Town's trolley station (another option) holds more spaces, at the northwest end. Admission is also free, although donations are encouraged. Old Town is open daily from 10 a.m. to 5 p.m.

Stop first at the **Robinson Rose Visitor Center,** the visitor center for Old Town State Park, on San Diego Avenue (☎ 619-220-5422), to get your bearings, join up with a walking tour (daily at 11 a.m. with an additional 2 p.m. tour Sat–Sun), or simply check out the old wagons, carriages, and stagecoaches. Other notable stops include

✔ **La Casa de Estudillo,** the 1827 adobe home of a wealthy family, furnished with typical upper-class furniture of the period

✔ **Robinson-Rose House,** built in 1853 and containing a scale model of Old Town the way it looked in 1872, before a fire destroyed much of the district

✔ The **San Diego Union Building,** where a forerunner to today's *Union-Tribune* began publishing in 1868

✔ The reproduction **Silvas-McCoy House,** currently under construction as an interpretive visitor center for Old Town

One of Old Town's top draws is its Mexican restaurants. See the "There's Mexican, Mexican, and also Mexican" sidebar, earlier in the chapter, for our top recommendations. See the "Shopping at the Top" section, later in the chapter, for the lowdown on Old Town shopping.

Hitting the beaches

San Diego's justifiably famous beaches are its second-biggest visitor draw (after the animal parks). Beach weather lasts virtually all year. Any sunny day is perfect for a walk, a little in-line skating, or a picnic.

Coronado Beach

If you're spending any time on Coronado, don't miss this wide, sparkling-sand paradise of a beach, framed by the fabulous Hotel Del Coronado and extending along Ocean Avenue up to grassy Sunset Park. It's a flat, benign beach (that can glitter with gold pyrite flakes) perfect for sunbathing, strolling, and wading. Street parking (some metered) is plentiful even in summer, and the beach includes lifeguards, restrooms, and a picnic area with a few fire rings. The islands visible from here — "Los Coronados" — are 18 miles away and belong to Mexico.

Ocean Beach

This beach sits just across the channel from Mission Bay. To reach it, take West Point Loma Boulevard all the way to the end. The northern end of **Ocean Beach Park** is known as **Dog Beach** after the pooches that frolic on the sand. Surfers generally congregate around **Ocean Beach Pier,** mostly in the water but often at the snack shack on the end. *Riptides* (dangerous currents) are strong here, so venturing in beyond waist depth is not a good idea. Facilities include restrooms, showers, picnic tables, and plenty of metered parking spots; the funky shops and food stands of Newport Avenue are a couple blocks away.

Mission Beach and Pacific Beach

These neighbors along Mission Boulevard share a popular boardwalk: **Ocean Front Walk,** a fun, free-for-all human parade. To the south, **Mission Beach** features several dozen blocks of narrow but popular sandy beach known for a youthful surf culture and beginner-friendly waves. Grassy **Belmont Park** sits at midpoint (at West Mission Bay Drive), offering rides and carnival-style entertainment.

Pacific Beach begins around Pacific Beach Drive, where the scene is only slightly more sophisticated, and the surfers a little more experienced. Waves break pretty far out, making this one of San Diego's best swimming beaches. One exception is **Tourmaline Surfing Park,** at the northernmost end of Pacific Beach, where the sport's old guard gathers to ride the waves. Swimming is prohibited, but come to watch the masters in action.

You can find metered spots spaced along Mission Boulevard's side streets, and maybe even a few curbside spaces, if you're lucky. Both beaches have lifeguards and well-spaced restroom facilities.

 Just east of Mission Beach is **Mission Bay,** whose labyrinth of calm waters and pretty peninsulas are ideal for exploring. Check with **Seaforth Boat Rental,** 1641 Quivera Rd. (☎ 619-223-1681; www.seaforthboat rental.com), which offers half- and full-day rentals on powerboats, sailboats, personal watercraft (PWCs), motorized skiffs, kayaks, or paddleboats. If you don't want to get your feet wet, **bikes are available for rent** at the **Marriott Hotel** (☎ 619-234-1500, ext. 6535) for $12 to $30 an hour, $30 to $50 a day. They also rent surreys starting at $20 an hour. You do not have to be a guest to rent. **Bike Tours San Diego** (☎ 619-238-2444) offers guided tours that vary in price depending on area covered; they also just rent bikes (about $22–$35 per day). For in-line skates or traditional quads, **Mission Beach Club,** 704 Ventura Place, at Ocean Front Walk (☎ 858-488-5050), can set you up with skates and all necessary safety gear.

La Jolla Cove

This scenic jewel appears regularly on La Jolla postcards and is worth the drive even if you're staying closer to downtown. Framed by grass-carpeted bluffs and sheltering a snorkel-friendly marine preserve just below the surface, the cove is also a terrific spot for swimmers of all abilities. It's on the small side, so avoid peak summer weekends if you can; the free parking spaces along Coast Boulevard tend to fill quickly, as well, but it's an easy walk from anywhere in the village.

 Many visitors never know about the seals that hang out about 4 blocks south of La Jolla Cove at **Children's Pool Beach,** a tiny cove originally named for the toddlers who could safely frolic behind a man-made seawall. These days, the sand is mostly off-limits to humans, who congregate along the seawall railing or onshore to admire the protected seals who sun themselves on the beach or on semi-submerged rocks. You can get surprisingly close — truly a mesmerizing sight.

Taking a Guided Tour by Trolley (And Other Means)

Not to be confused with the public-transit trolley trains, the fully narrated **Old Town Trolley** (☎ 619-298-8687) is a constant favorite. You can get a comprehensive look at the city — or just the parts that interest you — aboard the old-fashioned motorized trolley car as it follows a 30-mile circular route. Hop off at any one of a dozen stops (ticket sales reps are on hand at each), explore at leisure, and reboard when you please (check ahead of time — their operating schedule is different from day to day). Stops include the Embarcadero, Horton Plaza, Gaslamp Quarter, Coronado, San Diego Zoo, Balboa Park, and Heritage Park. The tour costs $30 for adults and $15 for kids 4 to 12 (free for kids 3 and younger) for one complete loop, no matter how many times you hop on and off; if you get on and stay on, the ride takes about two hours.

The old soft shoe (s)

Many parts of San Diego are quite walkable. The following are places that offer good walking tours:

- ✔ **The Gaslamp Quarter Historical Foundation** (☎ 619-233-4692; www.gaslampquarter.org) offers two-hour tours of San Diego's liveliest neighborhood. Tours of the Gaslamp neighborhood depart on Saturdays at 11 a.m. from the **William Heath Davis House Museum,** 410 Island Ave., at Fourth Avenue. A $10 donation is requested ($8 for seniors, military personnel, and students). Private group tours of six or more can be arranged.

- ✔ The **San Diego Natural History Museum Canyoneers** (☎ 619-255-0203; www.sdnhm.org/canyoneers) offer outdoor enthusiasts interpretive nature walks. Follow volunteers who are trained to teach appreciation of plants and animals in Southern California. Check the Web site for schedules and locations.

- ✔ **Coronado Touring** (☎ 619-435-5993) is a great way to learn a ton about charming Coronado. The 90-minute tour is upbeat and informative, including a delicious dose of local scandal and gossip. Tours leave at 11 a.m. on Tuesday, Thursday, and Saturday from the **Glorietta Bay Inn,** across the street from Hotel Del Coronado; the price is $12. Reservations are suggested, because walk-ins are subject to availability.

Bay cruises

When the weather's fine — which is most of the time — nothing says "San Diego" like a little waterborne sightseeing. **Hornblower Cruises** (☎ 800-668-4323 or 619-686-8715; www.hornblower.com) is the local big cheese. In addition to one- and two-hour narrated tours of San Diego

Bay, the company offers evening dinner/dance cruises, Sunday brunch cruises, and whale-watching trips in winter. Prices start at $17 for harbor cruises, $45 for meal cruises; kids are half-price.

Shopping at the Top

If you like to do your shopping in a mall, head to **Horton Plaza** in the **Gaslamp Quarter,** bounded by Broadway, First and Fourth avenues, and G Street (☎ **619-239-8180;** www.westfield.com). Although this multi-level complex is rather whimsical, the stores are conventional. The quarter is also known for its excellent art galleries, including **Many Hands,** 302 Island Ave. (☎ **619-557-8303;** www.manyhandscraftgallery.com), a cooperative with 35 artists working in a variety of crafts. **Le Travel Store,** 745 Fourth Ave., between F and G streets (☎ **619-544-0005;** www.letravelstore.com), offers a good selection of luggage, travel books and maps, and groovy travel accessories.

Depending on your tastes, you may think the Embarcadero's **Seaport Village,** 849 W. Harbor Dr. (☎ **619-235-4014;** www.spvillage.com), is quaintly appealing or completely contrived. This faux–New England–style village is big for souvenir shopping and dining with a view. It's worth the trip, though, for a ride on the 1890 Looff carousel imported from Coney Island, New York.

Hillcrest

Compact Hillcrest is an ideal shopping destination. You can browse a unique and sometimes wacky mix of independent boutiques, bookstores, vintage clothing stores, memorabilia shops, chain stores, bakeries, and cafes. Start at the neighborhood's hub — the intersection of University and Fifth avenues — and prepare yourself to drop a few dollars on parking (either meters or lots). Shops here tend to stay open later than in other parts of the city, and Tuesday nights, many local merchants offer 15 percent off all purchases.

Highlights include **Babette Schwartz,** 421 University Ave. (☎ **619-220-7048;** www.babette.com), a provocative pop-culture emporium named for a local drag queen. The **Village Hat Shop,** 3821 Fourth Ave. (☎ **619-683-5533;** www.villagehatshop.com), features headgear from straw hats to knit caps to classy fedoras, plus a minimuseum of vintage headwear.

If you love used and rare books, you'll want to poke around on Fifth Avenue between University and Robinson. This block is also home to **Off the Record,** 2912 University Ave. (☎ **619-298-4755**), a new-and-used record store with an alternative bent and the city's best vinyl selection. If vintage clothing is your passion, don't miss **Wear It Again Sam,** 3823 Fifth Ave. (☎ **619-299-0185**), a classy step back in time.

Aunt Teek's guide to vintage treasures

If you're a collectibles hound, this enormous antiques mall is guaranteed to leave you with dusty hands and a lighter wallet: **Cracker Factory Antiques,** 448 W. Market St., at Columbia Street, downtown (☎ **619-233-1669**). Merchandise ranges from kitschy collectibles to "real" antiques (you know, Louis the Whichever stuff).

Old Town

Yes, it's touristy (the local shopkeeper's motto is "ka-ching!"), but when you're looking for a classic souvenir of the cheesy variety — you know, San Diego–labeled T-shirts, baseball caps, snow domes, or those movable pens — this is the place to go. Milking the "old" even further, many of these shops boast a quasi-historic general-store theme. Look for artist's workshops and bona fide galleries tucked away from the commercialism, where higher quality commands higher prices.

With mariachi music and Mexican archways setting the stage for import shops with wares from Central and South America, colorful **Plaza del Pasado,** 2754 Calhoun St. (☎ **619-297-3100**; www.plazadelpasado. com), is a magnet. You won't find anything rare (or bargain-priced), but browsing can be fun.

La Jolla

Shopping is a major pastime here. Women's clothing boutiques tend to be conservative and costly, especially those lining Girard and Prospect streets. The many home-décor stores make for great window shopping, as do the ubiquitous jewelers — where Swiss watches, tennis bracelets, precious gems, and pearl necklaces sparkle in windows on every street. Affordable, trendy, boutiquish looking clothes, however, can be found at **Pink Zone,** 7880 Girard Ave. (☎ **858-456-2508**), where the friendly staff can help whip up the perfect disposable outfit. Pink Zone has locations in Pacific Beach and Gaslamp, too.

Nightlife

For a rundown of the latest performances and evening events, check the Entertainment Guide on the *Union-Tribune*'s **SignOnSanDiego.com** (www. signonsandiego.com). You can easily find copies of the free weekly *Reader* (www.sdreader.com) and *What's Playing?* (www.sandiego performs.com), the San Diego Performing Arts League's bimonthly guide, around town.

You can save a bundle on theater and musical events at the half-price **Arts Tix** kiosk in Horton Plaza Park, at Broadway and Third Avenue. It's open Tuesday through Thursday from 11 a.m. to 6 p.m., Friday and

---

Don't have time for Vegas?
Reservations recommended!

Have you noticed all of those casino billboards scattered around town? Have you also noticed that the majority of these establishments have Native American names attached to them? California allows Las Vegas–style gambling on Native reservations throughout the state. The casino rules vary slightly from those in Nevada, but the stakes are just as fun!

Barona Resort and Casino (☎ 619-443-2300; www.barona.com) and **Harrah's Rincon Casino & Resort** (☎ 760-751-3100; www.harrahs.com) are attracting more and more folks daily. Less than an hour from downtown, local favorite **Pala Casino Resort and Spa** (☎ 877-946-7252 or 760-510-2189; www.palacasino.com) consistently raises the proverbial bar because it's so darned nice — the hefty caliber of entertainers who take its stage isn't hurting it either.

Saturday from 10 a.m. to 6 p.m.; tickets are available day-of-show only (except for Sun and Mon shows, sold on Sat). They do not take credit cards. Call ☎ 619-497-5000 for more information and the daily offerings, or go online to www.sandiegoperforms.com and click on "Arts Tix." *Parking tip:* The Horton Plaza garage is most convenient, and Arts Tix will validate.

The play's the thing

It's well worth making the effort to catch a show at the Shakespearean-style **Old Globe Theatre** or its adjacent theaters, the open-air Lowell Davies Festival Theater and the intimate in-the-round **Cassius Carter Centre Stage.** Not only do these venues occupy a magical setting within lovely **Balboa Park,** but they attract expertly cast classics along with thought-provoking regional and experimental offerings. The season runs from January through October, with two to four plays going at any one time. Ticket prices range from around $23 to $59, with discounts for students and seniors. Call ☎ 619-239-2255 or the 24-hour hotline at ☎ 619-234-5623, or go online to www.oldglobe.org.

The **La Jolla Playhouse,** on the University of California–San Diego (UCSD) campus at 2910 La Jolla Village Dr., at Torrey Pines Road (☎ 858-550-1010; www.lajollaplayhouse.com), stages six productions each year, usually from April or May through November. Each one has something outstanding to recommend it, whether a nationally acclaimed director or a highly touted revival. Tickets range from $28 to $57. Any unsold tickets are available for $15 in a "public rush" sale ten minutes before the curtain goes up.

Play it loud: Live music

Cover charges and/or ticket prices vary widely for these hot spots, so it's best to call ahead to find out details — you're going to want to call ahead anyway to find out who's playing.

Belly Up

Another reason to head north to Solana Beach is the still-going-strong-after-over-30-years Belly Up, perhaps San Diego's best live venue, with acts ranging from locals to terrific out-of-towners, from rock to roots to regular Sunday-night salsa.

143 S. Cedros Ave., Solana Beach. ☎ *858-481-9022 (recorded schedule) or 858-481-8140 (information and tickets).* www.bellyup.com.

The Casbah

It may be a total dive, but this blaring downtown club has a well-earned rep for showcasing alternative and rock bands that are, were, or will be famous. Consider buying advance tickets to avoid disappointment.

See map p. 488. 2501 Kettner Blvd., near the airport. ☎ *619-232-4355.* www.casbahmusic.com.

Croce's Nightclubs

This loud, crowded gathering place is the cornerstone of the Gaslamp Quarter nightlife. Two separate clubs a couple doors apart offer traditional jazz (Croce's Jazz Bar) and rhythm and blues (Croce's Top Hat) nightly. The music blares onto the street, making it easy to decide whether to go in or not. The cover is waived if you eat at the restaurant (see the "Where to Dine in San Diego" section earlier in this chapter).

See map p. 488. 802 Fifth Ave. (at F Street). ☎ *619-233-4355.* www.croces.com.

Dizzy's

This no-frills performance space focuses on one thing and one thing only: showcasing talented jazz musicians. There is no alcohol, no smoking patio, and though they generally have cold water and soda for the price of a donation, music lovers are welcome to bring in snacks and drinks from local proprietors like PJ's Coffee & Tea Co. (at the corner of Fifth and K) who serves up an eye-opening cup o' joe and tasty treats. No age limit.

See map p. 488. 344 Seventh Ave. (between J and K streets), Gaslamp Quarter. ☎ *858-270-7467.* www.dizzyssandiego.com

4th & B

Haphazard seating (balcony theater seats, cabaret tables) and a handful of bar/lounge niches make this no-frills venue, housed in a former bank, comfortable. The genre is no genre; everyone from B.B. King to Dokken to local-girl-made-good Jewel has performed here (recently, James Brown, Rollins

Band, and X have all taken the stage), in between regular bookings of the San Diego Chamber Orchestra.

See map p. 488. 345 B St. (at Fourth Avenue). ☎ *619-231-4343.* www.4thandB.com.

Come here often? Bars and lounges

Altitude

On the 22nd floor of San Diego Marriott Gaslamp Quarter is this sublime sky bar and rooftop lounge — the highest, open-air rooftop bar in Southern California. Hot music, elegant surroundings, a view right into Petco, and two full bars keep partiers lining up at the street level elevators. If you want to keep the vibe going, the beautifully furnished hotel features chic retro rooms reminiscent of Lucy and Ricky's Hollywood travels, ultracomfy Marriott beds, and all the necessities a traveler could think of. Published rates begin at $425, but don't pay that — check the Web site for Internet specials.

660 K St. (between Sixth and Seventh avenues), Gaslamp Quarter. ☎ *619-446-6086.* www.altitudebar.com.

The Bitter End

With three floors, this self-important Gaslamp Quarter hot spot manages to be a sophisticated martini bar, after-hours dance club, and relaxing cocktail lounge all in one. Weekends are subject to velvet rope/dress code nonsense.

See map p. 488. 770 Fifth Ave. (at F Street). ☎ *619-338-9300.* www.thebitterend.com.

Jbar

Hotel Solamar's fourth floor is home to Jbar, a poolside lounge somewhat akin to the Mondrian's Los Angeles Skybar minus the attitude. Sure you can enjoy it during the day while you nibble on munchies crafted by Jsix, but at night, with its mood lighting, music flow, and genuine ambience, there's just something about it that stays with you long after you're back home.

See map p. 488. 616 J St. (at Sixth Avenue). ☎ *619-531-8744.* www.jsixsandiego.com.

Martini Ranch and Shaker Room

This Gaslamp Quarter crowd pleaser boasts a 30-martini menu that may stretch the definition of *martini* a bit; nevertheless, it features an impressive selection of vodkas and gins. Downstairs resembles an upscale sports bar, while upstairs is dotted with love seats and conversation pits. Dance Tuesday through Saturday in the Shaker Room.

See map p. 488. 528 F St. (between Fifth and Sixth avenues). ☎ *619-235-6100.* www.martiniranchsd.com.

Nunu's Cocktail Lounge

This is a perfect neighborhood place, provided you and your neighbors are more the cocktail-lounge hipster types. (We mean all this as a positive thing.) Though neither snooty nor tony — although someone sure paid attention to the details here — it's both increasingly fashionable (in terms of popularity — in terms of décor, it's over the top in its efforts to please all tastes). All things considered, it's just the right place to stick $5 in the jukebox and drink through your selections. They're noted for their Razzmatazz: raspberry Smirnoff mixed with cranberry juice.

See map p. 490. 3537 Fifth Ave., Hillcrest. ☎ *619-295-2878.*

Princess Pub & Grille

A local Anglophiles' haunt that's the place for a pint o' Bass, Fuller's, Watney's, or Guinness. This slice of Britain (in Little Italy, go figure) also serves up hearty pub grub.

See map p. 488. 1665 India St. (at Date Street). ☎ *619-702-3021.* www.princess pub.com.

Stingaree

This 22,000-square-foot place-to-be scene has caused quite a stir since its arrival. Set in a historic warehouse, this multilevel destination club comes complete with the restaurant, dance floors, and VIP areas, as well as the Oasis Rooftop Lounge. It pimps all the nuances of the new breed of pricey Vegas hot spots. See if your hotel concierge can swing you a spot on the VIP no-wait-but-not-free-admission list.

See map p. 488. 454 Sixth Ave., Gaslamp Quarter. ☎ *619-544-9500.* www.sting sandiego.com.

Thin/Onyx

Maybe it's a little too New York for the beachy Gaslamp types, but we were rather intrigued by this trendy spot. DJ-spun music ranging from deep house, mid- and down-tempo, acid jazz, trip and hip-hop, and mushroom jazz sets the mood upstairs at Thin, while Onyx hosts live music on Tuesdays and urban house beats the rest of the week. The beautifully crafted, not to mention potent, beverages make it that much better.

See map p. 488. 852 Fifth Ave., Gaslamp Quarter. ☎ *619-231-7529 or 619-235-6699.* www.thinroom.com or www.onyxroom.com.

Top of the Hyatt

What's that you say? You want to wet your whistle and see more of San Diego simultaneously? From this romantic, loungy, glassed-in venue 40 floors above the city's waterfront, you can do both.

See map p. 488. One Market Place (Manchester Grand Hyatt San Diego), Downtown. ☎ *619-232-1234.*

Fast Facts

AAA

Mission Valley at 2440 Hotel Circle N.
(☎ 619-233-1000; www.aaacalif.com).

American Express

Travel services are available at Anderson Travel & Cruises, 3545 Del Mar Heights Rd. #C6 (☎ 858-259-1995).

Baby Sitters

Check with your hotel's front desk or concierge.

Emergencies

For police, fire, highway patrol, or life-threatening medical emergencies, dial ☎ 911.

Hotel Docs (☎ 800-468-3537) is a 24-hour network of physicians, dentists, and chiropractors who claim they'll come to your hotel room within an hour to an hour and a half of your call.

Hospitals

The most conveniently located emergency room is at UCSD Medical Center–Hillcrest, 200 W. Arbor Dr. (☎ 619-543-6400); to get there, take First Avenue north, past Washington, and turn left on Arbor.

Newspapers and Magazines

The city's daily is the *San Diego Union-Tribune,* available from newsstands and vending machines around town. The free alternative weekly *Reader* is available at shops, restaurants, and public hot spots.

Police

Dial ☎ 911 in an emergency. For nonemergencies, contact the downtown precinct, 1401 Broadway (☎ 619-531-2000).

Post Office

Post offices are located downtown, at 815 E St. (at Eighth Avenue), and at 51 Horton Plaza (beside the Westin Hotel). Call ☎ 800-ASK-USPS or log on to www.usps.gov to find the branch nearest you.

Taxes

Sales tax in shops and restaurants is 7.75 percent. Hotel tax is 10.5 percent.

Taxis

Orange Cab (☎ 619-291-3333), San Diego Cab (☎ 619-226-TAXI), and Yellow Cab (☎ 619-234-6161).

Transit Info

☎ 619-685-4900 for 24-hour recorded info, ☎ 619-233-3004 daily from 5:30 a.m. to 8:30 p.m. to speak with a real live person.

Weather

For local weather and surf reports, call ☎ 619-289-1212.

Gathering More Information

The **San Diego Convention and Visitors Bureau's International Visitor Information Center** (☎ **619-236-1212**) is downtown on First Avenue at F Street, street level at Horton Plaza. It can provide you with the slick, glossy *San Diego Visitors Planning Guide,* as well as a money-saving coupon book. Open Monday through Saturday from 8:30 a.m. to 5 p.m., plus Sunday from 11 a.m. to 5 p.m. June through August.

A side trip to Tijuana

Tijuana (tee-*wah*-nah), the fourth largest city in Mexico, lies just half an hour south of San Diego. If you asked us, of course, we wouldn't go there on a bet. And yet, we would tell you to go. Why? Well, for starters, you've never been, and at all times, we're in favor of new experiences, to say nothing of any opportunity to cross any border. It's just that Tijuana is hardly the best that Mexico has to offer, and it's hardly the most authentic Mexican experience. It's a tourist trap of mass-produced crafts, knockoffs, and other dubious goods, and in between, there is mucho drinking going on (it's a sacred destination for rowdy frat boys). But it's an experience, to be sure, and easy to be had.

Getting to Tijuana from San Diego is simple and inexpensive, but beware: The crossing at the border takes longer and longer. Driving is also a bad idea because of the following:

✔ U.S. auto insurance, as well as many rental-car agreements, isn't valid across the border.

✔ Traffic is terrible in Tijuana.

✔ Getting through customs and back across the border can be more difficult if you're on your own.

✔ Having an accident in Mexico, major or minor, is a bad idea.

Note: Although a passport won't be required of U.S. citizens traveling overland from Mexico until January 1, 2008, carrying yours will speed up your return across the border. Be sure to at least have your driver's license handy.

Leave your car behind instead and hop aboard the **San Diego Trolley** (☎ 619-685-4900 or 619-233-3004; www.sdcommute.com), nicknamed the "Tijuana Trolley" for good reason. Get off at the last stop in San Ysidro. From there, just follow the signs to walk across the border. The one-way fare for the 40-minute trip is $2.50, and the trolleys run constantly, with the last return from San Ysidro after midnight. On Saturday nights (or should we say Sun mornings) there are two or three trolleys that run between midnight and 5 a.m. — because the schedule changes frequently, call and confirm as after a night in Tijuana, the trolley stop is probably the last place you want to hang out. Or leave your car at one of many **border parking lots**, which cost $8 to $10 for the day. Most lots are just a block or two away from the pedestrian walkway into Tijuana. Exercise caution, especially after dark, and don't be one of the last cars left.

After you're in Tijuana, getting around by walking or taking a taxi is easy. Tijuana's main event is bustling **Avenida Revolucion**, the city's original bawdy center for illicit fun. Changing times and civic improvement have toned it down a bit; shopping and drinking are now the main order of business. If a marketplace atmosphere and bargaining are what you're looking for, head to **Mercado de Artesanias (Crafts Market)**, at Calle 2 and Avenida Negrete, where vendors of pottery, clayware, and other crafts fill an entire block.

Before you go, get information and maps from **Baja California Tourism Information**, 7860 Mission Center Court #202, in Mission Valley (☎ 800-522-1516, 800-225-2786, or 619-299-8518; www.bajamexicovacations.com).

The **Mission Bay Visitor Information Center** (☎ 619-276-8200) is on Mission Bay Drive at the end of Clairemont Drive. Near the San Diego Zoo is the **Balboa Park Visitors Center** (☎ 619-239-0512), in the House of Hospitality on El Prado.

Information on La Jolla is distributed by the **La Jolla Town Council,** 7734 Herschel Ave., between Silverado and Kline streets (☎ 858-454-1444). You'll find all you need to know about Coronado at the **Coronado Visitors Bureau,** 1047 B Ave., near Orange Avenue (☎ 619-437-8788; www.coronadohistory.org).

You can find San Diego's official Web site at www.sandiego.org. A guide to Gaslamp Quarter dining and shopping is at www.gaslamp.org. Official Coronado information is available at www.coronado.ca.us.

A great source for club and show listings is the *San Diego Reader* site at www.sdreader.com. *San Diego* magazine's www.sandiego-online.com features listings for dining and events. CitySearch's www.signonsandiego.com, is run by the *Union-Tribune* and offers a mix of current news, entertainment listings, and visitor information. *Digital City San Diego* (www.digitalcity.com/sandiego) targets locals, making it great for off-the-beaten-tourist-path recommendations.

Part VI
The Part of Tens

The 5th Wave   By Rich Tennant

In this part . . .

Every *For Dummies* book contains a Part of Tens, and in this fun part, you can catch a whiff of West Coast craziness. In Chapter 28, you discover where you can get down and wacky the way real Californians do. If the folks back home demand a token of your travels — and if you're something of a penny-pincher — read Chapter 29 for tips on cheap trinkets and souvenirs.

Chapter 28

The Ten Wackiest Annual Events

- -

In This Chapter

▶ Having a one-of-a-kind California experience

▶ Jumping frogs, racing worms, and building sandcastles

▶ Celebrating garlic, showing weeds, telling tales — all the doo-dah-day

- -

California, in case you haven't heard, can be a kooky place. After all, strangeness is one of the Left Coast's most appealing qualities. The yearly festivities listed in this chapter — which hold their own on the annual statewide calendar next to such respected traditions as the **Tournament of Roses Parade** and the **Monterey Jazz Festival** — throw reserve to the wind and allow you to join in the nutty fun. Or you're welcome to just point and hoot from the sidelines, if you prefer.

Peg Leg Smith's Liars Contest

This tall-tale-telling competition (held the Sat nearest to April Fool's Day, of course) is the legacy of wooden-limbed yarn-spinner Thomas Long "Peg Leg" Smith, who, in 1829 or thereabouts (dates tended to be somewhat fluid in Peg Leg's world), found a few gold-specked rocks in the desert. Rather than actually looking for more, Peg Leg spent the next 35 years weaving an increasingly Bunyan-like tale about his lost Borrego Springs gold mine into Old West legend.

Storytellers and listeners make the trek to Borrego Springs in San Diego County. The annual gathering at the Peg Leg Monument in Anza Borrego Desert State Park honors Peg Leg's chutzpah. You're welcome to join the fun around the campfire and just listen or do some spinning yourself, as long as your tale has something to do with gold mining in the Southwest, doesn't last longer than five minutes, and contains nothing that any reasonable listener may actually mistake for the truth.

For details, contact the **Borrego Springs Chamber of Commerce** (☎ **800-559-5524** or 760-767-5555; www.borregosprings.org).

Calaveras County Fair and Jumping Frog Jubilee

Inspired by Mark Twain's joyful short story "The Celebrated Jumping Frog of Calaveras County," this yearly competition (held the third weekend in May) is the Olympics of frog jumping. Really. Frog jockeys (yep, that's what they're called) converge on Angels Camp in California's Gold Country from all over the globe with their lean-'n'-mean amphibians in tow, competing for cash prizes as large as 5,000 smackeroos. The races are a hoot, and the accompanying three days of festivities — including the crowning of Miss Calaveras (a human teenage beauty, not a frog) — are festive and fun. If you and your leaper dream of riches and glory, however, start training now: The current world frog-jumping record is 21 feet, 5¾ inches, set in 1986 by Rosie the Ribiter of Santa Clara. Sadly, the Pacific red-legged frog immortalized in Twain's story (which is what got his career, er, hopping) is an endangered species. Contact the **Calaveras County Fairgrounds** (☎ 209-736-2561; www.frogtown.org).

Ferndale Cross-Country Kinetic Sculpture Race

One of the country's coolest annual events is this ingenious race. Each Memorial Day weekend, wild and crazy people in wild and crazy people-powered sculptures race for three days and 38 miles across land, sand, and sea, from Arcata to the Victorian-cute town of Ferndale, in the Redwood Country's Humboldt County.

The mobile art must be entirely people powered, must measure no more than 8 by 14 feet, and cannot be inherently dangerous to driver or spectator. Otherwise, anything goes and usually does; in the 30-plus-year history of the race, contraptions have ranged from giant watermelons to amphibious armadillos. For more information, call ☎ 707-845-1717 or visit www.kineticsculpturerace.org.

International Worm Races

Launched in 1966 by a descendant of Mark Twain, this hugely popular event wins first prize for sheer ridiculousness. The "race" track is a 4-foot-square board with a 2-foot target painted on it. Two to five worms — either night crawlers or reds — are placed on the bull's-eye, and the first to inch its way across the edge of the outer circle wins. The day's grand champion wins a $500 cash prize (which begs the question, what do worms do with money, anyway?).

The ultimate worm-on-worm challenge takes place at Redbud Park in Clearlake (north of Napa Valley) immediately following the annual Lions Club Fourth of July Parade. Don't have your own red worm or night crawler to enter? No problem! You can rent fully trained worms from the worm "stable" (whatever that is) just prior to race time. Call ☎ 707-994-3600 for details and entry forms or visit www.clearlakechamber.ccm/wr.html.

Gilroy Garlic Festival

The city of Gilroy (east of Santa Cruz and south of San Jose) proclaims itself the Garlic Capital of the World and celebrates its cash crop with this ultrastinky food fest. This is one of the biggest, best, and most well-attended food festivals in the entire Golden State, ideal for garlic addicts (and you know whether you are). In addition to garlicky eats from all over the culinary map — garlic ice cream, yum! — the late-July festival features arts-and-crafts vendors, live bands, the Miss Gilroy Garlic pageant (a dubious honor if ever there were one), and a mouthwash table (just kidding). Attention, cooks: Enter the Great Garlic Cook-Off, and you could go home a thousand bucks richer. Call ☎ 408-842-1625 or visit www.gilroygarlicfestival.com for further details.

Pageant of the Masters

Think *The Last Supper* was too flat, the *Mona Lisa* too stiff, *The Blue Boy* a tad too, well, two-dimensional? Then this is the event for you. Watch master artworks spring to life in this truly bizarre yet awe-inspiring performance-art gala, first launched in artsy Laguna Beach in 1932 and going strong ever since. This serious affair (it runs through most of July and Aug) features trained actors working on intricate artist-designed sets to create living, breathing tableaux that remain remarkably faithful to the original, with dramatic narration and full orchestral accompaniment in a lovely alfresco setting. This pageant is fantastic, in the truest sense of the word.

You can, and should, order your pageant tickets way in advance by calling ☎ 800-487-3378 or 949-497-6582. Come early in the day so you can also enjoy the **Festival of the Arts,** an outdoor art show featuring first-rate artists working in all media. You can find additional details on the excellent Web site (www.foapom.com).

U.S. Open Sandcastle Competition

What's more fun than sandcastles? Nothing — especially when they're astoundingly complex, larger-than-life sand sculptures of everything from Noah's Ark to lobsters (complete with melted butter- and lemon-shaped sand on the side) to scenes from the San Diego skyline. This world-class competition in Imperial Beach (south of San Diego) may be the best of California's many beach events — the huge crowds think so. The throng comes out in full force not only for the main competition but also for the pancake breakfasts, food and music vendors, parade, and kids' sandcastle-building competition. Even if you don't make it for the actual event in July, you may be able to view the leftovers in the weeks that follow — as long as rain doesn't wash 'em away, that is. Call ☎ 619-424-6663 or 619-424-3151 or point your Web browser to www.usopen sandcastle.com.

Underwater Pumpkin-Carving Contest

Underwater pumpkin carving seems even a couple of notches less practical than underwater basket weaving, yet plenty of sporting divers have turned up in La Jolla for this 20-plus-year-old Halloween event each year. Nobody takes it very seriously — one year the panel of judges was the staff of a local dive shop, the next year five kids off the beach — but it's always a fun party, and the surfacing jack-o'-lanterns are mighty impressive. Even though the bulk of the action takes place below sea level, the event is still fun to watch. For details, call **Ocean Enterprises** at ☎ 858-565-6054.

Weed Show

No, this festival doesn't focus on *that* kind of weed. Still, you'll think the locals have been smokin' it, what with the mind-boggling sculptures they create in the name of art using found objects and, yes, weeds. Lest you think this desert event (held in the vicinity of Joshua Tree National Park), sponsored by the Twentynine Palms Historical Society, is small potatoes, think again: More than 250 entries are usually up for critique in multiple-judged categories during this weekend-long event in early November. Call ☎ 760-367-2366 for the exact date and additional details (including entry forms) or point your Web browser to www.msnusers. com/29palmshistoricalsociety.

Doo Dah Parade

This outrageous Thanksgiving-weekend event — referred to in host Pasadena as the "other" parade — was born way back in 1978 as a zany spoof of the city's New Year's Day annual Tournament of Roses promenade. Doo Dah has since grown into a left-of-center institution all its own, but age hasn't cost it an ounce of silliness.

Participants usually include the Synchronized Precision Briefcase Drill Team (whose twirling skills are unparalleled), drag-queen cheerleaders (representing West Hollywood, of course), the BBQ and Hibachi Marching Grill Team, and many more — plenty to make the Ministry of Silly Walks mighty proud. Radio personality Dr. Demento often serves as Master of Ceremonies. The ashes of one longtime fan have been crowned Doo Dah Queen in Perpetuity, and they ride on their own float. You get the idea. But be aware that the traditional throwing of tortillas at participants has been discouraged. Spoilsports. Call ☎ **626-440-4029** or visit www.pasadenadoodahparade.com.

Chapter 29

Top Ten Gifts for Cheapskates

In This Chapter

▶ Leaving more than your heart in San Francisco
▶ Contributing to California's worthless trinket economy
▶ Remembering (fondly?) the folks back home

*W*e don't know about you, but buying gifts for the folks back at the ranch who know we've been on vacation is sometimes more of a chore than a pleasure. Besides the fact that no one in the western world really needs another T-shirt, those souvenirs add up (and subtract from our shoe allowance). Understanding, however, that some people expect a little something, here are our best suggestions for portable, fun, somewhat useful gifts — and they're all (or almost all) under $10. This catalog of must-haves comprises only San Francisco–related knick-knacks — imagine the kind of list we could compile statewide!

Playing Bridge

Not to be outdone by the museum gift shops, our own Golden Gate Bridge hawks a variety of branded items sure to remind your nearest and dearest of one of the wonders of the modern world. We particularly like the $6 **Golden Gate Bridge playing cards,** printed with trivia about the construction and history of this beautiful landmark. A close second is the $7 **kitchen towel,** the gift of choice from thrifty shoppers. If you run out of time and can't get to the gift shop, you can actually purchase these things online at `http://store.goldengate.org`.

Riding High

This truly is a cheapskate souvenir, but being the practical sort, we find it elegant in its simplicity and usefulness. For a mere $5 at the Powell Street or Hyde Street Cable Car ticket booths, you can purchase one of four **limited-edition souvenir cable-car tickets.** The cards each picture a historic cable car and are good for a one-way ride. Collect all four and someone with a scrapbook will treasure them.

Smelling Salts

The Ferry Building Marketplace is full of places to find great gifts, but go on a Saturday when the Farmers' Market is in full tilt. Behind the building look for the **Eatwell Farms** booth and check out the attractive $5 jars of **lavender salt** or **rosemary salt.** They smell divine and add extra oomph to salads and roasts. Your friends who cook will be most impressed.

Bringing Good Fortune

The biggest producer of fortune cookies in town is **Mee Mee Bakery,** 1328 Stockton St. between Broadway and Vallejo streets in Chinatown (☎ **415-362-3204;** www.meemeebakery.com). Hand over $9.75 and you can delight . . . someone . . . with a **giant fortune cookie.** Okay, at roughly 5 inches in diameter, maybe it's not an actual giant, but it's still fairly large. Mee Mee also sells bags of chocolate- and strawberry-flavored fortune cookies for $6.50 per pound and almond cookies for $4.50 per pound. If you want to splurge on something more creative, for $25 per 100 cookies, the bakery will put your own custom fortunes inside the crispy little devils.

Lighting the Way

Intellectuals and all your friends who belong to book clubs will be thrilled to receive anything from **City Lights** (☎ **415-362-8193**), San Francisco's iconic bookstore in North Beach. Good budget-minded gifts are the very cool $8 **black-and-white posters** featuring the storefront, or those with Jack Kerouac and Neal Cassady looking rather James Deanish.

Writing Clearly

You can't have too many postcards, but there's something stressful about picking them out — after all, postcards are like greeting cards. They say something about the person who spent 20 minutes deciding between the one with the cat and the one depicting Einstein. Save your friends grief and gift them with a **book of 30 San Francisco postcards** featuring the photographs of Michal Venera. At $9.95 this is a deal. Find *San Francisco 30 postcards* at **Chronicle Books Metreon Store,** 101 Fourth St. (☎ **415-369-6271**) or **Cody's Books** at 2 Stockton St., near Market Street (☎ **415-773-0444**).

Spilling the Beans

You may not believe this, but B.S. (Before Starbucks), people in the Bay Area were drinking strong, delicious coffee! And many continue to do so. They purchase it at any of a number of **Peet's Coffee & Tea** stores, including the newest one in the Ferry Building (at the foot of Market Street on the Embarcadero), the shop in the Russ Building at 217 Montgomery St., or in the Marina at 2156 Chestnut St. A gift your coffee-loving pals will truly appreciate is a **pound of Peet's French Roast,** as this stuff is so strong it can bench-press the competition. Starting at around $12 per pound, it crosses the cheapskate limit, but not by much. Besides, it's worth it. And this is one souvenir gift that you can keep on giving — or keep for yourself — by ordering from Peet's online store (www.peets.com).

Ringing Your Bell

Useless ornaments . . . ah, where would commerce be without snow globes, pewter models, and plastic barista figurines? Well, San Francisco can supply its fair share and at the top of our list is a spiffy **tin cable car.** A mere $8.75, this little beauty actually moves using friction, and it ting-a-lings like the real thing while skittering over linoleum. These are among the many fine doodads available online and at the **Cable Car Museum** gift shop, 1201 Mason St. (☎ **415-474-1887;** www.cablecar museum.org). Admission to the museum is free and it's open every day from 10 a.m. to 5 p.m.

Nibbling Bliss

San Francisco has long attracted chocolate-makers to its shores, not for any reason we know of, but there was Ghirardelli to start and Joseph Schmidt (of the beautiful truffles) and most recently a former doctor and a former winemaker who have together produced some serious dark chocolate under the Scharffen Berger label. Free one-hour tours of the handsome brick factory located at 914 Heinz Ave., in Berkeley (☎ **510-981-4050;** www.scharffenberger.com), are offered by appointment daily at 10:30 a.m., 2:30 p.m., and 3:30 p.m. for people 10 and over. Scharffen Berger sells two gifts that we would be genuinely pleased to receive: the $8 **cylinder filled with chocolate-covered champagne grapes** and the $6 **rectangular acrylic package of a dozen 5-gram squares** (the mint flavor, if you're wondering).

Spreading the Love

Ten bucks may not seem like much to spend on a gift, but how often do you fork over that kind of money for a small jar of jam? Berkeley's June

Taylor does not make ordinary preserves from ordinary fruit; thus, her divine products created from organic fruits in small batches don't sell for chicken feed. And that's why an 8-ounce jar of her **white nectarine conserve** or **tangerine marmalade** (among many flavors that will cause your bread to sit up and take notice) is such a thoughtful and extravagant offering. June Taylor's jams can be purchased at **Yum,** 1750 Market St. (☎ **415-626-9866**), the Ferry Plaza Farmers' Market at the Embarcadero and Market Street, and other locations that you can find by clicking at www.junetaylorjams.com.

Quick Concierge

● ●

Fast Facts

American Automobile Association (AAA)

Call ☎ 800-564-6222 or visit www.aaa.com for national information. The California State AAA serves Northern California; call ☎ 800-922-8228 or visit www.csaa.com to locate the office nearest your current Northern California location. The Automobile Club of Southern California is AAA's Southern California arm; call ☎ 800-222-8794 or point your Web browser to www.aaa-calif.com for more information or to locate an office.

For roadside assistance, members can call AAA at ☎ 800-400-4AAA in California, ☎ 800-AAA-HELP anywhere else in the United States.

American Express

The San Francisco walk-in office is located at 455 Market St., at First Street (☎ 415-536-2600), open Monday through Friday from 9 a.m. to 5:30 p.m., Saturday from 10 a.m. to 2 p.m.

On the Central Coast, you'll find official Amex travel offices at two Santa Barbara Travel Bureau locations: 1028 State St., Santa Barbara (☎ 805-966-3116), and in neighboring Montecito at 1127 Coast Village Rd. (☎ 805-969-7746).

Los Angeles area locations include 8493 W. Third St., at La Cienega Boulevard, across from the Beverly Center (☎ 310-659-1682) and 327 N. Beverly Dr., between Brighton and Dayton ways, Beverly Hills (☎ 310-274-8277).

San Diego has an office at Anderson Travel & Cruises, 11952 Bernardo Plaza Dr. (☎ 858-487-7722).

In Palm Springs, Andersen Travel Service, 700 E. Tahquitz Canyon Way (☎ 760-325 2001), serves as an official travel office.

To make inquiries or to locate other branch offices, call ☎ 800-AXP-TRIP or visit www.americanexpress.com.

ATM

Unless you need dough in the backwoods of Big Sur, you'll have no trouble finding an ATM in California. Branches of the Golden State's most popular banks are everywhere, with virtually all connected to the global ATM networks that your home bank is affiliated with.

Emergencies

No matter where you are in California, dial ☎ 911 in any emergency, whether it requires police, the fire department, or an ambulance.

Highway Conditions

Call Cal-Trans at ☎ 800-427-ROAD or 916-445-7623, or point your Web browser to www.dot.ca.gov/hq/roadinfo for complete California highway information.

Whether you call or go online, keep the highway numbers you're interested in handy at all times.

Information

The California Division of Tourism (☎ 800-462-2543) can send you a free vacation planner that serves as a good introduction to the Golden State. Its extensive Web site (www.gocalif.com) is an equally useful source that can link you to local visitor bureaus throughout the state.

The state also runs convenient welcome centers in San Francisco at Fisherman's Wharf, Pier 39, at Beach and Embarcadero streets (☎ 415-956-3493), and in Los Angeles at 8500 Beverly Blvd. (☎ 310-854-7616).

See the "Gathering More Information" section in each destination chapter for the best local information sources for individual destinations.

Liquor Laws

The legal drinking age of 21 is strictly enforced throughout the state, so have your ID handy even if your college days were a decade or two ago. Liquor and grocery stores, as well as some drugstores, can legally sell packaged alcoholic beverages between 6 a.m. and 2 a.m., although in some communities the hours of sales may be less at certain outlets, such as grocery stores.

Maps

AAA supplies good maps of California to members only, and they're free if you're a card carrier. You can obtain a terrific freeway map covering the entire state and pick and choose city and regional maps to suit your needs. For more information on becoming a member or locating the nearest office in California, see the American Automobile Association (AAA) listing at the

beginning of this appendix (also check out Chapter 7).

If you're not going the AAA way or you just want other sources, a comprehensive road guide is the Thomas Bros. California Road Atlas. You can get this and other maps from major online booksellers and bookstores. We highly recommend acquiring a good state map before you leave home, but keep in mind that you'll often get the best local maps after you arrive, especially in smaller towns.

Safety

For general safety issues, use your common sense, just as you would at home or anywhere else. Avoid deserted and poorly lit areas, especially at night. Always lock the doors of your rental car and don't keep anything valuable inside; any thief worth his salt can get into your locked car quicker without a key than you can get in with one.

Be alert in hotels and don't let strange folks into your hotel room unless they are clearly personnel that you expect or have summoned. Don't hesitate to call the front desk to verify an employee's identity; nothing's too silly where your safety's concerned. And be sure to store your valuables and cash in the in-room or behind-the-front-desk safe; don't just leave them in your hotel room.

If you have a cellphone, bring it with you, or rent a phone after you're in California to avoid paying high roaming charges. You'll likely be doing a lot of driving, and having a cellphone with you can make all the difference in the world if your car breaks down or you get lost.

In the unlikely event of an earthquake, keep these basics in mind: Don't run outside; instead, move away from windows and toward the building's center. Crouch under a desk, table, or other sturdy piece of furniture or stand in a doorway. If you must leave the building, use the stairs, not the elevator. If you're in the car, pull over to the side of the road and stay in your car — but don't pull over until you're away from bridges, overpasses, telephone poles, and power lines. If you're out walking, stay in the open, away from trees, power lines, and buildings.

Smoking

California has the best and worst smoking laws in the United States, depending on your point of view. Basically, the rule is this: If you're indoors, you're not allowed to light up.

Smoking is prohibited in virtually all indoor public spaces — yes, including restaurants (hence the proliferation of patio dining, where smoking is usually allowed). Many bars and clubs openly defy the law, however.

A good number of hotels, especially smaller places, also prohibit in-room smoking, so be sure to ask, if it matters to you.

Taxes

California's statewide sales tax is 7.25 percent. Some cities tack on an additional percentage up to 1.25 percent. The base hotel tax is 10 percent, with some municipalities adding an additional surcharge (which is noted in the hotel section of each chapter of this book).

Time Zone

California lies in the Pacific time zone, which is eight hours behind Greenwich mean time, and three hours behind the East Coast. The entire state practices daylight saving time from April to October.

Weather

To check the weather forecasts online, log onto www.weather.com or www.cnn.com/weather. Also note that many local visitor bureaus have weather links, so you may want to check each city or region's official site (listed in the "Gathering More Information" section of each destination chapter) to get a local link.

Useful Toll-Free Numbers and Web Sites

Airlines

Air Canada
☎ 888-247-2262
www.aircanada.ca

Alaska Airlines
☎ 800-252-7522
www.alaskaair.com

Aloha Airlines
☎ 800-367-5250
www.alohaairlines.com

American Airlines
☎ 800-433-7300
www.aa.com

America West Airlines
☎ 800-235-9292
www.americawest.com

ATA Airlines
☎ 800-225-2995
www.ata.com

British Airways
☎ 800-247-9297
☎ 0845-77-333-77 in Britain
www.britishairways.com

Continental Airlines
☎ 800-525-0280
www.continental.com

Delta Air Lines
☎ 800-221-1212
www.delta.com

Hawaiian Airlines
☎ 800-367-5320
www.hawaiianair.com

Horizon Air
☎ 800-547-9308
www.horizonair.com

Northwest Airlines
☎ 800-225-2525
www.nwa.com

Southwest Airlines
☎ 800-435-9792
www.southwest.com

United Airlines
☎ 800-241-6522
www.united.com

US Airways
☎ 800-428-4322
www.usairways.com

Virgin Atlantic Airways
☎ 800-862-8621
www.virgin-atlantic.com

Car-Rental Agencies

Advantage
☎ 800-777-5500
www.advantagerentacar.com

Alamo
☎ 800-327-9633
www.goalamo.com

Avis
☎ 800-331-1212 in U.S.
☎ 800-TRY-AVIS in Canada
www.avis.com

Budget
☎ 800-527-0700
www.budget.com

Dollar
☎ 800-800-4000
www.dollar.com

Enterprise
☎ 800-325-8007
www.enterprise.com

Hertz
☎ 800-654-3131
www.hertz.com

National
☎ 800-CAR-RENT
www.nationalcar.com

Payless
☎ 800-PAYLESS
www.paylesscarrental.com

Rent-A-Wreck
☎ 800-535-1391
rent-a-wreck.com

Thrifty
☎ 800-367-2277
www.thrifty.com

Major Hotel & Motel Chains

Best Western International
☎ 800-528-1234
www.bestwestern.com

Clarion Hotels
☎ 800-CLARION
www.hotelchoice.com

Comfort Inns & Suites
☎ 800-228-5150
www.hotelchoice.com

Courtyard by Marriott
☎ 800-321-2211
www.courtyard.com

Days Inn
☎ 800-325-2525
www.daysinn.com

Doubletree Hotels
☎ 800-222-TREE
www.doubletree.com

Econo Lodges
☎ 800-55-ECONO
www.hotelchoice.com

Fairfield Inn by Marriott
☎ 800-228-2800
www.marriott.com

Four Seasons Hotels & Resorts
☎ 800-819-5053
www.fourseasons.com

Hampton Inn
☎ 800-HAMPTON (800-426-7666)
www.hampton-inn.com

Hilton Hotels
☎ 800-HILTONS (800-445-8667)
www.hilton.com

Holiday Inn
☎ 800-HOLIDAY (800-465-4329)
www.holiday-inn.com

Howard Johnson
☎ 800-654-2000
www.hojo.com

Hyatt Hotels
☎ 800-228-9000
www.hyatt.com

La Quinta Motor Inns
☎ 800-531-5900
www.laquinta.com

Marriott Hotels
☎ 800-228-9290
www.marriott.com

Motel 6
☎ 800-4-MOTEL6 (800-466-8536)
www.motel6.com

Quality Inns
☎ 800-228-5151
www.hotelchoice.com

Radisson Hotels International
☎ 800-333-3333
www.radisson.com

Ramada Inns
☎ 800-2-RAMADA (800-272-6232)
www.ramada.com

Red Carpet Inns
☎ 800-251-1962
www.reservahost.com

Red Lion Inns
☎ 800-RED-LION (800-733-5466)
www.redlion.com

Red Roof Inns
☎ 800-RED-ROOF (800-733-7663)
www.redroof.com

Residence Inn by Marriott
☎ 800-331-3131
www.marriott.com

Rodeway Inns
☎ 800-228-2000
www.hotelchoice.com

Sheraton Hotels & Resorts
☎ 800-325-3535
www.sheraton.com

Super 8 Motels
☎ 800-800-8000
www.super8.com

Travelodge
☎ 800-255-3050
www.travelodge.com

Vagabond Inns
☎ 800-522-1555
www.vagabondinns.com

W Hotels
☎ 877-946-8357
www.whotels.com

Wyndham Hotels & Resorts
☎ 800-822-4200 in Continental U.S.
and Canada
www.wyndham.com

Where to Get More Information

For information on the state as a whole, contact the **California Office of Tourism,** 801 K. St., Suite 1600, Sacramento, CA 95812 (☎ 800-462-2543; www.gocalif.com), and ask for a free information packet. For information on specific California cities or towns, contact that town's tourism bureau or chamber of commerce (see the appropriate chapter in this book for contact information). For information on California's national parks, contact the **Pacific West Center,** National Park Service, One Jackson Center, 1111 Jackson St., Suite 700, Oakland, CA 94607 (☎ 510-817-1300; www.nps.gov). For information on California state parks, contact the **Department of Parks and Recreation,** P.O. Box 942896, Sacramento, CA 94296 (☎ 916-653-6995; www.parks.ca.gov).

Index

BUSINESS, CAREERS & PERSONAL FINANCE

0-7645-5307-0   0-7645-5331-3 *†

Also available:

Accounting For Dummies †
0-7645-5314-3

Business Plans Kit For Dummies †
0-7645-5365-8

Cover Letters For Dummies
0-7645-5224-4

Frugal Living For Dummies
0-7645-5403-4

Leadership For Dummies
0-7645-5176-0

Managing For Dummies
0-7645-1771-6

Marketing For Dummies
0-7645-5600-2

Personal Finance For Dummies *
0-7645-2590-5

Project Management
For Dummies
0-7645-5283-X

Resumes For Dummies †
0-7645-5471-9

Selling For Dummies
0-7645-5363-1

Small Business Kit For Dummies *†
0-7645-5093-4

HOME & BUSINESS COMPUTER BASICS

0-7645-4074-2   0-7645-3758-X

Also available:

ACT! 6 For Dummies
0-7645-2645-6

iLife '04 All-in-One Desk Reference
For Dummies
0-7645-7347-0

iPAQ For Dummies
0-7645-6769-1

Mac OS X Panther Timesaving
Techniques For Dummies
0-7645-5812-9

Macs For Dummies
0-7645-5656-8

Microsoft Money 2004 For Dummies
0-7645-4195-1

Office 2003 All-in-One Desk
Reference For Dummies
0-7645-3883-7

Outlook 2003 For Dummies
0-7645-3759-8

PCs For Dummies
0-7645-4074-2

TiVo For Dummies
0-7645-6923-6

Upgrading and Fixing PCs
For Dummies
0-7645-1665-5

Windows XP Timesaving
Techniques For Dummies
0-7645-3748-2

FOOD, HOME, GARDEN, HOBBIES, MUSIC & PETS

0-7645-5295-3   0-7645-5232-5

Also available:

Bass Guitar For Dummies
0-7645-2487-9

Diabetes Cookbook For Dummies
0-7645-5230-9

Gardening For Dummies *
0-7645-5130-2

Guitar For Dummies
0-7645-5106-X

Holiday Decorating For Dummies
0-7645-2570-0

Home Improvement All-in-One
For Dummies
0-7645-5680-0

Knitting For Dummies
0-7645-5395-X

Piano For Dummies
0-7645-5105-1

Puppies For Dummies
0-7645-5255-4

Scrapbooking For Dummies
0-7645-7208-3

Senior Dogs For Dummies
0-7645-5818-8

Singing For Dummies
0-7645-2475-5

30-Minute Meals For Dummies
0-7645-2589-1

INTERNET & DIGITAL MEDIA

0-7645-1664-7   0-7645-6924-4

Also available:

2005 Online Shopping Directory
For Dummies
0-7645-7495-7

CD & DVD Recording For Dummies
0-7645-5956-7

eBay For Dummies
0-7645-5654-1

Fighting Spam For Dummies
0-7645-5965-6

Genealogy Online For Dummies
0-7645-5964-8

Google For Dummies
0-7645-4420-9

Home Recording For Musicians
For Dummies
0-7645-1634-5

The Internet For Dummies
0-7645-4173-0

iPod & iTunes For Dummies
0-7645-7772-7

Preventing Identity Theft
For Dummies
0-7645-7336-5

Pro Tools All-in-One Desk
Reference For Dummies
0-7645-5714-9

Roxio Easy Media Creator
For Dummies
0-7645-7131-1

SPORTS, FITNESS, PARENTING, RELIGION & SPIRITUALITY

0-7645-5146-9

0-7645-5418-2

Also available:

Adoption For Dummies
0-7645-5488-3

Basketball For Dummies
0-7645-5248-1

The Bible For Dummies
0-7645-5296-1

Buddhism For Dummies
0-7645-5359-3

Catholicism For Dummies
0-7645-5391-7

Hockey For Dummies
0-7645-5228-7

Judaism For Dummies
0-7645-5299-6

Martial Arts For Dummies
0-7645-5358-5

Pilates For Dummies
0-7645-5397-6

Religion For Dummies
0-7645-5264-3

Teaching Kids to Read
For Dummies
0-7645-4043-2

Weight Training For Dummies
0-7645-5168-X

Yoga For Dummies
0-7645-5117-5

TRAVEL

0-7645-5438-7

0-7645-5453-0

Also available:

Alaska For Dummies
0-7645-1761-9

Arizona For Dummies
0-7645-6938-4

Cancún and the Yucatán
For Dummies
0-7645-2437-2

Cruise Vacations For Dummies
0-7645-6941-4

Europe For Dummies
0-7645-5456-5

Ireland For Dummies
0-7645-5455-7

Las Vegas For Dummies
0-7645-5448-4

London For Dummies
0-7645-4277-X

New York City For Dummies
0-7645-6945-7

Paris For Dummies
0-7645-5494-8

RV Vacations For Dummies
0-7645-5443-3

Walt Disney World & Orlando
For Dummies
0-7645-6943-0

GRAPHICS, DESIGN & WEB DEVELOPMENT

0-7645-4345-8

0-7645-5589-8

Also available:

Adobe Acrobat 6 PDF
For Dummies
0-7645-3760-1

Building a Web Site For Dummies
0-7645-7144-3

Dreamweaver MX 2004
For Dummies
0-7645-4342-3

FrontPage 2003 For Dummies
0-7645-3882-9

HTML 4 For Dummies
0-7645-1995-6

Illustrator CS For Dummies
0-7645-4084-X

Macromedia Flash MX 2004
For Dummies
0-7645-4358-X

Photoshop 7 All-in-One Desk
Reference For Dummies
0-7645-1667-1

Photoshop CS Timesaving
Techniques For Dummies
0-7645-6782-9

PHP 5 For Dummies
0-7645-4166-8

PowerPoint 2003 For Dummies
0-7645-3908-6

QuarkXPress 6 For Dummies
0-7645-2593-X

NETWORKING, SECURITY, PROGRAMMING & DATABASES

0-7645-6852-3

0-7645-5784-X

Also available:

A+ Certification For Dummies
0-7645-4187-0

Access 2003 All-in-One Desk
Reference For Dummies
0-7645-3988-4

Beginning Programming
For Dummies
0-7645-4997-9

C For Dummies
0-7645-7068-4

Firewalls For Dummies
0-7645-4048-3

Home Networking For Dummies
0-7645-42796

Network Security For Dummies
0-7645-1679-5

Networking For Dummies
0-7645-1677-9

TCP/IP For Dummies
0-7645-1760-0

VBA For Dummies
0-7645-3989-2

Wireless All In-One Desk Referen
For Dummies
0-7645-7496-5

Wireless Home Networking
For Dummies
0-7645-3910-8

HEALTH & SELF-HELP

0-7645-6820-5 *†   0-7645-2566-2

Also available:
- Alzheimer's For Dummies
  0-7645-3899-3
- Asthma For Dummies
  0-7645-4233-8
- Controlling Cholesterol For Dummies
  0-7645-5440-9
- Depression For Dummies
  0-7645-3900-0
- Dieting For Dummies
  0-7645-4149-8
- Fertility For Dummies
  0-7645-2549-2

- Fibromyalgia For Dummies
  0-7645-5441-7
- Improving Your Memory For Dummies
  0-7645-5435-2
- Pregnancy For Dummies †
  0-7645-4483-7
- Quitting Smoking For Dummies
  0-7645-2629-4
- Relationships For Dummies
  0-7645-5384-4
- Thyroid For Dummies
  0-7645-5385-2

EDUCATION, HISTORY, REFERENCE & TEST PREPARATION

0-7645-5194-9   0-7645-4186-2

Also available:
- Algebra For Dummies
  0-7645-5325-9
- British History For Dummies
  0-7645-7021-8
- Calculus For Dummies
  0-7645-2498-4
- English Grammar For Dummies
  0-7645-5322-4
- Forensics For Dummies
  0-7645-5580-4
- The GMAT For Dummies
  0-7645-5251-1
- Inglés Para Dummies
  0-7645-5427-1

- Italian For Dummies
  0-7645-5196-5
- Latin For Dummies
  0-7645-5431-X
- Lewis & Clark For Dummies
  0-7645-2545-X
- Research Papers For Dummies
  0-7645-5426-3
- The SAT I For Dummies
  0-7645-7193-1
- Science Fair Projects For Dummies
  0-7645-5460-3
- U.S. History For Dummies
  0-7645-5249-X

Get smart @ dummies.com®

- **Find a full list of Dummies titles**
- **Look into loads of FREE on-site articles**
- **Sign up for FREE eTips e-mailed to you weekly**
- **See what other products carry the Dummies name**
- **Shop directly from the Dummies bookstore**
- **Enter to win new prizes every month!**

* Separate Canadian edition also available
† Separate U.K. edition also available

Available wherever books are sold. For more information or to order direct: U.S. customers visit www.dummies.com or call 1-877-762-2974.
U.K. customers visit www.wileyeurope.com or call 0800 243407. Canadian customers visit www.wiley.ca or call 1-800-567-4797.